Lecture Notes in Computer Science 1486

Edited by G. Goos, J. Hartmanis and J. van Leeuwen

Springer

Berlin
Heidelberg
New York
Barcelona
Budapest
Hong Kong
London
Milan
Paris
Singapore
Tokyo

Anders P. Ravn   Hans Rischel   (Eds.)

Formal Techniques in Real-Time and Fault-Tolerant Systems

5th International Symposium, FTRTFT'98
Lyngby, Denmark, September 14-18, 1998
Proceedings

Springer

Series Editors

Gerhard Goos, Karlsruhe University, Germany
Juris Hartmanis, Cornell University, NY, USA
Jan van Leeuwen, Utrecht University, The Netherlands

Volume Editors

Anders P. Ravn
Hans Rischel
Technical University of Denmark
Department of Information Technology
Building 344, DK-2800 Lyngby, Denmark
E-mail: {apr,rischel}@it.dtu.dk

Cataloging-in-Publication data applied for

Die Deutsche Bibliothek - CIP-Einheitsaufnahme

Formal techniques in real time and fault tolerant systems : 5th
international symposium ; proceedings / FTRTFT '98, Lyngby,
Denmark, September 14 - 18, 1998. Anders P. Ravn ; Hans Rischel
(ed.). - Berlin ; Heidelberg ; New York ; Barcelona ; Budapest ; Hong
Kong ; London ; Milan ; Paris ; Singapore ; Tokyo : Springer, 1998
  (Lecture notes in computer science ; 1486)
  ISBN 3-540-65003-2

CR Subject Classification (1991): D.3.1, F.3.1, C.1.m, C.3, B.3.4, B.1.3,
D.4.5, D.4.7

ISSN 0302-9743
ISBN 3-540-65003-2 Springer-Verlag Berlin Heidelberg New York

© Springer-Verlag Berlin Heidelberg 1998
Printed in Germany

Typesetting: Camera-ready by author
SPIN 10638813   06/3142 – 5 4 3 2 1 0   Printed on acid-free paper

Preface

Embedded systems have become a hot topic in computer science because technology has made computers very powerful and very inexpensive. Thus it becomes possible and economically feasible to embed sophisticated computational models for the control of physical systems even in common appliances, automobiles, etc. Such applications must conform to physical laws dictated by their construction and their intended use, i.e., the computations must interact with a dynamical system which has timing constraints on when certain actions must occur. The computations have hard real-time constraints. Furthermore, some of the applications must continue to work even in the presence of intermittent or permanent faults in the electronics, thus they must be fault tolerant.

Engineering of embedded systems must thus rely on models for real-time and fault-tolerant computing. Mathematical foundations for developing, understanding and applying such models are the topic of this school and symposium. It is the fifth in a line of international schools and symposia; the previous ones were held in Warwick 1989, at Nijmegen 1992, at Lübeck 1994, and in Uppsala 1996. The proceedings of the symposia are published in LNCS 331, 571, 863, and 1135.

The lectures at the school are given by Albert Benveniste (IRISA, Rennes, France), Gérard Le Lann (INRIA Le Chesnay, France), Jan Peleska (Bremen, Germany), Jørgen Staunstrup (Lyngby, Denmark), and Frits Vaandrager (Nijmegen, The Netherlands). Invited presentations at the symposium are given by Connie Heitmeyer (Naval Res. Lab., USA), John Knight (Virginia, USA), Amir Pnueli (Weizmann Inst., Israel), and Joseph Sifakis (VERIMAG, France). We thank the lecturers and speakers for their contributions.

The program committee selected 22 papers for presentation. In addition the symposium has 5 tool demonstrations with short presentations in this volume.

This school and symposium is supported by the Technical University of Denmark, in particular the Department of Information Technology, and by the Danish Technical Research Council. The school is also supported by The Danish Research Academy via The Graduate School in Microelectronics. Local publicity has been supported by DELTA and IFAD. We are very grateful for this support which has made this event possible.

We shall also like to thank the steering committee for valuable advice, and to thank Disa la Cour, Maria Hansen, and Karin S. Mogensen for their enthusiastic practical support.

Lyngby, July 1998   Anders P. Ravn, Hans Rischel

Program Committee

Ralph-Johan Back (Åbo Akademi, Turko)
A. Burns (Univ. of York)
C. Dwork (IBM Almaden)
T. Henzinger (Cornell Univ., Ithaca, N.Y.)
J. Hooman (Eindhoven Univ. of Technology)
B. Jonsson (Uppsala Univ.)
M. Joseph (Univ. of Warwick)
Y. Lakhnech (Kiel)
K. Larsen (Aalborg Univ.)
N. Leveson (Univ. of Washington)
J. Madsen (DTU, Lyngby)
D. Mandrioli (Pol. Milano)
A. Mok (Univ. of Texas, Austin)
E.-R. Olderog (Univ. of Oldenburg)
J. Parrow (Royal Inst. of Technology, Stockholm)
A. Pnueli (Weizmann Inst., Rehovot)
A.P. Ravn (co-chair) (DTU, Lyngby)
H. Rischel (co-chair) (DTU, Lyngby)
W.-P. de Roever (Univ. of Kiel)
J. Sifakis (IMAG-LGI, Grenoble)
J. Vytopil (Kath. Univ., Nijmegen)
Chaochen Zhou (UNU/IIST, Macau)

Steering Committee

M. Joseph (Univ. of Warwick)
A. Pnueli (Weizmann Inst., Rehovot)
H. Rischel (DTH, Lyngby)
W.-P. de Roever (Univ. of Kiel)
J. Vytopil (Kath. Univ., Nijmegen)

Referees

Henrik R. Andersen	Henrik Hulgaard	Erich Mikk	Hongyan Sun
Saddek Bensalem	Dang Van Hung	Simon Mørk	Luis Urbina
Henning Dierks	Wang Ji	Xu Qiwen	Poul F. Williams
Pablo Giambiagi	Burghard v. Karger	Kaisa Sere	Hanno Wupper
H. Griffioen	Johan Lilius	Michael Schenke	Wang Yi
Michael R. Hansen	Hans H. Løvengreen	Steve Schneider	
Anne Haxthausen	Angelika Mader	Jens U. Skakkebæk	

Contents

Invited Lectures

Selected Presentations

Temporal Logic

Requirements Engineering

Analysis Techniques

Verification

Tools Demonstrations

Invited Paper

Author Index

Challenges in the Utilization of Formal Methods

John C. Knight

Department of Computer Science, University of Virginia,
Charlottesville, VA 22903, USA

Abstract. Despite the established benefits of formal methods, they remain poorly accepted by industrial software developers. This paper examines the issues surrounding the use of formal methods in industrial software development. It is argued that the reason for their limited use is that the introduction of formalism into software development is a more complex undertaking than it appears to be. This idea is explored in three areas: the software lifecycle; software dependability analysis; and development tools and environments. It is shown that many capabilities must be present in order for formal methods to fit into the complete software lifecycle, that the results of formal methods are difficult to use in software dependability analysis, and that the development of tools to support formal methods comprehensively is a difficult undertaking.

1   Introduction

Many claims have been made that the use of formal methods in software development would bring significant benefits to industry. The benefits that have been cited include improved software quality and faster development. There have been many successful applications of formal methods [3, 9, 10, 12, 13, 15, 18] but, despite their popularity in academia, valuable examples, and the claimed benefits, formal methods are still not widely used by commercial software companies. Industrial authors have expressed frustration in trying to incorporate formal technologies into practical software development for many reasons including the perceptions: that they increase development time; that they require extensive personnel training; and that they are incompatible with other software packages.

Experts in formal methods have analyzed the situation and provided systematic insight into the reasons for this lack of acceptance [5, 8, 11]. One possibility is that present formal methods might be incomplete or inadequate for some applications, and evaluation criteria for formal methods have been proposed and used in a variety of ways. Rushby introduced a set of ideas intended to help practitioners select a verification system and also offered a set of evaluation criteria for specification notations [19]. Faulk also proposed a set of evaluation criteria for specification notations [6].

A comprehensive approach to evaluation and some results were presented by Ardis et al [1]. In that work, a set of criteria was established for the evaluation of formal specification notations and the set was then applied to several notations. The evaluation was performed on a sample problem from the field of telecommunications.

Some understanding of the lack of popularity of formal methods has been gained, but despite this, the use of formal methods remains the exception rather than the rule. Interestingly, the practical use of formal methods tends to be higher in some geographic regions, Europe for example, than in others such as the United States.

It is clear that there remain rather basic reasons why formal methods have not gained widespread acceptance. It is certainly not the case that the problem derives from something as simple as industrial practitioners merely being reluctant to change their current methods. There are, in fact, several well-known shortcomings that impede progress when industrial engineers attempt to use current formal techniques. For example, one of the difficulties that they encounter is the limited applicability of formal-specification languages. Such languages can usually describe only part of any particular system whereas natural languages can describe a system completely, albeit informally.

By looking at the evaluations and case studies that have been performed, one is led to an initial conclusion that formal methods must overcome a number of relatively mundane but important practical hurdles before their benefits can be realized. These practical hurdles arise from the current state of software-development practice. While the traditional methods used in industry are rarely formally based, they are reasonably well-developed, they are well-understood, and they are comprehensive in that they facilitate the development of real software systems. In order to be incorporated into industrial practice, it has been argued that formal methods must meet this current standard of industrial practice [14].

This assessment is quite valid but the problem is much more complex than this fairly straightforward explanation implies. As an example of why, consider the following question—a question that is posed by every software project manager who attempts to employ formal techniques:

How do formal techniques fit in with the other activities that are necessary in the development of a large software system?

The issue here is that formal techniques tend to be viewed in isolation. Software systems are developed through a complex lifecycle that has many interrelated elements all of which have to work correctly if a high-quality product is to be developed in a timely and cost-effective manner. Yet a lifecycle approach that incorporates formal methods is missing. Tools and techniques are not well integrated, for example, into production methods for system-wide documentation, configuration management, version control, and group development.

A second question that is raised frequently by software project managers is:

To which parts of a system should formal techniques be applied?

A common philosophy is that formal methods should be applied to "the most critical parts" of a software system. But what exactly are those parts and precisely how are they determined? This is not something that can be left to intuition or informal reasoning. A mistake in this determination would mean that some critical part or parts had been omitted from the formal analysis with possibly serious results.

Even if one knew which were the "the most critical parts", one is left wondering how the results of formal analysis are integrated into the development and analysis methods used for the remainder of the system. Suppose, for example, that an asynchronous real-time system were being developed for an embedded control application. Suppose further that a proof had been developed which showed that the tasking structure of the software was not subject to deadlock. This is a very useful result to have. But the developers need to be able to establish correct operation of the system for all of the expected inputs. Freedom from deadlock is just a part, albeit an important part, of the functional correctness of the system. The developers will always test such a system, and, often, they will seek quantitative assessment of the software; by bounding its mean time to failure for example. The problem then is to know how to use the fact that there is a proof that certain faults do not exist in such a quantitative analysis.

A third question that is raised frequently by software project managers is:

Where are the tools that support formal techniques and how do they fit in with the other tools used in large-scale software system development?

For a variety of reasons, the tools that have been developed to support formal techniques are not as comprehensive nor as easy to use as those that support traditional, non-formal methods.

In general, there are no satisfactory answers to the three questions posed above. In systems that are obvious candidates for the application of formalism, such as safety-critical systems, this presents a difficult dilemma. In this paper, a different and somewhat broader rationale for why formal methods are not more widely used is presented that is based on these three questions. ¿From this rationale, several challenges are developed that must be addressed before formal methods can become the preferred approach to software development.

I claim that the lack of use of formal methods arises because the introduction of formal methods into software development is a much more complex undertaking than it appears to be. Formalism is a completely different basis for software development from the informal and ad hoc methods that are typically used now. This difference in basis affects every aspect of software development, but the focus in this paper is on three main areas for purposes of illustration. These three areas are the impact of and the role of formal methods in:

– The software lifecycle.
– Software dependability analysis.
– Development tools and environments.

These topics are addressed in the remainder of this paper, and for each, a set of challenges is presented. These challenges are significant hurdles that must be overcome if a comprehensive formal basis for routine software development is to be achieved.

2   The Software Lifecycle

The first question that was posed above is about the software lifecycle:

How do formal techniques fit in with the other activities that are necessary in the development of a large software system?

If they are going to be used successfully, formal methods must work within the entire software development process as it is manifested in large-scale development. *It is not necessary for all aspects of development to be formalized.* But it is necessary that those aspects of development that are formalized be integrated seamlessly with those aspects that are not. And it is essential that the benefits of the formalism be clear and achieved relatively easily.

The real issue is *software development* and the associated *software lifecycle*. In other words, formal methods must contribute to software development and fit properly into the software lifecycle. The criteria used by developers when considering formal techniques inevitably reduce quickly to the question, "How will this help build better software?", where the definition of better is not restricted to a certain set of goals. There are two aspects to this question–first, what is needed to build software and, second, how can the use of formal methods augment the current development practices of industry to help build "better" software?

The question of what is needed to build software leads to an examination of current practice. Current methods of software development divide the activities into lifecycle phases. Such a division focuses the developers' attention on the tasks that must be completed. But the lifecycle alone is not sufficient to describe the current process of building software since development is guided by management activities. These activities continue throughout the lifecycle, monitoring and directing it.

A software development process that incorporates formal techniques can either be designed from scratch with this in mind or be adapted from existing processes. A process developed from scratch would almost certainly look very different from anything that most engineers have ever used or seen. It would, for example, almost certainly be based on reification for the development of executable code. Though such techniques exist and have been demonstrated successfully, it is clear that their widespread use is a remote possibility at this point.

If a process is developed by adapting an existing process to include formal methods, it is essential that their *compatibility* with current practice and the *actual benefits* they realize over the entire lifecycle be carefully analyzed. In order to be accepted by industrial practitioners, the introduction of formal methods has to meet the following four objectives:

- They must not detract from the accomplishments achieved by current methods.
- They must augment current methods so as to permit industry to build "better" software.
- They must be consistent with those current methods with which they must be integrated.

– They must be compatible with the tools and techniques that are in current use.

A complication that arises in trying to meet these objectives is that each project has different practical requirements. For instance, if the goal of a project is to be the first commercial vendor to develop a certain networked Java application, the reliability is less important than the speed of production. In this context, "better" software would probably imply a faster time to market, whereas in a safety-critical system, "better" would refer to greater dependability of the software.

In an experiment that was conducted recently, an evaluation framework based on these objectives was developed and from it a detailed set of criteria was derived in order to assess how well the four objectives outlined above are being met. As part of the experiment, four typical formal methods were evaluated using these criteria. The results of that experiment have been documented elsewhere [4, 7], but certain key aspects are repeated here to illustrate the breadth and depth of the impact that formalism has on the lifecycle.

The complete evaluation framework is in two major parts–one for formal specification and the other for mechanical analysis techniques. The framework is structured by the six phases of the software lifecycle–requirements analysis, requirements specification, design, implementation, verification, and maintenance–and for each phase a set of criteria that must be met was identified. Each criterion was documented along with its rationale. These criteria were derived from the basic goals of software development, and are, in fact, the essential requirements that formal techniques have to meet if they are to be integrated successfully into an existing software development process.

As an example of the way in which the framework operates, consider the oft-cited criterion that a formal specification language must be "readable". In practice, this is a completely inadequate criterion because it is not defined precisely and is untestable. In practice, a formal specification is read by engineers with different goals, skills, and needs in each phase of the lifecycle. What is readable to an engineer involved in developing a specification is not necessarily readable to an engineer using the specification for reference during implementation or maintenance. Thus, there are in fact many important criteria associated with the notion of a readable specification–the criteria are determined by the lifecycle phase and their relative importance by the product goals.

For purposes of illustration, the following are a small selection of the evaluation criteria developed for formal specification techniques as part of the experiment mentioned above [4]. It is important to keep in mind that although these are referred to as evaluation criteria, they are in no way intended to separate one formal technique from another–they are basic requirements that formal specification techniques have to meet:

– *Coverage.*
  Real systems are large and complex with many aspects. For a specification notation to serve well, it must either permit description of all of an application or be designed to operate with the other notations that will be required.

– *Integration with other components.*
The formal specification technology must be suited to the larger working environment. A specification is not developed in isolation, but rather as part of the larger software development process. Any specification technology must integrate with the other components of this process, such as comprehensive documentation, design, test, and management information. When developing a large software system, a system database and version control system are used, and a part or all of the specification might be inserted into other documents. The specification must be stored in a file format that is either the same as or interoperates easily with all of the other development tools.

– *Group development.*
Every software project involves more than one person. During the development of the specification, it must be possible for several people to work in parallel and combine their efforts into a comprehensive work product. This means that any specification technique must provide support for the idea of separate development–a notion equivalent to that of separate compilation of source programs in languages such as Ada that have syntactic structures and very precise semantics for separately compiled units.

– *Evolution.*
A specification is not built in one effort and then set in concrete; it is developed and changed over time. Specification technology must support the logical evolution of a specification and ease its change. Incompleteness must be tolerated. Functionality such as searching, replacing, cutting, copying, and file insertion must be available. Modularity and information hiding must be facilitated, so that, for example, a change in a definition is propagated to every usage of the definition automatically. Similarly, large scale manipulations must also be supported, such as moving entire sections or making them subsections.

– *Navigation.*
The ability to locate relevant information is a vital part of the utility of a specification. Being able to search, for example with regular expressions is valuable, but not sufficient. Structuring mechanisms to aid in navigation are also required since any specification document is likely to be large. In a natural language document, the table of contents and index assist in the location of information; many tools allow them to be generated automatically from the text. Another useful capability seen in text editing is the use of hypertext links to related sections or glossary entries. Finally, since a specification is intended to serve primarily as a means of communication, it is important to be able to annotate a specification with explanations, rationale, or assumptions for both the use of the specification in later phases and for modifications of the specification.

– *Compatibility with design methods and tools.*
Clearly, a very strong relationship exists between the specification of a system and its design, and specification technology must be compatible with popular design methods. A difficult transition from a formal specification to say

an object-oriented design is an unacceptable lifecycle burden. Similarly, the tools should also be closely related. It should not be necessary for the designer to re-enter parts of the specification that are also part of the design. Either the specification tool must also fully support the design phase or it must be compatible with common design tools.

– *Maintenance comprehension.*

An engineer responsible for maintenance should be able to study the specification and gain either a broad or detailed understanding of the system quickly. The documentation of non-functional requirements and design decisions is vital to a complete understanding of the system. The specification should be easy for the maintainer to navigate, accurate, complete, and easy to reference to find answers to questions. Structure, support for information hiding, and the ability to view the specification at different levels of abstraction are essential.

These criteria are merely examples but they illustrate the key point that, to be used effectively as part of a complete software development lifecycle, any formal technique has to address a wide range of practical issues. The challenges in this area are to ensure that the techniques and associated tools do address these issues.

3 Software Dependability Analysis

We now return to the second of the questions that was posed earlier:

To which parts of a system should formal techniques be applied?

A developer has to answer this question, but he or she has to answer a related questions also:

How are the results of applying formal techniques exploited in dependability analysis?

These are important questions because they focus attention on the reason why formal techniques are used.

We know that, on average, formal specification reduces the number of specification defects, and we know that formal verification allows the establishment of useful properties about a software system. But how do formal techniques help at the total system level? This is an important question because software does not execute in isolation. It executes as part of a system and provides functionality to the system. The dependability that is important is that of the system, not the software. Thus properties of software must be established, perhaps by formal techniques, because they are needed at the system level to facilitate establishment of some useful characteristic of the system itself.

An important approach to dependability assessment at the system level, i.e., including hardware, operators, the environment, etc., is *probabilistic risk analysis* [17]. This type of analysis is quite complex and provides a number of important results about engineered systems. Of particular importance is system modeling using fault-tree analysis [23]. A fault tree can be thought of as a graphic representation of a logical formula that shows how certain basic events and combinations of events can lead to system hazards. The system hazards are determined by hazard analysis, and, if probabilities of occurrence can be associated with the basic events, then the corresponding probabilities of the hazards arising can be estimated. If such probabilities are unacceptable, the system design can be modified so as to improve the situation.

Probabilistic risk analysis techniques are often limited to models of systems that only consider "chance" failures, i.e., the assumption is made that faults are due to component *degradation* [17]. This is a useful model of hardware faults. Software faults, however, are *design* faults because they do not arise from the software "wearing out", and this makes their inclusion in typical probabilistic risk analysis quite problematic. There is disagreement, for example, even about whether the effects of a software fault can be modeled stochastically [21].

In order to include software in the probabilistic risk analysis of a system, an approach that is sometimes used is to try to establish that the probability of failure of the entire software system is sufficiently small that it can be ignored. In this approach the software is treated as a black-box [16] and tests are performed with the goal of bounding the software's failure probability by life testing.

Systems that are the subject of probabilistic risk analysis will, in most cases, be systems for which the consequences of failure are extremely high, and the probability of software failure would have to be shown to be *very* small for it to be small enough to be ignored. The cost of obtaining a reliability estimate by testing for software in what is sometimes referred to as the ultra-dependable range is prohibitive because of the discrete nature of software [2].

An alternative approach is to retain the black-box model but to associate a probability distribution with software failure. In this way, the software in a system is treated as a single system component for purposes of analysis, and its failures are modeled in the same way that the failures of other system components, such as processors and memory units, are modeled.

Unfortunately, there is no way to integrate the results of formal techniques into this type of system dependability analysis because, typically, formal techniques do not produce stochastic results. Although a probability of one can be associated with a given software property if a proof of that property has been developed, that type of result cannot be included in traditional software dependability analysis.

The black-box approach is used in modeling software because the properties of a typical software system permit little else. Unlike hardware, it is usually not possible to base the analysis of the software on its structure, say the its functional structure, because faults typically lead to erroneous behavior across indeterminate regions of the software, the effects of which are essentially impossible to model.

This latter problem arises because a software fault can lead to correlated failures with high probability. A single software fault might cause one or more erroneous values to be produced but, if these values are used in subsequent computations, widespread damage to the system state can result very quickly as further data becomes corrupt. If the software in a system fails and is responsible for controlling a variety of devices, then the external effect could be a system failure in which several devices act improperly and these devices will appear to have failed in a correlated manner. Consider, for example, the effects of a fault in the scheduler of an operating system. Such a fault can cause multiple processes to be suspended at the same time, and if these processes are controlling different external devices, the failures that would appear in the system would, quite clearly, be correlated.

An approach to modeling software based on its structure is an essential step if better results are to be obtained. If it were possible to model software accurately as a set of connected components in the same way that the physical components of a system are usually modeled, the failure of individual components could appear, for example, as events in the system fault tree. The failure probabilities required of the components to achieve a certain system performance would then be determined in the same manner that such probabilities are bounded for physical components. In addition, assessing software components by testing would be simpler because a typical component would be considerably less complex than the entire system.

Modeling software as a set of components is only practical if it can be established that faults in one software component do not lead to failures in other software components or if the circumstances under which this occurs can be determined precisely. The benefits of this approach are considerable, however, and the approach would permit probabilistic risk analysis techniques to be applied to systems containing software with much greater fidelity.

Were it possible to model software as a connected set of components, it would provide an answer to the question posed at the beginning of this section. Software components (individual functions, subsystems, tasks, etc.) would be analyzed and events would appear in the fault tree that were associated with specific failures of specific elements of the software. Thus, for example, if it were possible for the embedded system mentioned earlier to fail as a result of a deadlock, this event would appear in the tree and be an explicit area of concern. Just as with hardware, were such an event likely to lead to a hazard, then its probability of occurrence would have to be shown to be sufficiently small. This is precisely what is required to identify "the most critical parts" of a software system, and provides both the system aspects to which formal methods should be applied and the means by which the results of the formal analysis can be exploited.

To be able to proceed with analysis based on the structure of a software system requires that progress be made in dealing with the correlated behavior of the various elements of a software system. The progress that is needed is in three areas:

− It is necessary to be able to identify precisely the causes of correlated behavior among software components.

- Design techniques need to be developed to minimize these correlations so that their effects can be isolated to the minimum number of components.
- Assessment techniques are required that will allow the various correlations that remain to be quantified.

We are investigating these issues in order to develop more comprehensive models of software reliability. The first step in the investigation is to determine how one software component can affect another. There are, of course, a multitude of ways that this can occur, but there is no basis in either models of computation or programming language semantics for performing a comprehensive analysis.

We chose to approach this problem by viewing component interaction as a *hazard* and basing our analysis on a fault tree for this hazard. In this way, we have documented, albeit informally, all possible sources of component interaction. Needless to say, the fault tree is quite large. The events in the fault tree are based on the semantics of a typical procedural programming language, and the results apply to all common implementation languages such as Fortran and C.

In order to reflect the syntactic structure of procedural languages accurately, we define the term component to mean either (a) a function in the sense of a function in C, (b) a class in the sense of a class in C++, or (c) a process in the sense of a task in Ada. No assumptions are made about how components can provide services to each other (in a client/server model) or collaborate with each other (in a concurrent model) or otherwise interact.

Fig. 1 shows the top of the component-interaction fault tree. With no loss of generality, in this fault tree we consider only two components because there can be no interaction between components if there is no pair-wise interaction. Since information flow between A and B is symmetric, only one of the cases needs to be considered.

In the first level, component interaction can be caused by erroneous information flow from A to B or by a common source of erroneous information. Thus, these are the two events shown. Note that component interaction does not necessarily mean *intended communication* in any format. Rather, it includes both intended and non-intended interaction between components. In addition, information flow does not mean just transfer of data. Flow of control is also information in the sense of the analysis that is needed.

The complete component-interaction fault tree permits the various sources of interaction to be documented. Illustrative examples of the interactions that are documented by this type of analysis are:

- *Global Variables:* Two or more components share a variable and its content are shared between them.
- *Memory Copying:* In some systems, it is possible for a component to request a copy of some other component's memory space.
- *Shared Memory:* Two components share data memory areas.
- *Function Calls:* A function in one component is called by a different component.
- *Parameter Passing:* When a function is invoked, parameters are passed from the caller to the called and return values are provided to the caller.

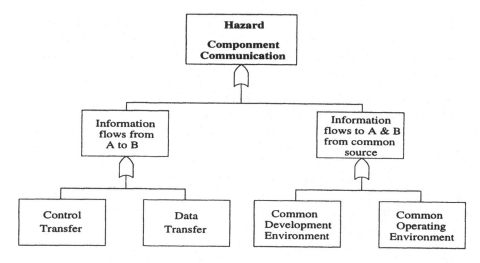

Fig. 1. Top level component-interaction fault tree.

- *Deadlocks:* More than one process cannot execute because they are dead-locked. This need not be the "fault" of all of the processes involved.
- *Deadlines:* Failure to meet a real-time deadline by one process can affect other processes.
- *Exception Handling:* An exception transfers control from one location to another, possibly in another component.
- *Common Compiler:* Multiple components are generated using the same compiler subjecting them all to any residual design faults in the compiler.
- *Common Linker:* Multiple components are combined by a linker subjecting them all to any residual design faults in the linker.
- *Common Operating Hardware:* Two or more components are executing on the same platform.
- *Common Operating Software:* Two or more components are executing using the services of common operating software such as an operating system.
- *Common Input Data:* Two or more components receive the same input datum from a third.

With the model of component interaction at hand, design techniques are being developed that will allow software to be designed that facilitates a component-based approach to dependability analysis. Formal techniques are introduced into this analysis by providing a mechanism for analyzing essential properties of specific components as mentioned earlier.

This is but one approach to the problem of integrating formal techniques for software development and analysis with system-level dependability analysis. Important challenges for the formal methods community are to provide comprehensive strategies for achieving this integration and to develop the associated analysis techniques. Without these strategies and techniques, formal methods remain outside and separate from the analysis that is central to system-level dependability assessment.

4 Support Tools

Finally, we turn to the third question that was posed in the Introduction:

Where are the tools that support formal techniques and how do they fit in with the other tools used in large-scale software system development?

The advantages that can accrue from machine-processable notations are only realized in full if suitable tools are available to perform the necessary processing. Several tools are in fact available in the formal methods area, but, for rather significant reasons, developing tools to support formal methods is unusually challenging.

One of the reasons derives from the rapid pace of development in formal methods. Because of this rapid pace, there tend to be numerous innovative concepts for new tools and tool enhancements from both researchers and developers. Lots of new tools are required. The innovation seen in new tool ideas is usually considerable, and making that innovation available is important. Researchers thus tend naturally to focus on implementing the core analysis idea in a new tool concept.

A major part of the challenge in developing tools in the formal methods area arises, however, from the need for new tools to provide a wide range of customarily-available features. To become available for regular use in engineering development, innovative tool ideas have to be combined with a multitude of routine facilities that, though routine, are essential. Formal specifications are complex documents, and, for notations like Z, they include both formal and informal content. Developers of such specifications appreciate the value of innovative analysis but must be able to perform routine manipulations conveniently.

It is at this point that a major difficulty arises. Implementing these routine facilities, the "superstructure" of a tool [22], requires enormous resources—frequently *much* more than are needed to implement the innovation that is at the heart of the tool. This has led to many tools being developed with only a limited superstructure thereby limiting the exploitation of their innovation.

An obvious manifestation of this problem can be seen in the widespread continued use of the ASCII representation of the Z character set. Many engineers developing Z specifications are required to work with the ASCII representation and to edit versions of their specifications that are substantially different from the printed forms. The primary text-manipulation tools at their disposal are an ASCII editor and LaTex. This is the case at a time when elaborate word-processing systems are in routine use that provide convenient access to operating system services and WYSIWYG editing for natural-language processing.

A second reason why tools to support formal methods are especially challenging is that the tools required are in many ways different from the majority of software tools that a developer uses in a traditional development process. Its not a case of making some enhancements to an existing tool or building a tool "like that one over there" but for a different notation or environment–completely different types of tools are needed. Dealing with a formal notation such as Z, for example, requires: (a) that a sophisticated text formatter be available to deal with the natural language; (b) that a syntax and type-checking system for Z be available; and (c) that a theorem-proving system be available if the full power of Z is to be realized.

The third reason that tools for formal methods are especially challenging is that all of the integration and interoperability issues raised in section 2 have to be addressed. These are significant issues since in many cases existing tools provide essential functionality and interfacing with them is a non-trivial undertaking.

In an effort to better understand what is required to support engineers who are working with formal specifications as part of the complete software lifecycle, we are developing a toolset (named Zeus) to facilitate the preparation and manipulation of specifications in Z. Zeus is designed to be the core of a system that can provide complete lifecycle support, and so it contains certain specialized tools along with facilities to allow interaction with other essential lifecycle-support tools.

A key part of the way that Zeus is being built is to incorporate large existing packages and tools to the extent possible rather than building them. Zeus uses, for example, the Framemaker desk-top publishing system produced by Adobe Systems, Inc. to provide desk-top publishing facilities. It also includes an easy-to-use interface to Z/EVES [20], an existing high-performance theorem-proving system, to permit sophisticated specification analysis. The current version of Zeus runs on the IBM PC/Microsoft Windows platform.

4.1 Zeus Basic Features

Since Zeus uses Framemaker, it provides all the document-processing features that Framemaker provides. These features include:

- WYSIWYG editing using the correct graphics for the Z character set. Editing includes cutting, pasting, and inserting both natural language and Z text, as well as find and replace.
- Access to the host operating system's file system thereby allowing specifications to be stored conveniently. Framemaker provides a "book" mechanism that allows a document to be stored in separate files that are linked to preserve page numbering and other parameters. Thus a specification can be developed and manipulated as a book.
- A wealth of formatting features permitting page layouts to be controlled, any compatible font to be used, paragraph formats to be controlled, and so on.
- The standard look and feel of Microsoft Windows applications including all window functions and standard keyboard shortcuts.

All of the Z graphic structures can be used with Zeus, and they are created simply by selecting a menu option. Thus, to insert a schema into a specification, the user merely places the insertion point at the desired location and selects the appropriate menu item.

Graphic structures are inserted automatically below the insertion point as anchored frames that move along with the text to which they are anchored. Thus, as text is added to or deleted from a specification, graphic structures remain with their associated natural language text (or with whatever the specifier wishes them to be associated). Graphic structures can, of course, be cut and pasted as desired to move them or copy them as the user desires.

As well as the display and searching facilities that Framemaker provides, Zeus includes a preliminary version of a more comprehensive browsing capability. A list of schemas in a specification can be displayed and any schema located by selecting the schema name with the mouse.

The Framemaker user interface is easily enhanced and it has been modified to provide access to Z/EVES. The interface consists of five separate Framemaker windows (three of which appear automatically when Zeus is started), and menu items that invoke relevant actions. The three initial windows are an editing window, an error window, and an output-display window. A fourth window is used for entering Z/EVES commands and appears when a menu item is selected. The fifth window appears whenever the user wishes to prepare a theorem for submission to Z/EVES.

In summary, the interface seen by the user of Zeus in its present form is a desk-top publishing system enhanced to permit convenient manipulation of Z text together with a relatively seamless connection to a powerful analysis capability. Other facilities can be added conveniently because of the system's design, and more comprehensive lifecycle tools will be integrated as development proceeds.

4.2 The Design Of Zeus

The high-level design of Zeus is shown in Fig. 2. Z/EVES is included in the figure for completeness although it is a separate system.

The design of Zeus is based on a set of central data structures that encapsulate all of the vital information about a specification and a functional structure that permits this information to be manipulated in a variety of ways. As well as synthesized information about a specification, such as the list of the schemas used in browsing navigation, the specification as displayed by Framemaker is treated as one of the central data structures. To provide user displays and controls, tools to be integrated with Zeus can either operate with an independent display, or operate through Framemaker. Thus, Zeus provides a flexible interface to which many relevant tools can be linked.

As an example of how tools can be linked and used, consider Z/EVES. Filters that translate between the Z character set and the LaTex ASCII sequences are included in the interface to the central data structures. In addition, access functions are available to acquire information about the Z text in a specification from the specification as displayed. Thus, type checking a specification using

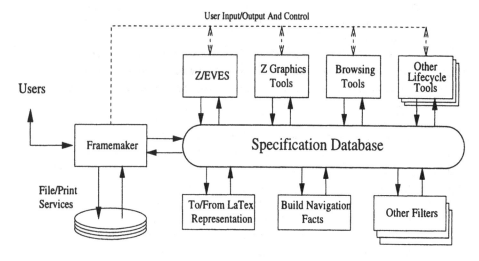

Fig. 2. The design of Zeus and its link to Z/EVES.

Z/EVES is accomplished by extracting the Z text from the specification as displayed, translating it to the LaTex representation, and passing the result to Z/EVES.

5 Conclusions

There are many benefits that accrue from the use of formal methods. The fact that they are not routinely used in industrial software development is not for any simple reason. The reason is that introducing formalism into software development is a complex task. It is a complex task because the majority of software technology at present is informal and it has been that way for a long time.

In this paper, three major areas of difficulty have been identified. They are: (1) the difficulty of integrating formal methods with all the lifecycle phases in existing development processes; (2) the difficulty of including the results of formal analysis in system-level dependability analysis; and (3) the difficulty of providing adequate support tools for formal methods in a typical modern development environment.

These are significant difficulties but they are not insurmountable. They present a set of significant challenges that must be addressed before formal techniques can become the development techniques of choice in large-scale software development.

6 Acknowledgments

It is a pleasure to thank Luis Nakano for many helpful discussions on the material discussed in this paper. This research was funded in part by NASA under grant number NAG1-1123-FDP.

References

1. Ardis, M., Chaves, J., Jagadeesan, L., Mataga, P., Puchol, C., Staskauskas, M., Von Olnhausen, J.: A framework for evaluating specification methods for reactive systems: Experience report. IEEE Trans. on Software Engr. 22(6) (1996) 378-389
2. Butler, R.: Finelli, G. The infeasibility of quantifying the reliability of life-critical real-time software. IEEE Trans. on Software Engr, 19(1) (1991) 3-12
3. Craigen, D., Gerhart, S., Ralston, T.: An international survey of industrial applications of formal methods. U.S. Department of Commerce, March (1993)
4. DeJong, C., Gibble, M., Knight, J., Nakano, L.: Formal specification: A systematic evaluation. Technical Report CS-97-09, Department of Computer Science, University of Virginia, Charlottesville, VA (1997)
5. Dill, D., Rushby, J.: Acceptance of formal methods: Lessons from hardware design. IEEE Computer 29(4) (1996) 23-24
6. Faulk, S.: Software requirements: A tutorial. Technical Report NRL/MR/ 5546–95-7775, Naval Research Laboratories, (November 1995)
7. Gibble, M., Knight, J., Nakano, L., DeJong, C.: Experience report using PVS for a nuclear reactor control system. Technical Report CS-97-13, Department of Computer Science, University of Virginia, Charlottesville, VA (1997)
8. Hall, A.: What is the formal methods debate about? IEEE Computer, 29(4) (1996) 22-23
9. Heitmeyer, C., McLean, J.: Abstract requirements specification: A new approach and its application. IEEE Trans. on Software Engr. 9(5) (1983)
10. Heninger, K.: Specifying software requirements for complex systems: New techniques and their application. IEEE Trans. on Software Engr, 6(1) (1980) 2-13
11. Holloway, M., Butler, R.: Impediments to industrial use of formal methods. IEEE Computer, 29(4) (1996) 25-26
12. Houstan, I., King, S.: CICS project report: Experiences and results from the use of Z in IBM. VDM '91. Formal Software Development Methods, Vol. 1: Conference Contribution. Lecture Notes in Computer Science, 552 Springer Verlag (1991) 588-596
13. iLogix, Inc.: http://www.ilogix.com/company/success.htm (1997)
14. Knight, J., DeJong, C., Gibble, M., Nakano, L.: Why are formal methods not used more widely? NASA Langley Formal Methods Workshop, Hampton, VA (1997)
15. Lutz, R., Ampo, Y.: Experience report: Using formal methods For requirements analysis of critical spacecraft software. 19th Annual Software Engineering Workshop, NASA Goddard Space Flight Center (1994) 231-248
16. Lyu, M. Handbook of Software Reliability Engineering, IEEE Computer Society Press, Los Alamitos, CA (1995)
17. Modarres, M.: What Every engineer should know about reliability and risk analysis. Marcel Dekker, New York, NY (1993)
18. Nobe, C., Warner, W.: Lessons learned from a trial application of requirements modeling using statecharts. Second International Conference on Requirements Engineering, IEEE Computer Society Press, Los Alamitos, CA (1996) 86-93
19. Rushby, J.: Formal methods and the certification of critical systems. Technical Report CSL-93-7, SRI International, Menlo Park, CA (1993)
20. Saaltink, M., Meisels, I.: The Z/EVES Reference Manual. Technical Report TR-97-5493, ORA Inc., Toronto, Canada (1997)
21. Singpurwalla, N.: The failure rate of software: does it exist? IEEE Trans. on Reliability, 44(3) (1995) 463 - 469

22. Sullivan, K., Knight, J.: Experience assessing an architectural approach to large-scale systematic reuse. International Conference on Software Engineering, IEEE Computer Society Press, Los Alamitos, CA (1997) 220 - 229
23. Vesely, W., Goldberg, F., Roberts, N., Haasl, F.: Fault Tree Handbook, NUREG-0492, U.S. Nuclear Regulatory Commission, Washington, DC (1981)

On the Need for *Practical* Formal Methods*

Constance Heitmeyer

Naval Research Laboratory, Code 5546, Washington, DC 20375, USA

Abstract. A controversial issue in the formal methods community is the degree to which mathematical sophistication and theorem proving skills should be needed to apply a formal method. A fundamental assumption of this paper is that formal methods research has produced several classes of analysis that can prove useful in software development. However, to be useful to software practitioners, most of whom lack advanced mathematical training and theorem proving skills, current formal methods need a number of additional attributes, including more user-friendly notations, completely automatic (i.e., pushbutton) analysis, and useful, easy to understand feedback. Moreover, formal methods need to be integrated into a standard development process. I discuss additional research *and* engineering that is needed to make the current set of formal methods more practical. To illustrate the ideas, I present several examples, many taken from the SCR (Software Cost Reduction) requirements method, a formal method that software developers can apply without theorem proving skills, knowledge of temporal and higher order logics, or consultation with formal methods experts.

1 Formal Methods in Practice: Current Status

During the last decade, researchers have proposed numerous formal methods, such as model checkers [6] and mechanical theorem provers [21], for developing computer systems. One area in which formal methods have had a major impact is hardware design. Not only are companies such as Intel beginning to use model checking, along with simulation, as a standard technique for detecting errors in hardware designs, in addition, some companies are developing their own in-house model checkers. Moreover, a number of model checkers customized for hardware design have become available commercially [17].

Although some limited progress has been made in applying formal methods to software, the use of formal methods in practical software development is rare. A significant barrier is the widespread perception among software developers that formal notations and formal analysis techniques are difficult to understand and apply. Moreover, software developers often express serious doubts about the scalability and cost-effectiveness of formal methods.

Another reason why formal methods have had minimal impact is the absence in practical software development of two features common in hardware design environments. First, hardware designers routinely use one of a small group of

---

* This work was supported by the Office of Naval Research and SPAWAR.

languages, e.g., Verilog or VHDL, to specify their designs. In contrast, precise specification and design languages are rarely used in software development.

Second, integrating a formal method, such as a model checker, into a hardware design process is relatively easy because other tools, such as simulators and code synthesis tools, are already a standard part of the design process at many hardware companies. In contrast, in software development, no standard software development environments exist. (Although "object-oriented design" has gained considerable popularity in recent years, this process is still largely informal and what "object-oriented design" means varies considerably from one site to the next.) Moreover, while a number of commercial Computer-Aided Software Engineering (CASE) tools have become available in recent years, few software developers are actually using the tools [18].

This paper distinguishes light-weight formal methods from heavy-duty methods and then describes two broad classes of problems in which formal methods have been useful. It concludes by proposing a number of guidelines for making formal methods more useful in practice.

2 Light-Weight vs. Heavy-Duty Techniques

A formal analysis technique may be classified as either "light-weight" or "heavy-duty". The user of a light-weight technique does not require advanced mathematical training and theorem proving skills. One example of a light-weight technique is an automated consistency checker, which checks a specification for syntax and type errors, missing cases, instances of nondeterminism, and circular definitions (see, e.g., [11, 10]). In contrast, the user of a heavy-duty technique must be mathematically mature, a person skilled in the formulation of formal arguments and clever proof strategies. The most common heavy-weight techniques are mechanical theorem provers, such as PVS [21] and ACL2 [16]. Other techniques which may be classified as heavy-duty are those that automatically generate state invariants from specifications (e.g., see [15, 3]). Such state invariants can be presented to system users for validation or, alternately, can be used as auxiliary invariants in proving new properties from the specifications.

Model checkers fall somewhere between light-weight and heavy-duty techniques. Once the user has defined the state machine model and the property of interest, the model checker determines automatically whether the property is satisfied. One problem with most current model checkers is that the languages available for representing the state machine model and the properties of interest can be difficult to learn. Usually, model checkers require the representation of a property is some form of temporal logic. Expressing certain properties in temporal logic is complex and error-prone, not only for practitioners but for formal methods experts as well. An additional problem with many current model checkers is that sometimes the counterexample produced by model checking is thousands of states long and extremely difficult to understand (see, e.g., [25]).

Fortunately, many of the current problems with model checkers are not inherent in the technology but simply limitations of the current implementations.

In Section 4, I suggest some improvements to model checkers, which should make them easier to use, more automatic, and hence more light-weight. I also suggest how automated, mathematically sound abstraction methods, a topic of current research, can help make model checking more accessible to practitioners.

3 Where Have Formal Methods Been Applied?

We can identify two large classes of problems where formal methods have had utility. First, formal methods have been used to formalize, debug, and prove the correctness of algorithms and protocols. Using formal methods to tackle such problems has proven useful in both hardware and software applications: once its correctness has been shown formally, the algorithm (or protocol) may be used with high confidence in many applications. While model checking has been used to analyze various protocols, such as cache coherence protocols and security protocols (see, e.g., [20]), the deep mathematical reasoning needed to verify most algorithms usually requires a heavy-duty theorem prover.

For example, recently, a microprocessor manufacturer, Advanced Micro Devices (AMD), developed a new algorithm for floating point division on the $AMD_5 86$, a new Pentium-class microprocessor. To increase confidence in the algorithm's correctness, AMD hired a team of formal methods experts to verify the $AMD_5 86$ microcode that implemented floating point division. The experts used ACL2, an extended version of the Boyer-Moore theorem prover, to formalize the algorithm and to check a relatively deep mathematical proof [16]. After nine weeks, the verification effort was successfully completed. Hiring the formal methods experts to construct the formal proof and mechanically check it using ACL2 was a relatively cheap means for AMD to gain confidence in the $AMD_5 86$ microcode for floating point division. Moreover, AMD can confidently reuse the algorithm in future microprocessors.

In a second class of problems, formal methods are used to demonstrate that a specification of a system (or system part) satisfies certain properties, or that a detailed description, such as a design or an implementation, of a system satisfies a given specification. In this latter case, the theorems proven have been referred to as "junk" theorems, since unlike theorems proven about algorithms and protocols, these theorems are not usually of interest outside the system that is being analyzed.

Experience applying formal methods to the requirements specifications of TCAS II [10], a collision avoidance system for commercial aircraft, and WCP [14], a safety-critical component of a U.S. military system, illustrates this second class of problems. In each case, the specification was analyzed for selected properties using both consistency checking and model checking. In both cases, the analysis exposed significant errors [10, 1, 14]. The properties analyzed included both application-independent properties (e.g., a given function is total) and application-dependent properties. In each case, the properties and their proofs were of little interest outside the analyzed systems.

The analysis of such specifications does not normally require deep reasoning. Hence, more light-weight methods, such as consistency checking and model checking, are more cost-effective than heavy-duty theorem proving. Yet, the analyses performed were often quite complex, especially for model checking, due to the enormous size of the state space that needed to be analyzed. Further, the presence in the specifications of logical expressions containing a mixture of boolean, enumerated types, integers, and reals as well as arithmetic and functions made automated consistency checking difficult, especially in the TCAS II specification. Two potential solutions to these problems, both of which are topics of current research, are automated abstraction methods and more powerful decision procedures.

4 Guidelines for Producing a Practical Formal Method

Presented below are a number of guidelines for making formal methods more practical. The objective of these guidelines is to make formal methods light-weight and thus more accessible to software developers. To a large extent, applying these guidelines is simply good engineering practice. However, in other cases, additional research is needed.

4.1 Minimize Effort and Expertise Needed to Apply the Method

To be useful in practice, formal methods must be convenient and easy to use. Most current software developers are reluctant to use current formal methods because they find the learning curve too steep and the effort required to apply a formal method too great. In many cases, deciding not to use a formal method is rational. The time and effort required to learn about and apply a formal method may not be worth the information and insight provided by the method; in some cases, the effort could be better spent applying another method, such as simulation. Suggested below are three ways in which the difficulty of learning and applying a formal method can be reduced.

Offer a language that software developers find easy to use and easy to understand. The specification language must be "natural"; to the extent feasible, a language syntax and semantics familiar to the software practitioner should be supported. The language must also have an explicitly defined formal semantics and it should scale. Specifications in this language should be automatically translated into the language of a model checker or even a mechanical theorem prover.

Our group and others (see, e.g., [14, 22, 7]) have had moderate success with a tabular notation for representing the required system behavior. Underlying this notation is a formal state-machine semantics [11]. Others, such as Heimdahl and Leveson [10], have proposed a hybrid notation, inspired by Statecharts [9], that combines tables and graphics; this notation also has a state-machine semantics.

Specifications based on tables are easy to understand and easy for software practitioners to produce. In addition, tables provide a precise, unambiguous basis for communication among practitioners. They also provide a natural organization which permits independent construction, review, modification, and analysis of smaller parts of a large specification. Finally, tabular notations scale. Evidence of the scalability of tabular specifications has been shown by Lockheed engineers, who used a tabular notation to specify the complete requirements of the C-130J Flight Program, a program containing over 230K lines of Ada code [8].

In addition to tabular notations, other user-friendly notations should also be explored. For example, one group is developing a set of tools which analyze message sequence charts, a notation commonly used in communication protocols [24]. Others are exploring a front-end for model checking based on the graphical notation Statecharts.

Make Formal Analysis as Automatic as Possible. To the extent feasible, analysis should be "pushbutton". One formal technique that is already largely pushbutton is automated consistency checking. To achieve this automation, consistency checking is implemented by efficient decision procedures, such as semantic tableaux [11] and BDDs (Binary Decision Diagrams) [10]. Moreover, a recent paper [23] shows how the Stanford Validity Checker (SVC), which uses a decision procedure for a subset of first-order logic with linear arithmetic, can check the validity of expressions containing linear arithmetic, inequalities, and uninterpreted function symbols.

More progress is needed, however. Specifications of many safety-critical applications contain logical expressions that mix booleans, enumerated types, integers, and reals. How to analyze such mixed expressions efficiently is an unsolved problem. New research is needed that shows how various decision procedures, such as term rewriting, BDDs, and constraint solvers, can be combined to check the validity of such expressions.

Another area where more automation is needed is model checking. Before practical software specifications can be model checked efficiently, the *state explosion* problem must be addressed—i.e., the size of the state space to be analyzed must be reduced. An effective way to reduce state explosion is to apply abstraction. Unfortunately, the most common approach is to develop the abstraction in ad hoc ways—the correspondence between the abstraction and the original specification is based on informal, intuitive arguments. Needed are mathematically sound abstractions that can be constructed automatically. Recent progress in automatically constructing sound abstractions has been reported in [4, 5].

Provide Good Feedback. When formal analysis exposes an error, the user should be provided with easy-to-understand feedback useful in correcting the error. Techniques for achieving this in consistency checking already exist (see, e.g., [12, 23]). As noted above, counterexamples produced by model checkers require improvement. One promising approach, already common in hardware design, uses a simulator to demonstrate and validate the counterexample.

4.2 Provide a Suite of Analysis Tools

Because different tools detect different classes of errors, users should have available an entire suite of tools. This suite may include a consistency checker, a simulator, a model checker, as well as a mechanical theorem prover [13]. The tools should be carefully integrated to work together. This is already happening in hardware design, where simulators, model checkers, equivalence checkers, and code synthesis tools are being used in complementary ways; moreover, some progress has been made in making tools, such as model checkers and simulators, work together [17]. One benefit of having a suite of tools is that properties that have been shown to hold using one tool may simplify the analysis performed with a second tool. For example, validating that each function in a specification is total can simplify subsequent verification using a mechanical prover.

4.3 Integrate the Method into the User's Development Process

To the extent feasible, formal methods should be integrated into the existing user design process. Techniques for exploiting formal methods in object-oriented software design and in software development processes which use semiformal languages, such as Statecharts, should also be explored. How formal methods can be integrated into the user's design process should be described explicitly.

4.4 Provide a Powerful, Customizable Simulation Capability

Many formal methods researchers underestimate the value of simulation in exposing defects in specifications. By symbolically executing the system based on the formal specification, the user can ensure that the behavior specified satisfies his intent. Thus, unlike consistency checking, model checking, and mechanical theorem proving, which formally check the specification for properties of interest, simulation provides a means of validating a specification. In running scenarios through the simulator, the user can also use the simulator to check properties of interest. Another use of simulation is in conjunction with model checking; as suggested above, simulation can be used to demonstrate and validate counterexamples obtained from a model checker.

One important approach to selling formal methods is to build customized simulator front-ends, tailored to particular application domains. For example, we have developed a customized simulator front-end for pilots to use in evaluating an attack aircraft specification. Rather than clicking on monitored variable names, entering values for them, and seeing the results of simulation presented as variable values, a pilot clicks on visual representations of cockpit controls and sees results presented on a simulated cockpit display. This front-end allows the pilot to move out of the world of the specification and into the world of attack aircraft, where he is the expert. Such an interface facilitates evaluation of the specification. Using a commercially available GUI (Graphical User Interface) Builder, one can construct a fancy simulator front-end in a few days.

5 More "Usable" Mechanical Theorem Provers

Although mechanical theorem provers have been used by researchers to verify various algorithms and protocols, they are rarely used in practical software development. For provers to be used more widely, a number of barriers need to be overcome. First, the specification languages provided by the provers must be more natural. Second, the reasoning steps supported by a prover should be closer to the steps produced in a hand proof; current provers support reasoning steps that are at too low and detailed a level. One approach to this problem is to build a prover front-end that is designed to support specification and proofs of a special class of mathematical models. An example of such a front-end is TAME, a "natural" user interface to PVS that is designed to specify and prove properties about automata models [2]. Although using a mechanical provers will still require mathematical maturity and theorem proving skills, making the prover more "natural" and convenient to use should encourage more widespread usage.

6 Conclusions

It is my belief that software practitioners who are not formal methods experts can benefit from formal methods research. However, to do so, they need formal methods that are user-friendly, robust, and powerful. To enjoy the benefits of formal methods, a user does not need to be mathematically sophisticated nor need he be capable of proving deep theorems. One analogy that I heard at CAV '98 is that beautiful music can come from either a good violin or a highly talented violinist. Light-weight techniques offer software developers good violins. A user need not be a talented violinist to benefit. This is in contrast to heavy-duty techniques where the user needs to be a good violinist.

Formal methods research has already produced a significant body of theory. Moreover, some promising research is currently in progress in automated abstraction and automatic generation of invariants (e.g., [19, 4, 15, 5]). However, to make formal methods practical, good engineering is needed. The user of formal methods should not need to communicate the required system behavior in some arcane language nor to decipher the meaning of obscure feedback from an analysis tool. What a practical formal method should do is liberate the user to tackle the hard problems that humans are good at solving, e.g.,

- What exactly is the required system behavior?
- What are the critical system properties?
- How can I make the specification easy for others to understand?
- What are the likely changes to the specification and how can I organize the specification to facilitate those changes?
- What should the missing behavior be? How can this nondeterminism be eliminated? How do I change the specification to avoid this property violation?

References

1. R. J. Anderson et al. "Model checking large software specifications." *Proc. 4th ACM SIGSOFT Symp. Foundations of Software Eng.*, October 1996.

2. M. Archer, C. Heitmeyer, and S. Sims. "TAME: A PVS Interface to Simplify Proofs for Automata Models." *Proc. User Interfaces for Theorem Provers 1998 (UITP 98)*, Eindhoven, Netherlands, July 13-15, 1998.

3. S. Bensalem, Y. Lakhnech, and Hassen Saïdi. "Powerful techniques for the automatic generation of invariants." *Proc. 8th Intern. Conf. on Computer-Aided Verification, CAV '96*, New Brunswick, NJ, July 1996.

4. S. Bensalem, Y. Lakhnech, and S. Owre. "Computing abstractions of infinite state systems compositionally and automatically." *Proc. 10th Intern. Conf. on Computer-Aided Verification, CAV '98*, Vancouver, BC, Canada, June-July 1998.

5. R. Bharadwaj and C. Heitmeyer. "Model checking complete requirements specifications using abstraction." *Automated Software Eng. Journal* (to appear).

6. E. M. Clarke, E. A. Emerson and A. P. Sistla. "Automatic verification of finite-state concurrent systems using temporal logic specifications." *ACM Transactions on Programming Languages and Systems* 8(2):244–263, 1986.

7. S. Easterbrook and J. Callahan. "Formal methods for verification and validation of partial specifications: A case study." *Journal of Systems and Software*, 1997.

8. S. Faulk et al. "Experience applying the CoRE method to the Lockheed C-130J." *Proc. 9th Annual Computer Assurance Conf. (COMPASS '94)*, June 1994.

9. D. Harel. "Statecharts: a visual formalism for complex systems." *Science of Computer Programming* 8(1): 231–274, Jan. 1987.

10. M. P. E. Heimdahl and N. Leveson. "Completeness and consistency analysis in hierarchical state-based requirements." *IEEE Trans. on Software Eng.* SE-22(6), pp. 363-377, Jun. 1996.

11. C. Heitmeyer, R. Jeffords, and B. Labaw. "Automated consistency checking of requirements specifications." *ACM Trans. Software Eng. and Method.* 5(3), 1996.

12. C. Heitmeyer, J. Kirby, and B. Labaw. "Tools for formal specification, verification, and validation of requirements." *Proc. 12th Annual Conf. on Computer Assurance (COMPASS '97)*, June 1997.

13. C. Heitmeyer, J. Kirby, B. Labaw, and R. Bharadwaj. "SCR*: A Toolset for specifying and analyzing software requirements." *Proc. 10th Intern. Conf. on Computer-Aided Verification, CAV '98*, Vancouver, BC, Canada, June-July 1998.

14. C. Heitmeyer, J. Kirby, and B. Labaw. "Applying the SCR requirements method to a weapons control panel: An experience report." *Proc. 2nd Workshop on Formal Methods in Software Practice (FMSP'98)*, St. Petersburg, FL, March 1998.

15. R. Jeffords and C. Heitmeyer. "Automatic generation of state invariants from requirements specifications." *Proc. 6th ACM SIGSOFT Symposium Foundations of Software Eng.*, November 1998 (accepted for publication).

16. M. Kaufmann and J S. Moore. ACL2: An industrial strength theorem prover for a logic based on common Lisp. *IEEE Trans. on Software Eng.* SE-23(4), Apr. 1997.

17. R. Kurshan. Formal verification in a commercial setting. *Proc. Design Automation Conference*, June 1997.

18. D. Lending and N. L. Chervany. "CASE tools: Understanding the reasons for non-use," *ACM Computer Personnel* 19(2), Apr. 1998.

19. C. Loiseaux, S. Graf, J. Sifakis, A. Bouajjani, and S. Bensalem. "Property preserving abstractions for the verification of concurrent systems." *Formal Methods in System Design* 6, 1–35, 1995.

20. G. Lowe. "Breaking and fixing the Needham-Schroeder Public-Key Protocol using FDR." In *Tools and Algorithms for the Construction of Systems*, Margaria and Steffen, eds., LNCS 1055, Springer-Verlag, 147-166, 1996.

21. Sam Owre, John Rushby, Natarajan Shankar, Friedrich von Henke. "Formal verification for fault-tolerant architectures: Prolegomena to the design of PVS." *IEEE Transactions on Software Engineering*, vol. 21, no. 2, pp. 107-125, Feb. 1995.

22. S. Miller. "Specifying the mode logic of a flight guidance system in CoRE and SCR." *Proc. 2nd Workshop on Formal Methods in Software Practice (FMSP'98)*, St. Petersburg, FL, March 1998.

23. D. Y. W. Park et al. "Checking properties of safety-critical specifications using efficient decision procedures." *Proc. 2nd Workshop on Formal Methods in Software Practice (FMSP'98)*, St. Petersburg, FL, March 1998.

24. D. Peled. "A toolset for message sequence charts." *Proc. 10th Intern. Conf. on Computer-Aided Verification, CAV '98*, Vancouver, BC, Canada, June-July 1998.

25. S. T. Probst. "Chemical process safety and operability analysis using symbolic model checking." PhD thesis, Carnegie-Mellon Univ., Pittsburgh, PA, 1996.

A General Framework for the Composition of Timed Systems *
Extended Abstract

Joseph Sifakis

Verimag
2, Rue Vignate
38610 Gières, France

It is recognized that there is no general methodology for writing correct timed specifications. Timed systems differ from untimed systems in that their runs are composed of alternating discrete transitions and time steps. When describing systems as the parallel composition of independent timed components, it is not in general easy to preserve this property, given that time progress must be synchronous in all components. We have shown in previous papers, that a source of problems is the fact that usually composition of timed formalisms, such as process algebras or timed automata, is defined by composing independently time steps and discrete (untimed) transitions.

We propose here a high level algebraic framework for the composition of timed systems that relies on the following basic ideas:

- The first idea is to use models where time progress conditions are associated with transitions. A class of timed automata, called Timed Automata with Deadlines (TAD), has been defined whose transitions have guards and resets as usually but also *deadlines* which are conditions that characterize states at which transitions become *urgent*. Deadlines are taken to imply the corresponding guards, which guarantees *time reactivity*: time progress cannot stop unless some action is enabled and urgent.
- The second idea is that timed systems are obtained by composition of *timed actions*. Timed actions are TAD consisting of one transition i.e., a pair of discrete states, a guard, a deadline and a reset set. The operators are timed extensions of the usual choice and parallel composition operators for untimed systems. However, composition rules are defined on timed actions, by composing guards and deadlines of the timed actions of the components and not in terms of labeled transition systems, as usually. This allows in particular, the definition of composition rules that preserve two essential properties: time reactivity and deadlockfreedom. The latter means that if some initial action of a component is possible from a state then some initial action of the product system is possible from this state. Time reactivity is guaranteed by construction.

---

* joint work with S. Bornot

We show that for timed systems, choice and parallel composition operators admit different kinds of extensions.

We define priority choice operators, parameterized by a priority order between actions. The priority order relates actions by means of integers representing degrees of priority. If some action a_1 has lower priority than another action a_2 by k then in the priority choice, action a_1 cannot be enabled if a_2 will be enabled within k time units. We give sufficient conditions for priority orders that guarantee deadlockfreedom preservation of the corresponding priority choice operators.

We define parallel composition operators by means of general synchronization and interleaving rules. As for untimed systems, the behavior of the product can be expressed as the choice between synchronizing and interleaving components by means of an expansion theorem. The main results are the following:

- Parallel composition operators preserve both deadlockfreedom and maximal progress. This is achieved by taking infinite priority of synchronization actions over interleaving actions that is, in the expansion theorem the usual non deterministic choice operator is replaced by priority choice.
- We apply for timed actions synchronization, the principle of composing actions by means of synchronization functions: the guards and the deadlines of synchronization actions are obtained by composing the guards and the deadlines of the synchronizing actions. We show that apart from conjunctive synchronization, other synchronization modes of practical interest can be defined, such as synchronization with waiting and synchronization with anticipation. These two synchronization modes correspond to powerful and "flexible" types of coordination.
- We show that the general framework can be drastically simplified by considering systems composed of timed actions with three types of urgency: lazy, delayable and eager. The rules for the composition of guards in the general model can be extended to rules on the corresponding types.

The proposed framework provides a unified view of the existing executable timed formalisms, such as timed automata, process algebras and the various timed extensions of Petri nets widely used for the specification of concurrent timed systems.

Operational and Logical Semantics for Polling Real-Time Systems

Henning Dierks[2,*], Ansgar Fehnker[1,**], Angelika Mader[1,***], and Frits Vaandrager[1]

[1] Computing Science Institute, University of Nijmegen, P.O. Box 9010, 6500 GL Nijmegen, the Netherlands
[2] University of Oldenburg, Germany

Abstract. PLC-Automata are a class of real-time automata suitable to describe the behavior of polling real-time systems. PLC-Automata can be compiled to source code for PLCs, a hardware widely used in industry to control processes. Also, PLC-Automata have been equipped with a logical and operational semantics, using Duration Calculus (DC) and Timed Automata (TA), respectively.

The three main results of this paper are: (1) A simplified operational semantics. (2) A minor extension of the logical semantics, and a proof that this semantics is *complete* relative to our operational semantics. This means that if an observable satisfies all formulas of the DC semantics, then it can also be generated by the TA semantics. (3) A proof that the logical semantics is *sound* relative to our operational semantics. This means that each observable that is accepted by the TA semantics constitutes a model for all formulas of the DC semantics.

1 Introduction

Programmable Logic Controllers (PLCs) are widely used in industry to control real-time embedded applications such as railway crossings, elevators, and production lines. PLCs are hardware devices that operate according to the simple but powerful architectural model of *polling real-time systems*. A polling real-time system behaves in cycles that can be split into three parts: the input values are polled, a new local state and output values are computed from the inputs and the old local state, and finally the new output values are written to the output ports. Depending for instance on the length of the computation, the duration of a cycle may vary, but some upper bound ϵ on the cycle time is assumed to be available.

* Supported by the German Ministry for Education and Research (BMBF), project UniForM, grant No. FKZ 01 IS 521 B3
** Research supported by Netherlands Organization for Scientific Research (NWO) under contract SION 612-14-004
*** Supported by the HCM Network EXPRESS and the Deutsche Akademischer Austauschdienst

In this paper we study the operational and denotational semantics of polling real-time systems, i.e., the relationships between the input and output signals of such systems that are induced when a program is executed in real-time. Our work builds on recent work within the UniForM-project [11] on PLC-Automata [5–7, 9]. PLC-Automata, basically an extension of classical Moore machines [10], can be viewed as a simple programming language for PLCs. In [5], a compilation scheme is given that generates runnable PLC-code for any given PLC-Automaton. Moreover, a logical (denotational) and an operational semantics of PLC-Automata are presented employing Duration Calculus (DC) [15, 14] and Timed Automata (TA) [1], respectively. However, in [5] the relationships between these semantics are not further investigated.

The three main results established in this paper are:

1. A simplified operational semantics for PLC-Automata based on Timed Automata.
2. A minor extension of the logical semantics with some additional formulas, and a proof that this (restricted) semantics is *complete* relative to our operational semantics. This means that if an observable satisfies all formulas of the DC semantics, then it can also be generated by the TA semantics.
3. A proof that the logical semantics is *sound* relative to our operational semantics. This means that each observable that is accepted by the TA semantics constitutes a model for all formulas of the (extended) DC semantics.

An advantage of our operational semantics is that it is very intuitive, and provides a simple explanation of what happens when a PLC-Automaton runs on PLC hardware. Clearly, the 8 rules of the operational semantics are easier to understand than the 26 formulas of the DC semantics, especially for readers who are not experts in duration calculus. The operational semantics can also serve as a basis for automatic verification, using tools for timed automata such as KRONOS [4] and UPPAAL [3]. Our timed automata semantics uses 3 clock variables, which makes it more tractable for such tools than the semantics of [5] which requires 2 clocks plus one clock for each input value.

The logical semantics also has several advantages. Rather than modelling the internal state variables and hidden events of PLC hardware, it describes the allowed *observable* behaviour on the input and output ports. Duration Calculus, an interval temporal logic for real-time, constitutes a very powerful and abstract specification language for polling real-time systems. Via the DC semantics, proving that a PLC-Automaton $\mathcal{A}$ satisfies a DC specification *SPEC* reduces to proving that the duration calculus semantics $[\mathcal{A}]_{DC}$ logically implies *SPEC*. For this task all the proof rules and logical machinery of DC can be used. In fact, in [6] an algorithm is presented that synthesizes a PLC-Automaton from an (almost) arbitrary set of *DC Implementables*, a subset of the Duration Calculus that has been introduced in [13] as a stepping stone for specifying distributed real-time systems. In [13] a fully developed theory can be found how Implementables can be obtained from general DC formulas. Hence, the synthesis algorithm provides a powerful means to design correct systems starting from specifications.

The fact that the TA and DC semantics are so different makes the proof of their equivalence interesting but also quite involved. In order to get the completeness result we had to extend the original DC semantics of [5] with 9 additional formulas of two lines each. These additional formulas, which express the presence of certain causalities between events, are not required for the correctness proof of the synthesis algorithm. This indicates that they may not be so important in applications. Nevertheless, we believe that the formulas do express fundamental properties of polling real-time systems and it is not so difficult to come up with an example of a situation in which the additional laws *are* used.

In this paper we only discuss the semantics of the simple PLC-Automata introduced in [5]. Meanwhile, PLC-Automata have been extended with a state charts like concept of hierarchy, in order allow for their use in the specification of complex systems [9]. We claim that it is possible to generalize the results of this paper to this larger class of hierarchical PLC-Automata. An interesting topic for future research is to give a low level operational semantics of PLCs, including hybrid aspects, clock drift, etc, and to prove that this low level semantics is a refinement of the semantics presented in this paper. Such a result would further increase confidence in the correctness of our semantic model.

2   PLC-Automata

In the UniForM-project [11] an automaton-like notion — called PLC-Automata — of polling real-time systems has been developed to enable formal verification of PLC-programs. Basically, Programmable Logic Controllers (PLCs), the hardware aim of the project, are just simple computers with a special real-time operating system. They have features for making the design of time- and safety-critical systems easier:

- PLCs have input and output channels where sensors and actuators, resp., can be plugged in.
- They behave in a cyclic manner where every cycle consists of three phases:
  - Poll all inputs and store the read values.
  - Compute the new values for the outputs.
  - Update all outputs.
- There is an upper time bound for a cycle, which depends on the program and on the number of inputs and outputs, that can be used to calculate an upper time bound for the reaction time.
- Convenient standardized libraries are given to simplify the handling of time.

The following formal definition of a PLC-Automaton incorporates the upper time bound for a polling cycle and the possibility of delay reactions of the system depending on state and input.

Definition 1. *A* PLC-Automaton *is a tuple* $\mathcal{A} = (Q, \Sigma, \delta, q_0, \varepsilon, S_t, S_e, \Omega, \omega)$, *where*

- Q *is a nonempty, finite set of* states,

- Σ *is a nonempty, finite set of* inputs,
- δ *is a function of type* $Q \times \Sigma \longrightarrow Q$ *(the* transition function*)*,
- $q_0 \in Q$ *is the* initial state,
- $\varepsilon \in \mathbb{R}_{>0}$ *is the* upper bound *for a cycle,*
- S_t *is a function of type* $Q \longrightarrow \mathbb{R}_{\geq 0}$ *that tells for each state q how long the inputs contained in $S_e(q)$ should be ignored (the* delay time*),*
- S_e *is a function of type* $Q \longrightarrow 2^{\Sigma}$ *that gives for each state q the set of* delayed inputs, *i.e., inputs that cause no state transition during the first $S_t(q)$ time units after arrival in q,*
- Ω *is a nonempty, finite set of* outputs,
- ω *is a function of type* $Q \longrightarrow \Omega$ *(the* output function*)*

We require that the two following conditions hold, for all $q \in Q$ and $a \in \Sigma$,

$$S_t(q) > 0 \wedge a \notin S_e(q) \Longrightarrow \delta(q,a) \neq q \tag{1}$$
$$S_t(q) > 0 \Longrightarrow S_t(q) > \varepsilon \tag{2}$$

Restriction (1) is technical and needed to ensure the correctness of the PLC-source-code representing a PLC-Automaton w.r.t. the semantics given in [5]. It can be trivially met by adding, for each q, all actions a with $\delta(q,a) = q$ to the set $S_e(q)$. Restriction (2) says that delay times are either 0 or larger than the cycle upper bound time ϵ.

In the picture an example of a PLC-Automaton is given. A box representing a state (e.g. q') is annotated with the output (e.g. $\omega(q') = T$) in the upper part of the box and the pair of the delay time and the delay set in the lower part of the box (e.g. $S_t(q') = 5$, $S_e(q') = \{0,1\}$). The system starts in state q with output N and remains in this state as long as the polled input is 0. The first time the polled input is not 0 the system changes state according

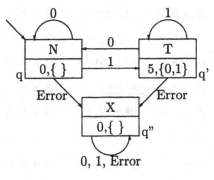

to the transition function. If, following a 1-input, state q' is entered then the system will start a timer. Now the following cases are possible.

- The polled input is 0. In this case the system checks the timer. Only if the timer says that $S_t(q') = 5$ time units are over, the system takes the 0-transition back to state q. Otherwise the system stays in q'.
- The polled input is 1. In this case the system remains in q' independently from the status of the timer due to the fact that the 1-transition leads to q' again.
- The polled input is *Error*. In this case the system takes the *Error*-transition independently from the status of the timer because $Error \notin S_e(q')$.

We would like to stress that the range of applicability of PLC-Automata is much wider than just PLCs. In fact, PLC-Automata are an abstract representation of a machine that periodically polls inputs and has the possibility of measuring time.

3   The Timed Automaton Semantics of PLC-Automata

In this section we give an operational semantics of PLC-automata in terms of timed automata. For the definition of timed automata the reader is referred to [12, 8]. We first present the components of the timed automaton $\mathcal{T}(\mathcal{A})$ that is associated to a given PLC-Automaton $\mathcal{A}$, and later give some intuition.

Each location[1] of $\mathcal{T}(\mathcal{A})$ is a 4-tuple (i, a, b, q), where $i \in \{0, 1, 2, 3\}$ describes the internal status of the PLC ("program counter"), $a \in \Sigma$ contains the current input, $b \in \Sigma$ contains the last input that was polled, and $q \in Q$ is the current state of the PLC-Automaton. There are three clocks in use: x measures the time that the latest input is stable, y measures the time spent in the current state, and z measures the time elapsed in the current cycle. The transitions of the timed automaton are defined in Table 1.

(i, a, b, q)	$\xrightarrow{c, \text{true}, \{z\}}$	(i, c, b, q)	if $c \neq a$	(ta-1)
$(0, a, b, q)$	$\xrightarrow{\text{poll}, 0 < z \wedge 0 < z, \emptyset}$	$(1, a, a, q)$		(ta-2)
$(1, a, b, q)$	$\xrightarrow{\text{test}, y \leq S_t(q), \emptyset}$	$(2, a, b, q)$	if $S_t(q) > 0 \wedge b \in S_e(q)$	(ta-3)
$(1, a, b, q)$	$\xrightarrow{\text{test}, y > S_t(q), \emptyset}$	$(3, a, b, q)$	if $S_t(q) > 0 \wedge b \in S_e(q)$	(ta-4)
$(1, a, b, q)$	$\xrightarrow{\text{test}, \text{true}, \emptyset}$	$(3, a, b, q)$	if $S_t(q) = 0 \vee b \notin S_e(q)$	(ta-5)
$(2, a, b, q)$	$\xrightarrow{\text{tick}, \text{true}, \{z\}}$	$(0, a, b, q)$		(ta-6)
$(3, a, b, q)$	$\xrightarrow{\text{tick}, \text{true}, \{z\}}$	$(0, a, b, q)$	if $q = \delta(q, b)$	(ta-7)
$(3, a, b, q)$	$\xrightarrow{\text{tick}, \text{true}, \{y, z\}}$	$(0, a, b, \delta(q, b))$	if $q \neq \delta(q, b)$	(ta-8)

Table 1: Transitions of timed automaton $\mathcal{T}(\mathcal{A})$

We now give some intuition about our semantics. Within the timed automaton we model the cyclic behaviour of a polling system. The events within one cycle are: polling input, testing whether input has to be ignored, producing new output (if necessary), and ending the cycle. The "program counter" models the phases of a cycle. The picture below shows how these events change the values of the program counter.

---

[1] Note that "locations" refer to the timed automaton and "states" to the PLC-Automaton.

- "0" denotes the first part of the cycle. The input has not yet been polled.
- "1" denotes that the polling has happened in the current cycle. The test whether to react has not been performed yet.
- "2" denotes that polling and testing have happened. The system decided to ignore the input.
- "3" denotes that polling and testing have happened. The system decided to react to the input.

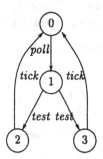

A clock z is introduced within the timed automaton to measure the time that has elapsed within the current cycle. This clock is not allowed to go above the time upper bound ε and is reset at the end of each cycle.

In the first phase of a cycle incoming input is polled. In the timed automaton model there are no continuous variables available by which we can model continuous input. We have to restrict to a finite set Σ of inputs, and introduce for each $a \in \Sigma$ a transition label a that models the discrete, instantaneous event which occurs whenever the input signal changes value and becomes a. In principle, the input signal may change value at any time, not only during the first cycle phase. The current value of the input is recorded in the second component of a location of the timed automaton. Within our semantic model the occurrence of input events is described by transition (ta-1) (see Table 1).

The timed automaton model allows inputs that last only for one point of time, i.e., it is not required that time passes in between input events. However, it is of course realistic to assume that polling input takes some (small) amount of time, and that an input can only be polled if persists for some positive amount of time. Technically, we require that input may only be polled, if it has remained unchanged throughout a left-open interval. In the semantics we model this by a clock x that is reset whenever an input event occurs. Polling is only allowed if x is non-zero (see transition (ta-2)). The polled input is recorded in the third component of a location of $\mathcal{T}(\mathcal{A})$.

Next, we have to deal with input delay. Whether input has to be ignored or not depends on the state of the PLC-automaton and on the time during which the system has been in this state. The state of the PLC-automaton is recorded in the fourth component of the locations of $\mathcal{T}(\mathcal{A})$. Furthermore, we introduce a clock y that measures how long the current state is valid. Transitions (ta-3), (ta-4) and (ta-5) describe the cases that the *test*-event has to distinguish: if a state requires no delay or if it requires delay but the delay time is over, then input is not ignored and in the subsequent location the program counter has value 3; otherwise the program counter is assigned value 2.

A cycle ends with an event *tick* (see (ta-6), (ta-7), (ta-8)). If the program counter has value 3 then the PLC-Automaton state is updated in the new location according to the function δ; otherwise the PLC-Automaton state remains unchanged. After a *tick*-event the program counter gets value 0 and clock z is reset to indicate that a new cycle has started. If the state changes then also clock y is reset. Formally, the timed automaton $\mathcal{T}(\mathcal{A})$ is defined as follows.

Definition 2. Let $\mathcal{A} = (Q, \Sigma, \delta, q_0, \varepsilon, S_t, S_e, \Omega, \omega)$ be a PLC-Automaton. We define $\mathcal{T}(A) \stackrel{df}{=} (\mathcal{S}, \mathcal{X}, \mathcal{L}, \mathcal{E}, \mathcal{I}, \mathcal{P}, \mu, S_0)$ with

- $\mathcal{S} \stackrel{df}{=} \{0, 1, 2, 3\} \times \Sigma \times \Sigma \times Q$ as locations,
- $\mathcal{X} \stackrel{df}{=} \{x, y, z\}$ as clocks,
- $\mathcal{L} \stackrel{df}{=} \Sigma \cup \{poll, test, tick\}$ as labels,
- $\mathcal{I}(s) \stackrel{df}{=} z \leq \varepsilon$ as invariant for each location $s \in \mathcal{S}$,
- $\mathcal{P} = \Sigma \cup Q \cup \Omega$ as the set of propositions,
- $\mu(i, a, b, q) \stackrel{df}{=} a \wedge q \wedge \omega(q)$ as propositions for each location $(i, a, b, q) \in \mathcal{S}$,
- $S_0 \stackrel{df}{=} \{(0, a, b, q_0) | a, b \in \Sigma\}$ as set of initial locations,
- the set of transitions $\mathcal{E}$ consists of the transitions in Table 1, for each $i \in \{0, 1, 2, 3\}$, $a, b, c \in \Sigma$, and $q \in Q$.

In [12,8], the operational behaviour of a timed automaton is defined in terms of accepting runs. An *accepting run* of a timed automaton $\mathcal{T} = (\mathcal{S}, \mathcal{X}, \mathcal{L}, \mathcal{E}, \mathcal{I}, \mathcal{P}, \mu, S_0)$ is an infinite sequence $r = ((s_i, v_i, t_i))_{i \in \mathbb{N}}$ where

- the $s_i \in \mathcal{S}$ are locations,
- the v_i are valuations of the clocks, i.e. $v_i \in [\mathcal{X} \longrightarrow \mathbb{R}_{\geq 0}]$,
- the $t_i \in \mathbb{R}_{\geq 0}$ form a diverging sequence of time stamps.

In order to be an accepting run, sequence r needs to satisfy a number of properties; we refer to [12,8] for the details. By $\mathcal{R}(\mathcal{T})$ we denote the set of accepting runs of a timed automaton $\mathcal{T}$.

4 The Duration Calculus Semantics of PLC-Automata

In this section we introduce logical semantics for PLC-Automata employing the Duration Calculus (see the Appendix for a brief introduction). It is based on the Duration Calculus semantics of [5].

We will give a set of formulae restricting the allowed interpretation of three observables input : Time $\longrightarrow \Sigma$, state : Time $\longrightarrow Q$, and output : Time $\longrightarrow \Omega$. We use q as abbreviation for state $= q$ and assume that $q \in Q$. By $A, B, C \subseteq \Sigma$ we denote nonempty sets of inputs and each formula should be interpreted over all possible assignments to A, B, C.

The following set of formulae describe the general behavior of PLCs. Only inputs that arrived since the system switched into q may produce transitions (dc-1). Moreover, due to the cyclic behavior a transition can only be the consequence of an input which is not older than ε time units (dc-2).

$$\lceil \neg q \rceil \,;\, \lceil q \wedge A \rceil \longrightarrow \lceil q \vee \delta(q, A) \rceil \qquad \text{(dc-1)}$$

$$\lceil q \wedge A \rceil \stackrel{\varepsilon}{\longrightarrow} \lceil q \vee \delta(q, A) \rceil \qquad \text{(dc-2)}$$

We write A for input $\in A$ and $\delta(q, A)$ for state $\in \{q' \in Q \mid \exists a \in A : \delta(q, a) = q'\}$.

To ensure that the delay is observed we add a pair of formulae that corresponds to (dc-1) and (dc-2). They allow state changes only due to input not contained in $S_e(q)$.

$$S_t(q) > 0 \Longrightarrow \lceil \neg q \rceil ; \lceil q \wedge A \rceil \xrightarrow{\leq S_t(q)} \lceil q \vee \delta(q, A \setminus S_e(q)) \rceil \qquad \text{(dc-3)}$$

$$S_t(q) > 0 \Longrightarrow \lceil \neg q \rceil ; \lceil q \rceil ; \lceil q \wedge A \rceil^\varepsilon \xrightarrow{\leq S_t(q)} \lceil q \vee \delta(q, A \setminus S_e(q)) \rceil \qquad \text{(dc-4)}$$

The formulae above do not force a transition, they only disallow some transitions. If we observe a change of the state, we know that another cycle will be finished within the next ε time units. In order to make this additional information exploitable we introduce formulae which force a reaction after at most ε time units depending on the valid input. First, two formulae for the case $S_t(q) = 0$:

$$S_t(q) = 0 \wedge q \notin \delta(q, A) \Longrightarrow \lceil \neg q \rceil ; \lceil q \wedge A \rceil^\varepsilon \longrightarrow \lceil \neg q \rceil \qquad \text{(dc-5)}$$

$$S_t(q) = 0 \wedge q \notin \delta(q, A) \Longrightarrow$$
$$\lceil \neg q \rceil ; (\lceil q \rceil^{>\varepsilon} \wedge \lceil A \rceil ; \lceil B \rceil) \longrightarrow \lceil \neg \delta(q, A) \setminus \delta(q, B) \rceil \qquad \text{(dc-6)}$$

Formula (dc-5) covers the case that $q \notin \delta(q, A)$ holds on the whole interval of length ε right after the state change, whereas formula (dc-6) takes care of the case that input which satisfies $q \notin \delta(q, A)$, is followed by arbitrary input. The next two formulae apply to the case delay in state q. Note that (1) and $a \notin S_e(q)$ implies $q \neq \delta(q, a)$.

$$S_t(q) > 0 \wedge A \cap S_e(q) = \emptyset \Longrightarrow \lceil \neg q \rceil ; \lceil q \wedge A \rceil^\varepsilon \longrightarrow \lceil \neg q \rceil \qquad \text{(dc-7)}$$

$$S_t(q) > 0 \wedge A \cap S_e(q) = \emptyset \Longrightarrow$$
$$\lceil \neg q \rceil ; (\lceil q \rceil^{>\varepsilon} \wedge \lceil A \rceil ; \lceil B \rceil) \xrightarrow{\leq S_t(q)} \lceil \neg \delta(q, A) \setminus \delta(q, B \setminus S_e(q)) \rceil \qquad \text{(dc-8)}$$

Figure 1 shows an impossible behavior of the automaton on page 2 according to the TA semantics. We know that at t_0 and t_3 a cycle ends. Since $t_3 - t_0 > \varepsilon$ holds, the interval $[t_0, t_3]$ must at least contain two cycles. The first cycle produces no state change, therefore input 0 has been polled, input from interval $[t_1, t_3]$. Consequently, input 0 has also to be polled in the successive cycles. This however implies that the change to state T at t_3 can not happen. In the DC semantics formula (dc-6) applies to this situation. There is no delay in state N, and the only element of set A is 1.

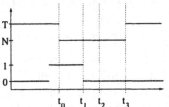

Fig. 1. Assume $t_1 - t_0 \leq \varepsilon$, $t_3 - t_1 \leq \varepsilon$ and $t_3 - t_0 > \varepsilon$

If the state changes we know that a cycle begins and will be completed within the next ε time units. The previous four DC formulae reflect that we have either two types of input or only one and there is a delay in current state or not. We have a set of formulae similar to (dc-5)-(dc-8) concerning intervals of length 2ε with a stable state. These intervals must also contain at least one cycle. However, for this situation we do not only have to consider the cases *no delay* and *delay active* but also the cases *delay has expired* and *delay expires*. If there is no delay active in state q then the following two formulae apply.

$$S_t(q) = 0 \wedge q \notin \delta(q, A) \implies \Box(\lceil q \wedge A \rceil \implies \ell < 2\varepsilon) \qquad \text{(dc-9)}$$

$$S_t(q) = 0 \wedge q \notin \delta(q, A) \implies$$
$$(\lceil q \rceil \wedge \lceil A \rceil^{>\varepsilon} ; \lceil B \rceil) \xrightarrow{2\varepsilon} \lceil \neg\delta(q, A) \setminus \delta(q, B) \rceil \qquad \text{(dc-10)}$$

In the case that $S_t(q) > 0$ holds and the delay time has not expired only inputs not contained in $S_e(q)$ can force a transition to happen.

$$S_t(q) > 0 \wedge A \cap S_e(q) = \emptyset \implies \Box(\lceil q \wedge A \rceil \implies \ell < 2\varepsilon) \qquad \text{(dc-11)}$$

$$S_t(q) > 0 \wedge A \cap S_e(q) = \emptyset \implies$$
$$\lceil \neg q \rceil ; \lceil q \rceil ; (\lceil q \rceil^{2\varepsilon} \wedge \lceil A \rceil^{>\varepsilon} ; \lceil B \rceil) \xrightarrow{\leq S_t(q)} \lceil \neg\delta(q, A) \setminus \delta(q, B \setminus S_e(q)) \rceil \quad \text{(dc-12)}$$

If the delay time is expired the system behaves like a system with no delay. The following formulae are consequently quite the same as (dc-9) and (dc-10), except that the state has to be stable for an additional $S_t(q)$ time units.

$$S_t(q) > 0 \wedge q \notin \delta(q, A) \implies \Box(\lceil q \rceil^{S_t(q)} ; \lceil q \wedge A \rceil \implies \ell < S_t(q) + 2\varepsilon) \quad \text{(dc-13)}$$

$$S_t(q) > 0 \wedge q \notin \delta(q, A) \implies$$
$$\lceil q \rceil^{S_t(q)} ; (\lceil q \rceil \wedge \lceil A \rceil^{>\varepsilon} ; \lceil B \rceil) \xrightarrow{S_t(q)+2\varepsilon} \lceil \neg\delta(q, A) \setminus \delta(q, B) \rceil \qquad \text{(dc-14)}$$

To express that the delay time expires during an interval we need some more complicated formulae, but the idea is the same as in the foregoing cases.

$$S_t(q) > 0 \wedge q \notin \delta(q, B) \wedge A \cap S_e(q) = \emptyset \implies$$
$$\Box(\lceil q \rceil \wedge (l = t_1); \lceil A \rceil^{t_2} ; \lceil B \rceil^{t_3} \wedge t_1 + t_2 = S_t(q) \implies t_2 + t_3 < 2\varepsilon) \quad \text{(dc-15)}$$

$$S_t(q) > 0 \wedge q \notin \delta(q, B) \wedge A \cap S_e(q) = \emptyset \implies$$
$$\lceil \neg q \rceil ; \left(\lceil q \rceil \wedge (l = t_1); \lceil A \rceil^{t_2} ; \lceil B \rceil^{t_3} ; \lceil C \rceil^{t_4} \wedge \begin{array}{c} \wedge \, t_2 + t_3 + t_4 = 2\varepsilon \\ t_1 + t_2 = S_t(q) \\ \wedge \quad t_2 + t_3 > \varepsilon \end{array} \right)$$
$$\longrightarrow \lceil \neg(\delta(q, A \cup B) \setminus \delta(q, C)) \rceil \qquad \text{(dc-16)}$$

The DC-semantics presented in this paper differs from the one presented in [5] by the additional formulae (dc-6), (dc-8), (dc-10), (dc-12), (dc-14), (dc-15), (dc-16). We also used $<$ instead of $\leq$ in the formulae (dc-9), (dc-11) and (dc-13). We did not mention two formulae that define the initial state and relate output to states. Those can be found together with the original semantics in [5, 8]. Some of the formulae given in this section are not applicable in the initial phase. The corresponding formulae for the initial phase can be found in the full paper [8].

5   Observables and Runs

In this section we establish the relationship between Duration Calculus and timed automata. The semantic objects of the Duration Calculus are interpretations of observables; the semantic objects of timed automata are accepting runs. We have to define suitable mappings between these semantic objects and show equi-expressiveness of both semantics.

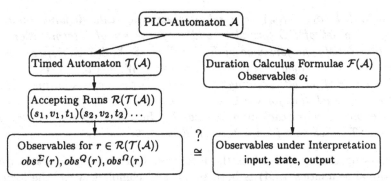

In order to compare timed automata and Duration Calculus within our setting, we need to relate sets of atomic propositions to observables. A sufficient condition for doing this is that, for each observable *obs* with domain P, elements of P are propositions of the timed automaton and P is a *league*.

Definition 3. *For a timed automaton $T = (S, X, L, E, I, P, \mu, S_0)$, we define a set $P \subseteq \mathcal{P}$ of propositions to be a* league, *if at each location one and only one proposition $p \in P$ is valid, i.e., $\forall s \in S \; \exists^1 p \in P : p \in \mu(s)$.*

For $T(A)$ as in Definition 2 there are three leagues corresponding to the three observables in the DC semantics $\mathcal{F}(A)$: Σ corresponds to input, Q to state, and Ω to output.

Recall that the interpretation of a DC observable is a function from time to the domain of this observable. In the case of accepting runs of a timed automaton time needs not to increase strictly monotonically. Therefore, when mapping an accepting run to an observable, we have to associate to each point of time a unique element of the domain, i.e., a proposition of a league. If in an accepting run there are consecutive states at the same point in time, we choose the last one as the unique interpretation.

Definition 4. *Let $T(A)$ be a timed automaton, $r = ((s_i, v_i, t_i))_{i \in \mathbb{N}}$ an accepting run of $T(A)$, and $P \subseteq \mathcal{P}$ a league. We define obs^P as a function from runs to observables as follows:*

$$obs^P \stackrel{df}{=} \begin{cases} \mathcal{R}(T(A)) \longrightarrow (\textit{Time} \longrightarrow P) \\ \quad r \qquad \mapsto \quad (t \quad \mapsto p \textit{ where } p \in \mu(s_i) \textit{ and } i = \max\{i \mid t_i \leq t\}). \end{cases}$$

Note that $obs^P(r)$ is finitely variable due to the divergence of time in the accepting run r.

In DC the truth of a formula is defined by integrals of functions over intervals. Functions that are identical up to zero-sets give the same truth values for all formulae and can be identified. We define two interpretations obs_I and $obs_{I'}$ of observable *obs* to be *equivalent*, notation $obs_I \cong obs_{I'}$, if the interpretations differ in at most countably many points. Hence, by definition of $\cong$ we have that, for each Duration Calculus formula F,

$$obs_1 \cong obs_2 \Longrightarrow (F \text{ holds for } obs_1 \Longleftrightarrow F \text{ holds for } obs_2).$$

Definition 5. *Let* $\{o_1, \ldots, o_n\}$ *be a set of observables with disjoint domains* $D_1, \ldots, D_n$, $\mathcal{F}$ *a set of DC formulae, and* $Int_{\mathcal{F}}$ *the set of interpretations of* $o_1, \ldots, o_n$ *that satisfy the formulae of* $\mathcal{F}$. *Let* $\mathcal{T} = (\mathcal{S}, \mathcal{X}, \mathcal{L}, \mathcal{E}, \mathcal{I}, \mathcal{P}, \mu, S_0)$ *be a timed automaton with leagues* $D_i \subseteq \mathcal{P}$ *for* $1 \leq i \leq n$. *We say that* $\mathcal{T}$ *is*

- *sound w.r.t.* $\mathcal{F}$ *if for all accepting runs* $r \in \mathcal{R}(\mathcal{T})$ *there exists an interpretation* $I \in Int_{\mathcal{F}}$ *such that for* $i = 1, \ldots, n$ *it is* $o_{i,I} \cong obs^{D_i}(r)$;
- *complete w.r.t.* $\mathcal{F}$ *if for each interpretation* $I \in Int_{\mathcal{F}}$ *there exists an accepting run* $r \in \mathcal{R}(\mathcal{T})$ *such that for* $i = 1, \ldots, n$ *it is* $o_{i,I} \cong obs^{D_i}(r)$.

The following theorem, which is the main result of this paper, states that the operational semantics $\mathcal{T}(\mathcal{A})$ is both sound and complete w.r.t. the logical semantics $\mathcal{F}(\mathcal{A})$. For the proof of this result we refer to [8].

Theorem 1. Let $\mathcal{A}$ be a PLC-Automaton. Then $\mathcal{T}(\mathcal{A})$ is sound and complete with respect to $\mathcal{F}(\mathcal{A})$, i.e.,
(i) for each accepting run $r \in \mathcal{R}(\mathcal{T}(\mathcal{A}))$ there exists an interpretation I of the observables input, state and output that satisfies all formulae of $\mathcal{F}(\mathcal{A})$, such that $\mathsf{input}_I \cong obs^{\Sigma}(r)$, $\mathsf{state}_I \cong obs^Q(r)$ and $\mathsf{output}_I \cong obs^{\Omega}(r)$;
(ii) for each interpretation I of the observables input, state and output that satisfies all formulae of $\mathcal{F}(\mathcal{A})$, there exists an accepting run $r \in \mathcal{R}(\mathcal{T}(\mathcal{A}))$ such that $\mathsf{input}_I \cong obs^{\Sigma}(r)$, $\mathsf{state}_I \cong obs^Q(r)$ and $\mathsf{output}_I \cong obs^{\Omega}(r)$.

References

1. R. Alur and D.L. Dill. A theory of timed automata. *Theoretical Computer Science*, 126:183–235, 1994.
2. R. Alur, T.A. Henzinger, and E.D. Sontag, editors. *Hybrid Systems III*, volume 1066 of *Lecture Notes in Computer Science*. Springer-Verlag, 1996.
3. J. Bengtsson, K.G. Larsen, F. Larsson, P. Pettersson, and Wang Yi. UPPAAL: a tool suite for the automatic verification of real-time systems. In Alur et al. [2], pages 232–243.
4. C. Daws, A. Olivero, S. Tripakis, and S. Yovine. The tool KRONOS. In Alur et al. [2], pages 208–219.
5. H. Dierks. PLC-Automata: A New Class of Implementable Real-Time Automata. In M. Bertran and T. Rus, editors, *ARTS'97*, volume 1231 of *Lecture Notes in Computer Science*, pages 111–125, Mallorca, Spain, May 1997. Springer-Verlag.
6. H. Dierks. Synthesising Controllers from Real-Time Specifications. In *Tenth International Symposium on System Synthesis*, pages 126–133. IEEE CS Press, September 1997.
7. H. Dierks and C. Dietz. Graphical Specification and Reasoning: Case Study "Generalized Railroad Crossing". In J. Fitzgerald, C.B. Jones, and P. Lucas, editors, *FME'97*, volume 1313 of *Lecture Notes in Computer Science*, pages 20–39, Graz, Austria, September 1997. Springer-Verlag.
8. H. Dierks, A. Fehnker, A. Mader, and F. Vaandrager. Operational and logical semantics for polling real-time systems. CSI-R9813, University of Nijmegen, april 1998.
9. H. Dierks and J. Tapken. Tool-Supported Hierarchical Design of Distributed Real-Time Systems. In *Proceedings of EuroMicro 98*, 1998. to appear.

10. Z. Kohavi. *Switching and Finite Automata Theory*. McGraw-Hill, Inc., 1970.
11. B. Krieg-Brückner, J. Peleska, E.-R. Olderog, D. Balzer, and A. Baer. UniForM — Universal Formal Methods Workbench. In U. Grote and G. Wolf, editors, *Statusseminar des BMBF Softwaretechnologie*, pages 357–378. BMBF, Berlin, March 1996.
12. O. Maler and S. Yovine. Hardware Timing Verification using Kronos. In *Proc. 7th Conf. on Computer-based Systems and Software Engineering*. IEEE Press, 1996.
13. A.P. Ravn. Design of Embedded Real-Time Computing Systems. Technical Report 1995-170, Technical University of Denmark, 1995.
14. Zhou Chaochen. Duration Calculi: An overview. In D. Bjørner, M. Broy, and I.V. Pottosin, editors, *Formal Methods in Programming and Their Application*, volume 735 of *Lecture Notes in Computer Science*, pages 256–266. Springer-Verlag, 1993.
15. Zhou Chaochen, C.A.R. Hoare, and A.P. Ravn. A Calculus of Durations. *Inform. Proc. Letters*, 40/5:269–276, 1991.

A   Duration Calculus

For a proper introduction to the DC see e.g. [15, 14].

Formulae of the DC are propositions about time-dependent variables *obs*, called *observables*. An interpretation I assigns to each observable *obs* a function $obs_I :$ Time $\longrightarrow D$, where Time $= \mathbb{R}_{\geq 0}$ and D is the type of *obs*.

Terms are built over observables and have a certain type. Terms of Boolean type are called *state assertions*, e.g., $obs = v$ for $v \in D$. For an interpretation I they denote functions $P_I :$ Time $\longrightarrow \{0, 1\}$.

Duration terms are of type real and their values depend on a given time interval $[b, e]$. The simplest duration term is the symbol ℓ denoting the length $e - b$ of $[b, e]$. For each state assertion P there is a duration term $\int P$ measuring the duration of P. Semantically, $\int P$ denotes $\int_b^e P_I(t)dt$ on the interval $[b, e]$. Real-valued operators applied to duration terms are also duration terms.

Duration formulae are built from boolean-valued operations on duration terms, the special symbols true and false, and they are closed under propositional connectives, the chop-operator ";", and quantification over rigid variables. Their truth values depend on a given interval. We use F for a typical duration formula. Constants true and false evaluate to true resp. false on every given interval. The composite duration formula $F_1; F_2$ holds in $[b, e]$ if this interval can be divided into an initial subinterval $[b, m]$ where F_1 holds and a final subinterval $[m, e]$ where F_2 holds.

Besides this basic syntax various abbreviations are used: $\lceil\rceil \stackrel{\mathrm{df}}{=} \ell = 0$ (point interval), $\lceil P \rceil \stackrel{\mathrm{df}}{=} \int P = \ell \wedge \ell > 0$ (everywhere), $\Diamond F \stackrel{\mathrm{df}}{=}$ true; F; true (somewhere), $\Box F \stackrel{\mathrm{df}}{=} \neg\Diamond\neg F$ (always), $F^t \stackrel{\mathrm{df}}{=} (F \wedge \ell = t)$, $F^{\sim t} \stackrel{\mathrm{df}}{=} (F \wedge \ell \sim t)$, where $\sim \in \{<, \leq, > , \geq\}$.

A duration formula F *holds* in an interpretation I if F evaluates to true in I and every interval of the form $[0, t]$ with $t \in$ Time.

The following so-called *standard forms* are useful to describe dynamic behaviour: $F \longrightarrow \lceil P \rceil \stackrel{\mathrm{df}}{=} \Box\neg(F; \lceil\neg P\rceil)$ (followed-by), $F \stackrel{t}{\longrightarrow} \lceil P \rceil \stackrel{\mathrm{df}}{=} (F \wedge \ell = t) \longrightarrow \lceil P \rceil$ (timed leads-to), $F \stackrel{\leq t}{\longrightarrow} \lceil P \rceil \stackrel{\mathrm{df}}{=} (F \wedge \ell \leq t) \longrightarrow \lceil P \rceil$ (timed up-to).

A Finite-Domain Semantics for Testing Temporal Logic Specifications

Alberto Coen-Porisini, Matteo Pradella, and Pierluigi San Pietro

Dipartimento di Elettronica ed Informazione, Politecnico di Milano
P.za Leonardo da Vinci, 32, 20133 Milano, Italia
{coen, pradella, sanpietr}@elet.polimi.it

Abstract. A method to achieve executability of temporal logic specifications is restricting the interpretation of formulas over finite domains. This method was proven to be successful in designing testing tools used in industrial applications. However, the extension of the results of these tools to infinite, or just larger, domains, requires an adequate definition of a "finite-domain semantics". Here we show the need for correcting previous semantics proposals, especially in the case of specifications of real-time systems which require the use of bounded temporal operators. We define a new semantics for the TRIO language, easily extendible to other linear metric temporal logic languages and show its adequateness on various examples.

1 Introduction

The use of formal executable specifications has many advantages: by executing formal specifications it is possible to observe the behavior of the specified system and check whether they capture the intended functional requirements. This kind of analysis, called *specification testing*, increases the confidence in the correctness of the specification in much the same way as testing a program may increase the confidence on its reliability, assessing the adequacy of the requirements before a costly development takes place. Moreover, execution may allow the generation of test data, that can be used for functional testing, that is for checking the correctness of the implementation against the specification [8, 9].

A specification formalism very suitable to real-time systems is Linear Temporal Logic with a metric of time [5]. Such a formalism allows one to express complex temporal conditions and properties in a precise, quantitative way, while its denotational style allows one to abstract from implementation details until the beginning of the development phase. However, specifications written using a first-order temporal logic with metric are in general not decidable.

Various proposals have appeared in the literature to define less powerful and less expressive, but decidable, temporal logics [1]. As a consequence many properties cannot be expressed in such languages. A different approach to overcome the undecidability problem consists in using finite domains to interpret (hence, test) first-order specifications [7]. The result is a decidable language as expressive as a first-order logic, although as powerful as a propositional logic.

Executability is achieved by defining a model-theoretic semantics (i.e., an interpretation schema) that, for any formula, builds its possible *models* (i.e., assignments of values to variables and predicates such that the formula evaluates to true), and by exploiting the idea of *finite approximation of infinite domains*. Original interpretation domains, which are usually infinite, are replaced by finite approximations thereof. For instance, the set of integers is replaced by the range 0..100.

In this way, every decision problem becomes decidable even though there is no *a priori* guarantee that the results obtained on the finite domain coincide with the theoretical results that would be obtained on the infinite domain. In practice, however, we may often rely on this type of prototyping, especially if the domains are large enough to contain all the "relevant facts" about the system under analysis, on the basis of the following considerations:

- Non-terminating reactive systems often have periodical behaviors. Thus it usually suffices to analyse them for a time period of, for instance, twice their periodicity.
- Using some common sense and experience one can tell whether all "relevant facts" about a system, whose dynamic behavior is in the order of magnitude of seconds, have been generated after having tested it for several hours.
- One may try several executions with different time domains of increasing cardinality. If the results do not change, one can infer that they will not change for larger domains.

Clearly, this approach is based on the assumption that it is possible to significantly evaluate formulas on a finite time domain, while a specifier usually makes the natural assumption of an *infinite* time domain. Hence, the finiteness is only a "trick" to enable specification execution and therefore it is crucial to provide a finite-domain semantics such that the results obtainable on finite histories may be easily extended to infinite behaviors of the system.

Execution algorithms based on a finite time semantics have been successfully designed for the TRIO language [4] and have been tested in the context of several industrial applications [2].

Various proposals of finite-domain semantics have appeared in the literature, for both TRIO and other temporal logic languages. In [5], a conventional *false* (or *true*) value is given to every formula (or part of a formula) whose evaluation time does not belong to the time domain. Very early it was recognised that this resulted in a very counterintuitive semantics. In [3] the language has two temporal distance operators: a strong operator Δ and a weak one ∇. $\Delta t F$ is true iff there exists a time instant whose distance from the current one equals t, in which F is true , while $\nabla t F$ is true iff there exists a time instant whose distance from the current one equals t, in which F is true, or if there is no such t. Using this approach the specification must be written taking into account the finite domains from the beginning. Moreover, the use of two different distance operators has proved to be confusing for most users.

The best proposal up to now is the model-parametric semantics (MPS) presented in [7]. MPS correctly interpretes many cases of practical interests that are not dealt with adequately by the other proposals. However, in this paper we show that MPS causes formulas with bounded temporal operators, which impose upper or lower bounds on the occurrence of events, to become counter-intuitive and has also some other minor problems. These problems in the interpretation of formulas over finite domains limit the validity and the use of the tools for executing specifications and hence may seriously hamper the validation phase. This is especially true for real-time systems since most of them require explicit time bounds, that is their specification must use bounded temporal operators. It is then of the outmost importance to define the semantics of such operators in the most general and intuitive way.

This paper presents a new semantics for the finiteness problem by modifying MPS. In particular, it provides a different semantics for the bounded temporal operators, along with some minor changes to the original definition in order to deal correctly with all temporal operators. Algorithms have been derived and already implemented from our definitions, and various experiments have been performed, showing the validity of our approach. It must be noticed that although our work has been carried out for the TRIO language, it can be easily extended to other temporal logic languages.

2 An Overview of TRIO

TRIO is a first order temporal logics that supports a linear notion of time: the *Time Domain* T is a numeric set equipped with a total order relation and the usual arithmetic relations and operators. The time domain represents the set of instants where a TRIO formula may be evaluated. Another special domain is the *distance domain* ΔT, a numeric domain composed of the distances between instants of the time domain.

TRIO formulas are constructed in the classical inductive way, starting from terms and atomic formulas. Besides the usual propositional operators and the quantifiers, one may compose TRIO formulas by using a single basic modal operator, called *Dist*, that relates the *current time*, which is left implicit in the formula, to another time instant: the formula $Dist(F, t)$, where F is a formula and t a term indicating a time distance, states that F holds at a time instant at t time units from the current instant.

For the sake of convenience, TRIO items (variables, predicates, and functions) are divided into time-independent (TI) ones, i.e., those whose value does not change during system evolution (e.g., the altitude of a reservoir) and time-dependent (TD) ones, i.e., those whose value may change during system evolution (e.g., the water level inside a reservoir).

TRIO formulas are evaluated on a *history*, that is a sequence of events. A model or behavior of a formula F is a history h such that F evaluates to *true* on h.

Several *derived temporal operators* can be defined from the basic *Dist* operator through propositional composition and first order quantification on variables representing a time distance. A sample list of such operators is given below, along with their definition and a short explanation. The variable d is over the distance domain ΔT.

- $Lasts(F, t) \triangleq \forall d(0 < d < t \to Dist(F, d))$, i.e. F holds over a period of length t in the future.
- $Lasted(F, t) \triangleq \forall d(0 < d < t \to Dist(F, -d))$, i.e. F held over a period of length t in the past.
- $Alw(F) \triangleq \forall d Dist(F, d)$, i.e. F always holds.
- $SomF(F) \triangleq \exists d(d > 0 \wedge Dist(F, d))$, i.e. sometimes in the future F will hold.
- $WithinF(F, t) \triangleq \neg Lasts(\neg F, t)$, i.e. F will occur within t time units.
- $Until(F1, F2) \triangleq \exists d(d > 0 \wedge Lasts(F1, d) \wedge Dist(F2, d))$, i.e. $F1$ will last until $F2$ occurs.
- $Becomes(F) \triangleq F \wedge Dist(\neg F, -1)$, i.e. F holds at the current instant but did not hold in the previous instant.

The traditional operators of linear temporal logics can be easily obtained as TRIO derived operators. For instance, $SomF$ corresponds to the *Eventually* operator of temporal logic. Moreover, it can be easily shown that the operators of several versions of temporal logic (e.g., interval logic) can be defined as TRIO derived operators. This argues in favour of TRIO's generality since many different logic formalisms can be described as particular cases of TRIO.

In what follows we provide two simple examples of a TRIO specification. Even though they are very simple they will be used in Section 3 to highlight the problems related to the current definition of TRIO's semantics.

Example: A transmission line Consider a simple transmission line, that receives messages at one end and delivers them at the opposite end with a fixed delay (e.g., 5"). The arrival of a message is represented by the time dependent predicate *in*, while its delivery is represented by predicate *out*. The following formula expresses that every received message is delivered after exactly 5 seconds from its arrival.

- (TL) $Alw(in \leftrightarrow Dist(out, 5))$.

The use of the equivalence operator '$\leftrightarrow$' ensures that no received message gets lost and no spurious message (i.e., an output without an input) is emitted. Figures 1 and 2 show examples of histories on which formula (TL) is verified.

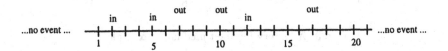

Fig. 1. A history for the transmission line example, representing a finite behavior

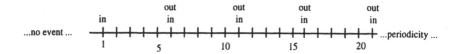

Fig. 2. A periodic (infinite) behavior for the transmission line example, where an in occurs forever exactly every 5 time instants, starting from instant 1

Example: A lamp with a timer Let us consider a lamp with a timer and a switch. When the lamp is off, pushing the button of the switch turns the lamp on. When the lamp is on, pushing the button turns the lamp off; moreover if the button is not pushed the lamp is turned off anyway by a timer after 4 time units. In the specification, the state of the lamp is modelled by the time dependent predicate *on*, which is true iff the lamp is on; the event of pushing the button is modelled by the time dependent predicate *push*. Finally, another time dependent predicate *timeout*, models the timer of the lamp. The specification of this system is the formula $Alw(A1 \land A2 \land A3)$, where $A1$, $A2$ and $A3$ are the following formulas:

- (A1) *timeout* $\leftrightarrow$ *Lasted*(*on*, 5).
- (A2) *Becomes*(*on*) $\leftrightarrow$ *push* $\land$ *Dist*($\neg on$, -1).
- (A3) *Becomes*($\neg on$) $\leftrightarrow$ (*push* $\land$ *Dist*(*on*, -1) $\lor$ *timeout*).

(A1) defines the timeout: the light has been on during the last 4 time units[1].

(A2) states that the lamp becomes on iff the button is pushed and the light was off.

(A3) states that the lamp becomes off iff either there is a timeout or the button is pushed while the light was on.

Let us consider the behavior shown in Figure 3 (where every predicate is false unless explicitly indicated): the button is pushed a first time at instant 3, and thus the light is on from instants 3 to 6, since the *timeout* occurs at instant 7. The light stays off until the next *push* (instant 10), remains on from 10 to 12, when another *push* occurs (instant 13), which finally turns the light off.

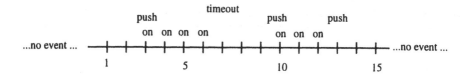

Fig. 3. A history for the timed lamp example

---

[1] The definition of *Lasted* does not consider the current time instant, hence *Lasted*(*on*, 5) requires *on* to be true in the previous four time instants.

2.1 The TRIO environment

The practical usefulness of a specification language depends not only on its inherent qualities (rigor, ease and naturalness of use, generality, etc.), but also on the availability of tools that favour its use. Thus, we are presently developing a complete environment of TRIO-based tools, that includes:

- An interactive, graphical editor for TRIO. The editor supports the incremental writing of TRIO-based specifications and histories.
- A TRIO interpreter which supports specification prototyping and verification of their properties such as consistency. Different operating modes allow the designer to manage a trade-off between generality and complexity.
- A test case generator, which allows the (semi)automatic i.e., user-driven generation of functional test cases associated with a given TRIO specification against which the designer can check the implementation. The core of the tool is the interpretation mechanism, tailored to the specialised use of test cases production, which generate models compatible with the given specifications.

The interpreter and the test case generator are based on the definition of a finite-domain semantics for TRIO.

3 TRIO's formal semantics: problems and solutions

Let us consider formula (TL) of example 1 (the transmission line), and the history depicted in Figure 1 restricted to the instants 1..20. This is certainly an acceptable behavior of the system. Notice that developing a finite-domain semantics adequate to this example is fairly easy; for instance, by providing a conventional evaluation to false for everything lying outside the time domain.

However, consider the history of Figure 2, again restricted to the instants 1..20, which is reported in Figure 4.

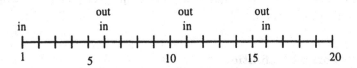

Fig. 4. The finite restriction of history of Figure 2 to the domain 1..20

In this case, *in* is true at instant 16 and there is no corresponding *out*, since it would occur at instant 21, which is outside the time domain. However, also this (finite) behavior should be considered acceptable because the *in* at instant 16 is a border event: it could be followed by an *out* at instant 21, that is there exists at least one infinite history containing all the events of Figure 4 which satisfies (TL). Obviously, there are also infinite histories that include the history of Figure 4 which do not satisfy (TL) (e.g. a history in which there is no *out* at instant 21).

Therefore, a finite-domain semantics should consider the history of Figure 4 as a model of (TL). The use of conventional truth values, however, does not work since it would conventionally assume that at instant 21 *out* is false (assuming a conventional true value outside the temporal domain would even worsen the situation). Enlarging or restricting the time domain does not solve this problem since: if the instant 21 is included in the time domain then also the instant 26 should be included and so on.

In order to enable the execution of TRIO specifications a model parametric semantics MPS was defined. The MPS may refer to any finite or infinite time domain T, the finite case being considered an approximation of the infinite one. If the finite time domain is large enough to include all relevant events, the corresponding finite history is included in an infinite behavior of the system.

As a consequence the size of the time domain is quite important: if it is too small some relevant event may not be included, and thus the finite restriction of an infinite history may not be meaningful. For instance, a specification such as $Som(in)$ is verified whenever there exists at least one occurrence of *in*. Every finite history in which no *in* occurs can hardly be considered to verify $Som(in)$; however, any such history can be extended to include an occurrence of *in*, and hence it is a sub-history of a behavior of the system.

The basic idea of MPS consists in not evaluating a formula in those instants in which the truth of the formula depends on what may or may not occur outside the time domain. For instance, the meaning of the *Alw* operator becomes: $Alw(A)$ is true iff A holds in every instant in which A may be evaluated. $Som(A)$ is true iff there exists an instant in which A can be evaluated and holds. If A cannot be evaluated in any instant, then $Alw(A)$ and $Som(A)$ are considered meaningless.

Hence, according to MPS, formula (TL), evaluated on the history of Figure 4 becomes true, since the subformula $in \leftrightarrow Dist(out, 5)$ is true where it can be evaluated, that is on the range 1..15. The truth value of the formula is not checked in 16, since $Dist(out, 5)$ cannot be evaluated.

To better understand MPS and its problems in what follows we summarize its formal definition given in [7].

3.1 MPS Formal Definition

For the sake of simplicity we consider only formulas where all variables are of the type distance domain (ΔT), which in MPS is interpreted as the interval $-|T| + 1..|T| - 1$, and there are no time dependent functions or constants.

A quantifier $\forall x$ in a formula of type $\forall x A$ is restricted to those values $a \in \Delta T$ such that A_x^a (the formula obtained from A by replacing every occurrence of x with the value a) can be evaluated without referencing time instants outside the time domain. This can be obtained by defining a function *Eval* that associates every formula with the subset of T on which it can be evaluated. The definition of *Eval* is:

1. $Eval(P) = T$, for an atomic formula P.
2. $Eval(\neg A) = \overline{Eval(A)}$.
3. $Eval(A \wedge B) = Eval(A) \cap Eval(B)$.
4. $Eval(Dist(A, t)) = \{i \in T | i + t \in Eval(A)\}$.
5. $Eval(\forall x A) = \bigcup_{a \in \Delta T} Eval(A_x^a)$.

A formula A is said to be not evaluable iff $Eval(A) = \emptyset$, that is it cannot be evaluated in any instant. In this case, the formula A is considered meaningless.

Notice that the evaluation of formulas following MPS differs from traditional evaluation only when quantifiers are involved. In fact, if a formula such as $\forall x A$ can be evaluated, (i.e., $Eval(\forall x A) \neq \emptyset$), then its truth value in an instant i is true if A_x^a is true in i for every $a \in \Delta T$ such that i belongs to $Eval(A_x^a)$, it is false otherwise.

3.2 Problems of MPS

While we believe that the general idea behind the MPS is very appealing, its definition is not completely satisfactory. Its main problems are discussed in what follows and concern the characterization of the distance domain ΔT, the treatment of the bounded operators and the semantics of propositional operators.

The distance domain ΔT Let us consider the timed lamp example and the restriction of the history depicted in Figure 3 to the time domain 1..15, as shown in Figure 5.

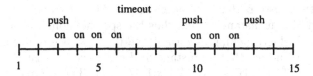

Fig. 5. A restriction of history 3 to 1..15

This behavior is intuitively correct and obviously includes every relevant event. However, according to MPS the subformula (A1), *timeout* $\leftrightarrow$ *Lasted(on, 5)*, is false at instant 1. In fact, the definition of *Lasted(on, 5)*, is $\forall d(0 < d < 5 \rightarrow Dist(on, -d))$, where d is a variable in the distance domain $\Delta T = $ -14..14. Thus, at instant 1 d can assume any value in the range -14..0^2, and the condition $0 < d < 5$ is false for every d. As a consequence, *Lasted(on, 5)* is true in 1, while *timeout* is not.

The problem does not disappear by extending the time domain: there is always a left border where (A1) can be false. Other similar counterexamples can be built for other TRIO operators, such as *Since* and *Until*, and are very puzzling for most users of the tools based on MPS.

---

^{2} The values greater than 0 are ruled off since $Dist(on, -d)$ cannot be evaluated

The problem arises from the use of non positive values in the distance domain $\Delta T = -|T| + 1..|T| - 1$, that may create undesired border effects. It can be solved by defining ΔT as $1..|T| - 1$. In this case, the subformula $\forall d(0 < d < 5 \rightarrow Dist(on, -d))$ becomes not evaluable at instant 1 and therefore instant 1 is ignored when evaluating (A1).

Bounded operators Let us further restrict the time domain of the previous example to the range 4..15 (Figure 6).

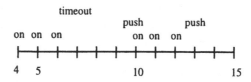

Fig. 6. A behavior for the timed lamp, where (A1), (A2) and (A3) are false

The history describes what can still be considered an intuitively acceptable behavior for the specification (A1): there is a border effect in the instants from 4 to 7, where the lamp has been on for less than 4 instants. Therefore we cannot know whether timeout should actually hold at instant 7. However, we expect the axiom (A1) to hold, because the left border 4..7 should not be considered for evaluation; at most, we could accept that the specification is not evaluable, thus signalling that we should have chosen a larger domain including at least instant 3. Unfortunately, also in this case according to MPS formula (A1) is false at instant 6 (and also at instant 5), and thus the specification $Alw(A1 \wedge A2 \wedge A3)$ does not hold. In fact, looking at formula $\forall d(0 < d < 5 \rightarrow Dist(on, -d))$, i.e. $Lasted(on, 5)$, we notice that at instant 6, d can have at least values 1 and 2 (both if $\Delta T = -|T| + 1..|T| - 1$ or $\Delta T = 1..|T| - 1$). Hence, $Lasted(on, 5)$ holds at instant 6, because $Dist(on, -1)$ and $Dist(on, -2)$ hold. But $timeout$ is false at 6.

The problem is that MPS evaluates $Lasted(on, 5)$ to true whenever on is true in every instant among the previous 4, in which $Dist(on, -d)$ can be evaluated. Near the border, on can be evaluated in less than 4 instants, and thus $Lasted(on, 5)$ becomes true even if on does not last for at least 4 instants.

This situation is typical of every bounded operator. A possible solution consists in regarding a bounded operator as not evaluable whenever its distance from the border is less than the stated bound. In the above example, $Lasted(on, 5)$ should not be evaluated in 4, 5, 6 and 7, that is the border should be ignored. In this way the specification becomes true. However, it is possible to improve further this solution as shown next.

Consider the history depicted in Figure 7, which is similar to the history of Figure 6 but in which on is false at instant 5. There is no finite or infinite behavior of the specified system that may include this one, since there cannot be a timeout at instant 6. The specification should evaluate to false when interpreted over this history. Hence, we should not ignore the border of the *Lasted* operator, but instead check if it is possible to establish its truth from the available data. Only when this is not possible, the *Lasted* operator should be regarded as not evaluable at the border.

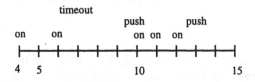

Fig. 7. An incorrect behavior of the timed lamp: there is a timeout but two instants before the lamp was off

Our proposal distinguishes the semantics of bounded operators from that of unbounded ones. Every quantification over the distance domain ΔT, defined as $1..|T|$, is assumed to be unbounded and hence treated as in MPS. Instead, in order to deal with the bounded operators, *Lasts* and the temporally symmetrical *Lasted* are added as primitive operators of the language. Their semantics is defined as follows:

- *Lasted*(A, t) is true in i iff $\forall j, 0 < j < t, i - j \in T$ and A holds in $i - j$;
- *Lasted*(A, t) is false in i iff $\exists j, 0 < j < t$, such that $i - j \in T$ and A does not hold in $i - j$;
- *Lasted*(A, t) is not evaluable in i otherwise.

Symmetrically for *Lasts*.

The meaning of these clauses is that *Lasted*(A, t) is true iff A can be evaluated and it is true in the previous $t - 1$ instants. It is false if A is false in at least one of the previous $t - 1$ instants, even if in some of these instants A cannot be evaluated. Finally, *Lasted*(A, t) cannot be evaluated if either A cannot be evaluated in any of the previous $t - 1$ instants or A can be evaluated only in some of them and the evaluation is true. Notice that the other bounded operators of TRIO can be derived from *Lasts* and *Lasted*.

The semantics of propositional operators According to MPS if a formula A cannot be evaluated at instant i, then also $A \wedge B$ is not evaluable at i, whatever the value of B is. This semantics of propositional operators may be called *strict*: a propositional formula is evaluable only if every part of the formula is evaluable. This leads to some unpleasant drawbacks. For instance, the semantics of *Lasted*$(on, 5)$ is not equivalent to $Dist(on, -1) \wedge Dist(on, -2) \wedge Dist(on, -3) \wedge Dist(on, -4)$ whatever semantics we choose for the *Lasted* operator (MPS or our proposal).

Another example is the history shown in Figure 8, which should not satisfy the specification of the timed lamp example since, at instant 1, the timeout occurs and the lamp is still on.

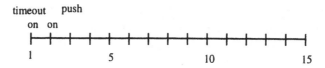

Fig. 8. An incorrect behavior of the timed lamp: there is a *timeout* and the lamp stays on

In fact, there is no finite or infinite behavior of the specified system that may include this one: the specification should evaluate to false when interpreted over this history. Instead, according to MPS the evaluation of $Alw(A1 \wedge A2 \wedge A3)$ gives the value *true*. In fact, formula (A3), $Becomes(\neg on) \leftrightarrow push \wedge Dist(on, -1) \vee timeout$, cannot be evaluated at instant 1, since $Becomes(\neg on)$ may not. As a consequence also formula $A1 \wedge A2 \wedge A3$ cannot be evaluated in 1, and therefore $Alw(A1 \wedge A2 \wedge A3)$ holds since $A1 \wedge A2 \wedge A3$ holds in every instant in which it can be evaluated (2..15 in the original MPS, 4..15 with our semantics of the bounded operators).

In order to overcome this problem, we use a different evaluation of propositional operators based on the introduction of a third truth value, called *unevaluable* (or *undefined*). The idea is that if A is false at instant i then $A \wedge B$ is false, even if B is not evaluable (i.e., it is not possible to establish whether B is true or false). This can be described as follows:

- $A \wedge B$ is true at an instant i iff both A and B are evaluable and true at i;
- $A \wedge B$ is false at an instant i iff either A is false (regardless of the possibility of evaluating B) or B is false (regardless of the possibility of evaluating A) at i;
- $A \wedge B$ is not evaluable at i otherwise.

This approach corresponds to adopting the Kleene's truth tables of three-valued logic [10], which are shown in Table 1. The main feature of Kleene's tables is that the value *true* or the value *false* is returned whenever possible. In this way the previous example is now satisfactorily dealt with: $push \wedge Dist(on, -1) \vee timeout$ is true at 1, since *timeout* holds; $Becomes(\neg on)$ is defined as $\neg on \wedge Dist(on, -1)$, and therefore is false since on holds at 1. Hence, (A3) is false and therefore also $A1 \wedge A2 \wedge A3$ is false at 1. As a consequence $Alw(A1 \wedge A2 \wedge A3)$ is false.

$a \to b$				$a \leftrightarrow b$				$a \vee b$				$a \wedge b$				a xor b				$\neg a$	
a \ b	T	F	U	a \ b	T	F	U	a \ b	T	F	U	a \ b	T	F	U	a \ b	T	F	U	a	
T	T	F	U	T	T	F	U	T	T	T	T	T	T	F	U	T	F	T	T	T	F
F	T	T	T	F	F	T	U	F	T	F	U	F	F	F	F	F	T	F	U	F	T
U	T	U	U	U	U	U	U	U	T	U	U	U	U	F	U	U	T	U	U	U	U

Table 1. Kleene's three-valued propositional tables. U stands for unevaluable

It is easy to verify that using the new definition for bounded and propositional operators $Lasted(on, 5)$ becomes equivalent to $Dist(on, -1) \wedge Dist(on, -2) \wedge Dist(on, -3) \wedge Dist(on, -4)$, that is universal bounded quantification can be treated as an extended conjunction.

4 The formalization of the revised semantics

In this section the formalization of our proposal is presented by using a notation based on a three-valued evaluation of a formula over a finite history. Let us first define the concept of history, that is a structure on which formulas are evaluated, then the evaluation function for terms and formulas is presented.

History A *history* (or *structure*) for a formula F is a triple $S = \langle T, D, \{\Phi_i : i \in T\} \rangle$, where:

- T is the time domain.
- D is a set of interpretation domains for all identifiers occurring in F. The distance domain, $\Delta T = 1..|T|$, is an element of D. The notation $D(d)$ denotes the interpretation domain associated with identifier d.
- $\{\Phi_i : i \in T\}$ is a set of functions, providing interpretations on the domains of D for the function and predicate names of F. Φ_i provides a different interpretation for every instant i of the time domain.

Time independent functions and predicates are treated as special cases for which the different Φ_i do not change with i. If p is the name of an n-place predicate with signature $c_1, ..c_n$, Φ_i assigns an n-ary relation to it, that is $\Phi_i(p) \subseteq D(c_1) \times .. \times D(c_n)$; if f is an n-place function name with signature $c_1, ..c_n \rightarrow c_{n+1}$, then it is assigned an n-ary operation $\Phi_i(f) : D(c_1) \times .. \times D(c_n) \rightarrow D(c_{n+1})$. Time independent and time dependent constants are also assigned values by this component since they are considered as special cases of time independent and time dependent functions, respectively.

In order to interpret a formula, we need a value assignment to every variable. An *assignment* σ for a structure S is a function mapping every variable x, declared of type c_i in formula F, to a value $\sigma(x) \in D(c_i)$. A reassignment of σ for variable x is defined as any assignment σ_x that differs from σ at most in the value assigned to x. The notation S^σ represents a structure S with an assignment σ.

Evaluation of terms We define inductively a function S_i^σ which determines the value of terms and formulas for each time instant $i \in T$. The index σ, conveying the dependence of S_i from an assignment, will be omitted when no confusion can arise. S_i is defined for terms according to the following clauses.

1. $S_i^\sigma(x) = \sigma(x)$, for every (time independent) variable x.
2. $S_i(f(t_1, .., t_n)) = \Phi_i(f)(S_i(t_1), .., S_i(t_n))$, for every application of function f.
3. $S_i(c) = \Phi_i(c)$, for every constant c.

Evaluation of formulas For formulas S_i^σ returns true, false or uneval, that stands for unevaluable. The main idea is that the truth value of an atomic formula is considered not evaluable at instant i whenever $i \notin T$: S_i in this case returns $uneval$. The value $uneval$ is propagated to formulas using Kleene semantics for propositional operators, a definition equivalent to MPS for the quantifiers over the distance domain, and a new definition for the bounded operators $Lasts$ and $Lasted$ and bounded quantifications.

1. $S_i(p(t_1, .., t_n)) =$ **if** $i \in T$ **then** (**if** $\langle S_i(t_1), .., S_i(t_n) \rangle \in \Phi_i(p)$ **then** $true$ **else** $false$) **else** $uneval$, for a predicate p.
2. $S_i(\neg A) =$ **if** $S_i(A) = false$ **then** $true$ **elsif** $S_i(A) = true$ **then** $false$ **else** $uneval$.
3. $S_i(A \wedge B) =$ **if** $(S_i(A) = true$ and $S_i(B) = true)$ **then** $true$ **elsif** $(S_i(A) = false$ or $S_i(A) = false)$ **then** $false$ **else** $uneval$.
4. $S_i(Dist(A, t)) = S_{i+S_i(t)}(A)$.
5. $S_i^\sigma(\forall x A) =$ **if** $\exists \sigma_x (S_i^{\sigma_x}(A) = false)$ **then** $false$ **elsif** $\forall \sigma_x (S_i^{\sigma_x}(A) = uneval)$ **then** $uneval$ **else** $true$, for a variable x of domain ΔT.
6. $S_i^\sigma(\forall x A) =$ **if** $\exists \sigma_x (S_i^{\sigma_x}(A) = false)$ **then** $false$ **elsif** $\forall \sigma_x (S_i^{\sigma_x}(A) = true)$ **then** $true$ **else** $uneval$, where x is a variable of a domain different from ΔT.
7. $S_i(Lasts(A, t)) =$ **if** $\forall j (0 < j < S_i(t) \Rightarrow S_{i+j}(A) = true)$ **then** $true$ **elsif** $\exists j (0 < j < S_i(t)$ and $S_{i+j}(A) = false)$ **then** $false$ **else** $uneval$.

Clause 4 allows the propagation of the $Dist$ operator; clause 6 is introduced to differentiate every domain different from ΔT, because ΔT is assumed to be the only unbounded domain: the other domains are bounded and are treated correspondingly. $Lasted$ may be defined symmetrically as in clause 7.

5 Conclusions

A key feature of the TRIO language is its *executability*, that allows the construction of semantic tools, to help validation and verification, by means of specification simulation and test case generation. Various applications to current industrial practice [2] have used these tools.

In general, the satisfability of arbitrary first-order TRIO formulas is undecidable: a general interpretation algorithm is not guaranteed to terminate with a definite answer. To achieve executability, in TRIO the original interpretation domains, which are usually infinite, are replaced by some finite approximation thereof. Of course validating a specification using finite domains does not provide answers for the corresponding problem in the infinite domain case, but still provides useful and effective validation methods.

The definition of algorithms for the finite domain case requires a suitable finite-domain semantics, that is a semantics on finite domains that approximates the results on infinite domains. In this paper we showed how the current semantics of the TRIO language (MPS) needs to be revised in order to overcome several major problems. Our improved version of the MPS introduces a distinction between bounded and unbounded quantifiers and operators, evaluates differently the propositional operators and corrects various other flaws of the original definitions of [7]. We believe our proposal to be an improvement also in terms of clarity and ease of comprehension.

Current work is being devoted to assert and prove approximation theorems. Satisfactory experiments have been already performed with the history checking tool, while others are currently being studied for the test case generator.

Acknowledgments
We thank Dino Mandrioli for the fruitful discussions.

References

1. R. Alur and T.A. Henzinger: Logics and Models of Real-Time: A Survey. Proc. of REX Workshop-Real-Time: Theory and Practice, Mook, The Netherlands, June 1991, LNCS 600, Springer Verlag, New York, 1992, pp. 74-106.
2. M. Basso, E. Ciapessoni, E. Crivelli, D. Mandrioli, A. Morzenti, P. San Pietro: Experimenting a Logic-based Approach to the Specification and Design of the Control System of a Pondage Power Plant. M. Wirsing (ed.), ICSE-17 Workshop on Formal Methods Application in Softw. Eng. Practice, Seattle, WA, April 1995.
3. E. Ciapessoni, E. Corsetti, A. Montanari, P. San Pietro: Embedding Time Granularity in a Logical Specification Language for Synchronous Real-Time Systems. Science of Computer Programming, 20(1993), pp. 141-171, Elsevier Publishing, Amsterdam, 1993.
4. M. Felder, A. Morzenti: Validating real-time systems by history-checking TRIO specifications. ACM TOSEM-Transactions On Software Engineering and Methodologies, vol.3, n.4, October 1994
5. C. Ghezzi, D. Mandrioli, and A. Morzenti: TRIO, a logic language for executable specifications of real-time systems. Journal of Systems and Software 12, 2 (May 1990), 107-123.
6. A. Morzenti, and P. San Pietro: Object oriented logic specification of time-critical systems. ACM TOSEM, Vol. 3, n. 1, January 1994, pp. 56-98.
7. A. Morzenti, D. Mandrioli, and C. Ghezzi: A Model Parametric Real-Time Logic. ACM Transactions on Programming Languages and Systems 14, 4 (October 1992), 521-573.
8. D. Mandrioli, S. Morasca, A. Morzenti: Generating Test Cases for Real-Time Systems from Logic Specifications. ACM Trans. On Computer Systems, Vol. 13, No. 4, November 1995. pp.365-398.
9. S. Morasca, A. Morzenti, P. San Pietro: Generating Functional Test Cases in-the-large for Time-critical Systems from Logic-based Specifications. Proc. of ISSTA 1996, ACM-SIGSOFT International Symposium on Software Testing and Analysis, Jan. 1996, San Diego, CA.
10. A. Urquhart: Many valued Logic. D. Gabbay and F, Guenthner (eds), Handbook of Philosophical Logic, Vol. III, Kluwer, London, 1986.

Duration Calculus of Weakly Monotonic Time

Paritosh K. Pandya[1] and Dang Van Hung[2]

[1] Tata Institute of Fundamental Research
Mumbai 400 005, India
email: pandya@tcs.tifr.res.in

[2] UNU/IIST
Macau
email: dvh@iist.unu.edu

Abstract. We extend Duration Calculus to a logic which allows description of *Discrete Processes* where several steps of computation can occur at the same time point. The resulting logic is called Duration Calculus of Weakly Monotonic Time (*WDC*). It allows effects such as *true synchrony* and *digitisation* to be modelled. As an example of this, we formulate a novel semantics of Timed CSP assuming that the communication and computation take no time.

1 Introduction

Many real-time systems are designed and analysed under the assumption that computation and communication do not take time. This assumption has been called **true synchrony** hypothesis [2]. Thus, only the waiting for external synchronisation or explicit delay statements take time. Such an abstraction provides an essential simplification in understanding the behaviour of real-time systems. Logics for real-time system must be capable of handling such abstractions.

One recent logic for real-time systems is the Duration Calculus (*DC*) [12]. The original duration calculus was intended as a logic for formulating requirements of real-time systems. At this level of description, the details of internal working of the system are hidden and only externally observable behaviour of the system is specified.

When behaviours under the true synchrony hypothesis are considered, it is quite natural that the system passes through a number of states within zero (negligible) time. To accommodate such behaviours, in this paper, we allow a discrete sequence of state changes to occur at a single "macro" time point. The resulting notion of time has been called in the literature as *weakly monotonic* [1]. We define an extension of Duration Calculus to weakly monotonic time. We also include the notion of point-intervals from the mean-value calculus [13].

Our extension, called *Duration Calculus of Weakly Monotonic Time* (*WDC*), has been largely motivated by our attempts to capture the *low level* semantics of a wide spectrum of distributed and timed programming notations in Duration Calculus. These include synchronous languages like ESTEREL, SL and State charts, hardware description languages like Verilog and VHDL, and models such as timed automata. In most of these languages, a causally connected sequence of events may occur at the same time point.

We believe that many new interesting features such as true synchrony and digitisation of signals with discrete clocks [5] can be handled within the generalised setting. As an example of this, we give a novel semantics to Timed CSP under the true synchrony assumption.

The rest of the paper is organised as follows. Section 2 defines the notion weakly monotonic time and gives the syntax and semantics of *WDC*. Section 3 gives the semantics of Timed CSP under the assumption of true synchrony. The report ends with a brief discussion.

2 Duration Calculus of Weakly Monotonic Time

We shall assume that the system execution consists of a sequences of *phases* where each phase may last for zero, finite or infinite time. In order to describe such an execution, we introduce the notion of a *stepped time frame*. Figure 1 depicts the nature of stepped time-frame.

The horizontal axis represents *macro* time whereas the vertical axis represents the *phase-count*. Macro time refers to the external view of time with respect to which the real-time properties like response and delay are measured. An execution of the system gives rise to a *path* within the two-dimensional plane, which always extends by steps in either up or the right direction. We shall identify such a path by a *stepped time frame* consisting of the set of points on the path. Each such point is called a *micro* time point and represented by a tuple (t, i) where t is the macro-time and i is the phase count.

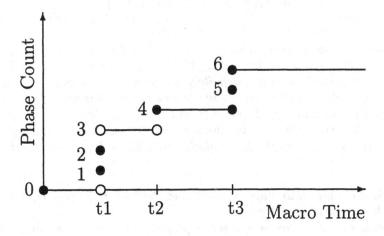

Fig. 1. Time Diagram

In the figure, solid circles indicates the presence of time-point whereas empty circles indicate the absence of time-point. We write the phase-count of each time point next to it. Thus, the diagram above represents the following stepped time frame:

$$\{(x,0) \mid 0 \leq x < t1\} \cup \{(t1,1), (t1,2)\} \cup \{(x,3) \mid t1 < x < t2\} \cup$$
$$\cup \{(x,4) \mid t2 \leq x \leq t3\} \cup \{(t3,5)\} \cup \{(x,6) \mid t3 \leq x\}$$

A behaviour of the system specifies the state of the system at each micro time point. Moreover, we shall assume the stability condition requiring that the state of the system remains unchanged throughout a phase. We shall now formalise the notion of a stepped time frame and behaviours over it.

2.1 Weakly-Monotonic Time

Macro-time We parameterise the logic with macro-time frame $TM = (T, <)$ where T is the set of time points and $<$ is "earlier than" order. It is assumed that TM is linearly ordered. The resulting logic is called $WDC(TM)$. In discrete time interpretation, TM is taken to be $(\omega, <)$, the set of natural numbers. In dense time interpretation, TM is taken to be $(\Re^0, <)$, the set of non-negative real numbers.

Every macro-time point is split into one or more micro-time point. Each micro-time point (t, i) consists of the macro-time t and a *phase-count* corresponding to the number of steps which have occurred *before* reaching this micro-time point.

Definition 1 (Stepped Time). *Given a time frame TM, a stepped time frame w.r.t. TM is a pair $WTM = (WT, <)$ satisfying the following conditions:*

- $WT \subseteq T \times \omega$. *Let* $\pi_1((t,i)) \overset{\text{def}}{=} t$ *and* $\pi_2((t,i)) = i$. *Define* $\pi_1(WT) = \{t \mid (t,i) \in WT\}$ *and* $\pi_2(WT) = \{i \mid (t,i) \in WT\}$.
- $<$ *is the lexicographic ordering on* WT, *i.e.* $(t_1, i_1) < (t_2, i_2)$ *iff* $t_1 < t_2 \vee (t_1 = t_2 \wedge i_1 < i_2)$. *Thus,* $(WT, <)$ *is a total order.*
- **(Phase Monotonicity)** $t_1 < t_2 \wedge (t_1, i_1) \in WT \wedge (t_2, i_2) \in WT \Rightarrow i_1 \leq i_2$.
- **(Progress)** $\pi_1(WT) = T \quad \vee \quad \pi_2(WT) = \omega$. *This states that either the macro-time must increase indefinitely, or the micro-time must increase indefinitely. Here we allow macro-time to stop in case there are infinitely many phase changes which occur within finite time (i.e. finite divergence [4]).*
- **(Past closure)** $\pi_2(WT)$ *is downward closed w.r.t.* $<$ *on* ω, *i.e.* $i_1 \in \pi_2(WT) \wedge i_2 < i_1 \Rightarrow i_2 \in \pi_2(WT)$. *Similarly,* $\pi_1(WT)$ *is downward closed w.r.t.* $(T, <)$.

We shall use b, e, m to range over WT. Let $Per(WT, i) \overset{\text{def}}{=} \{t \mid (t, i) \in WT\}$ denote the period of the ith phase.

Interpretation Let $Pvar$ be the set of propositional (state) variables. A behaviour over TM is a pair $I = (WTM, \theta)$, where WTM is a stepped time frame w.r.t. TM and the function θ assigns a boolean function of stepped time to each propositional variable $p \in Pvar$. Thus, $\theta(p) \in WT \to \{0,1\}$. Moreover, θ must satisfy the **stability** condition stating that for any $i \in \pi_2(WT)$, we have $\theta(p)(b) = \theta(p)(e)$ for all $b,e \in Per(WT,i)$.

We shall also assume that there are some global variables in the system, which do not change with time. Let $Gvar = Ivar \cup Rvar$ be the set global variables, which is partitioned into the disjoint subsets $Ivar$, of integer variables, and $Rvar$, of real variables. Finally, there are propositional interval variables, or formula variables, denoted by $X, Y \in Fvar$. Their value depends on the time interval.

The function θ also assigns a real-number to each global real variable $x \in Rvar$ and an integer to each integer variable. Thus,

$$\theta \in (Pvar \to WT \to \{0,1\}) \times (Ivar \to \omega) \times$$
$$(Rvar \to \Re) \times (Fvar \to Intv \to \{0,1\})$$

For each proposition P, we can define a partial function $\theta_c(P) \in \pi_1(WT) \mapsto Bool$ of macro-time as follows.

$$\theta_c(P)(t) = \theta(P)(t,i) \quad \{i \mid (t,i) \in WT\} \text{ is singleton}$$
$$= \perp \qquad\qquad \text{otherwise}$$

Note that $\theta_c(P)$ is undefined at a discrete set of points. However, for $TM = (\Re^0, <)$, the function $\theta_c(P)$ is piecewise continuous (in fact, constant) and bounded. Hence we can define the Riemann integral $\int_{t_1}^{t_2} \theta_c(P)(t)dt$ as usual.

2.2 Logic WDC

Given a time frame TM, notation $WDC(TM)$ will denote Duration Calculus with weakly monotonic time over the frame TM. In the rest of this paper we shall assume that the time is dense, i.e. $TM = (\Re^0, <)$.

Syntax We have a two sorted logic with terms of type integer and real. Let P, Q range over states, $ti_1, ti_2, \ldots$ over terms of type integer, $tr_1, tr_2, \ldots$ over terms of type real, and D_1, D_2 over formulae. We shall use t to denote term of either type.

Real Terms have the form:

$$c \mid xr \mid \ell \mid \int P \mid tr_1 \text{ op } tr_2$$

where $op \in \{+, -, *\}$ and xr denotes a real-variable.

Integer terms have the form:

$$k \mid xi \mid \eta \mid tr_1 \text{ op } tr_2$$

where $op \in \{+, -, *\}$ and xi denotes an integer variable.

Formulae have the form:

$$\lceil P \rceil^0 \mid Pt_l \mid t_1 = t_2 \mid t_1 < t_2 \mid \neg D \mid D_1 \wedge D_2 \mid \exists x.D \mid D_1 \frown D_2$$

In the above, care must be taken to compare terms t_1, t_2 of the same type.

Semantics The set of intervals over stepped time frame $WTM = (WT, <)$ is defined as $Intv(WTM) = \{[b, e] \in WT \times WT \mid b \le e\}$

A *model* is a pair $(I, [b, e])$ where I is an interpretation (WTM, θ) and $[b, e]$ is an interval from $Intv(WTM)$. We shall denote the value of a term t in a model $(WTM, \theta, [b, e])$ by $\mathcal{V}(t)(WTM, \theta, [b, e])$, and the satisfaction of a formula D by $(WTM, \theta, [b, e]) \models D$. We shall typically abbreviate these by $\mathcal{V}(t)(\theta, [b, e])$ and $(\theta, [b, e]) \models D$.

The semantics is inductively defined as follows:

$$\begin{aligned}
\mathcal{V}(\ell)(\theta, [b, e]) &= \pi_1(e) - \pi_1(b) \\
\mathcal{V}(\eta)(\theta, [b, e]) &= \pi_2(e) - \pi_2(b) \\
\mathcal{V}(\smallint P)(\theta, [b, e]) &= \int_{\pi_1(b)}^{\pi_1(e)} \theta_c(P)\, dt \\
\mathcal{V}(x)(\theta, [b, e]) &= \theta(x)
\end{aligned}$$

All the other cases are routine [12], and omitted.

$$\begin{aligned}
(\theta, [b, e]) &\models \lceil P \rceil^0 && \textbf{iff} && b = e \wedge \theta(P)(b) = 1 \\
(\theta, [b, e]) &\models t_1 = t_2 && \textbf{iff} && \mathcal{V}(t_1)(\theta, [b, e]) = \mathcal{V}(t_2)(\theta, [b, e]) \\
(\theta, [b, e]) &\models t_1 < t_2 && \textbf{iff} && \mathcal{V}(t_1)(\theta, [b, e]) < \mathcal{V}(t_2)(\theta, [b, e]) \\
(\theta, [b, e]) &\models X && \textbf{iff} && \theta(X)[b, e] = 1 \\
(\theta, [b, e]) &\models D_1 \frown D_2 && \textbf{iff} && \exists m \in WT : b \le m \le e. \\
& && (\theta, [b, m]) \models D_1 && \wedge \quad (\theta, [m, e]) \models D_2
\end{aligned}$$

The usual set of derived operators are defined as usual. Notably, we have $Pt_i \overset{\text{def}}{=} \lceil 1 \rceil^0$ and $Ext_i \overset{\text{def}}{=} \neg Pt_i$. Also, $Pt_l \overset{\text{def}}{=} \ell = 0$ and $Ext_l \overset{\text{def}}{=} \neg Pt_l$. Let $Unit \overset{\text{def}}{=} Ext_i \wedge \neg(Ext_i \frown Ext_i)$. Let $\lceil P \rceil^1 \overset{\text{def}}{=} \lceil P \rceil^0 \frown Unit$. Also, $\lceil P \rceil \overset{\text{def}}{=} \neg(Ext_i \frown \lceil \neg P \rceil^0 \frown Ext_i)$. It is easy to see that $(\theta, [b, e]) \models \lceil P \rceil$ iff $b < e$ and $\theta(P)(m)$ for all $m : b < m < t$.

Let $(WTM, \theta) \models D$ iff $(WTM, \theta, [b, e]) \models D$ for all $[b, e] \in Intv(WTM)$. Let $TM \models D$ iff $(WTM, \theta) \models D$ for all models (WTM, θ) over the macro time frame TM.

The axiomatisation and decidability results for WDC are similar to those for the Duration Calculus (see [9] for further details).

2.3 Extensions and Notation

State Quantification It is convenient to include the state quantification construct $\exists p.D$ where p is a state variable in the language. Its semantics is given below (see [6] for a detailed discussion of the state quantification construct).

$$(\theta, [b, e]) \models \exists p.D \text{ iff } (\theta', [b, e]) \models D \text{ for some } p\text{-variant } \theta' \text{ of } \theta.$$

The resulting logical may be called $QWDC$.

Notational Abbreviations

$$\lceil P \rceil^1 \overset{\text{def}}{=} \lceil P \rceil^0 \frown Unit \qquad \lceil\!\lceil P \rceil\!\rceil \overset{\text{def}}{=} \lceil P \rceil^0 \frown \lceil P \rceil$$

$$\lceil\!\lceil P \rceil\!\rceil^+ \overset{\text{def}}{=} \lceil\!\lceil P \rceil\!\rceil \vee \lceil P \rceil^0 \qquad \lceil\!\lceil P \rceil\!\rceil^- \overset{\text{def}}{=} \lceil\!\lceil P \rceil\!\rceil \vee \lceil \ \rceil$$

Similarly $\lceil P \rceil\!\rceil$, $\lceil P \rceil\!\rceil^+$, $\lceil P \rceil\!\rceil^-$, $\lceil\!\lceil P \rceil\!\rceil$, $\lceil\!\lceil P \rceil\!\rceil^+$, $\lceil\!\lceil P \rceil\!\rceil^-$.

3   Compositional Semantics of Timed CSP

In this section, we give semantics to programming notations under the *true synchrony hypothesis*. In this hypothesis, it is assumed that *computation, communication/shared memory access* take no time. We interpret this to mean that they starts and finishes at the same *macro* time point. Any elapsing of macro time must be explicitly modelled using the delay t construct. Time can also elapse when the process waits to synchronise with its environment.

Using the true synchrony abstraction, we define a compositional semantics of Timed CSP, a well-known notation for distributed real-time programs, where processes synchronise by handshake communication. The semantics is low-level and captures the details of scheduling and interleaving of concurrent processes at the micro-step level.

In this section, we shall assume that the time-frames are *left-right continuous*, i.e. the following axiom holds

$$\Box(\eta > 0 \Rightarrow true \,{}^\frown Unit \,{}^\frown true)$$

Let S, T range over processes, a, c over channels and d over real constants. Let $cc, cc_1, \ldots$ range over communication commands of the form $c?$ or $c!$. A Timed CSP process has the following form.

$$\text{stop} \mid \text{skip} \mid \text{tick} \mid cc \mid \text{delay } d \mid S; T \mid S \sqcap T \mid [\Box_{i \in I} cc_i \to S_i] \mid$$
$$S\|T \mid S \setminus c \mid \text{rec } X.F(X) \mid S \overset{t}{\triangleright} T \mid S\nabla_t T$$

Each process has the alphabet $\alpha = (In, Out)$ of input and output channels. Let $Ports(\alpha) = In \times \{?\} \cup Out \times \{!\}$.

Process stop represents a deadlocked process. skip terminates instantaneously without requiring any resources. On the other hand, tick takes one micro-step of computation to terminate. Processes $c?$ and $c!$ represent input and output communication over channel c. Process delay d waits for d time units before terminating. The nondeterministic choice $S \sqcap T$, the guarded choice $[\ldots]$, the sequential composition $S; T$, the parallel composition $S\|T$, hiding $S \setminus c$ and recursion $rec\ X.F(X)$ function in the same manner as in CSP. The "tireout" construct $S\nabla_t T$ allows S to execute for t time units. After that the process is interrupted and it terminates. The timeout construct $S \overset{t}{\triangleright} T$ is similar to the tireout, except that if process S performs any visible communication before time t then it is not interrupted. We refer the reader any standard work on Timed CSP, such as [3], for a detailed explanation of these constructs.

To record observable behaviour of a process, we use a state variable p for each $p \in Ports(\alpha)$ and a state variable c for each $c \in \alpha$. Variable p is true exactly when a process is waiting (ready) to communicate over the port p, and variable c is true exactly at those time points when a communication over c is taking place. We shall assume that communication takes no macro-time but requires one micro-step.

Notation For a set of states $C = \{c_1, \ldots, c_n\}$, let the state C denote $c_1 \vee c_2 \vee \ldots \vee c_n$. For a set of ports P and a set of channels C, let

$$enonly_\alpha(P) \stackrel{\text{def}}{=} (\forall p \in P.\ p) \quad \wedge \quad (\forall p \in (Ports(\alpha) - P).\ \neg p)$$
$$passive(C) \stackrel{\text{def}}{=} \neg C$$
$$await_\alpha(P) \stackrel{\text{def}}{=} enonly(P) \wedge passive(\alpha)$$
$$comm_\alpha(c) \stackrel{\text{def}}{=} c \wedge passive(\alpha - \{c\}) \wedge enonly_\alpha(\emptyset)$$
$$Idle_\alpha \stackrel{\text{def}}{=} enonly_\alpha(\emptyset) \wedge passive(\alpha)$$

For a process S over α we define a *WDC* formula $\mathcal{M}(S)$ capturing precisely the set of behaviours of S. Thus, $\mathcal{M}(S)$ gives the *strongest specification* of S. We use prefix-closed semantics. An interval temporal variable b records whether the execution is partial or terminated. Thus, $(\theta, [0, e]) \models \mathcal{M}(S)$ if and only if θ over the subinterval $[0, e]$ denotes a (partial) execution of S. Moreover, if $(\theta, [0, e]) \models \mathcal{M}(S) \wedge b$ then $(\theta, [0, e])$ denotes a complete execution where S has terminated. We shall use the following abbreviation:

$$fstep(D) \stackrel{\text{def}}{=} (Pt_i \wedge \neg b \quad \vee \quad Unit \frown D)$$

For example, the behaviour of process $(delay\ 2; c?)$ is given by the formula:

$$\lceil\!\lceil Idle \rceil\!\rceil^+ \wedge \ell < 2 \wedge \neg b$$
$$\vee\ (\lceil\!\lceil Idle \rceil\!\rceil^+ \wedge \ell = 2 \frown$$
$$\quad fstep(\lceil await(c?) \rceil^- \frown$$
$$\qquad (\lceil await(c?) \rceil^0 \wedge \neg b \quad \vee \quad \lceil comm(c) \rceil^0 \frown fstep(Pt_i \wedge b)))\ )$$

The behaviour of $(c? \stackrel{t}{\triangleright} d!)$ is given by:

$$\lceil\!\lceil await(c?) \rceil\!\rceil^+ \wedge \neg b \wedge \ell \le t$$
$$\vee\ (\lceil\!\lceil await(c?) \rceil\!\rceil^- \wedge \ell \le t) \frown \lceil comm(c) \rceil^0 \frown fstep(Pt_i \wedge b)$$
$$\vee\ (\lceil\!\lceil await(c?) \rceil\!\rceil^+ \wedge \ell = t) \frown fstep(\lceil\!\lceil await(d!) \rceil\!\rceil^+ \wedge \neg b \quad \vee$$
$$\qquad \lceil\!\lceil await(d!) \rceil\!\rceil^- \frown \lceil comm(d) \rceil^0 \frown fstep(Pt_i \wedge b))$$

Semantics

$$\mathcal{M}(stop) \stackrel{\text{def}}{=} \lceil\!\lceil Idle \rceil\!\rceil^+ \wedge \neg b$$
$$\mathcal{M}(skip) \stackrel{\text{def}}{=} b \wedge Pt_i$$

tick takes one micro-step. It is an abstraction of statements like assignment which represent internal steps.

$$\mathcal{M}(tick) \stackrel{\text{def}}{=} (\lceil Idle \rceil^0) \frown fstep(Pt_i \wedge b)$$

Delay consumes d units of macro-time. Below we give a loose semantics to this construct where there is no restriction on the number of micro-steps it may take once time d has elapsed.

$$\mathcal{M}(delay\ d) \stackrel{\text{def}}{=} (\lceil\!\lceil Idle \rceil\!\rceil^+ \wedge \ell < t \wedge \neg b$$
$$\vee\ (\lceil\!\lceil Idle \rceil\!\rceil^+ \wedge \ell = t) \frown fstep(Pt_i \wedge b)$$

An alternative semantics representing a "strong delay" construct can be given as

$$M(delay\ d) \stackrel{\text{def}}{=} (\llbracket Idle \rrbracket^+ \wedge \ell < t \wedge \neg b$$
$$\vee\ (\llbracket Idle \rrbracket^+ \wedge \ell = t \wedge \neg(true \frown (\ell = 0 \wedge Ext_i)))\ \frown \text{fstep}(Pt_i \wedge b)$$

The conjunct $\neg(true \frown (\ell = 0 \wedge Ext_i)))$ ensures that there no micro-steps at the endpoint. This forces the delay d to terminate as soon as time d has passed without consuming any micro-steps.

$$M(c?) \stackrel{\text{def}}{=} \begin{array}{l} \lceil await(c?) \rrbracket^+ \wedge \neg b \\ \vee\ \lceil await(c?) \rceil^- \frown \lceil comm(c) \rceil^0 \frown \text{fstep}(Pt_i \wedge b) \end{array}$$

The idea here is the process may be ready and wait for communication for arbitrary macro+micro time. The actual communication takes one micro-step.

$$M(c!) \stackrel{\text{def}}{=} \begin{array}{l} \lceil await(c!) \rrbracket^+ \wedge \neg b \\ \vee\ \lceil await(c!) \rceil^- \frown \lceil comm(c) \rceil^0 \frown \text{fstep}(Pt_i \wedge b) \end{array}$$
$$M(S; T) \stackrel{\text{def}}{=} M(S) \wedge \neg b \quad \vee \quad M(S)[true/b] \frown M(T)$$
$$M(S \sqcap T) \stackrel{\text{def}}{=} M(S) \vee M(T)$$

In the following guarded choice construct, we assume that the guard cc_i is of the form $c_i?$ or $c_i!$, and $G = \{c_i \mid i \in I\}$.

$$M([\square_{i \in I}\ cc_i \rightarrow S_i]) \stackrel{\text{def}}{=} \lceil await(G) \rrbracket^+ \wedge \neg b$$
$$\vee\ \bigvee_{i \in I}\ \lceil await(G) \rceil^- \frown \lceil comm(c_i) \rceil^0 \frown \text{fstep}(M(S_i))$$

Parallel Composition Let $M(PASS) \stackrel{\text{def}}{=} \lceil Idle \rceil^- \wedge b$. Then,

$$M(S \| T) \stackrel{\text{def}}{=} \exists b_1, b_2.\,(M(S; PASS)[b_1/b] \wedge M(T)[b_2/b]$$
$$\vee\ M(S)[b_1/b] \wedge M(T; PASS)[b_2/b]\,)$$
$$\wedge\ (b \Leftrightarrow b_1 \wedge b_2)\ \wedge\ COND$$

Here, $COND$ axiomatises the underlying assumptions about the nature of concurrency. For example, we can choose one of the following.

- $COND_1 = true$ places no restrictions.
- $COND_2 = \llbracket \neg(c? \wedge c!) \rrbracket^+$ states that the communication must occur as soon as it is possible (i.e. both sender and receiver become ready). Such semantics has been termed as maximum parallelism.
- $COND_3 = \square(\llbracket c? \wedge c! \rrbracket^+ \Rightarrow \ell = 0)$ states that the communication can remain ready for many micro-steps but it must be completed within 0 macro-time. This allows us to represent causal connections between multiple communications which occur at the same time, while giving maximum parallelism at the level of macro-time.
- $COND_4 = COND_3 \wedge (\bigwedge_{c, d \in \alpha, c \neq d} \llbracket c \Rightarrow \neg d \rrbracket^+)$ gives maximum parallelism at the macro-time level. But it also requires that only one communication can occur in a micro-step. Thus it enforces interleaving semantics at the micro-step level.

Timing Related Constructs The "tireout" construct $S\nabla_t T$ allows S to execute for t time units. After that the process is interrupted and it terminates. We define the loose semantics of tire-out construct below where there is no restriction on the number of micro-steps the process S may execute after time t.

$$\mathcal{M}(S\nabla_t T) \stackrel{\text{def}}{=} \quad \mathcal{M}(S) \wedge \ell < t \quad \vee \quad \mathcal{M}(S) \wedge \ell = t \wedge b$$
$$\vee \ ((\mathcal{M}(S)[false/b] \wedge \ell = t) ^\frown \text{fstep}(\mathcal{M}(T)))$$

An alternative semantics defining the "strong tireout" construct can be given as follows, where process S may not perform any micro-steps once time t has elapsed. The control must immediately be passed to process T.

$$\mathcal{M}(S\nabla_t T) \stackrel{\text{def}}{=} \quad \mathcal{M}(S) \wedge \ell < t$$
$$\vee \ ((\mathcal{M}(S)[false/b] \wedge \ell = t \wedge \neg(true ^\frown (\ell = 0 \wedge Ext_i))) ^\frown \text{fstep}(\mathcal{M}(T)))$$

The timeout construct is similar to above, except that if process S performs any visible communication before time t then it is not interrupted. We give the loose semantics below. Strong semantics can also be defined.

$$\mathcal{M}(S \stackrel{t}{\triangleright} T) \stackrel{\text{def}}{=} \quad \mathcal{M}(S) \wedge \ell \le t \vee \mathcal{M}(S) \wedge (\ell \le t ^\frown \lceil \neg passive(\alpha) \rceil^0 ^\frown true)$$
$$\vee \ ((\mathcal{M}(S)[false/b] \wedge \ell = t \wedge \lceil\lceil passive(\alpha) \rceil\rceil^+) ^\frown \text{fstep}(\mathcal{M}(T)))$$

Hiding Hiding is easily modelled using the state quantification construct.

$$\mathcal{M}(S \setminus c) \stackrel{\text{def}}{=} \exists c?, c!, c. \ \mathcal{M}(S)$$

Recursion Recursion cannot be directly handled within the logic *WDC*. However, the logic can be extended with least and greatest fixed point operators as in Pandya [8]. This can be used to give semantics of recursion as follows.

We represent a process variable X by a *WDC* formula variable X, $\mathcal{M}(X) \stackrel{\text{def}}{=} X$. Then, recursion can be handled using the greatest fixed point operator.

$$\mathcal{M}(rec \ X.F(X)) \stackrel{\text{def}}{=} \nu X.\mathcal{M}(F(X))$$

It is easy to see that the following laws holds:

$$\mathcal{M}(rec \ X.X) \Leftrightarrow true$$
$$\mathcal{M}(S; \text{skip}) = \mathcal{M}(S) = \mathcal{M}(\text{skip}; S)$$

Similar law does not hold for tick.

4   Discussion

We have defined a notion of weakly monotonic time where several state changes can occur at the same (macro) time point. We have given a straightforward extension of Duration Calculus for weakly monotonic time. The extension makes it possible to model interesting new phenomena like the behaviour of synchronous programs and digitisation. We have illustrated this by giving a novel semantics of Timed CSP assuming the true synchrony hypothesis. A more substantial example of the use of *WDC* may be found in [7], where a compositional semantics of the synchronous programming language *SL* has been defined, in [11] where assumption-commitment style verification of shared variable programs is investigated, and in [10] where semantics of a subset of Verilog has been formulated. We have not dealt with digitisation [5] in this paper, which is a topic of our on-going work.

One significant feature of *WDC* is that it preserves almost all the properties of the original Duration Calculus. Thus, most of the proof rules for durations remain unchanged. Decidability properties of *WDC* are also similar to those of the original *DC* [9].

Acknowledgements This paper is a revised version of the technical report [9] which has been available since August, 1996. We thank Anders Ravn, Hans Rischel, Xu Qiwen and Zhou Chaochen for their helpful comments which have helped in shaping this work to its present form.

References

1. R. Alur and T.A. Henzinger. Logics and models of real time: A survey. In *Proc. REX workshop on real-time: Theory in Practice*, volume 600 of *LNCS*. Springer-Verlag, 1991.
2. Gérard Berry and Georges Gonthier. The esterel synchronous programming language: Design, semantics, implementation. *Science of Computer Programming*, 19:87–152, 1992.
3. J. Davis and S. Schneider. A brief history of timed csp. *Theoretical Computer Science*, 138, 1995.
4. M.R. Hansen, P.K. Pandya, and Chaochen Zhou. Finite divergence. *Theoretical Computer Science*, 138:113–139, 1995.
5. T. Henzinger, Z. Manna, and A. Pnueli. What good are digital clocks. volume 623 of *LNCS*, pages 273–337. Springer-Verlag, 1992.
6. P.K. Pandya. Some extensions to mean-value calculus: expressiveness and decidability. In H. Kleine Buning, editor, *Proc. CSL'95*, volume 1092 of *LNCS*. Springer-Verlag, 1995.
7. P.K. Pandya. A compositional semantics of SL. Technical report, DeTfoRS Group, UNU/IIST, October 1997.
8. P.K. Pandya and Y.S. Ramakrishna. A recursive mean value calculus. Technical report, Computer Science Group, TIFR, Bombay, TCS-95/3, 1995.
9. P.K. Pandya and D.V. Hung. Duration Calculus of Weakly Monotonic Time. Technical Report 129, UNU/IIST, P.O. Box 3058, Macau, 1997.
10. G. Schneider and Qiwen Xu. Towards a formal semantics of Verilog using Duration Caculus. In *proc. of FTRTFT'98*, LNCS, 1998. (to appear).
11. Qiwen Xu and Swarup Mohalik. Compositional verification in duration calculus. Technical Report 136, UNU/IIST, P.O. Box 3058 Macau, 1997.
12. Chaochen Zhou, C.A.R. Hoare, and A.P. Ravn. A calculus of durations. *Information Processing Letters*, 40(5):269–276, 1991.
13. Chaochen Zhou and Xiaoshan Li. A mean value calculus of durations. In *A Classical Mind: Essays in Honour of C.A.R. Hoare, A.W. Roscoe (ed)*, pages 431–451. Prentice Hall International, 1994.

Reuse in Requirements Engineering: Discovery and Application of a Real-Time Requirement Pattern*

R. Gotzhein, M. Kronenburg, and C. Peper

University of Kaiserslautern, Germany
{gotzhein|kronburg|peper}@informatik.uni-kl.de

Abstract. We apply a reuse approach to formally specify system requirements. The approach is based on *requirement patterns*, which are related to *design patterns* well-known in object-oriented software development. The focus of this paper is on the application-driven discovery of an interesting, non-trivial real-time requirement pattern, and its subsequent application. In particular, we demonstrate how a given natural language requirement for a real-time system has been transformed into a precise and concise formal specification using real-time temporal logic. Finally, we motivate and illustrate the reuse potential of requirement specifications by a diverse collection of examples.

Keywords: requirements analysis, reuse, pattern discovery, formal specification, temporal logic, real-time, formal methods, case study

1 Introduction

Requirements analysis and specification are among the first steps of system development. In order to avoid later disagreements between customer and system developer, and to obtain a sound basis for subsequent development steps, it is essential that requirements be stated completely and precisely, while still being intelligible. In practice, requirements are often stated unprecisely – due to the use of natural language – and incompletely – due to the inherent difficulty to perceive all essential aspects of the problem to be solved. This could lead to disagreements during subsequent development stages including the acceptance of the final product by the customer. In order to avoid these problems, the use of formal description techniques (FDTs) for the specification of requirements is being advocated.

Especially for large and complex systems, the investment to obtain a "good" requirement specification is considerable. To reduce this effort, it is possible to benefit from earlier system developments by reusing developer experience as well as parts of already developed products. Recently, *design patterns* [2] have

---

* This work has been supported by the Deutsche Forschungsgemeinschaft (DFG) as part of the Sonderforschungsbereich (SFB) 501, "Development of Large Systems with Generic Methods".

been advocated as a promising reuse concept for the design phase, which is related to other well-known approaches such as *frameworks*, or *toolkits*. We have adopted this idea in [3, 4], where we have introduced and applied so-called SDL patterns for the development of communication protocols. Different from most reuse activities so far, which are informal, *SDL patterns* define building blocks that – when selected, adapted and composed properly – yield a formal protocol specification in SDL, an FDT that is internationally standardized and widely applied in industry.

It has been observed that the earlier the reuse, the larger the impact on a project [11]. It follows from this observation that reuse in the requirements phase may have a positive impact on subsequent development stages by an increased reuse of designs and implementations. While reuse has been well studied for systems *design*, less research is available on how to apply this principle to specify system *requirements*. In [10], we have introduced an approach that increases the reuse potential already in this early development stage. Our approach is based on so-called *requirement patterns*, which describe generic solutions for recurring problems and represent experience gained during previous system development activities.

In Section 2, we outline our reuse approach with emphasis on those aspects that are addressed in detail afterwards. In Section 3, we list an excerpt of a description of a real-time problem from the requirements document of a customer, which is stated in natural language augmented by a diagram as often found in this kind of document. In Section 4, we present our final result, consisting of a surprisingly concise formal specification using a real-time temporal logic with tailored operators. In Section 5, we extract the underlying requirement pattern, add it to our requirement pattern pool, and apply it to diverse requirements. We conclude with an outlook (Section 6).

2 Outline of Our Reuse Approach

In this section, we outline our reuse approach with emphasis on those aspects that are illustrated afterwards. The complete approach and additional details can be found in [10].

2.1 A Requirement Specification Development Model

System development usually starts with a *natural language requirement specification* (NLRS) consisting of an initial set of requirements that is supplied by the customer ("Customer NLRS" for short, see Figure 1a)). As already mentioned, natural language has no unique semantics. Therefore, these requirements should be formalized by the system developer, yielding a *formal requirement specification* (FRS).

As a result of this formalization, existing ambiguities of the natural language description are resolved in one particular way, which may differ from the original intentions of the customer. Therefore, the customer needs to check whether his

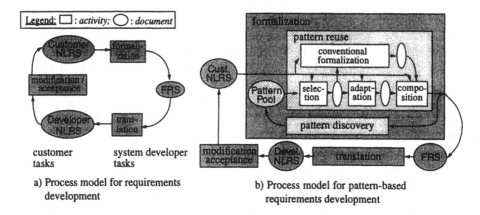

Fig. 1. Process models

intentions are correctly expressed in the FRS. Since the customer may not have a background in FDTs, we translate the FRS back to natural language resulting in a further document called "Developer NLRS" (see Figure 1a)). Since this natural language description is directly translated from a formal specification, we assume that it is more precise than the original Customer NLRS. The Developer NLRS may now serve as a basis for customer and developer to reach agreement on the system requirements.

If agreement is reached, the Developer NLRS replaces the previous Customer NLRS and serves as the basis for the acceptance of the final implementation. As another benefit, the new Customer NLRS already has a corresponding formalization, namely the FRS, which can be used as the starting point for subsequent development steps. If agreement is not reached, the customer supplies a modified Customer NLRS based on the Developer NLRS, and another cycle of the requirement specification development is started. Thus, the development of a requirement specification is an iterative process.

2.2 Reuse of Requirement Patterns

As we have argued, the described approach to the development of requirement specifications has a number of benefits. However, the effort to produce the FRS and its derived natural language description usually is considerable, especially if large and complex systems are to be characterized. To reduce this effort, we have proposed a *reuse approach* to the formalization of requirements. Our approach is based on a *pool of requirement patterns*. By *requirement pattern*, we refer to a generic description of a class of domain-specific requirements. Requirement patterns are related to *design patterns*, a well-known concept of object-oriented software development [2].

To describe requirement patterns, we use the format shown in Table 1, called *requirement pattern description template*. Instantiations of this template are termed *requirement patterns*, which, itself instantiated, form the constituents of a requirement specification. The contents of the template will depend on the application domain and the FDT used to specify patterns and their semantic properties.

Table 1. Requirement pattern description template

Name	The name of the requirement pattern.
Intention	An informal description of the kind of requirements addressed by this pattern.
Example	An example from the application domain illustrating the purpose of the requirement pattern.
Definition	The pattern is described both formally, using a suitable FDT, and in natural language. The formal description is the basis for subsequent development steps finally leading to the requirement specification (pattern selection, adaptation, and composition). The description in natural language will serve the translation of instantiated patterns of the FRS into informal requirements of the NLRS. Furthermore, the description provides some information about possible instantiations.
Semantic properties	Properties that have been formally proven from the pattern. By instantiating these properties in the same way as the requirement pattern, proofs can be reused, too.

Based on the pattern pool and the Customer NLRS, the formalization of requirements through pattern reuse consists of the following steps (see Figure 1b)):

Step 1. Requirement patterns are *selected* from the pattern pool. This selection is supported by information provided by pattern descriptions such as intention, definition, and semantic properties (see Table 1).

Step 2. The selected patterns are *adapted* by suitable instantiations. The same kind of adaptation is applied to the semantic properties. Already at this stage, it is possible to formally reason about single requirements.

Step 3. The adapted patterns are *composed* to yield the requirement specification. Composition can be supported by suitable operators.

The degree to which the formalization of requirements can be achieved through pattern reuse depends both on the Customer NLRS and the contents of the pattern pool. If the structure of an informal requirement follows a requirement pattern that is already contained in the pool, then its formalization can be achieved directly by instantiating the pattern. If the structure is different, then either transformations and/or modifications of the informal requirement (cf. Section 2.1) may lead to a structure that is already supported by the pattern pool, or the formalization must be done in the conventional way, i.e. without reuse (see Figure 1b)). The pool of requirement patterns should evolve over time. As a consequence, the portion of requirements that is developed from requirement patterns will increase, reducing the overall effort of requirement specification.

2.3 Discovery of Requirement Patterns

So far, we have assumed the existence of a pattern pool containing a set of already known domain specific patterns, where each entry follows the template defined in Table 1. The main difficulty here is that it is by no means obvious a priori what patterns will be useful later on, as this depends on the application domain as well as on the requirements to be specified. Therefore, building up the pattern pool will be an iterative process itself. This *pattern discovery* task can be modeled as a sub-cycle in the specification development model. Typically, each external specification development cycle triggers one or more internal pattern discovery/reuse cycles affecting both pattern pool and FRS, since each FRS modification can lead to new patterns or the improvement of existing patterns.

The discovery of new patterns is a difficult and time-consuming process. In general, many requirements have similarities in the way they restrict time bounds, delays, and dependences between system states or other domain specific properties. These similarities can be exploited in order to extract the underlying patterns. Below, we report on the discovery of a particular real-time requirement pattern in detail. The discovery of another real-time requirement pattern is presented in [10]. From these examples, it becomes evident that pattern discovery indeed is a considerable investment that will only pay off through extensive pattern reuse.

3 The Original Problem Description

The requirement discussed in the following is taken from the domain of building-automation. Building-automation systems usually exhibit reactivity, real-time behaviour, scalability, and distribution, and therefore qualify as instances of large software systems. Thus, requirements of such systems as well as methods and techniques to specify and analyse them can be evaluated in that domain.

Among the tasks of a building-automation system are the control of temperature, humidity, light, air flow, security, and safety. Depending on the type of a building (e.g. house, research lab, hospital, airport terminal), hundreds or thousands of sensors and actuators can be involved in maintaining required conditions in a building. Our approach in the requirements phase in general has been to use the initial informal problem description as delivered by the customer (initial Customer NLRS) in order to work out a precise and formal specification in real-time temporal logic (FRS) [10]. These formulae were then translated back to natural language, so that the resulting description (Developer NLRS) could be compared with the initial one and be discussed with the customer. When, after necessary revisions, full agreement with the customer was reached, the temporal formulae formed the basis for subsequent design activities.

In the following, we focus on the formalization of a real-time requirement, the extraction of the underlying requirement pattern, and its application. Our starting point is an excerpt of the original problem description, stated in natural language augmented by a diagram, which forms part of a larger document:

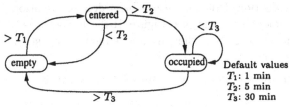

Default values
T_1: 1 min
T_2: 5 min
T_3: 30 min

Fig. 2. State diagram

The comfort temperature shall be maintained during preset comfort times or reached as fast as possible, when the room is occupied for a longer period of time. This state is called "occupied" and is explained in the state diagram. *This requirement shall be fulfilled during the heating period, and, if possible, also during the rest of the year. During the states "empty" and "entered", appropriate action has to be taken. We distinguish three time spans for detecting occupancy. If a person is in a room shorter than T_1 minutes, the control system does not try to reach the comfort temperature (state "empty", stand-by or off-time temperature, depending on the time period). If the person leaves the room before T_2 minutes, the system returns to the previous temperature. If the person occupies the room longer than T_2, the system enters the state "occupied", where the comfort temperature should be held, until this person leaves the room for at least T_3 minutes. Different settings for (T_1, T_2, T_3) may exist for each room, depending on the expected usage (day, night, vacation, etc.).*

4   The Final Formal Specification of the Real-Time Requirement

The final formal specification (FRS) is written in a propositional real-time temporal logic with tailored operators (for details, see [5] and [9]). Here we only give the informal semantics of the temporal operators used in this paper. Our basic model is a set of timed state sequences, as defined in [1]. Note that time is dense.

- $\Box\varphi$ means that φ is true now and will be true at all future points in time.
- $\blacksquare\varphi$ means that φ is true now and has always been true at all points in time of the current context in the past. The current context in the past usually covers the entire past, i.e. from the beginning of the timed state sequence. However, it may be limited using interval operators (see below).
- $\dot{\blacksquare}_{\leq T}\varphi$ means that φ is true now and has always been true in the preceeding time span T, limited by the current context in the past. I.e., if the current context in the past is shorter than T, φ is only required to be true during that context.
- $\blacklozenge\varphi \leftrightarrow_{Df} \neg\blacksquare\neg\varphi$; $\blacklozenge_{\leq T}\varphi \leftrightarrow_{Df} \neg\blacksquare_{\leq T}\neg\varphi$
- $[\varphi]$ (read "action of type φ") means that φ has just become true, i.e. φ is true now and has been false in the preceeding state (note that time is dense, however, the state sequence is discrete).
- $\langle[\varphi_1] \Rightarrow\rangle\varphi_2$ (read "φ_2 restricted on the context $[\varphi_1] \Rightarrow$") means that φ_2 holds in the context limited backwards by the last action of type φ_1; the formula is vacuously true if the context does not exist.
- $\langle *[\varphi_1] \Rightarrow\rangle\varphi_2 \leftrightarrow_{Df} \langle[\varphi_1] \Rightarrow\rangle\varphi_2 \wedge \blacklozenge[\varphi_1]$

Note that the final formal specification listed below has been done convention-ally, without the use of requirement patterns (see Figure 1b)). It uses several predicates considered atomic in the sense that they are not refined at this stage, with the following intuitive meaning:

roomEmpty — no person present (not to be confused with the state "empty"!)

comfortTime — current time within a time period where presence of persons is expected (e.g. during regular working hours)

comfortTemperature — valves of the heating system are currently controlled such that the comfort temperature is either reached within certain time bounds and maintained, or approximated, depending on outside temperatures

standByTemperature as before, w.r.t. stand-by temperature

offTimeTemperature as before, w.r.t. off-time temperature

Based on *roomEmpty*, the non-atomic (auxiliary) predicate *roomUsed* is defined:

D1. $roomUsed \leftrightarrow_{Df} \blacksquare_{\leq T_1} \neg roomEmpty \vee$
$\langle *[\blacksquare_{\leq T_1+T_2} \neg roomEmpty] \Rightarrow \rangle \blacksquare \blacklozenge_{\leq T_3} \neg roomEmpty$

Informally, a room is currently in use (written *roomUsed*) iff one of the following statements holds:

- during the past T_1 time units, a person has continuously been in the room;
- there has already been a time span of length $T_1 + T_2$ such that a person has continuously been in the room, and since this has been the case for the last time, periods where the room was empty were not longer than or equal to T_3.

The real-time requirement can then be formalized as follows:

R1. $\square(roomUsed \rightarrow comfortTemperature)$
R2. $\square(\neg roomUsed \wedge comfortTime \rightarrow standByTemperature)$
R3. $\square(\neg roomUsed \wedge \neg comfortTime \rightarrow offTimeTemperature)$

Informally, the comfort temperature has to be reached and/or maintained when-ever the room is used as defined by *roomUsed* (R1). During the remaining time periods, the stand-by or off-time temperatures apply, depending on the setting of *comfortTime* (R2, R3). Note that this requirement is stated on a high abstrac-tion level. It will, for instance, be necessary to refine the predicate *roomEmpty* by introducing a collection of sensors and by specifying how these sensors determine its value. Also, the predicates *comfortTime*, *comfortTemperature*, *standByTem-perature*, and *offTimeTemperature* have to be refined.

It is not obvious that the formal specification indeed captures the original problem description stated in Section 3. Actually, it doesn't, since natural lan-guage does not possess a formal semantics, and since the original description exhibits some ambiguities. So the goal must be to argue why the formal speci-fication captures the intentions of the informal description. The detailed justifi-cation and a proof of the soundness and completeness of the final formalization are presented in [7].

5 Extraction and Application of the Requirement Pattern

While working on application requirements in the domain of building-automation, we have found that most of them obey a small number of syntactic patterns [10]. One of the patterns we found has been extracted from the definition of roomUsed and is shown in Table 2. We have termed this pattern "LazyReaction", because it is applicable in cases where a reaction is not immediate, but is delayed by a specified time period.

Table 2. LazyReaction pattern

Name	LazyReaction (p, q, T_1, T_2, T_3)
Intention	Applicable if a reaction is not immediate, but contains some delay.
Example	$roomUsed \leftrightarrow_{Df} (\blacksquare_{\leq T_1} \neg roomEmpty \vee$ $(*[\blacksquare_{\leq T_1+T_2} \neg roomEmpty] \Rightarrow) \blacksquare \blacklozenge_{\leq T_3} roomEmpty)$
	A room is currently in use ($roomUsed$) iff one of the following holds: – during the past T_1 time units, a person has continuously been in the room; – there has already been a time span of length $T_1 + T_2$ such that a person has continuously been in the room, and since this has been the case for the last time, periods where the room was empty were not longer than or equal to T_3.
Definition	$p \leftrightarrow_{Df} \blacksquare_{\leq T_1} q \vee (*[\blacksquare_{\leq T_1+T_2} q] \Rightarrow) \blacksquare \blacklozenge_{\leq T_3} q$
	The predicate p holds iff one of the following statements holds: – during the past T_1 time units, q has continuously been true; – there has already been a time span of length $T_1 + T_2$ such that q has continuously been in the room, and since this has been the case for the last time, periods where q was false were not longer than or equal to T_3.
Semantic properties	$T_1 = T_2 = T_3 = 0 \rightarrow p \leftrightarrow q$; $T_2 = T_3 = 0 \rightarrow p \leftrightarrow \blacksquare_{\leq T_1} q$ $T_2 = 0 \rightarrow p \leftrightarrow (*[\blacksquare_{\leq T_1} q] \Rightarrow) \blacksquare \blacklozenge_{\leq T_3} q$; $T_1 = T_2 = 0 \rightarrow p \leftrightarrow \blacklozenge_{\leq T_3} q$

The pattern has the parameters p, q, T_1, T_2, and T_3, which have to be instantiated in order to obtain a particular requirement. By instantiating p and q with formulae, a more specific pattern is obtained. Therefore, pattern instantiation can be understood as an incremental process. The time parameters T_1, T_2, and T_3 can be replaced by specific values, and/or restricted by adding constraints (note that a replacement by a value is a special case of an added constraint). The entry "semantic properties" contains special cases of pattern instantiations, where based on a particular selection of time parameters, it is possible to transform the resulting formula into an even more concise expression. These expressions have been proven equivalent to the original pattern.

Below, we list some requirements occurring in air flow control, motion detection, and safety control. These requirements include applications of the *LazyReaction* pattern. Further applications of this pattern can be found in [7].

Motion detection

The specification of a motion detector on sale in a hardware store was obtained by instantiating p, q, T_1, T_2 with *personPresent, motion*, 0, and 0, respectively, by restricting T_3 as shown in D5, and by adding R5:

motion motion detected (implemented by an infrared sensor)
darkness light intensity below a threshold value, adjustable from 2 to 2000 lux
lightOn a light is switched on to illuminate the considered area

D4. $personPresent \leftrightarrow_{Df} \blacklozenge_{\leq T_3} motion$
D5. $T_3 \in [10 seconds, 15 minutes]$
R5. $\Box(darkness \wedge personPresent \leftrightarrow lightOn)$

Safety control

By instantiating p and q with *hazardousCondition* and *hazardousSituation*, respectively, and by adding R6, we obtain a safety control requirement (see also [6]). As already discussed, the time parameters can either be replaced by specific values, or restricted by additional properties.

hazardousSituation holds in case of heavy winds, heavy rainfall, etc.
upperSashClosed upper sash closed

D6. $hazardousCondition \leftrightarrow_{Df} \blacksquare_{\leq T_1} hazardousSituation \vee$
    $\langle *[\blacksquare_{\leq T_1 + T_2} hazardousSituation] \Rightarrow\rangle \blacksquare \blacklozenge_{\leq T_3} hazardousSituation$
R6. $\Box(hazardousCondition \mapsto_{\leq T} upperSashClosed)$

R6 uses a tailored operator, $\mapsto_{\leq}$, of the real-time temporal logic introduced in [9]. Informally, R6 states that each time *hazardousCondition* holds continuously for at least T time units, the upper sash must be closed within this time span and must then remain closed as long as *hazardousCondition* holds. R6 is an instantiation of another pattern occurring quite frequently in requirements on building-automation systems, namely $\Box(r \mapsto_{\leq T} s)$ (compare [10]).

6 Conclusions and Outlook

The focus of this paper has been on the discovery and the application of an interesting, non-trivial real-time requirement pattern called *LazyReaction* pattern. Starting with the description of a real-time problem in natural language augmented by a diagram, we have developed a precise and concise formal requirement specification in a step-by-step fashion.

It has become evident that pattern discovery is a time-consuming task and a major investment. *Good* requirement patterns are not just a by-product of specifying system requirements, but the result of rigorous development and continuous improvement. We have motivated and illustrated the reuse potential by a diverse collection of requirements in the domain of building-automation systems that we have formalized by applying the *LazyReaction* pattern. Thus, the original investment in developing a formal and rigorous specification pays off.

At the moment, only very few patterns have been reported, which keeps the reuse potential within narrow bounds. We expect that in the near future and with increasing experience, additional patterns will be discovered and added to the pattern pool. In fact, we perceive pattern discovery as a fertile field of future research.

Another benefit of pattern-based requirements engineering is that generic solutions that can be adapted to particular machine environments can be developed. We are currently developing distributed solutions for several real-time patterns, based on message passing. We expect that by a pattern-based development of systems and the resulting reuse, customized solutions can be developed with significantly less effort.

Acknowledgements

We are grateful for the stimulating environment provided by the SFB 501 and the discussions with other project members, in particular with Gerhard Zimmermann.

References

1. R. Alur, and T. A. Henzinger: Logics and Models of Real Time: A Survey. In: J. W. de Bakker, C. Huizing, W. P. de Roever, G. Rozenberg (Eds.), Real-Time: Theory and Practice, LNCS 600
2. E. Gamma, R. Helm, R. Johnson, J. Vlissides: Design Patterns - Elements of Reusable Object-Oriented Software. Addison-Wesley, 1995
3. B. Geppert, R. Gotzhein, F. Rößler: Configuring Communication Protocols Using SDL Patterns. in: A. Cavalli, A. Sarma (Eds.), SDL'97 - Time for Testing, Elsevier Science Publishers, Proceedings of the 8th SDL-Forum, Evry, France, Sept. 1997
4. B. Geppert, F. Rößler: Generic Engineering of Communication Protocols - Current Experience and Future Issues. Proceedings of the 1st IEEE International Conference on Formal Engineering Methods (ICFEM'97), Hiroshima, Japan, 1997
5. R. Gotzhein: Open Distributed Systems - On Concepts, Methods and Design from a Logical Point of View. Vieweg Wiesbaden, 1993
6. R. Gotzhein, B. Geppert, C. Peper, and F. Rößler: Generic Layout of Communication Subsystems - A Case Study. SFB 501 Report 14/96, University of Kaiserslautern, Germany, 1996
7. R. Gotzhein, M. Kronenburg, and C. Peper: Reuse in Requirements Engineering: Discovery and Application of a Real-Time Requirement Pattern. SFB 501 Report 8/98, University of Kaiserslautern, Germany, 1998
8. T. A. Henzinger, Z. Manna und A. Pnueli: Timed Transition Systems. In: J. W. de Bakker, C. Huizing, W. P. de Roever, and G. Rozenberg (Hrsg.), Real-Time: Theory in Practice, LNCS 600, Springer 1991, 226-251
9. M. Kronenburg, R. Gotzhein, and C. Peper: A Tailored Real-Time Temporal Logic for Specifying Requirements of Building-Automation Systems. SFB 501 Report 16/96, University of Kaiserslautern, Germany, 1996
10. C. Peper, R. Gotzhein, M. Kronenburg: A Generic Approach to the Formal Specification of Requirements. Proceedings of the 1st IEEE International Conference on Formal Engineering Methods (ICFEM'97), Hiroshima, Japan, 1997, pp. 252-261
11. R. E. Johnson: Frameworks = (Components + Patterns), Communications of the ACM, Vol. 40, No. 10 (October 1997), pp. 39-42

A Modular Visual Model for Hybrid Systems

Radu Grosu, Thomas Stauner* and Manfred Broy

Institut für Informatik, TU München, D-80290 München
Email: {grosu,stauner,broy}@informatik.tu-muenchen.de

Abstract. Visual description techniques are particularly important for the design of hybrid systems because specifications of such systems must usually be discussed between engineers from a number of different disciplines. Modularity is vital for hybrid systems not only because it allows to handle large systems, but also because hybrid systems are naturally decomposed into the system itself and its environment.

Based on two different interpretations for hierarchic graphs and on a clear hybrid computation model, we develop *HyCharts*, two modular visual formalisms for the specification of the architecture and behavior of hybrid systems. The operators on hierarchic graphs enable us to give a surprisingly simple denotational semantics for many concepts known from statechart-like formalisms. Due to a very general composition operator, HyCharts can easily be composed with description techniques from other engineering disciplines. Such heterogeneous system specifications seem to be particularly appropriate for hybrid systems because of their interdisciplinary character.

1 Introduction

Hybrid systems have been a very active area of research over the past few years and a number of specification techniques have been developed for such systems. While they are all well suited for closed systems, the search for hybrid description techniques for open systems is relatively new.

For open systems – as well as for any large system – modularity is essential. It is not only a means for decomposing a specification into manageable small parts, but also a prerequisite for reasoning about the parts individually, without having to regard the interior of other parts. Thus, it greatly facilitates the design process and can help to push the limits of verification tools, like model-checkers, further.

With a collection of operators on hierarchic graphs as tool-set, we follow the ideas in [6] and define a simple and powerful computation model for hybrid systems. Based on this model HyCharts, namely HySCharts and HyACharts, are introduced as two different interpretations of hierarchic graphs. HySCharts are a visual representation of hybrid, hierarchic state transition diagrams. HyACharts are a visual representation of hybrid data-flow graphs (or architecture graphs) and allow to compose hybrid components in a modular way. The behavior of

---

* The second author was supported with funds of the DFG, within the priority program *Design and design methodology of embedded systems* (reference number Br 887/9-1).

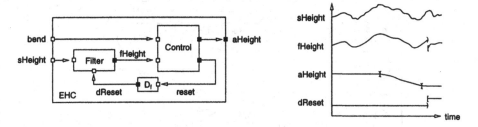

Fig. 1. The EHC: Architecture and a typical evolution.

these components can be described by using HySCharts or by any technique from system theory that can be given a semantics in terms of dense input/output relations. This includes differential equations. Dense input/output relations are a relational extension of hybrid FOCUS [10, 4].

Example 1 (An electronic height control system, EHC) The following example illustrates the kind of systems we want to regard. It will be used throughout the paper to demonstrate the use of HyCharts.

The purpose of the electronic height control system (EHC), which was originally proposed by BMW, is to control the chassis level of an automobile by a pneumatic suspension. The abstract model of this system which regards only one wheel was first presented in [12]. It basically works as follows: Whenever the chassis level is below a certain lower bound, a *compressor* is used to increase it. If the level is too high, air is blown off by opening an *escape valve*. The chassis level *sHeight* is measured by *sensors* and *filtered* to eliminate noise. The filtered value *fHeight* is read periodically by the *controller*. which operates the compressor and the escape valve and resets the filter when necessary. A further sensor *bend* tells the controller whether the car is going through a curve.

Here, we concentrate on the software part of the system. The environment is omitted. The basic components of the *system* are therefore the filter and the controller. The escape valve and the compressor are modeled within the controller. The diagrams in Figure 1 depict on the left the architecture of the EHC and on the right a typical evolution of the system over time. The architecture of the EHC is given by a HyAChart. Each component of this chart can be defined again by a HyAChart or by a HySChart or some other compatible formalism. The components only interact via clearly defined interfaces, or channels, in order to get modularity. The behavior of a component is characterized, as intuitively shown in Figure 1, right, by periods where the values on the channels change smoothly and by time instances at which there are discontinuities. In our approach the smooth periods result from the analog parts of the components. The discontinuities are caused by their combinational (or discrete) parts.

We specify the behavior of both the combinational and the analog part of a component by a HySChart, i.e., by a hybrid, hierarchic state transition diagram, with nodes marked by activities and transitions marked by actions. The transitions define the discontinuities, i.e., the instantaneous actions performed by the combinational part. The activities define the smooth periods, i.e., the time

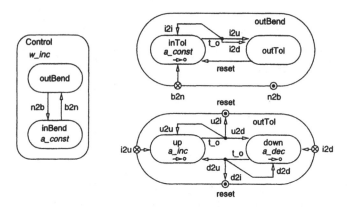

Fig. 2. The EHC's *Control* component.

consuming behavior of the analog part while the combinational part is idle. As
an example, Figure 2 shows the HySChart for the EHC's *Control* component. It
consists of three hierarchic levels. Figure 2, left, depicts the highest level. Figure
2, top right, refines the state *outBend* and Figure 2, bottom right, further refines
the state *outTol*. The states, transitions and activities (written in italics in the
figure) are explained in Section 5. □

In contrast to the well-known technique of hybrid automata [1], HyCharts are
fully modular and suitable for open systems. The hybrid modules from Alur
and Henzinger [2] are modular, but their utility suffers from the fact that it is
not obvious how to model feedback loops. For theoretical reasons, loops pose a
problem in our approach, too. Nevertheless we explicitly allow feedback loops, as
long as they introduce a delay. Demanding a delay is not unrealistic, as signals
cannot be transmitted at infinite speed. Another modular model, hybrid I/O
automata, is presented in [9]. While this model is promising from the theoretical point of view, we think it has some deficits in practice. Namely, there is
no graphical representation for hybrid I/O automata yet, there is no hierarchy
concept for them and finally, there is no visual formalism for the specification of
the architecture of a composed system. The same applies for the hybrid modules
mentioned above. From the systems engineering point of view our approach is
therefore more convenient. In contrast to the hybrid statecharts introduced in
[8] HyCharts not only permit hierarchic states, but also hierarchic activities.
HyCharts look largely similar to the description techniques used in the software
engineering method for real-time object-oriented systems ROOM [11] and may
therefore be seen as a hybrid extension of them.

The rest of the paper is organized as follows. In Section 2 we present an
abstract interpretation of hierarchic graphs. This interpretation provides the infrastructure for defining an unusually simple denotational semantics for the key
concepts of statecharts [7] offered in HyCharts, like hierarchy and preemption. It
is also the foundation for the denotational semantics of our hybrid computation
model, which is introduced in Section 3. Following the ideas developed in this
model, HyCharts are defined in Sections 4 and 5 as a multiplicative and respectively an additive interpretation of hierarchic graphs. Both interpretations are

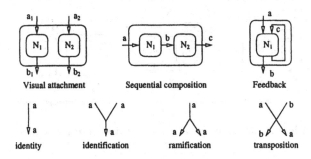

Fig. 3. The composition operators and the connectors

introduced in an intuitive way by using the example above. Finally, in Section 6 we summarize our results.

A version of this paper that goes into greater technical detail is available as a technical report [5].

2 Hierarchic Graphs as Relations

A *hierarchic graph* consists of a set of *nodes* connected by a set of *arcs*. For each node, the incoming and the outgoing arcs define the node's *interface*. In general, the arcs have associated some *type information*.

Suppose T is a set of *type names* and D is a *type function* mapping each name $t \in T$ to an associated *domain* of values D_t. Since we want to speak about incoming and outgoing arcs collectively we assume given a binary (monoidal) operation $\star$ with neutral element e, both on type names and on the corresponding domains. For types, we obtain the set of terms given by the grammar $a := t \in T \mid e \mid a \star a \mid (a)$. The $\star$ operation on type terms is assumed to be compatible with the $\star$ operation on domains, hence $D_{a \star b} = D_a \star D_b$ and $D_{a \star e} = D_{e \star a} = D_a$.

Now a node N with incoming arcs that collectively have type a and outgoing arcs that collectively have type b can be interpreted as a *relation* $N \subseteq D_a \times D_b$. Visually, this is represented by a box labeled by N, with an incoming arrow labeled by a and an outgoing arrow labeled by b. We shall also write $N : a \to b$.

Operators on nodes. In order to obtain graphs, we put nodes next to one another and interconnect them by using the following operators on relations: *visual attachment, sequential composition* and *feedback*. Their visual representation is given in Figure 3, top.

The *visual attachment* is achieved by extending $\star$ to an operation over nodes. Given $N_1 : a_1 \to b_1$ and $N_2 : a_2 \to b_2$ we define $N_1 \star N_2$ to be of type $a_1 \star a_2 \to b_1 \star b_2$. The *sequential composition* is the usual composition of relations. Given $N_1 : a \to b$ and $N_2 : b \to c$ we define $N_1 ; N_2$ to be of type $a \to c$. The *feedback* operation allows to connect the output of a node to the input of the same node, if both have the same type. Given $N : a \star c \to b \star c$ we define $N\uparrow_\star^c$ to be of type $a \to b$.

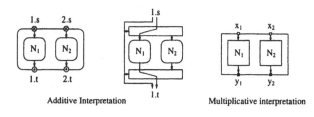

Fig. 4. The additive and multiplicative interpretations

Operators on arcs. Beside operators on nodes, we also have the following operators on arcs: *identity, identification, ramification* and *transposition*. The visual representation of these *connectors* is given in Figure 3, bottom.

The *identity* connector $I_a : a \to a$ copies its input to the output. The binary *identification* connector $\vee_a : a \star a \to a$ joins two inputs together. This operator is naturally extended to k inputs. In this case it is written $\vee_a^k$. The binary *ramification* connector $\wedge^a : a \to a \star a$ copies the input information on two outputs. For its natural extension to k outputs we write $\wedge_k^a$. Finally the *transposition* connector $^a\mathsf{X}^b : a \star b \to b \star a$ exchanges the inputs.

To be a precise formalization of graphs, the above abstract operators and connectors have to satisfy a set of laws, which intuitively express our visual understanding of graphs. These laws correspond to *symmetric monoidal categories with feedback* enriched with branching constants, see e.g. [13]. Such a category also contains *associativity isomorphisms* for $\star$. To simplify notation, they are never written explicitly and assumed present, when necessary.

[6] shows that the *additive* and the *multiplicative interpretations* of the operators and connectors are particularly relevant for computer science.

The additive interpretation. Here $\star$ is interpreted as the *disjoint sum* operation $+$ over the variable state space $\mathcal{S}$, i.e., $\mathcal{S}+\mathcal{S} = \{1\}\times\mathcal{S} \cup \{2\}\times\mathcal{S}$. In the following, we write the tuples $(1, s)$ and $(2, s)$ concisely as $1.s$ and $2.s$. Extending $+$ to an operation over nodes, we obtain $(N_1 + N_2)(i.s) = \{i.t \mid t \in N_i(s)\}$.

Its visual notation is given in Figure 4, left. The meaning of $(N_1 + N_2)(1.s)$ is intuitively shown in Figure 4, middle. Receiving the tuple $1.s$, the sum uses the control information 1 to "demultiplex" the input and select the corresponding relation N_1; this relation is then applied to the state s to obtain the next state t; finally, the output of the relation is "multiplexed" to $1.t$.

The effect of using the additive interpretation is that (composed) nodes closely correspond to *control states* and arcs to *transitions* of automata. A node receives control *on one* of its *entry points*, i.e., its incoming arcs, and passes control on *on one* of its *exit points*, i.e., its outgoing arcs. The whole graph models the control-flow in the automaton.

The other operators and connectors are defined consistently with $+$. Feedback in the additive interpretation allows loops. Hence, it has to be used with care in order to avoid non-termination, as in usual programming. For the additive connectors we write the symbols $I_{a,k} \rightarrow\bullet_a$, $_a\bullet\!\!<_k$ and $_a^b\mathsf{X}$.

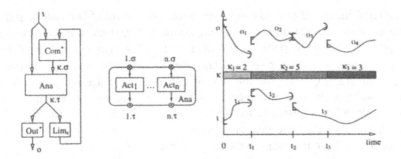

Fig. 5. The hybrid-machine computation model

The multiplicative interpretation. Here $\star$ is interpreted as the *product* operation $\times$ over sets of communication histories.[1] Extending $\times$ to an operation over nodes, we obtain $(N_1 \times N_2)(x_1, x_2) = \{(y_1, y_2) \mid y_i \in N_i(x_i)\}$.

Its visual notation is given in Figure 4, right. When we think of a system as consisting of interconnected components running in parallel, the effect of this interpretation is that arcs closely correspond to *data flow* and nodes to *system components*. A component receives data *on all* of its *input channels* and sends data along *all* of its *output channels*. Thus the graph models the data-flow in the system.

The other operators and connectors are defined consistently with $\times$. In the multiplicative interpretation, feedback allows to map the output of a component back to its input. It is defined as the greatest solution of a fixed-point equation. A unique solution is guaranteed to exist, if the output on the feedback channel c is delayed before it is fed back to the input. The multiplicative connectors are written as $I_a, \bigvee_a^k, \mathcal{R}_k^a$ and $^a X^b$.

3 The Hybrid Computation Model

We start this section by informally explaining how our hybrid computation model works. After that the model's constituents are introduced formally.

General idea. We model a *hybrid system* by a network of autonomous *components* that communicate in a *time synchronous* way. Time synchrony is achieved by letting time flow uniformly for all components.

Each component is modeled by a *hybrid machine*, as shown in Figure 5, left. This machine consists of three basic parts: a *combinational* (or discrete) part (*Com*), an *analog* (or continuous) part (*Ana*) and a *feedback* loop.[2] The feedback models the *state* of the machine. It allows the component to remember at each moment of time t the input received and the output produced "just before" t.

---

[1] Communication histories basically are functions from the time domain to some data domain M, a detailed definition follows in the next section.

[2] Note the similarity of this machine model with models from control theory [3].

The combinational part is concerned with the control of the analog part and has *no memory*. It instantaneously and nondeterministically maps the current input and the fed back state to the next state. The next state is used by the analog part to select an *activity* among a set of activities (or execution modes) and it is the starting state for this activity. If the combinational part passes the fed back state without modification, we say that it is *idle*. The combinational part can only select a new next state (different from the fed back state) at distinct points in time. During the intervals between these time instances it is idle and the selection of the corresponding activity is stable for that interval, provided the input does not change discretely during the interval. The analog part describes the input/output behavior of the component whenever the combinational part is idle. Hence, it adds to the component the temporal dimension. It may select a new activity whenever there is a discrete change in the input it receives from the environment or the combinational part.

Example 2 Figure 5, right, shows the exemplary behavior of a component. The shaded box κ indicates the time periods where the combinational part idles in node i. (κ can be regarded as the control state.) At time t_1 the discrete move of the environment triggers a discrete move of the combinational part. According to the new next state received from the combinational part, the analog part selects a new activity. The activity's start value at time t_1 is as determined by the combinational part. At time t_2 there is a discrete move of the environment, but the combinational part remains idle. The analog part chooses a new flow whose start value is the analog part's output just before t_2, because this is what it receives from the combinational part at time t_2. Thus, the output has a higher order discontinuity here. At time t_3 the environment does not perform a discrete move, but the combinational part does, e.g. because some threshold is reached. Again the analog part selects a new activity, which begins with the start value determined by the combinational part. During the intervals $(0, t_1), (t_1, t_3)$ and (t_3, ∞) the combinational part is idle. □

Feedback and state. Since the input received and the output produced may change abruptly at any time t, as shown in

Figure 5, right, we consider that the state of the component at moment t is the limit $lim_{x \nearrow t} \psi(x)$ of all the outputs $\psi(x)$ produced by the analog part when x approaches t. In other words, the feedback loop reproduces the analog part's output with an infinitesimal *inertia*. We say that the output is *latched*. The infinitesimal *inertia* is realized by the Lim_s part of the hybrid machine (Fig. 5, left). Its definition is $Lim_s(\psi)(t) = s$ if $t = 0$ and $Lim_s(\psi)(t) = lim_{x \nearrow t} \psi(x)$ for $t > 0$, where s is the initial state of the hybrid machine.

The *state* of the machine consists of a mapping of *latched* (or *controlled*) variable names to values of corresponding type. Let S denote the set of controlled variable names with associated domains $\{\sigma_v \mid v \in S\}$. Then the set of all possible states, i.e. the variable state space, is given by $\mathcal{S} = \prod_{v \in S} \sigma_v$. The set of controlled variable names can be split in two disjoint sets: a set P of *private* variable names and a set O of *output* (or *interface*) variable names. We write $\mathcal{S}_P$ for $\prod_{v \in P} \sigma_v$

and S_O for $\prod_{v \in O} \sigma_v$. Clearly, $S = S_P \times S_O$. The latched inputs are a subset of P.

The input is a mapping of *input* variable names to values of corresponding type. Let I denote the set of input variable names with associated domains $\{\sigma_v \mid v \in I\}$. Then the set of all possible inputs is given by $\mathcal{I} = \prod_{v \in I} \sigma_v$.

The combinational part. The combinational part is a relation from the current inputs and the latched state to the next state, formally:

$$Com \in (\mathcal{I} \times S_a) \to \mathcal{P}(S_a)$$

where a is a sum term and $\mathcal{P}(X) = \{Y \subseteq X \mid Y \neq \{\}\}$. The sum term is due to the additive interpretation of hierarchic graphs which defines Com and gives the number of leaf nodes in Com (see Section 5.1). The computation of Com takes no time.

An important property of the relation defining the combinational part is that it is defined for all states and inputs, i.e., it is *total*. To emphasize totality, we wrote it in a functional style. Furthermore, we want that the combinational part passes the next state to the analog part only if it cannot further proceed. In other words, if $s' \in Com(i, s)$ is the next state, then $Com(i, s') = \{s'\}$, i.e., no new state $s'' \neq s'$ can be computed starting in s' with input i. We say that Com is idle for i and s'. Finally, the set $E \subseteq \mathcal{I} \times S_a$ of inputs and states for which Com is not idle must be topologically closed. Together with the preceding property this guarantees that the extension of Com over time can only make discrete moves at distinct points in time. It is needed to ensure that the semantics of a hybrid machine is well-defined.

The analog part. Whenever the combinational part idles, the analog part performs an *activity*. We describe an activity by a relation Act with type

$$Act \in (\mathcal{I} \times S)^{\mathbf{R}_{c+}} \to \mathcal{P}(S^{\mathbf{R}_{c+}})$$

where $\mathbb{R}_+$ stands for the non-negative real line. For any set M, the set $M^{\mathbf{R}_{c+}}$ stands for the set of functions $\mathbb{R}_+ \to M$ that are *continuous* and *piecewise smooth*. We say that a function $f \in \mathbb{R}_+ \to M$ is piecewise smooth iff every finite interval on the nonnegative real line $\mathbb{R}_+$ can be partitioned into *finitely* many left closed and right open intervals such that on each interval f is infinitely differentiable (i.e., f is in C^∞) for $M = \mathbb{R}$ or f is constant for $M \neq \mathbb{R}$. Infinite differentiability is required for convenience. It allows us to assume that all differentials of f are well defined. A tuple of functions is infinitely smooth iff all its components are. We also call $M^{\mathbf{R}_{c+}}$ the set of *flows* over M.

To model analog behavior in a "well behaved" way, activities must be total and *time guarded*, that is at any moment of time t, the output at t should be completely determined by the input and the state received until that moment. Formally, for all $\varphi_1, \varphi_2, \sigma_1, \sigma_2$ and t:

$$(\varphi_1, \sigma_1){\downarrow}_{[0,t]} = (\varphi_2, \sigma_2){\downarrow}_{[0,t]} \quad \Rightarrow \quad Act(\varphi_1, \sigma_1){\downarrow}_{[0,t]} = Act(\varphi_2, \sigma_2){\downarrow}_{[0,t]}$$

where by $(\sigma, \varphi){\downarrow}_\delta$ we denote the restriction of σ and φ to the time interval δ.

The complete behavior of the analog part is described by a relation Ana with type:

$$Ana \in (\mathcal{I} \times \mathcal{S}_a)^{\mathbb{R}+} \to \mathcal{P}(\mathcal{S}_a^{\mathbb{R}+})$$

where $\mathcal{S}_a$ is the output type of Com and for any set M, $M^{\mathbb{R}+}$ denotes the set of *piecewise smooth* functions $\mathbb{R}_+ \to M$. Hence, the input and output of the analog part is not necessarily continuous. We call $M^{\mathbb{R}+}$ the set of *dense communication histories*.

The relation Ana is obtained by pasting together the flows of the activities associated to the nodes where the combinational part Com idles. Pasting is realized as shown in Figure 5, middle, by extending the sum operation to activities. Given a set of activities $ACT = \{Act_j \mid j \leq n\}$, their sum is defined as below[3]:

$$+_{j=1}^{n} Act_j \stackrel{\text{def}}{=} \{ (\iota, \kappa.\sigma, \kappa.\tau) \mid \forall \delta, m. \ \kappa|_\delta = m^\dagger \Rightarrow m \leq n \wedge (\iota, \sigma, \tau)|_\delta \in (Act_m)|_\delta \}$$

where δ is a left closed right open interval, $m^\dagger$ is the extension of m to a constant function over δ, $\iota \in \mathcal{I}^{\mathbb{R}+}$ and $\kappa.\sigma, \kappa.\tau \in \mathcal{S}_a^{\mathbb{R}+}$. The tuple $\kappa.\sigma$ consists of the control flow κ which gives at each moment of time the node where the combinational part idles (see Figure 5, right) and the state flow σ which gives at each moment of time the state passed by the combinational part. The tuple $\kappa.\tau$ consists of the same control flow κ and of the state flow τ computed by the sum. For each interval δ in which the combinational part idles, the sum uses the control information $\kappa|_\delta$ to demultiplex the input $\kappa.\sigma|_\delta$ to the appropriate activity and to multiplex the output $\tau|_\delta$ to $\kappa.\tau|_\delta$. Section 5.2 will show how Ana is constructed from the activities in a HySChart by using the $+$ operator.

Note that the type of Ana assures that $(\iota, \kappa.\sigma)$ is partitioned into pieces, where ι, κ and σ are simultaneously piecewise smooth. The output histories $\kappa.\tau$ of Ana are again piecewise smooth, by the definition of Ana.

As we demand that every activity is total and time guarded, the analog part also is total and time-guarded. Furthermore, for the analog part we demand that it is *resolvable*, which means that it must have a fixed point for every state $s_0 \in \mathcal{S}_a$ and every input stream $i \in \mathcal{I}^{\mathbb{R}_c+}$, i.e.,

$$\exists \sigma \in \mathcal{S}_a^{\mathbb{R}_c+}.\sigma(0) = s_0 \wedge \sigma \in Ana(\iota, \sigma)$$

Resolvability of the analog part is needed to prove that the semantics of a hybrid machine is well-defined [5].

The component. Given an initial state s_0, the behavior of the hybrid machine is a relation Cmp between its input and output communication histories. Writing the graph in Figure 5, left, as a relational expression with the multiplicative operators results in the denotational semantics of Cmp:

$$Cmp \quad \in \quad \mathcal{S}_a \to \mathcal{I}^{\mathbb{R}+} \to \mathcal{P}(\mathcal{O}^{\mathbb{R}+})$$

$$Cmp(s) = ((\mathcal{R}_2 \times I) \ ; \ (I \times Com^\dagger) \ ; \ Ana \ ; \ \mathcal{R}_2 \ ; \ (Out^\dagger \times Lim_s)) \uparrow_\times$$

where $R^\dagger$ trivially extends the combinational relation R in time, i.e., $R^\dagger(\iota) \stackrel{\text{def}}{=} \{o \mid o(t) \in R(\iota(t))\}$ for any $t \geq 0$. Out selects the output variables from the state stream.

---

[3] Here we use for convenience the relational notation $Act \subseteq \mathcal{I}^{\mathbb{R}_c+} \times \mathcal{S}^{\mathbb{R}_c+} \times \mathcal{S}^{\mathbb{R}_c+}$.

By definition, Cmp is a *time guarded* relation, because $Com^\dagger$, Ana, $Out^\dagger$, Lim_s, I and $\mathcal{R}_2$ are time guarded. [5] proves that Cmp is total if Com and Ana satisfy the properties required above and if Com in connection with Ana never performs infinitely many discrete actions within a finite interval. The central part of the proof is that, due to the properties of Com and Ana, some time $\delta > 0$ passes between any two discrete moves of Com.

4 System Architecture Specification - HyACharts

The system architecture specification determines the interconnection of a system's components.

Graphical syntax. The architecture specification is a hierarchic graph, a so called HyAChart (<u>Hy</u>brid <u>A</u>rchitecture <u>Chart</u>), whose nodes are labeled with component names and whose arcs are labeled with channel names. We use a graphical representation that is analogous to the structure specifications in ROOM [11].

Semantics. As a HyAChart is a hierarchic graph, it is constructed with the operators of Section 2. Writing the graph as the equivalent relational formula and interpreting the operators in it multiplicatively directly gives the HyAChart's semantics. As $\star$ is interpreted as the product operation for sets in this interpretation, visual attachment here corresponds to parallel composition. Hence, each node in the graph is a component acting in parallel with the other components and each arc in the graph is a channel describing the data-flow from the source component to the destination component, as explained in Section 2.

The component names in the graph refer to input/output behaviors specified in other HyACharts, in HySCharts (Section 5) or with other formalisms. The channel names are the input and output variable names used in the specification of the components. The variables' types must be specified separately.

Example 3 (The HyAChart of the EHC) We now return to the HyAChart of our example system given in the introduction in Figure 1, left, and develop its semantics.

The boolean-valued channel *bend* in the figure tells the controller whether the car is in a curve. The real-valued channel *sHeight* carries the chassis level measured by the sensors. The real-valued channel *fHeight* carries the filtered chassis level. The real-valued channel *aHeight* carries the chassis level as proposed by the actuators, compressor and escape valve, without environmental disturbances. The boolean-valued channels *reset* and *dReset* ("delayed reset") transfer the boolean reset signal to the filter. The delay component D_f ensures that the feedback is well-defined (see e.g. [10]).

The types of the filter, the control component and the delay component follow from the channels' types. The filter has type $Filter \in (\mathbb{R} \times \mathbb{B})^{\mathbb{R}+} \to \mathcal{P}(\mathbb{R}^{\mathbb{R}+})$, the controller's type is $Control \in (\mathbb{B} \times \mathbb{R})^{\mathbb{R}+} \to \mathcal{P}((\mathbb{R} \times \mathbb{B})^{\mathbb{R}+})$ and the delay has type $D_f \in \mathbb{B}^{\mathbb{R}+} \to \mathcal{P}(\mathbb{B}^{\mathbb{R}+})$. The semantics of the whole system EHC is defined as below. It is the relational algebra term corresponding to the HyAChart of

Figure 1, left.

$$EHC \in (\mathbb{B} \times \mathbb{R})^{\mathbf{R}+} \to \mathcal{P}(\mathbb{R}^{\mathbf{R}+})$$
$$EHC = ((\mathsf{I} \times Filter)\,;\, Control\,;\, (\mathsf{I} \times D_f)) \uparrow_\times$$

Note that the user only has to draw the HyAChart and define the types of the channels. □

5 Component Specification - HySCharts

A HySChart (Hybrid StateChart) defines the combinational and the analog part of a hybrid machine. The input/output behavior of the resulting component follows from these parts as explained in Section 3.

The Graphical Syntax of HySCharts. A HySChart is a hierarchic graph, where each node is of the form depicted in Figure 6, left. Each node may have sub-nodes. It is labeled with a node name, which only serves for reference, an activity name and possibly the symbols $\to\circ$ and $\circ\to$ to indicate the existence of an entry or exit action, which is executed when the node is entered or left. The outgoing edges of a node are labeled with action names. The action names stand for predicates on the input, the latched state and the next state. They are structured into a *guard* and a *body*. The activity names refer to systems of ordinary differential (in)equations. The specification of actions and activities and their semantics is explained in detail in the following. Transitions from composed nodes express preemption. Except for activities, HySCharts look similar to ROOM-charts [11].

The Semantics of HySCharts. The semantics of a HySChart is divided into a combinational and an analog part. The combinational part follows almost directly from the diagram. The analog part is constructed from the chart with little effort. In the following we will first explain how the combinational part is derived from a HySChart and how actions are specified. Then, the analog part and continuous activities are covered.

5.1 The Combinational Part

A HySChart is a hierarchic graph and therefore constructed from the operators in Section 2. As mentioned there, interpreting the graph additively leads to a close correspondence to automata diagrams.

We may view the graph as a network of autonomous *computation units* (the nodes) that communicate with each other over directed *control paths* (the arcs). Due to the additive interpretation, each time control resides in only one (primitive) computation unit.

In order to derive the combinational part from the HySChart we now give a semantics to its nodes, i.e., to its computation units. The semantics for hierarchy and actions follows.

Computation units. Each primitive node of the HySChart represents the graph given in Fig. 6, top right. It corresponds to the relational expression:

$$\mathtt{CompUnit} \stackrel{\text{def}}{=} (+_{i=1}^m \mathtt{entry} + \mathsf{I})\,;\, {}_{m+1}{\succ\!\!\bullet}\,;\, {\bullet\!\!\prec}_{n+1}\,;\, ((+_{i=1}^n (\mathtt{guard}_i\,;\, \mathtt{exit}\,;\, \mathtt{body}_i)) + \mathtt{wait})$$

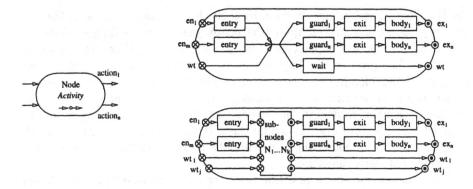

Fig. 6. Syntax and semantics of a computation unit.

According to the additive operators, it has the following intuitive meaning. A computation unit gets the *control* along one of its *entry points* en_i and gives the control back along one of its *exit points* ex_j.

After getting control along a regular entry point, i.e., an entry point different from *wait* wt, a computation unit may first execute an *entry action* entry. Then it evaluates a set of *action guards* $guard_k$. If one of the guards is true, then the corresponding *action* is said to be *enabled*, the *exit action* exit is executed, if present, and then the action's *body* $body_k$ is executed. After that, the computation unit passes control to another computation unit along the exit point corresponding to the executed action.

If more than one guard is true, then the computation unit *nondeterministically* chooses one of them. Guard wait in the diagram stands for the negation of the disjunction of the actions' guards $guard_k$. Hence, if none of the guards is true, then the discrete computation is completed, and the control leaves the combinational part along the designated wait exit point wt. The next section shows that the analog part takes advantage of the information about the exit point to determine the activity to be executed and gives control back along the corresponding wait entry point.

Hierarchy. A composed or *hierarchic* node in the HySChart stands for the graph in Figure 6, bottom right. A principal difference to primitive nodes is that the entry points are not identified, instead they are connected to the corresponding entry points of the sub-nodes. Similarly, the exit points of the sub-nodes are connected to the corresponding exit points of their enclosing hierarchic node. Furthermore, the hierarchic node has a wait entry and wait exit point for every wait entry/exit point of the sub-nodes. When it receives control on one of them, it is directly passed on to the wait entry point of the corresponding sub-node. Thus, the wait entry point identifies a sub-node. The hierarchic node is left along a wait exit point, if a sub-node is left along its corresponding wait exit point.

Actions. An *action a* is a relation between the current input, the latched state and the next state:

$$a \subseteq (\mathcal{I} \times \mathcal{S}) \times \mathcal{S}$$

For HySCharts, actions are specified by their characteristic predicate. They are the conjunction of a precondition (the *action guard*) on the latched state and the current input and a postcondition (the *action body*) that determines the next state. The precondition implies that the postcondition is satisfiable, hence the action is enabled iff the precondition is true. We use *left-quoted variables v'* to denote the current input, *right-quoted variables v'* to denote the next state and *plain variables* to denote the latched state. Moreover, we mention only the changed variables and always assume the necessary equalities stating that the other variables did not change. To simplify notation further, we associate a variable c with each channel c.

For example, the action resetting the filter is defined as $dReset' \neq dReset \wedge dReset' = dReset' \wedge fHeight' = 0$. It says that each time $dReset$ is toggled, $fHeight$ should be reset to 0. We abbreviate this by $dReset? \wedge fHeight' = 0$, where $e?$ for boolean variables e stands for $e' \neq e \wedge e' = e'$ and indicates that, toggling e is an event. Similarly, we define $e!$ for boolean variables e, to indicate the sending of an event. $e!$ stands for $e' \neq e$.

As mentioned in Section 3, the combinational part may only perform discrete state changes, on a topologically closed subset $\mathcal{I} \times \mathcal{S}$. This condition is satisfied by a HySChart defining the combinational part, if the precondition of every action in the chart identifies a topologically closed subset of $\mathcal{I} \times \mathcal{S}$. Note that in conjunction with hierarchy the action guards must be chosen with care in order to guarantee that the combinational part specified by the HySChart is total.

The additive interpretation of graphs also provides the infrastructure to easily model preemption, history variables and other concepts known from statecharts-like formalisms [6].

Semantics. If each node in the HySChart is replaced by the corresponding graph of Figure 6, right, we obtain a hierarchic graph whose nodes merely are relations. Writing the graph as the corresponding relational expression with the additive operators gives the denotational semantics of the HySChart's discrete part, i.e., the combinational part of a hybrid machine.

At the highest level of hierarchy, the hierarchic graph resulting from the HySChart has one wait entry/exit point pair for every primitive (or leaf) node in the chart. On the semantic level there is exactly one summand in the sum term a of the combinational part's type $(\mathcal{I} \times \mathcal{S}_a) \to \mathcal{P}(\mathcal{S}_a)$ for every entry/exit point pair. The analog part uses the entry/exit point information encoded in this disjoint sum to select the right activity for every node in the HySChart.

Example 4 (The EHC's Control component) To outline the utility of this approach for hybrid systems we now return to the HySChart for the controller given in the introduction. We describe the states and transitions in Figure 2 in a top-down manner. The activities, written in italics in the figure, are explained in the next section.

The computation unit Control. On the top level of the component *Control* we have two computation units, *outBend* and *inBend*. When the controller realizes that the car is in a curve, the computation unit *inBend* is entered. It is left again when the controller senses that the car no longer is in a curve. Sensing a curve is event driven. We use the boolean variable *bend* for this purpose. The actions $n2b$ and $b2n$ are identical and very simple: $n2b \equiv b2n \equiv bend$?

The computation unit outBend. The computation unit *outBend* is refined to *inTol* and *outTol* as shown in Figure 2, top right. Control is in *inTol* as long as the filtered chassis level is within a certain tolerance interval. The compressor and the escape valve are off then. If $fHeight$ is outside this interval at a sampling point, one of the sub-nodes of *outTol* is entered. These sub-nodes are left again, when $fHeight$ is inside the desired tolerance again and the filter is reset. The actions originating from *inTol* are defined as follows:

$$t\_o \equiv w = t_s, \qquad i2i \equiv lb \leq fHeight \leq ub$$
$$i2u \equiv fHeight \leq lb, \quad i2d \equiv fHeight \geq ub$$

An interesting aspect of *inTol* is the specification of the composed action started by the timeout t_o, which semantically corresponds to the ramification operator for hierarchic graphs. Of course, one could have used three separate transitions instead. However, in this case the visual representation would have failed to highlight the common enabling condition t_o.

Leaving the computation unit *outTol* along its exit point *reset* causes the execution of the *reset* action. This action is always enabled and defined by $reset \equiv reset!$. Note that we used here the same name for the action and its associated event. The transition $n2b$ originates from the composed node *outBend* (and from none of its sub-states). This expresses weak preemption, i.e., this transition can be taken from any sub-node of *outBend*, as long as it is not overwritten (see [5] for details).

The computation unit outTol. As shown in Figure 2, bottom right, the computation unit *outTol* consists of the computation units *up* and *down*. When the filtered chassis level is too low at a sampling point, node *up* is entered, where the compressor is on. When the level is too high, *down* is entered, where the escape valve is open. Control remains in these nodes until $fHeight$ is inside the desired tolerance again (actions $u2i$, $d2i$). These actions cause *outTol* to be left along the same exit point, *reset*. The actions originating from *up* and *down* are very similar to those of *inTol*, so we do not give them explicitly here.

As indicated by the symbol $\multimap$ the nodes *inTol*, *up* and *down* have an entry action. It is defined as $entry \equiv w' = 0$ and resets w. Together with action t_o and the activity w_inc it models sampling in these nodes.

Semantics. As explained, the combinational part follows directly from the HySChart by replacing the nodes by their corresponding graphs of Figure 6, right. As every wait entry/exit point pair at the highest hierarchic level of the resulting graph corresponds to an operand in the type of the combinational part, we get that the combinational part of *Control* has type $Com \in (\mathcal{I} \times S_a) \to \mathcal{P}(S_a)$, where $S_a = S + (S + (S + S))$.

Note that the user only has to draw the HySChart and give the definitions of the actions. The corresponding combinational part can be constructed automatically. $\qquad \Box$

5.2 The Analog Part

The second part of a HySChart's semantics is the analog part it defines. In the following we explain how this analog part is derived from the chart.

Activities. Each activity name in the HySChart refers to a system of ordinary differential (in)equations over the variables of the component. We demand that for any tuple of initial values $s \in S$ and any continuous, piecewise smooth input stream $i \in \mathcal{I}^{\mathbf{R}_c+}$, the resulting initial value problem is solvable. This ensures that the analog part that is constructed in the following is *resolvable* as required in Section 3.

Example 5 (The activities of Control) In our example from Figure 2 the activity names written in italics stand for the following differential (in)equations:

$$w\_inc \equiv \tfrac{d}{dt}w = 1 \qquad\qquad a\_inc \equiv \tfrac{d}{dt}aHeight \in [cp_-, cp_+]$$
$$a\_const \equiv \tfrac{d}{dt}aHeight = 0 \qquad\qquad a\_dec \equiv \tfrac{d}{dt}aHeight \in [ev_-, ev_+]$$

where $cp_-, cp_+ > 0$ and $ev_-, ev_+ < 0$ are constants. For w this means that it evolves in pace with physical time. Variable $aHeight$ either increases with a rate in $[cp_-, cp_+]$ (activity a_inc), it decreases (a_dec) or remains constant (a_const). Note that this is all the user has to provide to specify the analog part. □

The activity $Act \in (\mathcal{I} \times S)^{\mathbf{R}_c+} \to \mathcal{P}(S^{\mathbf{R}_c+})$ in every node is derived from the differential (in)equations in the following way: For the input stream i and the state stream s we take $s(0)$ as the initial value for the system of differential (in)equations. The activity's set of output streams then consists of the solutions of the resulting initial value problem for input stream i. For those controlled variables v, whose evolution is not determined by the initial value problem, the activity's output is equal to $s.v$, i.e., to the v component of the state stream the activity received. Hence, it remains unmodified.

Composition of Activities. To reflect the hierarchy in the HySChart the activities specified in the nodes are composed appropriately. Therefore, we extend the sequential composition operator ; to (disjoint sums of) activities:

$$Act_1 \,;\, Act_2 = \{(i, \sigma, \sigma') \mid \exists \tau. \, (i, \sigma, \tau) \in Act_1 \wedge (i, \tau, \sigma') \in Act_2\}$$

A HySChart can be seen as a tree with the primitive nodes as its leaves. The HySCharts in Figure 2, for example, has node *Control* as its root and the nodes *inBend*, *inTol*, *up* and *down* as leaves. Starting from the tree's root we derive the composed activity defined by the HySChart as follows: (We write Act_N for the (primitive) activity of node N and $CAct_N$ for the composed activity of node N, here.)

- if N has sub-nodes $M_1, \ldots, M_n$, $CAct_N \overset{\text{def}}{=} +_{i=1}^n (Act_N; CAct_{M_i})$
- if N is a primitive node, $CAct_N \overset{\text{def}}{=} Act_N$

The analog part is the composed activity of the HySChart's root node, i.e. $Ana = CAct_{root}$. Figure 7 and the following example explain this definition.

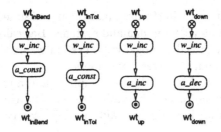

Fig. 7. The *Control* component's analog part.

Example 6 (The analog part of Control) The HySChart in Figure 2 has the analog part:

$$Ana \equiv (w\_inc; a\_const) + (w\_inc; (a\_const + (a\_inc + a\_dec)))$$

where we use the activity names to refer to the semantics of each activity, here. Figure 7 depicts the different paths in the associated tree. □

The entry and exit point symbols in the figure highlight that the analog part has one path for every primitive node in the HySChart. When we construct the combinational part from the HySChart, we also get one wait entry and wait exit point at its highest level of hierarchy for each primitive node. This allows to sequentially compose the combinational part with the analog part as in the semantics of a hybrid machine in Section 3. The distinct wait points allow both the combinational part and the analog part to know which node in the HySChart currently has control and to behave accordingly.

6   Conclusion

Based on a clear hybrid computation model, we were able to show that the ideas presented in [6] can smoothly be carried over to hybrid systems and yield modular, visual description techniques for such systems. Namely, the resulting techniques are HyACharts and HySCharts for the specification of hybrid system architecture and hybrid component behavior, respectively.

With an example we demonstrated the use of HyCharts and their features. Apart from many features known from statecharts-like formalisms, this in particular includes the ability to compose HySCharts with components specified with other formalisms. In our opinion such heterogeneous specifications are a key property for designing hybrid systems, as it allows to integrate techniques from different engineering disciplines.

Methodically we conceive a HySChart as a very abstract and precise mathematical model of a hybrid system. Knowing exactly the behavior of the analog part as given by a system of differential (in)equations allows us to develop more concrete models that can easily be implemented on discrete computers. For such models it is essential to choose a discretization which preserves the main properties of the abstract description.

Although this paper mainly aims at hybrid systems appearing in the context of disciplines like electrical and mechanical engineering, we think that the continuous activities in HySCharts also make them well suited for specifying multimedia systems, such as video on demand systems. Basically HyCharts seem to be appropriate for any mixed analog/digital system where the use of continuous time is more natural than a discrete time model.

In the future we intend to develop tool support and a requirement specification language for HyCharts. For the verification of HySCharts we believe that the techniques known for linear hybrid automata [1] can easily be adapted.

Acknowledgment. We thank Ursula Hinkel, Ingolf Krüger, Olaf Müller and Jan Philipps for their constructive criticism after reading draft versions of this paper.

References

1. R. Alur, C. Courcoubetis, N. Halbwachs, T.A. Henzinger, P.-H. Ho, X. Nicollin, A. Olivero, J. Sifakis, and S. Yovine. The algorithmic analysis of hybrid systems. *Theoretical Computer Science*, 138:3–34, 1995.
2. R. Alur and T.A. Henzinger. Modularity for timed and hybrid systems. In *CONCUR 97: Concurrency Theory*, LNCS 1243. Springer-Verlag, 1997.
3. M. Branicky, V. Borkar, and S. Mitter. A unified framework for hybrid control. Technical Report LIDS-P-2239, MIT, June 1994.
4. M. Broy. Refinement of time. In *ARTS'97*, LNCS 1231. Springer-Verlag, 1997.
5. R. Grosu and T. Stauner. Modular and visual specification of hybrid systems - an introduction to HyCharts. Technical Report TUM-I9801, Technische Universität München, July 1998.
6. R. Grosu, Gh. Stefănescu, and M. Broy. Visual formalisms revisited. In *Proc. Int. Conf. on Application of Concurrency to System Design (CSD)*. IEEE, 1998.
7. D. Harel. Statecharts: A visual formalism for complex systems. *Science of Computer Programming*, 8, 1987.
8. Y. Kesten and A. Pnueli. Timed and hybrid statecharts and their textual representation. In *Formal Techniques in Real-Time and Fault-Tolerant Systems, 2nd International Symposium*, LNCS 571. Springer-Verlag, 1992.
9. N.A. Lynch, R. Segala, F.W. Vaandrager, and H.B. Weinberg. Hybrid I/O automata. In *Hybrid Systems III*, LNCS 1066. Springer-Verlag, 1996.
10. O. Müller and P. Scholz. Functional specification of real-time and hybrid systems. In *Proc. Hybrid and Real-Time Systems (HART)*, LNCS 1201. Springer, 1997.
11. Bran Selic, Garth Gullekson, and Paul T. Ward. *Real-Time Object-Oriented Modeling*. John Wiley and Sons Ltd, Chichester, 1994.
12. T. Stauner, O. Müller, and M. Fuchs. Using HyTech to verify an automotive control system. In *Proc. Hybrid and Real-Time Systems (HART'97)*, LNCS 1201. Springer-Verlag, 1997.
13. Gh. Stefănescu. Algebra of flownomials. Technical Report TUM-I9437, Technische Universität München, 1994.

Integrating Real-Time Structured Design and Formal Techniques

D. Priddin* and A. Burns

Real-Time Systems Research Group,
Department of computer Science,
University of York, Y01 5DD, UK
Phone: (44) 1904 433241, Fax: (44) 1904 432767
E-mail: (darren,burns)@cs.york.ac.uk

Abstract. As most, if not all, real-time software is also critical, it is not unreasonable to expect developers to use best practice in the production of real-time software. But what is best practice? In terms of development, it would not be unreasonable to expect the use of structured analysis and design methods. In terms of verification of safety/liveness properties, it is not unreasonable to expect the use of a formalism. In general, however, structured methods and formal methods have different ways of modeling a system, so how can we be sure that properties that are proven of a formal model hold for a structured design? The answer is method integration. Method integration is a term commonly used to refer to the combination of a structured analysis or design method with a formal method. In this paper we shall present work on the integration of the structured real-time design method HRT-HOOD, and the real-time formal method Modecharts. We shall discuss the deficiencies of each of the methods, and show that when used together they co-optimize, enabling the user to produce a structured design that is amenable to scheduling analysis, which can also have properties about it verified.

1 Introduction

Method integration (MI) is a term commonly used to refer to the combination of a structured analysis or design method with a formal method. MI has a number of advantages over just using a structured method or a formal method. When we talk about a structured method the "method" is usually a recipe for capturing and structuring requirements or design properties. However when we talk about formal methods, the "method" is usually referring to a mathematical language with a property verification system or proof system. Clearly for the development of real-time systems that are nearly always critical, it is desirable to use a design method that constrains the developer to produce a design that is amenable to scheduling analysis, (as well as a design method that structures the design well) and a real-time formal method that enables the designer to prove that the design exhibits required properties. For example, the designer of

---

* Partly funded by a CASE award from the European Space Agency.

a railway crossing system may need a design method that enables him to define units that are responsible for: a) Periodically polling the track circuits every n time units, and b) Aperiodically controlling the opening and closing of the gate, dependant on the state of the track circuits. He may also be required to show that his design exhibits the bounded liveness property: that in all cases when a train enters a given track circuit, a barrier will be down within a defined time period.

HRT-HOOD [1] is a real-time design method that constrains the designer to produce a design that is amenable to scheduling analysis, i.e. at the final level the design is populated by a number of cyclic and sporadic tasks. However we note that HRT-HOOD lacked a rigorous definition of its object types, had no verification system, and has only one diagrammatic view of the system under development, (this diagrammatic view being a static entity relationship type diagram that also shows data flow between entities). Therefore HRT-HOOD lacks, (and so requires):

- A formal underpinning, to rigourously define the object types.
- A property verification system, to check the design has desired properties.
- A dynamic view of the design.

We chose to integrate Modecharts [4] with HRT-HOOD. Modecharts were chosen because they can fulfil the three requirements above. The integration does not only bring advantages to HRT-HOOD. It also gives Modecharts the benefits:

- Gives modecharts "structure in the large". It is easy to see how Modecharts can be used on small to medium sized problems, but it is difficult to see how large problems can be tackled. The HRT-HOOD design structures should give Modecharts "structure in the large" thus enabling them to be used more easily on large projects.
- Constrain a Modechart design so that it can be analysed for schedulability on a given processor set.
- Partial usage. Modecharts can be applied to only the most "important" parts of the design by applying them to the relative HRT-HOOD objects. Note: this could be a useful tool for controlling the state-space explosion problem that occurs during model checking.

The rest of this introduction gives an overview of HRT-HOOD and Modecharts. The relevant sections can be skipped by individuals who have knowledge of these methods.

1.1 HRT-HOOD

Hard Real-Time Hierarchical Object-Oriented Design (HRT-HOOD) [1] was developed between 1991 and 1993 at The University of York for the European Space Agency.

HRT-HOOD is a design method aimed at the logical and physical design stages. It is based on HOOD [6] and has been adapted for use with hard real-time systems. HRT-HOOD extends the types of objects in the system, where HOOD has Active and Passive objects, HRT-HOOD has Active, Passive, Sporadic, Periodic and Protected objects.

The primary aim of the HRT-HOOD process is to produce a design that can be analysed for schedulability.

The HRT-HOOD process starts with a single object, called the root object. This is decomposed into a set of child objects. This decomposition process continues until all the objects in the design that need to be analysed for scheduling are single threaded. This level of the design is called the terminal level.

A design at a terminal level, should consist of a number of single threaded cyclic and sporadic objects using protected and passive objects to access shared resources.

There are rules that govern the decomposition process, these preserve the nature of the parent object. For example, a passive object can only be decomposed into child passive objects, because if it contained a cyclic (or any other active object) then the parent could not be passive.

In this section we have given an informal description of HRT-HOOD. In the sections that follow we shall use the cyclic object as an example of a terminal object type. We shall examine the attributes of the object type, and use Modecharts to give a formal description of the structure of the object, and function of instances of the objects.

1.2 Modecharts

Modecharts [4] is a graphical formalism developed for the specification of real-time systems. Modecharts semantics are described in Real-Time Logic (RTL) [3]. A Modechart specification is hierarchically constructed from a set of primitive, serial and parallel modes. If a mode M is contained within a mode N then M is said to be the child of N, and N is said to be the parent of M. A primitive mode is a mode that has no children. If a parallel parent mode is entered then all of its immediate children are entered. If a serial parent mode is entered then exactly one of its immediate children is entered, this being defined as the initial mode of the parent. Similarly if a parent parallel mode is exited then all of its children are exited, and if a parent serial mode is exited, then whichever of its children the system is currently in is exited as well. Modecharts are very similar to Harel's statecharts [2] in that they use an event action model. Events are temporal markers that take zero time, and cause the transition between two groups of modes in the system.

The condition on each transition is of the form:

$$c_1 \lor c_2 \lor c_3 \lor ... \lor c_n$$

Where each disjunct c_m is a sub-condition that can be one of two types:

1. Triggering condition.
2. Lower/upper time bound condition.

A triggering condition is a conjunction of the occurrence of events and/or the truth values of predicates.

Events can be of any of the following:

1. An external event, ΩE.
2. An event denoting the start or stop of an action, $\uparrow A$, $\downarrow A$ respectively.
3. An event denoting a state variable becoming true or false, (S:=T), (S:=F) respectively.
4. An event denoting entry into or exit from a mode, (M1:=T), (M1:=F) or $\rightarrow$M1, M1$\rightarrow$ respectively or (M2-M1).

Predicates can specify a set of modes that the system has to be in (or not be in) for a transition to take place, and/or a set of state variables that must be true (or false) for the transition to take place.

Lower/upper time bound conditions are a sub-condition c_m of the form (r,d), where r is a delay (a nonnegative integer) and d is the deadline, (a nonnegative integer or ∞) with $r \leq d$. The transition is taken after the system has been in the source mode for at least r time units and before d time units have elapsed[1].

To break large, multi-layered modecharts up and to enable us to examine the structure and function of a HRT-HOOD object separately, we shall use the syntactic shorthand outlined in figures 1. In figure 1A there is a transition from X3 to a sibling of its parent X. The sibling is not shown.

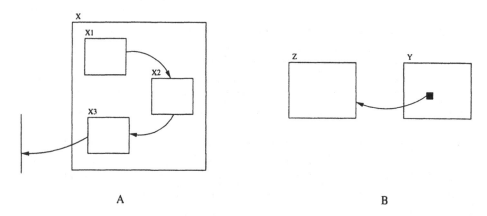

A   B

Fig. 1. Shorthand for transition (A) between a child of X and a sibling of X. (B) between a child of Y and Z, a sibling of Y

---

[1] If r=0 the shorthand (deadline d) is used and if r=d the shorthand (alarm r) is used.

In figure 1B there is a transition from a child of Y to Y's sibling Z. The child is not shown. In both cases if there is more than one transition, to avoid ambiguity an annotation convention will be employed.

2 Integration

At the terminal level, (as mentioned earlier) a HRT-HOOD design is made up of a number of single threaded cyclic and sporadic objects that use protected and passive objects. Each object in a design has a structure[2] which is dependant on the object type, (cyclic, sporadic or protected) and a function which is dependant on the purpose of the particular instance of that object. In this section we shall use the cyclic object as an example of an object type and define a modechart template for its structures. Then we shall look at the function of particular objects and see how this can be defined within the templates for the structure.

Using a number of the modechart templates for HRT-HOOD terminal objects with function modecharts defined within them, it is possible to product a modechart specification of the whole of a HRT-HOOD terminal design. This can then be used to verify that the design possesses the required properties.

2.1 Templates for HRT-HOOD object structure defined in Modecharts

The three types of object in a HRT-HOOD terminal design, Cyclic, Sporadic and Protected, each have a structure that is dependant on a number of attributes. In this section we shall use the cyclic as an example and look at the attributes that effect the structure of these objects, and then give an example of the simplest templates that capture the structure of the cyclic object. More complex templates can be created with different combinations of the attributes. (This work and the structure of the other object types are covered in more detail in [5]).

Cyclic. The attributes that affect the structure of a cyclic are:

- Period. Each cyclic must have a defined constant period per mode.
- Offset. Variations are: No offset or constant offset.
- Recovery routine. Variations are: No recovery routine or recovery routine.
- Deadline. Variations are: Hard deadline and soft deadline (whether the deadline is greater than or less than the period also affects the model).
- Clock jitter. Variations are: No clock jitter or varying clock jitter with a finite upper limit.
- Asynchronous transfer of control (ATC). Variations are: No ATC or a number of ATC's.

---

[2] Passive objects have no structure of their own and so need not be directly represented in modecharts. The only way they can be represented is in the function part of the objects that use the passive object.

– Thread budget (TB). All cyclic's must have one TB per mode.
– Thread worst case execution time (WCET). All cyclic's must have one WCET per mode.

Figure 2 shows the simplest template of a HRT-HOOD cyclic object. It has: no offset, no recovery routine, hard deadline (and deadline less than or equal to period), no clock jitter and no ATC's.

The event that triggers the cyclic to start its activity, is the event of the time controller entering mode X2, which occurs every T time units[3]. When X2 is entered the cyclic moves from its sleep mode to its work mode. The work mode is elaborated with the function of the instance of the particular object. Providing that the function is completed before the deadline or the WCET are exceeded, then the object returns to the sleep mode, alternatively the object transits to the Dead mode.

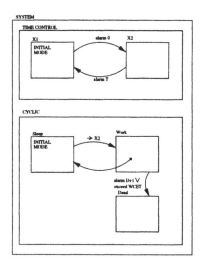

Fig. 2. Modechart template of a HRT-HOOD Cyclic object structure

2.2   HRT-HOOD object function defined in Modecharts

As mentioned earlier the "work" mode in figure 2 is intended to be elaborated using child modes to represent the function of a particular instance of that object type.

We define three basic building blocks for the functional part of the modechart, these are:

1. Action units. Action units are defined in modecharts as primitive modes that contain actions, i.e. the assignment of a value to a state variable. Figure 3

---

[3] T being the period of the cyclic.

shows the modechart representation of an action unit. The action "A" takes place in mode "X". The exit from mode X occurs at or before the deadline[4] of d has elapsed. In this work we assume that the action A has completed by the time the mode is exited[5]

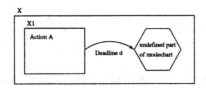

Fig. 3. modechart representation of an action

2. Asynchronous execution requests (ASER). An ASER is when one object requests another object to perform an operation, and once it has made the request it continues with its work. Figure 4 shows the modechart of object X requesting an ASER operation from object Y.

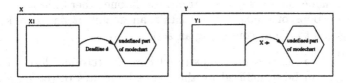

Fig. 4. modechart representation of an ASER (object X calling object Y)

3. Synchronous execution requests (SER). A SER is when one object requests another object to perform an operation, and then waits for the request to be completed before it continues with its work. Figure 4 shows the modechart of object X requesting a SER operation from object Y.
These three or variants of them, can be composed using a number of conditional edges to define any functionality that a object may undertake.

---

[4] Defining a deadline in Modecharts is to define a period with a lower limit of zero, however actions in modecharts must consume time, therefore there appears to be a contradiction here, as the action cannot take zero time. We take the view that it would be over-specifying to define a lower limit on an action in a design.

[5] For readers with background of RTL, this is to say, For all actions (A) within primitive modes X:
$\forall i, t_1, t_2 \; @(\rightarrow X, i) = t_1 \wedge @(X \rightarrow, i) = t_2 \Rightarrow \exists t_3, t_4 \; @(\uparrow A, i) = t_3 \wedge @(\downarrow A, i) = t_4 \wedge t_3 \geq t_1 \wedge t_4 \leq t_2$

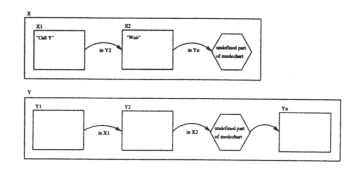

Fig. 5. modechart representation of a SER (object X calling object Y)

To preserve the nature of HRT-HOOD terminal objects, we impose the following rules on the construction of the functional part of the modechart representation:

1. All work modes are serial modes.
2. All children of the work mode must be either serial or primitive modes.
3. Only explicitly stated calling modes, i.e. modes with "call X" in them, can be used to cause an operation to begin in another object.
4. A calling mode can only cause a transition in one other object.
5. All closed loops of modes must contain an action mode or make a synchronous call to a unit containing an action mode.

The above two sections have illustrated how the terminal level of a HRT-HOOD design can be formalised by the use of templates of the object types, augmented with definitions of the function of the object instance in Modecharts. As expected during this formalisation, ambiguities in the semantics of HRT-HOOD were identified and clarified, leading to a more rigorous definition of the structured method, see [5] for more details.

3 Example

In this section we shall look at an object taken from a case study of the minepump problem. The HRT-HOOD solution to the minepump problem is presented in chapter 9 of [1]. We took this design and produced a formal design-specification of the whole system using the work outlined in this paper. Unfortunately space constraints prohibit us from presenting the whole design-specification here, and so we shall present just one of the objects in the minepump system as a partial example of how our method works. The object is the CH4 (methane) sensor.

3.1 CH4 sensor

The CH4 (methane) sensor is a cyclic object that is responsible for requesting and receiving CH4 level information from the CH4 measuring device. If the

CH4 measuring device does not reply to a request within a deadline, the CH4 sensor object informs the operator console. Providing that the CH4 device does reply, then the CH4 sensor object requests the motor status from the CH4 status object. If the mine pump motor status is safe, and the methane level is high then the motor object is called and informed that the motor should not be running. If the motor status is unsafe, and the methane is low, then the motor object is called and informed that the motor can run. The "data log" is then called with the methane level.

Figure 6 shows the modechart of the structure of the CH4 sensor. This is the same as the template for the cyclic given earlier, With the period (50) and the deadline (10) added and the names of the modes augmented with the name of the object.

Figure 7 shows the function of the CH4 sensor. This is made up of a number of asynchronous and synchronous requests as shown in figures 4 and 5. The external events ΩCH4A and ΩCH4D represent the external device accepting the request, and the external device completing the call, respectively. The state variables CH4 and MS represent the CH4 level, (low being safe level and high being unsafe), and Motor Safe to operate respectively.

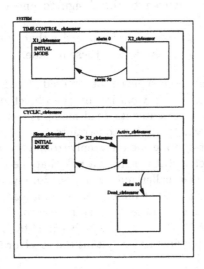

Fig. 6. structure of CH4 sensor object

4 Proving properties of a design

In the previous sections we have shown how a Modechart design-specification of a HRT-HOOD design can be produced. Once we have produced a formal description of the low level design, what properties do we want to be able to prove about it? In a purely formal development verification would either be immediate, (if refinement was used) or would involve proving the relationship between design and specification. This is possible because the specification is a

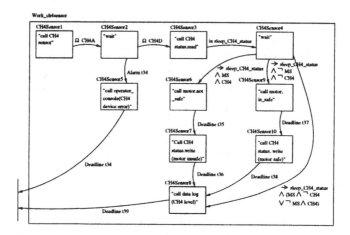

Fig. 7. function of CH4 sensor object

formal statement. In our integrated framework this is not necessarily the case, nevertheless we wish to interrogate the design to understand its subsequent behaviour.

There are a number of categories of properties that it would be desirable to be able to verify about any given design, these include:

- Check that dead modes can never be entered. Dead modes can only be entered if there is a timing violation by the object in question. To show that the object can never enter its dead mode, is to show that the objects function, never violates its timing constraints.
- Objects can never starve waiting on a reply from a protected. If a number of objects call a protected, then there is a risk that the load on the protected could be such that one caller may wait indefinitely for its request to be serviced. If you can show that under a maximum load the protected object has spare capacity, then no object can starve waiting.
- Violation of MAT or MAF. If a sporadic is called by a thread that is internally invoked,[6] it is possible to verify that the MAT or MAF of the sporadic will never be violated.
- End to end timing. If external event ΩX occurs, how long before the system causes a change in the environment? It is possible to verify that the maximum end to end timing does not exceed a given value.
- Freshness of data (data store). It is possible to examine the maximum separation between two calls to a data store to check that data is as fresh as required.
- Erroneous outputs. If an output occurs, you can verify that it was always proceeded by the system entering given modes.

---

[6] By an internally invoked thread we mean a timer invoked thread, as opposed to an interrupt invoked thread.

Using the model checking techniques proposed by Stuart, [7, 8] it is possible to verify all the types of properties given above. We are currently verifying these properties for the full mine pump example.

5 Conclusions

In this paper we have given a number of modechart templates for the terminal HRT-HOOD objects. We have also defined three basic building blocks in Modecharts for the function of instances of HRT-HOOD objects, and defined a set of rules that must be adhered to when constructing a design-specification. In doing this we have shown an approach to combining HRT-HOOD and Modecharts, that from the point of view of HRT-HOOD, has three main benefits:

1. The Modechart templates give an unambiguous definition of the objects that populate a HRT-HOOD design.
2. The designer is able to verify properties of the design.
3. The designer has an alternative and complimentary way of viewing the design.

And from the point of view of Modecharts, the following benefits:

1. The designer has a way of structuring large designs.
2. The design can be analysed for schedulability.
3. Modecharts can be used only on the most important objects or parts of the design.

The next stage in this work will be to present a full case study. The production of the design-specification of the Mine Pump has been completed (as mentioned earlier), and we are currently verifying properties of this system.

References

1. A. Burns and A.J. Wellings. *HRT-HOOD: A structured design method for hard real-time Ada systems*, volume 3 of *Real-Time Safty Critical Systems*. Elsevier, 1995.
2. D. Harel. Statecharts : A visual formalism for complex systems. *Science of computer programming*, 8(3):231–274, 1987.
3. Farnam Jahanian and Aloysius Ka lau Mok. Safty analysis of timing properties in real-time systems. *IEEE Transactions on software engineering*, 12(9):890–904, September 1986.
4. K. Mok and F. Jahanian. Modecharts: A specification language for real-time systems. *IEEE transactions in software engineering*, 20(12):933–947, December 1994.
5. D. Priddin and A. Burns. Using modecharts to define terminal hrt-hood object structure. Yellow YCS 293, University of York, 1997.
6. P.J. Robinson. *hierarchical object-oriented design*. prentice hall, 1992.
7. D. A. Stuart. A formal method for the verifying real-time properties of modechart specifications. URL: http://www.cs.utexas.edu/ users/cpg/RTS/pubs.html.
8. D.A. Stuart. *Formal Methods for real-time systems*. PhD thesis, The University of Texas at Austin, 1996.

Duration Calculus in the Specification of Safety Requirements

Veloudis, S. and Nissanke, N.

Department of Computer Science, The University of Reading
Whiteknights, P.O. Box 225, Reading RG6 2AY
United Kingdom
(tel: ++ 44 118 931 8608, fax: ++ 44 118 9751994
e-mail: S.Veloudis@reading.ac.uk, nn@reading.ac.uk)

Abstract. This paper investigates the effectiveness of Duration Calculus in the specification of safety, as well as, of functional requirements of critical systems. It is based on railway signalling – a case study which is realistic both in terms of complexity and in terms of the range of safety requirements covered by it. Duration Calculus is found to be a convenient medium of specification, firstly, due to its reliance on durations of states rather than on real time in explicit form and, secondly, due to the intuitive nature of its syntactic constructs.

1 Introduction

The design of critical systems involves two independent sets of requirements: *functional requirements* and *safety requirements*. Functional requirements address the expected service and, as characterized by the term *reliability*, usually allow some leeway with respect to the extent of the service provided over time. Although often associated with reliability, *safety* is quite a different notion. Safety requirements concern the behaviour patterns of the system forbidden on the grounds of danger to human life or property.

The given paper focuses on the classification and specification of safety requirements by using Duration Calculus. This is undertaken with two objectives, firstly, to establish the effectiveness of Duration Calculus in capturing the requirements of a given system and, secondly, to demonstrate the benefits of a formalism that does not rely on explicit references to real time. In comparison to other similar efforts such as [8, 9] based on Duration Calculus, the given work is devoted to the study of a system of reasonable complexity and, in particular, to railway signalling. For an introduction to the syntax and semantics of Duration Calculus (DC), the reader is referred to [3, 8, 9].

2 About the Case Study

We view any realtime system as consisting of the *controlling system*, usually a computer, and the *controlled system*, which in turn consists of *sensors* and *activators*. The communications of the latter with the controlling system are referred to as *sensor data* and *control signals* respectively. The signalling system is assumed to consist of two major components: the *permanent way* and the *interlocking*. The permanent way is the set of all the physical equipment: the *track circuits*, the *points* and the *signals*. The interlocking is a safety mechanism preventing certain undesirable combinations of events taking place. Let *TRACKS*, *POINTS*, *SIGNALS* be appropriate types for representing the components of the permanent way. Individual instances of these types are referred to by using variables with numerical subscripts. Therefore, variable $track_i \in TRACKS$ ($i \in \mathbb{N}$) for example, denotes the ith track in the system.

At any time t, a track can be in one of two possible states: either *clear* or *occupied*. A set of points can only be in two possible modes of operation: either *normal* or *reverse*. During the interval of time that a set of points is moving from the one position to the other, the points are defined as being *out of correspondence* since they are neither in the normal nor in the reverse positions and, moreover, no control action can be applied to them. The controlling system must also be able to lock a set of points to the normal or the reverse position. When a set of points is locked it cannot be moved into another position. It is assumed that a set of points is automatically locked to the desired position after the points have been controlled to that position.

A signal can typically display three colours: *red* (do not proceed beyond the signal), *yellow* (proceed and expect the next signal to be at red), *green* (proceed and expect the next signal to be at green or yellow). As far as the signalling system is concerned, all signals are normally at red unless they have explicitly been controlled to show a proceed aspect. Finally, the controlling system must also be able to monitor the state of the lamp in the head of a signal. Table 1 summarizes the DC state variables used in this paper in modelling the state of affairs described above.

DC variable	Description
$Occupied_i$	The ith track is occupied.
$PointsOp_i$	The ith set of points is operational (i.e. non-broken).
$InNor_i$, $InRev_i$	The ith set of points is in the normal or the reverse position.
$ReqToNor_i$, $ReqToRev_i$	There has been a request from the controlling system to move the ith set of points to the normal or the reverse position.
$OutOfCorr_i$	The ith set of points is out of correspondence.
$ReqToUnLock_i$	There has been a request from the controlling system to unlock the ith set of points.
$SignalOp_i$	The ith signal is operational.
$ProceedAspect_i$	The ith signal shows a proceed aspect.
$ReqToRed_i$, $ReqToYellow_i$ and $ReqToGreen_i$	There has been a request to the ith signal to display a red, yellow or green colour respectively.
$LampOn_i$	The ith lamp is alight (i.e. non-broken).

Table 1. Description of DC variables used in the paper

3 Functional Requirements

In this section we will focus on some of the *functional timing requirements*, that the system components may exhibit. Functional timing requirements express the desired evolution of each system component and they can be regarded as domain specific constraints that basically address the system liveness and hence guarantee the functionality and operability of the underlying system.

3.1 Functional Requirements on Points

First of all, once a request to move a set of points from the one position to the other has been issued, it is vital to ensure that this movement takes place within a certain amount of time (say ϵ_1). If after the expiration of ϵ_1 the points are not in the required position, they are considered to be broken (i.e. non–operational). This timing requirement can be expressed in DC for the normal position as follows:

$$FReq_1 \stackrel{def}{=} (\lceil ReqToNor_i \rceil \wedge \lceil PointsOp_i \rceil) \Rightarrow ((\lceil \rceil \sim \epsilon_1 \rightsquigarrow \lceil InNor_i \rceil) \\ \vee \, \Diamond PointsFail_i) \tag{1}$$

$$FReq_2 \stackrel{def}{=} PointsFail_i \Rightarrow \lceil \neg PointsOp_i \rceil \tag{2}$$

where,

$$PointsFail_i \stackrel{def}{=} \lceil OutOfCorr_i \rceil \Rightarrow \ell > \epsilon_2$$

and $\epsilon_1 > \epsilon_2$.

A request to move a set of points from the one position to the other should always result in the points being locked after at most ϵ_1' units of time. This requirement is a consequence of the fact that a request to move a set of points can only be issued as part of the process of setting a route and hence all points in the route should be locked. If after ϵ_1' units of time the points are still unlocked then the points are considered as broken:

$$FReq_3 \stackrel{def}{=} (\lceil ReqToNor_i \rceil \wedge \lceil PointsOp_i \rceil) \Rightarrow ((\lceil \rceil \sim \epsilon_1' \rightsquigarrow \lceil Locked_i \rceil) \\ \vee \, \Diamond PointsFail_i) \tag{3}$$

Note that $\epsilon_1 < \epsilon_1'$, since the points should first move into the correct position (within ϵ_1) and then become locked (within ϵ_1').

A similar timing requirement exists for the case that there has been a request from the controlling system to unlock an already locked set of points:

$$FReq_4 \stackrel{def}{=} (\lceil ReqToUnlock_i \rceil \wedge \lceil Locked_i \rceil) \Rightarrow ((\lceil \rceil \sim \epsilon_3 \rightsquigarrow \lceil \neg Locked_i \rceil) \\ \vee \, \Diamond PointsFail_i) \tag{4}$$

The above set of functional requirements concerns the normal position. As far as the reverse position is concerned, a similar set of timing requirements exists.

The general pattern for describing the process of moving a set of points to the desired position, and locking them in that position can now be specified in DC as the following set of transitions:

$$Pattern_i \stackrel{def}{=} \Box((((\lceil ReqToNor_i \rceil \wedge \lceil PointsOp_i \rceil) \rightarrow \lceil OutOfCorr_i \rceil) \wedge$$
$$(\lceil OutOfCorr_i \rceil \rightarrow (\lceil InNor_i \rceil \vee \lceil PointsFail_i \rceil)) \wedge$$
$$(\lceil InNor_i \rceil \rightarrow (\lceil Locked_i \rceil \vee \lceil PointsFail_i \rceil))) \tag{5}$$

As far as the reverse position is concerned, a similar set of transitions can be defined.

3.2 Functional Requirements on Signals

Once a request to display a red colour has been issued to a signal, it is important to ensure that the signal shows a *do–not* proceed aspect within a certain amount of time (say δ_1). If after δ_1 units of time the signal is still not displaying a *do–not* proceed aspect then it is assumed that the lamp is not on, and the signal should be considered as being out of order. This can be formally expressed as follows:

$$FReq_5 \stackrel{def}{=} (\lceil ReqToRed_i \rceil \wedge \lceil SignalOp_i \rceil) \Rightarrow$$
$$((\lceil \rceil \sim \delta_1 \rightsquigarrow \lceil \neg ProceedAspect_i \rceil) \vee \Diamond \lceil \neg LampOn_i \rceil) \tag{6}$$

$$FReq_6 \stackrel{def}{=} \lceil \neg LampOn_i \rceil \Rightarrow (\lceil \rceil \sim \delta_3 \rightsquigarrow \lceil \neg SignalOp_i \rceil) \tag{7}$$

where δ_3 is the maximum amount of time that is allowed to elapse before the signal is considered as non–operational. Similar timing requirements exist for the cases where there have been requests to display a yellow or green colour.

4 Route Setting

Unlike the components of the permanent way, routes do not physically exist: they are logical entities that only exist in the memory of the controlling system. In order to model routes, the state variable $RouteSet_i$ is introduced. We define $RouteSet_i$ to mean that the ith route is set. Also, we introduce the state variable $ReqToSet_i$ indicating whether there is a request from the controlling system to set the ith route. A route can be set by locking all points that lie on tracks that are part of the route in the required position, and controlling all signals in the route to display a proceed aspect.

The general process of setting an originally unset route can be formally described by the following set of transitions. It is important to note here that it is imperative to take into account the possibility of failures, in which case the whole route–setting process is cancelled:

$$SetRoute \stackrel{def}{=} (\lceil ReqToSet_j \rceil \wedge \lceil \neg RouteSet_j \rceil) \rightarrow$$
$$(\lceil SetPoints \rceil \wedge \lceil SetSignals \rceil) \rightarrow$$
$$(\lceil RouteSet_j \rceil \vee (\lceil PointFailure \rceil \vee \lceil SignalFailure \rceil)) \tag{8}$$

where *SetPoints*, *SetSignals*, *PointFailure* and *SignalFailure* are defined as

$$SetPoints \stackrel{def}{=} \forall i \bullet (InRoute(j, points_i) = 1) \Rightarrow (\lceil Pattern_i \rceil$$
$$\vee \lceil Pattern_i' \rceil)$$

$$SetSignals \stackrel{def}{=} \forall i \bullet (InRoute(j, signal_i) = 1) \Rightarrow$$
$$(\lceil ReqToGreen_i \rceil \vee \lceil ReqToYellow_i \rceil)$$

$$PointFailure \stackrel{def}{=} \exists i \bullet (InRoute(j, points_i) = 1) \Rightarrow (\lceil PointsFail_i \rceil)$$

$$SignalFailure \stackrel{def}{=} \exists i \bullet (InRoute(j, signal_i) = 1) \Rightarrow (\lceil \neg LampOn_i \rceil)$$

where $InRoute \in (\mathbb{N} \times \mathcal{X}) \rightarrow \{0, 1\}$, i.e. it is a predicate that determines whether a component of the permanent way is part of the route. $\mathcal{X}$ is a generic type and represents any possible component of the permanent way (signals, points or tracks).

Finally, in order for the system to be functional and achieve the required level of service, we require that

$$FReq_7 \stackrel{def}{=} (\lceil ReqToSet_i \rceil \wedge \lceil \neg RouteSet_i \rceil) \Rightarrow ((\lceil \rceil \sim \xi \rightsquigarrow \lceil RouteSet_i \rceil) \vee$$
$$(\lceil PointFailure \rceil \vee \lceil SignalFailure \rceil)) \tag{9}$$

where ξ is the predefined amount of time within which a route must be set (unless failures have occurred).

5 Safety timing requirements

Safety timing requirements are primarily concerned with ensuring that each item of equipment and, hence, the system as a whole operates in a safe manner and in the case that a failure occurs, either in the controlled or the controlling system, it is dealt with in a safe way. Safety timing requirements can be broadly classified into three categories:

5.1 Function–related safety timing requirements

The operation of any system inevitably involves transformations of the system's state from a state of relatively low risk to a state of relatively high risk. Function–related safety timing requirements are primarily concerned with how such transformations can be performed in a safe manner that ensures the safety of both the users of the system and the operators. There are two implicit assumptions in this type of requirements:

- The operation of the controlled system is 'controllable' both by the controlling system and the operators.
- The risks that are dealt with are considered acceptable in pursuing the benefits offered by the system.

Function–related safety timing requirements can be classified into two further subcategories of requirements:

1. Those describing under which conditions low to high risk state transformations should take place. This subcategory of requirements falls under the scope of *operational safety requirements* and is not going to be further examined in this paper.
2. Those describing under which conditions low to high risk state transformations should <u>not</u> take place, since it is speculated that such transformations could lead to potentially dangerous situations. This subcategory of requirements falls under the scope of *failure preventative requirements* whose general form can be defined as:

$$G \text{ prohibits } (P \rightsquigarrow Q) \overset{def}{=} \lceil G \rceil \Rightarrow \neg(\Diamond(\lceil P \rceil; \lceil Q \rceil)) \tag{10}$$

where P is the low risk state, Q is the high risk state of the item of equipment under consideration and G is a combination of states that describes the conditions under which the transformation $P \rightsquigarrow Q$ must not take place. Failure preventative timing requirements will be further examined in Section 7.

5.2 Failure–averting timing requirements

No matter how well a system is designed, one cannot rule out the possibility of failures. Failure–averting timing requirements are primarily concerned with avoiding an imminent failure. They usually involve transformations of the system's state from a state of relatively <u>high</u> risk (in which the system is operating in order to provide the required service) to a state of relatively <u>low</u> risk, in which the system is probably unable to provide the required service but this is deemed less important than averting the imminent failure.

The general form of a failure–averting timing requirement can be defined as:

$$G \wedge P \text{ requires } Q \text{ within } \theta \overset{def}{=} (\lceil G \rceil \wedge \lceil P \rceil) \sim \theta \rightsquigarrow \lceil Q \rceil \tag{11}$$

where P is the high risk state in which the system is initially operating, Q is the low risk state in which the system is required to fall back to, θ is the maximum amount of time within which the transformation from P to Q must take place and G is a set of states whose presence requires the high to low risk state transformation. Failure–averting timing requirements are further studied in Section 8.

5.3 Failure–handling timing requirements

Failure–handling timing requirements focus on safety procedures applicable amid failures. It is assumed that one or more item of equipment in the controlled system is no longer controllable either because of an equipment failure or a failure in the controlling system. The aim is to isolate the non–controllable item of equipment, and thus to limit the damage due to the failure. This results in degraded performance, or even a total shutdown in extreme situations, in order to minimize the potential risks. Failure–handling timing requirements are the subject of Section 6.

6 Dealing with failures

The existing solid state implementations of railway signalling systems do incorporate the approaches suggested by Leveson and Stolzy [4] for dealing with failures (namely, *fault–tolerant systems*, *fail–soft systems* and *fail–safe systems*), but in a varying degree and a highly selective manner. Fault–tolerant techniques are generally considered highly desirable, as far as railway signalling is concerned however, there must always be some predefined state to fall back on since there is always the possibillity that all backup resourses may fail.

6.1 Safe and Unsafe states

The distinction made in page 104 between sensor data and control signals is important with respect to the specification of safety requirements. Our intention is to associate the states of each piece of equipment either with the data of sensors attached to it, or with the control signals it receives. Degrees of risk for these states are then assessed, and on that basis, safe and unsafe states are defined. In general terms, the following can be stated:

- *Control signal failure:*
  Upon a failure of the controlling system, each item of equipment must be returned to its safe state which is defined as one of its lowest risk states (i.e. the *most restrictive* ones).
- *Sensor data failure:*
  Upon a sensor failure, the most sensible thing to do for the controlling system is to assume the worst possible scenario, i.e that the item of equipment being monitored is in its unsafe state (defined here as one of the *highest risk* states).

It is now time to associate each component of the permanent way with a set of safe and unsafe states. In order to do so, two predicates '*safe*' and '*unsafe*' are defined as $safe, unsafe : \mathcal{X} \rightarrow \mathbb{R}$.

Tracks. The controlling system cannot (directly) control a track to the one or the other state by means of a control signal. Therefore, a track can only be viewed as a source of sensor data. Following the discussion in the last section, the highest risk state, and hence the unsafe state, of a track is the one in which the track is occupied, since it is a potential risk to other trains approaching it. Therefore, $unsafe(track_i) = \lceil Occupied_i \rceil$.

Points. As opposed to tracks, a set of points is both the source of sensor data and the receiver of control signals. It is not appropriate to associate any level of risk with a set of points, when these points are operational and are either in the normal or the reverse position. However, the high risk state (and hence the unsafe state) may be considered as the one in which the points are broken, since in this case the points are no longer controllable. Therefore, in the case that the sensor attached to a set of points fails, the safest thing to do is to assume that the points are broken: $unsafe(points_i) = \lceil \neg PointsOp_i \rceil$.

Similarly, it does not make sense to control a set of points to the normal or the reverse position upon failure of the controlling system. In this case, the most restrictive state (and hence the safest one) is the one in which the points are locked. Therefore, $safe(points_i) = \lceil Locked_i \rceil$.

Signals. Following the same reasoning as above, we can associate the following safe and unsafe states with signals: $unsafe(signal_i) = \lceil \neg LampOn_i \rceil$ and $safe(signal_i) = \lceil \neg ProceedAspect_i \rceil$.

7 Low to High Risk State Transformations

Failure preventative requirements concern only those components of the system that are <u>directly</u> controllable by the controlling system (by means of control signals). Timing requirements are considered irrelevant in this case and, therefore, no reference to time intervals will be made when expressing such requirements.

Signals. In [7], it is stated that a signal (say the kth one) may 'clear' (i.e. go from a state where it shows a *do–not* proceed aspect to a state where it shows a proceed aspect) if the following conditions are true:

1. The route is set.
2. The signal ahead is alight.
3. All the tracks in the route are clear.

The circumstances under which it is prohibited for the kth signal to perform a low to high risk state transformation can be derived by negating the conjunction of the above conditions,

$$\neg\ States_1 \overset{def}{=} \neg\ ((\lceil RouteSet_j \rceil) \wedge (\lceil SignalOp_{F(j,k)} \rceil) \wedge$$
$$(\forall\, i \bullet (InRoute(j, track_i) = 1) \Rightarrow (\lceil \neg Occupied_i \rceil)))$$

leading to the following failure preventative requirement:

$$\lceil \neg States_1 \rceil \ \textbf{prohibits}\ (\lceil \neg ProceedAspect_i \rceil \rightsquigarrow \lceil ProceedAspect_i \rceil) \qquad (12)$$

where $F(j, k)$ is a predicate that yields the identifier of the next signal in the route. It can formally be defined as $F : (N \times N) \to N$.

Points. A set of points can go from the low risk state (i.e. the one in which the points are locked) to a high risk state (i.e. one in which the points are not locked), if the following condiotions are satisfied:

1. The mth route that passes over the kth set of points has been set.
2. The track on which the points lie is clear.
3. All the tracks in the route that <u>precede</u> the track on which the points lie are clear.

The circumstances under which the transformation is prohibited can be obtained by negating the conjunction of the above conditions:

$$\neg\ States_2 \overset{def}{=} \neg\ (\lceil RouteSet_m \rceil \wedge \lceil \neg Occupied_k \rceil \wedge \forall\, i \bullet$$
$$((InRoute(m, track_i) = 1) \wedge (i \leq k)) \Rightarrow \lceil \neg Occupied_i \rceil) \qquad (13)$$

Therefore, the following failure preventative requirement can be specified:

$$\lceil \neg States_2 \rceil \ \textbf{prohibits} \ (\lceil Locked_k \rceil \rightsquigarrow \lceil \neg Locked_k \rceil) \tag{14}$$

In the above definition it is assumed that the kth set of points lies on the kth track.

Routes. Despite the fact that routes do not exist in the physical sense and we have not associated with them safe and unsafe states, we will define a failure preventative requirement for prohibiting the controlling system from setting a specific route (it is assumed here that the high risk state is the one in which a route has been set, since in this case, trains are free to move along that route and this is potentially more dangerours than when the route is not set and no train movement is allowed along that route).

A route can be set (according to [7]) if no points in the route are locked and no track in the route is part of a different and already set route. Hence, the failure preventative requirement for routes takes the form:

$$\lceil \neg States_3 \rceil \ \textbf{prohibits} \ (\lceil \neg RouteSet_m \rceil \rightsquigarrow \lceil RouteSet_m \rceil) \tag{15}$$

where

$$\neg States_3 \stackrel{def}{=} \neg (\forall j \bullet \ \forall i \bullet \ (j \neq m) \ \land$$
$$(((InRoute(m, track_i) = 1) \Rightarrow (InRoute(j, track_{i_i}) = 0)) \Rightarrow$$
$$(\lceil \neg Occupied_i \rceil)) \land (\forall i \bullet (InRoute(m, points_i) = 1) \Rightarrow \lceil \neg Locked_i \rceil)) \tag{16}$$

Note that j ranges over the set of all possible routes, excluding, of course, the current route.

8 High to Low Risk State Transformations

Failure–averting timing requirements sacrifice the system's functionality and operability in order to avert an imminent failure. Timing requirements here are considered to be extremely important: failure to meet the timing requirements may result in the imminent failure not being averted and this could have catastrophic consequences for both the users of the system and its operators. We follow the same style as in Section 7 and define failure–averting timing requirements for individual components of the railway signalling system.

Signals. The set of states whose presence forces the kth signal to perform a high to low risk state transformation are exactly those defined in Section 7 as $States_1$. Therefore, if $\neg States_1$ evaluates to true at some point, and also $\lceil ProceedAspect_k \rceil$ holds (i.e. the kth signal is operating at a high risk level), the signal should return to its low risk state as quickly as possible. This can be expressed formally as

$$\lceil \neg States_1 \rceil \land \lceil ProceedAspect_k \rceil \ \textbf{requires} \ \lceil \neg ProceedAspect_k \rceil$$
$$\textbf{within} \ \theta_1 \tag{17}$$

where θ_1 is the time limit within which the transformation must be performed.

Points. Following the same reasoning as in the last subsection we can specify the following failure–averting timing requirement for the jth set of points:

$$\lceil \neg States_2 \rceil \wedge \lceil \neg Locked_j \rceil \textbf{ requires } \lceil Locked_j \rceil \textbf{ within } \theta_2 \qquad (18)$$

It should be noted here that the position in which the points get locked is irrelevant. What is important in this case is that the points are *not free* to move.

Remark: Due to their abstract nature, routes can become 'set' and 'unset' instanteneously. Therefore, no time is required for a route to 'jump' from the high risk state to the low risk state and hence we do not consider it appropriate to associate any failure–averting timing requirements with routes.

9   Conclusions

In addition to a refinement of a previous classification of safety requirements, the given paper has investigated the effectiveness of Duration Calculus in the specification of safety requirements in systems of realistic nature. Compared to our previous attempts [5, 6] based on predicate logic and deontic logic, the task of specification here has been considerably eased by the fact that timing issues can be specified without explicit reference to real time. Undoubtedly, this, as well as the use of Boolean–valued state variables only, has resulted in a more readable and abstract specification. Furthermore, the formalization has been able to maintain a clear separation between functional and safety concerns, which could greatly facilitate the process of validation and certification of critical systems.

References

1. J. Cullyer and W. Wong. Application of formal methods to railway signalling – a case study. *Computing & Control Engineering Journal*, Feb 1993.
2. K. M. Hansen. Formalising railway interlocking systems. Technical Report ID/DTH KMH3/1, ProCos II, Department of Computer Science, Technical University of Denmark, DK-2000 Lyngby, Denmark, 1994.
3. M. R. Hansen and Z. Chaochen. Duration calculus: Logical foundations. *Formal Aspects of Computing*, 9:283–330, 1997.
4. N. G. Leveson and J. L. Stolzy. Safety analysis using Petri nets. *IEEE Trans. on Software Engineering*, 13(3), 1987.
5. N. Nissanke and N. Robinson. Formal methods in safety analysis. In V. Maggioli, editor, *SAFECOMP'94*, International Conference on Computer Safety, Reliability and Security, pages 239–248, Anaheim, California, 1994. Instrument Society of America.
6. N. Nissanke. Safety specification in deontic logic. In *Proceedings*, 2nd IMA Conference on the Mathematics of Dependable Systems, York, England, pages 113–133. Oxford University Press, 1997.
7. Director of S & T Engineering and Director of Operations. *Standard Signalling Principles*. British Railways Board.
8. A. P. Ravn, H. Rischel, and K. M. Hansen. Specifying and verifying requirements of real-time systems. *IEEE Trans. on Software Engineering*, 19(1):41–55, 1993.
9. J. U. Shakkebæk, A. Ravn, H. Rischel, and Z. Chaochen. Specification of embedded, real–time systems. In *Proceedings*, Euromicro Workshop on Real Time Systems, pages 116–121. IEEE Computer Society, June 1992.

Automated Stream-Based Analysis of Fault-Tolerance*

Scott D. Stoller[1] and Fred B. Schneider[2]

[1] Computer Science Dept., Indiana University, Bloomington, IN 47405, USA
`stoller@cs.indiana.edu`
[2] Dept. of Computer Science, Cornell University, Ithaca, NY 14853, USA
`fbs@cs.cornell.edu`

Abstract. A rigorous, automated approach to analyzing fault-tolerance of distributed systems is presented. The method is based on a stream model of computation that incorporates approximation mechanisms. One application is described: a protocol for fault-tolerant moving agents.

1 Introduction

As computers are integrated into systems having stringent fault-tolerance requirements, there is a growing need for practical techniques to establish that these requirements are satisfied. This paper describes such an analysis method. Automated analysis methods address an important need, because informal arguments do not supply the desired level of assurance for critical systems, and practitioners often lack the background needed to construct the formal proofs required by proof-based methods, such as those in [ORSvH95,CdR93,PJ94,JJ96,Sch96]. Automated verification techniques based on exhaustive exploration of finite state-spaces [CGL94,Hol91,Kur94,CS96] have made great progress in the last decade. But relatively little work has been done on automated verification of fault-tolerant software systems, partly because exhaustive search of the state-space of these systems is infeasible in many cases.

This paper discusses a specialized approach to analysis of fault-tolerance properties for distributed systems. It is a novel hybrid of ideas from stream-processing (or data-flow) models of networks of processes [Kah74,Bro87] and abstract interpretation of programs [AH87]. An important feature of our approach is its emphasis on communication (rather than state), consistent with the thesis that distributed systems have natural descriptions in terms of communication.

In stream-processing models, each component of a system is represented by an *input-output function* describing its input/output behavior. For simplicity, we assume processes communicate only by messages transmitted along unbounded FIFO channels. Behaviors of a system can be determined from input-output functions describing its components by doing a fixed-point calculation; this provides a clean algorithmic basis for our analysis.

The fixed-point calculation produces a graph, called a *message flow graph* (MFG), representing possible communication behaviors of the system. Each node of the graph corresponds to a component, and each edge is labeled with a description of the sequence of messages sent from the source node to the target

---

* This material is based on work supported in part by NSF/DARPA Grant No. CCR-9014363, NASA/DARPA grant NAG-2-893, and AFOSR grant F49620-94-1-0198. Any opinions, findings, and conclusions or recommendations expressed in this publication are those of the authors and do not reflect the views of these agencies.

node. An exact computation of all possible sequences of messages that might be sent is generally infeasible. To help make automated analysis feasible, our framework supports flexible and powerful approximations, or abstractions, as they are called in the literature on abstract interpretation [AH87]. Traditionally, stream-processing models have not incorporated approximations. The approximations in our framework enable compact representation of the highly non-deterministic behavior characteristic of severe failures and also support abstraction from irrelevant aspects of a system's failure-free behavior. The latter reflects a separation of concerns that is crucial for making the fault-tolerance analysis tractable.

A common approach to modeling failures is to treat them as events that occur non-deterministically during a computation (e.g., [CdR93,PJ94,LM94]), but this makes it difficult to separate the effects of failures from other aspects of the system's behavior and, consequently, to model the former more finely than the latter. In particular, one often wants to avoid case analysis corresponding to non-determinism in a system's failure-free behavior, while case analysis corresponding to different combinations of failures appears unavoidable in general in automated analysis of fault-tolerance. A *failure scenario* for a system is an assignment of component failures to a subset of the system's components. In our approach, each input-output function is parameterized by possible failures in the corresponding component; system behavior is analyzed separately for each failure scenario of interest.

In our framework, possible communications (in a given failure scenario) between two components are characterized by approximations of *values* (the data transmitted in messages), *multiplicities* (the number of times each value is sent), and *message orderings* (the order in which values are sent). Values and multiplicities are approximated using a form of abstract interpretation and a form of symbolic computation. Message orderings are approximated using partial (instead of total) orders.

Our analysis method is implemented in a prototype tool called CRAFT [Sto97]. We have used CRAFT to analyze a protocol for fault-tolerant moving agents and the Oral Messages algorithm for Byzantine Agreement [LSP82].

A formal presentation of our analysis method, including a semantics and a proof of soundness with respect to that semantics, appears in [Sto97]. A discussion of related and future work, including comparisons with the abstraction methods of [CGL94,Kur94], can also be found there.

2 Analysis Method

We start by describing how data is approximated in our framework and then how sets and sequences of messages are approximated. This leads directly to definitions of MFGs and input-output functions.

Values. As in abstract interpretation, we introduce a set $AVal$ of *abstract values*. Each abstract value represents a set of concrete values. For example, we use abstract value N to represent the set of 64-bit numbers. In Section 3, we use abstract value $Arb(kcs, ms)$ to represent the concrete values that can be generated using encryption keys in the set kcs and ciphertexts in the set ms.

Abstract values alone capture too little information about relationships between concrete values. For example, consider a system containing a majority voter. The voter's outputs depend on equality relationships among its inputs. If two inputs both have abstract value N, there is no way to tell from this whether they are equal. So, we introduce a set *SVal* of *symbolic values*, which are expressions composed of constants and variables. All occurrences of a symbol (i.e., a constant or variable) in a single MFG represent the same value. For example, if two inputs of a 3-way voter contain the same symbolic value, then that symbolic values represents the majority value and therefore represents the voter's output.

A *constant* represents the same value in every execution of a system; most constants are typeset in a sans-serif font. The meaning of a constant is specified by an *interpretation*, which maps constants to concrete values. A *variable* represents values that may be different in different executions of a system. Variables are useful for modeling outputs that are not completely determined by a component's inputs. Such outputs commonly arise with components that interact with an environment that is not modeled explicitly; they also arise when a component's behavior is approximated. Each variable is *local to* a single component, whose outputs in a given execution determine the value represented by that variable. Making each variable local to a single component enables independent verification that each input-output function faithfully represents the behavior of the corresponding process (as described in [Sto97]). We also include in *SVal* a special *wildcard* symbol "_", which is used when a value is not known to have any interesting relationships to other values. Different occurrences of the wildcard in a MFG do *not* necessarily represent the same concrete value.

A symbolic value and an abstract value together are often sufficient to characterize the possible data in a message. Analysis of a non-deterministic system might yield multiple such pairs, each representing some of the possibilities for the data in a message. So, we use a set of such pairs to represent values, and define $Val \triangleq Set(SVal \times AVal) \setminus \{\emptyset\}$, where $Set(S)$ is the powerset of a set S. Since abstract values are analogous to types, we usually write $\langle s, a \rangle \in SVal \times AVal$ as $s:a$. We usually omit braces around singleton sets; for example, $\{\langle X, \mathbf{N} \rangle\} \in Val$ may be written $X:\mathbf{N}$. Since a wildcard is similar in meaning to omission of a symbolic value, we usually elide the wildcard; for example, $\{\langle \_, \mathbf{N} \rangle\} \in Val$ may be written $\mathbf{N}$.

Multiplicities. Uncertainty in the number of messages sent during a computation may stem from various sources, including non-determinism of components (especially faulty components), non-determinism of message arrival order, and approximation of values. For example, a component subject to Byzantine failures[1] might emit outputs with an arbitrary multiplicity. To compactly represent these possibilities, multiplicity (i.e., the number of messages) also needs to be approximated. Thinking of multiplicities as natural numbers suggests representing them in the same way as data. Thus, we define $Mul \triangleq Set(SVal \times AMul) \setminus \{\emptyset\}$, where the set $AMul \subseteq AVal$ of *abstract multiplicities* contains abstract values whose meanings are subsets of the natural numbers, excluding $\emptyset$ and $\{0\}$.

The symbolic values in multiplicities are useful for efficient analysis of systems with crash failures [SS97]. Abstract multiplicities are analogous to superscripts in regular expressions. To promote the resemblance, we assume *AVal* contains the following: 1, denoting $\{1\}$; ?, denoting $\{0,1\}$; +, denoting the set of positive natural numbers; and *, denoting the set of natural numbers. The notational conventions for *Val* also apply to *Mul*; for example, $\{\langle \_, * \rangle\} \in Mul$ may be written *.

---

[1] A *Byzantine failure* causes a component to exhibit arbitrary behavior.

Partially-ordered sets of messages. A set of messages is approximated in our framework by a *ms-atom* (mnemonic for "message-set atom"). Each ms-atom approximates a set of messages, using an element of *Val* to characterize the concrete values in the messages and an element of *Mul* to characterize the number of messages (i.e., the cardinality of the set). For example, a ms-atom with value $X : \mathbf{N}$ and multiplicity $*$ represents a set S of messages such that: (1) the concrete value in each message is an element of (the set represented by) $\mathbf{N}$ and is represented by variable X (hence all the messages in S contain the same concrete value), and (2) the number of messages in S is arbitrary (but finite). Similarly, a ms-atom with value $_- : \mathbf{N}$ and multiplicity $*$ represents an arbitrary-sized set of messages, with each message containing a (possibly different) element of $\mathbf{N}$.

A sequence of messages is approximated in our framework by a partially-ordered set (abbreviated as "poset") of ms-atoms. A poset over a set A is a pair $\langle S, \prec \rangle$, where $S \subseteq A$ and $\prec$ is an irreflexive, transitive, and acyclic binary relation on S. For a poset $\langle S, \prec \rangle$ of ms-atoms, the meaning of the partial order is: if $x \prec y$, then during an execution of the system, the messages represented by x would be sent (and received, since channels are FIFO) before the messages represented by y. As a technicality, in order to allow multiple ms-atoms with the same value and multiplicity to appear in a poset, we include in each ms-atom a tag from the set *Tag*. In examples, we take *Tag* to be the natural numbers. Thus, the signature of ms-atoms is $MSA \triangleq Val \times Mul \times Tag$. To promote the resemblance to regular expressions, we usually write an ms-atom $\langle val, mul, 0 \rangle$ as val^{mul}; if the multiplicity mul is 1, we usually elide it.

Message Flow Graphs. A system comprises a set of named components, with names from the set *Name*. The signature *Hist* of *histories* is $Hist \triangleq Name \rightarrow POSet(MSA)$, where $POSet(MSA)$ is the set of posets over MSA. When a history h is used to represent the inputs to a component x, $h(y)$ represents the sequence of messages sent by y to x; when a history h is used to represent as the outputs of a component x, $h(y)$ represents the sequence of messages sent by x to y. Possible behaviors of a system are represented by a MFG, which has signature $MFG \triangleq Name \rightarrow Hist$. A concrete MFG g is interpreted, by convention, as a labeled directed graph with nodes in *Name* and with edge $\langle x, y \rangle$ labeled with $g(y)(x)$. Thus, by convention, $g(y)$ is the input history of component y in g.

Input-output Functions. Since a component's behavior depends on what failures it suffers, input-output functions are parameterized by the possible failures of the corresponding component. Let *Fail* denote the set of all possible failures for the components of a system. For example, *Fail* might contain an element *Byz* corresponding to Byzantine failures. By convention, *Fail* contains an element *OK* corresponding to absence of failure. The behavior of a process is approximated by an input-output function with signature

$$IOF \triangleq \{ f \in Fail \rightharpoonup (Hist \rightarrow Hist) \mid tagUniform(f) \}, \qquad (1)$$

where the one-hooked arrow indicates a partial function and $tagUniform(f)$ asserts that renaming of tags in the input ms-atoms causes no change in the output ms-atoms except possibly renaming of tags (this requirement is sensible because tags do not appear in actual messages). For $f \in IOF$, domain(f) is the set of failures that the component might suffer, and for each $fail \in$ domain(f), $f(fail)$ characterizes the component's behavior when failure $fail$ occurs. Specifically, $f(fail)$ maps a history h representing a component's inputs to a history

$f(fail)(h)$ representing that component's outputs on those inputs. A failure scenario is a function in $FS \triangleq Name \to Fail$ that maps each component to one of its possible failures.

A system is represented by a function $nf \in Name \to IOF$ ("nf" is mnemonic for "name to input-output function"). A MFG representing a system's behavior is computed using the function

$$step_{nf,fs}(g) \triangleq (\lambda y : Name. \ (\lambda x : Name. \ nf(x)(fs(x))(g(x))(y))). \qquad (2)$$

Informally, $step_{nf,fs}(g)$ is the MFG representing the result of each component in system nf in failure scenario fs processing its inputs in the possibly-incomplete executions represented by MFG g and producing possibly-extended outputs. The behavior of a system nf in failure scenario fs is represented by the MFG $lfp(step_{nf,fs})$, if it exists, where lfp indicates the least fixed-point, and the partial ordering on MFG, defined in [Sto97], corresponds informally to the prefix ordering on sequences. This fixed-point might not exist; one reason, roughly, is that MFGs do not have canonical forms [Sto97]. The tool searches for a fixed-point by starting with the "empty" MFG $(\lambda x : Name. \ \lambda y : Name. \ \langle \emptyset, \emptyset \rangle)$ and repeatedly applying $step_{nf,fs}$. If the fixed-point does not exist, this procedure diverges.[2]

Fault-Tolerance Requirements. A fault-tolerance requirement is expressed in our framework as a function b such that for each failure scenario fs, $b(fs)$ is a predicate on MFGs. A system satisfies fault-tolerance requirement b if, for each failure scenario, the MFG computed as a fixed-point of $step_{nf,fs}$ satisfies $b(fs)$.

3 Analysis of Fault-Tolerant Moving Agent Protocol

An interesting paradigm for programming distributed systems is *moving agents*. In this paradigm, an agent moves from site to site in a network. For example, an agent that starts at site S might move to site S_1 in order to access some service (e.g., a database) available there. The agent might then determine that it needs to access a service located at site S_2 and move there. If the agent has gathered all of the information it needs, it might finish by moving to a final site A to deliver the result of the computation. The sequence of sites visited by a moving agent is generally not known when the computation starts, since it may depend on information obtained as the computation proceeds.

Replicated Two-Stage Moving Agent. To illustrate the fault-tolerance problems that arise with moving agents, we consider a "two-stage" moving agent that visits two replicated services. The moving agent starts at a source S, accesses service F, which is replicated at sites F_1, F_2, F_3, and then accesses service G, which is replicated at sites G_1, G_2, G_3. Since G is the last service it needs, the agent moves to a consolidator B, which is responsible for delivering the result of the computation to the destination, or "actuator", A. The consolidator computes the majority of the values it receives and sends the result to the actuator; in addition, as discussed below, the consolidator tests validity of received values and excludes invalid values from the vote.

---

[2] The user can interrupt the calculation and, by inspection of a few MFGs in the sequence, try to determine the "cause" of the divergence.

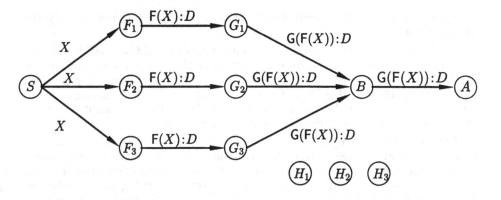

Fig. 1. MFG for replicated two-stage moving agent.

The failure-free behavior of this moving agent is represented by the MFG in Figure 1. Constants F and G represent the processing done by services F and G, respectively. A typical moving agent accesses only some of the available services. To reflect this, the system shown in Figure 1 includes a service H, replicated at sites H_1–H_3, which is not used by this particular agent. The fault-tolerance requirement is:

> **MA-FTR.** Inputs to the actuator should be unaffected by Byzantine failure of a minority of the replicas of each service used by the moving agent and by Byzantine failure of any number of replicas of each service not used by the moving agent.

Suppose faulty components can spoof (i.e., send messages that appear to be from other components) and eavesdrop (i.e., obtain copies of messages sent to other components). From the perspective of the recipient of a message, the possibility of spoofing causes uncertainty about the identity of the actual sender of the message. We model this uncertainty by using input-output functions that are independent of the names of the senders in the input history.

To eavesdrop on a component x, a faulty component (the "eavesdropper") sends a distinguished value *evsdrp* to x. The output history of a component that receives *evsdrp* must allow the possibility of sending copies of all subsequent outputs to the eavesdropper.[3] We assume that a faulty server is able to eavesdrop on all components except actuators.

Consider the consolidator B in Figure 1. How does it decide which inputs are valid? One might be tempted to say that B should treat messages from G_1–G_3 as valid and messages from other components as invalid. This criterion is inappropriate for moving agents, because it assumes B knows in advance that the last service visited by the moving agent will be service G; however, the sequence of services visited by a moving agent is generally not known in advance.

At the other extreme, suppose B considers all inputs valid: whenever B receives the same value from a majority of the replicas of some service, it sends that value to the actuator. (We assume every component knows which service is provided by each server.) It is easy to see that this scheme does not tolerate

---

[3] For this purpose, we allow an exception to the rule in the previous paragraph.

failure of a majority of the replicas of services (e.g., H_1–H_3) not used by the moving agent.

Informally, a message embodying a moving agent should be considered valid if it has visited the same sequence of services as the corresponding failure-free moving agent. We consider here a protocol in which digital signatures are used by the consolidator to determine validity. We assume digital signatures are implemented using public-key cryptography and that each component knows its own private key and the public key of every other component.

Each message sent by a source or server is signed and augmented with information about the sequence of services that should be visited. Each source or server includes in each outgoing message the name of the "destination", i.e., the next service or consolidator to be visited by the moving agent embodied in that message. A consolidator must verify the entire "history" of the moving agent (i.e., the entire sequence of visited services), so a server x also includes in the outgoing message the incoming message that embodied the arrival of that moving agent at x; by induction, that incoming message contains the history of the moving agent up to the arrival of the moving agent at x. The signatures on these recursively included messages provide a chain of evidence documenting the sequence of services actually visited by the moving agent.

A consolidator tests whether a message is valid by checking that it was originated by a (legitimate) source, that the consolidator itself is the declared destination of the message, and that the sequence of declared destinations (obtained from the included messages) are consistent with the chain of signatures on the included messages. Of course, the consolidator also verifies each of the signatures and considers the message invalid if any of those verifications fail. We say a set S of messages is valid if: (1) each message in S is valid; (2) all the messages in S contain the same sequence of declared destinations; (3) the final signatures on the messages in S are (collectively) from a majority of the replicas of some service. When the consolidator receives a valid set of messages, those messages should all contain the same data, which the consolidator forwards to the actuator.

To describe this protocol in our framework, we introduce some definitions. Let $D \in AVal$ be the "type" of data carried by moving agents. Let $Svc \subseteq Con$ denote the set of (names of) services that can be accessed by a moving agent. The processing done by a service $S \in Svc$ is represented by an operator $\mathsf{S} \in Con$, as in Figure 1. We assume component names can be used as constant symbols, i.e., that $Name \subseteq Con$. Let $Src \subseteq Name$ be the set of names of (legitimate) sources. For $x \in Name$, let $\mathsf{K}_x \in KC$ represents x's private key (used to sign messages); we assume each component's private key is unique. The set of constants representing private keys is $KC = \bigcup_{x \in Name} \mathsf{K}_x$.

To conveniently represent messages sent by sources, we introduce a constant $\mathsf{msg_0} \in Con$ with the following interpretation: symbolic value $\mathsf{msg_0}(k, data, dest)$ represents a message signed with key $k \in KC$, carrying data represented by symbolic value $data$, and with destination (either a service or the name of a consolidator) represented by symbolic value $dest$.

To conveniently represent messages sent by servers, we introduce a constant $\mathsf{msg} \in Con$ with the following interpretation: symbolic value $\mathsf{msg}(k, data, dest, msg)$ represents a message signed with key $k \in KC$, carrying data represented by symbolic value $data$, with destination (either a service or the name of a consolidator) represented by symbolic value $dest$, and with symbolic value msg representing a message that caused the server that received it to send this message.

120

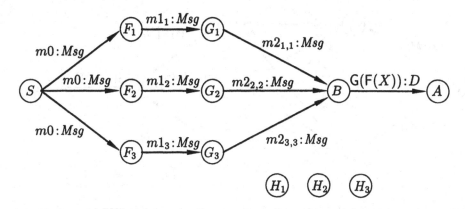

Fig. 2. Run of replicated two-stage moving agent, with authentication.

The MFG in Figure 2 shows the behavior of this protocol for the replicated two-stage moving agent described above, using the following abbreviations:

$$m0 = \mathsf{msg}_0(\mathsf{K}_S, X, F)$$
$$m1_i = \mathsf{msg}(\mathsf{K}_{F_i}, \mathsf{F}(X), G, m0)$$
$$m2_{i,j} = \mathsf{msg}(\mathsf{K}_{G_j}, \mathsf{G}(\mathsf{F}(X)), B, m1_i).$$

Tolerating Failure of Multiple Visited Services. The above protocol provides some fault-tolerance but does not satisfy MA-FTR. For example, the above protocol does not tolerate simultaneous failure of F_1 and G_2, because two of the consolidator's three inputs might be corrupted by these failures.

To make the moving agent more robust, each server sends its outgoing messages to *all* replicas of the next service, instead of just one, and validity tests and voting are incorporated into each stage of the computation after the first. The validity test and voting are as just described for consolidators.[4] Thus, a server sends messages only after receiving a valid set S of messages; to document the sequence of services visited by the moving agent, the server includes some message from S in the outgoing messages.[5] The behavior of the revised protocol is shown in Figure 3. Each server G_j might include any one of its three input messages in its output, so the value in its outputs is a set of three possibilities; specifically, the value is $(ms_j \times \{Msg\}) \in Val$, where

$$ms_j = \{m2_{1,j}, m2_{2,j}, m2_{3,j}\}.$$

Detailed input-output functions for this protocol appear in [Sto97].

3.1 Analysis Results

To determine whether the above protocol satisfies MA-FTR, an MFG representing the protocol's behavior is computed for each failure scenario in which a

---

[4] The only remaining differences between a server and a consolidator are: (1) a consolidator does not perform application-specific computation, i.e., does not apply an operator to the data carried by the moving agent; (2) a consolidator does not include authentication information in its outputs, because the channel between the consolidator and the actuator is assumed to be secure.

[5] The reader who wonders whether multiple messages from S should be included in the outgoing messages is referred to the comments in Section 3.1.

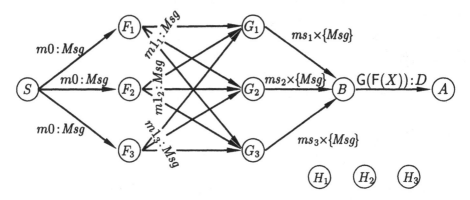

Fig. 3. Run of replicated two-stage moving agent, with authentication and with voting after each stage. Each skewed ms-atom labels each of the three edges it crosses.

minority of the replicas of each service used by the moving agent fail and any number of replicas of each service not used by the moving agent fail. MA-FTR is satisfied if, in each of these failure scenarios, the input to the actuator is represented by $G(F(X)):D$, as in the failure-free computation. We describe below the MFGs obtained for a few representative failure scenarios.

Failure of Visited Servers Only. Consider the failure scenario in which F_1 and G_2 fail. Let $N = \{F_1, F_2, F_3, G_1, G_2, G_3, H_1, H_2, H_3, B\}$. The fixed-point computed for this failure scenario is the same MFG as in Figure 3, except that the outputs of the faulty components are different, and other components send messages to the faulty components as a result of eavesdropping. Specifically, for $x \in \{F_1, G_2\}$, for $y \in N \setminus \{x\}$, edge $\langle x, y \rangle$ is labeled with the ms-atom

$$\{evsdrp, Arb(\{K_{F_1}, K_{G_2}\}, \{m0, m1_2, m1_3, m2_{2,1}, m2_{3,1}, m2_{2,3}, m2_{3,3}\})\}^*.$$

Arb was described in Section 2. Also, for $x \in \{F_1, G_2\}$ and $y \in N \setminus \{F_1, G_2\}$, edge $\langle y, x \rangle$ is labeled with all the output ms-atoms of component y in Figure 3, but with the multiplicities changed to ?.

Failure of Unvisited Servers Only. Consider the failure scenario in which H_1, H_2, and H_3 fail. The fixed-point computed for this failure scenario is the same MFG as in Figure 3, except that the outputs of the faulty components are different, and other components send messages to the faulty components as a result of eavesdropping. Specifically, for $x \in \{H_1, H_2, H_3\}$, for $y \in N \setminus \{x\}$, edge $\langle x, y \rangle$ is labeled with the ms-atom

$$\left\{evsdrp, Arb(\{K_{H_1}, K_{H_2}, K_{H_3}\}, \bigcup_{i,j \in \{1,2,3\}} \{m0, m1_i, m2_{i,j}\})\right\}^*.$$

Also, for $x \in \{H_1, H_2, H_3\}$ and $y \in N \setminus \{H_1, H_2, H_3\}$, edge $\langle y, x \rangle$ is labeled with all the output ms-atoms of component y in Figure 3, but with the multiplicities changed to ?.

Failure of Visited and Unvisited Servers. Consider the failure scenario in which F_1, H_1, and H_2 fail. As the reader may have suspected, the protocol violates

MA-FTR in this failure scenario. Tracing the first three iterations of the fixed-point computation shows why. Due to space limitations, we omit those MFGs and describe the behavior informally. F_1 includes $m0$ in a signed message m' with declared destination H and carrying arbitrary data and sends m' to H_1 and H_2, who each include m' in a signed message with declared destination B and carrying the same (but otherwise arbitrary) data and send that message to B. These two messages cause the consolidatorto send arbitrary data to the actuator. One way to fix the protocol is to have servers include in each output message input messages from a majority of the replicas of some service. The analysis of the corrected protocol is similar to the analysis sketched here.

References

[AH87]   S. Abramsky and C. Hankin, editors. *Abstract Interpretation of Declarative Languages.* Ellis-Horwood, 1987.

[Bro87]   M. Broy. Semantics of finite and infinite networks of concurrent communicating agents. *Distributed Computing*, 2(1):13–31, 1987.

[CdR93]   A. Cau and W.-P. de Roever. Using relative refinement for fault tolerance. In *Proc. 1st Intl. Symposium of Formal Methods Europe*, pages 19–41, 1993.

[CGL94]   E. M. Clarke, O. Grumberg, and D. E. Long. Model checking and abstraction. *ACM Trans. on Prog. Lang. and Sys.*, 16(5):1512–1542, 1994.

[CS96]   R. Cleaveland and S. Sims. The NCSU Concurrency Workbench. In *Proc. CAV '96*, volume 1102 of *LNCS*, pages 394–397. Springer-Verlag, 1996.

[Hol91]   G. J. Holzmann. *Design and Validation of Computer Protocols.* Prentice-Hall, 1991.

[JJ96]   T. Janowski and M. Joseph. Dynamic scheduling in the presence of faults: Specification and verification. In *Proc. FTRTFT '96*, volume 1135 of *LNCS*, pages 279–297. Springer-Verlag, 1996.

[Kah74]   G. Kahn. The semantics of a simple language for parallel programming. In J. L. Rosenfeld, editor, *Information Processing 74: Proc. IFIP Congress 74*, pages 471–475. North-Holland, 1974.

[Kur94]   R. P. Kurshan. *Computer-aided verification of coordinating processes: the automata-theoretic approach.* Princeton University Press, 1994.

[LM94]   L. Lamport and S. Merz. Specifying and verifying fault-tolerant systems. In *Proc. Formal Techniques in Real-Time and Fault-Tolerant Systems*, volume 863 of *LNCS*, pages 41–76. Springer-Verlag, 1994.

[LSP82]   L. Lamport, R. Shostak, and M. Pease. The Byzantine generals problem. *ACM Trans. on Prog. Languages and Systems*, 4(3):382–401, July 1982.

[MvRSS96] Y. Minsky, R. van Renesse, F. B. Schneider, and S. D. Stoller. Cryptographic support for fault-tolerant distributed computing. In *Proc. Seventh ACM SIGOPS European Workshop*, pages 109–114. ACM Press, 1996.

[ORSvH95] S. Owre, J. Rushby, N. Shankar, and F. von Henke. Formal verification for fault-tolerant architectures: Prolegomena to the design of PVS. *IEEE Transactions on Software Engineering*, 21(2):107–125, February 1995.

[PJ94]   D. Peled and M. Joseph. A compositional framework for fault-tolerance by specification transformation. *Theoretical Computer Science*, 128(1-2):99–125, 1994.

[Sch96]   H. Schepers. Real-time systems and fault-tolerance. In M. Joseph, editor, *Mathematics of Dependable Systems*, chapter 7. Prentice-Hall, 1996.

[SS97]   S. D. Stoller and F. B. Schneider. Automated analysis of fault-tolerance in distributed systems. In *Proc. First ACM SIGPLAN Workshop on Automated Analysis of Software*, pages 33–44, 1997. Available via http://www.cs.indiana.edu/~stoller/ .

[Sto97]   S. D. Stoller. *A Method and Tool for Analyzing Fault-Tolerance in Systems.* PhD thesis, Cornell University, May 1997. Available via http://www.cs.indiana.edu/~stoller/ .

Designing a Provably Correct Robt Control System Using a 'Lean' Formal Method[*]

Antonio Cau, Chris Czarnecki and Hussein Zedan

Software Technology Research Laboratory,
SERCentre, De Montfort University,
The Gateway, Leicester LE1 9BH, UK

Abstract. A development method for the construction of *provably correct* robot control systems together with its supporting tool environment are described. The method consists of four stages: 1. specification, 2. refinement, 3. simulation and 4. code. The method is centered around the notion of *wide-spectrum* formalism within which an abstract Interval Temporal Logic (ITL) representation is intermixed freely with the concrete Temporal Agent Model (TAM) representation of the system under consideration. The method with its associated tool support is applied to the design of a robot control system.

1 Introduction

Designing software to control *real-time, reactive embedded* applications is non-trivial. And as the complexity of such systems increases, the present industrial practice for their development gives cause for concern, especially, if they are to be used in safety-critical applications. In order for the design of these systems to be optimized, it is necessary to take into account the interdependence of the hardware and software. Thus, the system needs to be assessed at all stages of the development life-cycle in order to minimize the potential for errors. This has resulted in the development of a wide range of techniques which aim to support the analysis and design of both systems and their associated software. These vary from those with sound mathematical basis (*formal methods*) to *structured methodologies*. The later, while useful, do not provide a satisfactory and comprehensive solution. The former, on the other hand, are recognized as the most likely solution to the problem, but insufficient expertise and a lack of tool support have limited their deployment, specially in a highly specialized applications. For example, in the Automotive Industry, the MISRA *"Development Guidelines for Vehicle Based Software"* recommend the use of formal methods in the specification and analysis of systems at safety integrity levels 3 (difficult to control) and level 4 (uncontrollable). At present this represents an extremely difficult and costly step which has not yet been tried by system developers. These

---

[*] Funded by EPSRC Research Grant GR/K25922: A Compositional Approach to the Specification of Systems using ITL and Tempura.
E-mail: {`cau, cc, zedan`}`@dmu.ac.uk`

weaknesses in current analysis techniques therefore represent a significant threat for the deployment of advanced automotive electronics in the future.

The general objective should be therefore to bring real-time systems and software engineering activities to a similar level of maturity to that of traditional engineering disciplines. The key to this is predictability through the development of, what might be called, *'lean'* formal method which will be strongly supported by a suite of powerful and tightly integrated, practicable and affordable software tools.

In the present paper we outline our attempt to develop such *'lean'* formal method. The proposed formal design framework has an underlying abstract computational model leads to designs which can be analyzed for their schedulability. We will illustrate our technique by designing a *provably correct robot control system*.

The technique provides an integration between a logic-based formalism, namely, Interval Temporal Logic (*ITL*), Tempura (an executable subset of ITL) and a real-time refinement calculus, known as *TAM*. The technique is supported by various tools which forms the ITL-workbench.

1.1 Our Approach

The technique is depicted in Figure 1, and can be summarized as follows:

1. Specification is expressed as an ITL formula.
2. Refine specification into TAM code if possible otherwise revise the specification in 1.
3. Simulate the TAM code. If satisfactory then proceed otherwise either refine it in 2 to other TAM code or revise it in 1.
4. Translate TAM code into real programming language like C, ADA, etc.

We should note here that the TAM code represent the last stage in our formal development method. The TAM code could either be executed directly or be translated into an industrially accepted target programming language such as C, Ada, etc. Care must be taken however that the semantics of the target language is equivalent to TAM semantics.

Various observations are in order:

1. Once we completed the formal specification phase, various properties could be proven about the specification itself. This can provide an extra assurance that the final specification meets the required informal requirements. This is achieved within out ITL-workbench using PVS.
2. The ITL specification could directly be executed using Tempura. This gives an early confidence on the validity of the specification.
3. At each refinement step, we can simulate the resulting (sub)system. This gives some guidelines on the choice of the subsequent refinement rules.
4. The refinement calculus TAM used in this technique is based on *scheduling-oriented* model which was introduced in Lowe and Zedan [2]. It also uses *delayed specification* technique which we believe it makes formalizing many requirements much easier and less error prone.

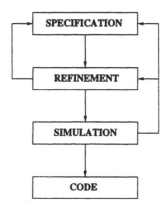

Fig. 1. The design strategy

1.2 Paper Structure

The format of the paper is as follows. In Section 2, we introduce the refinement calculus TAM together with its ITL semantics domain and some useful algebraic equations. Section 3 gives an informal description of the robot. The formal development of the robot control system will be given in Section 4. This section highlights the power of the simulation tool Tempura which supports the adopted design method.

2 Interval Temporal Logic and Temporal Agent Model

The formal development framework (TAM) proposed here provides the developer with:

1. a mathematical logic with which a formal description of the intended behaviors of the system under consideration could be precisely and unambiguously expressed. This is considered to be the highest level of abstraction of system development. For this purpose we have chosen a temporal logic known as Interval Temporal Logic (ITL) [3, 4] for its simplicity and the availability of an executable subset which assists in the simulation phase.
2. a wide-spectrum language (WSL) with formally defined syntax and semantics. The WSL allows the developer to intermix between abstract (i.e. logical) and concrete constructs giving greater flexibility in compositional design.
3. sound refinement rules which allows stepwise development of systems.

2.1 Interval temporal logic

This section introduces the syntax and informal semantics of Interval temporal logic (ITL). Our selection of ITL is based on a number of points. It is a flexible notation for both propositional and first-order reasoning about periods of time found in descriptions of hardware and software systems. Unlike most temporal logics, ITL can handle both sequential and parallel composition and offers powerful and extensible specification and proof techniques for reasoning about properties involving safety, liveness and projected time [5]. Timing constraints are expressible and furthermore most imperative programming constructs can be viewed as formulas in a slightly modified version of ITL [1]. Tempura provides an executable framework for developing and experimenting with suitable ITL specifications. In addition, ITL and its mature executable subset Tempura [4] have been extensively used to specify the properties of real-time systems where the primitive circuits can directly be represented by a set of simple temporal formulae.

$$\begin{aligned} \textit{Expressions} \quad & e ::= \mu \mid a \mid A \mid g(e_1, \ldots, e_n) \mid \imath a\!:\! f \\ \textit{Formulae} \quad & f ::= p(e_1, \ldots, e_n) \mid \neg f \mid f_1 \wedge f_2 \mid \forall v \bullet f \mid \mathsf{skip} \mid f_1 \,;\, f_2 \mid f^* \end{aligned}$$

Fig. 2. Syntax of ITL

An interval is considered to be a (in)finite sequence of states, where a state is a mapping from variables to their values. The length of an interval is equal to one less than the number of states in the interval (i.e., a one state interval has length 0).

The syntax of ITL is defined in Fig. 2 where μ is an integer value, a is a static variable (doesn't change within an interval), A is a state variable (can change within an interval), v a static or state variable, g is a function symbol and p is a predicate symbol.

The informal semantics of the most interesting constructs are as follows:

- $\imath a\!:\! f$: the value of a such that f holds.
- skip: unit interval (length 1).
- $f_1 \,;\, f_2$: holds if the interval can be decomposed ("chopped") into a prefix and suffix interval, such that f_1 holds over the prefix and f_2 over the suffix, or if the interval is infinite and f_1 holds for that interval.
- f^*: holds if the interval is decomposable into a finite number of intervals such that for each of them f holds, or the interval is infinite and can be decomposed into an infinite number of finite intervals for which f holds.

These constructs enable us to define programming constructs like assignment, if then else, while loops etc.

2.2 Temporal Agent Model

The temporal agent model (TAM) is a well established formalism [8, 9, 2] for the development real-time safety-critical systems.

$$A ::= w : f \mid \text{skip} \mid x := e \mid x \Leftarrow s \mid e \Rightarrow s \mid A \,;\, A' \mid \text{var}\, x \text{ in } A \mid$$
$$\text{shunt } s \text{ in } A \mid [t]\, A \mid \text{if}_t \;\; \underset{i \in I}{\square}\; g_i \text{ then } A_i \text{ fi} \mid A \sqcap A' \mid A \triangleright_i^s A' \mid$$
$$A \parallel A' \mid \Delta t \mid \text{loop for } n \text{ period } t \;\; A$$

Fig. 3. Syntax of TAM

At any instant in time a system can be thought of as having a unique *state*. The system state is defined by the values in the shunts (time-stamped variables) and the state variables of the system, the so called *frame*. This frame defines the variables that can possibly change during system execution, the variables outside this frame will certainly not change. *Computation* is defined to be a sequence of system states , i.e., an *interval* of states. ITL enables us to describe this set of computations in an eloquent way.

The syntax of TAM is defined in figure 3 where w is a set of computation variables and shunts; f is an ITL formula; t is a time; x is a variable; e is an expression on variables; s is a shunt; I is some finite indexing set; g_i is an ITL formula without temporal operators; and n is a natural number.

The informal semantics of some the TAM constructs is as follows:

- $w : f$ is a specification statement. It specifies that only the variables in the frame w may be changed, and the execution must satisfy f.
- The agent $x \Leftarrow s$ performs an input from shunt s, storing the value in x; the type of x must be a stamp–value pair.
- The agent $e \Rightarrow s$ writes the current value of expression e to shunt s, increasing the stamp by one.
- The agent $[t]\, A$ gives agent A a duration of t: if the agent terminates before t seconds have elapsed, then the agent should idle to fill this interval; if the agent does not terminate within t seconds, then it is considered to have failed.

TAM refinement and algebraic rules In this section we explore some of the algebraic properties of the TAM agents. But first, we define the *refinement* ordering relation $\sqsubseteq$ as logical implication:

$$f_0 \sqsubseteq f_1 \; \hat{=} \; f_1 \supset f_0$$

The following are some basic refinement rules:

$(\sqsubseteq -1) \vdash (f_0 \sqsubseteq f_1) \text{ and } \vdash (f_1 \sqsubseteq f_2) \quad \Rightarrow \quad \vdash (f_0 \sqsubseteq f_2)$

$(\sqsubseteq -2) \vdash (f_0 \sqsubseteq f_1) \text{ and } \vdash (f_2 \sqsubseteq f_3) \quad \Rightarrow \quad \vdash (f_0 \wedge f_2) \sqsubseteq (f_1 \wedge f_3)$

$(\sqsubseteq -3) \vdash (f_0 \sqsubseteq f_1) \text{ and } \vdash (f_2 \sqsubseteq f_3) \quad \Rightarrow \quad \vdash (f_0 \vee f_2) \sqsubseteq (f_1 \vee f_3)$

$(\sqsubseteq -4) \vdash f_1 \sqsubseteq f_2 \quad \Rightarrow \quad \vdash f_0 \,;\, f_1 \sqsubseteq f_0 \,;\, f_2$

$(\sqsubseteq -5) \vdash f_1 \sqsubseteq f_2 \quad \Rightarrow \quad \vdash f_1 \,;\, f_0 \sqsubseteq f_2 \,;\, f_0$

$(\sqsubseteq -6) \vdash f_0 \sqsubseteq f_1 \quad \Rightarrow \quad \vdash f_0^* \sqsubseteq f_1^*$

$(\sqsubseteq -7) \vdash f_0 \sqsubseteq f_1 \quad \Rightarrow \quad \vdash \forall v \cdot f_0 \sqsubseteq \forall v \cdot f_1$

Assignment: The assignment is introduced with the following law

$(:= -1)$ $x := exp$ $\equiv$ $\bigcirc x = exp$

If then–conditional: The conditional is introduced with the following law

(if −1) if f_0 then $f_1 \square f_2$ then f_3 fi $\equiv (f_0 \wedge f_1) \vee (f_2 \wedge f_3)$
(if −2) if f_0 then f_1 else f_2 fi $\equiv (f_0 \wedge f_1) \vee (\neg f_0 \wedge f_2)$
$\equiv$ if f_0 then $f_1 \square \neg f_0$ then f_2 fi

While loop: The following law introduces the while loop

(while −1) while f_0 do f_1 $\equiv (f_0 \wedge f_1)^* \wedge fin \neg f_0$
(while −2) while $true$ do f_1 $\equiv f_1^*$

Parallel: The following are some laws for the parallel agent.

$(\| -1)$ $f_0 \| f_1$ $\equiv$ $f_0 \wedge f_1$
$(\| -2)$ $f \| true$ $\equiv$ f
$(\| -3)$ $(f_0 \| f_1) \| f_2$ $\equiv$ $f_0 \| (f_1 \| f_2)$

Variable introduction: The following is the local variable introduction law.

$(var -1)$ var x in $\mathcal{A}$ $\equiv$ $\exists x \cdot \mathcal{A}$

The next section introduces the robot system which will be used as a case study.

3   Robot description

The tele-operated robot is a tracked device which was originally developed for military use. The carriage can easily traverse over rough terrain. The vehicle schematic is shown in Fig. 4. The vehicle has on-board a manipulator arm that has three degrees of freedom controlled by hydraulic actuators. The electric drive motors, manipulator actuators and on-board lamps are controlled manually by the operator via a control box that is linked to the vehicle. Currently one controller caters for the main control, one for the infrared sensor interfacing and processing, and a third for the on-board camera control.

The actual vehicle is driven by two motors, left and right, indicated as L and R in Fig. 4. Both of these motors can move forwards and in reverse. The vehicle is steered by moving one motor faster than the other.

From a control point of view, commands are issued to the motors via a operator joystick (L and R of the operator console in Fig. 4) which issues integers values in the range $0 \ldots 127$ for forward motion (127 max. speed) and $0 \ldots -128$ for reverse motion. It is possible to drive only one motor at a time, in such a case the robot will turn. The speed of the motors is directly proportional to the value written to them.

The robot is equiped with 8 infra red sensors. These return an integer value in the range $0 \ldots 255$ depending on whether an obstacle is present or not. 0

indicates no obstacle, 255 indicates obstacle very near. We normally operate with a threshold of around 100, above which we take notice of the sensor readings, i.e., an obstacle is of interest. At this point reactive control takes over from the manual control by moving the vehicle away from the obstacle until the 100 threshold is not set. The sensor positions are as follows: N, NE, E, SE, S, SW, W and NW, covering the body of the robot and shown in Fig. 4.

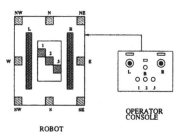

Fig. 4. The robot control system

4 Robot specification and design

This section presents the specification and the design (refinement) of the driving part of the robot control system. The hazardous nature of the task, coupled with the integration of reactive control and human commands presents a challenging safety critical application. We will use our design strategy of Sect. 1.1.

4.1 Specification

The specification of the robot control system consists of 3 parts:

1. Motor control: If the sensor detects an object then the control system takes over control otherwise if the operator requests a new movement then action this.

Let *l-i-c* and *r-i-c* denote respectively the left and right motor commands issued by the infra-red control. Let *i-act* denote the presence/absence of an object. Let *l-o-c* and *r-o-c* denote the left and right motor command issued by the operator and let *o-act* denote an active operator request. Let $move(l, r)$ denote the sending of left l and right r motor commands to the two motors.

The motor control is specified as:

$$MCS \mathrel{\widehat{=}} (\quad (i\text{-}act \wedge move(l\text{-}i\text{-}c, r\text{-}i\text{-}c)) \vee$$
$$(o\text{-}act \wedge move(l\text{-}o\text{-}c, r\text{-}o\text{-}c)) \vee$$
$$(\neg i\text{-}act \wedge \neg o\text{-}act) \qquad)^*$$

Note-1: if *i-act* and *o-act* are both enabled we have a non-deterministic choice. In the refinement process below we take the design decision that in this case the operator commands override.

2. Infra-red control: read the sensors and for each sensor that is greater than the threshold of 100 adjust the motor commands accordingly. For example if the north sensor detects an object we should move in the south direction as an avoidance strategy.

Let $ir\text{-}c(i)$ denote the sensor i (N: i=0, NE: i=1, E: i=2, SE: i=3, S: i=4, SW: i=5, W: i=6, NW: i=7). Let $mvl(i)$ and $mvr(i)$ denote respectively the left and right steering commands corresponding to sensor i.

The infra-red control is specified as:

$$ICS \cong (\quad i\text{-}act = (\bigvee_i ir\text{-}c(i) > 100) \wedge$$
$$l\text{-}i\text{-}c = (\textstyle\sum_i : ir\text{-}c(i) > 100 : mvl(i)) \wedge$$
$$r\text{-}i\text{-}c = (\textstyle\sum_i : ir\text{-}c(i) > 100 : mvr(i)) \quad)^*$$

3. Operator control: if the operator requests some changes then process them.

Let $l\text{-}o\text{-}c$ and $r\text{-}o\text{-}c$ denote respectively the left and right steering commands received from the operator. Let $ll\text{-}o\text{-}c$ and $lr\text{-}o\text{-}c$ denote respectively the last left and last right steering commands received from the operator.

The specification of operator control is as follows:

$$OCS \cong \exists ll\text{-}o\text{-}c, lr\text{-}o\text{-}c \bullet ($$
$$ll\text{-}o\text{-}c = 0 \wedge lr\text{-}o\text{-}c = 0 \wedge$$
$$(o\text{-}act = (l\text{-}o\text{-}c \neq ll\text{-}o\text{-}c \vee r\text{-}o\text{-}c \neq lr\text{-}o\text{-}c) \wedge$$
$$\bigcirc ll\text{-}o\text{-}c = l\text{-}o\text{-}c \wedge \bigcirc lr\text{-}o\text{-}c = r\text{-}o\text{-}c \qquad)^*$$
$$)$$

The overall specification is $\quad Robotcs \cong MCS \wedge ICS \wedge OCS$.

4.2 Refinement

In this section we show the refinement process. We will show only the refinement of MCS due to lack of space.

First we refine * into a while loop using law (while -2) and strengthened the guard of the infra-red move (only taken if the operator is also inactive):

$$MCS \sqsubseteq$$
while *true* do ($((i\text{-}act \wedge \neg o\text{-}act \wedge move(l\text{-}i\text{-}c, r\text{-}i\text{-}c)) \vee$
$\qquad (o\text{-}act \wedge move(l\text{-}o\text{-}c, r\text{-}o\text{-}c)) \vee$
$\qquad (\neg i\text{-}act \wedge \neg o\text{-}act)$
)

Then we introduce the if then with the (if -1) law.

$$\sqsubseteq$$
while *true* do (if $i\text{-}act \wedge \neg o\text{-}act$ then $move(l\text{-}i\text{-}c, r\text{-}i\text{-}c)$
$\qquad \square \ o\text{-}act \qquad\qquad$ then $move(l\text{-}o\text{-}c, r\text{-}o\text{-}c)$
$\qquad \square \ \neg i\text{-}act \wedge \neg o\text{-}act$ then *true*
$\qquad$ fi
)

The last refinement step consists of choosing a specific execution time for the body of the while loop. An execution time of t_m results in the following code.

```
⊑
while true do ( if_{t_m}  i-act ∧ ¬o-act   then move(l-i-c, r-i-c)
              □    o-act              then move(l-o-c, r-o-c)
              □   ¬i-act ∧ ¬o-act then true
              fi
)
```

ICS and OCS can be refined likewise. The results of each refinement are then composed together with rules ($⊑$ −2) and ($∥$ −1) resulting in the concrete TAM code of the robot control system.

4.3 Simulation

We use the Tempura[1] interpreter to simulate the TAM concrete code. This interpreter is written in C by Roger Hale and based on a Lisp version of Ben Moszkowski [4]. A graphical front end written in Tcl/Tk has been developed. Tempura offers a means for rapidly developing and testing suitable ITL/TAM specifications. As with ITL/TAM, Tempura can be extended to contain most imperative programming features and yet retain its distinct temporal feel. The use of ITL/TAM and Tempura combine the benefits of traditional proof methods balanced with the speed and convenience of computer-based testing through execution and simulation. The entire process can remain in one powerful logical and compositional framework. A practitioner can allocate his/her time and other resources to one or the other approach based on the merits of the system under consideration. Output from Tempura can be used as "documentation by example" to supplement other specification techniques.

4.4 Code

In this section we will translate TAM code into C. This translation is currently performed by hand but a tool that automatically converts to C, is under development. The choice of C is governed by the compiler available for the embedded target system. Other target languages such as Ada are equally valid.

5 Conclusion and future work

Designing software to control *real-time, reactive embedded* applications is non-trivial. As the complexity of such systems increases, the present industrial practice for their development gives cause for concern, especially, if they are to be used in safety-critical applications. Part of the reason for this can be considered

---

[1] available from http://www.cms.dmu.ac.uk/~cau/itlhomepage/index.html

due to the lack of appropriate *assurance* techniques. It is believed that the next generation of systems will indeed test our capabilities to the limit.

In this paper we have introduced a development method for the construction of *provably correct* robot control systems together with its supporting tool environment. The method is centered around the notion of *wide-spectrum* formalism within which an abstract (logical) representation is intermixed freely with the concrete representation of the system under consideration. The transformation from the abstract to the concrete representations is achieved by applying a series of correctness preserving refinement laws. In this way the resulting concrete representation is guaranteed to satisfy the required behavioral specification expressed at the logical level. At each stage of the refinement, the developer may *simulate* the resulting system. This will provide an extra level of assurance as well as a guideline to which refinement path the developer may wish to apply.

The choice of ITL was due to its simplicity and its capability of specifying various real-time reactive embedded requirements. Being a temporal logic, system's dynamics can be easily expressed and reasoned about. In addition, ITL is supported by an executable programming environment known as Tempura [4] which allows a fast prototyping and simulation of the design.

We believe that our method provides a very useful tool in developing provably correct real-time reactive systems. When combined with the *delayed specification* technique, introduced in [2], makes formalizing many requirements much easier and less error prone.

References

1. Cau, A. and Zedan, H.: *Refining Interval Temporal Logic Specifications*. In proc. of Fourth AMAST Workshop on Real-Time Systems, Concurrent, and Distributed Software (ARTS'97), LNCS **1231**, Mallorca, Spain, May 21–23, (1997) 79–94
2. Lowe, G. and Zedan, H.: *Refinement of Complex Systems: a Case Study*. The Computer Journal, **38**:10, (1995)
3. Moszkowski, B.: *A Temporal Logic for Multilevel Reasoning About Hardware*. IEEE Computer **18**, (1985) 10–19
4. Moszkowski, B.: *Executing Temporal Logic Programs*. Cambridge Univ. Press, UK, (1986)
5. Moszkowski, B.: *Some Very Compositional Temporal Properties*. In Programming Concepts, Methods and Calculi, Ernst-Rüdiger Olderog (ed.), IFIP Transactions, Vol. **A-56**, North-Holland, (1994) 307–326
6. Rushby, J.: *A Tutorial on Specification and Verification using PVS*. In proc. of the FME '93 symposium: Industrial-Strength Formal Methods, J.C.P. Woodcock and P.G. Larsen (eds.), LNCS **670**, Odense, Denmark, (1993) 357–406. Check homepage: http://www.csl.sri.com/pvs.html
7. Sheridan, T.B.: *Telerobotics, Automation, and Human Supervisory Control*. The MIT Press, Cambridge, Massachusetts, (1992)
8. Scholefield, D.J., Zedan, H. and He, J.: *Real-time Refinement: Semantics and Application*. LNCS **711**, (1993) 693–702
9. Scholefield, D.J., Zedan, H. and He, J.: *A Specification Oriented Semantics for the Refinement of Real-Time Systems*. Theoretical Computer Science **130**, (1994)

Static Analysis to Identify Invariants in RSML Specifications*

David Y.W. Park, Jens U. Skakkebæk, and David L. Dill

Computer Science Department, Gates Building 3A
Stanford University, Stanford, CA 94305, USA.
E-mail: {parkit,jus,dill}@cs.stanford.edu

Abstract. Static analysis of formal, high-level specifications of safety critical software can discover flaws in the specification that would escape conventional syntactic and semantic analysis. As an example, specifications written in the Requirements State Machine Language (RSML) should be checked for *consistency*: two transitions out of the same state that are triggered by the same event should have mutually exclusive guarding conditions. The check uses only behavioral information that is *local* to a small set of states and transitions.

However, since only local behavior is analyzed, information about the behavior of the surrounding system is missing. The check may consequently produce counterexamples for state combinations that are not possible when the behavior of the whole system is taken into account. A solution is to identify invariants of the global system that can be used to exclude the impossible state combinations. Manually deriving invariants from designs of realistic size is laborious and error-prone. Finding them by mechanically enumerating the state space is computationally infeasible. The challenge is to find *approximate* methods that can find fewer but adequate invariants from abstracted models of specifications.

We present an algorithm for deriving invariants that are used to exclude impossible counterexamples resulting from checking consistency of transitions in RSML. The algorithm has been implemented in an RSML prototype tool and has been applied successfully to the static checking of version 6.04a of the (air) Traffic alert and Collision Avoidance System (TCAS II) specification.

1   Introduction

Formal, high-level specifications of safety critical software are being advocated to reveal flaws in software early in the design phase [3,8,10,12]. In contrast to informal specifications, formal specifications can be checked for wellformedness beyond trivial syntactic properties [1,6,7,11]. For instance, specifications written in the Requirements State Machine Language (RSML) [10] should be checked to ensure that the specification is *consistent* [9]: two transitions out of the same state that are triggered by the same event should have mutually exclusive guarding conditions. An inconsistency inadvertently allows for several different implementations, which may complicate testing, verification, and reuse of the software.

---

* The research was supported by the Defense Advanced Research Projects Agency under contract number DABT63-96-C-0097-P00002.

Checking consistency using model checking is infeasible for designs of realistic size [6]. Instead, the guarding conditions can be converted into logical predicates and checked for mutual exclusion. We have specifically used the Stanford Validity Checker (SVC) [2], a decision procedure for a quantifier-free fragment of first-order logic [11]. The check is more efficient than model checking, since it uses only behavioral information that is *local* to a small set of states and transitions.

However, since only local behavior is analyzed, information about the behavior of the surrounding system is missing. The check may consequently produce counterexamples for state combinations that are not possible when the behavior of the whole system is taken into account. For example, a purely local check may report that two transitions can be enabled simultaneously whenever one component state machine is in state $s1$ and another is in state $s2$. However, a more global analysis might reveal that this combination of circumstances can not occur, indicating that the local check has reported a non-existent problem. A solution is to identify invariants of the global state that can be used to exclude some of the impossible state combinations. Manually deriving invariants from designs of realistic size is laborious and error-prone. Finding them by mechanically enumerating the state space is computationally infeasible.

The solution we propose is to find *approximate* methods that can find fewer but still sufficient invariants from abstracted models of specifications. Significant size reductions can be achieved by omitting information in the abstraction process. We present an algorithm for deriving invariants that rule out some of the impossible counterexamples when checking consistency in RSML. The algorithm has been integrated in an RSML prototype analysis tool and has been applied successfully to the static checking of part of version 6.04a of the specification of the (air) Traffic alert and Collision Avoidance System (TCAS II) [10]. It is likely that the algorithm can be generalized to other variations of statecharts [4,5].

2 Motivating Example

We illustrate our approach with an example. An RSML Component State Machine (CSM), shown in Figure 1, consists of a set of input variables, a hierarchical state machine, and a set of output variables. When an external event arrives at the boundary of the CSM, the state machine executes using the values of the input variables, assigning new values to the output variables.

As in statecharts, individual states may themselves contain state machines. A state is *active* if control resides in that state, and *inactive* otherwise. The predicate $in(s)$ means that state s is active. State *Root* is of type *and*, so its immediate substates A, B, C, D, and E (outlined by dotted lines) must be active simultaneously if *Root* is active. State A is of type *or*, so at most one of its immediate substates may be active. A *basic* state has no children.

A transition is annotated with *trigger [guard]/output-event* and is taken if and only if its guarding condition is true when its trigger event occurs. If taken, the transition may generate an output event that triggers other transitions in the CSM. The guarding conditions are logical expressions over the values of the input variables and the active/inactive status of the states inside the CSM.

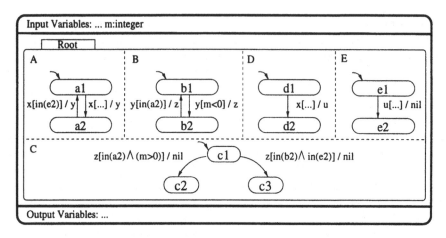

Fig. 1. An RSML component state machine to be checked for consistency.

The CSM executes in *supersteps*. A superstep begins when an external event arrives at the boundary of the CSM. The external event begins a chain of internally generated events that trigger transitions within the CSM. In our example, external event x triggers transitions in states A and D in parallel. If taken, these transitions trigger transitions in states B and E. The transition in state B may, in turn, trigger transitions in state C, concluding the superstep. The event ordering scheme is shown in Figure 2(a).

Transitions in the CSM are *consistent* if and only if every pair of transitions out of the same state with the same trigger event has guarding conditions that can not be enabled simultaneously. For instance, transitions $c1{\to}c2$ and $c1{\to}c3$ are inconsistent under the condition $in(b2) \wedge in(e2) \wedge in(a2) \wedge (m > 0)$ since both guarding conditions are satisfied. Thus, the local check indicates that the transitions are potentially inconsistent. In such a situation, we say that the transitions are *locally inconsistent*.

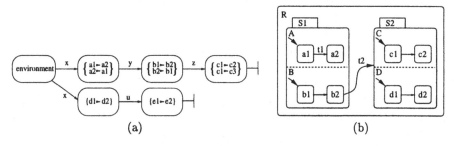

Fig. 2. (a) Event flow in the CSM. (b) Illustration of source and target completions.

However, a static analysis of a superstep can show that $in(a2)$ and $in(b2)$ can not be true at the same time, invalidating the inconsistency condition. Assume that the inconsistency condition holds when the two transitions in state C are triggered. Given the event tree in Figure 2(a), this assumption implies the following. First, predicate $(m > 0)$ must be true from the beginning of the superstep since it is an input variable. Second, predicate $in(a2)$ was either true from the beginning of the superstep, or it recently became true if transition a1→a2 was taken. In either case, predicate $in(a2)$ must be true after transitions in state A are triggered since this is the last opportunity in which it can be made true before transitions in state C are triggered. Similarly, predicate $in(e2)$ must be true after transitions in state E are evaluated.

Finally, predicate $in(b2)$ must be true after state B evaluates. However, a stronger claim can be made since the guarding condition of transition b1→b2 is $[(m < 0)]$. Since predicate $(m > 0)$ must be true from the beginning of the step, this transition could not have been enabled and thus predicate $in(b2)$ must also have been true from the beginning of the superstep.

From the upper branch of the event tree in Figure 2(a) we know that transitions in state A evaluate before those in B. Therefore, $in(a2)$ must be true when transitions in state B are triggered. But this means that transition b2→b1 with guarding condition $[in(a2)]$ is enabled, making $b2$ no longer active. This contradicts the requirement that $in(b2)$ must be true from the beginning of the superstep. The inconsistency condition is therefore invalidated, and we derive the invariant: $(in(a2) \land (m > 0)) \Rightarrow \neg in(b2)$.

3   RSML

An RSML specification is a collection of CSMs which communicate through asynchronous message passing. Refer to [10] for a comprehensive description of the syntax and semantics. We focus on the internal behavior within a CSM and introduce concepts used later in the explanation of the approach.

3.1   Transitions

The explicit source and destination states of a transition are the states connected by the tail and head of the transition arrow. In Figure 2(b), the explicit source state and target state of transition $t2$ are $b2$ and $S2$ respectively.

Due to the hierarchical nature of the states, the explicit source and target states may not be the only states that are left and entered on a transition. In Figure 2(b), transition $t2$ not only leaves state $b2$, it also leaves $S1$ and all of its substates. This is because state $S1$ can not be active when the explicit target state $S2$ is active (they are both children of an *or* state). Similarly, state $S2$ is not the only state that is entered. $S2$ is an *and* state, so states C and D are also entered. Since C is an *or* state and no child state is specified to be the target, we enter state $c1$ by default. Default states are indicated by a transition arrow without a source. Likewise, state $d1$ is entered by default.

The set of all states that can not be active after taking a transition t is denoted *source-completion(t)* and the set of all states that may become active is denoted *target-completion(t)*. Both sets can be determined statically. Informally, *source-completion(t)* is the set of all substates of the highest level state exited on the transition, and *target-completion(t)* is the set of default substates and explicitly targeted substates of the highest level state entered.

Identity transitions may be specified, although they are not shown in the CSM diagram. They are taken when no other transition out of the state is enabled. By the RSML semantics used in TCAS II, identity transitions do not cause any state changes, and their sole purpose is to propagate trigger events.

3.2 Behavior of the CSM

A *superstep* takes the CSM from one global state to the next, where a global state is represented by the values of variables and the set of active states in the hierarchical state machine. A superstep is decomposed into a series of *microsteps*. A microstep can intuitively be thought of as a wavefront of transitions that are taken concurrently, in an arbitrary interleaving. The transitions in each microstep generate the set of events that trigger the transitions in the subsequent microstep. Transitions in a microstep are evaluated only after all transitions in the preceding microstep have been evaluated. An external trigger event from the environment begins the first microstep. The superstep ends when there is a microstep in which no more transitions are triggered.

4 Overview of the Algorithm

Given a local inconsistency condition, we look for an invariant that shows that the condition is unsatisfiable. Since this condition is a conjunction of predicates, it suffices to show that at least one predicate fails to hold, given the others.

First, the behavior of the CSM is abstracted, resulting in a model delineating which transitions can be triggered at each microstep. In *Backward Pass*, we begin by assuming that the local inconsistency condition holds at the last microstep (the microstep in which the locally inconsistent transitions are triggered). We then determine the earliest microstep from which each predicate must hold if it is to hold at the last microstep. In *Forward Pass*, we try to establish a contradiction by showing that some predicate in the inconsistency condition can not hold in the last microstep given other predicates determined to hold from prior microsteps. An invariant is formulated from the results of the analysis.

5 The Causality Model

The behavior of the CSM is abstracted as a model called the *causality tree* that delineates which transitions can be triggered at each microstep. Figure 3a is the causality tree for the superstep initiated by external event x in the CSM from Section 2. A node in the tree represents a set of transitions with the same input and output triggers. The directed edge into a node represents the trigger event to transitions associated with the node, and the directed edge out of the node represents the output event (possibly empty).

Beginning with the external trigger event from the environment node, we add nodes containing transitions triggered by the event. These new nodes may have their own output triggers which become directed edges to subsequent nodes with transitions triggered by them. Nodes are added until all leaves of the tree have the empty output trigger. Circularities in the event propagation are not allowed, since they lead to infinite paths in the causality tree. The algorithm trivially checks for circularities each time a new node is added, and aborts the tree construction if a circularity is detected.

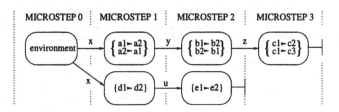

Fig. 3. Causality tree for the CSM in Figure 1.

The depth of a node in the tree denotes the microstep number in which its transitions may be triggered. Hence, grouping all of the nodes in the tree by their depth effectively determines the set of those and only those transitions that can be triggered in each microstep. Transitions in states B and E, for instance, may be triggered simultaneously in microstep 2. Note that the causality tree is a conservative model: it captures what events *may* be generated at each microstep, without information about whether guarding conditions are enabled. Identity transitions are not included in the model since they are not important to our analysis. However, they must be considered in the construction of the tree since they also have output events.

A *causality path* is a path in the tree from the environment node to the node with the locally inconsistent transitions. Every trigger in this path must fire if the locally inconsistent transitions are to be triggered. In Figure 3, there is only one causality path to transitions in state C, the upper branch. All causality paths to the node with the locally inconsistent transitions in every causality tree must be checked. The Backward Pass and the Forward Pass stages of the algorithm analyze each causality path separately in the context of the causality tree in which it resides.

6 Backward Pass: Predicate Positioning

Backward Pass begins by assuming that the inconsistency condition holds in the last microstep of the causality path in which the locally inconsistent transitions are triggered. It then determines the earliest microstep from which each predicate must hold if it is to hold at the last microstep. Let $\mathcal{P}$ be the set of predicates in the local inconsistency condition. In our running example from Section 2, the transitions $c1{\to}c2$ and $c1{\to}c3$ have guarding conditions that are both enabled under $in(b2) \wedge in(e2) \wedge in(a2) \wedge (m > 0)$ so $\mathcal{P} = \{in(b2), in(e2), in(a2), (m > 0)\}$.

Before proceeding, we introduce the notion of a *suspect* transition. A transition t is suspect if and only if it can cause a predicate p to become true.

$$Suspect(t,p) \equiv \begin{cases} s \in target\text{-}completion(t) & \text{if } p = in(s) \\ s \in source\text{-}completion(t) & \text{if } p = \neg in(s) \end{cases}$$

For a given predicate, we define its *microstep assignment* to be the microstep after which it can safely be assumed to be true if it is true at the last microstep. Each predicate is initially assigned to the last microstep. Backward pass then assigns each predicate p to the first preceding microstep that contains a suspect transition. If no suspect transition exists, p is assigned to microstep zero. This

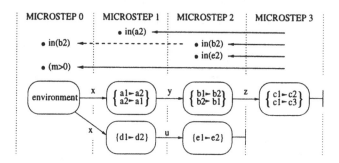

Fig. 4. The solid black lines show the result after the initial predicate assignments. The dotted line illustrates the reassignment of predicate *in(b2)* to a previous microstep.

is a sound process since a predicate's truth value can only change at a microstep that contains a suspect transition.

The solid black lines in Figure 4 show the state after all of the predicates have been assigned. Predicate *in(a2)* is assigned to microstep 1 since transition a1→a2 is suspect. Hence, *in(a2)* can safely be assumed to be true in microsteps 2 and 3. Predicate *in(b2)* can become true in microstep 2, so it can only be safely asserted in microstep 3. Likewise, predicate *in(e2)* is assigned to microstep 2. Predicate $(m > 0)$ involves an input variable so it must have been true from the beginning of the superstep (microstep zero).

Next, we determine whether predicates can be reassigned to earlier microsteps. A predicate p is reassigned if all suspect transitions in its currently assigned microstep have guarding conditions that are unsatisfiable in the context of predicates assigned to previous microsteps. In such a case, p must have become true in an earlier microstep. It is thus reassigned to the next preceding microstep with a suspect transition. The reassignment of predicates is an iterative process since a reassignment may affect the microstep assignments of other predicates. This process is guaranteed to terminate since the number of preceding microsteps is finite and predicates can only be moved in one direction. The dotted line in Figure 4 shows the reassignment step. Predicate *in(b2)* can be reassigned because the suspect transition b1→b2 has guarding condition $[(m < 0)]$ which is negated by predicate $(m > 0)$ assigned to a previous microstep.

Note that backward pass conservatively considers all of the nodes in the entire causality tree at each microstep, and not only the transitions triggered in the node in the causality path. In Figure 4, for instance, *in(e2)* would be assigned to microstep zero if we do not consider nodes outside the causality path. This is not sound since transition e1→e2 may have made it true.

7   Forward Pass: Deriving a Contradiction

In the Forward Pass stage, we try to derive a contradiction based on the predicate assignments. Beginning with the first microstep, we look for transitions that (1) must be taken, and (2) falsify a predicate that was determined to be true at that microstep in the backward pass stage. We will refer to such transitions as *violating* transitions.

140

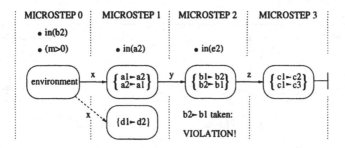

Fig. 5. Illustration of the Forward Pass stage. Predicate *in(a2)* enables a transition from state *b2* to *b1* violating predicate *in(b2)*. (Although transition d1→d2 is not explicitly in the causality path, it is still considered since it is triggered by an event in the path.)

Unlike backward pass which examines the entire causality tree, forward pass looks only at the causality path and analyzes transitions triggered by trigger events in the path. This is because all trigger events in the causality path must fire in order for the locally inconsistent transitions to be ultimately triggered, and hence these are the only events that we can safely assume to have occurred.

The procedure for forward pass begins at microstep one and executes the following steps for each subsequent microstep:

1. Construct set *MustHold* that consists of all of the predicates assigned to previous microsteps. These predicates must be true in the current microstep in order for the local inconsistency condition to be valid. In Figure 5, *MustHold* for microstep 2 is $\{(m > 0), in(b2), in(a2)\}$.
2. Construct set *EnabledT* that consists of transitions triggered in the current microstep of the causality path and whose guarding conditions are enabled by asserting predicates in *MustHold*. In Figure 5, *EnabledT* for microstep 2 is $\{b2 \rightarrow b1\}$ since this transition has guarding condition $[in(a2)]$.
3. For each $p \in MustHold$ do
   – If p is of type *in(s)*: If there exists a transition t in *EnabledT* such that (1) the predicates in *MustHold* imply that we are in the source state of t, and (2) s is a member of *source-completion(t)*, then report violation.
   – If p is of type $\neg in(s)$: If (1) predicates in *MustHold* imply that we are in the parent state p of s and (2) *EnabledT* contains transitions from all child states of p other than s back to s, then report violation.

Note that if p is of type $\neg in(s)$, the fact that p, the parent state of s, is active guarantees that some child state of p other than s is active. Since we do not know which child state is active, we must ensure that there are enabled transitions from all child states of p other than s back to s.

In microstep 2 of Figure 5, transition b2→b1 must be taken since (1) predicate *in(b2)* assigned to microstep 0 implies that we are in the source state of the transition, and (2) the guarding condition of the transition is satisfied by predicate *in(a2)* assigned to microstep 1. Transition b2→b1 causes *b2* to be inactive in microstep 3. This invalidates the local inconsistency condition. The constraint

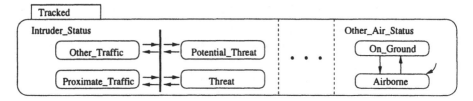

Fig. 6. Threat Detection Logic in CAS.

we can derive for this causality path is $[in(a2) \wedge (m > 0)] \Rightarrow \neg in(b2)$. Predicate $(m > 0)$ is included in the constraint only because it contributes to the reassignment of the violated predicate $in(b2)$. We have thus proven by contradiction that the local inconsistency condition can not hold for this causality path.

8 Deriving the Invariant

Since we must consider all causality paths to the locally inconsistent transitions, a violation must be found for each path. Otherwise, no invariant can be safely formulated. Suppose we have the following violation constraints for n causality paths: $(P_1 \Rightarrow \neg p_1, P_2 \Rightarrow \neg p_2, ..., P_n \Rightarrow \neg p_n)$, where P_i denotes the conjunction of predicates which once asserted, guarantees the negation of predicate p_i for the ith causality path. The invariant is then the conjunction of the n violation constraints: $(P_1 \wedge P_2 \wedge ... \wedge P_n) \Rightarrow (\neg p_1 \vee \neg p_2 \vee ... \vee \neg p_n)$. This invariant applies only when the trigger event to the locally inconsistent transitions occurs.

9 Application to TCAS II

Our method was applied to a part of the TCAS II ([air] Traffic alert and Collision Avoidance System) specification version 6.04A written in RSML. It was used to supplement consistency checking in the Collision Avoidance Subsystem (CAS). CAS models intruding aircraft and classifies them as one of *Threat, Potential_Threat, Proximate_Traffic,* or *Other_Traffic.* Figure 6 shows a part of CAS that models the intruding aircraft. The transition bar in state *Intruder_Status* is shorthand notation for transitions between any two states. State *Other_Air_Status* models the intruding aircraft as either being close to the ground (state *On_Ground*), or airborne (hence more of a threat).

Using the Stanford Validity Checker (SVC), we discovered a local inconsistency condition for transitions *Proximate_Traffic* to *Potential_Threat* and *Proximate_Traffic* to *Other_Traffic.* It includes, in part, the predicates $in(On\_Ground)$ and $\neg Other\_Alt\_Reporting$. This means that the intruding aircraft is not reporting altitude but it is classified as being close to the ground.

By applying the analysis described in this paper, our tool generated the invariant $\neg Other\_Alt\_Reporting \Rightarrow \neg in(On\_Ground)$. This invariant, as well as another one that was critical in consistency checking the specification, were found in no more than two seconds using our prototype tool written in LISP. However, the runtime is an underestimate since we did not fully expand all causality trees; the entire specification was not available in an electronic format. The parts that were left unspecified were nevertheless determined to be irrelevant to our analysis.

10 Discussion

We analyze a conservative approximation of the execution that statically determines all possible changes that can occur in the system at any given time with any given input. Since the approximation has less information than the original specification, we may overlook properties that are in fact true of the specification. On the other hand, the limited size of the approximation makes it computationally feasible to analyze. The algorithm has been integrated into a general consistency checking prototype tool. We expect to extend it with other static analysis tools as they become available.

Acknowledgements

We have benefitted greatly from the collaboration with Mats Heimdahl, University of Minnesota, who has provided us with insights into RSML in general and comments to an earlier draft of the paper.

References

1. R.J. Anderson, P.Beame, S. Burns, W. Chan, F. Modugno, Notkin D, and J.D. Reese. Model checking large software specifications. In D. Garlan, editor, *Proceedings of the Fourth ACM SIGSOFT Symposium on the Foundations of Software Engineering (SIGSOFT'96)*, pages 156–166, October 1996.
2. C. Barrett D.L. Dill and J. Levitt. Validity checking for combinations of theories with equality. In M. Srivas and A. Camilleri, editors, *Formal Methods in Computer Aided Design (FMCAD)*, number 1166 in Lecture Notes in Computer Science, pages 197–201. Springer-Verlag, November 1996.
3. S. Gerhart, D. Craigen, and T. Ralston. Formal methods reality check: Industrial usage. *IEEE Transactions on Software Engineering*, 21(2):90–98, February 1995.
4. D. Harel. Statecharts: A visual formalism for complex systems. *Science of Computer Programming*, 8:231–274, 1987.
5. D. Harel and A. Pnueli. On the development of reactive systems. In K.R. Apt, editor, *Logics and Models of Conc. Systems*, pages 477–498. Springer-Verlag, 1985.
6. M. P.E. Heimdahl and N.G. Leveson. Completeness and consistency analysis of state-based requirements. *IEEE TSE*, 22(6):363–377, June 1996.
7. C. L. Heitmeyer, R. D. Jeffords, and B. G. Labaw. Automated consistency checking of requirements specifications. *TOSEM*, 5(3):231–261, July 1996.
8. D.N. Hoover and Zewei Chen. Tablewise, a decision table tool. In J. Rushby, editor, *Proceedings of 10th Annual Conference on Computer Assurance (COMPASS '95)*, pages 97–108, Gaithersburg, MD, USA, June 1995. IEEE.
9. M. S. Jaffe, N. G. Leveson, M. P.E. Heimdahl, and B. Melhart. Software requirements analysis for real-time process-control systems. *IEEE Transactions on Software Engineering*, 17(3):241–258, March 1991.
10. N.G. Leveson, M. P.E. Heimdahl, H. Hildreth, and J.D. Reese. Requirements specification for process control systems. *IEEE Transactions on Software Engineering*, 20(9):694–707, September 1994.
11. D. Y.W. Park, J.U. Skakkebæk, M. P.E. Heimdahl, B.J. Czerny, and D.L. Dill. Checking properties of safety critical specifications using efficient decision procedures. In *Formal Methods in Software Practice*, pages 34–43. ACM Press, 1998.
12. D. L. Parnas, G. J. K. Asmis, and J. Madey. Assessment of safety-critical software in nuclear power plants. *Nuclear Safety*, 32(2):189–198, April–June 1991.

Partition Refinement in Real-Time Model Checking

Ronald Lutje Spelberg, Hans Toetenel and Marcel Ammerlaan

Delft University of Technology
Faculty of Information Technology and Systems
Zuidplantsoen 4, NL-2628 BZ Delft, The Netherlands
r.f.lutjespelberg@twi.tudelft.nl

Abstract. Many successful model checking tools for real-time systems are based on pure forward or backward reachability analysis. In this paper we present a real-time model checker that is based on a different approach, namely partition refinement. Partition refinement was applied before in real-time model checking, but never resulted, to our knowledge, in tools with competitive performance. Our partition refinement algorithm is inspired by currently existing ones for real-time systems, and operates on a product structure of a system specification and a property specification. A key aspects of our approach is that, unlike other real-time model checking approaches, we do not use a canonical representation like DBM's to manipulate regions. Instead we solely use the splitting history generated by the partition refinement algorithm. This paper presents our model checking technique, and reports on first experiences with a first implementation, comparing its performance to that of other model checkers.

1 Introduction

Most published real-time model checking algorithms are based on either backward/forward reachability analysis, compositional techniques, or partition refinement techniques. The first approach has been applied successfully and is implemented in several successful verification tools [4, 11], and recently successes were reported in using compositional techniques [10]. Several approaches based on partition refinement have been described, but seem not to have lead to tools that match the performance of the reachability analysis-based tools. However, we will show that partition refinement is also a powerful approach to real-time model checking.

The use of a partition refinement technique allowed us to use an unconventional approach in representing state sets. A representation for state sets that is efficient in storage and in manipulation is essential for a symbolic model checking technique. In non-real-time model checking, Binary Decision Diagrams (BDD's) have proven to be very successful [12], while for real-time systems Difference Bound Matrices (DBM's) [6] are often used. The time and data resources needed for maintaining such canonical representation have great impact on the performance of the model checking techniques. Problems furthermore arise when non-convex regions have to be modeled. There is no efficient canonical representation for them: disjunctions are simply represented by sets of DBM's.

Most model checking approaches require several involved operations on regions, which justifies the burden of using a canonical representation, because all these operations are performed more efficiently on such a representation. When using a partition refinement technique, this is not such a natural approach, because these techniques need only one operation: splitting a region according to a simple constraint. This operation can be implemented fairly simple on an unstructured set of constraints. In this case, there is no advantage in using structures like DBM's, because the time and space their manipulation requires, is not justified by the gain in the splitting operation.

Real-time model checking techniques based on partition refinement build a symbolic state space that is as coarse as possible. Starting from some (implicit) initial partition, the partition is iteratively refined until the verification problem can be decided. To our knowledge, the minimization algorithm of [1] was the first to apply partition refinement in real-time model checking. An alternative minimization algorithm was presented in [15]. Our approach was inspired Sokolsky's technique named MCT [14], that applies partition refinement to a structure that models the 'product' of the symbolic state space and a mu-calculus specification. The partition refinement algorithm that is applied to this structure is related to the earlier mentioned minimization algorithm of [1]. Sokolsky used the idea of [15] to keep the splitting history of regions in splitting trees, allowing a more efficient implementation of operations on regions. In these trees, leaves represent regions and internal nodes are associated with the splitting of a region in two subregions. Like Sokolsky's algorithm we use a splitting tree to record the splitting history of a region, but we do not keep an additional canonical region data structure with each reachable node.

The next section describes our system and property modeling formalism. Section 3 and 4 discuss our model checking approach, first at an abstract level, and that at a some more detail. Section 5 presents some early results, while the final section presents some conclusions.

2 Specifying systems

For modeling real-time systems, we defined an extension of timed automata [3], called XTG (eXtended Timed Graphs). Essentially, timed automata [3] are finite state machines augmented with clocks and data. Clocks are non-negative real-valued variables that uniformly increase. The increasing of clocks models the progress of time. Conditions on clocks and data can be used to constrain (by guards on edges) and enforce (by invariants on locations) the execution of transitions. Upon execution, a transition may update clocks and data. One key feature of XTG is that it provides a general form of urgency. Transitions can either be marked normal or urgent, indicating that they have to be executed immediately upon enabling, without letting time pass. This general form of urgency allows easy modeling of transitions that trigger on data and time conditions The communication model is based on the synchronous value passing model of CCS [13]. Briefly, a transition labeled with a synchronization $l!e$ must synchronize with a transition labeled with $l?v$, where l is a synchronization label (or channel name), e is value expression, and v is a variable. As a consequence the value of e is assigned to the variable v. Furthermore processes can communicate through shared data. The XTG notation is intended to offer the possibility to model rich data structures. The first version of our tool however, is only able to deal with systems that (besides clocks) have floats, integers, and enumerated variables.

Core syntax. We define a core syntax for XTG systems, on which the dynamic semantics are based. In core syntax, an XTG system is defined as a single, global graph. In the following, we use some abstract syntax domains that are assumed to be provided by the data model:

- *Val*: values
- *Vexpr*: value expressions
- *Bexpr*: boolean value expressions (*Bexpr* $\subset$ *Vexpr*)
- *StateMan*: state manipulations

Let *ClockId*, *VarId* and *LocId* denote the sets of clock names, state variable names, and location identifiers, respectively. An XTG system is a tuple $\langle$*Data, Clocks, Locations, Invar, Init, Edges, Urgent*$\rangle$, where:

- *Data* $\subseteq$ $\mathcal{P}$(*VarId* $\times$ *Val*) defines the state. Each tuple $\langle$*name, init*$\rangle$ $\in$ *State* defines a variable, together with its type and initial value.
- *Clocks* $\subseteq$ *ClockId* defines a set of clocks.
- *Locations* $\subseteq$ *LocId* is a set of vertices.
- *Invar* : *Locations* $\rightarrow$ *Bexpr* assigns to each location a location invariant.
- *Init* $\in$ *Locations* is an initial location.
- *Edges* is a set of edges. An edge is a tuple $\langle$*source, destin, constraint, update*$\rangle$ where *source, destin* $\in$ *Locations*, *constraint* $\in$ *Bexpr* is the constraint of the edge, and *update* $\in$ *StateMan* is the update of data and clock values associated with the transition.
- *Urgent* : *Edges* $\rightarrow$ $\mathbb{B}$ identifies the subset of urgent edges.

Semantics. Let *Env* denote the set of environments, an environment (also referred to as valuation) being a map from identifiers to values. A labeled transition system $\langle S, s_0, \longrightarrow \rangle$ corresponding to an XTG system consists of:

- A set of states $S \subseteq LocId \times Env \times Env$. A state is tuple (l, ρ, ξ) where l is a location, ρ is a data valuation, and ξ is a clock valuation.
- An initial state $s_0 \in S$.
- A transition relation $\longrightarrow \subseteq S \times \mathbb{R}^{\geq 0} \cup \{\iota\} \times S$. A transition can either be a *step transition* denoted $s \xrightarrow{\iota} s'$ or a *time transition* written as $s \xrightarrow{d} s'$, where d is a nonnegative real indicating the duration of the transition. The ι is often omitted from a step transition.

To define the dynamic semantics of XTG, the following two denotational semantic functions for evaluating value expressions and state manipulations are needed:

$$EvalC: \ Vexpr \times Env \times Env \rightarrow \mathbb{B}$$
$$EvalS: \ StateMan \times Env \times Env \rightarrow Env \times Env$$

$EvalC[\![c]\!](\rho, \xi)$ evaluates the constraint c in a data valuation ρ, and a clock valuation ξ. $EvalS[\![u]\!](\rho, \xi)$ evaluates the update u in ρ and ξ and returns two new valuations ρ' and ξ' in which the effect of the update is incorporated.

In the following, $\xi[+\delta]$ denotes the application of a function $Env \times \mathbb{R}^{\geq 0} \rightarrow Env$, that increases each clock in ξ with δ. The transition relation $\longrightarrow$ for a XTG system is defined as the least relation satisfying the following two rules:

$$\frac{l \xrightarrow{g,u} l' \in E \ \wedge \ (\rho', \xi') = EvalS[\![u]\!](\rho, \xi) \ \wedge}{EvalC[\![g]\!](\rho, \xi) \ \wedge \ EvalC[\![inv(l')]\!](\rho', \xi')}{\langle l, \rho, \xi \rangle \xrightarrow{\iota} \langle l', \rho', \xi' \rangle}$$

$$\frac{\forall 0 \leq d \leq \delta \cdot EvalC[\![inv(l)]\!](\rho, \xi[+d]) \ \wedge}{\forall 0 \leq d < \delta \cdot \forall l \xrightarrow{g,u} l' \in E \cdot Urgent(l \xrightarrow{g,u} l') \Rightarrow}{\neg(EvalC[\![g]\!](\rho, \xi[+d]) \ \wedge \ EvalC[\![inv(l')]\!](EvalS[\![u]\!](\rho, \xi[+\delta])))}{\langle l, \rho, \xi \rangle \xrightarrow{\delta} \langle l, \rho, \xi[+\delta] \rangle}$$

The first rule states that a transition corresponding to an edge can be performed if its constraint is satisfied, and the invariant of the destination location is satisfied. As a consequence of transition, the clock and data valuations are changed according to the update. The second rule governs the passing of time. According to the rule, time may pass in a location as long as the invariant is satisfied and no urgent transitions are enabled.

Definition 1. *The next relation* $\longmapsto \subseteq S \times \mathbb{R}^{\geq 0} \times S$ *of a transition system* $\langle S, s_0, \longrightarrow \rangle$ *is transition relation on* S *defined as follows. For all states* $s, s' \in S$, $t \in \mathbb{R}^{\geq 0}$:

$$s \xmapsto{t} s' \iff s \xrightarrow{t} s' \ or \ \exists s'' \in S \cdot (s \xrightarrow{t} s'' \xrightarrow{\iota} s')$$

Thus $s \xmapsto{t} s'$ *means that* s' *can be reached from* s *by the passing of* t *time units and possibly performing a subsequent action transition. It is this relation that our model checking technique is be based on. The* t *will at times be omitted in cases it is irrelevant. A run is a possibly infinite sequence of states:* $s_0 \xmapsto{t_0} s_1 \xmapsto{t_1} s_2 \xmapsto{t_2} \cdots$. $\Pi(G)$ *denotes the set of runs of a graph* G.

The above given semantics gives a meaning to global XTG systems. A semantics for parallelism can be defined using either a syntactic transformation or by defining direct semantic rules for the parallel composition. Either way, such a definition is relatively straightforward and is not given here.

In the first version of the model checker, state manipulations can be sequences of assignments of the form: $\{v_1 := c_1, \ v_1 := v_2 + c_1, \ v_1 := c_1 * v_1 + c_2\}$, and constraints are conjunctions of inequalities of the form $\{v_1 \sim c_1,\ v_1 - v_2 \sim c_1\}$, where v_1, v_2 are float or integer variables, c_1, c_2 are integer constants, and $\sim \in \{<, \leq, \geq, >\}$. We will refer to constraints in which no conjunctions appear, simple constraints. Simple constraints as well as their negation always define convex regions.

Specifying properties. Our property specification language is a temporal logic based on CTL (Computation Tree Logic) [5] and TCTL (Timed CTL) [8]. The usage of these logics is strongly connected with the application of model checking verification. TCTL variants are real-time extensions of CTL. These extensions either augment temporal operators with time bounds, or use reset quantifiers. We use a similar approach by replacing the reset quantifier by assignments to specification clocks and variables. In our CTL variant (referred to as CTL_{XTG} or simply CTL), $z := 0.AF(p \wedge z \leq 10)$. would express that p will always become true sometime within ten time-units. A secondary benefit from this approach is that we can use symbolic constants in our property formulae (as suggested in [7]). Consider for example, the CTL formula $AG(t := count.AF(count = t + 1))$ in which $count$ is a system variable and t is property specification variable.

The core syntax defines two temporal operators, AU and EU. The formula $(\phi_1 AU \phi_2)$ is satisfied in a state if for all computation paths starting from that state, there is a state along it which satisfies ϕ_2, and until that time ϕ_1 is satisfied. $(\phi_1 EU \phi_2)$ is satisfied if there is at least one such computation path. Derived operators are: $EF\phi$ (There is path on which there is state satisfying ϕ), $EG\phi$ (There is a path of which every state satisfies ϕ), $AF\phi$ (On all paths there is some state satisfying ϕ), and $AG\phi$ (On all paths every state satisfies ϕ). There are two types atomic properties in our CTL variant: boolean expressions over values of variables and clocks of both the system and the property, and location expressions. The latter are of the form $g@l$, and express the fact that the graph g of the system is currently at location l.

A property specification is defined by a tuple $\langle C_p, V_p, \phi \rangle$, where C_p is a set of clocks, V_p is a set of variables, and ϕ is a CTL formula. Formulae are defined by the following syntax:

$$\phi ::= p \mid g@l \mid \neg\phi \mid \phi \vee \phi \mid \phi \wedge \phi \mid \phi AU \phi \mid \phi EU \phi \mid u.\phi$$

$p \in Bexpr$ (boolean expressions from data language), $u \in StateMan$ is a state manipulation assigning new values to variables from V_p or clocks from V_c. $g \in GraphId$, and $l \in LocId$, and in $g@l$, l has to identify a location of the graph identified by g. Furthermore, property specification variables and clocks in boolean value expressions p have to be bound by some earlier assignment operation.

The formal semantics definition is to some extend analogous to that of TCTL given in [2]. Given an XTG system G, let the extension of G with V_p and C_p, denote a XTG system G', derived from G by adding V_p to the set of variables, and C_p to the set of clocks. An XTG system G satisfies a property specification

$\langle C_p, V_p, \phi \rangle$ if the initial state s_0 of the transition system defined by the extension of G with C_p and V_p satisfies ϕ, written as $s_0 \models \phi$. The latter satisfaction relation is inductively defined as follows:

$$\langle l, \rho, \xi \rangle \models p \iff EvalC[\![p]\!](\rho, \xi)$$
$$\langle l, \rho, \xi \rangle \models g@ll \iff Location(l)(g)=ll$$
$$\langle l, \rho, \xi \rangle \models \phi_1 \vee \phi_2 \iff \langle l, \rho, \xi \rangle \models \phi_1 \text{ or } \langle l, \rho, \xi \rangle \models \phi_2$$
$$\langle l, \rho, \xi \rangle \models \phi_1 \wedge \phi_2 \iff \langle l, \rho, \xi \rangle \models \phi_1 \text{ and } \langle l, \rho, \xi \rangle \models \phi_2$$
$$\langle l, \rho, \xi \rangle \models \phi_1 AU\phi_2 \iff \text{for all runs } \pi \in \Pi(G)$$
$$\text{starting at } \langle l, \rho, \xi \rangle, \pi \models \phi_1 U\phi_2$$
$$\langle l, \rho, \xi \rangle \models \phi_1 EU\phi_2 \iff \text{for at least one run } \pi \in \Pi(G)$$
$$\text{starting at } \langle l, \rho, \xi \rangle, \pi \models \phi_1 U\phi_2$$
$$\langle l, \rho, \xi \rangle \models u.\phi \iff \langle l, \rho', \xi' \rangle \rangle \models \phi, \text{ with } (\rho', \xi') = EvalS[\![u]\!](\rho, \xi)$$

Let π denote a run $\langle l_0, \rho_0, \xi_0 \rangle \overset{t_0}{\longmapsto} \langle l_1, \rho_1, \xi_1 \rangle \overset{t_1}{\longmapsto} \langle l_2, \rho_2, \xi_2 \rangle \overset{t_2}{\longmapsto} \cdots$, then:

$\pi \models \phi_1 U\phi_2 \iff$ there is a state $\langle l_i, \rho_i, \xi_i \rangle$ and a $t < t_i$ such that
$\quad \langle l_i, \rho_i, \xi_i[+t] \rangle \models \phi_2$ and
$\quad$ for all $t' < t$, $\langle l_i, \rho_i, \xi_i[+t'] \rangle \models \phi_1 \vee \phi_2$ and
$\quad$ for all $j < i$, for all $t < t_j$, $\langle l_j, \rho_j, \xi_j[+t] \rangle \models \phi_1$

where the function *Location: LocId → (GraphId → LocId* returns for each global location a mapping from graphs to (local) locations.

3 Region product graphs and model checking

Our model checking algorithm operates on a structure called a *region product graph*. This structure can be viewed as the product of a graph representing the property (called formula graph) and a symbolic graph of a system. A *formula graph* is a graph representation of a CTL formula, that decomposes a formula in subformulae and defines their relationship. This decomposition is based on the fixed point characterizations of CTL formulae.

Each node of a region product graph is a tuple $\langle \phi, l, R \rangle$, that represents a subproperty (a formula graph node) ϕ and a set of states defined by the location l and region R. A region product graph that satisfies certain criteria, can be used the decide the verification problem. To that end nodes are assigned values that express whether or not the states defined by (l, R) satisfy the subproperty ϕ. This value may depend on values of other nodes, which is represented by edges to these nodes. A node can either be conjunctive, disjunctive, or terminal. The value of the conjunctive node is the conjunction of the values of its successors, that of a disjunctive node is the disjunction of those of its successors, while the value of a terminal node can be decided immediately, because it does not depend on values of other nodes.

The goal of our model checking algorithm is to construct a region product graph that is as small as possible, but still allows the verification problem to be decided. The latter means deciding the value of the initial node. This verification process is done by an iterative refinement algorithm based on depth-first search.

Formula graph nodes are identified by syntactic constructs taken from the CTL syntax extended with some derived constructs, namely $\phi AU'\phi$, $\phi AU''\phi$, $\phi EU'\phi$, and $\phi EU''\phi$. These have no formal meaning, but are used to identify nodes in a convenient way. Edges are labeled by tuples $\langle type, u \rangle$ where $type \in \{P, T\}$, and $u \in StateMan$. Let XF be the set of mentioned extended syntax constructs: the set of CTL constructs augmented with the four additional constructs.

Definition 2. *A formula graph is a tuple $\langle F, \phi_0, E \rangle$, where $F \subseteq XF$ is a set of nodes, $\phi_0 \in F$ is an initial node, and E is a set of edges $\phi_1 \stackrel{type, upd}{\longrightarrow} \phi_2$, with $\phi_1, \phi_2 \in F$, $type \in \{P, T\}$, and $upd \in StateMan$. The set of edges of the formula graph corresponding to a CTL formula ϕ is given by the following inductive definition.*

- *if $\phi = \phi_1 \vee \phi_2$ then $\phi \stackrel{\langle P, - \rangle}{\longrightarrow} \phi_1$ and $\phi \stackrel{\langle P, - \rangle}{\longrightarrow} \phi_2$*
- *if $\phi = \phi_1 \wedge \phi_2$ then $\phi \stackrel{\langle P, - \rangle}{\longrightarrow} \phi_1$ and $\phi \stackrel{\langle P, - \rangle}{\longrightarrow} \phi_2$*
- *if $\phi = \phi_1 AU \phi_2$ then $\phi \stackrel{\langle P, - \rangle}{\longrightarrow} \phi_1 AU' \phi_2$ and $\phi \stackrel{\langle P, - \rangle}{\longrightarrow} \phi_2$*
- *if $\phi = \phi_1 AU' \phi_2$ then $\phi \stackrel{\langle P, - \rangle}{\longrightarrow} \phi_1 AU'' \phi_2$ and $\phi \stackrel{\langle P, - \rangle}{\longrightarrow} \phi_1$*
- *if $\phi = \phi_1 AU'' \phi_2$ then $\phi \stackrel{\langle T, - \rangle}{\longrightarrow} \phi_1 AU \phi_2$*
- *if $\phi = \phi_1 EU \phi_2$ then $\phi \stackrel{\langle P, - \rangle}{\longrightarrow} \phi_1 EU' \phi_2$ and $\phi \stackrel{\langle P, - \rangle}{\longrightarrow} \phi_2$*
- *if $\phi = \phi_1 EU' \phi_2$ then $\phi \stackrel{\langle P, - \rangle}{\longrightarrow} \phi_1 EU'' \phi_2$ and $\phi \stackrel{\langle P, - \rangle}{\longrightarrow} \phi_1$*
- *if $\phi = \phi_1 EU'' \phi_2$ then $\phi \stackrel{\langle T, - \rangle}{\longrightarrow} \phi_1 EU \phi_2$*
- *if $\phi \stackrel{\langle P, u1 \rangle}{\longrightarrow} \phi'$ then $u2.\phi \stackrel{\langle P, u2; u1 \rangle}{\longrightarrow} \phi'$*

To facilitate the definition of the region product graph, first the *timed product graph* (t.p.g.) structure is defined. A timed product graph models the product structure of a formula graph and the transition system induced by the *next* relation of definition 1.

Definition 3. *The timed product graph corresponding to a transition system $\langle S, s_0, \longrightarrow \rangle$ (with $S \subseteq L \times Env_1 \times Env_2$) and a formula graph $\langle F, \phi_0, E_F \rangle$ is a graph $\langle T, t_0, \longrightarrow \rangle$, where $T \subseteq F \times L \times Env_1 \times Env_2$, and the transition relation $\longrightarrow \subseteq V_T \times V_T$ is defined as follows: $\langle \phi, l, \rho, \xi \rangle \longrightarrow \langle \phi', l', \rho', \xi' \rangle$ iff either*

- *$\phi \stackrel{type, upd}{\longrightarrow} \phi' \in E_F$, $type = P$, $l = l'$, and $(\rho', \xi') = EvalS[\![u]\!](\rho, \xi)$, or*
- *$\phi \stackrel{type, -}{\longrightarrow} \phi' \in E_F$, $type = T$ and $\langle l, \rho, \xi \rangle \longmapsto \langle l', \rho', \xi' \rangle$.*

We can now define the concept of a *region product graph* (r.p.g.), which is a quotient structure of a timed product graph. Each node in a region product graph represents a set of timed product graph nodes. These nodes share the same formula component and location component, but differ in the valuations of data and clocks.

Definition 4. *Let $\langle V_T, t_0, \longrightarrow \rangle$ be a timed product graph with $V_T \subseteq V_F \times V_G \times Env_1 \times Env_2$. Then a region product graph corresponding to this timed product* graph is a graph $\langle V_R, r_0, \longrightarrow \rangle$, where $V_R \subseteq V_F \times V_G \times \mathcal{P}(Env_1 \times Env_2)$, and $\longrightarrow \subseteq V_R \times V_R$ is defined as follows:

$$\langle \phi, l, R \rangle \longrightarrow \langle \phi', l', R' \rangle \text{ iff } \exists (\rho, \xi) \in R, (\rho', \xi') \in R' \cdot \langle \phi, l, \rho, \xi \rangle \longrightarrow \langle \phi', l', \rho', \xi' \rangle$$

We write that $\langle \phi, l, \rho, \xi \rangle \in \langle \phi, l, R \rangle$ if $(\rho, \xi) \in R$. Furthermore $succ(s)$ denotes the set of successor nodes of a node s in an r.p.g.: $succ(s) = \{t \mid s \longrightarrow_r t\}$.

As mentioned earlier nodes of a formula graph are classified as either *terminal*, *disjunctive*, or *conjunctive*. The *type* of a node $\langle \phi, l, \rho, \xi \rangle$ is defined as follows:

- if $\phi \in \{p, g@l\}$ then $type(\phi) = terminal$
- if $\phi \in \{\phi_1 \vee \phi_2, \phi_1 AU \phi_2, \phi_1 EU \phi_2, \phi_1 EU'' \phi_2\}$ then $type(\phi) = disjunctive$
- if $\phi \in \{\phi_1 \wedge \phi_2, \phi_1 AU' \phi_2, \phi_1 EU' \phi_2, \phi_1 AU'' \phi_2\}$ then $type(\phi) = conjunctive$
- if $\phi = u.\phi'$ then $type(\phi) = type(\phi')$

We refer to edges that correspond to 'T' edges of the formula graph as *transition edges* (edges corresponding to next transitions in the system), while edges corresponding to 'P' edges of the formula graph are referred to as *property edges* (edges corresponding to dependencies in the property graph).

Given an XTG and a formula graph, there is a class of corresponding r.p.g.'s, differing in the region component of the nodes. We are interested in r.p.g.'s that are *stable*, because these region graphs allow us to decide values of nodes.

Definition 5. *A node $\langle \phi, l, R \rangle$ of a region product graph is stable with respect to an outgoing edge $\langle \phi, l, R \rangle \longrightarrow \langle \phi', l', R' \rangle$ if for all $(\phi, l, \rho, \xi) \in \langle \phi, l, R \rangle$ there is an edge in the timed product graph $\langle \phi, l, \rho, \xi \rangle \longrightarrow \langle \phi', l', \rho', \xi' \rangle$ with $\langle \phi', l', \rho', \xi' \rangle \in \langle \phi', l', R' \rangle$. A node $\langle \phi, l, R \rangle$ is stable if it is stable with respect to all its outgoing edges, and, if it is the case that ϕ is an atomic property, then all $(\rho, \xi) \in R$ either satisfy or do not satisfy ϕ. A region product graph is stable if all its nodes are.*

Thus if an r.p.g. is stable then all timed product graph nodes represented by the same r.p.g. node are equivalent with respect to the current partition, and satisfy the same subset of predicates used in the property specification.

Values of r.p.g. nodes are defined by means of a marking $val : S \to \mathbb{B}$. In a stable region product graph this marking can be determined by iteratively applying a function that improves a marking until the fixed point is reached.

Definition 6. *Let $\langle S, s_0, \longrightarrow \rangle$ be a region product graph, and $val : S \to \mathbb{B}$ be a marking. Then val is a marking of $\langle S, s_0, \longrightarrow \rangle$ if it is the least fixed point of a function $f : (S \to \mathbb{B}) \to (S \to \mathbb{B})$, defined as follows: $f(val)(s) =$*

- $\exists \langle \phi, l, \rho, \xi \rangle \in s \cdot \langle l, \rho, \xi \rangle \models \phi$, *if type(s) = terminal*
- $\bigvee \{val(t) \mid t \in succ(s)\}$, *if type(s) = disjunctive*
- $\bigwedge \{val(t) \mid t \in succ(s)\}$, *if type(s) = conjunctive*

The following intuitive meaning can be given to this. Initially, all terminal nodes are given their appropriate value, while all other nodes are assigned the value *false*. Then, nodes are iteratively set to *true* until the fixed point is reached. A conjunctive node can be set to *true* if all of its successors have this value, a disjunctive node can be set to *true* if at least one of its successors has this value.

The following proposition justifies the use of r.p.g. for model checking.

Proposition 1. *Let G be an XTG system and ϕ be an CTL formula. Then if $\langle S, s_0, E \rangle$ is a stable region product graph derived from G and ϕ, and val is a corresponding marking, then $G \models \phi \iff val(s_0) = true$.*

4 The model checking algorithm

The model checking algorithm is based on a depth-first search. Starting from the initial r.p.g. node, the r.p.g. is constructed in an iteration of three steps: (1) explore a new edge (and possibly a new node), (2) stabilize the r.p.g., and (3) use the new information to decide values of nodes. This iteration ends if the value of the initial node becomes decided. Note that the r.p.g. is constructed from the compositional description of the XTG system. The composition is thus made on-the-fly, without constructing the global XTG model. We will often write that an r.p.g. node is split according to a constraint, meaning that the node is split in subnodes of which the values in associated region either all satisfy the constraint, or all dissatisfy the constraint. With each node, the following values are associated:

- *decided* indicates whether or not the value of the node has been decided
- *val* holds the value of a decided node
- *reachable* indicates whether or not a node is reachable
- *inaccessible* indicates whether edges to this node are allowed

Each time the r.p.g. is extended, it is refined until all reachable nodes are stable. This is done by splitting unstable nodes into stable subnodes. There are four causes for such a splitting. Firstly, in case an outgoing edge of an (already explored) node is explored, this node is split in the following way:

A if an outgoing edge has a guard, the node is split according to this guard.

This rule ensures that the node from which the edge leaves is stabilized with respect to the outgoing edge. Exploring a new edge may result in exploring a new node, in which case the new node is immediately split in the following way:

B if the node is a terminal node, it is split according to the corresponding atomic property.
C if the node has a location invariant, it is split according to this invariant.

Rule B stabilizes the newly explored node by separating state values that do satisfy the atomic property from those that do not. Rule C separates inaccessible t.p.g. nodes from accessible ones. New subnodes that do not satisfy the invariant are marked *inaccessible*, indicating that edges to these nodes are not allowed.

Splitting a node according to one of the three rules described until now may cause predecessors of this node to become unstable, because t.p.g. nodes corresponding to these predecessor nodes may have successors in different r.p.g. nodes. This leads to the fourth cause of node splitting:

D Whenever a node has an outgoing edge to a splitted node, the node is split in such a way that the resulting subnodes are stable with respect to the edge.

Node splitting is thus initiated by of one of the first three rules, while the fourth rule defines the propagation of the splits back through the earlier explored nodes, to ensure that the already explored portion of the state space remains stable. The backward propagation technique is combined with a reachability analysis technique, to avoid unnecessary splitting of unreachable nodes. When splitting a reachable node, one of the two subnodes may become unreachable.

In the model checking process, values of nodes are decided on-the-fly. Initially all values are set to false. If a terminal node is encountered its value can immediately be decided to true or false, depending on the value of the atomic property. These values are then reported to its predecessors, which may in turn also become decided. This propagation is done according to the function of definition 6: the value of a conjunctive (disjunctive) node can be set to true (false) if all of its successors have this value, it can be set to false (true) if one of its successors has this value. Whenever the value of node is set, *decided* is set to true. If no cycles occur, this procedure can be shown to be conform the value assignment of definition 6.

For cycles an additional mechanism is needed. Cycles of undecided nodes may occur, which will not become decided using the above procedure. If this happens there is an *interference-free cycle*: a cycle of undecided nodes of which all successors that are not on the cycle have been decided already. In this case the value of all nodes can be decided to false. From definition 6 it can be seen that no node on an interference-free cycle of undecided nodes can ever be set to true. Therefore these nodes get the value false.

Once the value of a node is decided, there is no use in splitting it again, so splits are never propagated through decided nodes. Therefore, values are propagated as soon as possible, to avoid unnecessary splitting. Note that the propagation of values has to be done after propagating splits, since values can only be decided on stable r.p.g.'s. By reporting values on-the-fly, the verification may complete before the full reachable product graph is built, because irrelevant portions of this graph are not refined.

Figure 1 presents an abstract pseudo-code description of the algorithm. *search* identifies the search stack of not yet fully explored reachable nodes. If a node is encountered of which the value has already been decided, then this node is not explored further. Otherwise, if there are still unexplored outgoing edges, one of these is taken, and the node is split according to rule A by the *trans_split* function. Because guards are restricted to be conjunctions of simple constraints, there will be exactly one subnode that satisfies the guard (namely that with the region in which all conjuncts of the guard are satisfied). This subnode is returned by *trans_split*. If the destination node was not yet visited, then it is initialized and added to the region product graph. It is immediately split according to rules B and C, by the *initial_split* function. If the new node was a terminal node, the values of its subnodes can be decided. After adding the edge to the region product graph, the splitting of the destination node is propagated back through the graph. This splitting, which corresponds to rule D, is performed by the *propagate_split* function, which is depicted in fig. 2. Note that this func-

modelcheck:

> *push(search, s_0)*; *initial_split(s_0)*; *reachable(s_0)* := *true*
> **while** *search* $\neq \emptyset$ **do**
>> *s* := *top(search)*
>> **if** *decided(s)* **then**
>>> *pop(search)*
>>
>> **else if** *S* has unexplored outgoing edges **then**
>>> let *t* be an outgoing edge of *s*, let *s'* be the destination of *t*
>>> *ss* := *trans_split (s, t)*
>>> **if** *s'* was not yet visited **then**
>>>> add *s'* to r.p.g.; *initial_split(s')*
>>>> **if** *s'* is a terminal node **then**
>>>>> **for each** subnode *ss'* of *s'* **do**
>>>>>> set *val(ss')* to value of A.P.; *decided(ss'):=true*;
>>>
>>> add *ss → s'* to r.p.g.
>>> *propagate_split (s')*
>>> *propagate_values (s')*
>>
>> **else**
>>> *push(cycle,pop(search))*
>>> **if** *top(search)* and *top(cycle)* correspond to different temporal ops **then**
>>>> **for each** node *n* in the interference-free cycle **do**
>>>>> *decided(n)* := *true*; remove *n* from *search*

Fig. 1. the abstract algorithm

tion incorporates a mechanism to keep track of the nodes that reachable. Only reachable nodes are pushed onto the search stack.

After that, any decided values of subnodes of *s'* are propagated back through the graph by the *propagate_value* function. With each non-terminal node a counter is associated that keeps track of the number of outgoing edges that have not yet been decided. When initializing a node, this counter is made equal to the number of outgoing edges of the node. If a successor of a disjunctive node is set to true, then the node itself can be decided to true. If a successor is decided to false, the counter is decremented. In case the counter reaches zero, the node is decided to false, since all its successor nodes are false. For conjunctive nodes dual rules apply.

Finally, if a node has no unexplored outgoing edges left and still is not decided, it is pushed onto the *cycle* stack. This stack is used to detect interference-free cycles. To detect that a complete interference-free cycle is on the *cycle* stack, we use the fact that the formula component of all nodes in a cycle must originate from the same temporal operator in the property specification, since the formula graph is acyclic. If top node of *stack* and the top node of *cycle* correspond to different temporal operators, we know that there is a set of nodes on top of the *cycle* stack that forms an interference-free cycle. In that case all undecided nodes on the cycle stack belonging to this temporal operator can be decided to their standard value.

---

propagate_split (s):

    for each predecessor node *s'* of *s* for which *reachable(s')* **do**
        split *s'* in subnodes that are stable with respect to *s*
        if *s'* was split **then**
            propagate_split (s')
            for each subnode *ss'* of *s'* **do**
                if *ss'* has a predecessor *ss* such that *reachable(ss)*
                or *ss'* contains the initial state **then**
                    reachable(ss') := *true*
            if *s'* is on *search* **then**
                replace *s'* on *search* with all its reachable subnodes

---

Fig. 2. the propagation of splits

To implement the algorithm, a representation is needed for regions. The representation we use is based on a simple idea. In a partition refinement approach, regions are the consequence of repeated splitting. This leads to using a forest structure in which for every (ϕ, l) pair, a *splitting tree* is kept, which holds the splitting history of its regions. Internal nodes are labeled with constraints and represent the splitting of a region into two subregions by this constraint, while leaf nodes correspond to actual r.p.g. nodes. The set of constraints defining the region associated with an r.p.g. node is obtained by collecting all constraints while traversing the tree upwards from the node. The constraints that split a region are always simple constraints. This guarantees that the resulting regions are always convex. Unlike other approaches that use splitting trees, we do not use any additional representation to store the regions. As explained in the introduction, this approach avoids the burden of building and manipulating canonical representations like DBM's. On the other hand the operations on state sets that are needed for our algorithm can be be implemented relatively efficient. In particular, a mechanism is needed to avoid the extension of splitting tree with useless constraints: if a constraint is always satisfied or never satisfied in a region, then splitting with that constraint is obviously not needed.

For clock constraints this mechanism, which we refer to as constraint reduction, is applied whenever a region split is considered. The reduction procedure integrates two tests, one checking whether or not $R \Rightarrow c$, and one checking $R \Rightarrow \neg c$. If either condition is the true, then no splitting is performed. These checks are performed by a variant of a shortest path algorithm. A convex region can conceptually be represented by a graph in which vertices are variables and edges are constraints on clocks: an edge $x \xrightarrow{3} y$ means that $x - y < 3$. An additional node '0' is introduced to represent constraints on single variables: an edge $x \xrightarrow{3}$ '0' represents the fact that $x < 3$. Checking $R \Rightarrow x - y < v$ then means checking whether or not there is a path from x to y with an accumulated weight less than c. This approach is easily extended to also deal with non-strict constraints. The idea of using a splitting tree is independent of the kind of data that is represented. This makes the incorporation of other data types in the input language of our model checker relatively easily. As far as the representation of state sets is concerned, adding a new data type would only mean adding a reduction procedure for the new data type.

The splitting of nodes according to rules A, B, and C is straightforward. Given a node and a constraint, the node is subsequently split by all simple constraints of the constraint. Before splitting a node by a simple constraint, the reduction procedure of the previous subsection is applied. If the constraint proves to be no splitting, an edge is added from s' to either the left or the right subnode of s, depending on the result of the reduction. The splitting caused by rule D is more complex. Given an r.p.g. node s', an r.p.g. node s that is split by a constraint c, and an edge $s' \longrightarrow s$, split s' into a set of subnodes that are stable with respect to s. In this case the propagation of splits must take in account the possible passing of time, since the t.p.g. nodes of s' and s are related by a next relation $\longmapsto$.

The size of the formula graph has great impact on the size of the resulting region product graph. In the formula graph each temporal operator $\phi_1 AU \phi_2$ and $\phi_1 EU \phi_2$ results in three formula graph nodes. However, these nodes are strongly related. Therefore, it is worthwhile to operate on more complex nodes that integrate nodes that result from a single temporal operator. Thus all three nodes of an AU or EU operator are integrated into a single node, in which the edges are not related by simple conjunctions or disjunctions, but more complex expressions. This means that a slightly more complex decision procedure is needed, in which the outgoing edges have different roles. This considerable improves performance both in space and time. We can take the reduction suggested here one step further by making the number of nodes of the formula graph as small as possible. In that case exactly one node is needed for each temporal operator in the specification. For example, the formula $(p \vee q)AU(r \wedge (sEUt))$ would only result in two nodes, one associated with $(p \vee q)AU(r \wedge (...))$, and one associated with $sEUt$.

5   Results and Discussion

The algorithm described in this paper has been implemented in a prototype model checking tool called PMC (a Prototype Model Checker). We defined a concrete syntax for XTG systems which offers some additional powerful constructs to model systems more easily. Given a ASCII description of the XTG system which includes a set of CTL properties to be verified, the tool returns, if feasible within available resources, a positive or negative result for each property. The tool is furthermore able to generate traces that may clarify the verification result – for example a counterexample in case of a negative verification result for a safety property.

To obtain confidence in the correctness of the implementation, our first experiments concentrated on existing case studies taken from real-time model checking literature. The Fischer protocol [9] is a mutual exclusion protocol that is a popular and easily scalable benchmark for real-time model checking techniques.

156

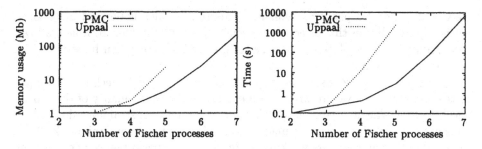

Fig. 3. Time and memory usages for the Fischer's protocol

Figure 3 compares (on a logarithmic scale) the performance in time and space with that of a leading model checking tool called Uppaal[11]. The experiments were done on a Pentium II at 300MHz with 512Mb of memory. The version of Uppaal that was used was 2.17.1. The generalised railroad crossing models a railroad crossing with a gate that must only be closed when a train is in the gate. Several versions of such a system exist which mainly differ in the way how the control is implemented and whether the controller can handle an arbitrary number of trains. The version of GRC used here models the control as a separate automaton and uses a counter to handle any number of trains in the system. Figure 4 shows the resource usage for both tools, for different numbers of trains.

First experiments thus show that our model checking technique performs relatively well. Although these positive results are only based on limited experience with the tool, we believe that further experiments will show that they are of a more general character. This would show that partition refinement is a useful approach to real-time model checking, that could be at least as valuable as the currently followed approaches.

#trains	Uppaal time	Uppaal memory	PMC time	PMC memory
2	0.1s	1.0Mb	0.1s	1.8Mb
3	1.6s	1.0Mb	1.2s	1.9Mb
4	553.6s	11.9Mb	365.0s	47.0Mb

Fig. 4. Time and memory usage for GRC

Summarizing, we can say that we developed an efficient model checking technique based on partition refinement. One of the key aspects of our technique is that we experimented with an approach that does not use DBM or another canonical representation, but splitting trees. This is, to our knowledge, a new approach in real-time model checking, that is motivated by the fact that for partition refinement this might be a more natural approach than the DBM's originating from the reachability-based model checking approach. Furthermore we use an improved partition refinement approach which is derived from some earlier approaches in this direction especially [1] and [14]. Our approach allows the verification of a relatively large set of properties as they can be specified in real-time extension of CTL.

Currently we are focusing on the extension of our model checking technique in two ways. Firstly, we are working on extending the functionality of the model checking tool. The next version will allow more complex constraints and updates. This extension will for example make it possible to express constraints like $2x - 4y - z > 10$. Secondly we are working on improving the performance of our model checking technique. To that end, techniques based on partial order reduction and exploiting symmetry, have been investigated.

References

1. R. Alur, C. Courcoubetis, D. Dill, N. Halbwachs, and H. Wong-Toi. Minimization of timed transition systems. In *Concur'92*, volume 630 of *LNCS*, pages 340–354. Springer-Verlag, 1992.
2. R. Alur, C. Courcoubetis, N. Halbwachs, T.A. Henzinger, P.-H. Ho, X. Nicollin, A. Olivero, J. Sifakis, and S. Yovine. The algorithmic analysis of hybrid systems. *Theoretical Computer Science*, 138:3–34, 1995.
3. R. Alur and D. Dill. The theory of timed automata. *Theoretical Computer Science*, 126:183–235, 1994.
4. R. Alur, T.A. Henzinger, and P.-H. Ho. Automatic symbolic verification of embedded systems. *IEEE Transactions on Software Engineering*, 22:181–201, 1996.
5. E.M. Clarke, E.A. Emerson, and A.P. Sistla. Automatic verification of finite-state concurrent systems using temporal logic specifications. *ACM TOPLAS*, 8(2):244–263, 1986.
6. D.L. Dill. Timing assumptions and verification of finite-state concurrent systems. In *CAV'89*, volume 407 of *LNCS*, pages 195–212. Springer-Verlag, 1989.
7. T.A. Henzinger. The theory of hybrid automata. In *LICS'96*, pages 278–292. IEEE Computer Society Press, 1996.
8. T.A. Henzinger, X. Nicollin, J. Sifakis, and S. Yovine. Symbolic model checking for real-time systems. *Information and Computation*, 111:193–244, 1994.
9. K.J. Kristoffersen, F. Laroussinie, K.G. Larsen, P. Pettersson, and Wang Yi. A compositional proof of a real-time mutual exclusion protocol. In *Proceedings of the 7th International Joint Conference on the Theory and Practice of Software Development*, 1997.
10. K.G. Larsen, P. Petterson, and Wang Yi. Compositional and symbolic model checking of real-time systems. In *16th IEEE Real-Time Systems Symposium*, 1995.
11. K.G. Larsen, P. Petterson, and Wang Yi. Model checking for real-time systems. In *Proceedings of Fundamentals of Computation Theory*, volume 965 of *LNCS*, pages 62–88. Springer-Verlag, 1995.
12. K.L. McMillan. *Symbolic model checking*. Kluwer, 1993.
13. R. Milner. *Communication and Concurrency*. Prentice Hall, 1989.
14. O.V. Sokolsky and S.A. Smolka. Local model checking for real-time systems. In *CAV'95*, volume 939 of *LNCS*, pages 211–224. Springer-Verlag, 1995.
15. M. Yannakakis and D. Lee. An efficient algorithm for minimizing real-time transition systems. In *CAV'93*, volume 697 of *LNCS*, pages 210–224. Springer-Verlag, 1993.

Formal Verification of Stabilizing Systems

M. Siegel

University of Kiel, Germany
Dept. of Applied Mathematics and Computer Science
E-mail: mis@informatik.uni-kiel.de

Abstract. This paper links too formerly rather disjoint areas: formal verification and stabilization. Stabilization is a vitally emerging paradigm in fault tolerant distributed computing; formal verification investigates mathematically rigorous techniques to reason about systems.
We give an introduction to the principles and the design of stabilizing systems and present a fully syntactical formal framework for phased, i.e. modular, verification of stabilizing systems.

1 Introduction

Stabilization is a concept which has gained its importance computer science as a vitally emerging paradigm in fault tolerant distributed computing [13].

In this paper we explain the principles of stabilization and the main design pattern for stabilizing systems. This design pattern, which suggests to construct stabilizing systems from simpler stabilizing phases [13], is our guideline for a set of verification rules which support phased, i.e. modular, verification of composed stabilizing systems. These proof rules replace the hitherto informal reasoning in the field of stabilization and constitute the basis for machine-supported verification of an important class of distributed algorithms.

The notion of stabilization has been introduced to the field of distributed computing by E. W. Dijkstra [4] in 1974. Nine years later Leslie Lamport rediscovered stabilization as a paradigm for fault-tolerant computing. He observed that stabilizing systems show the remarkable property of being capable to automatically recover from transient errors, i.e. errors which do not continue to occur during the period of recovery [13]. So, the concept of stabilization allows to construct extremely robust fault-tolerant systems (see [17] for an extensive list of articles).

But stabilization comes at a high price. Stabilizing algorithms are amongst the most complicated objects studied in the field of distributed computing. Their intricacy stems from an extremely high degree of parallelism which is inherent to *all* stabilizing systems – details are given in Section 3. The involvement of stabilizing systems makes tool support for their verification desirable if not indispensable. In order to allow tool-support we need a formal model to describe stabilizing systems, a formal specification language to describe properties of stabilizing systems, and mechanisms to establish that a certain system obeys some specific properties.

Such a formal basis has first been introduced in [11] where fair transition systems have been used to describe stabilizing systems and where is has been demonstrated that linear temporal logic (LTL) [12] is an adequate specification language for this class of systems.

The temporal proof rules for stabilizing systems presented in [11] exploit the *semantical* properties of stabilizing systems and were proven to be sound and relative complete while being considerably simpler than the general proof rules for program validity. Completeness of these rules is fully satisfactory only from a theoretical point of view. However, a satisfactory proof system – now from a practical point of view – also has to support the *verification strategies* applied in the field of stabilization. The main observation in this respect is, that correctness arguments for stabilizing systems which are constructed as parallel compositions of smaller stabilizing phases (most systems are designed this way), address the correctness of the phases in isolation and give additional evidence that despite interference between phases they still perform their tasks. Such a decomposition of proofs – based on the *structural* properties of stabilizing systems – into *phase correctness* and *interference freedom* is the guideline for the proof rules presented in this paper. The combination of the proof rules as presented in [11] and the forthcoming proof rules gives a convenient and powerful framework for the formal verification of stabilizing systems as will be demonstrated.

This article is organized as follows: In Section 2 we present fair transition systems and linear temporal logic. An introduction to the principles of stabilization and the design of stabilizing systems is given in Section 3. The verification rules are presented in Sections 4 and 5. An example and conclusions are given in Sections 6, 7.

Remark: All proofs of results presented in this paper can be found in [15].

2 Preliminaries

We use fair transition systems [12] to describe stabilizing systems. For a given set V of typed variables a *state* s is a function $s : V \longrightarrow Val$ assigning type-consistent values to all variables in V. The set of all states interpreting variables in V is denoted by Σ_V.

Definition 1. *A* fair transition system *(fts)* $A = (V, \Theta, T, WF, SF)$ *consists of a finite set* V *of variables, an assertion* Θ *characterizing* initial states, *a finite set* $T = \{t_1, \ldots, t_n\}$ *of transitions as well as* weak *and* strong *fairness constraints expressed by set* $WF \subseteq T$ *resp.* $SF \subseteq T$.

□

The state space of A is denoted by Σ_A and defined by $\Sigma_A \overset{\text{def}}{=} \Sigma_{V_A}$. Each transition $t \in T$ is represented by a first order assertions $\rho_t(V, V')$, called a *transition predicate* [12]. A transition predicate relates the values of the variables V in a state $s \in \Sigma_V$ to their values in a successor state s' obtained by applying the transition to s. It does so by using two disjoint copies of set V. The occurrence of variable $v \in V$ refers to its value in state s while an occurrence of v' refers to the value of v in s'. Assuming that $\rho_t(V, V')$ is the transition predicate of transition t, state s' is called a *t-successor* of s iff $(s, s') \models \rho_t(V, V')$. A transition t is *enabled* in state s if there exists s' with $(s, s') \models \rho_t(V, V')$; otherwise it is *disabled*. We require that T contains the *idling* transition t_{idle} whose transition relation is $\rho_{t_{idle}} : (V = V')$.

Definition 2. *A computation of an fts $A = (V, \Theta, T, WF, SF)$ is an infinite sequence $\sigma = \langle s_0, s_1, s_2, \ldots \rangle$ of states $s_i \in \Sigma_A$, s.t.*

1. *$s_0 \models \Theta$,*
2. *for all $i \in \mathbf{N}$ state s_{i+1} is a t-successor of s_i for some transition $t \in T$,*
3. *if transition $t \in WF$ is continuously enabled from some point onwards in σ, there are infinitely many $i \in \mathbf{N}$ with $(s_i, s_{i+1}) \models \rho_t(V, V')$,*
4. *if transition $t \in SF$ is infinitely often enabled in σ, there are infinitely many $i \in \mathbf{N}$ with $(s_i, s_{i+1}) \models \rho_t(V, V')$.*

□

The set of computations generated by an fts A is denoted by $[\![A]\!]$. Parallel composition of ftss is defined as:

Definition 3. *For $S_1 = (V_1, \Theta_1, T_1, WF_1, SF_1)$ and $S_2 = (V_2, \Theta_2, T_2, WF_2, SF_2)$ the parallel composition $S_1 \| S_2 = (V, \Theta, T, WF, SF)$ is defined by:*

$$V \stackrel{def}{=} V_1 \cup V_2 \quad \Theta \stackrel{def}{=} \Theta_1 \wedge \Theta_2 \quad T \stackrel{def}{=} T_1 \cup T_2 \quad WF \stackrel{def}{=} WF_1 \cup WF_2$$
$$SF \stackrel{def}{=} SF_1 \cup SF_2.$$

As specification language we use a future fragment of Linear Temporal Logic [12] without next-operator, referred to as LTL$^-$. Formulas are constructed from state formulas of some first order language $\mathcal{L}$, the temporal operator $\Diamond$ (eventually), and boolean operators $\wedge, \neg$ applied to formulas. Temporal formulas are denoted by $\varphi, \psi, \ldots$ and state formulas by $p, q, \ldots$. Temporal formulas are interpreted over infinite sequences of states [12].

Definition 4. *Given an infinite sequence $\sigma = \langle s_0, s_1, s_2, \ldots \rangle$ of states and $\varphi \in LTL^-$. We define that σ satisfies φ, denoted by $\sigma \models \varphi$, as:*

$$
\begin{array}{lll}
\sigma \models p & \text{iff} & \sigma_0 \models p, \\
\sigma \models \varphi \wedge \psi & \text{iff} & \sigma \models \varphi \text{ and } \sigma \models \psi, \\
\sigma \models \neg\varphi & \text{iff} & \sigma \not\models \varphi, \\
\sigma \models \Diamond\varphi & \text{iff} & \exists i \geq 0.\ \sigma_{\geq i} \models \varphi.
\end{array}
$$

□

We use the standard abbreviation $\Box\varphi \stackrel{def}{=} \neg\Diamond\neg\varphi$ (always). An fts A satisfies a formula $\varphi \in$ LTL$^-$, denoted by $A \models \varphi$, if all its computations satisfy φ. Furthermore, we denote the set of free variables of some state predicate p by V_p.

3 Stabilization for Fault-Tolerance

Stabilization is studied as an approach to cope with the *effects* of faults (i.e. not with a specific fixed set of faults as usual) as long as these effects do not violate some indispensable prerequisites for recovery, characterized by a so-called *fault-span* [3]. Such prerequisites may require, e.g., that the actual code is not affected. Fault-tolerance by stabilization ensures the continued availability of systems by correctly restoring the system state whenever the system exhibits incorrect behavior due to the occurrence of transient faults – i.e. faults that do not continue to occur during recovery of the system – within the fault-span.

When talking about stabilization there is always an environment that acts as an adversary producing transient faults thus affecting the consistency of variables upon which the actual stabilization depends. Generally, the adversary is not explicitly modeled in publications on stabilization. In the analysis of stabilizing systems the influence of transient faults is indirectly taken into account by considering any state in stabilizing systems as being a potential initial state. This models the situation that a fault-action just occurred – the stabilizing system is in an arbitrary state – and now time is given to the stabilizing system to reestablish a legal state if the pre-requisites for recovery are satisfied (else the system can not guarantee recovery).

The formal definition of stabilization is based on the following three distinct kinds of behavior that a fault-tolerant system displays. As long as no fault occurs it performs the task that it is designed for. As soon as a fault occurs which results in a state within the fault-span of the system, the system re-converges to a so-called *legal* state [4] from which point on it displays the original fault free behavior. For a fault, resulting in a state where the prerequisites for recovery are no longer given, i.e. outside the fault-span, nothing can be guaranteed.

Based on the above informal description and [3], stabilization can be formally defined as follows. Let predicate *le* characterize the set of legal system states and predicate *fs* the fault-span and let S^T denote the system obtained by substituting the initial condition of fts S by predicate T (true).

Definition 5. *Given fts S, fault span fs and predicate le, with $\models le \rightarrow fs$. System S is stabilizing w.r.t. fs and le iff S^T satisfies the following properties:*

convergence: $S^T \models \Box(fs \rightarrow \Diamond le)$
closure: $\quad S^T \models \Box(fs \rightarrow \Box fs)$
$\quad\quad\quad\quad S^T \models \Box(le \rightarrow \Box le)$.

$\Box$

The first clause states that system S converges from any state in *fs* back to a legal state. The second and third clause state that the predicates *fs*, *le* are invariant under transitions of S.

Note, that the convergence clause is not equivalent to $S \models \Box(fs \rightarrow \Diamond le)$ due to the possibility of unreachable *fs*-states in S. However, $S^T \models \Box(fs \rightarrow \Diamond le)$ is equivalent to $S^T \models fs \rightarrow \Diamond le$ due to suffix closure of $[S^T]$. We nevertheless stick to the formulation given in the definition because Theorem 1 and the proof rules presented in [11] address the more general convergence properties $\Box(p \rightarrow \Diamond q)$. Next, we elaborate on the structural properties of stabilizing systems and explain the corresponding verification strategy.

Design of Stabilizing Systems

Most publications on stabilization built complex stabilizing systems by composing simpler stabilizing systems referred to as the *phases* of the complex system (see [15] for an extensive list of references). Instead of constructing one monolithic system that solves the overall stabilization requirement, a number of stabilizing phases are constructed, each of them solving a well defined subproblem. These phases are built such that the computation of phase S_i, $i \in \{1, \ldots, n\}$, depends on the computation of the phases $S_j, j < i$, which temporally precede S_i. The fault-span of S_i is constructed to be a superset of the set of legal states of phase S_{i-1}. Thus, in order to converge to its set of legal states, S_i depends on S_{i-1} in the sense that S_{i-1} has to establish a state within S_i's fault span, since otherwise convergence of S_i can not be guaranteed. The convergence of such a composed system can be described by a *convergence stair*, cf. [7].

Definition 6. *Given fts S. A sequence of state predicates $\langle p_0, p_1, p_2, \ldots p_n \rangle$ with $\models p_i \to p_{i-1}$ for $1 \leq i \leq n$ is a convergence stair for S iff S^{T} satisfies the following properties:*

convergence: $S^{\mathrm{T}} \models \Box(p_{i-1} \to \Diamond p_i)$ *for $1 \leq i \leq n$*
closure: $S^{\mathrm{T}} \models \Box(p_i \to \Box p_i)$ *for $0 \leq i \leq n$*

□

It is simple to show that a system S stabilizes w.r.t. *fs* and *le* iff there exists a convergence stair for S which satisfies the so called *boundary condition* $\models p_0 \leftrightarrow fs$ and $\models p_n \leftrightarrow le$. The idea of Definition 6 is the following: Starting in a state where predicate *fs* ($= p_0$) holds, the system establishes in a first phase predicate p_1 which is closed under system execution; having established p_1, eventually p_2 will be established. This pattern is repeated till finally *le* ($= p_n$) is established.

Constructing stabilizing systems by means of phases results in a natural and appealing decomposition of the initial stabilization requirement into simpler stabilization requirements. But decomposing a stabilization requirement into simpler stabilization requirements, then constructing phases which meet the simpler requirements, and finally composing these phases *sequentially* does not solve the problem of obtaining overall stabilization. Though there exists a *virtual* temporal ordering between the phases of stabilizing systems the phases actually have to be executed in *parallel*, i.e., without explicit sequencing [13] which results in a very high degree of parallelism in those systems. Assume system S is sequentially composed of two phases. If S indeed satisfies the convergence requirement in Definition 5 – which requires that the system converges no matter in which state (including program counters) it currently resides – then the first phase is obviously superfluous, since S guarantees convergence already by the second phase. If the first phase is not superfluous, S would not satisfy Definition 5, because started on the control location between the two phases, S could not guarantee convergence.

So, we observe:

- The phases of a stabilizing system have to be constructed such that they perform their task when executed in isolation. This issue is referred to as *phase correctness.*
- The phases have to be constructed – because they execute in parallel – such that they do not prevent the other phases from converging which considerably complicates their design. This issue is referred to as *interference freedom* of the phases.

The main verification strategy applied by designers of stabilizing systems is to give (typically informal) correctness proofs for the phases in isolation and to give evidence that phases are indeed interference free. In the next section we extend the set of proof rules presented in [11] by rules which allow to deal with phase correctness and interference freedom separately.

4 Phased Composition and Proof Rules

Assume we are given a system which consists of a set of phases whose execution overlap. We refer to this system as the *distributed system.* We divide the convergence proof – this is the hard part of the stabilization proof – of the distributed system into two parts:

1. **Phase Correctness:** We abstract the distributed system to a so-called *phased system* which performs the phases in a strict temporal order. The first part of the convergence proof then consists of verifying convergence of the phased system.
2. **Interference Freedom of Phases:** The second part of the proof requires to establish a *link* between the phased and the distributed system which allows to conclude convergence of the distributed system from the convergence of the phased system. This link is formulated by means of a convergence preserving refinement relation [14].

4.1 Phased Composition

We advocate a composition operator that allows to combine stabilizing phases into a stabilizing compound system such that the phases are actually executed in *strict temporal order*, i.e. without any interference. In the definition of phased composition we use an operator $\{p\} \rightarrow$ which adds state predicate p as additional guard to the transitions of a fair transition system. So, system $\{p\} \rightarrow S$ is identical to fts S besides the fact that all transition predicates $\rho \in T_s$ are replaced by $p \wedge \rho$ in $T_{\{p\} \rightarrow S}$. Now, phased composition can be defined as follows.

Definition 7. *Given systems $S_i, i \in \{1, \ldots, n\}$, and a sequence of predicates $\langle p_0, \ldots, p_n \rangle$. The phased composition of $S_i, i \in \{1, \ldots, n\}$, w.r.t. $\langle p_0, \ldots, p_n \rangle$ is defined by*

$$(S_1 \bullet \ldots \bullet S_n)_{\langle p_0, \ldots, p_n \rangle} \stackrel{def}{=} \{p_0 \wedge \neg p_1\} \rightarrow S_1 \| \ldots \| \{p_{n-1} \wedge \neg p_n\} \rightarrow S_n$$

□

Phased composition plays the same role in our setup as sequential composition and layered composition in approaches for phased reasoning (see [16] for references). However, phased composition cannot enforce the ordered execution of arbitrary systems. It is constructed to compose stabilizing phases.

Proposition 1. *Given systems $S_i, i \in \{1, \ldots, n\}$, where S_i is stabilizing w.r.t. p_{i-1}, p_i and $\models p_i \rightarrow p_{i-1}$ for $1 \leq i \leq n$. Then, the sequence $\langle p_0, \ldots, p_n \rangle$ is a convergence stair for $(S_1 \bullet \ldots \bullet S_n)^{\mathsf{T}}_{\langle p_0, \ldots, p_n \rangle}$, i.e.:*

$$\text{convergence: } (S_1 \bullet \ldots \bullet S_n)^{\mathsf{T}}_{\langle p_0, \ldots, p_n \rangle} \models \Box(p_{i-1} \rightarrow \Diamond p_i) \ \text{ for } 1 \leq i \leq n$$
$$\text{closure: } \quad (S_1 \bullet \ldots \bullet S_n)^{\mathsf{T}}_{\langle p_0, \ldots, p_n \rangle} \models \Box(p_i \rightarrow \Box p_i) \ \text{ for } 0 \leq i \leq n \ .$$

□

As a corollary we obtain that system $(S_1 \bullet \ldots \bullet S_n)_{\langle p_0, \ldots, p_n \rangle}$ is stabilizing w.r.t. p_0, p_n. According to the definition of $\{p\} \rightarrow$, the phased composition operator adds guards to the transitions of the systems $S_i, i \in \{1, \ldots, n\}$. These predicates $p_0, \ldots, p_n$ generally refer to *global* state information in system $(S_1 \bullet \ldots \bullet S_n)_{\langle p_0, \ldots, p_n \rangle}$. A guard $p_{i-1} \wedge \neg p_i$ enforces phase S_i to await the convergence of phases $S_j, j < i$, before it starts manipulating the state space in order to establish a state that satisfies predicate p_i. As soon as p_i has been established the next phase becomes activated. This pattern repeats till finally a p_n-state is reached. So, without introducing control locations the added guards enforce that phases are executed in strict temporal order without any interference. Note, that the phased system terminates (indefinitely stutters) once it reaches a p_n-state, rather than displaying some fault-free behavior. We could eliminate the guard $\neg p_n$ from transitions of phase S_n in Definition 7, but in this paper we are only interested in the mechanisms which provide the convergence towards some set of legal states and not in any kind of fault-free behavior which is displayed afterwards.

System $(S_1 \bullet \ldots \bullet S_n)_{\langle p_0, \ldots, p_n \rangle}$ is only interesting as an abstraction of a system where the execution of the S_i overlap. No algorithm designer would use phased composition as a composition operator to construct stabilizing compound system from simpler stabilizing phases, because the resulting transition guards use *global* (i.e. not locally detectable) information about the overall state space. Such global guards are extremely costly to implement and result in rather inefficient systems so they are generally avoided at the price of interference between phases.

4.2 Proof Rules for Convergence

In the forthcoming rules the premises are of the form $\models p$ (validity of state predicate p), $S \models \varphi$ (program validity for temporal formula φ), and $S \sqsubseteq_i S'$. The last kind of premise refers to a refinement relation $\sqsubseteq_i$ which will be introduced formally in Section 5. This refinement relation is shown to support convergence preserving refinement. So, to exploit the structural characteristics of stabilizing systems we leave the framework of assertional and temporal reasoning as introduced in [11] and incorporate refinement arguments.

We first investigate the convergence of the phased system. By convention we omit the range of indices if it is clear from the context.

$$
\begin{array}{l}
S_i \text{ stabilizing w.r.t. } p_{i-1}, p_i \\
\models p_i \rightarrow p_{i-1} \\
\hline
(S_1 \bullet \ldots \bullet S_n)^{\mathrm{T}}_{\langle p_0, \ldots, p_n \rangle} \models \Box(p_0 \rightarrow \Diamond p_n)
\end{array}
\qquad \text{Conv-PS}
$$

Convergence of Phased System

Rule Conv-PS is a consequence of Proposition 1. This rule is the primary objective for the definition of phased composition. Rule Conv-PS is compositional by considering the convergence of the phases S_i in isolation.

The second part of the convergence proof for the distributed system consists of proving that convergence of the phases, when executed overlapped, is not spoiled.

$$
\begin{array}{l}
S_i \text{ stabilizing w.r.t. } p_{i-1}, p_i \\
\models p_i \rightarrow p_{i-1} \\
(S_1 \| \ldots \| S_n)^{\mathrm{T}} \sqsubseteq_i S_i^{\mathrm{T}}, \quad \text{for } i \in \{1, \ldots, n\} \\
\hline
(S_1 \| \ldots \| S_n)^{\mathrm{T}} \models \Box(p_0 \rightarrow \Diamond p_n)
\end{array}
\qquad \text{Conv-DS}
$$

Convergence Distributed System

The idea in this rule is the following: From the first premise of rule Conv-DS we have that $S_i^{\mathrm{T}} \models \Box(p_{i-1} \rightarrow \Diamond p_i)$. The premise $(S_1 \| \ldots \| S_n)^{\mathrm{T}} \sqsubseteq_i S_i^{\mathrm{T}}$ is supposed to guarantee that S_i establishes the convergence from p_{i-1}-states to p_i-states despite the interference of other phases, i.e. that $(S_1 \| \ldots \| S_n)^{\mathrm{T}} \models \Box(p_{i-1} \rightarrow \Diamond p_i)$ holds, too. Relation $\sqsubseteq_i$ is defined as inclusion of observable behavior as standard refinement relations but with a different notion of observability. In order to decide whether a computation σ satisfies a convergence property $\varphi = \Box(p \rightarrow \Diamond q)$ we need not observe all states in the computation. The fact that $\sigma \models \varphi$ holds is witnessed or disproved by the subsequence of states in σ, restricted to set $V_p \cup V_q$, that satisfy predicate $p \vee q$. Now, informally $(S_1 \| \ldots \| S_n)^{\mathrm{T}} \sqsubseteq_i S_i^{\mathrm{T}}$ states for a computation of system $S_1 \| \ldots \| S_n$: if we consider the subsequence of states which witness or disprove the satisfaction of $\Box(p_{i-1} \rightarrow \Diamond p_i)$—these are all p_{i-1}-states— then we may observe the same subsequence in a computation of S_i. Since all computations in S_i satisfy the convergence property $\Box(p_{i-1} \rightarrow \Diamond p_i)$ we conclude that $(S_1 \| \ldots \| S_n)^{\mathrm{T}} \models \Box(p_{i-1} \rightarrow \Diamond p_i)$ holds, too. So, proving $(S_1 \| \ldots \| S_n)^{\mathrm{T}} \sqsubseteq_i S_i$ establishes interference freedom of phases $S_j, j \neq i$, w.r.t. convergence of S_i. Technical details of relation $\sqsubseteq_i$ as well as the soundness of rule Conv-DS are given next.

5   The Refinement Relation

We use the refinement approach presented in [14]. While standard refinement approaches typically preserve all temporal properties of the system which is refined, the approach presented here also allows the preservation of only specific temporal properties. This generality is need in order to formulate the relation between the phased and the distributed system.

In most existing refinement setups the definition of observable behavior of computations is fixed. This definition is a parameter of our refinement relation.

Definition 8. *An observer $\mathcal{O}$ is characterized by a tuple $\mathcal{O} = (p, E)$ consisting of a state predicate p and a set E of externally visible variables. We define the set of free variables of $\mathcal{O}$ as $V_{\mathcal{O}} \stackrel{def}{=} V_p \cup E$.* □

An observer observes a set E of externally visible variables but only in those states of a computation that satisfy the so-called *filter predicate* p. The idea is – in the context of this paper – that the filter predicate is used to characterize states which witness or disprove that a computation satisfies some convergence property. The observer notion in Definition 8 induces the following definitions of observable behavior of computations. Here, operator Π_p, for state predicate p, projects a sequence of states to its subsequence of states which satisfy p and operator Π_E denotes restriction of states to the set E of variables. Operator Π_E acts point-wise on sequences of states.

Definition 9. *Let σ be a computation of system A. For observer $\mathcal{O} = (p, E)$ with $V_{\mathcal{O}} \subseteq V_A$ the observable behavior of σ w.r.t. $\mathcal{O}$ is $beh_{\mathcal{O}}(\sigma) \stackrel{def}{=} \Pi_E(\Pi_p(\sigma))$.*

The induced notion of observable behavior for systems is $beh_E(A) \stackrel{def}{=} \{beh_E(\sigma) | \sigma \in [A]\}$. Refinement is generally defined as inclusion of observable behaviors modulo *stuttering* [1]. We say that a sequence of states $seq = \langle s_0, s_1, s_2, s_3 \ldots \rangle$ is *stutter free* if $s_{i-1} \neq s_i$ for all $0 < i < |seq|$ where $|seq|$ denotes the length of seq. Operator $\natural$ assigns to each sequence seq its stutter free version, i.e. the stutter free sequence obtained by replacing every maximal subsequence $\langle s_i, s_{i+1} \ldots \rangle$ of identical elements in seq by element s_i. Two sequences σ, τ are *stutter equivalent*, denoted by $\sigma \simeq \tau$, if $\natural(\sigma) = \natural(\tau)$. The *stutter closure* of a set A of sequences is defined as $\Gamma(A) \stackrel{def}{=} \{\tau \mid \exists \sigma \in [A]. \sigma \simeq \tau\}$.

Definition 10. *Given systems A, C and observer $\mathcal{O} = (p, E)$ with $V_{\mathcal{O}} \subseteq V_A \cap V_C$. C refines A w.r.t. $\mathcal{O}$, denoted by $C \sqsubseteq_{\mathcal{O}} A$, iff $\Gamma(beh_{\mathcal{O}}(C)) \subseteq \Gamma(beh_{\mathcal{O}}(A))$.*

The main result which enables us to use this parameterized refinement relation for modular verification of stabilizing systems is stated in the following theorem.

Theorem 1. *Given ftss A, C and $\varphi = \square(p \rightarrow \Diamond q)$ for state predicates p, q. If $A \models \square(p \rightarrow \Diamond q)$ and $C \sqsubseteq_{\mathcal{O}_\varphi} A$ for $\mathcal{O}_\varphi = (p \vee q, V_p \cup V_q)$ then $C \models \square(p \rightarrow \Diamond q)$.*

This theorem states that the notion of observability induced by observer $\mathcal{O}_\varphi$ suffices to conclude from $A \models \square(p \rightarrow \Diamond q)$ and $C \sqsubseteq_{\mathcal{O}_\varphi} A$ that also $C \models \square(p \rightarrow \Diamond q)$ holds. Observer $\mathcal{O}_\varphi$ observes the sequence of states in a computation that witness or disprove the satisfaction of φ. These relevant states in a computation are those satisfying $p \vee q$ and the relevant state information which needs to be preserved during refinement are the values of variables in set $V_p \cup V_q$. Based on the previous theorem we can now be more precise in the formulation of rule Conv-DS.

Theorem 2. *Given S_i where $i \in \{1, \ldots, n\}$. For $\mathcal{O}_i \stackrel{def}{=} (p_{i-1}, V_{p_{i-1}} \cup V_{p_i})$ with $i \in \{1, \ldots, n\}$ the following rule is sound:*

$$
\begin{array}{l}
S_i \text{ stabilizing w.r.t. } p_{i-1}, p_i \\
\models p_i \to p_{i-1} \\
\underline{(S_1 \| \ldots \| S_n)^{\mathrm{T}} \sqsubseteq_{\mathcal{O}_i} S_i^{\mathrm{T}}, \quad \text{for } i \in \{1, \ldots, n\}} \\
(S_1 \| \ldots \| S_n)^{\mathrm{T}} \models \Box(p_0 \to \Diamond p_n) \\
\\
\text{Convergence Distributed System}
\end{array}
\qquad \text{Conv-DS}
$$

This rule allows the following two kinds of non-malicious interference of phases $S_j, j \neq i$, w.r.t. convergence of S_i:

- The state changes caused by S_j are non-observable w.r.t. $\mathcal{O}_i$, i.e. either stutter steps or steps resulting in states that do not satisfy p_{i-1}.
- The state changes caused by S_j are indeed observable w.r.t. $\mathcal{O}_i$; then they must be possible state changes of S_i w.r.t. set $V_{p_{i-1}} \cup V_{p_i}$.

According to our experience, this comprises the kind of non-malicious interference encountered in stabilizing systems. More material on $\sqsubseteq_{\mathcal{O}}$, in particular a proof method, is elaborated in [15].

6 Example

In this section we apply the advocated framework to the verification of a stabilizing graph coloring algorithm which is a generalization of the one presented in [6].

The objective of the algorithm is to assign colors to the nodes of so-called *admissible* graphs – a superset of the set of planar graphs – so that adjacent nodes get different colors.

We prove that the algorithm is fault tolerant w.r.t. adversaries which change the colors of nodes and which change the topology of the graph by adding and/or removing edges between nodes. However, edges may only be rearranged as long as the resulting graph is still admissible. This constitutes the fault-span in our investigations. The algorithm in [6] considers the smaller class of *planar* graphs and demonstrates fault-tolerance w.r.t. adversaries which solely change colors of nodes.

The algorithm that we consider consists of two phases (cf. [6]):

1. A **redirection phase** which transforms any given admissible graph into a directed acyclic graph (DAG) with an out-degree of less than six. Such graphs will be called *properly directed*.
2. A **coloring phase** which colors properly directed graphs with no more than six colors.

The rest of the section is organized as follows. First we define formally the set of admissible graphs. Then we present the algorithm composed from the two phases mentioned above and prove its stabilization by means of the advocated framework.

6.1 Admissible and properly colored graphs

In order to characterize the set of admissible graphs we use the following definitions. We assume that there exists a fixed, finite set of nodes $\mathcal{V}$. Each node is identified with an element in set $\{1, 2, \ldots, m\}$, where m is the number of nodes in $\mathcal{V}$. The adjacency relation among nodes is described by a function $adj : \{1, 2, \ldots, m\} \times \{1, 2, \ldots, m\} \longrightarrow \{T, F\}$ with $\forall i, j \in \mathcal{V}.\ adj(i, j) = adj(j, i)$ since adj is supposed to describe an undirected graph.

The following predicate ag (admissible graph) specifies that the graph described by $\mathcal{V}$ and adj has two properties: 1) it contains no self-loops and 2) each of its non-empty sub-graphs contains at least one node with less than six neighbors.

$$(\text{adm. graph})\, ag \stackrel{\text{def}}{=} \forall i \in \mathcal{V}.\ \neg adj(i, i)$$
$$\wedge \forall \mathcal{V}' \subseteq \mathcal{V}.\ (\mathcal{V}' \neq \emptyset \rightarrow (\exists i \in \mathcal{V}'.\ |\{j \in \mathcal{V}' \mid adj(i, j)\}| \leq 5))$$

Predicate ag constitutes the fault span of our system. Each node $i \in \mathcal{V}$ maintains a variable c_i to record its color $col \in \{col_1, \ldots, col_6\}$. Let $Col \stackrel{\text{def}}{=} \{col_1, \ldots, col_6\}$ and $C \stackrel{\text{def}}{=} \{c_1, \ldots, c_m\}$. Assuming that the underlying graph is admissible, the task of the system is to eventually establish the following property and to keep it invariant afterwards:

$$(\text{colored})\quad clrd \stackrel{\text{def}}{=} \forall i, j \in \mathcal{V}.\ adj(i, j) \rightarrow c_i \neq c_j.$$

6.2 The redirection phase

The redirection phase uses a set $X \stackrel{\text{def}}{=} \{x_1, \ldots, x_m\}$ of integer variables, cf. [6]. The x_i serve to give direction to edges of the graph. Each node i in the graph maintains a corresponding variable x_i. We introduce a predicate $i \longmapsto j$ to denote that there exists an edge in the graph directed from node i to node j. Formally $i \longmapsto j$ is defined as $i \longmapsto j \stackrel{\text{def}}{=} adj(i, j) \wedge [(x_i < x_j) \vee (x_i = x_j \wedge i < j)]$. Note, that the variables $x_i, i \in \{1, \ldots, m\}$, specify a directed acyclic graph irrespectively of their values.

The redirection phase is supposed to establish an admissible graph which is a DAG with out-degree of at most five. This is characterized by predicate pd.

$$(\text{properly directed})\quad pd \stackrel{\text{def}}{=} ag \wedge \forall i \in \mathcal{V}.\ |\{j \in \mathcal{V} \mid i \longmapsto j\}| \leq 5$$

We introduce the abbreviation $out_i \stackrel{\text{def}}{=} \{j \in \mathcal{V} \mid i \longmapsto j\}$. The redirection phase works as follows: whenever a node finds that it has more than five outgoing edges, it redirects all edges towards itself. So, phase $Ph_1 \stackrel{\text{def}}{=} (V_1, \Theta_1, T_{red}, WF_1, SF_1)$ is defined by $V_1 = X \cup \{adj\}, \Theta_1 = ag, T_{red} = \{t_{red_1}, \ldots, t_{red_m}\}, WF_1 = \{t_{red_1}, \ldots, t_{red_m}\}$, and $SF_1 = \emptyset$ with

$$\rho_{t_{red_i}} \stackrel{\text{def}}{=} |out_i| > 5 \wedge x_i' = 1 + max\{x_j | j \in out_i\}.$$

By convention, variables which do not occur primed in transition predicates do not change their value.

6.3 The coloring phase

The task of the coloring phase Ph_2 is to assign colors to the nodes of a properly directed graph in order to turn it into a properly colored graph, defined as follows:

$$\text{(properly colored)} \quad pc \stackrel{\text{def}}{=} ag \wedge pd \wedge clrd$$

We use the abbreviation $outcol_i \stackrel{\text{def}}{=} \{col \in Col \mid \exists j \in out_i. \; c_j = col\}$ and define the second phase $Ph_2 \stackrel{\text{def}}{=} (V_2, \Theta_2, T_{col}, WF_2, SF_2)$ by: $V_2 = X \cup C \cup \{adj\}, \Theta_2 = pd, T_{col} = \{t_{col_1}, \ldots, t_{col_m}\}, WF_2 = \{t_{col_1}, \ldots, t_{col_m}\}$, and $SF_2 = \emptyset$ with

$$\rho_{t_{col_i}} \stackrel{\text{def}}{=} \exists j \in out_i. \; (c_j = c_i \wedge c_i' \in any(Col \setminus outcol_i)).$$

Here, $any(C)$, for $C \subseteq Col$, selects an arbitrary element of set C with the convention $any(\emptyset) = any(Col)$. Now, we investigate the stabilization of $Ph_1 \| Ph_2$ w.r.t. the fault-span ag and the set pc of legal states.

6.4 Stabilization proof for $Ph_1 \| Ph_2$

We observe that the execution of phases in system $Ph_1 \| Ph_2$ indeed overlap, since the coloring of nodes starts before a properly directed graph is established. According to Definition 5 we need to establish the convergence and closure of system $(Ph_1 \| Ph_2)^{\top}$ w.r.t. predicates ag, pc.

The closure part is easily established by proving $ag \wedge \rho_t \to ag'$ (resp. $pc \wedge \rho_t \to pc'$) for all transitions $t \in T_{Ph_1 \| Ph_2}$ (see [15] for details). In order to prove the convergence part we use system $(Ph_1 \bullet Ph_2)_{\langle ag, pd, pc \rangle}$ as abstraction of $Ph_1 \| Ph_2$ and apply the introduced rules.

Application of rule Conv-PS leaves us with the proof obligation that Ph_1 stabilizes w.r.t. ag, pd and that Ph_2 stabilizes w.r.t. pd, pc. Since neither Ph_1 nor Ph_2 are themselves constructed from phases we can establish the proof obligation for the phases by application of the closure and convergence rules presented in [11].

Proposition 2.

– $Ph_1 \models \Box(ag \to \Diamond pd) \wedge \Box(ag \to \Box ag) \wedge \Box(pd \to \Box pd)$.

$-$ $Ph_2 \models \Box(pd \to \Diamond pc) \land \Box(pd \to \Box pd) \land \Box(pc \to \Box pc).$ $\qquad$ $\Box$

Now we are left with the interference freedom of Ph_1 and Ph_2. Application of rule Conv-DS and Theorem 2 gives two further proof obligations.

Proposition 3. $(Ph_1 \| Ph_2)^{\mathsf{T}}$ *refines* Ph_1^{T} *w.r.t.* $\mathcal{O} = (ag, X \cup \{adj\})$.

Informally, this proposition states: Only observing the redirection of edges in an admissible graph in system $(Ph_1 \| Ph_2)^{\mathsf{T}}$ yields a possible behavior of Ph_1^{T} w.r.t. $\mathcal{O}$.

Proposition 4. $(Ph_1 \| Ph_2)^{\mathsf{T}}$ *refines* Ph_2^{T} *w.r.t.* $\mathcal{O} = (pd, X \cup C \cup \{adj\})$.

This proposition states: Only observing state changes in system $(Ph_1 \| Ph_2)^{\mathsf{T}}$ if adj and X describe a properly directed graph yields a possible behavior of Ph_2^{T} w.r.t. observer $\mathcal{O}$. Since we have no space to elaborate on *delayed simulation* – the proof method for $\sqsubseteq_{\mathcal{O}}$ – we refer for the proof of these two propositions to [15].

From the above results we conclude:

Theorem 3. *System* $Ph_1 \| Ph_2$ *stabilizes w.r.t.* ag, pc.

So, we proved that system $Ph_1 \| Ph_2$ is fault-tolerant w.r.t. adversaries that:

- arbitrarily change colors of nodes, i.e. variables in set C,
- arbitrarily change direction of edges, i.e. variables in set X, and
- change edges between nodes, but only to the extent that the resulting graph is still admissible.

7 Conclusion and Related Work

In this paper we presented a formal framework for the modular verification of stabilizing systems. The framework allows to use computer-aided-verification machinery for correctness proofs of stabilizing systems.

Our framework resembles those for phased reasoning about distributed systems as presented [5, 9, 10, 18]. In [16] we demonstrate that these approaches are not applicable for stabilizing systems because they are based on a notion of *independence* between phases which does not exist in stabilizing systems. Furthermore, in [15] we prove that a slight variant of the presented approach (where phased composition is replaced by standard sequential composition) extends all previous approaches for phased reasoning.

Stomp gives in [19] a common proof pattern resorting to phases to show that the parallel composition of phases actually converges as specified in the convergence stair. The work by Stomp mixes arguments concerning stabilization of phases with arguments concerning interference freedom of phases. We consider it to be essential to separate these two issues in order to structure the verification and in order to apply those formal techniques which are best suited for the different tasks (program verification for phase correctness and refinement techniques for the interference freedom). In particular, our separation allows to *reuse* phase correctness proofs of standard phases (such as spanning tree constructions, leader election, clock synchronization diffusing computations and many more).

Furthermore, there exist stratification techniques for stabilizing systems whose phases do not write variables of logically preceding phases, see [8, 2]. It is not difficult to prove that for such systems the third proof obligation in rule Conv-DS is always satisfied, however the converse is not true. Thus, the presented approach is more general.

Acknowledgments: I thank A. Arora, A. Pnueli, E.R. Olderog and W.P. de Roever for many valuable comments on [15] from where I have taken most of the presented material.

References

1. M. Abadi and L. Lamport. The existence of refinement mappings. *Theoretical Computer Science*, 82(2), 1991.
2. A. Arora, P. Attie, M. Evangelist, and M.G. Gouda. Convergence of iteration systems. *Distributed Computing*, 7, 1993.
3. A. Arora and M.G. Gouda. Closure and convergence: a foundation of fault-tolerant computing. *IEEE Transactions on Software Engineering*, 19, 1993.
4. E.W. Dijkstra. Self stabilizing systems in spite of distributed control. *Communications of the ACM*, 17(11), 1974.
5. T. Elrad and N. Francez. Decomposition of distributed programs into communication closed layers. *Science of Computer Programming*, 2, 1982.
6. S. Ghosh and M.H. Karaata. A self stabilizing algorithm for graph coloring. In *Proceedings of the 29th Allerton Conference on Control, Communication, and Computing*, October 1991.
7. M.G. Gouda and N. Multari. Stabilizing communication protocols. *IEEE Transactions on Computers*, 40, 1991.
8. T. Herman. *Adaptively through Distributed Convergence*. PhD thesis, Department of Computer Science, University of Texas Austin, USA, 1991.
9. W. Janssen, M. Poel, and J. Zwiers. Action systems and action refinement in the development of parallel systems. volume 527 of *LNCS*. Springer-Verlag, 1991.
10. S. Katz and D. Peled. Interleaving set temporal logic. *Theoretical Computer Science*, 75(3), 1990.
11. Y. Lakhnech and M. Siegel. Temporal logic for stabilizing systems. In *ICTL 97: International Conference on Temporal Logic*. Kluwer Academic Publishers, 1997.
12. Z. Manna and A. Pnueli. *The Temporal Logic of Reactive and Concurrent Systems*. Springer Verlag, 1991.
13. M. Schneider. Self-stabilization. *ACM Computing Surveys*, 25, 1993.
14. M. Siegel. A refinement theory that supports both 'decrease of non-determinism' and 'increase of parallelism'. In S. Smolka, editor, *CONCUR '95 (Conference on Concurrency Theory)*, volume 962 of *LNCS*, 1995.
15. M. Siegel. *Phased Design and Verification of Stabilizing Systems*. PhD thesis, Christian Albrechts University of Kiel, Germany, 1996.
16. M. Siegel and F. Stomp. Extending the limits of sequentially phased reasoning. In P. S. Thiagarajan, editor, *FST&TCS 14 (Foundations of Software Technology & Theoretical Computer Science)*, volume 880 of *LNCS*, 1994.

17. Stabilization Research at Iowa, http://www.cs.uiowa.edu/ftp/selfstab/main.html.
18. F. Stomp and W.P. de Roever. A principle for sequentially phased reasoning about distributed algorithms. *Formal Aspects of Computing*, 6(6), 1994.
19. F.A. Stomp. Structured design of self-stabilizing programs. In *Proceedings of the 2nd Israel Symposium on Theory of Computing and Systems*, 1993.

Synchronizing Clocked Transition Systems

Mannes Poel and Job Zwiers

University of Twente, Department of Computer Science,
P.O. Box 217, 7500 AE Enschede, The Netherlands
E-mail: {mpoel,zwiers}@cs.utwente.nl

Abstract. A model related to the CTS model of [KMP96] is introduced that deals with distributed systems with clocks that are not perfectly synchonized. The basis of the system is temporal logic of actions [Lam91], which ensures that the model is easily integrated with other formalisms. Verification rules and refinement rules for timed modules are proposed, and applied to a clock synchronization algorithm derived from [CAS86].

Real-time systems are often *distributed* systems. Real-time protocols for such systems cannot assume that clocks and timers at different network sites run at the same speed. In fact, one often runs clock synchronization algorithms to ensure that the difference in clock readings does not grow arbitrarily large. When one wants to reason formally about such algorithms, then the underlying model must cope with *local clocks*, each running at its own speed. In [AL94,JPXZ94,KMP96] a rather simple model for real-time systems is used, based on the idea that "clocks" can be seen as system variables that are updated periodically, and that "time" itself can be seen as a special master clock that is never reset or modified otherwise by the program. This model lends itself well for generalization to the case with many local clocks. In essence, one introduces *several* master clocks that cannot be modified by the program, one for each local time scale so to say. A so called *clock assumption* is used to state what relationship between local clock readings is guaranteed, despite differences in clock speed. When time progresses, all clocks advance at different rates, but always such that the clock assumption is satisfied. Clock assumptions were defined in [Zwi92] for a partial order model of concurrency. Here we use a simpler model, based on interleaving of ordinary transitions and synchronization of timed transitions. We discuss two concrete examples of clock assumptions, called the "ϵ-synchronization, and "bounded drift". For the former, master clocks are assumed to stay within a bound ϵ from one each other. For the bounded drift assumption this is not the case; all that is assumed is that the different clock *rates* stay within a certain bound from each other. In [AH94] the bounded drift assumption is mentioned, in the form of differential constraints on clock variables. Such constraints are introduced in our framework by incorporating them in a timed module called the clock assumption. The latter is seen as a process that runs in parallel with the rest of the program. We illustrate the formal verification of systems with clock assumptions by providing a correctness proof for a clock synchronization algorithm. The algorithm starts off with a set of clocks satisfying only the bounded drift clock assumption, and establishes via synchronization messages a set of ϵ-synchronized clocks [CAS86].

An interesting question is what sort of formalism should be used to deal with multiple time scales. The problem is not only to invent an appropriate model, but also how to integrate it with existing formalisms. Here we have taken the approach advocated in, for instance, [Heh84,Hoa85,ZdR89,Lam91], where the use of plain logic as a universal basis is advocated. Thanks to this approach we are able to define so called timed modules as a simple abbreviation of temporal logic formulae. Timed modules can be compared to the timed automata of [AD91,AD94] and to the clocked transition systems in [KMP96], except that the transition relation is split into an asynchronous part, describing the "ordinary" transitions caused by the program, and a synchronous part that is used here solely to describe progress of time. The reason for this separation is that a parallel composition operator can easily be defined for timed modules, in terms of simple logic operations. We provide a number of verification rules for timed modules, all of which can be seen as derived rules from temporal logic and predicate logic. Because we define timed modules as abbreviations of temporal formulae, rules for verifying temporal formulae or for refinement of timed modules can be mixed freely. An interesting rule is the auxiliary variables rule [OG76], that can be seen here as a derived rule for hiding variables. The difference between hidden variables and auxiliary variables is that the former are just "not visible" anymore, whereas the latter type of variables can be completely removed from the program, after one has verified its correctness.

The paper is organized as follows. In section 1 we recall some basic facts from temporal logic. In section 2 we introduce transition systems, timed modules and clock assumptions. In section 3 we discuss refinement and verification rules for timed modules. Finally in section 4 we discuss the clock synchronization algorithm and the strategy of the correctness proof. Detailed proofs have been included in the appendix.

1 Timed Modules

The formalism that we use is temporal logic of actions, much like [Lam91]. On top of this logic we define transition systems, specifications, and real-time transition systems, as abbreviations of logic formulae. The advantage of this approach is that we have only a small set of basic constructs and proof rules, and that more elaborate proof rules follow as derived rules. This approach becomes in particular important when dealing with constructs and proof rules for real-time with multiple (not fully synchronized) clocks. Rather than inventing a whole new logic we show here that proof rules for such systems follow easily from first principles. The basis of the logic is predicate logic for actions and states. This is just ordinary predicate logic except that one distinguishes between primed and unprimed variables. Informally, a predicate logic formula $\Phi(\bar{x}, \bar{x}')$ describes the execution of a single action, where the unprimed variables refer to the old state and the primed variables refer to the new state. A special case are predicate formulae $\phi(\bar{x})$ without free occurrences of primed variables. These will be used for instance as program invariants. The syntax of the logic is given in figure 1. For a formal treatment of the semantics we refer to [Lam91]. We define the *correctness formula* of the form F_1 sat F_2, which denotes that $F_1 \rightarrow F_2$ is a *valid* temporal formula.

$$\phi ::= e_1 = e_2 \mid e_1 \leq e_2 \mid \phi_1 \wedge \phi_2 \mid \phi_1 \rightarrow \phi_2 \mid \exists x . \phi_1$$
$$F ::= \phi \mid \Box F_1 \mid F_1 \wedge F_2 \mid F_1 \rightarrow F_2 \mid \exists x . F_1$$

Fig. 1. Syntax of predicate formulae ϕ and temporal formulae F

Transition systems

A *transition system* $S = (\bar{x}, \Theta, \Phi)$ is a triple, consisting of:

- a finite list of (unprimed) variables $\bar{x}$,
- an initial state predicate $\Theta(\bar{x})$,
- a transition predicate $\Phi(\bar{x}, \bar{x}')$.
- we assume that $var(\Theta) \cup var(\Phi) = \{\bar{x}\}$.

We identify a transition system $S = (\bar{x}, \Theta, \Phi)$ with the temporal formula $\Theta \wedge \Box \Phi$, and we use the generic term *system* for transition systems and temporal formulae. It follows that S_1 sat S_2 denotes the validity of the temporal formula $(\Theta_1 \wedge \Box \Phi_1) \rightarrow (\Theta_2 \wedge \Box \Phi_2)$. For systems S we use *variable hiding* notation $S \backslash \{\bar{y}\}$ for the formula $\exists \bar{y} . S$. A formula like S_1 sat S_2 is actually equivalent to $S_1 \backslash \mathbf{y}$ sat S_2, where $\mathbf{y}$ is the set of variables that occur free in S_1 but not in S_2. In this situation we say that S_1 *implements* S_2, where the variables in $\mathbf{y}$ are *hidden*.

Timed Modules

A *timed module*, which has the form $(\bar{x}; \bar{T}; \bar{c}, \Theta, \Phi^A, \Phi^S)$, is a special kind of transition system. The variables have been split into three disjoint lists: a list $\bar{x}$ of *system variables*, a list $\bar{T}$ of *master clocks*, and a list $\bar{c}$ of *timers*. Both master clocks and timers are referred to as "clocks". Clocks are variables ranging over non-negative real numbers, and their value increases when time progresses. The difference between master clocks and timers is that timers can be set to a new value by the program, whereas master clocks only change by passage of time. For any system we assume that there is at least one master clock, but unlike [KMP96] we allow for *more* than one such clock. The reason is that we consider distributed systems where each independent module has its own physical master clock. We assume a certain degree of synchronization between the master clocks, formalized by means of a so called *clock assumption*, but we won't assume perfect synchrony here. The *initial state condition* Θ is the same as for general transition systems. The *asynchronous transition relation* Φ^A is a predicate formula that determines the possible state transitions for which the master clocks do not change, whereas the *synchronous transition relation* Φ_T determines the transitions where clock variables (both master clocks and timers) are increased. The idea of transitions that either increase time or change system variable, but not both, is custom in the theory of timed automata [XN92]. In many approaches to timed automata, it is assumed that all the program can do with timers (during an asynchronous transition) is to reset certain timers to zero, but that assumption need not be made here. Actually, our example concerns a clock synchronization algorithm where timers can be set to a *larger* value than their current value. When we view a timed module as a generic transition system, than the transition predicate of the latter is simply the disjunction $\Phi_A \vee \Phi_S$. The main reason for splitting the transition predicate into a synchonous and asynchronous part for timed modules is that we want to *compose* two timed modules $S_1 = (\bar{x}_1, \bar{T}_1, \bar{c}_1, \Theta_1, \Phi_1^A, \Phi_1^S)$ and $S_2 = (\bar{x}_2, \bar{T}_2, \bar{c}_2, \Theta_2, \Phi_2^A, \Phi_2^S)$. Here the intuition is that an asynchronous transition is taken by *either* S_1 *or* S_2, whereas a timed, i.e. synchronous, transition is taken by *both* S_1 *and* S_2 in a joint step. Let $\bar{l}_i$ denote the list of S_i variables that are not shared with S_{2-i}, for $i = 1, 2$. We define parallel composition

$$S_1 \parallel S_2 = (merge(\bar{x}_1, \bar{x}_2), merge(\bar{T}_1, \bar{T}_2), merge(\bar{c}_1, \bar{c}_2), \Theta_1 \wedge \Theta_2, \Phi^A, \Phi_1^S \wedge \Phi_2^S),$$

where Φ^A denotes the predicate formula $(\Phi_1^A \wedge \bar{l}_2' = \bar{l}_2) \vee (\Phi_2^A \wedge \bar{l}_1' = \bar{l}_1)$.

Globally synchronized clocks

At first we discuss a model based on the assumption of *globally synchronized clocks*. This is a simple model where all clocks progress *uniformly*. That is, when some clock variable t_1 increases by an amount of δ, then all other clocks increase by exactly the same amount. These systems are characterized by the fact that there is just a *single* master clock "T", that is used by all concurrent modules. Let us consider the effect of this on the parallel composition of transition modules. So, consider a system S of the form $S_1 \parallel S_2$, where

$$S_1 = (\bar{y}_1; T; \bar{c}_1, \Theta_1, \Phi_1^A, \Phi_1^S), \text{ and } S_2 = (\bar{y}_2; T; \bar{c}_2, \Theta_2, \Phi_2^A, \Phi_2^S)$$

An asynchronous transition of S boils down to an asynchronous transition of either S_1 or S_2. For instance, an asynchronous transition caused by S_1 might change some variables in $\bar{y}_1$ and might change some clocks from $\bar{c}_1$. A *synchronous transition* is specified by $\Phi_1^S \wedge \Phi_2^S$. Φ_1^S specifies that all clocks in $\bar{c}_1$ must increase by the same amount as T, and similarly Φ_2^S specifies that all clocks in $\bar{c}_2$ musts also increase by the same amount as T. A synchronous transition therefore must increase all clocks in $\bar{c}_1$ and in $\bar{c}_2$ by the same amount, and so *all* clocks run at the same speed.

Distributed clocks

Next, we discuss a timed model where we relax the global synchrony assumption. Rather, we assume that a distributed system is divided into a number of network nodes, where each node runs one or more processes. For each node $Node_j$ there must be one master clock variable T_j. We assume that each timer c is allocated at one of the network nodes, say at $Node_j$, and therefore runs at the same speed as the master clock T_j. However, we do *no longer assume* that all master clocks are perfectly synchronized. That is, the rate of increase for one network node might be different from the rate for another network node. Instead of this global synchrony, we allow for a more refined *clock assumption* relating the master clocks of the nodes $Node_1, \ldots, Node_m$. A simple example of a clock assumption is the notion of ϵ-synchronized clocks. Here, the clock assumption is in essence determined by an invariant

$$sync_\epsilon = \bigwedge_{1 \leq i < j \leq m} |T_i - T_j| \leq \epsilon.$$

An invariant like this is not guaranteed by the processes running at the various network nodes. Rather, for a given system one simply postulates that a certain clock assumption holds. Sometimes, a clock assumption can be justified by considering the physical structure of the underlying hardware that is used to implement clocks and timers. In more interesting cases, clocks are not simply hardware devices, but a combination of low-level hardware and on top of that, software that implements high-level clocks. High-level clocks typically have nicer features than their lower level counterparts, and a typical example of this is the ϵ-synchonization assumption. Such ϵ synchronized clocks have the desirable property that they will not drift apart farther and farther over time, since their difference is bounded by some constant ϵ. Unfortunately it is clear that physically decoupled timer devices will never behave like ϵ-synchronized clocks. A weaker, but more realistic, assumption is so called *bounded drift*, where one only assumes that that the *rates of increase* of time for different network nodes do not differ by more than a given amount ρ. This is captured by a clock assumption of the form:

$$drift_\rho = \bigwedge_{1 \leq i,j \leq m} \Delta T_i \leq (1 + \rho)\Delta T_j,$$

where for any clock T, we use ΔT to denote $T' - T$. With this clock assumption, clocks T_i and T_j can drift apart an arbitrary amount, but the maximal difference grows linearly over time. One of our aims is to study clock synchronization algorithms. Here one starts off with drifting clocks T_i and tries to implement timers c_i that behave as ϵ synchronized clocks. After this has been done one can treat these synchronized timers as the master clocks on a higher level of abstraction. Programs operating at this higher level can read, but not modify, the c_i variables.

Clock assumptions in general

Inspired by the two examples of clock assumption above, we now postulate that a clock assumption $\mathcal{CA}$ is, in general, a timed module of the form

$$\mathcal{CA} = (\langle T_1, \ldots, T_m \rangle, \Theta_{\mathcal{CA}}, false, \Phi_{\mathcal{CA}}).$$

Note that all we assume is that a clock assumption $\mathcal{CA}$ has as its list of variables just the list of all master clocks, and that we assume that no asynchronous transitions originate from $\mathcal{CA}$. Finally we define parallel composition of timed modules S_1 and S_2 with a clock assumption $\mathcal{CA}$ simply as the threefold parallel composition

$$S_1 \parallel \mathcal{CA} \parallel S_2.$$

Examples of clock assumptions
In the example in this paper we use clock assumptions based on the predicate formulae $sync_\epsilon$ and $drift_\rho$, defined as follows:

$$\mathcal{CA}sync(\epsilon) = (\langle T_1, \ldots, T_n \rangle, sync_\epsilon, false, sync'_\epsilon)$$

$$\mathcal{CA}drift(\delta, \rho) = (\langle T_1, \ldots, T_n \rangle, sync_\delta, false, drift_\rho)$$

The clock assumption of the form $\mathcal{CA}drift(\delta, \rho)$ is based on two parameters: a constant δ for the synchronization in the initial state, and a constant ρ determining the actual drift. We remark that neither of the two clock assumptions above is (with suitable choice for ϵ, δ, ρ) stronger than the other one. For instance, for a collection of ϵ-synchronized clocks it is possible that, for a short period of time, one of the clocks progresses much faster than other clocks. Actually, the clock synchronization algorithm that we discuss below cause clocks that are "lagging behind" to *jump* to a larger clock value. In [CAS86] a variation of our algorithm is discussed where such "jumps" are replaced by temporarily speeding up a clock that lags behind. The result is a set of clocks that satisfy both a $\mathcal{CA}sync(\epsilon)$ and a $\mathcal{CA}drift(\delta, \rho)$ assumption. (Of course this can be represented easily as a single clock assumption in our framework.)

Urgency conditions
The typical form of a clock transition relation is that clocks $\bar{t}$ can be increased by a nondeterministically determined amount, but limited by so called *urgency conditions*, also called time progress conditions in [KMP96]. The latter are conditions that can disable clock transitions and therefore, implicitly, force an ordinary transition to occur. We discuss how such urgency conditions are modelled. A *simple urgency condition* for a timed module with clocks $t_1, \ldots, t_n$ is a predicate formula of the form $t_i \leq C$, for some $i, 1 \leq i \leq n$, and some constant C. An *urgency condition* is a predicate formula U of the form

$$\bigwedge_{i \in I} (p_i \rightarrow \bigwedge_{j \in J_i} U_{i,j}),$$

where the assertions p_i do not contain free occurrences of clocks, and where each of the $U_{i,j}$ is a simple urgency condition. The corresponding timed transition relation for a timed module with system variables $\bar{x}$ is the following formula:

$$\Phi^S = \exists \delta > 0 \,.\, (\bar{t}' = \bar{t} + \bar{\delta} \wedge U(\bar{t}') \wedge \bar{x}' = \bar{x})$$

Here we, used the following "vector" notation: For a list $\bar{t} = \langle t_1, \ldots, t_n \rangle$ and a value δ we define $\bar{t} + \bar{\delta}$ as the list $\langle t_1 + \delta, \ldots, t_n + \delta \rangle$. For lists $\bar{t} = \langle t_1, \ldots, t_n \rangle$ and $\bar{t}' = \langle t'_1, \ldots, t'_n \rangle$ we define $\bar{t} \leq \bar{t}'$ as $t_1 \leq t'_1 \wedge \cdots \wedge t_n \leq t'_n$. Other "vector" operations" are defined in a similar style.

2 Refinement and verification

In principle, verification for timed modules boils down to verifying the validity of temporal formulae. In practice one aims at simpler derived rules that take the structure of transition systems and timed modules into account. Proof rules for temporal logic and for TLA are well known [KMP96,Lam91]. Here we provide a few *derived* rules that we used in the proof of the clock synchronization algorithm.

Theorem 1 (Verification of invariants).
Let $S = (\bar{x}, \bar{T}, \bar{c}, \Theta, \Phi^A, \Phi^S)$ be a timed module, and let I be a predicate formula without occurrences of primed variable names, with $var(I) \subseteq \{\bar{x}, \bar{T}, \bar{c}\}$. In order to check the correctness formula S *sat* $\Box I$ it suffices to check the validity of the following three verification conditions:

$$\Theta \to I, \quad (\Phi^A \wedge I) \to I', \quad \text{and} \ (\Phi^S \wedge I) \to I'. \qquad \Box$$

Next we present a rule for systems with with a *clock assumption* $\mathcal{CA}$.

Theorem 2 (Parallel composition).
Let

- $S_i = (\bar{x}_i, \bar{T}_i, \bar{c}_i, \Theta_i, \Phi_i^A, \Phi_i^S)$, for $i = 1, 2$,
- $\Phi_i^S = \exists \delta_i > 0 \,.\, \wedge \bar{t}'_i = \bar{t}_i + \bar{\delta}_i \wedge U_i(\bar{t}'_i) \wedge \bar{x}'_i = \bar{x}_i$, for $i = 1, 2$, where $\bar{t}_i = T_i, \bar{c}_i$,
- $\mathcal{CA} = (\bar{T}_1; \bar{T}_2, \Theta_{\mathcal{CA}}, \text{false}, \Phi_{\mathcal{CA}})$
- I a predicate formula without primed variables,
- $\bar{l}_i$ denote the variables in $\bar{x}_i, \bar{c}_i$ but not in $\bar{x}_j, \bar{c}_j$, for $i, j = 1, 2, i \neq j$.

In order to check that $S_1 \parallel \mathcal{CA} \parallel S_2$ *sat* $\Box I$, it suffices to check the validity of the following verification conditions:

- $(\Theta_1 \wedge \Theta_2 \wedge \Theta_{\mathcal{CA}}) \to I$
- $(\Phi_1^A \wedge \bar{l}'_2 = \bar{l}_2 \wedge I) \to I'$
- $(\Phi_2^A \wedge \bar{l}'_1 = \bar{l}_1 \wedge I) \to I'$
- $(\delta_1 > 0 \wedge \delta_2 > 0 \wedge \bar{t}'_1 = \bar{t}_1 + \bar{\delta}_1 \wedge \bar{t}'_2 = \bar{t}_2 + \bar{\delta}_2 \wedge U'_1 \wedge U'_2 \wedge \Phi_{\mathcal{CA}} \wedge \bar{x}' = \bar{x} \wedge I) \to I'$

$\Box$

In [OG76] *auxiliary variables* are defined as variables that do not occur in boolean tests nor in the right hand sides of assignments to other (non-auxiliary) variables. Let $(\bar{x}, \Theta, \Phi)$ be a transition system. Let the list of variables we separated into two disjoint lists $\bar{x} = \bar{y}, \bar{z}$. The list $\bar{z}$ is a list of auxiliary variables if the following holds.

$$\forall \bar{y}, \bar{z}, \bar{y}', \bar{z}' \,.\, \Phi(\bar{y}, \bar{z}, \bar{y}', \bar{z}') \to \forall \bar{w} \,.\, \exists \bar{w}' \,.\, \Phi(\bar{y}, \bar{w}, \bar{y}', \bar{w}')$$

The intuition is that the values of the $\bar{z}$ variables does not affect the enabledness of some transition, nor does it affect the values of the other variables. So, if from a state with values $\bar{y}, \bar{z}$ a transition is possible to some state $\bar{y}', \bar{z}'$, then changing the values $\bar{z}$ into $\bar{w}$ does not disable the transition, nor does it affect the possible outcome $\bar{y}'$.

Theorem 3 (Auxiliary variables). *If a list of variables $\bar{z}$ classifies as "auxiliary" for a transition system $S = (\bar{y}, \bar{z}, \Theta, \Phi)$, then the system $S \backslash \bar{z}$ can be represented as the transition system $(\bar{y}, \exists \bar{z} . \Theta, \exists \bar{z}, \bar{z}' . \Phi)$*

We remark that when transition systems or timed modules are represented as program texts or timed automata, then the notion of auxiliary variable as defined above, and the standard notion as for instance in [OG76] coincide.

3 A clock synchronization algorithm

As an example we consider a clock synchronization algorithm. Consider n processes $S_1, \cdots, S_n$, where S_i executes on a node with masterclock $T(i)$ and where the masterclocks satisfy the $CA_{drift}(\delta, \rho)$ clock assumption. Processes S_i can send messages to process S_j via a one-place buffer, $Buff(i, j)$. Each process S_i has a timer $C(i)$. Through a synchronization protocol we want to achieve that these local timers $C(i)$ behave as ϵ-synchronized clocks for a certain ϵ, i.e. $Sync_\epsilon(C(1), \cdots, C(n))$ should hold. So the idea is that, although the $C(i)$ variables are timers that can be modified by the clock synchronization algorithm, these variables could act as master clocks for a higher level program that satisfy the $CA_{sync}(\epsilon)$ assumption. Each process S_i sends regularly its timer value $C(i)$ to processes S_j by writing $C(i)$ in the variable $Buff(i, j)$. It uses a timer $ts(i, j)$ to guarantee that the value in $Buff(i, j)$ lags at most a time period *pers* behind the current $C(i)$ value.

Also each process S_j reads the $Buff(i, j)$ buffers regularly, using a timer $tr(i)$ to guarantee that this is done within a period *perr*. If the maximum of the values in $Buff(i, j)$, where i ranges over all processes except S_j itself, is larger than $C(j)$ than the latter is reset to this maximum value. The claim is that the protocol as sketched above induces a clock synchronization such that

$$Sync_\epsilon(C(1), \cdots, C(n))$$

with

$$\epsilon = pers \cdot (1 + \rho) + perr \cdot \rho$$

We use the following abbreviations:

- $Buff(i, *) = Buff(i, 1); \cdots; Buff(i, i - 1); Buff(i, i + 1); \cdots; Buff(i, n)$,
- $Buff(*, j) = Buff(1, j); \cdots; Buff(j - 1, j); Buff(j + 1, j); \cdots; Buff(n, j)$,
- $Buff$ denotes a list containing $Buff(i, j)$ for all $1 \leq i, j \leq n$, with $i \neq j$.
- $ts(i, *) = ts(i, 1), \ldots, ts(i, n)$.
- $max(max\{Buff(j, i) \mid 1 \leq j \leq n, j \neq i\}, C(i))$ is abbreviated by $MaxBuff(i)$.
- $Unchanged(x)$ denotes $x' = x$, where x can be any expression. Also, $Unchanged(x, y, \ldots)$ denotes $Unchanged(x) \wedge Unchanged(y) \wedge \ldots$.

The processes S_i are modelled as timed modules of the form $S_i = (\bar{x}_i, \Theta_i, \Phi_i^A, \Phi_i^S)$ with the list of variables $\bar{x}_i = \langle Buff(i, *), T(i), ts(i, *), tr(i), C(i) \rangle$

$\Theta_i = ((\forall j \,.\, Buff(i,j) = 0 \wedge ts(i,j) = 0) \wedge T(i) = 0 \wedge tr(i) = 0 \wedge C(i) = 0)$,
the asynchronous transition relation

$$\Phi_i^A = \begin{cases} \quad (C'(i) = MaxBuff(i) \wedge tr(i)' = 0 \\ \qquad\qquad\qquad \wedge \\ (\forall j \neq i \,.\, Unchanged(Buff(i,j), ts(i,j), T(i)))) \\ \qquad\qquad\qquad \vee \\ (\exists j \neq i \,.\, (Buff(i,j) = C(i) \wedge ts(i,j)' = 0) \\ \qquad\qquad\qquad \wedge \\ \forall k \neq i,j \,.\, Unchanged(Buff(i,k), ts(i,k)) \\ \qquad\qquad\qquad \wedge \\ \qquad Unchanged(C(i), T(i), tr(i))), \end{cases}$$

and the time transition relation

$$\Phi_i^S = \begin{cases} (\exists \delta > 0.\, T(i)' = T(i) + \delta \wedge (\forall j \neq i \,.\, ts(i,j)' = ts(i,j) + \delta) \\ \qquad\qquad\qquad \wedge \\ \qquad tr(i)' = tr(i) + \delta \wedge C(i)' = C(i) + \delta \\ \qquad\qquad\qquad \wedge \\ (\forall j \neq i \,.\, ts(i,j)' \leq pers \wedge tr(i)' \leq perr) \wedge Unchanged(Buff(i,j))). \end{cases}$$

Now the global protocol is given by

$$ClockSync = S_1 \parallel S_2 \parallel \cdots \parallel S_n \parallel CA_{drift}(\delta, \rho)$$

Theorem 4.
Let $\epsilon = pers \cdot (1 + \rho) + perr \cdot \rho$ then

$$ClockSync \ sat \ \Box Sync_\epsilon(C(1), \cdots, C(n))$$

In other words, the timers $C(1), \cdots, C(n)$ behave as ϵ-synchronized clocks.

A sketch of the Correctness proof
In order to prove theorem 4 we introduce a number of abbreviations and auxiliary variables:

- $MaxC$ abbreviates $max\{C(i) \mid i = 1, \ldots, n\}$.
- $IdMaxC$ abbreviates the index of a process r such that $C(r) = MaxC$, i.e. $IdMaxC = j$ with $C(j) = MaxC$. For concreteness we assume that $IdMaxC$ denotes the process with the smallest index with this property.
- $LMaxC(i,j)$ is an auxiliary variable that keeps track of the value of $MaxC$ at the moment when process S_i executed its last broadcast to S_j.
- $IdLMaxC(i,j)$ is an auxiliary variable that denotes the $IdMaxC$ at the moment when process S_i executed its last broadcast to S_j.
- $MinLMaxC(j)$ abbreviates $min\{LMaxC(i,j) \mid i = 1, \ldots, n, \ i \neq j\}$.
- $Count$ is a global auxiliary variable that is used to number broadcast events.
- $LCount(i,j)$ is an auxiliary variable that contains a copy of $Count$ at the moment process S_i executed its last broadcast to S_j.

The algorithm is changed by adding assignments to auxiliary variables. The only actions that are affected are the assignments to $Buff(i, j)$; these actions become as follows:

$$Buff(i, j), ts(i, j), LMaxC(i, j), IdLMaxC(i, j), LCount(i, j), Count :=$$
$$C(i), 0, MaxC, IdMaxC, Count, Count + 1$$

The augmented timed transition system
In order to define the timed transition system $ClockSync^\dagger$ which is $ClockSync$ augmented with the auxiliary variables defined above, we introduce the following abbreviation:

- $auxvar_i$ is the list of variables of $S_i{}^\dagger$ which don't occur in S_i, i.e.

$$auxvar_i = LMaxC(i, *); IdLMaxC(i, *); LCount(i, *); Count.$$

The initial state predicate $\Theta^\dagger{}_i$ for the augmented component $S_i{}^\dagger$ is given by

$$\Theta^\dagger{}_i = \begin{cases} \Theta_i \wedge (\forall j, \ j \neq i. \ LMaxC(i, j) = 0 \ \wedge \ LCount(i, j) = -i \\ \qquad\qquad\qquad \wedge \\ IdLMaxC(i, j) = 1) \ \wedge \ Count = 0. \end{cases}$$

The asynchronous transition predicate for the component $S_i{}^\dagger$ is given by

$$\Phi^{\dagger A}_i = \begin{cases} (C(i)' = MaxBuff \wedge (\forall j, \ i \neq j. Unchanged(Buff(i, j), ts(i, j))) \\ \wedge \\ tr(i)' = 0 \ \wedge \ Unchanged(T(i), auxvar_i)) \\ \vee \\ ((\exists j, \ i \neq j. \ Buff(i, j)' = C(i) \wedge LMaxC(i, j)' = MaxC \\ \wedge \\ IdLMaxC(i, j)' = IdMaxC \wedge LCount(i, j)' = Count \\ \wedge \\ ts(i, j)' = 0 \wedge Count' = Count + 1 \\ \wedge \\ (\forall k \neq i, j. \ Unchanged(Buff(i, k), LMaxC(i, k), IdLMaxC(i, k))) \\ \wedge \\ (\forall k \neq i, j. Unchanged(, LCount(i, k), ts(i, k)))) \wedge Unchanged(C(i), tr(i), T(i))), \end{cases}$$

and the time transition part almost equals the time transition relation Φ^S_i, except for the auxiliary variables $auxvar_i$ which remain unchanged,

$$\Phi^{\dagger S}_i = \Phi^S_i \ \wedge \ Unchanged(auxvar_i).$$

Now the total augmented timed transition system $ClockSync^\dagger$ is defined by

$$ClockSync^\dagger = S^\dagger{}_1 \ \|_{CA} \ S^\dagger{}_2 \ \|_{CA} \ \cdots \ \|_{CA} \ S^\dagger{}_n$$
$$= S^\dagger{}_1 \ \| \ S^\dagger{}_2 \ \| \ \cdots \ \| \ S^\dagger{}_n \ \| \ CA_{drift}(\delta, \rho)$$

Proof of the synchronization theorem

The proof of theorem 4 consists of showing the validity of a number of invariants for $ClockSync^\dagger$, and afterwards using the auxiliary variable rule, 3 to obtain the desired invariant for $ClockSync$. The relevant invariants, and an (informal) explanation of their correctness, for $ClockSync^\dagger$ are:

$$I_1 = \forall i,j,\ j \neq i.\ LCount(i,j) < Count$$
$$I_2 = \forall i,j,r,s,\ i \neq j \ \wedge\ s \neq r \ \wedge\ i \neq r.\ LCount(i,j) \neq LCount(r,s)$$

$Count$ is the number of the next communication (update of the variable $Buff$) and $LCount(i,j)$ is the number of the last communication from processor i to process j, i.e. the update of $Buff(i,j)$.

$$I_3 = \forall i,j,r,\ i \neq j.\ IdLMaxC(i,j) = r \to C(r) \geq LMaxC(i,j)$$
$$I_4 = \forall i,j,r, j \neq i \wedge j \neq r. \begin{cases} (LCount(i,j) < LCount(r,j) \ \wedge\ IdLMaxC(i,j) = r) \\ \to \\ Buff(r,j) \geq LMaxC(i,j) \end{cases}$$

The premises $LCount(i,j) \leq LCount(r,j) \ \wedge\ IdLMaxC(i,j) = r$ means that process i assigned his clock value $C(i)$ to the buffer $Buff(i,j)$ and copied the value of $C(r)$ in $lastmax(i,j)$ before process r assigned the clock value $C(r)$ to $Buff(r,j)$. Since clock values don't decrease one deduces $Buff(r,j) \geq lastmax(i,j)$.

$$I_5 = \forall j.\ MaxBuff(j) \geq MinLMaxC(j)$$

The validity of this invariant follows from the invariants, I_3 and I_4. Let p be the process with the lowest $LCount(i,j)$ index, and let $s = IdLMaxC(p,j)$. If $s = j$ then by invariant I_3 we get $C(j) \geq LMaxC(p,j) \geq MinLMaxC(j)$. The last inequality follows straightforward from the definition of $MinLMaxC(j)$. By the definition of $MaxBuff(j)$, the maximum value of the $Buff(*,j)$ variables and $C(j)$ one gets the desired result. On the other hand if $s \neq j$ then by invariant I_4 we deduce $Buff(s,j) \geq lastmax(p,j) \geq MinLMaxC(j)$ and again I_5 follows.

$$I_6 = \forall i,j,\ i \neq j.\ C(i) \geq Buff(i,j)$$

$Buff(i,j)$ contains a copy of $C(i)$ and since clocks don't decrease one gets I_6.

$$I_7 = \forall i,j,\ i \neq j.\ LMaxC(i,j) \geq MaxC - ts(i,j) \cdot (1 + \rho)$$

At the moment process i updates $LMaxC(i,j)$ with the value of $MaxC$, one has the equality $LMaxC(i,j) = MaxC$. But afterwards $MaxC$ increases with speed at most $1 + \rho$ times the speed of the local timer (i,j), due to the clock assumption. Hence the inequality $LMaxC(i,j) \geq MaxC - ts(i,j) \cdot (1 + \rho)$.

$$I_8 = \forall j.\ MinLMaxC(j) \geq MaxC - (1 + \rho) \cdot max\{ts(i,j) \mid i,j = 1,\ldots,n,\ j \neq i\}$$

This invariant follows straightforward from I_7, by taking the maximum at the right-hand side and afterwards the minimum at the left-hand side.

$$I_9 = \forall j.\ MaxBuff(j) \leq MaxC - (1 + \rho) \cdot max\{ts(i,j) \mid i,j = 1,\ldots,n,\ j \neq i\}$$

I_9 follows directly from I_5 and I_8.

$$I_{10} = \forall i.\ C(i) \geq MaxC - pers \cdot (1 + \rho) - tr(i) \cdot \rho$$

First observe that $max\{ts(i,j) \mid i,j = 1, \ldots, n,\ j \neq i\} \leq pers$ due to the urgency condition on the timers $ts(i,j)$. Hence the clock update $(C'(i) = MaxBuff(i)\ \wedge\ tr(i)' = 0$ preserves the invariant due to invariant I_9. Since C and $MaxC$ are clocks there values can drift apart by a factor ρ. But this drifting is compensated by the term $-tr(i) \cdot \rho$, since $tr(i)$ runs at the same speed as $C(i)$.

$$I_{11} = \forall i.\ C(i) \geq MaxC - pers \cdot (1 + \rho) - perr \cdot \rho$$

I_{11} follows straightforward from I_{10} and the urgency condition $tr(i) \leq perr$ From invariant I_{11} we can conclude, by the definition of $MaxC$, that

$$\forall i.\ MaxC - pers \cdot (1 + \rho) - perr \cdot \rho \leq C(i) \leq MaxC$$

i.e. all local clocks are between $MaxC - pers \cdot (1 + \rho) - perr \cdot \rho$ and $MaxC$. Hence $ClockSync^\dagger$ satisfies

$$\Box sync_{pers \cdot (1+\rho)+perr \cdot \rho}(C(1), \cdots, C(n)).$$

By the auxiliary variables rule, theorem 3, we conclude

$$ClockSync\ sat\ \Box sync_{pers \cdot (1+\rho)+perr \cdot \rho}(C(1), \cdots, C(n)),$$

which finishes the proof of theorem 4. A proof of the validity of the above invariants can be found in the full version of the paper.

4 Conclusion

We have introduced a model for real-time systems based upon a logical extension of temporal logic and TLA. This has resulted in a simple yet powerful proof system. The feasability of the proof system has been shown by means of an example of a clock synchronization algorithm. As always with hand verification the construction and validity proofs of verification conditions is somewhat laborious. Our plans are to use theorem provers for temporal logic, like the STeP system [Man94], to automate this process. The STeP system already deals with real-time, although not with multiple clocks and clock assumptions. Yet the basic STeP system appears to be a suitable candidate, due to the fact that timed modules are just subclass of transition systems, which can be handled by the STeP system directly. A second possibility for mechanized support might be the use of generic theorem provers for (higher order) logic. What would work best remains a topic for future research.

References

[AD91] R. Alur and D. Dill. The theory of timed automata. In de Bakker, Huizing, de Roever, and Rozenberg, editors, *Real-Time: Theory in Practice*, pages 45–73. Springer-Verlag, 1991.

[AD94] R. Alur and D. Dill. A theory of timed automata. *Theor. Comp. Sci.*, 126:183–235, 1994.

[AH94] R. Alur and T.A. Henzinger. Real-time system = discrete system + clock variables. In T. Russ and C. Rattray, editors, *Theories and Experiences for Real-time System Development*, volume 2 of *AMAST Series in Computing*, pages 1–29. World Scientific, 1994.

[AL94] M. Abadi and L. Lamport. An old-fashioned recipe for real time. *ACM Toplas*, 5:1543–1571, 1994.

[CAS86] F. Cristian, H. Aghili, and R. Strong. Clock synchronization in the presence of ommision and performance faults, and processor joins. In *Proceedings 16th International Symposium on Fault-Tolerant Computing*, pages 218–223, 1986.

[Heh84] E.C.R. Hehner. Predicative programming, part i and ii. *CACM*, 27:134–151, 1984.

[Hoa85] C.A.R. Hoare. Programs are predicates. In Hoare and Sheperdson, editors, *Mathematical Logic and Programming Languages*. Prentice-Hall, 1985.

[JPXZ94] W. Janssen, M. Poel, Q. Xu, and J. Zwiers. Layering of real-time distributed processes. In H. Langmaack, W.-P. de Roever, and J. Vytopil, editors, *Proceedings Formal Techniques in Real Time and Fault Tolerant Systems, LNCS 863*, pages 393–417. Springer-Verlag, 1994.

[KMP96] Y. Kesten, Z. Manna, and A. Pnueli. Verifying clocked transition systems. In E. Sontag R. Alur, T. Henzinger, editor, *Proceedings Hybrid Systems III, LNCS 1066*, pages 13–40. Springer-Verlag, 1996.

[Lam91] L. Lamport. The temporal logic of actions. Technical Report 79, Digital Equipment Corporation, Systems Research Center, 1991.

[Man94] Z. Manna et. al. Step: The stanford temporal prover. Technical report, Stanford University, 1994.

[OG76] S. Owicki and D. Gries. An axiomatic proof technique for parallel programs. *Acta Informatica*, 6:319–340, 1976.

[XN92] S. Yovine X. Nicollin, J. Sifakis. From atp to timed graphs and hybrid systems. In de Bakker, de Roever, and Rozenberg, editors, *Real-Time: Theory in Practice, LNCS 600*, pages 549–572. Springer-Verlag, 1992.

[ZdR89] J. Zwiers and W.-P. de Roever. Predicates are predicate transformers: a unified theory for concurrency. In *Proceedings of the ACM conference on Principles of Distributed Computing*, Edmonton, Canada, august 14-16 1989. ACM.

[Zwi92] J. Zwiers. Layering and action refinement for timed systems. In de Bakker, Huizing, de Roever, and Rozenberg, editors, *Real-Time: Theory in Practice, LNCS 600*, pages 687–723. Springer-Verlag, 1992.

Some Decidability Results for Duration Calculus under Synchronous Interpretation

Manoranjan Satpathy
Indian Institute of Technology, Guwahati - 781 001, India
Dang Van Hung
UNU/IIST, Post Box 3058, Macau
Paritosh K Pandya
Tata Institute of Fundamental Research, Mumbai - 400 005, India.
email(s): ms@iitg.ernet.in, dvh@iist.unu.edu, pandya@tcs.tifr.res.in

Abstract. Duration Calculus (or DC in short) presents a formal notation to specify properties of real-time systems and a calculus to formally
prove such properties. Decidability is the underlying foundation to automated reasoning. But, excepting some of its simple fragments, DC has
been shown to be undecidable.

DC takes the set of real numbers to represent time. The main reason of
undecidability comes from the assumption that, in a real-time system,
state changes can occur at any time point. But an implementation of
a specification (for a class of applications) is ultimately executed on a
computer, and there states change according to a system clock. Under
such an assumption, it has been shown that the decidability results can
be extended to cover relatively richer subsets of DC. In this paper, we
extend such decidability results to still richer subsets of DC.

1 Introduction

Duration Calculus (DC) [11] is a logic for reasoning about real-time systems.
It presents a formal notation to specify properties of real-time systems and a
calculus to formally prove such properties. It uses real numbers to model the
continuous time, and time-dependent boolean state expressions to model the
behaviours of real-time systems. DC is an extension of *interval logic* (IL) [2] in
the sense that it introduces duration constraints on time-dependent boolean state
expressions into IL. Intuitively, duration of a state expression in a time interval
tells, for what amount of time in the interval, the state expression holds. Since
there is no explicit mention of time and timing of state changes, DC provides
an ideal platform for reasoning about the requirements of real-time systems at
an abstract level, and hence does not have to deal with implementation details.
DC has been successfully used to specify and verify many real-time systems; e.g.
the deadline driven scheduler [10], a gas burner [4], a railway crossing [8] and
a mine pump controller [5]. One would always hope that such verification be
checked mechanically by a model-checker. Decidability is the underlying foundation to model-checking; but, it has been shown that DC in its fullest generality

is undecidable. Whatever decidability results have been shown are only for some simple subsets of DC [12]. The main reason of undecidability comes from the assumption that, in a real-time system, a state change can occur at any time point. And the density of real numbers mostly brings in the undecidabilty.

When a design reaches a certain lower level, then it satisfies some extra properties. To illustrate it, let REQ and $IMPL$ be DC formulas representing respectively the requirement and the implementation of a real-time system. What we need to show is whether: $IMPL \longrightarrow REQ$ is valid in DC. But the implementation (for a class of applications) has to be ultimately executed in a computer. In such a case, states have to change at clock points. We can then take clock ticks to be integer points and hence assume that states only change at such integer points [1]. But we will still allow the set of real numbers to represent time. This is because at specification level, the requirements are typically formulated with respect to the real-valued time without any reference to the clock period enforced by the implementation. Let us term the assumption that states do change only at integer points as the *synchronous assumption* (SA). Any interpretation of a DC formula with SA is termed a *synchronous interpretation* (SI), and if formulas of DC are interpreted by SIs only, then it is termed *Synchronous Duration Calculus* (SDC). Since at implementation level SA always holds, we can now rewrite the above formula as: $IMPL \wedge SA \longrightarrow REQ$ and ask whether it is a valid DC formula. In terms of SDC, we can then ask whether $IMPL \longrightarrow REQ$ is valid in SDC?

If SDC is decidable, then the validity of the above formula could be checked mechanically. Thus, a good decision procedure for SDC would enable us to carry out mechanical verification of many systems of interest. With this motivation, in this paper, we study the decidability of SDC. Under SI, some decidability results have been shown for reasonable subsets of DC [3]. In this paper, we extend such decidability results to richer subsets of DC.

The organisation of the paper is as follows. The remaining part of this section briefly describes the syntax and the semantics of DC, and also various subsets of DC whose decidability issues have been addressed in literature. It also defines DC subsets DC^Q and DC^N whose decidabilities, under SI, are proved respectively in Section 2 and Section 3. Section 4 discusses the importance of the subset DC^Q, and Section 5 concludes the paper.

1.1   The DC syntax

A state expression S is defined by the following BNF.
$$S ::= 0 \mid 1 \mid v \mid \neg S \mid S \vee S$$
where 0 and 1 are boolean constants representing *true* and *false*, and $v \in SVar$, the set of state variables.
A term t in DC is defined by: $\quad t ::= c \mid x \mid \int P$
where, c stands for a constant (usually a real number), x is a global variable (independent of time) and P is a state expression.

---

[1] Later in the paper, we will generalize this to the case where clock period is any fixed rational number

A formula D is defined by: $\quad D ::= true \mid t_1 \circ t_2 \mid \neg D \mid D \vee D \mid D \frown D \mid \forall x.D$, where x is a global variable, and $\circ$ stands for any binary relational operator.

In this paper we will be concerned with propositional fragments of duration calculus. So we omit global variables and quantified formulas from the definitions of terms and formulas respectively.

1.2 The Semantics of DC

We will take $\mathcal{R}^+$, the set of non-negative reals, as the time domain and shall refer to it by $Time$. A time interval $[b, e]$ with $b, e \in Time$ is defined by $\{t \mid b \leq t \leq e\}$. $Intv$ denotes the set of time intervals. The set $\{tt, ff\}$ is denoted by $Bool$. Q^+ denotes the set of non-negative rational numbers.

An interpretation Θ associates a total function $\Theta_v : (Time \Rightarrow Bool)$ with each state variable v. It is assumed that such functions have only finite number of discontinuity points in any finite interval [11]. An interpretation Θ can be extended to $\Theta[S] : Time \Rightarrow Bool$, for any state S. The semantics of term t in an interpretation Θ is a function $\Theta[t] : Intv \rightarrow \mathcal{R}$.

$\Theta[c][b, e] = c$

$\Theta[\int S][b, e] = \int_b^e \Theta[S](t)dt$

Semantics of a formula D in an interpretation Θ is a function $\Theta[D] : Intv \rightarrow \{tt, ff\}$ defined by:

$\Theta[true][b, e] = tt$

$\Theta[t_1 \circ t_2][b, e] = tt \qquad$ iff $\Theta[t_1][b, e] \circ \Theta[t_2][b, e] = tt$

$\Theta[\neg D][b, e] = tt \qquad$ iff $\Theta[D][b, e] = ff$

$\Theta[D_1 \vee D_2][b, e] = tt \qquad$ iff $\Theta[D_1][b, e] = tt$ or $\Theta[D_2][b, e] = tt$

$\Theta[D_1 \frown D_2][b, e] = tt \qquad$ iff $\Theta[D_1][b, m] = tt$ and $\Theta[D_2][m, e] = tt$
$\qquad\qquad\qquad\qquad\qquad$ for some $m \in Time$ and $b \leq m \leq e$.

A formula D holds in interpretation Θ (written as $\Theta \models D$) iff $\Theta[D][b, e] = tt$ for every interval $[b, e]$. D is *valid* (written as $\models D$) iff $\Theta \models D$ for every interpretation Θ. A formula D is *satisfiable* iff there exists an interpretation Θ and an interval $[b, e]$ such that $\Theta[D][b, e] = tt$. It is trivial to show that D is satisfiable iff $\neg D$ is not valid.

The following abbreviations for certain duration formulas are heavily used.

$\ell \overset{\text{def}}{=} \int 1 \qquad\qquad\qquad\qquad$ denotes "length of an interval".

$\lceil \rceil \overset{\text{def}}{=} \ell = 0 \qquad\qquad\qquad$ denotes "a point interval".

$\lceil P \rceil \overset{\text{def}}{=} (\int 1 > 0) \wedge (\neg \int \neg P > 0) \quad$ denotes "P holds almost everywhere in a non-point interval"

$\Diamond D \overset{\text{def}}{=} true \frown D \frown true \qquad$ denotes "D holds in some subinterval"

$\Box D \overset{\text{def}}{=} \neg \Diamond(\neg D) \qquad\qquad$ denotes "D holds in every subinterval"

1.3 Subsets of DC

Various subsets of DC are defined by restricting formulas. In subset $\{\lceil P \rceil\}$, its formulas are generated from primitive formulas of the form $\lceil P \rceil$ and by using connectives $\neg, \vee$ and $\frown$. Similarly, the subsets $\{\lceil P \rceil, \ell = k\}$ and $\{\int P = \int Q\}$ are defined. Formulas in subset $\{\int P < k, \int P > k\}$ include primitive formulas of the form $\int P < k, \int P > k$ and the formulas obtained from them by using operators $\neg, \vee$ and $\frown$. Formulas in subset $\{\forall x, \lceil P \rceil, l = x\}$ are built from primitive formulas $\lceil P \rceil$ and $\ell = x$, using connectives $\neg, \vee, \frown$ and $\forall x$.

In this paper, we will concentrate on the subset of DC whose formulas are described by: $\quad D ::= \int P < k \mid \int P > k \mid \neg D \mid D \vee D \mid D \frown D$
When $k \in \mathcal{N}$, we will address the above set of formulas as DC^N, and when $k \in Q^+$, we will address the same subset as DC^Q. This subset properly includes $\{\lceil P \rceil, \ell = k\}$ [3].

1.4 Related work

The following table tabulates the decidability results of the original DC under discrete and dense time DC [12]. Dense time DC is the DC we have described earlier. Under discrete time interpretation, states change only at integer points, and the set of intervals is defined by $\{[b, e] \mid (b, e \in \mathcal{N}) \text{ and } (b \leq e)\}$.

DC subset	$\lceil P \rceil$	$\lceil P \rceil, \ell = k$	$\int P = \int Q$	$\lceil P \rceil, \forall x, \ell = x$
Discrete time	Decidable	Decidable	Undecidable	Undecidable
Dense time	Decidable	Undecidable	Undecidable	Undecidable

1.5 Our work

Under SI, Fränzle [3] has shown the decidability of the subset $\{\int P < k, \int P > k\}$ $(k \in \mathcal{N})$, and it is the best decidability result shown so far. In this paper, we make an extension to this subset. we remove the restriction that $k \in \mathcal{N}$, and show that, even when $k \in Q^+$, the resulting subset, i.e. DC^Q, is also decidable under SI. Then, we give an independent proof of Fränzle's result that is simpler than the proof in [3].

2 Decidability of DC^Q

In the following discussion, for integers $a \geq 0$ and $b > 0$, $gcd(a, b)$ denotes the *greatest common divisor* of a and b. And for two positive integers a and b, $lcm(a, b)$ denoted the *least common multiple* of a and b. For two positive rational numbers p_1/q_1 and p_2/q_2, we define their $gcd(p_1/q_1, p_2/q_2)$ as follows. Let $p_1/q_1 = p_1'/lcm(q_1, q_2)$ and $p_2/q_2 = p_2'/lcm(q_1, q_2)$.

Then, $\qquad gcd(p_1/q_1) \overset{\text{def}}{=} p_1/q_1$.
$$gcd(p_1/q_1, p_2/q_2) \overset{\text{def}}{=} gcd(p_1', p_2')/lcm(q_1, q_2),$$
$gcd(p_1/q_1, \ldots, p_m/q_m) \overset{\text{def}}{=} gcd(gcd(p_1/q_1, \ldots, p_{m-1}/q_{m-1}), p_m/q_m)$ (for $m > 2$).
For a formula $D \in DC^Q$, let $r_1, r_2 \ldots, r_m$ be the set of rational numbers occurring in D. Let $p_1/q_1, p_2/q_2 \ldots, p_m/q_m$ be respectively their fractional parts; i.e. $\forall i, \; p_i/q_i < 1$. We will term $gcd(p_1/q_1, \ldots, p_m/q_m, 1)$ as $gcd(D)$.
As an illustration, consider, $D = (\int P > 15/22) \frown (\int P < 5/8) \frown (l = 5/11)$
Then $gcd(D) = gcd(15/22, 5/8, 5/11, 1) = 1/88$

Definition 1. Let g be any positive rational and Θ is any interpretation (not necessarily synchronous). Then define a new interpretation Θ_g by:
$$\Theta_g(P)(t) = \Theta(P)(gt) \qquad \text{for all } t \in Time \text{ and for all states } P.$$

Definition 2. Let g be any positive rational and $D \in DC^Q$. Then from D obtain a new formula $D[g] \in DC^Q$, where each k in D gets replaced by k/g.

Theorem 3. *Let g be a positive rational, $D \in DC^Q$, Θ be an interpretation and $[b, e] \in Intv$. Then* $\qquad \Theta, [b, e] \models D$ *iff* $\Theta_g, [b/g, e/g] \models D[g]$

Proof: By induction over the structure of D. We consider two important cases.

Case 1: D is of the form $\int P < k$ (k is a positive rational).
Define for $t \in Time$, $t = gt'$. Then $dt = gdt'$.
Now $\Theta, [b, e] \models \int P < k$
iff $\int_b^e \Theta(P)(t)dt < k$
iff $\int_{b/g}^{e/g} \Theta(P)(gt')gdt' < k$
iff $\int_{b/g}^{e/g} \Theta_g(P)(t')dt' < k/g$
iff $\Theta_g, [b/g, e/g] \models \int P < k/g$.

Case 2: D is of the form $D_1 \frown D_2$
Assume $\Theta, [b, e] \models D_1 \frown D_2$
i.e. $\exists m : b \le m \le e$ such that $\Theta, [b, m] \models D_1$ and $\Theta, [m, e] \models D_2$
Using hypothesis, $\Theta_g, [b/g, m/g] \models D_1[g]$ and $\Theta_g, [m/g, e/g] \models D_2[g]$
i.e. $\Theta_g, [b/g, e/g] \models D_1[g] \frown D_2[g]$
Proof of the converse is similar. $\qquad\qquad\qquad\qquad\qquad\qquad\qquad\qquad\qquad\qquad\square$

Lemma 4. *For any positive rational r and for any interpretation Θ under which states change only at points in $\{ir \mid i \in N\}$, Θ_r is synchronous.*

Proof: Under interpretation Θ, if states change at ticks of a clock with period r, then Θ_r just scales the clock period by $1/r$. $\qquad\qquad\qquad\qquad\qquad\square$

Theorem 5. *Let $D \in DC^Q$, Θ be a SI, $[b, e] \in Intv$. Then*
$$\Theta, [b, e] \models D \quad \text{iff} \quad \Theta_{gcd(D)}, [b/gcd(D), e/gcd(D)] \models D[gcd(D)],$$
where $D[gcd(D)] \in DC^N$ and $\Theta_{gcd(D)}$ is synchronous.

Proof: For any constant k occurring in D as length, from the definition of $gcd(D)$, it is obvious that $k/gcd(D)$ is an integer. So $D[gcd(D)] \in DC^N$. The rest of the theorem is a direct consequence of Theorem 3 and Lemma 4. $\qquad\square$

Definition 6. Let r be a positive rational, Θ be an interpretation. If states change only at points in $\{ir \mid i \in N\}$ under Θ, then the interpretation Θ is termed r–synchronous.

Definition 7. (i) A formula $D \in DC^Q$ is s–valid iff for all SI Θ; $\Theta \models D$.
(ii) A formula $D \in DC^Q$ is rs-valid iff for all r-synchronous interpretation Θ_r; $\Theta_r \models D$

Theorem 8. *For all $D \in DC^Q$, s–validity of D is decidable.*

Proof: For a formula $D \in DC^N$ and for SI, validity of D is known to be decidable (proof in next section). And from Theorem 5, validity of $D \in DC^Q$ under SI can be reduced to validity of $D[gcd(D)] \in DC^N$ under SI. □

Theorem 9. $\forall D \in DC^Q$, *rs–validity of D is decidable.*

Proof: Let Θ be a r–synchronous interpretation. Then from Theorem 3 and Lemma 4: $\quad \Theta, [b, e] \models D$ iff $\Theta_r, [b/r, e/r] \models D[r]$,
where Θ_r is synchronous and $D[r] \in DC^Q$. Now take $g = gcd(D[r])$. From Theorem 5, $\quad \Theta_r, [b/r, e/r] \models D[r]$ iff $\Theta_{rg}, [b/rg, e/rg] \models D[r][g]$,
where Θ_{rg} is synchronous and $D[r][g] \in DC^N$. So rs–validity of a formula $D \in DC^Q$ could be reduced to the s-validity of formula $\quad D[r][gcd(D)] \in DC^N$. □

3 Decidability of DC^N

Fränzle [3] has shown that the DC subset $\{\int P < k, \int P > k\}$ is decidable under SI. In this section, we present an independent proof of the same result but it is much simpler. To keep our proof simple, we will first prove the decidability result for a subset of DC^N (and call it DC^s) whose formulas are described by:
$$D ::= \lceil P \rceil \mid \neg D \mid D \vee D \mid D^\frown D \mid \ell = k \quad /* k \in \mathcal{N} */.$$
Then we will extend the decidability of DC^s to that of DC^N.

Definition 10. Let $[b, e], [b', e'] \in Intv$. We say that $[b', e'] \approx [b, e]$ iff

(i) $\lceil b' \rceil = \lceil b \rceil$ and $\lfloor b' \rfloor = \lfloor b \rfloor$ (ii) $\lceil e' \rceil = \lceil e \rceil$ and $\lfloor e' \rfloor = \lfloor e \rfloor$
(iii) $\lfloor e - b \rfloor = \lfloor e' - b' \rfloor$ *and* (iv) $\lceil e - b \rceil = \lceil e' - b' \rceil$

It is easy to see that $\approx$ is an equivalence relation. We will now state the following lemma without proof. The proof is given in [7].

Lemma 11. *For arbitrary intervals $[b, e]$ and $[b', e']$ such that $[b, e] \approx [b', e']$, for any real number $m \in [b, e]$ (i.e. $b \leq m \leq e$) there exists a real number $m' \in [b', e']$ such that $[b, m] \approx [b', m']$ and $[m, e] \approx [m', e']$* □

Lemma 12. *Let D be a formula in DC^s, $[b', e']$ and $[b, e]$ be intervals such that $[b', e'] \approx [b, e]$, and Θ be SI. Then*
$$\Theta, [b, e] \models D \quad \Leftrightarrow \quad \Theta, [b', e'] \models D.$$

Proof: By structural induction over D [7]. □

3.1 Decidability of DC^s

Given a formula $D \in DC^s$, we build a regular language $\mathcal{L}(D)$. Then we show that a SI Θ satisfies D in an interval $[b, e]$ iff there exists a word $w \in \mathcal{L}(D)$ corresponding to the interpretation Θ in $[b, e]$. The formula D is satisfiable iff $\mathcal{L}(D)$ is non-empty. Since emptiness problem of a regular language is decidable, we obtain a decision procedure for the satisfiability of D.

Let S be the set of state variables in formula D. Each word w in language $\mathcal{L}(D)$ will consist of a string s made up of characters in alphabet $\Sigma = 2^S$ (power set of S). The intention is that we let $a \in \Sigma$ represent that all state variables in a hold for one time unit (from one integer point to next).

Definition 13. Let $s = a_1 a_2 \ldots a_n$ be a string over Σ. s corresponds to a SI Θ in interval $[b, e]$, $b \neq e$ iff $n = \lceil e \rceil - \lfloor b \rfloor$ and for all $i = 1, \ldots, n$; $\Theta \llbracket \lceil P \rceil \rrbracket(t) = true$ for all $t \in [\lfloor b \rfloor + i - 1, \lfloor b \rfloor + i]$ iff $P \in a_i$. Thus, the string corresponding to a SI Θ in $[b, e]$ is defined uniquely and will be denoted by $word(\Theta, [b, e])$. By our convention, $word(\Theta, [b, b]) = \epsilon$.

Clearly, for each string $s = a_1 a_2 \ldots a_n$ over Σ, $n \geq 0$, we can find a SI Θ and an interval $[b, e]$ such that $s = word(\Theta, [b, e])$. For the following discussion, let Δx denote the fraction of the real number x, i.e. $x = \lfloor x \rfloor + \Delta x$. Further, let for a real number x, δx denote $\lceil x \rceil - x$ (thus, $x = \lfloor x \rfloor + \Delta x = \lceil x \rceil - \delta x$). Let us define: $\quad \Sigma_\delta = \{\delta_{01H}, \delta_{01R}, \delta_{01L}, \delta_{01}, \delta_{12}, \delta_{00}, \delta_{11}, \delta_\epsilon\}$
Any interval $[b, e]$ should be of one of the following types.

- δ_{01H} : $b, e \notin \mathcal{N}$; $\lfloor b \rfloor = \lfloor e \rfloor$; $\lceil b \rceil = \lceil e \rceil$ and $b \neq e$ (i.e. $\lfloor b \rfloor = \lfloor e \rfloor$ and $\Delta b < \Delta e$)
- δ_{01R} : $b \in \mathcal{N}$ and $e \notin \mathcal{N}$ (or, equivalently, $0 = \Delta b < \Delta e$)
- δ_{01L} : $b \notin \mathcal{N}$ and $e \in \mathcal{N}$ (or, equivalently, $0 = \Delta e < \Delta b$)
- δ_{01} : $b, e \notin \mathcal{N}$ and $0 < \delta b + \Delta e < 1$ (or, equivalently, $0 < \Delta e < \Delta b$)
- δ_{12} : $b, e \notin \mathcal{N}$ and $1 < \delta b + \Delta e < 2$ (or, equivalently, $0 < \Delta b < \Delta e$)
- δ_{00} : $b, e \in \mathcal{N}$ and $b \neq e$ (or, equivalently, $0 = \Delta b = \Delta e$ and $b \neq e$).
- δ_{11} : $b, e \notin \mathcal{N}$; $b \neq e$ and $\delta b + \Delta e = 1$ (or, equivalently, $0 < \Delta b = \Delta e$)
- δ_ϵ : Point intervals.

Note that if an interval is of type δ then any other interval equivalent to it is also of type δ. Conversely, all intervals of the same type with the same floor of the beginning point and with the same floor of the ending point are equivalent.

3.2 The Language definition

For a formula D, for each $\delta \in \Sigma_\delta$ we are now going to construct a language $\mathcal{L}_\delta(D)$ such that for SI Θ, for interval $[b, e]$ of type δ, it holds that $\Theta, [b, e] \models D$ iff $word(\Theta, [b, e]) \in \mathcal{L}_\delta(D)$. Let us denote by $\mathcal{L}_\delta$ the set of all strings that can correspond to a SI in an interval of the type δ:

$$\mathcal{L}_{\delta_{00}} = \Sigma^+ \qquad\qquad \mathcal{L}_{\delta_{01H}} = \Sigma$$
$$\mathcal{L}_{\delta_{01R}} = \Sigma^* \Sigma \qquad\qquad \mathcal{L}_{\delta_{01L}} = \Sigma \Sigma^*$$
$$\mathcal{L}_{\delta_\epsilon} = \{\epsilon\} \qquad\qquad \mathcal{L}_{\delta_{01}} = \Sigma \Sigma^* \Sigma$$
$$\mathcal{L}_{\delta_{11}} = \Sigma \Sigma^* \Sigma \qquad\qquad \mathcal{L}_{\delta_{12}} = \Sigma \Sigma^* \Sigma$$

$\mathcal{L}_\delta(D)$ are defined over the structure of D.

$$\mathcal{L}_i(\lceil\,\rceil) = \begin{cases} \{\epsilon\} \text{ if } i = \delta_\epsilon \\ \emptyset \quad \text{otherwise} \end{cases}$$

In the context of formula $\lceil P\rceil$, let $DNF(P)$ stand for the set of conjuncts in the *disjunctive normal form* of predicate P. So if $a \in DNF(P)$ is *true*, it also implies that P is true.

$$\mathcal{L}_i(\lceil P\rceil) = \begin{cases} DNF(P)^+ & \text{if } i \in \{\delta_{00}, \delta_{01R}, \delta_{01L}\} \\ DNF(P) & \text{if } i = \delta_{01H} \\ DNF(P).DNP(P)^*.DNF(P) & \text{if } i \in \{\delta_{01}, \delta_{12}, \delta_{11}\} \\ \emptyset & \text{if } i = \delta_\epsilon \end{cases}$$

$$\mathcal{L}_i(\ell = k) = \begin{cases} \Sigma^k & \text{if } i = \delta_{00} \\ \Sigma.\Sigma^{k-1}.\Sigma & \text{if } i = \delta_{11} \\ \emptyset & \text{otherwise} \end{cases}$$

$$\mathcal{L}_i(\neg D) = \mathcal{L}_i - \mathcal{L}_i(D)$$
$$\mathcal{L}_i(D_1 \vee D_2) = \mathcal{L}_i(D_1) \cup \mathcal{L}_i(D)$$

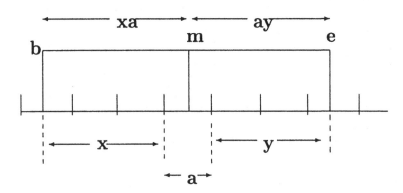

Fig. 1. A string represents chopped intervals

When a formula D is of the form $D_1\frown D_2$, an interval of type γ satisfying D will be chopped into an interval of type α satisfying D_1 and an interval of type β satisfying D_2. All the possibilities of γ, β, α are given in the table in figure 2. If an interval is chopped into two subintervals such that the first interval is of type $\alpha = \delta_{01L}$ and then the second is of type $\beta = \delta_{01R}$ then γ, the type of the original interval, must be either of δ_{01}, δ_{11} or δ_{12}. That is why the corresponding entry for γ in the table has three such entries.

For an interval $[b, e]$ ($b \neq e$), for any SI Θ; $\Theta, [b, e] \models D$ iff for some $m \in [b, e]$; $\Theta, [b, m] \models D_1$ and $\Theta, [m, e] \models D_2$. If $b < m < e$, for each unit

	δ_ϵ	δ_{01H}	δ_{01R}	δ_{01L}	δ_{01}	δ_{12}	δ_{00}	δ_{11}
δ_ϵ	δ_ϵ	δ_{01H}	δ_{01R}	δ_{01L}	δ_{01}	δ_{12}	δ_{00}	δ_{11}
δ_{01H}	δ_{01H}	δ_{01H}	$\times$	δ_{01L}	$\delta_{01},\delta_{11},\delta_{12}$	δ_{12}	$\times$	δ_{12}
δ_{01R}	δ_{01R}	δ_{01R}	$\times$	δ_{00}	δ_{01R}	δ_{01R}	$\times$	δ_{01R}
δ_{01L}	δ_{01L}	$\times$	$\delta_{01},\delta_{11},\delta_{12}$	$\times$	$\times$	$\times$	δ_{01L}	$\times$
δ_{01}	δ_{01}	$\delta_{01},\delta_{11},\delta_{12}$	$\times$	δ_{01L}	δ_{01}	$\delta_{01},\delta_{11},\delta_{12}$	$\times$	δ_{01}
δ_{12}	δ_{12}	δ_{12}	$\times$	δ_{01L}	$\delta_{01},\delta_{11},\delta_{12}$	δ_{12}	$\times$	δ_{12}
δ_{00}	δ_{00}	$\times$	δ_{01R}	$\times$	$\times$	$\times$	δ_{00}	$\times$
δ_{11}	δ_{11}	δ_{12}	$\times$	δ_{01L}	δ_{01}	δ_{12}	$\times$	δ_{11}

Fig. 2. Table for all possibilities of α, β, γ for $\frown$ operator: The entry of row α and column β gives the corresponding γ('s)

interval inside $[\lfloor b \rfloor, \lceil m \rceil]$ and $[\lfloor m \rfloor, \lceil e \rceil]$, there is a character in Σ representing Θ. Thus, if $\lfloor m \rfloor < \lceil m \rceil$ ($[b,m]$ is one of $\delta_{01}, \delta_{12}, \delta_{11}, \delta_{01R}, \delta_{01H}$ and $[m,e]$ is one of $\delta_{01}, \delta_{12}, \delta_{11}, \delta_{01L}, \delta_{01H}$), the character in Σ to represent Θ for the unit interval $[\lfloor m \rfloor, \lceil m \rceil]$ is the last character of the string corresponding to Θ in the interval $[b,m]$ and also the first character of the string corresponding to Θ in the interval $[m,e]$ (see Figure 1). Furthermore, the string representing point intervals can only be ϵ. Therefore, we define $\mathcal{L}(D)$ as follows.

$$\mathcal{L}_\gamma(D_1 \frown D_2) = \bigcup_{\alpha \text{ and } \beta \text{ correspond to } \gamma \text{ in Fig. 2}} \mathcal{L}_\alpha(D_1) \# \mathcal{L}_\beta(D_2)$$

where

$$\mathcal{L}_\alpha(D_1) \# \mathcal{L}_\beta(D_2) = \begin{cases} \left\{ \begin{matrix} xay \mid xa \in \mathcal{L}_\alpha(D_1), \\ ay \in \mathcal{L}_\beta(D_2), \\ a \in \Sigma \end{matrix} \right\} & \begin{matrix} \text{if } \alpha \in \{\delta_{01}, \delta_{12}, \delta_{11}, \delta_{01R}, \delta_{01H}\} \\ \text{and } \beta \in \{\delta_{01}, \delta_{12}, \delta_{11}, \delta_{01L}, \delta_{01H}\} \end{matrix} \\ \left\{ \begin{matrix} xy \mid x \in \mathcal{L}_\alpha(D_1), \\ y \in \mathcal{L}_\beta(D_2) \end{matrix} \right\} & \begin{matrix} \text{if } \alpha \in \{\delta_{00}, \delta_{01L}, \delta_\epsilon\} \text{ and} \\ \beta \in \{\delta_{00}, \delta_{01R}, \delta_\epsilon\} \end{matrix} \end{cases}$$

Regular languages are closed under union, intersection, concatenation, Kleene closure and complementation. Further it is also known that: if L_1 and L_2 are regular languages then the *quotient language* $L_1/L_2 \overset{\text{def}}{=} \{x \mid \exists y \in L_2 \text{ such that } x.y \in L_1\}$ is regular. From these properties, it could be easily verified that, for all $\delta \in \Sigma_\delta$, $\mathcal{L}_\delta(D)$ is regular [7].

Lemma 14. *Let Θ be a SI of formula $D \in DC^s$. Then D is satisfiable in interval $[b,e]$ of type δ, iff $word(\Theta, [b,e])$ belongs to $\mathcal{L}_\delta(D)$.*

Proof: By induction over the structure of D it can be shown [7] that for all Θ, for all $[b,e]$ of type δ, $\Theta, [b,e] \models D$ iff $word(\Theta, [b,e]) \in \mathcal{L}_\delta(D)$. $\square$
As a consequence of this lemma, we have the following theorem.

Theorem 15. *The validity of a formula $D \in DC^s$ under SI is decidable.* $\square$

3.3 Decidability of DC^N

DC^N is the set of DC formulas, which contains, in addition to the formulas of DC^s, the formulas $\int P < k$ and $\int P > k$, where $k \in \mathcal{N}$. We will show that the validity of a formula in this set is decidable under SI.

The definitions of Σ and $DNF(P)$ remain same as above. We will now define Σ_1 as: $\Sigma_1 = \Sigma \backslash DNF(P)$. So, when $a \in \Sigma_1$ holds in an interval, it is obvious that P will not hold in that interval. $\mathcal{L}_i(\int P < 1)$, $i \in \Sigma_\delta$ are defined as:

$$\mathcal{L}_{\delta_e}(\int P < 1) = \{\epsilon\}$$
$$\mathcal{L}_{\delta_{01H}}(\int P < 1) = \Sigma$$
$$\mathcal{L}_{\delta_{01}}(\int P < 1) = \{a_1.a_2 \ldots a_{n-1}.a_n \mid n \geq 2; a_1, a_n \in \Sigma \text{ and } a_2, \ldots, a_{n-1} \in \Sigma_1\}$$
$$\mathcal{L}_{\delta_{11}}(\int P < 1) = \{a_1.a_2 \ldots a_{n-1}.a_n \mid (n \geq 2; (a_1 \in \Sigma \text{ and } a_2, \ldots, a_n \in \Sigma_1) \text{ or}$$
$$(a_n \in \Sigma \text{ and } a_1, a_2, \ldots, a_n \in \Sigma_1)\}$$
$$\mathcal{L}_{\delta_{12}}(\int P < 1) = \mathcal{L}_{\delta_{11}}(\int P < 1)$$
$$\mathcal{L}_{\delta_{00}}(\int P < 1) = \{a_1.a_2 \ldots a_{n-1}.a_n \mid n \geq 1; a_1, a_2, \ldots, a_n \in \Sigma_1\}$$
$$\mathcal{L}_{\delta_{01R}}(\int P < 1) = \{a_1.a_2 \ldots a_{n-1}.a_n \mid n \geq 1; a_n \in \Sigma \text{ and } a_1, \ldots, a_{n-1} \in \Sigma_1)\}$$
$$\mathcal{L}_{\delta_{01L}}(\int P < 1) = \{a_1.a_2 \ldots a_{n-1}.a_n \mid n \geq 1; a_1 \in \Sigma \text{ and } a_2, \ldots, a_n \in \Sigma_1)\}$$

$\mathcal{L}_i(\int P > 0)$ can be defined on similar lines.
Based on a case analysis, when the atomic formulas $\int P < 1$ and $\int P > 0$ hold, it can be easily verified that Lemma 12 holds when the structural induction is extended over to such formulas. Moreover, with the above translation schema, lemma 14 holds for cases when D is of the forms $\int P < 1$ and $\int P > 0$. Further, formulas $\int P < k$ and $\int P > k$, when $k \in \mathcal{N}$, could be generated from the above atomic formulas [3]. So we have the following theorem.

Theorem 16. *The validity of a formula in DC^N, where $k \in \mathcal{N}$, under SI is decidable.* □

The complexity of our decision procedure is non-elementary. The argument for this is same as the one given by Skakkebaek & Sestoft in [9].

4 Importance of the subset DC^Q

In this section, we illustrate two important systems to show that the subset DC^Q is strong enough to to specify and verify many real-time systems.

4.1 The Mine Pump Controller

In a mine, water gets accumulated in a mine shaft which is pumped out of the mine. The water level inside the mine shaft is measured using H_2O sensor. The pump controller is supposed to keep the water level in the shaft below a critical level, called the $DangerH_2O$. If the water in the shaft exceeds this level a boolean state variable DH_2O is set to 1. For implementation purposes, a water level called the $HighH_2O$ is selected which is slightly lower than the level $DangerH_2O$. Boolean state variable HH_2O is set to 1 when water level exceeds

HighH_2O. When HH_2O flag remains set for δ amount of time, the monitor sets the boolean state variable H_2O-flag.

Similarly the methane level in the mine shaft is measured by CH_4-sensor. Boolean variable DCH_4 is set to one if methane level in the shaft crosses a critical level, called the DangerCH_4. Like the previous case, HighCH_4 is selected which is slightly lower than DangerCH_4. A flag HCH_4 is set when methane level crosses HighCH_4 level. The monitor sets boolean variable CH_4-flag if the flag HCH_4 remains set for δ amount of time.

The pump controller sets ALARM flag when either HH_2O or HCH_4 remains set for δ amount of time. The pump controller takes the values of HH_2O and HCH_4 to decide when to turn the pump on or off.

The requirement of the mine pump system is that, in any observation interval of 1000 time units or less, the amount of time for which DH_2O flag remains set should not exceed 1 time unit. In terms of DC the above requirement is specified as: **Req** $= \square\,(l \leq 1000 \rightarrow \int DH_2O \leq 1)$.

There are two design decisions DES_1 and DES_2, and the proof that the they meet the requirement, could be stated through the following two theorems [5].

Theorem 1: $AS_1 \wedge AS_2 \wedge DES_1 \rightarrow$ **Req**

Theorem 2: $AS_3 \wedge AS_4 \wedge AS_5 \wedge Monitor \wedge DES_2 \rightarrow DES_1$

Here, $AS_1, \ldots AS_5$ are the specifications of the assumptions about the environment under which the system will operate. $Monitor$ is the specification of the actions of the monitor. The coding of the assumptions, the design decisions and the *monotor* have all been done in [5]. It is to be noted that the coding of assumptions use some constants like the parameters of the pump, the minimum time for which methane-level remains low, and the minimum time required for the water level to reach from HH_2O to reach DH_2O. So all such constants can be assumed to be rational numbers. Since they are either dependent on natural phenomena and the design of the pump, we cannot take them to be natural numbers. So we cannot specify the above theorems by using the subset DC^N. But from the codings in [5], it can be seen that such theorems could be specified by the subset DC^Q. So our decision procedure for subset DC^Q can verify the validity of the above two theorems.

4.2 Gas Burner System

Computer controlled gas burner system is a widely quoted example in the context of specification and verification of real-time systems. In [6], the requirements and the design decisions of the gas burner system have been specified by using the subset DC^Q. The refinement of the design decisions there have been proved manually by using the axioms and inference rules of DC. Now that DC^Q is decidable under synchronous interpretation, our decision procedure could be used to prove the refinement. Since the specifications of the system as in [6] require rational numbers in the form of constants, DC^N will not serve the purpose.

5 Conclusion

The (i) synchronous assumption (ii) k as a rational number in the subset DC^Q have enough practical significance. The significance of (i) lies in the fact that at implementation level, the synchronous assumption holds. Though the set of real numbers is taken as the time domain, hardly anybody ever uses irrational numbers in a formula as a specification. That is why (ii) has much practical significance. So, in conclusion, the decidability result of DC^Q under synchronous assumption is a significant step towards automatic verification of the properties of real-time systems.

Acknowledgements

Prof. Zhou Chaochen has been a constant source of guidance throughout this research work. Martin Fränzle has gone through an earlier version of this paper and offered many valuable suggestions. Swarup Mohalik and Xu Qiwen have checked most of the proofs. Thanks to all of them.

References

1. Bouajjani A., Lakhnech Y. & Robbana R., From Duration Calculus to Linear Hybrid Automata, Proc. of 7th Intnl. Conf. on *Computaer Aided Verification* (CAV '95), LNCS No. 939, 1995.
2. Dutertre B., Complete Proof systems for First Order Interval Logic, Tenth Anual IEEE Symposium on *Logic in Computer Science*, pp. 36-43, IEEE Press, 1995.
3. Fränzle M., *Controller Design from Temporal Logic: Undecidability need not matter*, Dissertation, University of Kiel, 1996.
4. Hansen M.R. & Zhou Chaochen, Duration Calculus: Logical Foundations, To appear in *Formal Aspects of Computing*, Springer Verlag.
5. Joseph M., Real-Time Systems:*Specification, Verification and Analysis*, Printice Hall Intl. Series in Computer Science, 1996.
6. Ravn A.P., Rischel H. & Hansen K.M., Specifying and Verifying Requirements of Real-Time Systems, IEEE Tr. on Software Engineering, Vol 19(1), January 1993.
7. Satpathy M., Hung D.V. & Pandya P.K., Some Results on the Decidability of Duration Calculus under Synchronous Interpretation, TR No. 86, UNU/IIST, Macau, 1996.
8. Skakkebaek J.U., Ravn A.P., Rischel H. & Zhao Chao Chen, Specification of Embedded real-time systems, Proc. of Euromicro Workshop on real-time systems, IEEE Computer Society Press, 1992.
9. Skakkebaek J.U. & Sestoft P, Checking Validity of Duration Calculus Formulas, Report ID/DTH/ JUS 3/1, Technical University of Denmark, Denmark, 1994.
10. Yuhua Z. & Zhou Chaochen, A Formal Proof of the Deadline Driven Scheduler, Third International Symp. on *Formal Techniques in Real-Time and Fault-Tolerant Systems*, Lubeck (Germany), LNCS No. 863, Springer Verlag, 1994, pp. 756-775.
11. Zhou Chaochen, Hoare C.A.R. & Ravn A.P., A calculus of durations, *Information Processing Letters*, Vol 40(5), pp. 269-276, 1991.
12. Zhou Chaochen, Hansen M.R. & Sestoft P, Decidability and Undecidability Results in Duration Calculus, Proc. of the 10th Annual Symposium on *Theoretical Aspects of Computer Science (STACS 93)*, LNCS No. 665, Springer Verlag, 1993.

Fair Synchronous Transition Systems and Their Liveness Proofs[*]

A. Pnueli[1]   N. Shankar[2]   E. Singerman[2]

[1] Weizmann Institute of Science, Rehovot, Israel
[2] SRI International, Menlo Park, California, USA

Abstract. We present a compositional semantics of synchronous systems that captures both safety and progress properties of such systems. The *fair synchronous transitions systems* (FSTS) model we introduce in this paper extends the basic αSTS model [KP96] by introducing operations for parallel composition, for the restriction of variables, and by addressing fairness. We introduce a weak fairness (justice) condition which ensures that any communication deadlock in a system can only occur through the need for external synchronization. We present an extended version of linear time temporal logic (ELTL) for expressing and proving safety and liveness properties of synchronous specifications, and provide a sound and compositional proof system for it.

1   Introduction

Synchronous languages are rapidly gaining popularity as a high-level programming paradigm for a variety of safety-critical and real-time control applications and for hardware/software co-design. Synchronous languages are used to define systems that are:

- Reactive: Engaged in an ongoing interaction with an environment.
- Event-triggered: System computation is triggered by the arrival and absence of external inputs.
- Concurrent: A system is composed of subsystems that are computing and interacting concurrently.
- Synchronous: The system response to input stimuli is "instantaneous".

---

[*] This research was supported in part by the Minerva Foundation, by an infrastructure grant from the Israeli Ministry of Science, by US National Science Foundation grants CCR-9509931 and CCR-9712383, and by US Air Force Office of Scientific Research Contract No. F49620-95-C0044. Part of this research was done as part of the European Community project SACRES (EP 20897). The views and conclusions contained herein are those of the authors and should not be interpreted as necessarily representing the official policies or endorsements, either expressed or implied, of NSF, AFOSR, the European Union, or the U.S. Government. We are grateful to Sam Owre for lending assistance with PVS.

There are two major classes of synchronous languages [H93]. The *imperative* languages like ESTEREL [BG92] and STATECHARTS [Har87], and *declarative* languages like LUSTRE [CHPP87] and SIGNAL [BGJ91].

The present paper presents a unifying compositional transition system model for synchronous languages based on *fair synchronous transition systems* (FSTS) that can be used as a semantic basis for synchronous languages. Such a unifying semantic model can be used to specify the temporal behavior of synchronous systems and to relate different synchronous system descriptions. The semantics is given in terms of the model of fair synchronous transitions systems (FSTS), which is based on the αSTS model [KP96]. The αSTS model has been used as a common semantic domain for both SIGNAL programs and the C-code generated by compiling them, for proving the correctness of the translation (compilation) [PSiS98]. It has also been used in [BGA97] as a semantics which is "...fully general to capture the essence of the synchronous paradigm."

The FSTS model presented here extends αSTS by introducing operations for parallel composition, for the restriction of variables, and by addressing fairness. It can be used to answer questions such as:

- What is the valid set of runs corresponding to a given synchronous specification?
- How can we characterize a set of fair computations corresponding to a given synchronous specification?
- How can linear time temporal logic be adapted to reasoning about fair synchronous specifications?
- What is a sound compositional proof system for proving temporal safety and liveness properties of synchronous specifications?

The FSTS model is designed to be simple and general. It extends the classical notion of transition systems with *signals* that can be present or absent in a given state, communication as *synchronization* by means of signals, *stuttering* as the absence of signals, and local progress through weak fairness constraints. The fairness condition ensures that any communication deadlock in a module can only occur through the need for external synchronization. Except for the fairness condition, the presence or absence of a signal is treated in a symmetrical manner as is the case in synchronous languages. The use of weak fairness constraints ensures that a module can satisfy these constraints without the cooperation of the environment, i.e., the module is *receptive* [AL95].

The FSTS model, the compositionality proofs, the extended linear temporal logic, and the accompanying soundness proofs have all been formally verified using PVS [Ow95]. The PVS verification pointed out a number of gaps in our earlier formalization and led to sharper definitions of the basic concepts, and elegant and rigorous proofs.[1]

The paper is organized as follows. In Section 2 we introduce the FSTS computational model. In Section 3 we define two important operations on FSTS

---

[1] The PVS formalization and proofs can be obtained from the URL `www.csl.sri.com/~singermn/fsts/`.

modules, *parallel composition* and *restriction*, and motivate the definitions by an intuitive example of progress (liveness). In Section 4 we present a formal method for proving temporal properties of synchronous systems by introducing an appropriate logic for expressing these properties and a system of deductive proof rules. We demonstrate the use of these rules by formalizing the intuitive arguments used in the example of Section 3. In Section 5 we outline the FSTS semantics of the most expressive synchronous language – SIGNAL. (The FSTS semantics of ESTEREL and LUSTRE can be obtained in a similar way.)

2 Fair Synchronous Transition Systems

In this section, we introduce the notion of *fair synchronous transition systems*.

The Computational Model

We assume a vocabulary V which is a set of typed variables. Variables which are intended to represent signals are identified as *volatile*, and their domain contains a distinguished element $\perp$ used to denote the absence of the respective signal. In the translation of synchronous programs to FSTS specifications (see Section 5), we shall also use *persistent* variables to simulate the "memorization" operators of the synchronous languages (e.g., **current** in LUSTRE, "$\$$" in SIGNAL).

Some of the types we consider are the *booleans* with domain $B = \{T, F\}$, the type of *integers* whose domain Z consists of all the integers, the type of *pure signals* with domain $S_\perp = \{T, \perp\}$, the type of *extended booleans* with domain $B_\perp = \{T, F, \perp\}$, and the type of *extended integers* with domain $Z_\perp = Z \cup \{\perp\}$.

We define a *state* s to be a type-consistent interpretation of V, assigning to each variable $u \in V$ a value $s[u]$ over its domain. We denote by Σ the set of all states. For a subset of variables $V \subseteq V$, we define a *V-state* to be a type-consistent interpretation of V.

Following [MP91] and [KP96], we define a *fair synchronous transition system* (FSTS) to be a system

$$\Phi: \quad \langle V, \Theta, \rho, E, S \rangle,$$

consisting of the following components:

- V : A finite set of typed *system variables*.
- Θ : The *initial condition*. A satisfiable assertion characterizing the initial states.
- ρ : A *transition relation*. This is an assertion $\rho(V, V')$, which relates a state $s \in \Sigma$ to its possible successors $s' \in \Sigma$ by referring to both unprimed and primed versions of the system variables. An unprimed version of a system variable refers to its value in s, while a primed version of the same variable refers to its value in s'. For example, the assertion $x' = x + 1$ states that the value of x in s' is greater by 1 than its value in s. If $\rho(s[V], s'[V]) = T$, we say that state s' is a *ρ-successor* of state s.

Remark: As implied by the notation $\rho(V, V')$, ρ can only refer to the variables of Φ, and therefore cannot distinguish between two possible Φ-successors that agree on the values of all the variables of Φ. That is, for all $s, s_1, s_2 \in \Sigma$,

$$s_1|V = s_2|V \;\rightarrow\; (\rho(s, s_1) \Leftrightarrow \rho(s, s_2)).$$

- $E \subseteq V$: The set of *externally observable variables*. These are the variables that can be observed outside the module. We refer to $L = V - E$ as the *local variables*. Local variables cannot be observed outside the module.
- $S \subseteq E$: The set of *synchronization variables*. These are the signal variables on which the module may (and needs to) synchronize with its environment. We refer to $C = V - S$ as the *controllable variables*. These are the variables on whose values the module has full control.

For states $s, s' \in \Sigma$ and assertion $\varphi(V, V')$, we say that φ holds over the *joint interpretation* $\langle s, s' \rangle$, denoted $\langle s, s' \rangle \models \varphi$, if $\varphi(V, V')$ evaluates to T over the interpretation which interprets every $x \in V$ as $s[x]$ and every x' as $s'[x]$.

For an FSTS Φ, a state s' is called a Φ-*successor* of the state s if $\langle s, s' \rangle \models \rho$.

Definition 1. *An* FSTS Φ *is called* realizable *if every state* $s \in \Sigma$ *has a* Φ-*successor in which all the synchronization variables assume the value* $\bot$. *This requirement expresses the possibility that the environment might not be ready to co-operate with the module* Φ *in the current state.*

From now on, we restrict our attention to realizable FSTS specifications.

Computations of an FSTS

Let $\Phi = \langle V, \Theta, \rho, E, S \rangle$ be an FSTS. A *computation* of Φ is an infinite sequence

$$\sigma: \quad s_0, s_1, s_2, \ldots,$$

where, for each $i = 0, 1, \ldots,$ $s_i \in \Sigma$, and σ satisfies the following requirements:

- *Initiation:* s_0 is initial, i.e., $s_0 \models \Theta$.
- *Consecution:* For each $j = 0, 1, \ldots,$ s_{j+1} is a Φ-successor of s_j.
- *Justice* (weak fairness): We say that a signal variable $x \in C$ is *enabled with respect to* S at state s_j of σ if there exists a Φ-successor s of s_j, such that $s[x] \neq \bot \wedge s[S] = \{\bot\}$. The *justice* requirement is that for every signal variable $x \in C$, it is not the case that x is enabled w.r.t. S in all but a finite number of states along σ, while $s_j[x] \neq \bot$, for only finitely many states s_j in the computation.

Remark: In the sequel, we shall sometimes use the term "enabled w.r.t. Φ" instead of "enabled w.r.t. S_Φ".

The requirement of justice with respect to a controllable signal variable x demands that if x is continuously enabled to assume a non-$\bot$ value from a certain point on, without the need to synchronize with the environment, it will eventually assume such a value. The fact that a variable x is enabled to become non-$\bot$ without 'external assistance' is evident from the existence of a Φ-successor s such that $s[x] \neq \bot \wedge s[S] = \{\bot\}$.

A *run* of a system Φ is a finite or an infinite sequence of states satisfying the requirements of initiation and consecution, but not necessarily the requirement of justice.

An FSTS is called *viable* if every finite run can be extended into a computation. From now on, we restrict our attention to viable FSTS specifications.

For the case that Φ is a finite-state system, i.e., all system variables range over finite domains, there exist (reasonably) efficient symbolic model-checking algorithms for testing whether Φ is viable.

A state s' is a *stuttering variant* of a state s if all volatile (i.e., signal) variables are undefined in s' and s' agrees with s on all persistent variables. A state sequence $\widehat{\sigma}$ is said to be a *stuttering variant* of the state sequence $\sigma : s_0, s_1, \ldots$, if $\widehat{\sigma}$ can be obtained from σ by repeated transformations where a state s in σ is replaced with s, s' in $\widehat{\sigma}$, or a pair of adjacent states s, s' in σ is replaced with s in $\widehat{\sigma}$ where s' is a stuttering variant of s. A set of state sequences S is called *closed under stuttering* if, for every state sequence σ, $\sigma \in S$ iff all stuttering variants of σ belong to S. An FSTS Φ is called *stuttering robust* if the set of Φ-computations is closed under stuttering.

3 Operations on FSTS Modules

There are two important operations on FSTS modules: *parallel composition* and *restriction*.

3.1 Parallel Composition

Let Φ_1: $\langle V_1, \Theta_1, \rho_1, E_1, S_1 \rangle$ and Φ_2: $\langle V_2, \Theta_2, \rho_2, E_2, S_2 \rangle$ be two FSTS modules. These systems are called *syntactically compatible* if they satisfy

$$C_1 \cap V_2 = V_1 \cap C_2 = \emptyset \text{ (or equivalently } V_1 \cap V_2 = S_1 \cap S_2).$$

That is, only synchronization variables can be common to both systems. We define the *parallel composition* of syntactically compatible Φ_1 and Φ_2, denoted $\Phi = \Phi_1 \parallel \Phi_2$, to be the FSTS Φ: $\langle V, \Theta, \rho, E, S \rangle$, where

$$V = V_1 \cup V_2$$
$$\Theta = \Theta_1 \wedge \Theta_2$$
$$\rho = \rho_1 \wedge \rho_2$$
$$E = E_1 \cup E_2$$
$$S = S_1 \cup S_2$$

The following theorem (whose proof can be found in [PShS98]) indicates the relation between computations of a composed system and computations of its constituents.

Theorem 1. *Let Φ_1: $\langle V_1, \Theta_1, \rho_1, E_1, S_1 \rangle$ and Φ_2: $\langle V_2, \Theta_2, \rho_2, E_2, S_2 \rangle$ be two compatible FSTS modules, and σ: $s_0, s_1, s_2, \ldots$ a sequence of states.*

σ is a computation of $\Phi_1 \parallel \Phi_2 \iff \sigma$ is both a computation of Φ_1 and of Φ_2.

3.2 Restriction

In the operation of restriction, we identify a set of synchronization variables and close off the system for external synchronization on these variables.

Let $W \subseteq S$ be a set of synchronization variables of the FSTS Φ: $\langle V, \Theta, \rho, E, S \rangle$. We define the *$W$-restriction* of Φ, denoted [**own** W: Φ], to be the FSTS $\widetilde{\Phi}$: $\langle \widetilde{V}, \widetilde{\Theta}, \widetilde{\rho}, \widetilde{E}, \widetilde{S} \rangle$, where $\widetilde{V} = V$, $\widetilde{\Theta} = \Theta$, $\widetilde{\rho} = \rho$, $\widetilde{E} = E$, and $\widetilde{S} = S \setminus W$.

Thus the effect of W-restricting the system Φ amounts to moving the variables in W from S to C. This movement may have a considerable effect on the computations of the system.

Example 1 Consider the FSTS Φ, where

$$V = E = S : \{x : \{\text{T}, \bot\}\}$$
$$\Theta : x = \text{T}$$
$$\rho : x' = \text{T} \ \lor \ x' = \bot.$$

Let $\widetilde{\Phi}$: [**own** x. Φ] denote the x-restriction of Φ. The sequence below, in which next to each state appears the set of all possible successors,

$$\sigma: \quad s_0: \langle x: \text{T} \rangle, \quad \{\langle x: \bot \rangle, \langle x: \text{T} \rangle\}$$
$$s_1: \langle x: \bot \rangle, \quad \{\langle x: \bot \rangle, \langle x: \text{T} \rangle\}$$
$$s_2: \langle x: \bot \rangle, \qquad \cdots$$

is a computation of Φ but is not a computation of $\widetilde{\Phi}$. Note that x assumes a non-$\bot$ value only at s_0. The sequence σ is a computation of Φ since x is not in C ($x \in S$), and therefore is not enabled w.r.t. S in any state of σ. On the other hand, x is no longer a synchronization variable in $\widetilde{\Phi}$, since it belongs to $\widetilde{C}$. The sequence σ is not a computation of $\widetilde{\Phi}$ since it is unfair to x. This is because now, x is enabled w.r.t. $S_{\widetilde{\Phi}}$ in every state of σ, but $s[x] \neq \bot$ only in s_0. From this we can deduce that all computations of $\widetilde{\Phi}$ contain infinitely many states in which $x \neq \bot$, but this is not necessarily the case for computations of Φ.

The following lemma (whose proof is left for the journal version) describes the relation between computations of unrestricted and restricted systems.

Lemma 1. *The infinite sequence σ: $s_0, s_1, s_2, \ldots$ is a computation of [**own** W. Φ] iff*

- σ *is a computation of Φ, and*
- σ *satisfies the justice requirement w.r.t. $S \setminus W$.*

Thus, the computations of [**own** $W. \Phi$] can be obtained from those of Φ.

Example 2 Consider the FSTS Φ_1 defined by

$$V_1 = E_1 : \{x, y : Z_\bot\}$$
$$S_1 : \{x\}$$
$$\Theta_1 : x = y = \bot$$
$$\rho_1 : (y' = 3) \wedge (x' = 4) \ \vee \ (y' = \bot) \wedge (x' \neq 4)$$

and the FSTS Φ_2 defined by

$$V_2 = E_2 = S_2 : x : Z_\bot$$
$$\Theta_2 : x = \bot$$
$$\rho_2 : (x' = 4) \vee (x' = 5) \vee (x' = \bot).$$

Both of these FSTS modules have computations satisfying $\Box \Diamond (y = 3)$. There exists, however, a computation of both Φ_1 and Φ_2 which by Theorem 1 is therefore also a computation of $\Phi_1 \parallel \Phi_2$, which does not satisfy $\Box \Diamond (y = 3)$. This computation is

$$\sigma: \quad s_0 : \langle \overset{x}{\bot}, \overset{y}{\bot} \rangle, \ \{\langle \bot, \bot \rangle, \langle 4, 3 \rangle, \langle 5, \bot \rangle\}$$
$$s_1 : \langle \bot, \bot \rangle, \ \{\langle \bot, \bot \rangle, \langle 4, 3 \rangle, \langle 5, \bot \rangle\}$$
$$s_2 : \langle \bot, \bot \rangle, \qquad \cdots$$

In σ, the variable y does not get the value 3 even once. This is fair, since y is not enabled w.r.t. $S_{\Phi_1 \parallel \Phi_2}$ in any state of σ. This is because $y' \neq \bot \wedge x' = \bot$ is false in every state of σ. Now, suppose we close off Φ with respect to x, to get the FSTS module $\widetilde{\Phi}$: [**own** $x. [\Phi_1 \parallel \Phi_2]$]. In $\widetilde{\Phi}$, x is no longer a synchronization variable, and therefore y is continuously enabled w.r.t. $S_{\widetilde{\Phi}}$ in σ (in every state, in fact). However, it is obviously not the case that $y \neq \bot$ is satisfied infinitely often in σ, and hence σ is not a computation of $\widetilde{\Phi}$. In conclusion, we see that only the restriction of x guarantees $\Box \Diamond (y = 3)$.

4 Compositional Verification of FSTS Modules

In this section we show how to construct compositional verification of the temporal properties of FSTS's, concentrating on liveness properties.

First, we define an appropriate temporal logic. Let ELTL be LTL extended with the unary predicate *ready*. An ELTL *model* is a pair $M = (\sigma, L)$, where σ is an infinite sequences of the form

$$\sigma: \quad s_0, s_1, s_2, \ldots, \text{ where } s_j \in \Sigma, \text{ for every } j \geq 0,$$

and $L : \Sigma \to 2^\Sigma$. ELTL formulas are interpreted as follows.

- For a state formula p, $(M, j) \models p \leftrightarrow s_j \models p$.

- $(M, j) \models \neg p \leftrightarrow (M, j) \not\models p$.
- $(M, j) \models p \vee q \leftrightarrow (M, j) \models p$ or $(M, j) \models q$.
- $(M, j) \models \bigcirc p \leftrightarrow (M, j + 1) \models p$.
- $(M, j) \models p \mathcal{U} q \leftrightarrow (M, k) \models q$ for some $k \geq j$ and $(M, i) \models p$ for all i, $j \leq i < k$.
- For a state formula p, $(M, j) \models ready(p) \leftrightarrow \exists s \in L(s_j)$ s.t. $s \models p$.

As usual, we use the abbreviations $\Diamond p$ for $\mathtt{T} \mathcal{U} p$ and $\Box p$ for $\neg \Diamond \neg p$.

We say that a model M *satisfies* an ELTL formula p, written $M \models p$, if $(M, 0) \models p$.

Notation: For an ELTL model $M = (\sigma, L)$, we denote by $\sigma(i)$, the $i + 1$-th element of σ.

For an FSTS Φ, the ELTL model $M = (\sigma, L)$ is called a Φ-*model*, if

- σ is a computation of Φ, and
- For every $j = 0, 1, 2, \ldots$, $L(\sigma(j))$ is the set of all possible Φ-successors of $\sigma(j)$, i.e., $L(\sigma(j)) = \text{image}(\rho, \{\sigma(j)\})$.

We write $\Phi \models p$, and say that p *is valid over* Φ, if $M \models p$, for every Φ-*model* M.

Definition 2. *An* ELTL *formula is called* universal, *if it does not contain ready or if each occurrence of ready appears under an* odd *number of negations.*

We present our method by formalizing the intuitive arguments used in Example 2. In the proof, we introduce several deductive rules that we believe may be useful in typical liveness proofs.

Let us begin by noting that

$$\Phi_1, \Phi_2 \models \Box ready(y = 3 \wedge x = 4), \tag{1}$$

can be verified independently for Φ_1 and for Φ_2. From (1) and the temporal tautology $q \rightarrow \Diamond q$, we can derive

$$\Phi_1, \Phi_2 \models \Diamond \Box ready(y = 3 \wedge x = 4). \tag{2}$$

Applying rule READY, presented in Fig. 1, to (2) yields

$$\Phi_1 \parallel \Phi_2 \models \Diamond \Box ready(y = 3 \wedge x = 4). \tag{3}$$

From the latter, we can easily derive

$$\Phi_1 \parallel \Phi_2 \models \Diamond \Box ready(y \neq \bot). \tag{4}$$

By applying rule OWN (Fig. 2) to (4), with $W = \{x\}$, we get

$$\underbrace{[\mathbf{own}\ x.\,[\Phi_1 \parallel \Phi_2]]}_{\Phi} \models \Diamond \Box ready(y \neq \bot). \tag{5}$$

$$
\boxed{
\begin{array}{l}
1.\ \Phi_1 \models \Diamond\Box\, ready(z_1 = c_1 \wedge \ldots \wedge z_n = c_n),\ \text{where } \{z_1, \ldots, z_n\} \supseteq S_{\Phi_1} \cap S_{\Phi_2} \\
2.\ \Phi_2 \models \Diamond\Box\, ready(z_1 = c_1 \wedge \ldots \wedge z_n = c_n) \\
\hline
\quad \Phi_1 \parallel \Phi_2 \models \Diamond\Box\, ready(z_1 = c_1 \wedge \ldots \wedge z_n = c_n)
\end{array}
}
$$

Fig. 1. Rule READY.

$$
\boxed{
\begin{array}{c}
\Phi \models p,\ \text{where } p \in \text{ELTL} \\
\hline
[\mathbf{own}\ W.\Phi] \models p
\end{array}
}
$$

Fig. 2. Rule OWN.

Now, since $S_\Phi = \emptyset$, we can use axiom CONT (Fig. 3), and (5) with $z = y$, to derive

$$\Phi \models \Box\Diamond(y \neq \bot). \tag{6}$$

It is not difficult to prove

$$\Phi_1 \models \Box(y = 3 \vee y = \bot). \tag{7}$$

By applying rule COMP (Fig. 4) to the latter, we get

$$\Phi_1 \parallel \Phi_2 \models \Box(y = 3 \vee y = \bot). \tag{8}$$

We now apply rule OWN (Fig. 2) to (8), to get

$$\Phi \models \Box(y = 3 \vee y = \bot). \tag{9}$$

The latter, together with (6) implies $\Phi \models \Box\Diamond(y = 3)$ which completes the proof.

The soundness of the deductive rules we have introduced is stated in the following theorem whose proof is omitted due to lack of space. A detailed proof can be found in [PShS98].

Theorem 2. *The rules* READY, OWN, CONT *and* COMP *are sound.*

We conclude with a practical remark. Verification of FSTS specification can be done by using existing symbolic model-checking algorithms. Computing the L-sets comes at no extra cost, since the predicate $ready(p)$ is equivalent to the CTL formula EXp which every model checker knows how to compute very efficiently.

5 The FSTS semantics of SIGNAL

As mentioned in the introduction, the FSTS model is a significant extension of the previous, more basic αSTS model [KP96] obtained by introducing operations

$$\Phi \models \Diamond \Box \, ready(z \neq \bot \wedge S_\Phi = \bot) \rightarrow \Box \Diamond (z \neq \bot), \text{ where } z \in C_\Phi$$

Fig. 3. Axiom CONT.

$$\Phi_1 \models p, \text{ where } p \in \text{ELTL is universal}$$

$$\Phi_1 \parallel \Phi_2 \models p$$

Fig. 4. Rule COMP.

(parallel composition and restriction) and by addressing fairness. The translation from SIGNAL programs to corresponding FSTS specifications, however, is not affected by these extensions, and can be carried out exactly as with αSTS simply by taking the input/output variables as the *externally observable* variables and also as the *synchronization* variables. Nevertheless, to make the paper more self-contained, we sketch below an outline of the translation given by Kesten and Pnueli [KP96].

In the following, we describe how to construct an FSTS Φ_P corresponding to a given SIGNAL program P.

Notation: For a variable v, $clocked(v)$ denotes the assertion $v \neq \bot$.

System Variables

The system variables of Φ are given by $V = U \cup X$, where U are the SIGNAL variables explicitly declared and manipulated in P, and X is a set of auxiliary variables. An auxiliary variable by the name of $x.v$ is included in X for each expression of the form v \$ appearing in P. The value of $x.v$ is intended to represent the value of v at the previous instance (present excluded) that v was different from $\bot$.

Externally observable and synchronization variables

The externally observable variables E and also the synchronization variables S are those explicitly declared in P as input/output variables.

Initial Condition

The initial condition for Φ is given by

$$\Theta: \bigwedge_{u \in U} u = \bot \quad \wedge \quad \bigwedge_{x.v \in U} x.v = \bot$$

As will result from our FSTS translation of SIGNAL programs, they are all stuttering robust. Consequently, we can simplify things by assuming that the first state in each run of the system is a stuttering state.

Transition Relation

The transition relation ρ will be a conjunction of assertions, where each SIGNAL statement gives rise to a conjunct in ρ. We list below several representative statements of SIGNAL and, for each statement S, we present the conjunct contributed to ρ by S. For a complete discussion see [KP96] and [PShS98].

- Consider the SIGNAL statement $y := f(v_1, \ldots, v_n)$, where f is a state-function. This statement requires that the signals $y, v_1, \ldots, v_n$ are present at precisely the same time instants, and that at these instants $y = f(v_1, \ldots, v_n)$. Its contribution to ρ is given by:

$$clocked(y') \equiv clocked(v_1') \equiv \ldots \equiv clocked(v_n')$$
$$\wedge\ (clocked(y') \rightarrow y' = f(v_1', \ldots, v_n'))$$

- The contribution of $y := v\$\ \mathbf{init}\ v_0$, stating that the value of y is that of v shifted by one time unit (initialized with v_0) and that both variables have the same clock, is given by:

$$x'.v = \mathbf{if}\ clocked(v')\ \mathbf{then}\ v'\ \mathbf{else}\ x.v$$
$$\wedge\ y' = \begin{pmatrix} \mathbf{if} & \neg clocked(v')\ \mathbf{then}\ \bot \\ \mathbf{else\ if}\ x.v = \bot & \mathbf{then}\ v_0 \\ \mathbf{else} & x.v \end{pmatrix}$$

- The contribution of $y := v\ \mathbf{when}\ b$, stating that y is present and has the value of v only when v is present and b is true, is given by:

$$y' = \mathbf{if}\ (b' = \mathrm{T})\ \mathbf{then}\ v'\ \mathbf{else}\ \bot.$$

- The contribution of $y := u\ \mathbf{default}\ v$, stating that the value of y is that of v if v is present, or else it is the value of v if v is present and otherwise it is $\bot$, is given by:

$$y' = \mathbf{if}\ clocked(u')\ \mathbf{then}\ u'\ \mathbf{else}\ v'.$$

6 Conclusions and Future Work

We have presented FSTS, a compositional semantics of synchronous systems that captures both safety and progress properties. We have motivated the fairness requirement and the operations of parallel composition and of restriction of variables by means of intuitive examples.

We have then introduced an extended version of linear temporal logic (ELTL), in which it is convenient to express safety and liveness properties of synchronous specifications, and have presented (and demonstrated) a sound compositional proof system for it.

We have concluded by specifying how to translate programs written in an expressive representative of the synchronous school, namely SIGNAL, to FSTS.

Directions in future work which we intend to pursue are

- Specifying in detail the FSTS semantics of LUSTRE, ESTEREL and STATECHARTS.
- Apply the deductive proof system developed here together with existing symbolic model-checking algorithms to the verification of FSTS specifications that result from actual synchronous programs.

References

[AL95]   M. Abadi and L. Lamport. Conjoining Specifications. *TOPLAS*, 17(3), pages 507–534, 1995.

[BGA97]   A. Benveniste, P. Le Guernic, and P. Aubry. Compositionality in dataflow synchronous languages: specification & code generation. *Proceedings of COMPOS'97*.

[BGJ91]   A. Benveniste, P. Le Guernic, and C. Jacquemot. Synchronous programming with event and relations: the SIGNAL language and its semantics. *Science of Computer Programming*, 16, pages 103–149, 1991.

[BG92]   G. Berry and G. Gonthier. The ESTEREL Synchronous Programming Language: Design, semantics, implementation. *Science of Computer Programming*, 19(2), 1992.

[CHPP87]   P. Caspi, N. Halbwachs, D. Pilaud, and J. Plaice. LUSTRE, a Declarative Language for Programming Synchronous Systems. *POPL'87*, ACM Press, pages 178–188, 1987.

[H93]   N. Halbwachs. *Synchronous Programming of Reactive Systems*. Kluwer, Dordrecht, The Netherlands, 1993.

[Har87]   D. Harel. Statecharts: A Visual Formalism for Complex Systems. *Science of Computer Programming*, 8, pages 231–274, 1987.

[KP96]   Y. Kesten and A. Pnueli. An αSTS-based common semantics for SIGNAL and STATECHARTS, March 1996. Sacres Manuscript.

[MP91]   Z. Manna and A. Pnueli. *The Temporal Logic of Reactive and Concurrent Systems: Specification*. Springer-Verlag, New York, 1991.

[Ow95]   S. Owre, J. Rushby, N. Shankar, and F. von Henke. Formal Verification for Fault-Tolerant Architectures: Prolegomena to the Design of PVS. IEEE trans. on software eng., 21(2), pages 107–125, 1995.

[PSiS98]   A. Pnueli, M. Siegel, and E. Singerman. Translation Validation. *TACAS'98*, LNCS 1384, pages 151–166, 1998.

[PShS98]   A. Pnueli, N. Shankar, and E. Singerman. Fair Synchronous Transition Systems and their Liveness Proofs. Technical Report SRI-CSL-98-02, http://www.csl.sri.com/csl-98-2.html, 1998.

Dynamical Properties of Timed Automata

Anuj Puri
Bell Laboratories
Murray Hill, NJ 07974
anuj@research.bell-labs.com

Abstract. Timed automata are an important model for specifying and analyzing real-time systems. The main analysis performed on timed automata is the reachability analysis. In this paper we show that the standard approach for performing reachability analysis is not correct when the clocks drift even by a very small amount. Our formulation of the reachability problem for timed automata is as follows: we define the set $R^*(T, Z_0) = \cap_{\epsilon>0} Reach(T_\epsilon, Z_0)$ where T_ϵ is obtained from timed automaton T by allowing an ϵ drift in the clocks. $R^*(T, Z_0)$ is the set of states which can be reached in the timed automaton T from the initial states in Z_0 when the clocks drift by an infinitesimally small amount. We present an algorithm for computing $R^*(T, Z_0)$ and provide a proof of its correctness. We show that $R^*(T, Z_0)$ is robust with respect to various types of modeling errors. To prove the correctness of our algorithm, we need to understand the dynamics of timed automata — in particular, the structure of the limit cycles of timed automata.

Keywords: Timed Automata, Dynamical Systems, Verification

1 Introduction

Real-time systems play an increasingly important role in applications ranging from telecommunications to computer controlled physical systems. An important model for analyzing real-time systems is the timed automata model [1]. A timed automaton is an automaton coupled with a finite number of continuous clocks. The clocks move uniformly at rate one and a jump is made from one control location of the automaton to another based on the value of the clocks. Timed automata have been used for specifying and analyzing numerous real-time systems from a variety of application domains and a number of computer tools are now available for their analysis [1, 3–5, 7–9, 12, 17].

The main analysis performed on timed automata is the reachability analysis. The reachability analysis checks whether some undesirable states of the system are reachable from the initial state. In [1], it was shown that a finite *region graph* can be constructed from the timed automata and the reachability problem can be solved using this graph. In this paper we show that the approach of [1] is not robust. Reachability analysis done using the approach of [1] will not be correct under the assumption of a small drift in clocks. This is disturbing because the behavior of a system when the clocks drift even a little bit maybe quite different from what happens when the system has perfect clocks. This is the issue we address in this paper.

Let us describe the problem we want to solve. Define $Reach(T, Z_0)$ to be the reachable states in the timed automaton T starting from the initial states in Z_0. Similarly define $Reach(T_\epsilon, Z_0)$ to be the reachable states in T_ϵ where T_ϵ is obtained by allowing an ϵ drift in the clocks in T. Now $Reach(T, Z_0) \subset Reach(T_\epsilon, Z_0)$. We will be interested in computing the limit $R^*(T, Z_0) = \cap_{\epsilon > 0} Reach(T_\epsilon, Z_0)$. The set $R^*(T, Z_0)$ is the limit of $Reach(T_\epsilon, Z_0)$ as $\epsilon \to 0$. So $R^*(T, Z_0)$ is the set of states which can be reached in the timed automaton T from the initial states in Z_0 when the clocks drift by an infinitesimally small amount. In general, $R^*(T, Z_0) \neq Reach(T, Z_0)$. In this paper we present an algorithm for computing $R^*(T, Z_0)$. To prove the correctness of our algorithm, we will need to understand the dynamics of timed automata — in particular, the structure of the limit cycles of timed automata. We will show that unlike $Reach(T, Z_0)$, $R^*(T, Z_0)$ is robust against various types of modeling errors and drifts in clocks.

Our main contributions in this paper are as follows:

1. We present an algorithm for computing $R^*(T, Z_0)$ and a proof of its correctness.
2. We present an analysis of the dynamics of timed automata. In particular, we present a complete analysis of the limit cycles of timed automata.
3. We provide a method for establishing the relationship between the trajectories of the timed automaton T and the perturbed model T_ϵ.

In other related work, [1] presented an algorithm for computing $Reach(T, Z_0)$. The complexity of this algorithm is $O(|L|(n!)2^n M^n)$ where the state space of the timed automaton is $Q_T \subset L \times [0, M]^n$. This result was extended in [11] which presented an algorithm for computing $Reach(T_\delta, Z_0)$ for a fixed $\delta = \frac{k}{l}$. The complexity of this algorithm was $O(|L|(2n!)2^{2n}(Ml)^{2n})$. We define $R^*(T, Z_0)$ to be the limit of $Reach(T_\delta, Z_0)$ as $\delta \to 0$. In general, $R^*(T, Z_0) \neq Reach(T, Z_0)$. We present an algorithm for computing $R^*(T, Z_0)$ and a proof of its correctness. The complexity of our algorithm for computing $R^*(T, Z_0)$ is $O(|L|(n!)2^n M^n)$. In particular, the complexity for computing $R^*(T, Z_0)$ does not depend on δ.

In Section 2, we introduce our notation. In Section 3, we describe the timed automata model and review the work of [1]. In Section 4, we show that the reachability analysis based on the approach of [1] is not robust. We then present our formulation of the reachability problem. In Section 5, we present the algorithm for computing $R^*(T, Z_0)$. Proving correctness of the algorithm relies on understanding the structure of the limit cycles of timed automata and on understanding the relationship between the trajectories of T and T_ϵ. In Section 6, we discuss the relationship between zones and regions. In Section 7, we provide a complete analysis of the limit cycles of timed automata. In Section 8, we discuss the relationship between the trajectories of T and T_ϵ. In Section 9, we show that $R^*(T, Z_0)$ is a robust set. Section 10 discusses the complexity of computing $R^*(T, Z_0)$ and Section 11 is the conclusion.

A complete version of this paper is available as [16].

2 Notation

2.1 Preliminaries

The set $\mathbb{R}$ ($\mathbb{R}^+$) are the (positive) reals and $\mathbb{Z}$ ($\mathbb{Z}^+$) are the (positive) integers. For $x \in \mathbb{R}^n$, we write x_i for the ith component of x. For $x, y \in \mathbb{R}^n$, define $\|x - y\| = \max_i |x_i - y_i|$. For a set $S \subset \mathbb{R}^n$ and $x \in \mathbb{R}^n$, define $dist(x, S) = \inf_{s \in S} \|x - s\|$. For $S \subset \mathbb{R}^n$, $cl(S)$ is the closure of S and $conv(S)$ is the convex hull of S. For sets X and Y, $X + Y = \{x + y \mid x \in X, \ y \in Y\}$. A set-valued map is $f : A \longrightarrow B$ where $f(a)$ is a set. We define $f^{i+1}(x) = \{z \mid z \in f(y) \text{ and } y \in f^i(x)\}$.

2.2 Graphs

A graph is $G = (V, \longrightarrow_G)$ where V is the set of vertices and $\longrightarrow_G \subset V \times V$ is the set of edges (i.e., there is an edge from v to w provided $v \longrightarrow_G w$). We write $v \Longrightarrow_G w$ provided there is a path from v to w in G.

A non-trivial strongly connected component (SCC) of G is a maximal set $S \subset V$ such that for any $v, w \in S$, $v \Longrightarrow_G w$ and each vertex $v \in S$ is contained in a cycle. In this paper we will only be interested in non-trivial strongly connected components. There are well known algorithms for computing the non-trivial strongly connected components of a graph [6].

2.3 Zones

A $\mathbb{Z}$-zone ($\mathbb{R}$-zone) $Z \subset \mathbb{R}^n$ is a closed set defined by inequalities of the form

$$x_i - x_j \leq u_{ij}, \qquad l_i \leq x_i \leq u_i \tag{1}$$

where $i, j \in \{1, \ldots, n\}$ and $u_{ij}, l_i, u_i \in \mathbb{Z}$ ($u_{ij}, l_i, u_i \in \mathbb{R}$). We will refer to $\mathbb{Z}$-zones simply as zones.

3 Timed Automata

A timed automaton [1] is an automaton with a finite number of real-valued clocks, a finite number of control locations and edges between the control locations. In the control locations, the clocks move uniformly at rate one. A jump from one location to another can be made when the clocks satisfy the guards on the edges. During the jump, some of the clocks may get reset to zero.

More formally, a timed automaton is $T = (L, E)$ where L is the set of control locations and E is the set of edges. The state of a timed automaton with n clocks is (l, x) where l is a control location and $x \in \mathbb{R}^n$. An edge from location

l to location m is $e = (l, g, j, m)$ where g is the guard and $j \subset \{1, \ldots, n\}$ are the clocks which are reset on the jump from l to m. The guard g is a closed zone in $\mathbb{R}^n$. The state space of the timed automaton is $Q_T \subset L \times [0, M]^n$ where $Q_T = \cup_{l \in L} (l, Z_l)$ and Z_l is a closed zone. Notice the state space of our timed automaton is a closed bounded set and the guards are closed sets.

Figure 1 is an example of a timed automaton with clocks a and b, control locations A and B, and state space $Q_T = (A, 0 \leq b \leq a \leq 2) \cup (B, 0 \leq a \leq b \leq 2)$.

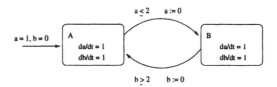

Fig. 1. A Timed Automaton

We now review the work of [1] who presented a method for solving the reachability problem in timed automata.

3.1 Transition System

The transition system of the timed automaton describes how the state of the timed automaton moves. The transition system of the timed automaton is $T = (Q_T, \longrightarrow, \Sigma)$ where Q_T is the state space of the timed automaton, $\longrightarrow \subset Q_T \times \Sigma \times Q_T$ is the transition relation and $\Sigma = \mathbb{R}^+ \cup \{d\}$ is the set of moves.

The state of the timed automaton moves by either staying in the same control location and letting time elapse, or by making a jump from one control location to another.

Definition 31 *The transition system of timed automaton* $T = (L, E)$ *is* $T = (Q_T, \longrightarrow, \mathbb{R}^+ \cup \{d\})$ *where*

1. $(l, x) \xrightarrow{t} (l, y)$ *provided* $y = x + t$.
2. $(l, x) \xrightarrow{d} (m, y)$ *provided* $(l, g, j, m) \in E$, $x \in g$, $y_i = 0$ *when* $i \in j$, *and* $y_i = x_i$ *for* $i \notin j$.

We define the relation $\longrightarrow \subset Q_T \times Q_T$ where $q \to q'$ provided $q \xrightarrow{t} q'$ or $q \xrightarrow{d} q'$. We define the relation $\Rightarrow$ to be the reflexive and transitive closure of $\to$. So $q_0 \Rightarrow q_N$ provided there are $q_1, \ldots, q_{N-1}$ such that $q_i \to q_{i+1}$ for $i = 0, \ldots, N - 1$.

Definition 32 *For a timed automaton* $T = (L, E)$ *and an initial closed zone* Z_0, *define* $Reach(T, Z_0) = \{ q \mid q_0 \Rightarrow q, q_0 \in Z_0 \}$.

$Reach(T, Z_0)$ is the set of states which can be reached in the timed automaton T starting from a state in the initial zone Z_0. The *reachability problem* is to determine whether a state $q \in Reach(T, Z_0)$.

3.2 Trajectories of Timed Automata

A trajectory of the timed automaton is $\pi = (q_0, t_0)(q_1, t_1)$ $\ldots (q_k, t_k)$ where either $q_i \xrightarrow{d} q_{i+1}$ and $t_{i+1} = t_i$, or $\tau_i = t_{i+1} - t_i$ and $q_i \xrightarrow{\tau_i} q_{i+1}$. We will sometimes also refer to this trajectory as $\pi[t_0, t_k]$ and write $\pi(t_i)$ instead of q_i. The trajectory is *stutter-free* provided it is not the case that $q_i \xrightarrow{\tau_i} q_{i+1}$ and $q_{i+1} \xrightarrow{\tau_{i+1}} q_{i+2}$ for some i.

Example 1. A trajectory of the timed automaton of Figure 1 is $(A, a = 1, b = 0)(A, a = 1.5, b = 0.5)(B, a = 0, b = 0.5)(B, a = 1.5, b = 2.0)(A, a = 1.5, b = 0)$.

3.3 Equivalence Classes

For $c \in \mathbb{R}$, define $\lfloor c \rfloor$ to be its integer part and $\langle c \rangle$ to be its fractional part.

Definition 33 *Define a relation* $\sim \subset [0, M]^n \times [0, M]^n$ *where* $x \sim y$ *provided for every i and j*

- $\langle x_i \rangle < \langle x_j \rangle$ *iff* $\langle y_i \rangle < \langle y_j \rangle$
- $\langle x_i \rangle = \langle x_j \rangle$ *iff* $\langle y_i \rangle = \langle y_j \rangle$
- $\lfloor x_i \rfloor = \lfloor y_i \rfloor$ *for every i*

It can be checked that $\sim$ is an equivalence relation. We next describe the equivalence classes of the relation $\sim$. For a vector $x \in \mathbb{R}^n$, we define $\langle x \rangle$ to be the ordering of the fractional parts of its components. For example, for $x = (0.3 \; 4.7 \; 3.2 \; 8.3)$, $\langle x \rangle = (0 < \langle x_3 \rangle < \langle x_1 \rangle = \langle x_4 \rangle < \langle x_2 \rangle)$. Similarly, $\lfloor x \rfloor$ is a vector of integer parts of the components. For $x = (0.3 \; 4.7 \; 3.2 \; 8.3)$, $\lfloor x \rfloor = (0 \; 4 \; 3 \; 8)$.

Lemma 1. *For the relation* $\sim$, *the equivalence class* $]x[= \{ y \mid \langle x \rangle = \langle y \rangle$ *and* $\lfloor x \rfloor = \lfloor y \rfloor \}$.

Because in this paper, we have assumed that the guards, the initial set and the state space of the timed automaton are closed, we only need to deal with the closure of the equivalence classes. Let us *define* $[x] = cl(]x[)$. For example, for $x = (0.3 \; 4.7 \; 3.2 \; 8.3)$, $[x] = \{ y \mid \lfloor y \rfloor = (0 \; 4 \; 3 \; 8)$ and $(0 \leq \langle y_3 \rangle \leq \langle y_1 \rangle = \langle y_4 \rangle \leq \langle y_2 \rangle) \}$.

The relation $\sim$ and $[\;]$ extends in a natural manner to Q_T. For $q \in Q_T$, we call $[q]$ a region. Let us define $\mathcal{C} = \{ [q] \mid q \in Q_T \}$ to be the set of regions. Because Q_T is bounded, $\mathcal{C}$ is a finite set.

For a zone $Z \subset Q_T$, we define $[Z] = \{ [q] \mid q \in Z \}$. For a set $K \subset \mathcal{C}$, we define $(K) \subset Q_T$ to be the states making up the regions in K. When it is clear from the context that we are talking about (K), we may simply write it as K.

The following theorem states the basic property of regions.

Theorem 1. *[1] Suppose $q \to q'$ for $q, q' \in Q_T$. Then for any $s \in [q]$, there exists $s' \in [q']$ such that $s \to s'$; and for any $r' \in [q']$, there exists $r \in [q]$ such that $r \to r'$.*

3.4 The Region Graph

The equivalence relation $\sim$ partitions the state space Q_T into a finite set. Taking closure of the elements of this set, we obtain C. We call the members of C regions. Associated with a timed automaton is a finite *region graph* whose vertices are C and there is an edge from vertex $[q]$ to vertex $[q']$ provided some point in $]q[$ can move to a point in $]q'[$.

Definition 34 *For the timed transition system $T = (Q_T, \longrightarrow, \Sigma)$, we define the region graph $G = (C, \longrightarrow_G)$ where the vertices are C and the edges are $\longrightarrow_G \subset C \times C$. We define $[q] \longrightarrow_G [q']$ provided $q \to q'$ and $[q] \neq [q']$.*

Let us define $\Longrightarrow_G$ to be the reflexive and transitive closure of $\longrightarrow_G$. So $u \Longrightarrow_G w$ provided there is a path in the graph G from vertex u to the vertex w.

Definition 35 *For the graph $G = (C, \longrightarrow_G)$, define $Reach(G, S) = \{ v \mid v_0 \Longrightarrow_G v, v_0 \in S \}$.*

$Reach(G, S)$ is the set of vertices which can be reached in the graph G starting from a vertex in S. The region graph G is in some sense a finite description of the underlying timed automaton. In particular, as the next theorem of [1] shows the reach set of the timed automaton can be computed using the region graph G.

Theorem 2. *[1] For a timed automaton $T = (L, E)$, let $G = (C, \longrightarrow_G)$ be the underlying region graph. Then $Reach(T, Z_0) = Reach(G, [Z_0])$.*

Figure 2 shows the states which are reached in the timed automaton of Figure 1 starting from the initial state $(A, (a = 1) \wedge (b = 0))$. This set can be computed by finding the reachable vertices in the region graph G of the timed automaton of Figure 1 from the initial vertex $(A, (a = 1) \wedge (b = 0))$.

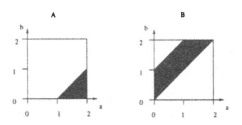

Fig. 2. The set $Reach(T, Z_0)$ for timed automaton of Figure 1

Definition 36 *A progress cycle in the region graph is a cycle in which each clock is reset at least once.*

Assumption 31 *We make the assumption that for the timed automata we consider, every cycle in the region graph is a progress cycle.*

4 A Problem with Timed Automata

In this section, we discuss a problem with computing the reach set of the timed automata using the approach of the previous section. We show that even an infinitesimally small drift in the clocks can invalidate the results obtained using the analysis of the previous section. We then present our formulation of the reachability problem for timed automata.

4.1 Problem

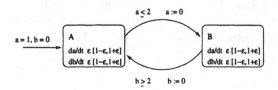

Fig. 3. The Timed Automaton T_ϵ

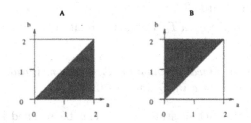

Fig. 4. The set $R^*(T, Z_0)$ for timed automaton of Figure 1

Consider again the timed automaton of Figure 1. Let us now assume that clocks a and b are not perfect, but they may drift a little bit. We model the clocks as $\dot{a} \in [1 - \epsilon, 1 + \epsilon]$ and $\dot{b} \in [1 - \epsilon, 1 + \epsilon]$ where ϵ bounds the amount of drifting. Let us call this new automaton shown in Figure 3, T_ϵ.

We will now compute the reachable states in T_ϵ. Clearly all the states in $Reach(T, Z_0)$ can also be reached in T_ϵ. In addition, the following phenomenon occurs: in the first jump from A to B, the state $(B, (b = 1+\epsilon) \wedge (a = 0))$ is reached; and on the subsequent jump from B to A, the state $(A, (a = 1 - \epsilon) \wedge (b = 0))$ is reached. In the next jump from A to B, the state $(B, (b = 1 + 2\epsilon) \wedge (a = 0))$ is reached; and on the jump from B to A, the state $(A, (a = 1 - 2\epsilon) \wedge (b = 0))$ is reached. Continuing is this manner, we find that any state $(B, (b = 1+k\epsilon) \wedge (a = 0))$ and $(A, (a = 1 - k\epsilon) \wedge (b = 0))$ can be reached. In fact, it can be checked that the whole set $R^*(T, Z_0)$ shown in Figure 4 can be reached under the assumption of drifting clocks for any $\epsilon > 0$. On the other hand, if $\epsilon = 0$ then the set of reachable states is exactly the one shown in Figure 2.

Assuming perfect clocks in a timed system is clearly not a reasonable assumption. Therefore, an analysis based on the approach of the previous section can lead to an incorrect conclusion about the behaviour of the system (as for example in the timed automaton of Figure 1).

4.2 Problem Formulation

Let us now appropriately formulate the problem we want to solve in this paper. For a timed automaton T, let us define the timed automaton T_ϵ. The timed automaton T_ϵ is obtained from T by replacing the clock $\dot{a} = 1$ in T with the drifting clock $\dot{a} \in [1 - \epsilon, 1 + \epsilon]$ in T_ϵ. Figure 3 shows the timed automaton T_ϵ obtained from the timed automaton T in Figure 1.

Definition 41 *The transition system of timed automaton T_ϵ is $T_\epsilon = (Q_T, \longrightarrow, \mathbb{R}^+ \cup \{d\})$ where*

1. $(l, x) \xrightarrow{t} (l, y)$ *provided $(1 - \epsilon)t \le y_i - x_i \le (1 + \epsilon)t$ for each i.*
2. $(l, x) \xrightarrow{d} (m, y)$ *provided $(l, g, j, m) \in E$, $x \in g$, $y_i = 0$ when $i \in j$, and $y_i = x_i$ for $i \notin j$.*

For the timed automaton T_ϵ, define the relation $\rightarrow \subset Q_T \times Q_T$ where $q \rightarrow q'$ provided $q \xrightarrow{t} q'$ or $q \xrightarrow{d} q'$ in T_ϵ. Define the relation $\Rightarrow$ to be the reflexive and transitive closure of $\rightarrow$.

Definition 42 *For a timed automaton T_ϵ and an initial zone Z_0, define $Reach(T_\epsilon, Z_0) = \{ q \mid q_0 \Rightarrow q \text{ in } T_\epsilon \text{ and } q_0 \in Z_0 \}$.*

$Reach(T_\epsilon, Z_0)$ is the set of states which can be reached in T_ϵ. Clearly for $\epsilon_2 \le \epsilon_1$, $Reach(T_{\epsilon_2}, Z_0) \subset Reach(T_{\epsilon_1}, Z_0)$. We will be interested in computing the set $R^*(T, Z_0) = \cap_{\epsilon > 0} Reach(T_\epsilon, Z_0)$. The set $R^*(T, Z_0)$ is the limit of $Reach(T_\epsilon, Z_0)$ as $\epsilon \rightarrow 0$. The set $R^*(T, Z_0)$ for the timed automaton of Figure 1 is shown in Figure 4. As this example shows, $R^*(T, Z_0)$ is not necessarily equal to $Reach(T, Z_0)$.

Our main result in this paper is an algorithm for computing $R^*(T, Z_0)$ for a timed automaton T and an initial zone Z_0. In Section 5, we will present the algorithm for computing $R^*(T, Z_0)$. In Section 9, we will show that unlike $Reach(T, Z_0)$, $R^*(T, Z_0)$ is robust against errors in guards, drifts in clocks and other types of modeling errors.

5 The New Algorithm

We now present the algorithm for computing $R^*(T, Z_0)$ for a timed automaton T and a closed initial zone Z_0. The algorithm works on the underlying region graph $G = (\mathcal{C}, \longrightarrow_G)$ of the timed automaton T.

Algorithm for computing $R^*(T, Z_0)$:

   1. Construct the region graph $G = (\mathcal{C}, \longrightarrow_G)$ of timed automaton T
   2. Compute $SCC(G) = $ non-trivial strongly connected components of graph G
   3. $J^* := [Z_0]$
   4. $J^* := Reach(G, J^*)$
   5. If for some $S \in SCC(G)$, $S \not\subset J^*$ and $(J^*) \cap (S) \neq \emptyset$
         then $J^* := J^* \cup S$
           Goto 4
       else STOP

The set J^* is computed using two operations: if a SCC S is "touching" J^*, then the new $J^* := J^* \cup S$; and from a given set J^*, the new $J^* := Reach(G, J^*)$. Starting from the set $[Z_0]$, these two operations are repeated until no new states are added to J^*.

For a timed automaton T, the set J^* computed by our algorithm is exactly $R^*(T, Z_0)$. The correctness of the algorithm relies on the following two theorems. We assume that the timed automaton T has state space $Q_T \subset L \times [0, M]^n$ and W is the number of regions in Q_T.

Theorem 7 *Suppose S is a SCC of the region graph G, and x, y are two points in (S). Then $x \Rightarrow y$ in T_ϵ for any $\epsilon > 0$.*

Proof: See Section 7

Theorem 10 *Suppose $x \in (J^*)$ and $x \Rightarrow y$ in timed automaton T_ϵ with $\epsilon < \frac{\alpha}{4(n+W+1)(M+1)}$ where $\alpha < \frac{1}{4}$. Then $dist(y, J^*) < \alpha$.*

Proof: See Section 8

Theorem 7 says that in a SCC S of the region graph G of timed automaton T, it is possible to move from any point $x \in (S)$ to any other point $y \in (S)$ in the timed automaton T_ϵ. To prove this result, we will need to understand the structure of the limit cycles of the timed automaton. We do this in Section 7.

Theorem 10 states that from a point $x \in (J^*)$, it is not possible to get to any other point which is more than distance α away from J^* in the timed automaton T_ϵ for sufficiently small ϵ. To prove this, we need to better understand the relationship between trajectories of T_ϵ and T. We do this in Section 8.

The correctness of our algorithm for computing $R^*(T, Z_0)$ follows straightforwardly from Theorem 7 and Theorem 10.

Theorem 3. $R^*(T, Z_0) = J^*$.

Proof: For $K \subset \mathcal{C}$, if $K \subset R^*(T, Z_0)$ then $Reach(G, K) \subset R^*(T, Z_0)$. And if $K \subset R^*(T, Z_0)$ and $(K) \cap (S) \neq \emptyset$ for a SCC S, then from Theorem 7, $K \cup S \subset R^*(T, Z_0)$. Since $[Z_0] \subset R^*(T, Z_0)$ and J^* is obtained from $[Z_0]$ by only repeated application of the above two operations, it follows that $J^* \subset R^*(T, Z_0)$.

Since (J^*) is a closed set containing Z_0, from Theorem 10, for any $y \in Reach(T_\epsilon, Z_0)$,

$dist(y, J^*) \leq \alpha$ where α can be made arbitrarily small. It follows that $R^*(T, Z_0) \subset J^*$. ∎

Lemma 2. *The set $R^*(T, Z_0)$ can be computed in time $O(W)$ where W is the number of regions in Q_T.*

From [1] W is at most $n!2^n M^n |L|$.

6 Properties of Zones and Regions

We defined zones in Section 2.3 and regions in Section 3.3. Here we make the relationship between zones and regions, and discuss some of their properties. We will need these results in Sections 7 and 8.

6.1 Regions

A region $r = \{x \mid \lfloor x \rfloor = \alpha$ and $\langle x \rangle = \beta\,\}$ where $\alpha \in \mathbb{Z}^n$ and β is an ordering of the fractional components. Each region r can be equivalently described by a set of inequalities.

Example 2. Consider the region $r = \{y \mid \lfloor y \rfloor = (0\ 4\ 3\ 8)$ and $(0 \leq \langle y_3 \rangle \leq \langle y_1 \rangle = \langle y_4 \rangle \leq \langle y_2 \rangle))\}$. The region r is equivalently described by the following set of inequalities:

$$3 \leq y_3, \quad y_3 - 3 \leq y_1 - 0, \quad y_1 - 0 = y_4 - 8, \quad y_4 - 8 \leq y_2 - 4,$$

$$y_2 \leq 5.$$

The vertices of a region can be determined from the description of the region. The vertices of the region r in Example 2 are $Vertex(r) = \{(0\ 4\ 3\ 8), (0\ 5\ 3\ 8), (1\ 5\ 3\ 9), (1\ 5\ 4\ 9)\}$. A m-dimensional region has $m + 1$ vertices.

Theorem 4. *Each region is a simplex and every face of a region is itself a region.*

Two consequences of Theorem 4 are of interest: in a region r, a point $x \in r$ is a unique convex combination of the vertices of r; and for any $V \subset Vertex(r)$, $conv(V)$ is a face of r and hence is a region.

6.2 Zones

A zone ($\mathbb{R}$-zone) $Z \subset \mathbb{R}^n$ is defined by a set of inequalities of the form

$$x_i - x_j \leq u_{ij}, \qquad l_i \leq x_i \leq u_i \tag{2}$$

where $i, j \in \{1, \ldots, n\}$ and $u_{ij}, l_i, u_i \in \mathbb{Z}$ ($u_{ij}, l_i, u_i \in \mathbb{R}$).

Lemma 3. *The following properties relate zones and regions:*

1. *Each region is a zone.*
2. *If Z is a zone then $Z = \cup_i r_i$ where each r_i is a region.*
3. *If $W = \cup_i Z_i$ is convex and each Z_i is a zone, then W is a zone.*

The next lemma states that for two non-intersecting zones, the points in the two zones are at least $\frac{1}{2}$ distance away.

Lemma 4. *Suppose Z_1 and Z_2 are zones such that $Z_1 \cap Z_2 = \emptyset$. Then for any $x \in Z_1$ and $y \in Z_2$, $\|x - y\| \geq \frac{1}{2}$.*

6.3 Zones and Trajectories

Consider a path $p = p_0 p_1 \ldots p_N$ in the region graph of the timed automaton T. Define the set-valued map $R : p_0 \to p_N$ where $R(q_0) = \{ q_N \mid \pi = (q_0, t_0)(q_1, t_1) \ldots (q_N, t_N)$ is a trajectory of T and $q_i \in p_i \}$. For $q_0 \in p_0$, $R(q_0)$ is the set of points which can be reached in p_N from q_0 by passing through the regions $p_1 \ldots p_N$.

Lemma 5. *For $q_0 \in p_0$, $R(q_0)$ is a $\mathbb{R}$-zone, and for a region $r_0 \subset p_0$, $R(r_0)$ is a region.*

Definition 61 *For $p = p_0 p_1 \ldots p_N$ where $p_i \in C$, define the set $F_T(p) =$*
$$\{ \qquad\qquad (-q_0, t_0, t_1, \ldots, t_N) \qquad\qquad \mid$$
$\pi = (q_0, t_0)(q_1, t_1) \ldots (q_N, t_N)$ *is a trajectory of T and $q_i \in p_i \}$.*

Lemma 6. *$F_T(p)$ is a zone.*

7 Limit Cycles of Timed Automata

In this section, we will study the limit cycles of timed automata. Our main result will be Theorem 7. The theorem states that in a SCC S of the region graph G of the timed automaton T, it is possible to move from any state $x \in (S)$ to any other state $y \in (S)$ in the timed automaton T_ϵ. To prove this result, we will need to understand the structure of the limit cycles of the timed automaton T.

A state q has a limit cycle through it provided there is a trajectory $\pi[0, t]$ with $t > 0$ such that $\pi(0) = q$ and $\pi(t) = q$. We call $\pi[0, t]$ a limit cycle [13]. Clearly for state q to have a limit cycle through it, there must be a cycle through $[q]$ in the region graph.

Our approach to analyzing the limit cycles will be to focus on a cycle $c = c_0 c_1 \ldots c_N$ with $c_N = c_0$ in the region graph. We then look at the return map $R : c_0 \to c_0$ where $R(x)$ is the set of states in c_0 to which it is possible to return after one cycle starting from state $x \in c_0$. We analyze the limit cycles using the return map R. One of our main results is that the set of points in c_0 with limit cycles forms a region. Theorem 7 will be a simple consequence of our results about limit cycles and the return map R.

In Section 7.1, we define the return map. Section 7.2 shows some examples of limit cycles. Section 7.3 describes the properties of the return map. In Section 7.4, we show that the behavior of the return map is described completely by its behavior on the vertices of the region c_0. We also show that the set of points with limit cycles forms a region. In Section 7.5 we prove Theorem 7

7.1 The Return Map

Consider a cycle $c = c_0 c_1 c_2 \ldots c_N$ in the region graph where $c_N = c_0$. Define the *return map* $R : c_0 \to c_0$ where $R(q_0) = \{\ q_N \mid \pi = (q_0, t_0)(q_1, t_1) \ldots (q_N, t_N)$ is a trajectory of the timed automaton and $q_i \in c_i\ \}$. R is a set-valued map where for $x \in c_0$, $R(x)$ is the set of points to which it is possible to return in c_0 after passing through the regions $c_1, \ldots, c_N$. From Lemma 5, we know that for $x \in c_0$, $R(x)$ is a $\mathbb{R} - zone$, and for a region $r_0 \subset c_0$, $R(r_0)$ is a region.

We define $L_1 = \{\ x \mid x \in R(x)\ \}$, $L_2 = \{\ x \mid x \in R^2(x)\ \}$ and more generally $L_m = \{\ x \mid x \in R^m(x)\ \}$. So L_m is the set of points which can return back to themselves after m cycles. The set of points with limit cycles is $L = \cup_i L_i$.

7.2 Examples of Limit Cycles

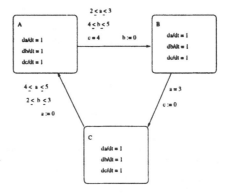

Fig. 5. A Timed Automaton

Figure 5 shows a timed automaton. Consider the region $c_0 = (A, r)$ where $r = \{x \mid \lfloor x \rfloor = (0\ 2\ 1)$ and $\langle x \rangle = (0 = \langle a \rangle \le \langle b \rangle \le \langle c \rangle)\ \}$. The reader can check that the region c_0 has only one cycle through it in the region graph which goes through the control locations A, B and C only once.

Now consider the return map $R : c_0 \to c_0$. The set $L_1 = \{A\} \times \{x \mid 2c = b+1$ and $x \in c_0\ \}$ and $L_2 = c_0$. The sets L_1 and L_2 are shown in Figure 6. Since $L = L_2 = c_0$, every point of c_0 has a limit cycle through it.

7.3 Properties of the Return Map

We next note some basic properties of the return map and the set L.

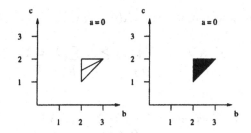

Fig. 6. The sets L_1 and L_2

Theorem 5. $R(\lambda x + (1 - \lambda)y) = \lambda R(x) + (1 - \lambda)R(y)$ *for* $0 \le \lambda \le 1$.

Lemma 7. *L is a convex set.*

7.4 Orbit Graph of Vertices of a Region

Consider again a cycle $c = c_0 c_1 \ldots c_N$ in the region graph. Define the orbit graph $\Theta = (V_\theta, \rightarrow_\theta)$ where the vertices V_θ are the vertices of the region c_0 and for $v, w \in V_\theta$, there is an edge $v \rightarrow_\theta w$ provided $w \in R(v)$.

Lemma 8. *Suppose $r \longrightarrow_G r'$ in the region graph G. Then for each vertex u of region r, there exists a vertex v of region r' such that $u \rightarrow v$; and for each vertex v' of r', there exists a vertex u' of r such that $u' \rightarrow v'$.*

From Lemma 8, each vertex of Θ has at least one incoming edge and at least one outgoing edge.

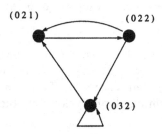

Fig. 7. Orbit Graph

Example 3. Consider again the timed automaton of Figure 5 and the region $c_0 = (A, r)$ where $r = \{x \mid \lfloor x \rfloor = (0\ 2\ 1)$ and $\langle x \rangle = (0 = \langle a \rangle \le \langle b \rangle \le \langle c \rangle) \}$. The vertices of region c_0 are $V_\theta = \{A\} \times \{(0\ 2\ 1), (0\ 2\ 2), (0\ 3\ 2)\}$. The orbit graph for this example is shown in Figure 7.

Lemma 9. *For $v \in V_\theta$, $R(v)$ is a region and $R(v) = conv\{w | v \rightarrow_\theta w\}$.*

From Theorem 5, $R(x)$ is then a convex combination of $R(v_i)$, $v_i \in V_\theta$.

Lemma 10. *Suppose* $y \in R(x)$ *where* $x = \sum_i \lambda_i v_i$, $v_i \in V_\theta$, $\lambda_i \geq 0$, $\sum_i \lambda_i = 1$. *Then* $y = \sum_i \lambda_i \sum_j p_{ij} w_{ij}$ *where* $w_{ij} \in V_\theta$, $p_{ij} \geq 0$, $\sum_j p_{ij} = 1$ *and* $p_{ij} = 0$ *if there is no edge from* v_i *to* w_{ij} *in* Θ.

Proof: $y \in R(\sum_i \lambda_i v_i) = \sum_i \lambda_i R(v_i)$ from Theorem 5. So $y = \sum_i \lambda_i s_i$ where from Lemma 9 $s_i = \sum_j p_{ij} w_{ij}$ where $w_{ij} \in V_\theta$ and $p_{ij} = 0$ if there is no edge from v_i to w_{ij} in Θ. Thus $y = \sum_i \lambda_i \sum_j p_{ij} w_{ij}$. ∎

The limit cycles of points in c_0 can also be described in terms of the limit cycles of points in V_θ.

Theorem 6. $L = conv(V)$ *where* $V \subset V_\theta$ *are the vertices of* Θ *with a cycle.*

From Theorem 4, it follows that L is a region.

7.5   Main Result

We now show that in a strongly connected component S of the region graph of T, $x \Rightarrow y$ in T_ϵ for any $x, y \in (S)$.

Lemma 11. *Consider a cycle* $c = c_0 c_1 \ldots c_N$ *in the region graph. Then for any* $x \in c_0$, *there exist* $u, v \in L$ *such that* $x \Rightarrow u$ *and* $v \Rightarrow x$ *in* T.

Proof: Using Lemma 10. ∎

Lemma 12. *Consider a cycle* $c = c_0 c_1 \ldots c_N$ *in the region graph. Then for* $u, v \in L$, $u \Rightarrow v$ *in* T_ϵ.

Proof: L is a convex set in which each point has a limit cycle through it. From Assumption 31, cycle c is a progress cycle. So each point in L has a limit cycle with a positive period. In timed automaton T_ϵ, we can reach state $v \in L$ from state $u \in L$ by drifting from one limit cycle to another until we reach state v. ∎

Lemma 13. *For* $x, y \in c_0$, $x \Rightarrow y$ *in timed automaton* T_ϵ.

Proof: Using Lemma 11 and Lemma 12. ∎

Theorem 7. *Suppose* S *is a SCC of the region graph* G, *and* x, y *are two points in* S. *Then* $x \Rightarrow y$ *in* T_ϵ *for any* $\epsilon > 0$.

Proof: By considering a cycle of S which contains x and y and using Lemma 13. ∎

8 Relationship Between Trajectories of T and T_ϵ

In this section we discuss the relationship between the trajectories of T and T_ϵ. We show that for any trajectory of T_ϵ, there is a trajectory of T which is close to it. In particular, we show that in a timed automaton with state space $Q_T \subset L \times [0, M]^n$, for any trajectory π' of T_ϵ which makes k jumps, there is a trajectory π of T which makes the same k jumps and is at most $4(k+n)(M+1)\epsilon$ distance away from π'.

We will use this result to prove Theorem 10: starting from a point in J^*, for any $\alpha > 0$, it is not possible to get more than distance α away from J^* in T_ϵ for sufficiently small ϵ.

8.1 Zones Z and Z_β

In proving our results, we will need to understand the relationship between the solutions to the zone Z and the solutions to the $\mathbb{R}$-zone Z_β. Z_β is obtained from Z by replacing each inequality $x_i - x_j \le u_{ij}$ $(l_i \le x_i \le u_i)$ in Z with the inequality $x_i - x_j \le u_{ij} + \beta$ $(l_i - \beta \le x_i \le u_i + \beta)$ in Z_β. The following theorem makes the relationship between solutions of Z and Z_β.

Theorem 8. *Suppose Z is a zone with variables $x_i, i = 1, \ldots, K$. We define the $\mathbb{R}$-zone Z_β where each inequality $x_i - x_j \le u_{ij}$ $(l_i \le x_i \le u_i)$ in Z is replaced with the inequality $x_i - x_j \le u_{ij} + \beta$ $(l_i - \beta \le x_i \le u_i + \beta)$ in Z_β. Then for $\beta < \frac{1}{2K+1}$, for any $d \in Z_\beta$, there exists a $d' \in Z$ such that $\|d - d'\| \le K\beta$.*

8.2 Trajectories of T_ϵ and $F_{T_\epsilon}(p)$

For $p = p_0 p_1 \ldots p_k$ where each p_i is a region, define $F_{T_\epsilon}(p) = \{(-q'_0, t'_0, \ldots, t'_k) \mid \pi' = (q'_0, t'_0)(q'_1, t'_1) \ldots (q'_k, t'_k)$ is a trajectory of T_ϵ and $q'_i \in p_i \}$. It can then be shown that if the variables $(-q_0, t_0, \ldots, t_k)$ satisfy the inequalities

$$a \le t_i - t_j \le b, \quad a \le t_i - (-q_{0j}) \le b$$

in $F_T(p)$, then the variables $(-q'_0, t'_0, \ldots, t'_k)$ satisfy the inequalities

$$a - 2(M + 1)\epsilon \le t'_i - t'_j \le b + 2(M + 1)\epsilon,$$

$$a - (M + 1)\epsilon \le t'_i - (-q'_{0j}) \le b + (M + 1)\epsilon$$

in $F_{T_\epsilon}(p)$ for sufficiently small ϵ. Lemma 14 is a consequence of this observation.

Lemma 14. *Suppose $Z = F_T(p)$ where $Q_T \subset L \times [0, M]^n$. Then for sufficiently small ϵ, $Z \subset F_{T_\epsilon}(p) \subset Z_\beta$ for $\beta \ge 2(M + 1)\epsilon$.*

We will now make the relationship between the trajectories of T and T_ϵ.

Theorem 9. *Suppose we are given a $0 < \delta < 1$ and a trajectory $\pi' = (q'_0, t'_0) \ldots (q'_k, t'_k)$ of T_ϵ where $\epsilon < \frac{\delta}{4(k+n)(M+1)}$. Then there is a trajectory $\pi = (q_0, t_0) \ldots (q_k, t_k)$ of T such that $q_i \in [q'_i], |t'_i - t_i| < \frac{\delta}{2}$ and $|q'_i - q_i| < \delta$.*

Proof: Consider $p = p_0 p_1 \ldots p_k$ where $p_i = [q_i']$. The result follows by making the relationship between $F_{T_\epsilon}(p)$ and $F_T(p)$ using Lemma 14 and Theorem 8. ∎

A consequence of Theorem 9 is that for a state $q \in R^*(T, Z_0)$ but $q \notin Reach(T, Z_0)$, the time it takes to reach q in T_ϵ becomes longer as ϵ becomes smaller.

8.3 Main Result

We are now ready to prove the main result of this section: starting from a point in J^*, it is not possible to get more than α distance away from J^* in the timed automaton T_ϵ for sufficiently small ϵ.

The state space of timed automaton T is $Q_T \subset L \times [0, M]^n$ and W is the number of regions in Q_T.

Theorem 10. *Suppose $x \in J^*$ and $x \Rightarrow y$ in timed automaton T_ϵ with $\epsilon < \frac{\alpha}{4(n+W+1)(M+1)}$ where $\alpha < \frac{1}{4}$. Then $dist(y, J^*) < \alpha$.*

Proof: Suppose $\pi' = (q_0', t_0')(q_1', t_1') \ldots (q_m', t_m')$ is a stutter-free trajectory of T_ϵ where $q_0' = x$, $q_m' = y$ and $q_0' \in J^*$. We need to show that $dist(q_m', J^*) < \alpha$. The proof will be by using induction. Using Theorem 9, $dist(q_i', J^*) < \alpha$ for $i \leq W + 1$. Now assume that $dist(q_i', J^*) < \alpha$ for $i \leq N$ where $N \geq W + 1$. By our induction hypothesis $dist(q_j', J^*) < \alpha$ for $j = (N + 1) - (W + 1)$. Consider $p = p_j p_{j+1} \ldots p_{N+1}$ where $p_i = [q_i']$. From Theorem 9, there is a trajectory $\eta = (q_j, t_j)(q_{j+1}, t_{j+1}) \ldots (q_{N+1}, t_{N+1})$ in T where for $j \leq i \leq N+1$, $\|q_i - q_i'\| < \alpha$ and $q_i \in [q_i']$. Now $dist(q_j, J^*) < \frac{1}{2}$ because $dist(q_j', J^*) < \alpha$ and $\|q_j - q_j'\| < \alpha$. Therefore from Lemma 4 $[q_j] \cap (J^*) \neq \emptyset$. By construction of J^* (since the path $[q_j][q_{j+1}] \ldots [q_{N+1}]$ contains a cycle, $[q_{N+1}] \subset J^*$), it follows that $q_{N+1} \in J^*$. Therefore $dist(q_{N+1}', J^*) < \alpha$. ∎

9 Robustness of $R^*(T, Z_0)$ and Approximations

In Section 5, we presented an algorithm for computing the set $R^*(T, Z_0)$. We next show that $R^*(T, Z_0)$ is robust against various types of modeling errors. We then describe an approximation method which allows us to determine whether a control location l_f is reachable in T_ϵ without computing $R^*(T, Z_0)$.

9.1 Modeling Errors

Consider a timed automaton T with state space $Q_T \subset L \times [0, M]^n$ and W regions. We first show that control location l_f is reachable in T_ϵ for sufficiently small ϵ iff it is reachable in $R^*(T, Z_0)$.

Lemma 15. *In a timed automaton T, control location l_f is reachable in T_ϵ for $\epsilon < \frac{1}{16(n+W+1)(M+1)}$ iff l_f is reachable in $R^*(T, Z_0)$.*

Proof: Using Lemma 4 and Theorem 10. ∎

Define the automaton T_ϵ^δ as being obtained from the timed automaton T by replacing clock $\dot{x} = 1$ with the clock $\dot{x} \in [1 - \epsilon, 1 + \epsilon]$ and by replacing the guard $a \leq x \leq b$ in T with the guard $a - \delta \leq x \leq b + \delta$.

Theorem 11. $\cap_{\delta > 0} \cap_{\epsilon > 0} Reach(T_\epsilon^\delta, Z_0) = R^*(T, Z_0)$.

Proof: The proof is similar to that of Theorem 3. ∎

The theorem states that for sufficiently small ϵ and δ, $Reach(T_\epsilon^\delta, Z_0)$ is close to $R^*(T, Z_0)$. Hence, $R^*(T, Z_0)$ is robust against errors in guards and drifts in clocks.

9.2 Approximations

We next show that for the control location reachability problem, if the control location l_f is not reachable in T_0^δ then for sufficiently small ϵ, it is also not reachable in T_ϵ^0. This implies that to check that l_f is not reachable in T_ϵ^0, it is sufficient to check this for T_0^δ.

Lemma 16. *Suppose the control location l_f is not reachable in the timed automaton T_0^δ. Then l_f is also not reachable in T_ϵ^0 for $\epsilon \leq \frac{\delta}{2(M+1)}$.*

Proof: Using Lemma 14. ∎

10 Complexity

We next consider the complexity of computing $R^*(T, Z_0)$. In [7], it is shown that determining whether a state $q \in Reach(T, Z_0)$ is PSPACE-Complete. The same result can be modified to prove the following results.

Theorem 12. *For a timed automaton T and an initial zone Z_0, determining whether a state $q \in R^*(T, Z_0)$ is PSPACE-Complete.*

Theorem 13. *For a timed automaton T and an initial zone Z_0, determining whether $Reach(T, Z_0) = R^*(T, Z_0)$ is PSPACE-Complete.*

Although for a timed automaton T, determining whether $R^*(T, Z_0) = Reach(T, Z_0)$ is PSPACE-hard, it is of interest to find some simple sufficient conditions which guarantee this.

11 Conclusion

Our main contribution in this paper is an algorithm for computing $R^*(T, Z_0)$ and a proof of its correctness. We showed that unlike $Reach(T, Z_0)$, $R^*(T, Z_0)$ is robust against various types of modeling errors. We also presented an analysis of the dynamics of timed automata. In particular, we presented a complete analysis of the limit cycles of timed automata.

Although in this paper we have focused on timed automata, the same methods can be used to analyze robustness issues in the class of decidable hybrid systems [14, 15]. Open issues which require further study include designing efficient algorithms for computing $R^*(T, Z_0)$ and finding simple sufficiency conditions which guarantee that $R^*(T, Z_0) = Reach(T, Z_0)$.

References

1. R. Alur and D. Dill, Automata for modeling real-time systems, *Proc. 17th ICALP*, LNCS 443, Springer-Verlag, 1990.
2. R. Alur et. al., The algorithmic analysis of hybrid systems, *Theoretical Computer Science*, Feb. 1995.
3. R. Alur, A. Itai, R. Kurshan and M. Yannakakis, Timing verification by successive approximation, *Information and Computation* 118, 142-157, 1995.
4. R. Alur and R. Kurshan, Timing analysis in COSPAN, *Hybrid Systems III*, LNCS 1066, Springer-Verlag, 1996.
5. J. Bengtsson, K. G. Larsen, F. Larsson, P. Pettersson and W. Yi, UppAal: a tool-suite for automatic verification of real-time systems, *Hybrid Systems III*, LNCS 1066, Springer-Verlag, 1996.
6. T.H. Cormen, C.E. Leiserson and R.L. Rivest *Introduction to Algorithms*, MIT Press, 1990.
7. C. Courcoubetis and M. Yannakakis, Minimum and maximum delay problems in real-time systems, *Formal Methods in System Design*, Dec. 1992, vol. 1, pp. 385-415.
8. C. Daws, A. Olivero, S. Tripakis and S. Yovine, The tool Kronos, *Hybrid Systems III*, LNCS 1066, Springer-Verlag, 1996.
9. D. Dill, Timing assumptions and verification of finite state concurrent systems, *Automatic Verification Methods for Finite-State Systems*, Springer-Verlag LNCS 407, 1989.
10. T. Henzinger, P.-H. Ho and H. Wong-Toi, HyTech: A model checker for hybrid systems, *Computer Aided Verification*, LNCS 1254, Springer-Verlag, 1997.
11. T. Henzinger, P. Kopke, A. Puri and P. Varaiya, What's decidable about hybrid automata ?, *Proc. 27th ACM Symp. on Theory of Computing*, 1995.
12. T. Henzinger, X. Nicollin, J. Sifakis and S. Yovine, Symbolic model-checking for real-time systems, *Proc. 7th IEEE Symp. on Logic in Computer Science*, 1992.
13. M. W. Hirsh and S. Smale *Differential Equations, Dynamical Systems, and Linear Algebra*, Academic Press, Inc., 1974.
14. A. Puri and P. Varaiya, Decidable hybrid systems, *Computer and Mathematical Modeling*, June 1996, vol. 23, 191-202.
15. A. Puri, Theory of hybrid systems and discrete event systems, PhD thesis, University of California, Berkeley, 1995.
16. A. Puri, Dynamical Properties of Timed Automata, Bell Labs Technical Memo, August, 1997.
17. M. Yannakakis and D. Lee, An efficient algorithm for minimizing real-time transition systems, *Computer Aided Verification*, Springer-Verlag, 1993.

An Algorithm for the Approximative Analysis of Rectangular Automata

J. Preußig[‡*], S. Kowalewski[‡*], H. Wong-Toi[¶], T.A. Henzinger[†**]

‡ Dept. of Chemical Engineering, University of Dortmund, Germany.
¶ Cadence Berkeley Labs, Berkeley, CA.
† Dept. of EECS, University of California, Berkeley, CA.

Abstract. Rectangular automata are well suited for approximate modeling of continuous–discrete systems. The exact analysis of these automata is feasible for small examples but can encounter severe numerical problems for even medium-sized systems. This paper presents an analysis algorithm that uses conservative overapproximation to avoid these numerical problems. The algorithm is demonstrated on a simple benchmark system consisting of two connected tanks.

1 Introduction

Embedded systems consist of digital controllers operating in analog environments. They are often used in safety-critical situations, such as for transportation control or logic control for processing systems, where correct behavior is essential. The interaction between the controller and its environment is hybrid, in that it involves both discrete and continuous aspects of behavior. Numerous models for specifying and analyzing such hybrid systems have been proposed: see, for example, the volumes [2, 10].

This paper is concerned with hybrid systems verification using automated techniques. A system is modeled as a finite control graph augmented with real-valued variables subject to differential inclusions [7]. This model is far too expressive for immediate automatic verification. Previously, we proposed the following approach: given a complex hybrid system H, we construct a simpler abstraction H', and then automatically analyze H' instead [7]. We require the abstraction H' to be conservative, *i.e.* if H' is correct, then H is correct. Furthermore, the abstraction must be amenable to automated analysis. Typically, this is achieved by ensuring that the abstraction belongs to a restricted class of automata.

In previous work, we proposed that the abstractions H' be *linear hybrid automata* [1], in which the continuous dynamics are given as constant polyhedral

* Supported by the German Research Council (DFG) under grant Ko1430/3 in the special program KONDISK ('Continuous-discrete dynamics of technical systems').
** This research was supported in part by the ONR YIP award N00014-95-1-0520, by the NSF CAREER award CCR-9501708, by the NSF grant CCR-9504469, by the DARPA/NASA grant NAG2-1214, by the ARO MURI grant DAAH-04-96-1-0341, and by the SRC contract 97-DC-324.041.

differential inclusions. For these automata, reachable state sets can be represented exactly using linear constraints, and generated automatically using the model-checking tool HYTECH [8]. Experience, however, shows that this subclass of automata may be still too expressive, and hence too computationally expensive to analyze efficiently and robustly [11, 12]. HYTECH manipulates linear constraints over n variables as sets of n-dimensional polyhedra using a polyhedral library that performs exact computation over rationals stored using integers for numerator and denominator [6]. However the geometric algorithms over polyhedra require internal computations that quickly surpass the limits of integer precision when presented with systems with nontrivial continuous dynamics.

The main contribution of this paper is a numerically robust, specialized algorithm for computing (a superset of) the reachable states of a subclass of linear hybrid automata. The algorithm operates on *rectangular automata* [9], subject to a few additional restrictions. In rectangular automata, the continuous dynamics must be defined using constant lower and upper bounds on the individual rates of variables. Given an arbitrary hybrid system, it is often easy to obtain a rectangular automaton as a conservative abstraction by bounding the rates of each variable. The key to efficient analysis is to avoid HYTECH's computation over arbitrary polyhedra. Rather, sets of hybrid states are represented using *face-regions*—convex hulls of sets of $2n$ rectangular faces of dimension $n - 1$. By restricting attention to rectangular faces, in which the continuous variables are decoupled, one obtains simpler algorithms for computing sets of successors states. The idea behind the algorithm is to determine, from a given reachable face, the minimal and maximal times it may take to reach some extremal bound, and to use this range of times to compute bounds on the new values of the variables. The algorithm is exact for systems with two continuous variables. It is inaccurate for higher dimensional systems, where it returns a superset of the reachable states. Consider the example of a three-dimensional system with x having rate $\dot{x} \in [1, 2]$, and both y and z having rate 1. The states that are reachable from the origin and for which $x \leq 2$ are $0 \leq x \leq 2 \wedge x/2 \leq y = z \leq x$. But this set is not definable using a face-region, and must be overapproximated by one. Thus, the drawback of the algorithm is its inaccuracy: it leads to a further approximation beyond that already inherent in translating the original hybrid system into a rectangular automaton, c.f. following an approximation step to a linear hybrid automaton, HYTECH's algorithms over arbitrary polyhedra would return, if successful, the exact reachable set of that linear hybrid automaton.

The benefits of our algorithm are two-fold: efficiency and robustness. The simple structure of face-regions yields efficient algorithms for finding successor states. Furthermore, the simplicity of manipulating rectangles versus arbitrary polyhedra means that our algorithm can be made robust far more easily than HYTECH's algorithms for analyzing linear hybrid automata: rectangular faces can be conservatively approximated using rounding in the appropriate direction.

In the next section, we review basic definitions and concepts related to rectangular automata, and then introduce our algorithm in Section 3. In Section 4, we demonstrate the algorithm on a simple two-tank example, and Section 5 contains conclusions and a short discussion of related work.

2 Rectangular Automata

We review basic definitions and concepts related to rectangular automata [9].

2.1 Syntax

Let $Y = \{y_1, \ldots, y_k\}$ be a set of variables. A *rectangular inequality* over the set Y is an inequality of the form $y_i \sim c$, for some $y_i \in Y$, some relation $\sim \in \{\leq, =, \geq\}^1$ and some rational $c \in \mathbb{Q}$. A *rectangular predicate* over Y is a conjunction of rectangular inequalities over Y. The set of rectangular predicates over Y is denoted $\mathcal{R}(Y)$. We adopt the convention that for a boldfaced vector $\mathbf{a} \in \mathbb{R}^k$, its ith component is denoted by a_i. For a rectangular predicate φ over Y, let $[\varphi]$ denote the set of points $\mathbf{a} \in \mathbb{R}^k$ for which φ is true when each y_i is replaced by a_i for each i. A set B is a *rectangle* if there exists a rectangular predicate φ such that $B = [\varphi]$. Given a rectangle B, let $b_i^{min}, b_i^{max} \in \mathbb{Q} \cup \{-\infty, \infty\}$ denote the bounds on the individual variables such that $B = \Pi_{i=1..k}[b_i^{min}, b_i^{max}]$.

A *rectangular automaton* A is a system $(X, V, inv, flow, init, E, guard, reset\_vars, reset)$ consisting of the following components [9]:

Variables: A finite set $X = \{x_1, \ldots, x_n\}$ of variables.

Control modes: A finite set V of control modes.

Invariant conditions: A function inv that maps every control mode to an invariant condition in $\mathcal{R}(X)$. Control of the automaton may remain in a control mode only when its invariant is satisfied.

Flow conditions: A function $flow$ that maps every control mode to a flow condition in $\mathcal{R}(\dot{X})$, where $\dot{X} = \{\dot{x}_1, \ldots, \dot{x}_n\}$ with $\dot{x}_i$ representing the first derivative of x_i with respect to time. While control remains in a given mode, the variables evolve according to the differential inclusion specified by the mode's flow condition.

Initial conditions: A function $init$ that maps every control mode to an initial condition in $\mathcal{R}(X)$.

Control switches: A finite multiset E of control switches in $V \times V$. For a control switch (v, v'), we say that v denotes the *source mode* and v' the *target mode*.

Guard conditions: A function $guard$ that maps every control switch to a guard condition in $\mathcal{R}(X)$. Intuitively, the guard must be satisfied before the mode switch can be taken.

Resets: A function $reset\_vars$ that maps every control switch to an *update set* in 2^X, and a function $reset$ that maps every control switch e to a reset condition in $\mathcal{R}(X)$. We require that for every control switch e and for every $x \in X$, if $x \in reset\_vars(e)$, then $reset(e)$ implies $x = c$ for some constant c, which,

---

[1] For simplicity, we consider only nonstrict inequalities.

by abuse of notation, will be denoted $reset(e)(x)$. Intuitively, after the mode switch, the variables must satisfy the reset condition. Variables that appear in the update set must be reset to the fixed value indicated by the reset condition. Furthermore, all other variables must be unchanged.

2.2 Semantics

A *configuration* of a rectangular automaton is a pair $(v, \mathbf{a})$ that consists of a control mode v, together with a point $\mathbf{a} \in \mathbb{R}^n$. A configuration $(v, \mathbf{a})$ is *admissible* if $\mathbf{a} \in [inv(v)]$. Let $Config(A)$ denote the admissible configurations of A. A configuration $(v, \mathbf{a})$ is *initial* if it is admissible and $\mathbf{a} \in [init(v)]$. Let $Init(A)$ denote the set of initial configurations of A. There are two kinds of transitions between admissible configurations: jump transitions, which correspond to instantaneous control switches, and flow transitions, which correspond to the variables continuously evolving while time elapses. For every control switch $e \in E$, we define the binary *jump transition* relation $\xrightarrow{e}$ by $(v, \mathbf{a}) \xrightarrow{e} (v', \mathbf{a}')$ iff the following four conditions hold: (1) $e = (v, v')$, (2) $\mathbf{a} \in [guard(e)]$, (3) $\mathbf{a}' \in [reset(e)]$, and (4) for every $x_i \in X \setminus reset\_vars(e)$, $a_i = a_i'$. For every nonnegative real $\delta \geq 0$ and for every rectangular flow condition $\varphi \in \mathcal{R}(\dot{X})$, we define the binary flow relation $\xrightarrow{\delta}_{\varphi} \subseteq \mathbb{R}^n \times \mathbb{R}^n$ over states in $\mathbb{R}^n$ by $\mathbf{a} \xrightarrow{\delta}_{\varphi} \mathbf{a}'$ iff either (a) $\delta = 0$ and $\mathbf{a} = \mathbf{a}'$ or (b) $\delta > 0$ and $(\mathbf{a}' - \mathbf{a})/\delta \in [\varphi]$. From this, we derive a relation expressing the flows of the automaton. For every nonnegative real $\delta \geq 0$, we define the binary *flow transition* relation $\xrightarrow{\delta} \subseteq Config(A) \times Config(A)$ by $(v, \mathbf{a}) \xrightarrow{\delta} (v', \mathbf{a}')$ iff (1) $v = v'$, and (2) $\mathbf{a} \xrightarrow{\delta}_{flow(v)} \mathbf{a}'$. The second condition states that the continuous variables evolve at a rate consistent with the flow condition.

The transition relation $\rightarrow_A$ for the rectangular automaton A is $\bigcup_{e \in E} \xrightarrow{e} \cup \bigcup_{\delta \in \mathbb{R}_{\geq 0}} \xrightarrow{\delta}$. A *trajectory* is a finite sequence $q_0, q_1, \ldots, q_m$ of admissible configurations such that q_0 is an initial configuration, and $q_i \rightarrow_A q_{i+1}$ for $i = 0..m - 1$. A configuration is *reachable* if it appears on some trajectory. The set of reachable configurations of A is denoted $Reach(A)$.

2.3 Reachability analysis

Reachability analysis consists of determining the set of reachable configurations. It is commonly used to validate the correctness of a system. Safety properties intuitively assert that nothing bad happens during system execution. Violations of safety properties can be expressed via a designated set of unsafe configurations. Safety properties can then be verified by performing reachability analysis and checking whether any unsafe configurations are reached. We review a familiar procedure for computing $Reach(A)$. We define the successor operator $Post : 2^{Config(A)} \rightarrow 2^{Config(A)}$ by $Post(W) = Post_{time}(W) \cup Post_{evt}(W)$, where $Post_{time}(W) = \{q' \mid \exists q \in W. \exists \delta \in \mathbb{R}_{\geq 0}. q \xrightarrow{\delta}_A q'\}$ and $Post_{evt}(W) = \{q' \mid \exists q \in W. \exists e \in E. q \xrightarrow{e}_A q'\}$. Let $Post^i$ represent the composition of i $Post$ operations. Then $Reach(A) = \bigcup_{i=0}^{\infty} Post^i(Init(A))$. Iterating $Post$ until convergence yields a semialgorithm for computing $Reach(A)$. If the procedure terminates, one obtains $Reach(A)$, but in general, termination is not guaranteed.

2.4 Simple rectangular automata

A rectangular predicate φ is *bounded* if $[\![\varphi]\!]$ is bounded. A rectangular automaton is *simple* if the following two properties hold:

1. Its invariant, initial, flow, guard, and reset conditions are bounded.
2. For every control switch $e = (v, v')$, if $[\![inv(v)]\!] = B = \Pi_{i=1..n}[b_i^{min}, b_i^{max}]$, and if $[\![inv(v')]\!] = B' = \Pi_{i=1..n}[b_i^{min'}, b_i^{max'}]$, then there exists a variable $x_i \in X$ such that either

   (a) (i) $x_i \in reset\_vars(e)$, and (ii) the guard condition $guard(e)$ implies $x_i = b_i^{min}$ or $x_i = b_i^{max}$, and (iii) $reset(e)(x_i) \in \{b_i^{min'}, b_i^{max'}\}$,

   (b) (i) $x_i \notin reset\_vars(e)$, and (ii) the guard condition $guard(e)$ implies $x_i = b_i^{min}$, and (iii) $b_i^{min} \in \{b_i^{min'}, b_i^{max'}\}$, or

   (c) (i) $x_i \notin reset\_vars(e)$, and (ii) the guard condition $guard(e)$ implies $x_i = b_i^{max}$, and (iii) $b_i^{max} \in \{b_i^{min'}, b_i^{max'}\}$.

The second condition states that guard conditions include tests for equality for one of the variables' bounding values in the source mode's invariant. Furthermore, if the variable is reset, then it is reset to a bounding value for the target mode's invariant (condition 2a). Finally, if it is not reset, then its value in the guard must be a bounding value in the target mode's invariant (conditions 2b and 2c).

Simple rectangular automata often arise naturally when approximating more complex hybrid systems. In order to conservatively overapproximate the flow field of nontrivial continuous dynamics, one may partition the state space into rectangular blocks, and for each variable provide constant lower and upper bounds on the flow within each block [7]. A control mode is split into several control modes, one for each block of the partition. Crossing from one block in the state space to another is modeled by mode switches among the blocks, with the guards being tests for equality across common boundaries. For example, a mode v with the invariant $1 \leq x \leq 3$ may be split into two modes — v_1 with the invariant $1 \leq x \leq 2$ and v_2 with the invariant $2 \leq x \leq 3$ — with mode switches between them having the guard $x = 2$.

3 Approximative Analysis Algorithm

In this section we define an algorithm for the approximative reachability analysis of simple rectangular automata. The algorithm is built on top of a conservative $\widehat{Post}$ operator and based on some other concepts that are defined first.

3.1 Face-regions

A *face* is a rectangular predicate with one dimension fixed to a certain value. Our rationale for introducing faces is to use rectangular faces to represent non-rectangular sets. A *face-region* $\mathcal{F}$ is a set $\{F_1, \ldots, F_k\}$ where each F_i is a face. The semantics of $\mathcal{F}$ is the convex hull over its k faces, i.e. $[\mathcal{F}] = convexhull\{[F_1], \ldots, [F_k]\}$. This is shown for an example in Fig.1 where a face-region $\mathcal{F}$ is represented by the two faces F_1 and F_2. In practice, the faces of a face-region over n variables are derived from $2n$ constraints of the form $x_i = l_i$ or $x_i = u_i$. In the example, the face F_1 corresponds to $x_1 = 1$ and the face F_2 to $x_2 = 7$, with the empty faces for $x_1 = 7$ and $x_2 = 1$ being omitted.

3.2 The operator $Post^{x_d=b}$

Our algorithm is based on the fact that face-regions are bounded by their faces. We present an operator $Post^{x_d=b}$ that takes a face F and a flow φ of the variables and returns a conservative approximation $Post^{x_d=b}(F, \varphi)$ of the states for which $x_d = b$ that are reachable from F by following φ.

Let F be the face $\bigwedge_{i=1}^{n}(x_i^{min} \leq x_i \leq x_i^{max})$ and let φ be the flow condition in $\mathcal{R}(\dot{X})$ defining the possible rates of the x_i as $\bigwedge_{i=1}^{n}(\dot{x}_i^{min} \leq \dot{x}_i \leq \dot{x}_i^{max})$. We want to compute a new face $\bigwedge_{i=1}^{n}(x_i^{min'} \leq x_i \leq x_i^{max'})$ that defines the reachable states where $x_d^{min'} = x_d^{max'} = b$. The idea behind the operator is simple. We look at the time that x_d needs at least and at most to reach the bound b from its possible values in F and then see

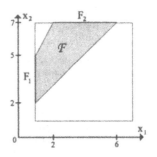

Fig. 1. Face-Region

how much the values of the other dimension's variables possibly change in these times, thereby computing the new values for x_i^{min} and x_i^{max}.

So at first we compute an interval $T = [t_{min}, t_{max}]$ of the times in which x_d can reach the bound b according to its current value and its possible rates. The maximal time of the interval can also be set to the symbol '*infinite*' to express that a bound can be reached within any arbitrarily large amount of time. The interval is empty if the bound b can not be reached at all. This is the case if b is less than x_d^{min} and no negative rate is possible or if b is greater than x_d^{max} and no positive rate is possible. Formally:

$$T = \emptyset \quad \text{if} \quad (b < x_d^{min} \wedge \dot{x}_d^{min} \geq 0) \vee (b > x_d^{max} \wedge \dot{x}_d^{max} \leq 0)$$

If T is not empty its interval bounds t_{min} and t_{max} are given as follows.

$$t_{min} = \begin{cases} \frac{x_d^{min}-b}{-\dot{x}_d^{min}} & \text{if } b < x_d^{min} \wedge \dot{x}_d^{min} < 0 \\[2mm] \frac{b-x_d^{max}}{\dot{x}_d^{max}} & \text{if } b > x_d^{max} \wedge \dot{x}_d^{max} > 0 \\[2mm] 0 & \text{if } x_d^{min} \leq b \leq x_d^{max} \end{cases}$$

$$t_{max} = \begin{cases} infinite & if \begin{array}{l} (b < x_d^{min} \wedge \dot{x}_d^{min} < 0 \wedge \dot{x}_d^{max} \geq 0) \\ \vee (b > x_d^{max} \wedge \dot{x}_d^{max} > 0 \wedge \dot{x}_d^{min} \leq 0) \\ \vee (x_d^{min} \leq b \leq x_d^{max} \wedge \dot{x}_d^{min} \leq 0 \leq \dot{x}_d^{max}) \end{array} \\[2em] \frac{x_d^{max} - b}{-\dot{x}_d^{max}} & if \ (b \leq x_d^{max} \wedge \dot{x}_d^{max} < 0) \\[1.5em] \frac{b - x_d^{min}}{\dot{x}_d^{min}} & if \ (b \geq x_d^{min} \wedge \dot{x}_d^{min} > 0). \end{cases}$$

We now give an intuitive explanation of these formulas. To compute T, we first check on which side of the current values of x_d the new bound b lies. Three cases are possible:

1. $b < x_d^{min}$: If no negative rate is possible, i.e. $\dot{x}_d^{min} \geq 0$, then T is empty. So consider the case that a negative rate is possible, i.e. $\dot{x}_d^{min} < 0$. The maximal time is either '*infinite*', if a positive or zero rate is also possible, or else computed by using the slowest rate possible to clear the greatest possible distance to b. The minimal time is computed by using the fastest rate possible to clear the smallest possible distance to b.

2. $b > x_d^{max}$: If no positive rate is possible, i.e. $\dot{x}_d^{max} \leq 0$, then T is empty. So consider the case that a positive rate is possible, i.e. $\dot{x}_d^{max} > 0$. The maximal time is either '*infinite*', if a negative or zero rate is also possible, or else computed by using the slowest rate possible to clear the greatest possible distance to b. Again, the minimal time is computed by using the fastest rate possible to clear the smallest possible distance to b.

3. $x_d^{min} \leq b \leq x_d^{max}$: In this case the bound b is already part of the old face. So we have $t_{min} = 0$. The maximal time is '*infinite*', if a zero rate is possible. Otherwise there are only positive or only negative rates and the maximal time is computed using the slowest rate possible to clear the greatest possible distance to b.

We use the computed interval T to compute the new bounds $x_i^{min'}$ and $x_i^{max'}$ of the other dimensions' variables that give the new face where $x_d^{min'} = x_d^{max'} = b$. If T is empty, then no face can be computed and *Post* returns an empty face. Otherwise, let us first assume that the computation of t_{max} did not yield '*infinite*'. To compute $x_i^{min'}$ we take the old x_i^{min} and subtract as much as possible, if there are negative rates for x_i, or add as little as possible, if there are only positive rates. To compute $x_i^{max'}$ we take the old x_i^{max} and add as much as possible, if there are positive rates for x_i, or subtract as little as possible, if there are only negative rates. Then we obtain:

$$x_i^{min'} = \begin{cases} x_i^{min} + \dot{x}_i^{min} \cdot t_{max} & if \ i \neq d \wedge \dot{x}_i^{min} < 0 \\ x_i^{min} + \dot{x}_i^{min} \cdot t_{min} & if \ i \neq d \wedge \dot{x}_i^{min} \geq 0 \\ b & if \ i = d \end{cases}$$

$$x_i^{max'} = \begin{cases} x_i^{max} + \dot{x}_i^{max} \cdot t_{max} & \text{if } i \neq d \wedge \dot{x}_i^{max} > 0 \\ x_i^{max} + \dot{x}_i^{max} \cdot t_{min} & \text{if } i \neq d \wedge \dot{x}_i^{max} \leq 0 \\ b & \text{if } i = d \end{cases}$$

If t_{max} has previously been found to be '*infinite*', then the computations with t_{max} also yield $\pm$'*infinite*'. For the variable x_d, constant $b \in \mathbb{Q}$, face F, and flow condition φ, we define the new face as

$$Post^{x_d=b}(F,\varphi) = \bigwedge_{1 \leq i \leq n} x_i^{min'} \leq x_i \leq x_i^{max'}.$$

Considering the example in Fig.1, the operator could be used to compute the face F_2 from F_1. Let $F_1 = \{x_1 = 1 \wedge 2 \leq x_2 \leq 5\}$, $F_2 = \{2 \leq x_1 \leq 6 \wedge x_2 = 7\}$ and $\varphi = \{\dot{x}_1 = 1 \wedge 1 \leq \dot{x}_2 \leq 2\}$. Then $F_2 = Post^{x_2=7}(F_1,\varphi)$ with $T = [1,5]$.

In two dimensions, the operator $Post^{x_d=b}$ is exact. For any number of dimensions, the operator is conservative.

Lemma 1. *Let x_d be a variable and b a constant in $\mathbb{Q}$. For every face F and flow condition φ, the operator $Post^{x_d=b}$ computes a superset of the points at which $x_d = b$ that are reachable according to φ from the points given by F, i.e. $[Post^{x_d=b}(F,\varphi)] \supseteq \{\mathbf{x}'|\exists \mathbf{x} \in [F].\exists \delta \in \mathbb{R}_{\geq 0}.\mathbf{x} \xrightarrow{\delta}_\varphi \mathbf{x}'\} \cap [x_d = b]$.*

Proof. We outline the proof. Assume $\mathbf{x}'$ satisfies $x_d = b$ and there exists an $\mathbf{x} \in [F]$ and $\delta \in \mathbb{R}_{\geq 0}$ such that $\mathbf{x} \xrightarrow{\delta}_\varphi \mathbf{x}'$. By a tedious check on the construction of interval T in the definition of the $Post^{x_d=b}$ operator, we see that $\delta \in T$, and hence by construction of the bounds $x_i^{min'}$ and $x_i^{max'}$, each x_i lies in $[x_i^{min'}, x_i^{max'}]$.

3.3 An algorithm for approximative reachability analysis

The algorithm described here makes use of the fact that the invariants in a control mode of a rectangular automaton form a rectangular region. So, a reachable face-region within the invariants can be represented by faces that lie on the invariant's bounds. Let $\mathcal{F}^v$ be a reachable face-region in a control mode v. Now we want to compute the new $\mathcal{F}^k$ in another control mode k, for which there is a mode switch from v. The algorithm performs an event-step evolution from each face of $\mathcal{F}^v$, checking the guard and possibly applying a reset operation to compute each face F_i^k lying on one of the faces of the invariant of k. Then the algorithm does a time-step evolution from each F_i^k using the $Post^{x_d=b}$ operator for each of the bounds defining the invariant of k, thereby computing $\mathcal{F}^k$. Being able to compute a successor face-region for a face-region, we can apply standard fixpoint analysis to find the set of all reachable face-regions in a given automaton.

We now give a more formal description of the algorithm. Let the invariant in a control mode v be of the form $\bigwedge_{i=1}^n (x_i^{min} \leq x_i \leq x_i^{max})$. Let a *region* R be a set of pairs $(v, \mathcal{F})$ of a mode v and a face-region $\mathcal{F}$ in v. The semantics of a region

R is a set of configurations defined by $[R] = \{(v, \mathbf{a}) | \exists (v, \mathcal{F}) \in R.\mathbf{a} \in [\mathcal{F}]\}$. We define $\widehat{Post}(R)$ as follows:

$$\widehat{Post}(R) = \bigcup_{(v, \mathcal{F}) \in R} \widehat{Post}_{time}(v, \mathcal{F}) \cup \widehat{Post}_{evt}(v, \mathcal{F})$$

where

$$\widehat{Post}_{time}(v, \mathcal{F}) = \{(v, \bigcup_{F \in \mathcal{F}} \left(\begin{array}{c} \bigcup_{1 \leq i \leq n} \{[Post^{x_i = x_i^{min}}(F, flow(v))] \cap [inv(v)]\} \cup \\ \bigcup_{1 \leq i \leq n} \{[Post^{x_i = x_i^{max}}(F, flow(v))] \cap [inv(v)]\} \end{array} \right))\}$$

and

$$\widehat{Post}_{evt}(v, \mathcal{F}) = \bigcup_{e = (v, k) \in E} \bigcup_{F \in \mathcal{F}} \{(k, \left\{ \left[\!\!\left[\begin{array}{c} (\exists x_i \in reset\_vars(e).(guard(e) \wedge F)) \\ \wedge \ reset(e) \wedge inv(k) \end{array} \right]\!\!\right] \right\})\}.$$

The way in which the operator $\widehat{Post}_{time}$ is built on top of the conservative operator for faces insures that it conservatively overapproximates $Post_{time}$.

Lemma 2. *For all regions R, $[\widehat{Post}_{time}(R)] \supseteq Post_{time}([R])$.*

The operator $\widehat{Post}_{evt}$ is exact, since it simply requires existential quantification and intersection of faces with guards, reset conditions, invariants, and hyperplanes of the form $x = b$.

Lemma 3. *For all regions R, $[\widehat{Post}_{evt}(R)] = Post_{evt}([R])$.*

The operator $\widehat{Post}$ can be used in the procedure in Section 2.3 in place of the exact operator $Post$. Since $\widehat{Post}(R)$ contains $Post(R)$, the resultant fixpoint contains the set of reachable configurations.

Theorem 1. *Let A be a rectangular automaton, and let the region R_{init} represent the initial configurations of A, i.e. $[R_{init}] = Init(A)$. Then the fixpoint computed by $\widehat{Post}$ from R_{init} is a superset of reachable configurations of A, i.e.*

$$[\bigcup_{0 \leq i \leq \infty} \widehat{Post}^i(R_{init})] \supseteq \bigcup_{0 \leq i \leq \infty} Post^i(Init(A)) = Reach(A).$$

3.4 Tighter approximations

The operator $\widehat{Post}$ is exact in two dimensions. In higher dimensions, however, it can compute vast overapproximations. Consider a box $[0, 2] \times [0, 2] \times [0, 4]$ in the three dimensions x, y, and t. Let $F_I = \{0 \leq x \leq 1 \wedge y = t = 0\}$ and $\varphi = \{\dot{x} = \dot{y} = \dot{t} = 1\}$. Computing $F_R = Post^{x=2}(F_I, \varphi)$ results in $F_R = \{x = 2 \wedge 1 \leq y \leq 2 \wedge 1 \leq t \leq 2\}$. Now we divide the original box according to the hyperplanes $x = 1$ and $y = 1$. Fig.2a displays the partitioned box projected on the plane spanned by x and y. From an initial face F_I the algorithm would now compute via F_1 and F_2 the face $F_R = Post^{x=2}(Post^{y=1}(Post^{x=1}(F_I, \varphi), \varphi), \varphi)$. This F_R gives a vast overapproximation for the value of t. The faces are:

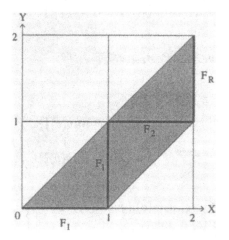 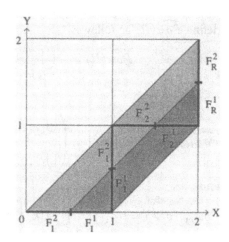

(a) Computation without splitting

(b) Computation using face splitting

Fig. 2. Face splitting

$$F_I: (0 \leq x \leq 1, y = t = 0) \qquad F_1: (x = 1, 0 \leq y \leq 1, 0 \leq t \leq 1)$$
$$F_2: (1 \leq x \leq 2, y = 1, 0 \leq t \leq 2) \qquad F_R: (x = 2, 1 \leq y \leq 2, 0 \leq t \leq 3)$$

An attempt to solve this problem is *face splitting*. The idea of face splitting is, not to compute the successor faces from a whole face, but to split a face into several parts, and then to compute the successors for these parts. In Fig.2b the face F_I is split into two pieces F_I^1 and F_I^2. Assuming the same partitioning as before, this leads to a better approximation, namely the faces F_R^1 and F_R^2, instead of F_R. The faces are:

$$F_I^1: (0.5 \leq x \leq 1, y = t = 0) \qquad F_I^2: (0 \leq x \leq 0.5, y = t = 0)$$
$$F_1^1: (x = 1, 0 \leq y \leq 0.5, 0 \leq t \leq 0.5) \qquad F_1^2: (x = 1, 0.5 \leq y \leq 1, 0.5 \leq t \leq 1)$$
$$F_2^1: (1.5 \leq x \leq 2, y = 1, 0.5 \leq t \leq 1.5) \qquad F_2^2: (1 \leq x \leq 1.5, y = 1, 0.5 \leq t \leq 1.5)$$
$$F_R^1: (x = 2, 1 \leq y \leq 1.5, 0.5 \leq t \leq 2) \qquad F_R^2: (x = 2, 1.5 \leq y \leq 2, 1 \leq t \leq 2.5)$$

Note that the same result could not be achieved by simply choosing a finer grid. A finer grid may be useful to obtain rates that are better approximations for the underlying differential equations but as we have shown in this example, somewhat unintuitively, there are cases in which finer grids lead to worse overapproximations in the analysis procedure. However, the drawback of face splitting is that it contributes to state explosion in larger systems.

4 Two-Tank Example

The analysis method is demonstrated on a small laboratory plant [12]. First, the dynamics of the system are approximated by a rectangular automaton. Then this

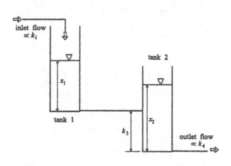

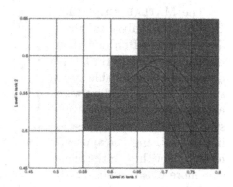

(a) Scheme of the two-tank plant

(b) Reachability analysis for the two-tank example

Fig. 3. Two-Tank example

automaton is analyzed using the approximative analysis algorithm. The plant consists of two tanks which are connected as illustrated in Fig.3a. The first tank is fed by an inflow characterized by the parameter k_1. The inlet stream of the second tank is the outflow of the first one. The stream from tank 1 to tank 2 depends on the difference between the tanks' liquid levels, the geometric properties of the connecting pipe (characterized by parameter k_2) and its height k_3 above the bottom of tank 2. The liquid level in this tank and the dimensions of its outlet pipe (characterized by constant k_4) determine the flow out of tank 2. The resulting model for the dynamics of the two tank levels is given by equation (1), where $\mathbf{x} = (x_1, x_2)$ is the continuous state vector of the system. Equation (1) defines a flow $\dot{\mathbf{x}} = \mathbf{f}(\mathbf{x}, k_1, ..., k_4)$ which moves the system to an equilibrium point $\mathbf{x_s}$ for all $k_j > 0$, $x_i \geq 0$, and $x_1 \geq x_2 - k_3$.

$$\begin{pmatrix} \dot{x}_1 \\ \dot{x}_2 \end{pmatrix} = \begin{cases} \begin{pmatrix} k_1 - k_2\sqrt{x_1 - x_2 + k_3} \\ k_2\sqrt{x_1 - x_2 + k_3} - k_4\sqrt{x_2} \end{pmatrix} & \text{if } x_2 > k_3 \\[2ex] \begin{pmatrix} k_1 - k_2\sqrt{x_1} \\ k_2\sqrt{x_1} - k_4\sqrt{x_2} \end{pmatrix} & \text{if } x_2 \leq k_3 \end{cases} \tag{1}$$

A MATLAB script was developed to generate an approximative rectangular automaton of the dynamics given by (1) for arbitrary partition grids. By refining the partition grid, arbitrarily accurate automata can be generated. The script estimates upper and lower bounds for the derivatives of x_1 and x_2 in each partition cell by evaluating equation (1) for a finite number of grid points. While the automata generated by this procedure are not conservative approximations, they are sufficiently accurate for testing the approximative analysis algorithm on realistic systems.

The MATLAB script calls HYTECH to analyze the rectangular automaton and then graphically displays HYTECH's output of the reachable state space. The finest grid we were able to run on the exact version of HYTECH can be seen in Fig.3b. Using our approximative algorithm for the analysis more exact models with much finer grids could be analyzed, as is shown in Fig.4.

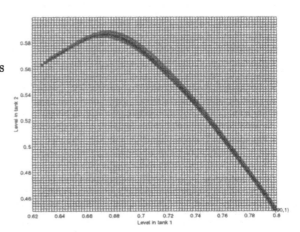

Fig. 4. Reachability analysis for the two-tank example on a finer grid

The main purpose of our example was the demonstration of the approximation technique. From the analysis point of view, the example is not very challenging, since simulation can achieve more accurate results rather easily. The application of the algorithm to a more realistic example can be found in [13].

5 Conclusion and Related Work

We have introduced an algorithm for the approximative analysis of rectangular hybrid systems. Though the approximations are accurate in two dimensions, the approximation technique seems to be of limited use in higher dimensions.

The idea of computing reachable regions only from the bounds of the predecessor regions, instead of looking at the whole regions, is not new. It also appears in [4, 5], where the bounding edges of a region are 'bloated' outward with an integration routine on the original differential equations of a system to compute the edges of the successor region. Reachable sets may be represented by a set of non-convex polyhedral 2-dimensional projections. The idea of 'bloating' is referred to as 'face lifting' in [3]. The state space is partitioned a priori into hypercubes, and a face is then 'lifted' to a successor region, by computing successors for all hypercubes associated with that face. The current methodology uses a fixed partition which can lead to computational inefficiency. The authors have also identified the problem of potentially large overapproximations during the analysis.

There are a number of extensions that could be made to our algorithm. Instead of allowing only rectangular bounds for the derivatives of continuous variables the $\widehat{Post}$ operator could also deal with differential equations. In a different direction, the algorithm could be made accurate over higher dimensions at the cost of increased computation. Each face could be represented as the convex hull of a set of points instead of a rectangle. Then we could compute the successor faces F^i of a given face F^k pointwise, i.e. to compute F^i at $x_d = b$, we collect from each point in F^k the successor points for which $x_d = b$. This would avoid unwanted overapproximation during the analysis. However, from a computational standpoint, we confront two problems. First, we compute redundant points, and have to minimize face representations (i.e. solve the convex hull problem). Second, intersection with face invariants is no longer as efficient.

Acknowledgement. We thank Tiziano Villa for many helpful comments and Olaf Stursberg for his help with the MATLAB script.

References

1. R. Alur, C. Courcoubetis, N. Halbwachs, T.A. Henzinger, P.-H. Ho, X. Nicollin, A. Olivero, J. Sifakis, and S. Yovine. The algorithmic analysis of hybrid systems. *Theoretical Computer Science*, 138:3–34, 1995.
2. P. Antsaklis, A. Nerode, W. Kohn, and S. Sastry, editors. *Hybrid Systems IV*. Lecture Notes in Computer Science 1273. Springer-Verlag, 1997.
3. T. Dang and O. Maler. Reachability analysis via face lifting. In T.A. Henzinger and S. Sastry, editors, *HSCC 98: Hybrid Systems—Computation and Control*, Lecture Notes in Computer Science 1386, pages 96–109. Springer-Verlag, 1998.
4. M.R. Greenstreet. Verifying safety properties of differential equations. In R. Alur and T.A. Henzinger, editors, *CAV 96: Computer Aided Verification*, Lecture Notes in Computer Science 1102, pages 277–287. Springer-Verlag, 1996.
5. M.R. Greenstreet and I. Mitchell. Integrating projections. In T.A. Henzinger and S. Sastry, editors, *HSCC 98: Hybrid Systems—Computation and Control*, Lecture Notes in Computer Science 1386, pages 159–174. Springer-Verlag, 1998.
6. N. Halbwachs, P. Raymond, and Y.-E. Proy. Verification of linear hybrid systems by means of convex approximation. In B. LeCharlier, editor, *SAS 94: Static Analysis Symposium*, Lecture Notes in Computer Science 864, pages 223–237. Springer-Verlag, 1994.
7. T.A. Henzinger, P.-H. Ho, and H. Wong-Toi. Algorithmic analysis of nonlinear hybrid systems. *IEEE Transactions on Automatic Control*, 43(4):540–554, 1998.
8. T.A. Henzinger, P.H. Ho, and H. Wong-Toi. HyTech: A model checker for hybrid systems. *Software Tools for Technology Transfer*, 1(1,2):110–122, 1997.
9. T.A. Henzinger, P.W. Kopke, A. Puri, and P. Varaiya. What's decidable about hybrid automata? In *Proceedings of the 27th Annual Symposium on Theory of Computing*, pages 373–382. ACM Press, 1995. Full version to appear in *Journal of Computer and System Sciences*.
10. T.A. Henzinger and S. Sastry, editors. *HSCC 98: Hybrid Systems—Computation and Control*. Lecture Notes in Computer Science 1386. Springer-Verlag, 1998.
11. T. Stauner, O. Müller, and M. Fuchs. Using HyTech to verify an automotive control system. In O. Maler, editor, *HART 97: Hybrid and Real-Time Systems*, Lecture Notes in Computer Science 1201, pages 139–153. Springer-Verlag, 1997.
12. O. Stursberg, S. Kowalewski, I. Hoffmann, and J. Preußig. Comparing timed and hybrid automata as approximations of continuous systems. In P. Antsaklis, W. Kohn, A. Nerode, and S. Sastry, editors, *Hybrid Systems IV*, Lecture Notes in Computer Science 1273, pages 361–377. Springer-Verlag, 1996.
13. T. Villa, H. Wong-Toi, A. Balluchi, J. Preußig, A. Sangiovanni-Vincentelli, and Y. Watanabe. Formal verification of an automotive engine controller in cutoff mode. 1998. Submitted.

On Checking Parallel Real-Time Systems for Linear Duration Properties

Zhao Jianhua* and Dang Van Hung**

The United Nations University
International Institute for Software Technology, P.O.Box 3058, Macau
email: {zjh, dvh}@iist.unu.edu

Abstract. The major problem of checking a parallel composition of real-time systems for a real-time property is the explosion of untimed states and time regions. To attack this problem, one can use bisimulation equivalence w.r.t. the property to be checked to minimise the system state space. In this paper, we define such equivalence for the integrated linear duration properties of real-time automaton networks with shared variables. To avoid exhaustive state space exploration, we define a compatibility relation, which is a one-direction simulation relation between configurations. Based on this technique, we develop an algorithm for checking a real-time automaton network with shared variables w.r.t. a linear duration property. Our algorithm can avoid exhaustive state space exploration significantly when applied to Fischer's mutual exclusion protocol.

1 Introduction

In the last few years, some verification tools have been developed for timed systems [10, 11, 3]. The verification engines of most of these tools are based on reachability analysis of timed automata following the pioneering work of Alur and Dill [2].

A series of techniques have been developed to attack the potential state explosions arising not only from the control-structure but also from the region space. Efficient data structures and algorithms have been sought to represent and manipulate timing constraints over clock variables [9] and to avoid exhaustive state space exploration.

In this paper, we show how to apply and to improve these techniques for a class of model-checking problems for real-time systems. Namely, we use linear duration properties (a kind of simple Duration Calculus [4] formulas) as system specifications and real-time automaton networks with shared variables as real-time system models. Checking linear duration properties is difficult because

---

* On leave from Department of Computer Science, Nanjing University, Nanjing 210093, P.R. China. email: seg@nju.edu.cn. Partly supported by National NSF.
** On leave from the Institute of Information Technology, Nghia Do, Tu Liem, Hanoi, Vietnam.

the durations of states are defined on the history of the systems. Actually, the problem has been solved for real-time automata (real-time automaton networks of single process) in [5] by using linear programming technique. In that paper, an algorithm was given for reducing the problem to a finite set of very simple linear programming problems. This technique has been generalised for verifying a subset of timed automata in [6], and for verifying a parallel composition of real-time automata in [12]. This technique has also been generalised for verifying a subset of hybrid automata in [7]. For timed automata, it has been shown in [14] that the problem can be solved but ones have to use the mixed integer and linear programming techniques, which are very complicated. In [1], an algorithm has been developed for checking duration-bounded reachability which asks whether there is a run of an automaton from a start state to a target state along which the accumulated duration of system states satisfies a constraint. In that paper, the coefficients corresponding to the state durations are restricted to non-negative integers only.

In this paper, we consider the problem for a network of real-time automata with shared variables. We show that a linear duration property is satisfied by a real-time automaton network iff it is satisfied by all the integer behaviours of the network. Then, we define a so-called compatibility relation between configurations and apply the technique in [13] for that relation to develop a model-checking algorithm for real-time automaton networks that can avoid exhaustive state space exploration in some cases. We apply our technique to Fischer's mutual exclusion protocol and find that this technique results in a significant space-reduction.

The paper is organised as follows. In Section 2 real-time automaton networks with shared variables are formally defined. Linear duration properties and their satisfaction by a network are described in Section 3. Our basic idea and the algorithm are given in Section 4. Section 5 is devoted to the verification of Fischer's mutual exclusion protocol using our algorithm. The last section is the conclusion of the paper.

2 Real-Time Automaton Networks with Shared Variables

In this section, we give a formal definition of real-time automaton networks with shared variables and their behaviours. Let *Nat* denote the set of nonnegative integers, and *Intv* denote the set of intervals on *Nat*.

Definition 1. *A real-time automaton [5] is a pair* $\langle \mathbf{A}, \Gamma \rangle$, *where*

1. $\mathbf{A} = \langle S, s_0, \mathcal{E} \rangle$ *is a conventional automaton,*
2. Γ *is a mapping from $\mathcal{E}$ to Intv; Γ assigns to each transition $e \in \mathcal{E}$ a time interval $[a_e, b_e]$ or $[a_e, \infty)$, where a_e, b_e are integers and $0 \le a_e \le b_e$, which express the delay a_e and the deadline b_e or ∞ of the transition e.*

For a given state $s \in S$, we use U_s to denote the value $\max\{b_e \mid (\overleftarrow{e} = s)\}$. $\Gamma(e)$ is denoted by $[a_e, b_e]$, or $[a_e, \infty)$ when $b_e = \infty$. The empty word ϵ is considered as a special transition of all the real-time automata in this paper.

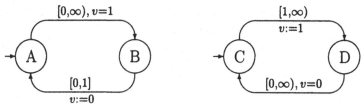

v : shared variable

Fig. 1. A real-time automaton network with shared variables

Definition 2. *A real-time automaton network with shared variables (real-time automaton network for short) is a tuple $\mathcal{N} = \langle \mathcal{P}, \mathcal{V}, \mathcal{G}, \mathcal{R} \rangle$, where*

1. $\mathcal{P} = \{\mathcal{A}_1, \mathcal{A}_2, \ldots, \mathcal{A}_n\}$ *is a finite set of real-time automata; for $i = 1, 2, \ldots, n$ let $\mathcal{A}_i = \langle \mathbf{A}_i, \Gamma_i \rangle$ and $\mathbf{A}_i = \langle \mathcal{S}_i, q_0^i, \mathcal{E}_i \rangle$,*
2. $\mathcal{V} = \{v_1, v_2, \ldots, v_m\}$ *is a finite set of shared variables,*
3. $\mathcal{G}$ *is a mapping from $(\mathcal{E}_1 \cup \mathcal{E}_2 \cup \ldots \cup \mathcal{E}_n)$ to VarGuard (defined below)which assigns to each transition of the automata in $\mathcal{P}$ a boolean expression on the values of the shared variables in $\mathcal{V}$,*
4. $\mathcal{R} \in (\mathcal{E}_1 \cup \mathcal{E}_2 \cup \ldots \cup \mathcal{E}_n) \to (\mathcal{V} \to Nat)$; $\mathcal{R}$ *expresses the values of shared variables reset by the transitions; when a transition e takes place, each shared variable v in the domain of $\mathcal{R}(e)$ is assigned the value $\mathcal{R}(e)(v)$.*

VarGuard ranged over by ψ is generated by the following grammar:

$$\psi \triangleq true \mid v = c \mid \psi_1 \wedge \psi_2,$$

where v stands for a shared variable, and c stands for an integer constant. A guard $\psi \in VarGuard$ is evaluated to be true on a valuation V iff for each equation $v = c$ appeared in ψ, the value of v is c.

For a vector $\overline{x}$, let x_i denote the ith element of $\overline{x}$, and let $\overline{x}[x_i'/i]$ denote the vector obtained from $\overline{x}$ by replacing the ith element with x_i'.

Definition 3. *Let $\mathcal{N} = \langle \mathcal{P}, \mathcal{V}, \mathcal{G}, \mathcal{R} \rangle$ be a real-time automaton network. An untimed state $\overline{s}$ of $\mathcal{N}$ is an n-dimensional vector of local states (s_i is a state of $\mathcal{A}_i$ for $1 \leq i \leq n$). A configuration of $\mathcal{N}$ is a tuple $\langle \overline{s}, \overline{t}, V \rangle$, where $\overline{s}$ is an untimed state of $\mathcal{N}$, $\overline{t}$ is an n-dimensional vector of nonnegative reals. The value t_i expresses how long the automaton $\mathcal{A}_i$ has been staying at s_i and V is a valuation of the shared variables.*

The transition system of a real-time automaton network is described as follows.

Definition 4. *Let $\mathcal{N} = \langle \mathcal{P}, \mathcal{V}, \mathcal{G}, \mathcal{R} \rangle$ be a real-time automaton network, $\langle \overline{s}, \overline{t}, V \rangle$ and $\langle \overline{s}', \overline{t}', V' \rangle$ be its configurations. We define:*

1. $\langle \overline{s}, \overline{t}, V \rangle \xrightarrow{e^i} \langle \overline{s}', \overline{t}', V' \rangle$ *(e^i is a transition of $\mathcal{A}_i$) iff*
   (a) $(s_i = \overleftarrow{e^i}) \wedge (\overline{s}' = \overline{s}[\overrightarrow{e^i}/i])$, *and*

(b) $t_i \in [a_{e^i}, b_{e^i}] \wedge \bar{t}' = \bar{t}[0/i]$, *and*
(c) $\mathcal{G}(e^i)(V) \wedge V' = V \dagger \mathcal{R}(e^i)$.

2. $\langle \bar{s}, \bar{t}, V \rangle \xrightarrow{\epsilon,d} \langle \bar{s}, \bar{t}', V \rangle$ $(d \geq 0)$ *iff* $(t_i' = t_i + d) \wedge (t_i' \leq U_{s_i})$ *for* $1 \leq i \leq n$.

Given two configurations C_1 and C_2, we write $C_1 \xrightarrow{e,d} C_2$ iff there exists a configuration C' such that $C_1 \xrightarrow{\epsilon,d} C'$ and $C' \xrightarrow{e} C_2$. For a configuration C, for a transition e (can be ϵ) and for an integer d, there is at most one configuration C' satisfying $C \xrightarrow{e,d} C'$. We denote this configuration by $Succ(C, e, d)$ in the case it exists.

An execution α of the network $\mathcal{N}$ is defined as

$$\alpha = C_0 \xrightarrow{e_1,d_1} C_1 \xrightarrow{e_2,d_2} \ldots \xrightarrow{e_m,d_m} C_m \xrightarrow{\epsilon,d_{m+1}} C_{m+1},$$

where C_0 is the initial configuration of $\mathcal{N}$. We call the timed sequence $\tau = (e_1, t_1)\hat{\,}(e_2, t_2)\hat{\,}\ldots\hat{\,}(e_m, t_m)\hat{\,}(\epsilon, t_{m+1})$ the behaviour corresponding to the execution α and C_{m+1} the final configuration of α, where for each $1 \leq i \leq m + 1$, $t_i = \sum_{j=1}^{i} d_j$. A configuration $\langle \bar{s}, \bar{t}, V \rangle$ is called an integer configuration iff for each i $(1 \leq i \leq n)$ t_i is an integer. The execution α is said to be an integer execution iff all C_i's $(0 \leq i \leq m + 1)$ are integer configurations.

3 Linear Duration Properties

Let, from now on in this paper, $\mathcal{N}$ be a real-time automaton network as defined in Definition 2. The linear duration properties (LDPs) are simple Duration Calculus formulas used to express requirements of real-time systems. An LDP is a linear inequality of the state-durations of the form $\Psi \leq M$, where $\Psi = \sum_{i=1}^{k} c_i \int S_i$, and for each i $(1 \leq i \leq k)$, S_i is a predicate on untimed states of $\mathcal{N}$, c_i and M are real numbers (c_i is called the coefficient corresponding to S_i and $\int S_i$ the duration of S_i).

Let $\alpha = C_0 \xrightarrow{e_1,d_1} C_1 \xrightarrow{e_2,d_2} \ldots \xrightarrow{e_m,d_m} C_m \xrightarrow{\epsilon,d_{m+1}} C_{m+1}$ be an execution of $\mathcal{N}$. The duration $\int S_i$ of system state S_i over the behaviour α is defined by

$$\int S_i(\alpha) = \sum_{u \in \beta_i} d_{u+1},$$

where $\beta_i = \{u | (0 \leq u \leq m) \wedge (\bar{s}_u \text{ is the untimed state of } C_u) \wedge (\bar{s}_u \Rightarrow S_i)\}$. Thus, given an LDP $\Psi \leq M$, the value of Ψ evaluated over α, denoted $\Psi(\alpha)$, is calculated as

$$\Psi(\alpha) = \sum_{i=1}^{k} c_i \int S_i(\alpha) = \sum_{i=1}^{k} c_i \left(\sum_{u \in \beta_i} d_{u+1} \right) = \sum_{j=0}^{m} C_{\bar{s}_j} d_{j+1},$$

where $C_{\bar{s}_j} = \sum_{i \in \{i | \bar{s} \Rightarrow S_i\}} c_i$, and $\bar{s}_j$ $(0 \leq j \leq m)$ is the untimed state of C_j.

Definition 5. *An LDP $\Psi \leq M$ is satisfied by an execution α iff $\Psi(\alpha) \leq M$, and is satisfied by $\mathcal{N}$, denoted $\mathcal{N} \models \Psi \leq M$, iff it is satisfied by all executions of $\mathcal{N}$.*

For example, the property that the time the first automaton in Figure 1 stays at the state A is longer than the time it stays at the state B can be expressed by the LDP $\int \mathbf{at}_B - \int \mathbf{at}_A \leq 0$ where $\mathbf{at}_A$ and $\mathbf{at}_B$ are predicates on untimed states such that $\langle A, C \rangle \Rightarrow \mathbf{at}_A$, $\langle A, D \rangle \Rightarrow \mathbf{at}_A$, $\langle B, C \rangle \Rightarrow \mathbf{at}_B$, $\langle B, D \rangle \Rightarrow \mathbf{at}_B$.

4 The Algorithm

4.1 Some Properties of Real-Time Automaton Networks and LDPs

Let, in this section, $\Psi \leq M$ be an LDP. The observation leading to our algorithm is formulated in the following lemma.

Lemma 1. *For any execution α of $\mathcal{N}$, there is an integer execution α' of $\mathcal{N}$ such that $\Psi(\alpha) \leq \Psi(\alpha')$.*

From Lemma 1, the network $\mathcal{N}$ satisfies the LDP $\Psi \leq M$ iff all the integer behaviours of $\mathcal{N}$ satisfy the LDP. In fact, we do not have to check all the integer executions. Let $\mathcal{C}_1$ and $\mathcal{C}_2$ be configurations for which each behaviour starting from $\mathcal{C}_1$ can be simulated by a behaviour starting from $\mathcal{C}_2$. Let α and α' be integer executions with $\mathcal{C}_1$ and $\mathcal{C}_2$ as their final configurations. If $\Psi(\alpha') \geq \Psi(\alpha)$ holds, We do not need to consider the right extensions of α. In order to formalise this idea we introduce the compatibility relation between configurations as follows.

Definition 6. *Let $\mathcal{C}_1 = \langle \bar{s}, \bar{t}, V \rangle$ and $\mathcal{C}_2 = \langle \bar{s}, \bar{t}', V \rangle$ be configurations of $\mathcal{N}$. $\mathcal{C}_1$ is said to be compatible with $\mathcal{C}_2$, denoted by $\mathcal{C}_1 \preceq \mathcal{C}_2$, iff for $1 \leq i \leq n$ the following holds,*

$$(t_i = t_i') \vee (t_i \geq RgBnd_{s_i} \wedge t_i' \geq RgBnd_{s_i}) \vee$$
$$(LowBnd_{s_i} \leq t_i < t_i') \vee (t_i > t_i' \wedge \forall e \bullet (\overleftarrow{e} = s_i \Rightarrow b_e = \infty)),$$

where $RgBnd_{s_i} = \max(\{a_e | \overleftarrow{e} = s_i\} \cup \{b_e + 1 | (\overleftarrow{e} = s_i) \wedge (b_e < \infty)\})$ and $LowBnd_{s_i} = \max(\{a_e | \overleftarrow{e} = s_i\})$.

Since for each local state s, $\forall e \bullet (\overleftarrow{e} = s \Rightarrow b_e = \infty)$ means $RgBnd_s = LowBnd_s$, the compatibility relation is transitive and reflexive.

Lemma 2. *Let $\mathcal{C}_1$, $\mathcal{C}_2$ be integer configurations of $\mathcal{N}$. $\mathcal{C}_1 \preceq \mathcal{C}_2$ implies that for arbitrary transition e (e can be ϵ), for arbitrary integer d and for arbitrary configuration $\mathcal{C}_2'$, if $\mathcal{C}_2 \xrightarrow{e,d} \mathcal{C}_2'$ then for some configuration $\mathcal{C}_1'$, it holds $\mathcal{C}_1 \xrightarrow{e,d} \mathcal{C}_1' \wedge \mathcal{C}_1' \preceq \mathcal{C}_2'$.*

This lemma means that given configurations $\mathcal{C}_1$ and $\mathcal{C}_2$, if $\mathcal{C}_1 \preceq \mathcal{C}_2$, then each behaviour starting from $\mathcal{C}_2$ can be simulated by a behaviour starting from $\mathcal{C}_1$.

Definition 7. *Integer configurations $\mathcal{C}_1$ and $\mathcal{C}_2$ are equivalent, denoted $\mathcal{C}_1 \equiv \mathcal{C}_2$, iff $(\mathcal{C}_1 \preceq \mathcal{C}_2) \wedge (\mathcal{C}_2 \preceq \mathcal{C}_1)$.*

It is obvious that $\equiv$ is an equivalence relation, and furthermore, of finite index. Indeed, let $\mathcal{R}_\mathcal{N}$ be $\{[\mathcal{C}] \,|\, (\mathcal{C} \text{ is a reachable integer configuration of } \mathcal{N})\}$, where $[\mathcal{C}]$ denote the equivalence class of $\equiv$ containing $\mathcal{C}$.

Lemma 3. *$\mathcal{R}_\mathcal{N}$ is a finite set.*

4.2 Weighted Directed Graphs

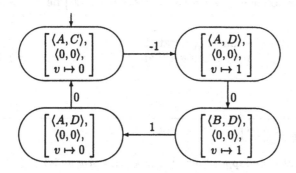

Fig. 2. A weighted directed graph

A *weighted directed graph* of the real-time automaton network $\mathcal{N}$ corresponding to the LDP $\Psi \leq M$ is defined as follows. The set of nodes is $\mathcal{R}_{\mathcal{N}}$. There is an arc a with weight D_a from a node n to a node n' iff there exist a transition e and configurations $C \in n$ and $C' \in n'$ for which $C \xrightarrow{e,d} C'$ for some d and $D_a = \max\{C_{\bar{s}}d \mid \exists C_1, C_1' \bullet (C_1 \in n \wedge C_1' \in n' \wedge C_1 \xrightarrow{e,d} C_1')\}$, where $\bar{s}$ is the untimed state of C. From definition, D_a may be ∞, and if $D_a < \infty$, there is an integer d such that $C_{\bar{s}}d = D_a$. (Figure 2 shows such a graph for the network in Figure 1)

The initial node of the graph is the node containing the initial configuration of the network. From the definition of $\equiv$, there is an algorithm to enumerate all the successive nodes of any node n.

For a configuration $C = \langle \bar{s}, \bar{t}, V \rangle$, let L_C denote the value $\min(\{U_{s_i} - t_i \mid 1 \leq i \leq n\})$. L_C is the longest time the network can stay at $\bar{s}$ once it reaches the configuration C. From the definition of the weighted graph, we have the following lemma.

Lemma 4. *Let* $p = [C_0] \xrightarrow{a_1} [C_1] \xrightarrow{a_2} \ldots \xrightarrow{a_m} [C_m]$ *be an arbitrary path of the graph. Let* $\widehat{\Psi}(p)$ *denote the length of* p, *i.e.* $\widehat{\Psi}(p) = \sum_{i=1}^{m} D_{a_i}$. *Let* $\alpha = C_0' \xrightarrow{e_1,d_1} C_1' \xrightarrow{e_2,d_2} \ldots \xrightarrow{e_m,d_m} C_m' \xrightarrow{\epsilon,d_{m+1}} C_{m+1}'$ *be an execution of* $\mathcal{N}$ *satisfying that for* $0 \leq i \leq m$, $C_i' \in [C_i]$. *Then*

1. $\Psi(\alpha) \leq \widehat{\Psi}(p) + \max(0, C_{\bar{s}} L_{C_m})$.
2. *If* $\widehat{\Psi}(p) + \max(0, C_{\bar{s}} L_{C_m}) = \infty$, *then for any constant* M, *there is an execution* α' *satisfying* $\Psi(\alpha') > M$. *Else there is an execution* α'' *satisfying* $\Psi(\alpha'') = \widehat{\Psi}(p) + \max(0, C_{\bar{s}} L_{C_m})$.

4.3 Algorithm

From Lemma 4, for checking whether the network $\mathcal{N}$ satisfies the LDP $\Psi \leq M$, we can check whether there is a path in the graph the length of which is greater than M. We can use the depth-first method to generate and check the paths starting from the initial node of the graph. It performs back-tracking once it finds that one of the following two conditions holds (let $[\mathcal{C}]$ be the last node of the path).

1. No new successive node can be generated.
2. A previously checked path p reaches $[\mathcal{C}']$ and $\mathcal{C}' \preceq \mathcal{C}$, the length of p is greater the current length.

$G := \{\langle [\mathcal{C}^0], 0\rangle\}$; $p :=\ll [\mathcal{C}^0]\gg$;
while $True$ **do**
      $flg := NextNode$;{append p with a new successive node}
      while $flg = False$ **do**
      begin
              Delete the last element from p; {back-tracking}
              if (p is empty) **return** $True$;
              {No more paths can be generated and checked}
              $flg := NextNode$;
      end
      $\mathcal{C} :=$ a configuration in the last node of p;
      if $\widehat{\Psi}(p) + \max(0, C_{\bar{s}}L_C) > M$, where $\bar{s}$ is the untimed state of $\mathcal{C}$
              then return $False$;
      if there is a prefix p' of p such that
          $\mathcal{C}$ is compatible with the configuration in the last node of p'
          and $\widehat{\Psi}(p) > \widehat{\Psi}(\alpha')$
              then return $False$;
      if $\exists \langle [\mathcal{C}'], l'\rangle \in G \bullet (\mathcal{C}' \preceq \mathcal{C}) \wedge (l' \geq \widehat{\Psi}(p))$ **then**
              delete the last element of p;{ back-tracking}
      else begin
              Add the tuple $\langle [\mathcal{C}], \widehat{\Psi}(p)\rangle$ to G;
              Delete all the tuples $\langle [\mathcal{C}'], l'\rangle$ from G satisfying $\widehat{\Psi}(p) \geq l' \wedge \mathcal{C} \preceq \mathcal{C}'$.
      end; {of else}
end; {of while}

Fig. 3. The Algorithm

The algorithm for checking whether the network $\mathcal{N}$ satisfies the LDP $\Psi \leq M$ is given in Figure 3. It uses auxiliary variables G and p. The variable G is used to record the nodes reached by previously checked paths together with the length of the longest paths reaching them. The variable p is used to record the currently generated path. In this algorithm $NextNode$ is a procedure used to generate a new successive node of the currently generated path in p. It returns $False$ if no such node can be generated. Otherwise, $NextNode$ generates a new node and appends it to p. Besides, $\mathcal{C}$ is a variable ranging over the set of configurations, flg is a boolean variable, l is a variable of real.

Let p be the currently generated path and $[\mathcal{C}]$ be its last node. Let p' be a prefix of p and the last node of p' is also $[\mathcal{C}]$. If $\widehat{\Psi}(p') < \widehat{\Psi}(p)$, we can repeat the segment of p from the end of p' to the end of p for making the Ψ value unlimitedly large. So the LDP is violated in this case. If $\widehat{\Psi}(p') \geq \widehat{\Psi}(p)$, the tuple $\langle [\mathcal{C}], \widehat{\Psi}(p') \rangle$ must have been stored in G, so the algorithm performs back-tracking. Therefore, the algorithm generates only paths with at most one circle, there are only finite number of such paths. The algorithm terminates.

The body of the algorithm is written in a Pascal-like language, where $[\mathcal{C}^0]$ denotes the initial node of the graph.

5 Fischer's Mutual Exclusion Protocol: A Case Study

We have implemented the algorithm presented in the previous section in the C language and tried the program with Fischer's mutual exclusion protocol. To our knowledge, Fischer's protocol is well studied and the size of the example can be scaled up by increasing the number of processes in the protocol.

The protocol is to guarantee mutual exclusion in a concurrent system consisting of a number of processes, using clock constraints and a shared variable. The protocol can be modelled as a real-time automaton network with a shared variable v. The ith process has its own identifier i and can be modelled as a real-time automaton shown in Figure 4.

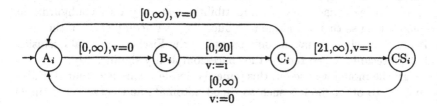

Fig. 4. The real-time automaton of the ith process

We need to verify formally that at any moment at most one process can be in its critical section. This requirement can be formalised as the following linear duration property:

$$\int Error \leq 0$$

where $Error$ is a predicate on the untimed states, and $\bar{s} \Rightarrow Error$ iff there exist j and i such that $j \neq i$ and $s_i = CS_i \wedge s_j = CS_j$.

Running on a SparcStation 5 with 48MB of primary memory, our program has verified the mutual exclusion property of Fischer's protocol for the cases $n = 2, 3, \ldots, 11$. The space requirements for these cases are listed in Table 1, these requirements are represented in term of the number of nodes generated and stored by the algorithm. It can be seen that for $k \leq 10$ the space requirement

n =	2	3	4	5	6	7	8	9	10	11
nodes	18	65	220	727	2378	7737	25080	81035	260998	837949

Table 1. Space requirements on checking Fischer's protocol using our algorithm

n =	2	3	4	5
space	16	237	3528	59715

Table 2. Space requirements on checking Fischer's protocol using UPPAAL

for the case $n = k + 1$ is approximately 4 times of the one for the case $n = k$. The run time requirement for the case $n = 11$ is about 15 minutes. The well-known verification tool UPPAAL can only check the Fischer's protocol with up to 8 processes by state space exploration [8]. The performance statistics data in Table 2 [9] shows that adding a new process makes the space requirement of UPPAAL rise to more than 12 times of the original one. The similar results have been reported for the tool HyTech.

6 Conclusion

In this paper, we have presented an algorithm to check the validity of a real-time automaton network with respect to a linear duration property, which is a linear inequality of integrated state-durations. To attack the state space explosion caused by time-constraints, a compatibility relation $\preceq$ over configurations is introduced. We use this technique to reduce the space-complexity of the algorithm. It has been shown that in some cases like the Fischer's mutual exclusion protocol, this technique can reduce the space-complexity significantly.

Although the model we used in this paper is simple, we believe that this idea can be applied to other models such as timed automata and networks of timed automata.

References

1. R. Alur, C. Courcoubetis, and T.A. Henzinger. Computing accumulated delays in real-time systems. In *Proceedings of the Fifth Conference on Computer-Aided Verification*, LNCS 693, pages 181–193. Springer-Verlag, 1993.
2. R. Alur and D. Dill. Automata for Modelling Real-Time Systems. In *Proc. of ICALP'90*, LNCS 443, 1990.
3. C.Daws, A.Olivero, S.Tripakis, and S.Yovine. The tool Kronos. In *Hybrid Systems III, Verification and Control*, number 1066 in Lecture Notes in Computer Science. Springer-Verlag, 1996.
4. Zhou Chaochen, C.A.R. Hoare, and A.P.Ravn. A Calculus of Durations. In *Information Processing Letter 40,5*, pages 269–276, 1991.
5. Zhou Chaochen, Zhang Jingzhong, Yang Lu, and Li Xiaoshan. Linear Duration Invariants. Research Report 11, UNU/IIST, P.O.Box 3058, Macau, July 1993.

Published in: Formal Techniques in Real-Time and Fault-Tolerant systems, LNCS 863, 1994.

6. Li Xuan Dong and Dang Van Hung. Checking Linear Duration invariants by Linear Programming. Research Report 70, UNU/IIST, P.O.Box 3058, Macau, May 1996. Published in Joxan Jaffar and Roland H. C. yap (Eds.), *Concurrency and Palalellism, Programming, Networking, and Securiry* LNCS 1179, Springer-Verlag, Dec 1996, pp. 321–332.

7. Li Xuan Dong, Dang Van Hung, and Zheng Tao. Checking Hybrid Automata for Linear Duration Invariants. Research Report 109, UNU/IIST, P.O.Box 3058, Macau, June 1997. Published in R.K.Shamasundar, K.Ueda (Eds.), Advances in Computing Science, Lecture Notes in Computer Science 1345, Springer-Verlag, pp.166-180.

8. Kere J. Kristoffersen, Francois Larroussinie, Kim G.Larsen, Paul Pettersson, and Wang Yi. A Compositional Proof of a Real-Time Mutual Exclusion Protocol. In *Proceedings of TAPSOFT'97, the 7th International Joint Conference on the Theory and Practice of Software Development*, pages 14–18, April 1997.

9. Kim G. Larsen, Fredrik Larsson, Paul Pettersson, and Wang Yi. Efficient Verification of Real-Time Systems: Compact Data Structure and State-Space Reduction. December 1997. Accepted for presentation at the 18th IEEE Real-Time Systems Symposium. San Francisco, California, USA.

10. Kim G Larsen and Paul Pettersson Wang Yi. UPPAAL: Status & Developments. In Orna Grumberg, editor, *Proceedings of the 9th International Conference on Computer-Aided Verification. Haifa, Israel,*, LNCS 1254, pages 456–459. Springer-Verlag, June 1997.

11. T.A.Henzinger, P.-H. Ho, and H. Wong-Toi. A Users Guide to HyTech. Technical report, Department of Computer Science, Cornell University, 1995.

12. Pham Hong Thai and Dang Van Hung. Checking a regular class of Duration Calculus Models for Linear Duration Invariants. Technical Report 118, UNU/IIST, P.O.Box 3058, Macau, July 1997. Published in the Proceedings of the International Symposium on Software Engineering for Parallel and Distributed Systems (PDSE'98), 20 - 21 April 1998, Kyoto, Japan, Bernd Kramer, Naoshi Uchihira, Peter Croll and Stefano Russo (Eds), IEEE Computer Society Press, 1998, pp. 61 - 71.

13. Mihalis Yannakakis and David Lee. An Efficient Algorithm for Minimizing Real-Time Transition Systems. *Formal Methods in System Design*, 11(2):113–136, August 1997.

14. Y.Kesten, A.Pnueli, J.Sifakis, and S.Yovine. Integration Graphs: A Class of Decidable Hybrid Systems. In *Hybrid System*, number 736 in LNCS, pages 179–208, 1993.

A Practical and Complete Algorithm for Testing Real-Time Systems

Rachel Cardell-Oliver and Tim Glover

Department of Computer Science University of Essex
Colchester CO4 3SQ United Kingdom
Tel. +44-1206-873586 Fax. +44-1206-872788
{cardr,glovtv}@essex.ac.uk

Abstract. This paper presents a formal method for generating conformance tests for real-time systems. Our algorithm is complete in that,
under a test hypothesis, if the system being tested passes every test generated then the tested system is bisimilar to its specification. Because
the test algorithm has exponential worst case complexity and finite state
automata models of real-time systems are typically very large, a judi-
cious choice of model is critical for the successful testing of real-time
systems. Developing such a model and demonstrating its effectiveness
are the main contributions of this paper.
Keywords: real-time systems, black-box testing, timed automata

1 Introduction

An idealistic description of a formal development method from requirements to
an implementation in hardware and software runs as follows. Construct successive refinements of the requirements until a detailed design is produced, verifying
formally at each stage that the refinement satisfies the requirements imposed by
its predecessor. Finally, implement the design in hardware and software. Each
of the stages from requirements to design is a textual description, and formal
verification can be carried out by symbol manipulation. However, the final implementation is not a description, and its properties can only be determined
by performing experiments upon it. Thus the last stage in any formal development is a formal test method which ensures that an implementation meets its
specification.

A formal test method has four stages: checking the test hypothesis, generating
test cases, running the tests and evaluating test results. The *test hypothesis*
defines the assumptions necessary to draw conclusions about the correctness
of the implementation from the evidence of test results. For example, our test
hypothesis requires that the system under test can be viewed, at some level of
abstraction, as a deterministic finite state automata. A test case is an experiment
to be performed on the implementation resulting in a pass or fail result for
each test. The test generation algorithm constructs a set of test cases from a
formal specification. A test method is *complete* if its test generation algorithm
determines a finite set of test cases sufficient to demonstrate that the formal

model of the implementation under test is equivalent to its specification. For the method to be *practical* the number of tests generated must not be too large.

Previously proposed theories for testing reactive systems [8, 9, 11] are incomplete in this sense because the set of test cases required is infinite and so the outcome of testing a finite number of cases only approximates a complete test. Springtveld *et al* present a complete test generation algorithm for dense real-time automata based on [3, 6], but acknowledge the algorithm is not practical [10]. Indeed, all the test methods cited have a worst case exponential complexity. The main contribution of this paper is the development of a complete test method which is also practical.

The advantage of a complete test method is that results from test and verification can be combined seamlessly and the assumptions under which this is done are explicit in the test hypothesis. The *test justification theorem* states that,

> IF the specification and implementation satisfy the test hypothesis THEN the implementation passes every test generated for the specification if and only if the implementation is equivalent to the specification.

A proof of the test justification theorem for the testing theory developed in this paper may be found in [2].

The paper is organised as follows. In Section 2 we define our specification language and a model of timed action automata for testing real-time systems. Section 3 presents our adaptation for real-time systems of Chow's test generation algorithm for Mealy automata [3, 6]. Test generation examples are presented in Section 4.

2 Specification Language and Test Model

In this section we recall the real-time specification language of timed transition systems (TTSs) [5, 1] and define *timed action automata* to model TTS computations for testing. It is straightforward to adapt our test method for different real-time specification languages, including those with synchronous communication such as timed CSP, but that is beyond the scope of this paper.

Specifications will be given by two explicit TTS processes: a system process, S, and its environment, E. The implementation under test is represented by an unknown TTS process I. The aim of testing is to show that, at a suitable level of abstraction, I corresponds to S when executed in the same environment E. We write $S \parallel E$ for the specification and $I \parallel E$ for the system to be tested. It is a notable feature of our test method that the environment itself is described by a TTS process, and that correctness only has to be demonstrated with respect to this environment. This allows a large process to be decomposed into manageable pieces without requiring the behaviour of each component to be defined in arbitrary contexts.

A TTS **process** consists of a collection of variables, each with an associated range of values. Each variable is tagged as **public** or **hidden**. All environment variables are public since the tester controls the environment for all tests. The public variables of S (and I) correspond to those whose values the tester can *observe*. A process **state** is a binding of a legal value to each process variable. An **action** is a list of variable bindings. The idea is that the actions of the process represent (multiple) assignments of values to variables. Thus an action can be seen as a relation between states.

A **timed transition system (TTS) specification** consists of a unique initial state and a set of **timed transition rules** t each of the form

$$\text{If } C_t \text{ Then } B_t \text{ Between } L_t \text{ And } U_t$$

where C is a guard (a state predicate), B is an action, and U and L are upper and lower time bounds respectively. Each rule defines a possible timed state transition from any state meeting the guard conditions. Each rule belongs to either the environment or the system process and the corresponding actions are regarded as inputs and outputs respectively. Associated with each transition rule is a special clock variable which takes discrete time values. The requirement that an action take place between the upper and lower time bounds is a guard condition on the associated clock.

The computations of a TTS are defined in terms of states and labelled transitions. Whenever an action can be inferred between two states, there will be a labelled transition between them. Labels $\delta/\alpha/\nu$ denote an action α occurring after discrete time delay δ. The tag ν is i for an input action or o for an output action. Each computation of a TTS is an infinite sequence of states and labels

$$\sigma_0 \to \delta_0/\alpha_0/\nu_0 \to \sigma_1 \to \delta_1/\alpha_1/\nu_1 \to \sigma_2 \to \ldots$$

In any state σ the clock variable associated with transition rule t has the value c_t^σ. The rule is said to be **enabled** on σ if its guard C_t is true in that state. The rule must become disabled after it is **taken**, that is after the assignment bindings B_t are applied to σ.

We say state σ' is a $(\delta/\alpha/\nu)$-**successor** of state σ iff there is a timed transition rule t such that,

- t is enabled on σ
- σ' is obtained by applying the bindings B_t to σ;
- $\nu = i$ if t is a transition rule of environment E and $\nu = o$ if t is a rule of the system process S;
- the time step δ must be chosen so that no enabled rule's upper time bound is exceeded: $c_s^\sigma + \delta \leq U_s$ for all rules s enabled in σ;
- the clock variables of each transition rule are set in σ' as follows:
  - the clocks of all rules (including t) which are disabled in σ' are set to -1;
  - the clocks of all rules disabled in σ but enabled in σ' are set to 0;
  - the clocks of all rules enabled in both σ and σ' are incremented by the delay δ;

Each specification action may change both public and hidden variables. Actions that affect only hidden variables are not observable directly, and can be thought of as silent actions. Since we assume implementations to be deterministic these silent actions can simply be elided from the model. This is the motivation behind the following definitions.

The function *seen* returns the public variable bindings of any action. If there are no public variables changed in output action α then the action is **silent** and $seen(\alpha) = \Lambda$, the null action. Otherwise, α is **observable**. State σ_n is a $(\Delta/A/V)$-**successor** of state σ_0 iff there exist states $\sigma_1, \ldots \sigma_{n-1}$ and labels $\alpha_0/\delta_0/\nu_0 \ldots \alpha_{n-1}/\delta_{n-1}/\nu_{n-1}$ such that

- each σ_{i+1} is a $(\delta_i/\alpha_i/\nu_i)$-successor of σ_i
- all but the last action are silent: $seen(\alpha_i) = \Lambda$ for $i : 0..n-2$
- the final action is an observable one: $A = \alpha_{n-1} \neq \Lambda$
- $\Delta = \sum_{i=0}^{n-1} \delta_i$
- $V = \nu_{n-1}$

The $(\Delta/A/V)$-successors of the initial state binding for a timed transition system determine a labelled transition system (LTS). For testing purposes we require that the LTS be finite and we call the resulting labelled graph of states a **timed action automata**. The timed action automata for a TTS, $P \parallel E$, is denoted $\mathcal{A}(P \parallel E)$.

We can now define the test hypothesis. A specification S, an implementation I and environment E satisfy the **test hypothesis** iff

1. $S \parallel E$ and $I \parallel E$ are timed transition systems whose computations can be characterised, using the $\Delta/A/V$ rules, as (finite state) timed action automata.
2. Any two input actions or two output actions of $\mathcal{A}(S \parallel E)$ or $\mathcal{A}(I \parallel E)$ must be separated by at least one time unit. This constraint is necessary so that a tester can observe each output action correctly and can offer input actions at the right time. For example, an input could be offered just before an output or just after. We also demand the standard TTS constraint that time must behave reasonably [5]: Zeno specifications are not allowed.
3. $S \parallel E$ must be deadlock and livelock free. This is because it is not possible to verify permanent inactivity by finite experiments. Note however that the implementation may contain deadlocks or livelocks in which case that $\mathcal{A}(I \parallel E) \not\approx \mathcal{A}(S \parallel E)$ will be detected by the tests generated.
4. I and S are deterministic when executed in environment E. If this is not the case then, even if the IUT passes every test, we can not deduce that the system will always behave correctly. This means that for all timed transition rules of I and S the upper and lower time bounds must be equal and enabling conditions must be mutually exclusive. The environment E, however, can be (and usually is) non-deterministic. This is reasonable since the tester can simulate (deterministically) any chosen environment behaviour. In practice, limited freedom about the precise time an action occurs can be provided by allowing a certain tolerance in the times outputs are observed [10].
5. After each test case is executed the implementation under test can be reset to its initial state within a finite time.

6. The number of states in $\mathcal{A}(I \parallel E)$ does not exceed $n + k$ where n is the number of states in the specification, $\mathcal{A}(S \parallel E)$

The tester must postulate a suitable k, which is usually selected on pragmatic grounds. As k grows the number of tests grows exponentially and so this is the limiting factor in producing a complete test set. The problem of exponential growth of number of tests is also present in other formal test methods [9, 11] although for different reasons.

3 Test Generation Algorithm

The test generation algorithm takes the timed action automata $\mathcal{A}(S \parallel E)$ associated with a TTS specification and constructs a finite set of test cases which will test each timed action edge of the automata. Each test is simply a sequence of timed actions. Input actions are to be offered by the test harness and output actions are to be observed. The test set has the property that if all tests succeed then the implementation and specification automata are trace equivalent where trace equivalence corresponds to bisimilarity under our test hypothesis.

The N transitions of $\mathcal{A}(S \parallel E)$ are labelled t1 to tN. The number of states in $\mathcal{A}(S \parallel E)$ is n and k is the maximum number of *extra* states which may be used in the automata $\mathcal{A}(I \parallel E)$. The tests will actually be *applied* in a breadth first manner, to ensure that errors are detected as soon as possible, but we can *generate* the test cases in any order - in our tool depth first. Trace concatenation mapped over sets is written ++.

Algorithm 1 (Test Generation)
```
T:=EMPTY;
for j:=0 to k do
  for i:=1 to N do
    T:=T UNION
      ( {reach(src(ti))} ++ {test(ti)} ++
        step(dst(ti),j,x) ++ cs(x) ++ {reset} )
```

Each test case consists of four components. The first part, reach(src(ti)) followed by test(ti), exercises the transition to be tested. The second part, step(dst(ti),j,x), performs a number of transition sequences which allow for the possibility that the implementation may possess extra states. The third part, cs(x), resolves any ambiguity in the final state reached by exercising a set of sequences of transitions which distinguishes the expected state from any other state with which it might be confused. The final timed action, reset, returns the implementation to its initial state within a fixed time in readiness for the next test [10].

The sequence reach(s) can be any one of the possible sequences of timed actions starting in the initial state and finishing in state s, in this case the source state of the transition being tested: src(ti). In the context of real-time systems, the important test parameter is the total time elapsed rather than the number of observations in each test, and so a least-time path rather than a least-edge path to src(ti) is constructed. The timed action label of the transition ti being tested is given by test(ti).

After the sequence {reach(src(ti))} ++ {test(ti)} the implementation should be in state dst(ti). To ensure this is the case, each state of the specification automata has a set of timed action sequences cs(x) called the **characterising set** for state x. Its sequences distinguish that state from any of the n-1 other states in the specification automaton. Characterising sequences may be empty but otherwise they must end with a visible output action. Each characterising sequence has a pass or fail result (explained below).

Alternatively, the implementation might go to one of the k extra states for which there is no equivalent in the specification. We ensure that this has not happened by checking that every implementation timed action sequence from that state of length 0 to k matches those of the specification. Furthermore, the final state reached by each such sequence must pass the characterising set tests for that state. Every possible sequence of length j from state s in the graph is given by the set step(s,j,x) where x is the state reached after these j steps and j ranges from 0 to k.

Checking that specification and implementation agree on *every* sequence of length 0 up to k ensures that the implementation's version of transition ti matches the specification's transition ti. For example, compare a sequence of two inputs followed by an output from state s_1 allowed by a specification

$$s_1 \rightarrow \delta_1/\alpha/i \rightarrow s_2 \rightarrow \delta_2/\beta/i \rightarrow s_3 \rightarrow \delta_3/\gamma/o \rightarrow s_4$$

with this one of an implementation model which has 2 extra states

$$r_1 \rightarrow \delta_1/\alpha/i \rightarrow r_{102} \rightarrow \delta_2/\beta/i \rightarrow r_{103} \rightarrow \delta_3/\zeta/o \rightarrow r_4$$

That the states s_1 and r_1 are not equivalent is detected by tests from the set step(s1,2,s3)++cs(s3) which detect that states s_3 and r_{103} produce different outputs γ and ζ.

Characterising Sequences The timed action automata we generate from timed transition system specifications contain not only labelled transition information but also information about the values of all public variables in each state. This differs from the finite state automata of Chow's test algorithm where transition actions can be observed but nothing is known about the state.

Using this information, it is possible to simplify the standard algorithms for constructing a characterising set. First, it is not necessary to use a sequence to distinguish two states whose public variable values differ. For example, a state just reached by a "turn-red" action could not be confused with a "green" state. Second, since the environment is entirely under the tester's control, two states which have different environment parts need no further comparison.

Algorithm 2 (Characterising Sequences) *For the timed action automata* $M = \mathcal{A}(S \parallel E)$,

1. *Partition the states which occur in M so that within each partition, every state shares the same values for all public variables. If any of these partitions contains only one element, then that configuration is characterised by its observable sub-part and its characterising sequence is the empty sequence.*
2. *For the remaining partitions, take any pair of states σ_j, σ_k from the same partition p_i. These states are not distinguished by their observable parts. Construct a (minimal) sequence of timed actions ending in a visible output action: $t_0/\alpha_0/\nu_0, ..., t_s/\alpha_s/\nu_s, t_{s+1}/\alpha_{s+1}/o$ such that $t_0/\alpha_0/\nu_0, ..., t_s/\alpha_s/\nu_s$ is a possible sequence for both σ_j and σ_k. The final timed output action $t_{s+1}/\alpha_{s+1}/o$ should be a possible after the pre-sequence from σ_j but fail (see below) after the same sequence from σ_k or vice versa. Use this sequence to partition all states in p_i. Add the sequence $t_0/\alpha_0/\nu_0, ..., t_{s+1}/\alpha_{s+1}/o$ to the characterising sequence set and note for each state whether the check condition is True or False.*
3. *Repeat step 2 until every pair of configurations is distinguished either by their different observable parts or by their response to one of the characterising sequences.*

The same characterising sequence may be used to distinguish different state pairs. For a finite state automata with n states, $n - 1$ characterising sequences will suffice to distinguish all states [6]. However, since the test for transition ti must be run with each of the characterising sequences for dst(ti) it is obviously important to make characterising sets as small as possible. The results of Section 4 confirm that by using observable differences to characterise state pairs we obtain many fewer than $n - 1$ sequences.

Applying the Tests Each test in the test set is performed on the implementation under test by a test driver. The driver offers each timed input in the test case in sequence and observes that all timed outputs occur at the correct time.

The implementation may fail a test by failing to produce any expected output from the test sequence at the expected time or by producing an unexpected output. That is, a system under test **fails a test** iff for an expected output $\delta/\alpha/o$ we observe any of

1. an early output $\delta'/\alpha/o$ where $\delta' < \delta$
2. an incorrect output action $\delta'/\beta/o$ where $\beta \neq \alpha$ and $\delta' \leq \delta$
3. a late or missing output $\delta/\beta/o$ for $\delta < \delta'$
4. an incorrect characterising sequence check. That is, $t_{s+1}/\alpha_{s+1}/o, True$ fails conditions 1 to 3 or $t_{s+1}/\alpha_{s+1}/o, False$ does *not* do so.

If any test from the set of test cases is failed then the implementation under test does not satisfy its specification.

4 Examples

We plan to use a variety of case studies to identify a practical methodology for testing real-time systems. In this section we describe our first experiments in this area. We have implemented a tool to generate test cases from timed transition system specifications. The first version of this tool was implemented in Miranda, and the current version in SML. The results presented this section were generated using the SML tool.

The first example is a traffic light controller for a pelican crossing [5]. The system has two public variables namely, light, which may take the values red and green, and request which may be True or False. In addition it possesses a hidden location variable cloc. By default the controller keeps the light red, but it guarantees to set the light green within 1 second of a request being made, and to maintain the light green until no further request has been received for some pre-determined time period δ, taken to be 5 in this example. A specification which meets these requirements is as follows.

```
Initially:   Public req=F;   Public light=red;   Hidden cloc=0;
Implementation:
If req=T and cloc=0 Then req:=F and cloc:=1 Between 0 And 0;
If cloc=1 Then light:=green and cloc:=2 Between 1 And 1;
If cloc=2 Then cloc:=3 Between 5 And 5;
If cloc=3 and req=T Then req:=F and cloc:=2 Between 0 And 0;
If cloc=3 and req=F Then cloc:=0 and light:=red Between 1 And 1;
```

The controller operates in an environment which may make requests. In general requests may be received at any time;

```
If req=F Then req:=T Between 1 And infinity;
```

It turns out that, on the assumption that the implementation has no more states than its specification, no extra interesting behaviour is observed by waiting more than 10 seconds between requests, and the specification of the environment may be modified accordingly;

```
If req=F Then req:=T Between 1 And 10;
```

We place a further restriction on the environment that there is a minimum delay γ which can be expected between requests. This can be modelled by the following environment.

```
If req=F Then req:=T Between γ And 10;
```

The size of the timed action automata generated from this specification for different values of γ are shown in figure 1. The interesting point is that the behaviour of the combined system depends critically on the delay between requests. If γ takes a value larger than 7 then it is never possible for a request to be received whilst the light is green, and the combined system is degenerate. Between these values there is a complex interaction between the values of γ and δ. Clearly, if the environment is restricted there is a reduction in the number of tests that must be performed. Details of the tests generated are available [2].

gamma	1	2	3	4	5	6	7	8
edges	47	41	37	33	29	24	18	9
nodes	15	13	12	11	10	9	8	5
tests	90	51	40	31	24	17	14	6

Fig. 1. Number of test cases for the traffic light under different environments

Recall that a characterising sequence distinguishes a pair of states in a timed action automata. Frequently the state reached by a test sequence can be determined unambiguously since the values of all public variables are known. In the present example, taking γ to be 1, 4 out of the 15 states can be determined unambiguously. The remaining 11 states can be distinguished by just 6 distinct characterising sequences, each consisting of a single observation.

It is clear that the test algorithm described in Section 3 will result in a certain amount of redundancy, since many test sequences will be subsequences of other tests. This is particularly true when extra states are allowed for. In the present case, if we assume k=0 then the 127 test sequences generated can be reduced to 90 by subsuming short sequences into longer ones. If we allow for the possibility of two extra implementation states, the figures are 41,079 and 12,702 respectively. The number of tests required for different values of k are shown below. The tests for k=p include all those for k<p.

k	0	1	2	5
$tests$	90	224	494	12,702

The second example concerns the controller of a mine pump [7], which must keep the water level in a mine between fixed maximum and minimum bounds, with the proviso that the pump must be switched off if the methane concentration within the mine reaches a dangerous level. The implementation of the controller is given by the following three rules;

```
If highm=F and level=maxlevel and pump=off Then pump:=on
   Between 3 And 3;
If highm=F and level=1 and pump=on Then pump:=off
   Between 3 And 3;
If highm=T and pump=on Then pump:=off Between 1 And 1;
```

Water is assumed to flow into the mine at a variable rate, which however never exceeds the discharge capacity of the pump, so the water level may always be reduced as long as the methane concentration is low.

```
If pump=off and level ≠ maxlevel Then level:=level+1
   Between 2 And 3;
If pump=on and level ≠ 1 Then level:=level-1 Between 2 And 4;
```

The methane concentration may become dangerous at any time, but it can always be made safe within 10 time units.

```
If highm=T Then highm:=F Between 5 And 10;
If mloc=0 and highm=F Then mloc:=1 Between 1 And 1;
If mloc=1 and highm=F Then highm:=T and mloc:=0
   Between 1 And 1;
If mloc=1 and highm=F Then mloc:=0 Between 1 And 1;
```

The interest of this example arises from the fact that the pump may be switched off at any time due to the methane concentration. Whilst the pump is off the water level rises; once the mine has been made safe the pump can be switched on again and the water level falls. In order to model the behaviour of the mine it is necessary to keep track of the water level. In our specification language the real water level is approximated to a number of discrete water levels. The greater the number of levels used the more accurate the model, but the larger the graph generated, and so the greater the number of tests necessary.

Some figures relating to this model are given in figure 2, which shows the size of the graph and the number of tests required for different numbers of water levels. In this particular example, if we assume no extra states then all states can be distinguished by inspection, so there is exactly one test for each edge of the graph. However, there is a dramatic increase in the number of tests required if the implementation is assumed to have up to 2 extra states.

levels	2	4	6	10	20	20
k	0	0	0	0	0	2
nodes	33	92	154	278	588	588
tests	82	235	339	727	1,547	14,115

Fig. 2. Number of test cases for the mine pump under different environments

5 Future Work

We have presented a complete test algorithm for timed transition system specifications and some results of using the algorithm to generate tests for real-time systems. The main advantage of a complete test algorithm is that results from formal verification and testing can be combined. The major difficulty is that the number of tests required may be very large.

One way of reducing the number of tests is to look for redundancy. The results of the previous section show that the number of distinct tests required for completeness is much smaller than the total number of tests computed since any test that is a subsequence of another is redundant. There are some obvious ways in which the number of tests can be reduced still further. For example, it is often possible to find a single *unique identifying sequence* that can distinguish a given state from any other, and where these exist their use should result in fewer tests than a set of characterising sequences. It may also be possible to develop heuristics for minimising the total number of distinct tests, rather than computing a set of shortest-time tests and then removing any redundancy.

Even with these improvements it will only be possible to perform exhaustive testing on large systems by dividing the system into manageable pieces. In principle our approach is well suited to such decomposition. Each module need only be tested within the environment defined by the remaining components. Internal interactions between the parts of this environment can be hidden. Our next step will be to test the effectiveness of this strategy by applying it to a significant case study.

Acknowledgment This work is supported by EPSRC grant GR/L26087: Integrating Test and Verification for Real-Time and Fault-Tolerant Systems in a Trustworthy Tool. We are grateful to the anonymous referees for their comments.

References

1. Cardell-Oliver, R.: An Equivalence Theorem for the Operational and Temporal Semantics of Real-Time, Concurrent Programs, To appear in *Journal of Logic and Computation* Vol 8, 23 pages (1998)
2. Cardell-Oliver, R. and Glover, T.: *A Practical and Complete Algorithm for Testing Real-Time Systems*, Technical Report CSM-306, Department of Computer Science, University of Essex, February 1998. source http://cswww.essex.ac.uk/FSS/projects/test.html
3. Chow, T.S.: Testing Software Design Modeled by Finite-State Machines, In *IEEE Transactions on Software Engineering* Vol SE-4, No.3, 178–187 (1978)
4. Hennessy, M.C.: *Algebraic Theory of Processes*, MIT Press (1988).
5. Henzinger, T., Manna, Z. and Pnueli, A.: Temporal Proof Methodologies for Timed Transition Systems. *Information and Computation*, **112**, 273–337 (1994).
6. Holzmann, G.J.: *Design and Validation of Computer Protocols*, Prentice Hall (1991).
7. Joseph, M. (ed.): *Real-Time Systems: Specification, Verification and Analysis*, Prentice-Hall (1996).
8. Mandioli, Morasca and Morzenti: Generating Test Cases for Real-Time Systems from Logic Specifications, *ACM Trans on Computer Systems* **13**(4), 365–398 (1995).
9. Peleska, J. and Siegel, M.: Test Automation of Safety-Critical Reactive Systems, *South African Computer Journal* **19** 53–77 (1997).
10. Springtveld, J., Vaandrager, F., and D'Argenio, P.: *Testing Timed Automata*, CSI-R9712, Computing Science Institute, University of Nijmegen, August 1997. source http://www.cs.kun.nl/~fvaan/publications
11. Tretmans, J.: Test Generation with Inputs, Outputs and Quiescence In T Margaria and B Steffan (eds.) *Tools and Algorithms for the Construction and Analysis of Systems*, LNCS 1055, Springer Verlag (1996)

Mechanical Verification of Clock Synchronization Algorithms *

D. Schwier and F. von Henke

schwier,vhenke@informatik.uni-ulm.de
Universität Ulm, Fakultät für Informatik,
D-89069 Ulm, Germany

Abstract. Clock synchronization algorithms play a crucial role in a variety of fault-tolerant distributed architectures. Although those algorithms are similar in their basic structure, the particular designs differ considerably, for instance in the way clock adjustments are computed. This paper develops a formal generic theory of clock synchronization algorithms which extracts the commonalities of specific algorithms and their correctness arguments; this generalizes previous work by Shankar and Miner by covering non-averaging adjustment functions, in addition to averaging algorithms. The generic theory is presented as a set of parameterized PVS theories, stating the general assumptions on parameters and demonstrating the verification of generic clock synchronization. The generic theory is then specialized to the class of algorithms using averaging functions, yielding a theory that corresponds to those of Shankar and Miner. As examples of the verification of concrete, published algorithms, the formal verification of an instance of an averaging algorithms (by Welch and Lynch [3]) and of a non-averaging algorithm (by Srikanth and Toueg [14]) is discussed.

1 Introduction

Clock synchronization is one of the central elements of distributed dependable real-time systems. Many mechanisms for realizing dependability properties in distributed real-time systems rely on the fact that the different processes or computing 'nodes' can be synchronized tightly enough for satisfying the real-time requirements of the system. A major concern is the ability to synchronize the local clocks of the different nodes in such a way that the readings of any two local clocks differ by no more than a small fixed amount. The synchronization algorithms for achieving this are required to compensate for the drift of physical clocks. Furthermore, they must be able to tolerate different kinds of failures, so that even if a limited number of processes fail the clocks of the remaining, properly functioning processes maintain the required synchrony.

Clock synchronization is thus a basic service that warrants careful analysis. The case for applying formal methods, including mechanized theorem proving,

---

* This work has been supported in part by ESPRIT LTR Project 20072 "Design for Validation (DeVa)" and ESPRIT Project 20716 "GUARDS'.

to this task has been made in the past (cf. [10]; see also [6] for a summary of previous work). Reasoning about fault-tolerant clock synchronization algorithms is inherently difficult because of the possibility of subtle interactions involving failed components. A proof with the assistance of a mechanized proof system thus offers a higher degree of assurance that the verification of a claimed property of a synchronization algorithm is indeed correct. However, since such proof efforts require substantial skill and effort, it appears to be very desirable to have available a reusable formal framework that assists in verifying the specific clock synchronization algorithms used in particular practically relevant contexts, such as [8, 1, 2].

Clocks are synchronized by the periodical application of an adjustment to the local clock value. The required bound between different clock values can be reached either by variation of the re-synchronization period length or by variation of the amount of adjustment. Clock synchronization algorithms can be classified as either averaging or non-averaging. *Averaging* algorithms synchronize clocks by variation of clock adjustments at regualr intervals. In contrast, *non-averaging* algorithms use a fixed clock adjustment and a varying period between clock adjustments.

Schneider [11] was the first to observe that correctness of averaging algorithms depends on common general assumptions about the applied convergence function. Subsequently, Shankar [13] verified Schneider's proof with the help of the EHDM system, a predecessor of the PVS verification system [7, 6, 5]. Miner [4] was able to relax some of the assumptions and extended the reasoning about recovery from transient faults. The theories developed by Shankar and Miner allow for a generic verification of algorithms that use an averaging function. The formalization of these clock synchronization algorithms takes a convergence function as a generic parameter; the underlying algorithm and its correctness argument remain fixed. In contrast, non-averaging algorithms like the one presented in [14] do not fit Miner's and Shankar's theories because they use a different algorithm and do not rely on a convergence function.

In this paper, we report on the formal analysis of a broader class of clock synchronization algorithms than those formally analyzed before. Our original starting point was a direct formalization of the non-averaging algorithm of Srikanth and Toueg [14] and of the averaging algorithm of Welch and Lynch [3]. Several commonalities and similarities between both types of algorithms became apparent, at the level of basic concepts (faulty/non-faulty processing nodes, interval clocks, rounds etc.) as well as at the abstract level of correctness arguments. This led to the development of a set of PVS theories, including a generic theory that generalizes the previous formalization of averaging clock synchronization algorithms by covering non-averaging algorithms, in addition to the more specialized theory of Shankar and Miner that deals with averaging algorithms. We regard as original contributions of this paper this more general theory and, as an instance of this theory, the formal, mechanically checked verification of the algorithm of Srikanth and Toueg [14], which, to our knowledge, is the first and so far only one for a non-averaging clock synchronization algorithm.

The remainder of this paper is organized as follows. The next section summarizes the basic concepts and the overall structure. Section 3 presents the generic theory and its specialization for the averaging case; Section 4 briefly describes the instantiation to concrete algorithms. The concluding section gives a summary and discusses ongoing work.

2 Overview

Clock synchronization algorithms operate on a cluster of nodes. Each node maintains a physical clock, typically a discrete counter that is incremented periodically; the *logical* clock of a node indicates its logical time, which is computed by adding an adjustment to its physical clock. The aim of clock synchronization is to keep the individual logical clocks of the nodes sufficiently well synchronized among each other (*agreement*). This is achieved by each node locally running an implementation of the clock synchronization algorithm and thereby periodically adjusting the clock. (We do not discuss accuracy, the second important property, in this paper.)

There are several ways to determine the clock adjustment. Averaging algorithms read the clock values of all or some of the nodes in the cluster to be synchronized. Then they calculate the adjustment from an average of all or some of the clock values read [11]. Non-averaging algorithms synchronize the clocks upon a special event, such as upon receipt of an explicit synchronization message on the network [14].

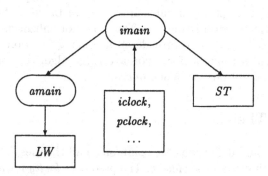

Fig. 1. Theory dependencies

The nodes communicate through an interconnection network. Each pair of nodes is able to exchange messages either directly or indirectly through remote nodes. Depending on the algorithm, different interconnection network architectures may be used. Furthermore, the network may or may not loose or fake messages. The general theories make no assumptions about the underlying network. This is left to the instances which formalize concrete algorithms.

The PVS formalization is structured into several theories. Each theory formalizes a certain concept and states the relevant theorems. Figure 1 shows the most important theories and their relationships. The auxiliary theories are not considered further in this paper; details can be found in the technical report that contains the full PVS specifications [12].

The PVS theories fall into three groups. The first group (*imain*, *iclock*, *pclock*, etc.) formalizes the basic concepts and theorems common to all synchronization algorithms. In theory *imain*, the central agreement property is stated and proved from fairly general assumptions. The proof is rather abstract and relies essentially on geometrical reasoning.

The second group of theories, consisting of PVS theory *amain* and auxiliary theories, formalizes averaging algorithms as a specialization of *imain*. Here, the central generic parameter is the convergence function, and a simpler set of assumptions is essentially sufficient to derive the agreement property. The assumptions about the convergence function are equivalent to those given by Miner [4]. The agreement theorem is obtained by instantiating the generic theory *imain*; this requires demonstrating that the generic assumptions of *imain* are satisfied by the actual parameters – which in turn is achieved by derivation from the assumptions on the convergence function.

The final theory formalizes the algorithm of Srikanth and Toueg [14] as an example of a non-averaging algorithm. Compared to the journal-level proof in ref. [14] which reasons about sets of nodes, our formulation of the lemmas is more appropriate for mechanized reasoning (e.g. by decision procedures) and enables PVS to find the required proofs largely automatically.

The validation of a concrete synchronization algorithm proceeds in two steps. First, the algorithm must be formalized; then an instance of the assumptions of one of the generic theories is derived from that formalization. For an averaging algorithm it is sufficient to provide an averaging function that satisfies the assumptions of theory *amain*; for a non-averaging algorithm one has to supply proofs for the assumptions of theory *imain*.

3 Generic Theories

Some PVS types and definitions are common to all theories. The type *nodeid* is the set of nodes that form the cluster. The predicate *faulty* formalizes the notion of faulty nodes. A node is faulty if it deviates from the algorithm or if its physical clock drifts too far from real time. Re-synchronization rounds are represented by the type *round*, which is equivalent to the type of natural numbers.

3.1 Clock Definitions

Each node maintains a physical clock which marks the passage of time. Real time is assumed to correspond to a Newtonian time frame. A physical clock typically is a discrete counter which is incremented periodically. $PC_i(t)$ is the physical clock value of node i at real time t. Clocks are modeled as functions from *realtime* to *localtime*, where the type *localtime* is isomorphic to the natural numbers. The assumption *bounded drift* reflects the expected physical properties of the system. The rate at which a non-faulty clock can drift from real time is bounded by a small positive constant ρ:

$$\lfloor (t_2 - t_1)/(1 + \rho) \rfloor \leq PC_i(t_2) - PC_i(t_1) \leq \lceil (t_2 - t_1)(1 + \rho) \rceil$$

To simplify the presentation and analysis, the standard convention of interval clocks is adopted. Each of these interval clocks on a node is indexed by the number of rounds since the beginning of the run. At the r-th synchronization a node i starts a new interval clock, denoted by $IC_i^r(t)$. These interval clocks are derived from the physical clock by adding a round-specific adjustment.

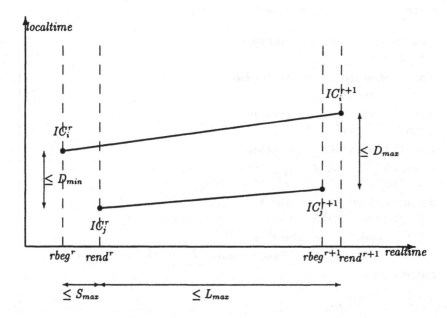

Fig. 2. *imain* constants

The symbol t_i^r denotes the real-time instant at which the interval clock IC_i^r starts. For every round there exists a first and a last node which start their new interval clocks. $rbeg^r$ and $rend^r$ are the minimum respectively the maximum of all t_i^r. At real time $rbeg^r$ the first node starts a new interval clock, while at real time $rend^r$ the last node does so. The discontinuously re-synchronizing interval clocks can be easily transformed into a single continuous logical clock. This can be achieved by spreading out each adjustment over the next re-synchronization period. Several possible schemes for this are being discussed in ref. [14]; however, none of those has been formalized so far.

3.2 General Agreement

In theory *imain*, the main agreement theorem is stated and proved from the assumptions on the generic parameters. The parameters are various upper and lower bounds for time intervals. Figure 2 graphically illustrates the relationships among bounds and clock values.

$imain[\ldots, D_{min}, D_{max}, S_{max}, L_{max}, \ldots]$: **theory**
begin

  assuming
  % Less significant assumptions and parameters
  % and imports of auxiliary theories are omitted.
  $\ldots$

  $rend\_rbeg\_upperbound$: **assumption**
    $rend^r - rbeg^r \leq S_{max}$

  $rend\_rend\_lowerbound$: **assumption**
    $rend^r \leq rend^{r+1}$

  $rend\_rend\_upperbound$: **assumption**
    $rend^{r+1} - rend^r \leq L_{max}$

  $startclock\_bounded$: **assumption**
    $\left| IC_i^r(t_i^{r+1}) - IC_j^r(t_j^{r+1}) \right| \leq D_{max}$
    $\rightarrow \left| IC_i^{r+1}(t_i^{r+1}) - IC_j^{r+1}(t_j^{r+1}) \right| \leq D_{min}$

  $init\_assumption$: **assumption**
    $\left| IC_i^0(t_i^0) - IC_j^0(t_j^0) \right| \leq D_{min}$

  $const\_assumption$: **assumption**
    $S_{max}(1 + \rho) + D_{min} + (S_{max} + L_{max})\rho(2 + \rho)/(1 + \rho) \leq D_{max} - 2$

  endassuming
  $\ldots$

  $agreement$: **theorem**
    $\left| IC_i^r(t) - IC_j^r(t) \right| \leq D_{max}$

end *imain*

The first assumption ($rend\_rbeg\_upper\_bound$) constrains the length of the re-synchronization periods. Each correct node starts its r-th clock not later than S_{max} after the first one does so. The algorithm determines the point in time at which the next re-synchronization round begins. For *imain* an upper bound L_{max} for the period between re-synchronizations is sufficient ($rend\_rbeg\_upper\_bound$). The inherent ordering of re-synchronization periods with respect to real time is reflected by assumption $rend\_rend\_lowerbound$. We assume that all logical clocks initially start at most a positive number D_{min} apart ($init\_assumption$).

Assumption *start_clocks_bounded* is a precision enhancement condition: if all non-faulty clocks are at most D_{max} apart at the end of the previous round, the new clocks are started within the bound D_{min}.

The assumptions given in theory *imain* are sufficient to prove agreement of interval clocks. The proof is inductive on the round r. From the induction hypothesis that all non-faulty nodes were sufficiently synchronized during the previous round and the assumptions, one has to show synchronization for the current round. By the induction principle it follows that all non-faulty nodes are synchronized during all rounds. The induction step builds on a lemma (cf. Fig. 2) which states that if non-faulty clocks were at most D_{max} apart at the end of the previous round then they will also be at most D_{max} apart at the end of the current round. This lemma could be proved by the PVS system automatically without user interaction.

3.3 Averaging Algorithms

The generic theory of averaging algorithms is an instance of theory *imain*. The agreement theorem is inherited from *imain* by importing an apropriate instance. An averaging algorithm uses a convergence function *cfn* to calculate the adjustment for the next round. *cfn* is a parameter of *amain*. The averaging algorithm assumes a mechanism to read clock values of remote nodes. Θ_i^r is the vector of all estimates at node i during round r. α and π are functions which calculate upper bounds for the convergence function.

Assumptions *start_clock_assumption* and *bound_on_read_error* reflect properties of the averaging algorithm. Whenever the local clock value is a multiple of the length R of a round, the adjustment is recalculated and applied. Even if the value of a remote clock can not be observed directly, the communication protocol allows a fairly accurate estimate (*bound_on_read_error*).

Two definitions simplify the notation of further assumptions. $read1(r, i, Y)$ constrains the difference between clock readings at a particular node. Clock readings on different nodes are constrained by $read2(r, i, j, X)$.

The next assumptions, describing properties of the convergence function *cfn*, are Miner's [4] conditions 3, 4 and 5, except for minor notational differences. *precision_enhancement* is a formalization of the concept that, after application of the convergence function, clocks should be close together. *accuracy_preservation* formalizes the notion that their should be a bound on the amount of correction applied in any synchronization interval. *translation_invariance* describes the insensitivity of the convergence function on absolute values of its arguments. More precisely, adding X to the result of the convergence function should be the same as adding X to each of the clock readings used in calculating the convergence function. The agreement theorem is obtained by importing theory *imain*.

4 Algorithm Instances

Two concrete algorithms serve as examples. The first one is the non-averaging algorithm described in [14]. The second is an averaging algorithm described in [3]. For the instantiation of *imain* and *amain*, respectively, concrete values for the required functions and constants must be supplied. The assumptions of *imain* and *amain* must be derived from the formal description of the algorithms.

$amain[\dots,\ cfn, \alpha(X), \pi(X,Y), \Delta, \beta, \dots]$: **theory**
begin

  assuming
  % Less significant assumptions and parameters
  % and imports of auxiliary theories are omitted.
  ...

  start_clock_assumption : **assumption**
$$(r+1)R = IC_i^r(t_i^{r+1})$$

  bound_on_read_error : **assumption**
$$\left|IC_j^r(t_i^{r+1}) - \Theta_i^{r+1}(j)\right| \le \Delta$$
$$read1(r,i,Y) := \forall l,m \cdot |\Theta_i^r(l) - \Theta_i^r(m)| \le Y$$
$$read2(r,i,j,X) := \forall l \cdot |\Theta_i^r(l) - \Theta_j^r(l)| \le X$$

  precision_enhancement : **assumption**
$$\exists X, Y \cdot read1(r,i,Y) \wedge read1(r,j,Y) \wedge read2(r,i,j,X)$$
$$\rightarrow \left|cfn(i,\Theta_i^r) - cfn(j,\Theta_j^r)\right| \le \pi(X,Y)$$

  accuracy_preservation : **assumption**
$$\exists Y \cdot read1(r,i,Y)$$
$$\rightarrow \left|cfn(i,\Theta_i^r) - IC_j^r(t_j^r)\right| \le \alpha(Y)$$

  translation_invariance : **assumption**
$$cfn(i,\Theta_r^i + X)) = cfn(i,\Theta_i^r) + X$$

  initialization : **assumption**
$$\left|t_i^0 - t_j^0\right| \le \beta$$
  endassuming
...
importing $imain[\dots, \alpha(\beta + 2\delta)/(2\rho R + \beta), \alpha(\beta + 2\delta),$
$$2\rho R + \beta, (1+\rho)R + \beta, \dots]$$
end *amain*

4.1 Srikanth-Toueg Algorithm

The clock synchronization algorithm of Srikanth and Toueg [14] relies on authenticated synchronization messages and broadcasting. During every round, a synchronization message (*round r*) is processed. Whenever the local clock is a multiple of R, a node prepares a (*round r*) message, signs it, and broadcasts it on the net. Concurrently, each node accepts and processes messages originating from remote nodes. Whenever a node has received at least $f+1$ (*round r*) messages, it starts a new clock and relays all $f+1$ messages to all other nodes.

Because both activities run concurrently, a node may start a new clock before it becomes ready. Roughly speaking, this algorithm leads to a synchronization with the fastest logical clock.

This algorithm tolerates at most f faulty nodes if the number n of all nodes is larger than $2f + 1$. A non-faulty node which has received more than $f + 1$ messages has received at least one synchronization message originated from a non-faulty node; even if there where f faulty messages on the net. Relaying all received messages ensures that all non-faulty nodes start there new interval clocks. For details of the algorithm see [14] and the formalization in [12].

The agreement property is obtained by instantiating theory *imain* with the following concrete values: $\lfloor t_{del}(1 + \rho) \rfloor$ for D_{min}, $\lfloor S_{max}(1 + \rho) \rfloor + D_{min} + \lfloor S_{max} + L_{max} \rfloor (\rho(2 + \rho)/(1 + \rho)) + 2$ for D_{max}, t_{del} for S_{max} and $(P - \alpha)(1 + \rho)$ for L_{max}. Because of space limitation, only the proof of *rend_rbeg_upperbound* is sketched. The first non-faulty node starts its clock at $rbeg^r$. At this point in time the node has received $f + 1$ messages. Since it relays all these messages, every correct node receives at least $f + 1$ messages and starts its clock by time $rbeg^r + t_{del}$, where t_{del} is the maximal network delay. Thus $rend^r - rbeg^r \leq t_{del}$. The other assumptions are proved in a similar manner.

4.2 Averaging Instance: Fault-Tolerant Midpoint

Agreement for the Lynch/Welch algorithm is attained by instanting theory *amain* with concrete parameters: $(\lfloor \theta_{(f+1)} + \theta_{n-f} \rfloor)/2$ for *cfn*, the identity function for $\alpha(X)$ and $Y/2 + X$ for $\pi(X, Y)$. The proofs of the instantiated assumptions *precision_enhancement*, *accuracy_preservation* and *translation_invariance* where essentially follow Miner's [4]. Details can be found in [12].

5 Conclusion

This paper has describes PVS theories that give a unified framework for proving agreement for averaging and non-averaging clock synchronization algorithms. Agreement is proved in the general theory from a set of generic assumptions. The general theory has been specialized to a theory for averaging algorithms which inherits the agreement theorem from the general theory. Two concrete algorithms [3, 14] were given a of the main theories. A full report [12], including the complete PVS specifications, will be made available online.

There are several directions in which the current work can be expanded. The present formalization does not consider initialization and re-integration of clocks. Also, further specific clock synchronization algorithms and convergence functions should be examined as to how well they fit into the general framework presented here. We are currently working on fitting the clock synchronization of the Time-Triggered Architecture (TTA) [1, 2] into the framework; this requires a slight modification of the theories because of the different way in which the clock values of other nodes are gathered. A further direction of current work is an examination of how the clock synchronization theories can be combined with

Rushby's general approach to verifying fault-tolerant time-triggered systems [9], which is based on, and assumes, synchronized clocks.

Acknowledgements. We would like to thank Ercüment Canver and Holger Pfeifer for valuable discussions; Ercüment Canver also contributed directly to this work in an early stage.

References

1. H. Kopetz and G. Gruensteidl. Ttp – a time triggered protocol for fault-tolerant real-time systems. *IEEE Computer*, 27(1):14–23, January 1994.
2. Hermann Kopetz. The time-triggered approach to real-time system design. In B. Randell, J.-C. Laprie, H. Kopetz, and B. Littlewood, editors, *Predictably Dependable Computing Systems.* Springer, 1995.
3. J. Lundelius Welch and N. Lynch. A new fault-tolerant algorithm for clock synchronization. *Inf. and Comp.*, 77(1):1–36, 1988.
4. P. S. Miner. Verification of fault-tolerant clock synchronization systems. NASA Technical Paper 3349, NASA Langley Research Center, Nov. 1993.
5. S. Owre, S. Rajan, J.M. Rushby, N. Shankar, and M.K. Srivas. PVS: Combining specification, proof checking, and model checking. In R. Alur and T.A. Henzinger, editors, *Computer-Aided Verification, CAV '96*, volume 1102 of *Lecture Notes in Computer Science*, pages 411–414, New Brunswick, NJ, July/August 1996. Springer-Verlag.
6. S. Owre, J. Rushby, N. Shankar, and F. von Henke. Formal Verification for Fault-Tolerant Architectures: Prolegomena to the Design of PVS. *IEEE Trans. on Software Engineering*, 21(2):107–125, February 1995.
7. S. Owre, J. M. Rushby, and N. Shankar. PVS: A prototype verification system. In D. Kapur, editor, *11th International Conference on Automated Deduction (CADE)*, volume 607 of *Lecture Notes in Artificial Intelligence*, pages 748–752, Saratoga, NY, June 1992. Springer-Verlag.
8. D. Powell. A Generic Upgradable Architecture for Real-Time Dependable Systems. In *IEEE Intern. Workshop on Embedded Fault-Tolerant Systems, Boston.* May 1998.
9. J. Rushby. Systematic formal verification for fault-tolerant time-triggered algorithms. In M. Dal Cin, C. Meadows, and W. H. Sanders, editors, *Dependable Computing for Critical Applications—6*, pages 203–222. IEEE Computer Society, March 1997.
10. J. M. Rushby and F. von Henke. Formal verification of algorithms for critical systems. *IEEE Trans. on Software Engineering*, 19(1):13–23, Jan. 1993.
11. F. B. Schneider. Understanding protocols for byzantine clock synchronization. Technical Report 87-859, Cornell University, Aug. 1987.
12. D. Schwier and F. von Henke. Mechanical verification of clock synchronization algorithms. Ulmer Informatik Berichte, Universität Ulm, 1998 (forthcoming).
13. N. Shankar. Mechanical verification of a schematic byzantine clock synchronization algorithm. Technical Report CR-4386, NASA, 1991.
14. T. K. Srikanth and S. Toueg. Optimal clock synchronization. *Journ. of the ACM*, 34(3):626–645, July 1987.

Compiling Graphical Real-Time Specifications into Silicon*

Martin Fränzle and Karsten Lüth**

Carl von Ossietzky Universität Oldenburg, Dept. of Computer Science
P.O. Box 2503, D-26111 Oldenburg, Germany

Abstract. The basic algorithms underlying an automatic hardware synthesis environment using fully formal graphical requirements specifications as source language are outlined. The source language is *real-time symbolic timing diagrams* [3], which are a *metric-time temporal logic* such that hard real-time constraints have to be dealt with.
While automata-theoretic methods based on translating the specification to a finite automaton and constructing a winning strategy in the resulting ω-regular game could in principle be used, and do indeed provide the core algorithm, complexity withstands practical application of these methods. Therefore, a compositional extension is explored, which yields modular synthesis of multi-component controllers. Based on this, a second extension is proposed for efficiently dealing with hard real-time constraints.

1 Introduction

As embedded systems become more and more complex, early availability of unambiguous specification of their intended behaviour has become an important factor for quality and timely delivery. Consequently, the quest for rapid prototyping methods for specifications arises. This quest becomes even more pronounced if specifications are to be formal, because formal specifications are often found to be particularly hard to write and maintain. On the other hand, formal specifications are — if complexity of the prototyping process can be kept reasonably low — an ideal starting point for reliable rapid prototyping, as they bear an unambiguous semantics.

Addressing these issues, the computer architecture group of Oldenburg University has dedicated part of its rapid prototyping project 'EVENTS' [10] towards automatic prototyping of embedded control hardware from fully formal specifications given as *real-time symbolic timing diagrams*. Real-time symbolic timing diagrams (RTSTDs, for short), as introduced in [3], are a graphical formalism for specifying behavioural requirements on hard real-time embedded systems. They are a full-fledged *metric-time temporal logic*, but with a graphical syntax reminiscent of the informal timing diagrams widely used in electrical engineering.

---

* This article reflects work that has been partially funded by the German Research Council DFG under grant no. Da 205/5-1.
** Email: {Martin.Fraenzle|Karsten.Lueth}@Informatik.Uni-Oldenburg.De

Fig. 1. An RTSTD specifying a simple handshaking protocol. The black arcs represent strong constraints, while weak constraints (i.e., assumptions on the environment) are printed in grey. The perpendicular line to the far left indicates the activation mode of the diagram, which here is the so-called invariant mode, meaning that the diagram has to apply whenever its activation condition fires. The activation condition is the state condition crossed by the perpendicular line, i.e. ¬Req ∧ ¬Ack.

Mapping such specifications to prototype hardware involves two steps: first, the generation of a set of interacting state machines that satisfy the specification and second, their implementation by a given target technology, e.g. FPGAs. The latter is by now standard: if the state machines are encoded in a suitable subset of VHDL this can be done through so-called high-level synthesis by e.g. the Synopsys tools [5], and we have indeed integrated our tools with the Synopsys tools to achieve this. Therefore, we will in the remainder concentrate on the first step and will sketch different specification-level synthesis procedures yielding sets of interacting Moore machines from RTSTD specifications. The procedures differ in the methods used for dealing with timing constraints and in the number and shapes of the interacting Moore machines generated, which affects the average-case complexity of the synthesis procedure and the size of the hardware devices delivered.

In sections 2 to 4 we introduce real-time symbolic timing diagrams and the controller synthesis problem and outline a classical controller synthesis framework based on the effective correspondence of propositional temporal logic to finite automata on infinite words and on the theory of ω-regular games [14]. A compositional variant of this approach, which is more suitable for rapid prototyping purposes due to its reduced complexity, is shown in section 5. This is our current synthesis method, which has been fully implemented in the ICOS tools [9]. The results obtained using this method on e.g. the FZI production cell [8] indicate that the compositional extension yields a significant enhancement for reactive systems, yet a further compositional treatment of timing is necessary for real-time systems. Section 6 sketches the basic design decisions underlying such an extension which will be implemented in a new release of ICOS, while section 7 compares this to the state of the art.

2 Real-time symbolic timing diagrams

The RTSTD language is a metric discrete-time temporal logic with an — as we hope — intuitive graphical syntax and with a declarative semantics which is formalized through a mapping to propositional temporal logic (PTL). In contrast to some other approaches using timing diagrams, e.g. those described in [1, 6], symbolic timing diagrams do *not* have any imperative control structure like iteration or sequencing. Instead, the recurrence structure of RTSTDs is expressed in terms of the modalities of linear-time temporal logic, thus providing a direct logical interpretation. In fact, RTSTDs provide a declarative rather than an operational specification style, even despite their intuitive syntax: an RTSTD is interpreted as a constraint on the admissible behaviours of a component, and a typical specification consists of several small RTSTDs, with the individual constraints being conjoined. The main consequence is that RTSTDs are well-suited for incremental development of requirements specifications. However, they pose harder problems than more operational timing diagrams when used as source language for code generation. Fig. 1 shows an example RTSTD, specifying a simple handshaking protocol using two signals Ack and Req.

A basic[1] RTSTD consists of the following parts:

- An *entity declaration* defining the interface of the component (not shown in figure 1). It specifies the signals (e.g. Req, Ack), their data types (e.g. Bit) and access modes (in or out, i.e. being driven by the environment or the component, resp.).
- A set of *waveforms* (here Req,Ack). A waveform defines a sequence of Boolean expressions associated with a signal (e.g. ~Req, then Req, then ~Req in the upper waveform of figure 1). The point of change from validity of one expression to another is called an *event*. A distinguished *activation event*, which specifies a precondition for applicability of the diagram, is located to the left over the waveforms.
- A set of *constraints*, denoted by constraint arcs, which define a partial order on events. We distinguish between *strong constraints* and *weak constraints*. Strong constraints are those which have to be satisfied by the system under development, while weak constraints denote assumptions on the behaviour of the environment. Violation of a weak constraint implies that the remainder of the timing diagram poses no further design obligations. Table 1 summarizes the different kinds of constraints.
- An *activation mode*. *Initial diagrams* describe requirements on the initial system states whereas an *invariant diagrams* expresses requirements which must be satisfied at any time during system lifetime. Invariant mode corresponds to the 'always' modality of linear-time temporal logic, implying that — in contrast to timing diagram formalisms employing iteration — multiple incarnations of the diagram body may be simultaneously active if the activation condition fires again before the end of the body has been reached.

More details about syntax and semantics of RTSTDs are given in [3].

3 The synthesis problem

We pursue the following approach to rapid prototyping with RTSTDs: after each item of a requirement set has been formalised through a symbolic timing dia-

---

[1] there is some syntactic sugar available for making large specifications more concise.

Table 1. Basic strong constraint types of symbolic timing diagrams and a compound constraint. Each of these has a weak counterpart, denoted by a shaded constraint arc.

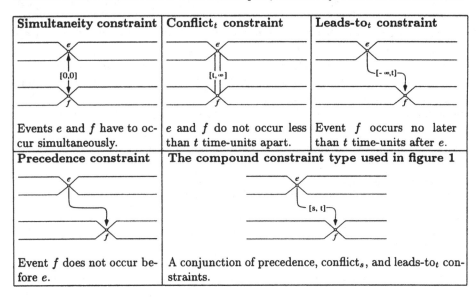

Simultaneity constraint	Conflict$_t$ constraint	Leads-to$_t$ constraint
Events e and f have to occur simultaneously.	e and f do not occur less than t time-units apart.	Event f occurs no later than t time-units after e.
Precedence constraint	**The compound constraint type used in figure 1**	
Event f does not occur before e.	A conjunction of precedence, conflict$_s$, and leads-to$_t$ constraints.	

gram, we employ an automatic synthesis algorithm which tries to construct a Moore automaton satisfying all stated requirements. However, no such Moore automaton need exist due to a contradictory specification in which case the algorithm creates error paths to help the programmer refine the specification. Otherwise, the generated Moore automaton is automatically translated to VHDL code. The subset of VHDL used as target language is synthesizable by the Synopsys tools [5] such that this synthesis path constitutes a fully automatic translation from requirements specification level down to an actual hardware implementation.

Given a specification ϕ, the problem of constructing a Moore automaton satisfying the specification, called the *synthesis problem*, is to find a Moore automaton A_ϕ which is

1. *well-typed wrt.* ϕ, i.e. has the inputs and outputs that the entity declaration of ϕ requires, and accepts any input at any time (i.e., only the outputs are constrained),
2. *correct wrt.* ϕ, i.e. the possible behaviours of A_ϕ are allowed by the specification ϕ, formally $\mathcal{L}_{A_\phi} \subseteq \mathcal{M}[\![\phi]\!]$, where $\mathcal{M}[\![\phi]\!]$ is the set of behaviours satisfying ϕ and $\mathcal{L}_{A_\phi}$ is the set of possible behaviours of A_ϕ.

By adoption of logical standard terminology, an algorithm solving the synthesis problem is called *sound* iff, given any specification ϕ, it either delivers an automaton that is well-typed and correct wrt. the specification ϕ, or no automaton at all. It is called *complete* iff it delivers an automaton whenever a well-typed and correct automaton wrt. the specification exists.

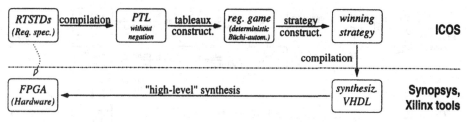

Fig. 2. The basic synthesis chain.

4 Classical controller synthesis and RTSTDs

If the requirements specification language is a classical, non-graphical, discrete-time temporal logic, like propositional temporal logic (PTL) [11], then algorithms for solving the synthesis problem are well-known: there is an effective mapping of these logics to infinite regular games which, together with the firmly developed theory of strategy construction in infinite regular games yields a fully automatic procedure for generating finite-state winning strategies, i.e. finite-state controllers, from temporal logics specifications of the allowable behaviour [14].

As there is an effective mapping of RTSTDs to PTL, which is fully explored in [7], this approach can be extended to deal with RTSTDs also. Soundness and completeness of the synthesis method then is directly inherited from the corresponding properties of winning strategy construction in regular games. In fact, this chain of algorithms, depicted in figure 2, forms the backbone of the ICOS tool set [4, 9].

However, this basic synthesis chain suffers from complexity problems if the specification is large, i.e. is a conjunction of multiple timing diagrams, as the regular games constructed then tend to suffer from state explosion. With the basic method, game graphs grow exponentially in the number of timing diagrams due to the automaton product involved in dealing with conjunction. As this would render application for rapid prototyping impractical, the ICOS tools offer modified procedures which reduce the complexity of dealing with large specifications. Obviously, such extensions cannot deal efficiently with arbitrary RTSTD specifications, but they are, however, carefully designed to cover the typical specification patterns.

5 Modular synthesis

The first such variant is a compositional extension of the basic algorithm. Within this approach, which is sketched in figure 3, the specification is first partitioned into a maximal set of groups of formulae $\mathcal{G}_1, ..., \mathcal{G}_n$ such that each output is constrained by the formulae of at most one group. Then synthesis down to a winning strategy is performed for each group individually, yielding for each group $\mathcal{G}_i$ a Moore automaton A_i that has just the outputs constrained by $\mathcal{G}_i$ as outputs, and all other ports as inputs. The individual Moore automata are then compiled to synthesizable VHDL and composed by parallel composition.

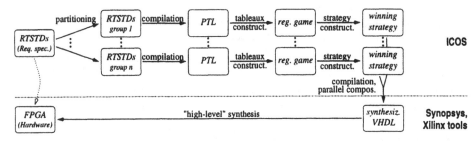

Fig. 3. Modular synthesis.

With this compositional method, grows of the game graph is linear in the number of groups, and exponential grows is only encountered in the maximal size of the individual groups. [4] reports that when synthesizing a controller for the FZI production cell [8], the compositional approach saves over 99% of the transitions in the game graphs of the major components.

Soundness of this modular synthesis technique is easily established:

Theorem 1. *Let $\mathcal{G}_1, ..., \mathcal{G}_n$ be groups of RTSTDs with O_i, $1 \leq i \leq n$, being the outputs constrained by $\mathcal{G}_i$, and with $O_i \cap O_j = \emptyset$ for $i \neq j$. Let A_i be the Moore automaton synthesized for $\mathcal{G}_i$. Then $A_1 \parallel \ldots \parallel A_n$ is well-typed and correct wrt. $\mathcal{G}_1 \wedge \ldots \wedge \mathcal{G}_n$, where $\parallel$ denotes parallel composition of Moore automata.*

Proof. Correctness of $A_1 \parallel \ldots \parallel A_n$ wrt. $\mathcal{G}_1 \wedge \ldots \wedge \mathcal{G}_n$ is straightforward, as parallel composition of Moore automata with disjoint output alphabets semantically yields language intersection, as does conjunction of RTSTDs. Thus, soundness of the basic synthesis algorithm, which yields $\mathcal{L}_{A_i} \subseteq \mathcal{M}[\mathcal{G}_i]$ for the individual groups, implies $\mathcal{L}_{A_1 \parallel ... \parallel A_n} = \mathcal{L}_{A_1} \cap \ldots \cap \mathcal{L}_{A_n} \subseteq \mathcal{M}[\mathcal{G}_1] \cap \ldots \cap \mathcal{M}[\mathcal{G}_n] = \mathcal{M}[\mathcal{G}_1 \wedge \ldots \wedge \mathcal{G}_n]$.
Similarly, well-typedness of $A_1 \parallel \ldots \parallel A_n$ wrt. $\mathcal{G}_1 \wedge \ldots \wedge \mathcal{G}_n$ follows from soundness of the basic synthesis procedure since the composition rules for interfaces agree for Moore automata and RTSTDs if outputs occur at most once in a parallel composition. ◻

Completeness is, however, lost using modular synthesis. The problem is that a certain group may not be synthesizable without knowledge about the behaviour of another group. Such problems are regularly encountered within compositional methods, and we propose to solve them by just the same techniques that proved to be helpful in compositional verification: the necessary information on the other components can be formalized via assumptions (i.e., weak constraint arcs). It should be noted that ICOS helps in finding adequate assumptions, as an error path is supplied whenever synthesis of a component fails.

6 Synthesizing hardware clocks

However, there still is some reason for dissatisfaction: as timing annotations have to be unwound to an according number of next-operators of PTL by the translation of RTSTDs to PTL, which introduces corresponding chains of unit-delay transitions in the game graphs, the modular synthesis method remains

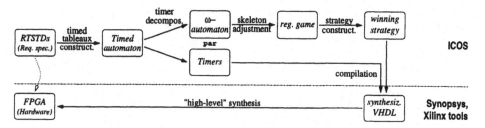

Fig. 4. Synthesis chain employing timer decomposition.

exponential in the number of potentially overlapping timing constraints. This makes dealing with timing constraints of more than a handful time units hardly affordable — realistic real-time system programming cannot be done with such code generation methods. Therefore, we are heading for an algorithm that is of linear complexity in the number of timing constraints, even though completeness is thereby necessarily sacrificed. What is thus needed is a synthesis method that separates generation of timers controlling the allowable passage of time from synthesis of an untimed control skeleton. In the remainder, we sketch a synthesis technique to be integrated into ICOS in the near future, which offers the desired separation. In this hybrid approach, small — and thus harmless wrt. the state explosion problem — time constants are treated by purely ω-automata-theoretic means, whereas large-scale timing constraints, if found to be sufficiently independent, are directly mapped to hardware timers.

The new approach starts by using timed automata for representing the semantics of real-time symbolic timing diagrams: every RTSTD ϕ is assigned a timed automaton A_ϕ that accepts exactly the *counterexamples* of ϕ, i.e. all those traces that are *not* models of ϕ. An example of a timed automaton recognizing the counterexamples of an RTSTD can be seen on the left hand side of figure 5, where the conjunction of a precedence and a leads-to$_t$ constraint between events e and f is dealt with.

Once a timed automaton accepting counterexamples to the specification is constructed, synthesis of a controller satisfying the specification can commence: in a first step, all clocks implementing delays of more than a handful time units are removed from the timed automaton and replaced by external timer components acting in parallel, as shown in figure 5. Thereafter, the remaining clocks are removed by expanding their effect to an appropriate number of unit-delay transitions. This results in an untimed automaton, called sequential skeleton in the remainder, which communicates with the environment and with the timer components. The novelty of our approach is that from then on, synthesis will treat the timers similar to environment components, which means that the behaviour of these components is left untouched during synthesis. The advantages are twofold: first of all, the fixed behavioural description of timers allows for the use of pre-fabricated, optimized hardware components, and second, controller synthesis can concentrate on solving the control problem described by the small, untimed automaton that remains.

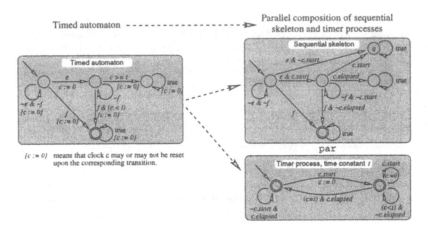

Fig. 5. Converting clocks to timer components.

Note that the parallel composition (alas automaton product, thus yielding language intersection) of the sequential skeleton and the timer processes derived thus far recognizes the counterexamples to the specification. Now, we would like to implement the timers in hardware and to remove them from the synthesis problem, i.e. we want to synthesize wrt. the skeleton *only* without, however, risking erroneous behaviour of the synthesized controller. As the timer communications are only internal to the controller, the correctness criterion involved is

$$(\mathcal{L}_C \cap \mathcal{L}_{timer}) \setminus [t.start, t.elapsed] \subseteq \overline{(\mathcal{L} \cap \mathcal{L}_t) \setminus [t.start, t.elapsed]} , \qquad (1)$$

where $\mathcal{L}_C$ and $\mathcal{L}_{timer}$ are the trace sets of the controller and the timers, resp., $\mathcal{L}$ is the language accepted by the skeleton automaton, '$\setminus [t.start, t.elapsed]$' denotes hiding of the timer communications, and the overbar denotes language complement.

It might seem that straightforward synthesis wrt. the complement of the skeleton, which yields a controller C satisfying the language inclusion property $\mathcal{L}_C \subseteq \overline{\mathcal{L}}$, suffices. Unfortunately, $\mathcal{L}_C \subseteq \overline{\mathcal{L}}$ is in general not a sufficient condition for (1) due to the existential quantification involved in hiding,[2] which changes to universal quantification under the complementation involved in (1).

However, this can be repaired by synthesizing wrt. an appropriately adjusted variant *skel'* of the skeleton automaton that enforces a certain usage of timers. The key issue is that the synthesized controller is forced to start a timer and not interfere its run whenever a violation of the corresponding timing constraint could possibly occur. The new skeleton *skel'* is generated by taking the same state set, same initial states, and same transition relation as in the original skeleton, yet expanding the set of accepting states by states like state q in figure 5, which is entered if the timer signalling the possible violation of the leads-to$_t$

---

[2] For a language $\mathcal{L} \subseteq (\alpha \times (\{t.start, t.elapsed\} \to \mathbb{B}))^\omega$ and some string $w \in \alpha^\omega$, $w \in \mathcal{L} \setminus [t.start, t.elapsed]$ holds if some sequence $ts \in (\{t.start, t.elapsed\} \to \mathbb{B})^\omega$ of timer actions exists with $w \oplus ts \in \mathcal{L}$.

constraint is not properly activated. The detailed construction, which we cannot provide due to lack of space, is s.t. if a timer action sequence ts exists with $w \oplus ts \in \mathcal{L} \cap \mathcal{L}_{timer}$ then $w \oplus ts' \in \mathcal{L}_{skel'}$ for each $ts' \in \mathcal{L}_{timer}$. Note that furthermore $\mathcal{L}_{skel'} \supseteq \mathcal{L}$ by construction.

If we now synthesize a controller with inputs $I \cup \{t.elapsed\}$, outputs $O \cup \{t.start\}$ (where I and O are the original in- and outputs) that is correct wrt. the adjusted control problem, i.e. satisfies $\mathcal{L}_C \subseteq \overline{\mathcal{L}_{skel'}}$, then we have obtained a correct solution:

Lemma 1. *Correctness of C wrt. $\overline{\mathcal{L}_{skel'}}$, i.e. $\mathcal{L}_C \subseteq \overline{\mathcal{L}_{skel'}}$, implies (1).*

Proof. Assume that $\mathcal{L}_C \subseteq \overline{\mathcal{L}_{skel'}}$ holds and (1) is false, i.e. there exists some $w \in (\mathcal{L}_C \cap \mathcal{L}_{timer}) \setminus [t.start, t.elapsed] \cap (\mathcal{L} \cap \mathcal{L}_{timer}) \setminus [t.start, t.elapsed]$. By definition of hiding this implies that there are two timer action sequences ts_1, ts_2 with

$$w \oplus ts_1 \in \mathcal{L}_C \cap \mathcal{L}_{timer} \quad \wedge \quad w \oplus ts_2 \in \mathcal{L} \cap \mathcal{L}_{timer} .$$

Then, by construction of $skel'$, $w \oplus ts_1 \in \mathcal{L}_{skel'}$. But on the other hand $w \oplus ts_1 \in \mathcal{L}_C$ and $\mathcal{L}_C \subseteq \overline{\mathcal{L}_{skel'}}$, which yields a contradiction. □

Consequently, synthesis wrt. the adjusted control problem is sound. Furthermore, by directly mapping all timing constraints of significant size to hardware timers, this method is linear in the number of timing constraints. If it is furthermore combined with modular synthesis then super-linear blow-up can only occur through individual timing diagrams containing unusually large numbers of events or through large groups of formulae controlling the same outputs. These situations are, however, atypical, rendering the new method a practical rapid-prototyping tool for real-time embedded controllers.

7 Discussion

We have presented an approach towards fully automatic synthesis of embedded control hardware from requirements specifications that are formalised through real-time symbolic timing diagrams, a metric-time temporal logic with a graphical syntax akin to the informal timing diagrams used in electrical engineering [3]. While the underlying algorithms have been derived from the well-established theory of winning-strategy construction in ω-regular games, the overall approach is — being targeted towards rapid prototyping — mostly pragmatic, weighing efficiency higher than completeness. Two key issues have been identified in this respect: first, the necessity of compositional synthesis of parallel components and second, early decomposition of timing issues from the synthesis problem. The result is a synthesis method that is essentially linear in the size of the specification and thus suitable as a development tool in rapid prototyping contexts.

Due to the obvious necessity of treating timing mostly independent from algorithmic aspects within any reasonably efficient synthesis method for hard real-time controllers, quite a few other research groups work on this theme. However, most approaches are based on primarily operational rather than declarative specification styles (e.g. [15]). Closest to our approach is [12], where Dierks and Olderog detail a direct mechanism for deriving timer actions from specifications formalised through a very restrictive subset of Duration Calculus [16], the so-called DC-implementables [13]. Dierks' algorithm is extremely efficient, but at the price of a very restrictive specification format: the processable specifications are confined to be 'phased designs' in the sense of the ProCoS projects [2], which are akin to RTSTDs featuring just three events. While our formalism is more expressive in this respect, Dierks and Olderog do, on the other hand, go ahead by dealing with a dense-time logic and analysing certain kinds of switching latency.

References

1. G. Borriello. Formalized timing diagrams. In *The European Conference on Design Automation*, pages 372–377, Brussels, Belgium, Mar. 1992. IEEE Comp. Soc. Press.
2. J. P. Bowen, M. Fränzle, E.-R. Olderog, and A. P. Ravn. Developing correct systems. In *Proc. 5th Euromicro Workshop on Real-Time Systems, Oulu, Finland*, pages 176–189. IEEE Comp. Soc. Press, June 1993.
3. K. Feyerabend and B. Josko. A visual formalism for real time requirement specification. In *Transformation-Based Reactive System Development*, volume 1231 of LNCS, pages 156–168. Springer Verlag, 1997.
4. K. Feyerabend and R. Schlör. Hardware synthesis from requirement specifications. In *Proceedings EURO-DAC with EURO-VHDL 96*. IEEE Comp. Soc. Press, 1996.
5. S. Golsen. State Machine Design Techniques for Verilog and Vhdl. *Synopsys Journal of High Level Design*, Sept. 1994.
6. P. Khordoc, M. Dufresne, and E. Czerny. A Stimulus/Response System based on Hierarchical Timing Diagrams. Technical report, Univ. de Montreal, 1991.
7. F. Korf. *System-Level Synthesewerkzeuge: Von der Theorie zur Anwendung*. Dissertation, Fachbereich Informatik, Universität Oldenburg, Germany, 1997.
8. C. Lewerentz and T. Lindner, editors. *Formal Development of Reactive Systems: Case Study Production Cell*, volume 891 of LNCS. Springer-Verlag, Jan. 1995.
9. K. Lüth. The ICOS synthesis environment. These proceedings.
10. K. Lüth, A. Metzner, T. Peikenkamp, and J. Risau. The EVENTS approach to rapid prototyping for embedded control systems. In *Zielarchitekturen eingebetteter Systeme (ZES '97)*, Rostock, Germany, Sept. 1997.
11. Z. Manna and A. Pnueli. *The Temporal Logic of Reactive and Concurrent Systems*, volume 1. Springer-Verlag, 1992.
12. E.-R. Olderog and H. Dierks. Decomposing real-time specifications. In H. Langmaack, W. de Roever, and A. Pnueli, editors, *Compositionality: The Significant Difference*, LNCS. Springer-Verlag, to appear 1998.
13. A. P. Ravn. *Design of Embedded Real-Time Computing Systems*. Doctoral dissertation, Dept. of Comp. Science, Danish Technical University, Lyngby, DK, 1995.
14. W. Thomas. Automata on infinite objects. In J. v. Leeuwen, editor, *Handbook of Theoretical Computer Science*, volume B: Formal Models and Semantics, chapter 4, pages 133–191. North-Holland, 1990.
15. P. Vanbekbergen, G. Gossens, and B. Lin. Modeling and synthesis of timed asynchronous circuits. In *Proceedings EURO-DAC with EURO-VHDL 94*. IEEE Comp. Soc. Press, 1994.
16. Zhou Chaochen, C. A. R. Hoare, and A. P. Ravn. A calculus of durations. *Information Processing Letters*, 40(5):269–276, 1991.

Towards a Formal Semantics of Verilog Using Duration Calculus

Gerardo Schneider* and Qiwen Xu

International Institute for Software Technology
United Nations University
P.O.Box 3058, Macau
{gss,qxu}@iist.unu.edu

Abstract. We formalise the semantics of V^-, a simple version of Verilog hardware description language using an extension of Duration Calculus. The language is simple enough for experimenting formalisation, but contains sufficient features for being practically relevant. V^- programs can exhibit a rich variety of computations, and it is therefore necessary to extend Duration Calculus with several features, including Weakly Monotonic Time, infinite intervals and fixed point operators. The semantics is compositional and can be used as the formal basis of a formal theory of Verilog.

1 Introduction

Modern hardware design typically uses hardware description languages to express designs at various levels of abstraction. A hardware description language is a high level programming language, with the usual programming constructs such as assignments, conditionals and iterations, and appropriate extensions for real-time, concurrency and data structures suitable for modelling hardware. The common approach is to first build a high level design using programming constructs. The high level design is then recoded using a subset of the description language which is closer to implementation. This process may be repeated several times until the design is at a sufficiently lower level such that the hardware can be synthesised from it.

For ensuring correctness of the development, precise understanding of the description language used is apparently important. Verilog is a hardware description language widely used in industry, but its standard semantics [7] is informal. A formal semantics will also be the basis of further formal support for the language. This includes methods to prove that the highest level description satisfies the overall requirements and that a lower level description correctly implements a higher level one.

Verilog programs can exhibit a rich variety of computations, when several features of the language are intertwined. The features include

---

* On leave from Catholic University of Pelotas, Cx.Postal 402 (96010-000), Pelotas-RS, Brazil. Email: gerardo@atlas.vcpel.tche.br

- shared states, updated by possibly instantaneous assignments from different processes;
- delay statements;
- synchronisation by waiting for some conditions to become true;
- recursion.

It is therefore a non-trivial task to give an adequate semantics to the language. In contrast to many attempts to formalise semantics of VHDL, another popular but reportedly less used hardware description language, there is only a little work on formal semantics of Verilog [6, 13].

In this paper, we give a formal semantics to a large subset of Verilog using an extension of the Duration Calculus, aiming to achieve a satisfactory level of abstraction and a more faithful modelling of concurrency. The logic is called Duration Calculus of Weakly Monotonic Time with Infinite Intervals and Fixed Point Operator, abbreviated as μWDCI, and it has incorporated features from several recent extensions of Duration Calculus [16, 15, 17, 20].

This paper is organised as follows. In Section 2, we introduce μWDCI. The semantics of V^- is presented in Section 3. The paper is concluded with a short discussion of related work.

2 Duration Calculus of Weakly Monotonic Time with Infinite Intervals and Fixed Point Operators

Duration Calculus [1, 4], is an extension of Interval Temporal Logic (ITL) [11] to dense time domains. The classical Duration Calculus [1], abbreviated as DC, was developed to reason about piece-wise continuous Boolean functions of time (called states in literature), which model the status of the system. This view is not adequate for describing semantics of Verilog programs. The standard semantics of Verilog [7], being defined for simulation, uses a discrete event execution model. In such a model, discrete events do not take any real-time, and subsequently several of them may happen at the same real-time point governed possibly by a causal order. Such abstraction, proposed also in the work on synchronous languages, provides substantial simplification in verification of real-time systems. To reason about discrete events and their compositions, one needs a more involved logic. Koymans [9] suggested that a time point can be defined as a pair (r, n), with r denoting the real-time and n the causal order, and following the terminology in the work on synchronous languages, we call r the macro-time and n the micro-time. A variant of Duration Calculus, called Weakly Monotonic Time Duration Calculus, abbreviated as WDC, was formed by Pandya and Dang over such time structures [15]. A similar logic was suggested by Liu, Ravn and Li [10].

Both DC and WDC are defined over finite intervals. However, timed systems in general and Verilog programs in particular often exhibit infinite behaviours. In [2], an extension of DC was studied by Zhou, Dang and Li, where infinite behaviours are described by their finite approximations. This approach avoids direct interpretation of formulae over infinite intervals but has the disadvantage that properties are somewhat cumbersome to express. As an alternative formulation, infinite intervals have been directly included in DC [19] following an approach by Moszkowski [12] for ITL. In [20], WDC is extended with infinite intervals along both macro-time and micro-time. To describe recursive computations, Pandya and Ramakrishna [16] introduced fixed point operators in DC. Properties of the fixed points have been further studied in [17]. Our logic, μWDCI, is obtained by incorporating all these features.

We next give an overview of μWDCI.

Definition 1. *A* time domain *is a total order* $(\mathcal{T}, <)$, *where*

- $\mathcal{T} \subseteq (\Re^+ \cup \{\infty\}) \times (\aleph \cup \{\infty\})$, *with* $(0,0) \in \mathcal{T}$,
- $(r_1, n_1) < (r_2, n_2)$
  iff $(r_1 \neq \infty \wedge r_1 \leq r_2 \wedge n_1 < n_2) \vee (r_1 < r_2 \wedge n_1 \neq \infty \wedge n_1 \leq n_2)$,
- *for any* $t \notin \mathcal{T}$, *there exists* $t' \in \mathcal{T}$, *such that* $t \not\leq t'$ *and* $t' \not\leq t$,
- $lim((r_i, n_i)) \in \mathcal{T}$.

where $\Re^+$ is the set of non-negative real numbers and $\aleph$ is the set of natural numbers.

The first and second conditions define the set and the order relationship $(<)$. The third condition says that a time domain is maximal, in the sense that adding any other time point will cause the set to be no longer a total order. By the definition, exactly one of (r, ∞), (∞, n) and (∞, ∞) is in a time domain and it is the maximal element. The last condition implies that if the time domain has an infinite sequence of time points of the form $(r, n_0), (r, n_1), \ldots, (r, n_n), \ldots$ for the same real number r, then (r, ∞) must be in the sequence. This in turn by the third condition ensures that in this case any other infinite time point, either (r', ∞) where $r \neq r'$ or (∞, ∞) is not in the domain. For any $t = (r, n)$, let $\pi_1(t) \overset{\text{def}}{=} r$ and $\pi_2(t) \overset{\text{def}}{=} n$. We write $t = \infty$ iff $n = \infty$ or $r = \infty$. An interval on $\mathcal{T}$ is a pair of time points $[b, e]$ of $\mathcal{T}$, where $b \neq \infty$ and $b \leq e$.

The logic contains the following sets of symbols: global variables $GVar=\{x, y, \ldots\}$, state variables $SVar=\{P, Q, \ldots\}$ and temporal propositional letters $PLetter = \{X, Y, \ldots\}$. State expressions are defined as

$$S ::= c \mid x \mid P \mid op_1 S \mid S_1 \; op_2 \; S_2$$

where c is a constant, $op_1 \in \{-, \neg\}$ and $op_2 \in \{\wedge, \vee, +, -, *, =, <\}$ are unary and binary operators of appropriate types. The syntax of terms is

$$T ::= c \mid x \mid \int S \mid \hat{\int} S \mid T_1 \; op \; T_2 \mid \mathbf{b}.S \mid \mathbf{e}.S$$

where $op \in \{\wedge, \vee, +, -, *\}$, $\mathbf{b}.S$ and $\mathbf{e}.S$ denote respectively the values of S at the beginning and the end of the interval. When S is Boolean, represented as $\{0, 1\}$, $\int S$ and $\hat{\int} S$ denote respectively durations of the expression along macro-time and micro-time.

The syntax of μWDCI formulae is

$$X \mid t_1 = t_2 \mid t_1 < t_2 \mid \neg\phi \mid \phi_1 \wedge \phi_2 \mid \exists x . \phi \mid \phi_1 \,^\frown \phi_2 \mid \mu X.\phi$$

where x is a global variable, and the occurrence of bounded propositional letter X in the fixed point formula is positive (i.e., X is preceded by even number of negation symbols).

Definition 2. *A* model **M** *is a tuple* $((\mathcal{T}, <), \mathcal{I}, \mathcal{J}, \mathcal{V}, [b, e])$, *where*

- $(\mathcal{T}, <)$ *is a time domain,*
- $\mathcal{I} :$ SVar $\rightarrow \mathcal{T} \rightarrow$ Values *is an interpretation of state variables where* Values $= \Re^+ \cup \aleph \cup$ Bool,
- $\mathcal{J} :$ Pletter $\rightarrow$ *Intv* $\rightarrow$ Bool *is an interpretation of propositional letters, where Intv is the set of all intervals,*
- $\mathcal{V} :$ GVar $\rightarrow$ Values *is an interpretation of global variables,*
- $[b, e]$ *is an interval on* $\mathcal{T}$.

Let t be a time point. The interpretation of state expressions is

- $[\![x]\!](\mathcal{T}, \mathcal{I}, \mathcal{V}, t) \stackrel{\text{def}}{=} \mathcal{V}(x)$
- $[\![P]\!](\mathcal{T}, \mathcal{I}, \mathcal{V}, t) \stackrel{\text{def}}{=} \mathcal{I}(P)(t)$
- $[\![op_1\, S]\!](\mathcal{T}, \mathcal{I}, \mathcal{V}, t) \stackrel{\text{def}}{=} op_1^* [\![S]\!](\mathcal{T}, \mathcal{I}, \mathcal{V}, t)$
- $[\![S_1\, op_2\, S_2]\!](\mathcal{T}, \mathcal{I}, \mathcal{V}, t) \stackrel{\text{def}}{=} [\![S_1]\!](\mathcal{T}, \mathcal{I}, \mathcal{V}, t)\, op_2^* [\![S_2]\!](\mathcal{T}, \mathcal{I}, \mathcal{V}, t)$

where op_i^* is the interpretation of the operator op_i. Let

$$[\![\bar{S}]\!](\mathcal{T}, \mathcal{I}, \mathcal{V}, r) \stackrel{\text{def}}{=} \begin{cases} [\![S]\!](\mathcal{T}, \mathcal{I}, \mathcal{V}, (r, n)) & \text{if } \{n | (r, n) \in \mathcal{T}\} \text{ is singleton} \\ 0 & \text{otherwise} \end{cases}$$

$$[\![\hat{S}]\!](\mathcal{T}, \mathcal{I}, \mathcal{V}, n) \stackrel{\text{def}}{=} \begin{cases} [\![S]\!](\mathcal{T}, \mathcal{I}, \mathcal{V}, (r, n)) & \text{if } (r, n), (r, n+1) \in \mathcal{T} \\ 0 & \text{otherwise.} \end{cases}$$

The first definition is well-formed because if $\{n | (r, n) \in \mathcal{T}\}$ is singleton, then obviously $n_1 = n_2$ for any $(r, n_1) \in \mathcal{T}$ and $(r, n_2) \in \mathcal{T}$. The second definition is also well-formed because for any $(r_1, n) \in \mathcal{T}$, $(r_2, n) \in \mathcal{T}$, $(r_1, n+1) \in \mathcal{T}$ and $(r_2, n+1) \in \mathcal{T}$, it is easy to prove $r_1 = r_2$. The interpretation of terms is

- $[\![\int S]\!](\mathcal{T}, \mathcal{I}, \mathcal{V}, [b, e]) \stackrel{\text{def}}{=} \int_{\pi_1(b)}^{\pi_1(e)} [\![\bar{S}]\!](\mathcal{T}, \mathcal{I}, \mathcal{V}, r) dr$
- $[\![\hat{\int} S]\!](\mathcal{T}, \mathcal{I}, \mathcal{V}, [b, e]) \stackrel{\text{def}}{=} \sum_{n=\pi_2(b)}^{\pi_2(e)-1} [\![\hat{S}]\!](\mathcal{T}, \mathcal{I}, \mathcal{V}, n)$
- $[\![T_1\, op\, T_2]\!](\mathcal{T}, \mathcal{I}, \mathcal{V}, [b, e]) \stackrel{\text{def}}{=} [\![T_1]\!](\mathcal{T}, \mathcal{I}, \mathcal{V}, [b, e])\, op^* [\![T_2]\!](\mathcal{T}, \mathcal{I}, \mathcal{V}, [b, e])$
- $[\![b.S]\!](\mathcal{T}, \mathcal{I}, \mathcal{V}, [b, e]) \stackrel{\text{def}}{=} [\![S]\!](\mathcal{T}, \mathcal{I}, \mathcal{V}, b)$
- $[\![e.S]\!](\mathcal{T}, \mathcal{I}, \mathcal{V}, [b, e]) \stackrel{\text{def}}{=} [\![S]\!](\mathcal{T}, \mathcal{I}, \mathcal{V}, e)$

where op^* is the interpretation of op. The lengths of an interval along macro-time and micro-time are denoted by $\ell \stackrel{\text{def}}{=} \int 1$ and $k \stackrel{\text{def}}{=} \hat{\int} 1$. It is easy to show that

$$- [\![\ell]\!](\mathcal{T},\mathcal{I},\mathcal{V},[b,e]) = \pi_1(e) - \pi_1(b)$$
$$- [\![k]\!](\mathcal{T},\mathcal{I},\mathcal{V},[b,e]) = \pi_2(e) - \pi_2(b)$$

To define the fixed point operators by Knaster-Tarski theorem, we give the semantics of μWDCI in the complete lattice $(2^{\text{Intv}}, \subseteq)$, where Intv is the set of all intervals. In this setting, an interpretation of propositional letters $\mathcal{J}$ is regarded as a function from propositional letters to 2^{Intv}. For a given time domain $(\mathcal{T}, <)$, an interpretation of state variables $\mathcal{I}$, an interpretation of propositional letters $\mathcal{J}$, a valuation of global variables $\mathcal{V}$, we define a function $\mathcal{E}_{\mathcal{V},\mathcal{T}}^{\mathcal{I},\mathcal{J}}$ from the set of μWDCI formulae to 2^{Intv}.

$$\mathcal{E}_{\mathcal{V},\mathcal{T}}^{\mathcal{I},\mathcal{J}}(X) \overset{\text{def}}{=} \mathcal{J}(X)$$
$$\mathcal{E}_{\mathcal{V},\mathcal{T}}^{\mathcal{I},\mathcal{J}}(T_1 = T_2) \overset{\text{def}}{=} \{[b,e] \mid \{b,e\} \subset \mathcal{T} \wedge [\![T_1]\!](\mathcal{T},\mathcal{I},\mathcal{V},[b,e]) = [\![T_2]\!](\mathcal{T},\mathcal{I},\mathcal{V},[b,e])\}$$
$$\mathcal{E}_{\mathcal{V},\mathcal{T}}^{\mathcal{I},\mathcal{J}}(T_1 < T_2) \overset{\text{def}}{=} \{[b,e] \mid \{b,e\} \subset \mathcal{T} \wedge [\![T_1]\!](\mathcal{T},\mathcal{I},\mathcal{V},[b,e]) < [\![T_2]\!](\mathcal{T},\mathcal{I},\mathcal{V},[b,e])\}$$
$$\mathcal{E}_{\mathcal{V},\mathcal{T}}^{\mathcal{I},\mathcal{J}}(\neg\phi) \overset{\text{def}}{=} 2^{\text{Intv}} - \mathcal{E}_{\mathcal{V},\mathcal{T}}^{\mathcal{I},\mathcal{J}}(\phi)$$
$$\mathcal{E}_{\mathcal{V},\mathcal{T}}^{\mathcal{I},\mathcal{J}}(\phi_1 \wedge \phi_2) \overset{\text{def}}{=} \mathcal{E}_{\mathcal{V},\mathcal{T}}^{\mathcal{I},\mathcal{J}}(\phi_1) \cap \mathcal{E}_{\mathcal{V},\mathcal{T}}^{\mathcal{I},\mathcal{J}}(\phi_2)$$
$$\mathcal{E}_{\mathcal{V},\mathcal{T}}^{\mathcal{I},\mathcal{J}}(\exists x.\phi) \overset{\text{def}}{=} \bigcup_{a \in \text{Values}} \mathcal{E}_{\mathcal{V}(x \mapsto a),\mathcal{T}}^{\mathcal{I},\mathcal{J}}(\phi)$$
$$\mathcal{E}_{\mathcal{V},\mathcal{T}}^{\mathcal{I},\mathcal{J}}(\phi_1 \frown \phi_2) \overset{\text{def}}{=} \{[b,e] \mid \exists m . \{b,e,m\} \subset \mathcal{T} \wedge b \leq m \leq e \wedge (m \neq \infty$$
$$\wedge [b,m] \in \mathcal{E}_{\mathcal{V},\mathcal{T}}^{\mathcal{I},\mathcal{J}}(\phi_1) \wedge [m,e] \in \mathcal{E}_{\mathcal{V},\mathcal{T}}^{\mathcal{I},\mathcal{J}}(\phi_2)) \vee (e = \infty \wedge [b,e] \in \mathcal{E}_{\mathcal{V},\mathcal{T}}^{\mathcal{I},\mathcal{J}}(\phi_1))\}$$
$$\mathcal{E}_{\mathcal{V},\mathcal{T}}^{\mathcal{I},\mathcal{J}}(\mu X.\phi) \overset{\text{def}}{=} \bigcap \{A \mid \mathcal{E}_{\mathcal{V},\mathcal{T}}^{\mathcal{I},\mathcal{J}(X \mapsto A)}(\phi) \subseteq A\}$$

where $\mathcal{J}(X \mapsto A)$ is the interpretation of the propositional letters that is the same as $\mathcal{J}$ except mapping X to A. The greatest fixed point operator can be defined from the the least fixed point in the usual way

$$\nu X.\phi \overset{\text{def}}{=} \neg\mu Y.\neg\phi[\neg Y/X]$$

where $\phi[\neg Y/X]$ is the substitution of $\neg Y$ for all the occurrences of the propositional letter X in formula ϕ.

The notions of *satisfaction* and *validity* are defined as follows:

$$- (\mathcal{T},\mathcal{I},\mathcal{J},\mathcal{V},[b,e]) \models \phi \text{ iff } [b,e] \in \mathcal{E}_{\mathcal{V},\mathcal{T}}^{\mathcal{I},\mathcal{J}}(\phi)$$
$$- \models \phi \text{ iff } \mathcal{E}_{\mathcal{V},\mathcal{T}}^{\mathcal{I},\mathcal{J}}(\phi) = 2^{\text{Intv}} \text{ for any } \mathcal{T},\mathcal{I},\mathcal{J},\mathcal{V}.$$

The following two theorems give the semantics of two fixed point formulae which will be used in defining the semantics of iteration statement.

Theorem 1. *Let* ϕ_1, ϕ_2 *be two* μ*WDCI formulae. If both* ϕ_1 *and* ϕ_2 *do not contain any free occurrence of the propositional variable symbol* X, *then for any* $\mathcal{T},\mathcal{I},\mathcal{J},\mathcal{V}$, $[b,e] \in \mathcal{E}_{\mathcal{V},\mathcal{T}}^{\mathcal{I},\mathcal{J}}(\mu X.(\phi_1 \frown X)) \vee \phi_2)$ *iff there is a natural number* n *(may be 0) and a non-descending sequence of time points* $b_0, b_1, \ldots, b_n$ *such that*

$$- b_0 = b, b_1, \ldots, b_n \in \mathcal{T} - \{\infty\},$$
$$- [b_i, b_{i+1}] \in \mathcal{E}_{\mathcal{V},\mathcal{T}}^{\mathcal{I},\mathcal{J}}(\phi_1) \text{ for all } i < n,$$

– $[b_n, e] \in \mathcal{E}^{\mathcal{I},\mathcal{J}}_{\mathcal{V},\mathcal{T}}(\phi_2)$, or $e = \infty$ and $[b_n, e] \in \mathcal{E}^{\mathcal{I},\mathcal{J}}_{\mathcal{V},\mathcal{T}}(\phi_1)$.

Theorem 2. *Let* ϕ_1, ϕ_2 *be two* $\mu WDCI$ *formulae. If both* ϕ_1 *and* ϕ_2 *do not contain any free occurrence of the propositional variable symbol* X, *then for any* $\mathcal{T}, \mathcal{I}, \mathcal{J}, \mathcal{V}$,

$$\mathcal{E}^{\mathcal{I},\mathcal{J}}_{\mathcal{V},\mathcal{T}}\left(\nu X.((\phi_1 \frown X) \vee \phi_2)\right) = \mathcal{E}^{\mathcal{I},\mathcal{J}}_{\mathcal{V},\mathcal{T}}\left(\mu X.((\phi_1 \frown X) \vee \phi_2)\right) \cup E$$

where $[b, e] \in E$ *iff there is an infinite non-descending sequence of time points* $b_0, b_1, \ldots, b_n, \ldots$ $(n \geq 0)$ *such that:*

– $b_0 = b$, $b_n \leq e$ *for all* $n \geq 0$,
– $[b_n, b_{n+1}] \in \mathcal{E}^{\mathcal{I},\mathcal{J}}_{\mathcal{V},\mathcal{T}}(\phi_1)$ *for all* $n \geq 0$.

Details about these theorems and other properties about fixed points can be found in [18]. We next introduce some derived modalities that will be useful when defining the semantics of V^-.

$$\Diamond A \stackrel{\text{def}}{=} \text{true} \frown A \frown \text{true}$$
$$\Box A \stackrel{\text{def}}{=} \neg \Diamond \neg A.$$

A model satisfies $\Diamond A$ and $\Box A$ if respectively a sub-interval and all sub-intervals satisfy A. Let

$$\text{fin} \stackrel{\text{def}}{=} \exists x. (\ell < x \wedge k < x)$$
$$\widehat{\text{fin}} \stackrel{\text{def}}{=} \exists x. k < x$$
$$\text{inf} \stackrel{\text{def}}{=} \neg \text{fin}$$
$$\text{point} \stackrel{\text{def}}{=} \ell = 0 \wedge k = 0.$$

They characterise intervals which respectively are finite, finite on micro-time, infinite and points. For a Boolean expression S, define

$$\lceil S \rceil \stackrel{\text{def}}{=} \neg((\ell > 0 \vee k > 0) \frown (\text{point} \wedge \neg \mathbf{b}.S) \frown (\ell > 0 \vee k > 0)).$$

This denotes that S holds everywhere inside the interval. Let

$$\lceil S \rceil \stackrel{\text{def}}{=} \lceil S \rceil \wedge \mathbf{b}.S \wedge \mathbf{e}.S.$$

This specifies that S holds everywhere inside and at both the beginning and the end of the interval. Let

$$\text{dint} \stackrel{\text{def}}{=} \ell = 0 \wedge k = 1$$
$$\text{cint} \stackrel{\text{def}}{=} \ell > 0 \wedge k = 0.$$

Intervals that satisfy cint and dint are called respectively continuous and discrete.

3 Semantics of V^-

Gordon [6] suggested a simple version of Verilog which he called V. In this paper, we consider a subset of it which we denote by V^-, that has essentially the same statements as V except the function definition, the non-blocking assignment, the `disable` statement and the assignment statements with delays. The language is simple enough for experiments in formalisation, but contains sufficient features for being practically relevant.

In the literature, the semantics usually is considered as for the program concerned defining a set of *runs*, each of which is a sequence

$$\sigma : (\sigma_0, r_0)(\sigma_1, r_1) \cdots (\sigma_i, r_i) \cdots$$

where σ_i is a valuation of variables and r_i is a real number denoting the macro-time that the variables are updated. Between two consecutive time points, variables are not changed. If there are several discrete events happening at the same macro-time, they will have the same time stamps and micro-time is denoted by the order in the sequence. A run σ can be regarded as the interpretation of the variables over a time domain. For example, assume the variable is x, and for a run

$$\sigma : (\sigma_0, 0)(\sigma_1, 2)(\sigma_2, 2)(\sigma_3, 2)(\sigma_4, 3) \cdots$$

the corresponding time domain is illustrated by the following diagram

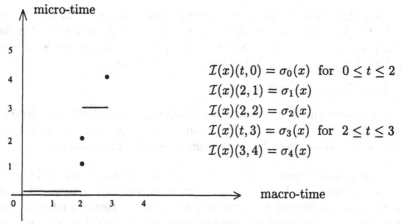

Time domain corresponding to σ

Therefore a μWDCI formula can be regarded as characterising a set of runs, and consequently, can be used to define the semantics of V^- programs. This gives the abstraction and reasoning facilities provided by a logic system.

At the top level, a V^- program can be considered as a collection of concurrent processes, communicating through shared variables. When there are discrete transitions enabled, one of them will be selected for execution. When none of the discrete transitions are enabled, time may advance until a discrete transition is enabled.

It is desirable to define the semantics compositionally, that is, define the semantics of a compound statement as a function of the semantics of the components. The standard way to give a compositional semantics to shared variable programs, suggested first by Aczel (cited e.g., in [5]), is to define the semantics as a set of labelled state transition sequences, where the label records whether the transition is from the environment or from the component. This can be expressed in the setting of μWDCI by introducing a variable, say ∂, in the state, to record the transition agent. More precisely, let $\{P_i \mid i \in I_{Proc}\}$ be the set of processes, where I_{Proc} is a set of indexes. If there is a transition at $[(r, n), (r, n + 1)]$, then the transition is from process P_i iff $\mathcal{I}(\partial)(r, n + 1) = i$. To define the semantics compositionally, a component process P_i should be viewed as an open system, with its semantics containing all the potential actions from its environment processes. Runs with unmatching environment actions are removed by the semantics of the parallel composition.

Let Var be the set of variables from the concerned program and $Var^+ \overset{\text{def}}{=} Var \cup \{\partial\}$. The semantics contains a general formula

Ax$_1$: $\forall x \in Var^+ . \quad \Box(\text{cint} \Rightarrow \text{b}.x = \text{e}.x)$

This says that none of the variables are changed if there are no transitions. The semantics of the whole system, considered as a closed system contains the formula:

Ax$_2$: $\exists i \in I_{Proc} . \Box(\text{dint} \Rightarrow \text{e}.\partial = i)$.

This says that any transition is caused by one of the constituent process.

In the following, we assume that the considered sequential statements are from process P_i. As the semantics of an open system, it is necessary to include possible behaviours from other processes. The formula

$\text{idle}_i \overset{\text{def}}{=} \Box(\text{dint} \Rightarrow \text{e}.\partial \neq i)$

says that over the interval, process P_i does not contribute any discrete transitions. There is no restriction over transitions by processes other than P_i, or in other words, transitions from other processes can be arbitrary.

Procedural Assignment. This is the usual assignment, denoted by $v = e$. It is called *procedural* in Verilog to distinguish it from other forms of assignments such as the continuous assignment which will be discussed later. Evaluation of expression e is assumed to take one micro-time, and the value is assigned to variable v, with other variables unchanged. Before the assignment is executed, its environment processes may perform an arbitrary, including infinite, number of instantaneous actions.

$$\mathcal{M}(v = e) \overset{\text{def}}{=} \ell = 0 \wedge (\text{idle}_i \frown (\text{dint} \wedge \text{e}.v = \text{b}.e \wedge unchanged_{Var-\{v\}} \wedge \text{e}.\partial = i))$$

where $unchanged_{Var-\{v\}} \overset{\text{def}}{=} \bigwedge_{x \in Var-\{v\}} \exists a. \lceil x = a \rceil$, denoting that any variable in $Var - \{v\}$ is not changed. A vacuous assignment like $x = x$ is denoted as skip.

Sequential Composition. The execution of sequential composition begin $S_1; \ldots;$ S_n end is that of S_1 followed by the execution of begin $S_2; \ldots; S_n$ end.

$$\mathcal{M}(\text{begin } S_1; S_2; \ldots; S_n \text{ end}) \stackrel{\text{def}}{=} \mathcal{M}(S_1) \frown \mathcal{M}(\text{begin } S_2; \ldots; S_n \text{ end})$$

Parallel Composition. The parallel composition of the processes is defined roughly as the conjunction

$$\mathcal{M}(P_1 \parallel \ldots \parallel P_n) \stackrel{\text{def}}{=}$$
$$\bigvee_{i=1}^{n} ((\mathcal{M}(P_1) \frown \text{idle}_1) \wedge \ldots \wedge \mathcal{M}(P_i) \wedge \ldots \wedge (\mathcal{M}(P_n) \frown \text{idle}_n)).$$

Boolean Expressions. Successful evaluation of a Boolean expression is defined as:

$$\mathcal{M}(eb) \stackrel{\text{def}}{=} \ell = 0 \wedge (\text{idle}_i \frown (b.eb \wedge \text{dint} \wedge \textit{unchanged}_{Var} \wedge e.\partial = i)).$$

Like a procedural assignment, successful evaluation of a Boolean expression takes one micro-time, and its environment processes may perform an arbitrary number of instantaneous actions before the expression is evaluated. Evaluation has no side-effect. For Boolean constants true and false, we have

- $\mathcal{M}(\text{true}) = (\ell = 0 \wedge (\text{idle}_i \frown (\text{dint} \wedge \textit{unchanged}_{Var} \wedge e.\partial = i)))$
- $\mathcal{M}(\text{false}) = (\ell = 0 \wedge (\text{idle}_i \frown \text{false})) = (\ell = 0 \wedge \text{idle}_i \wedge \text{inf}).$

Conditional. In if (eb) S_1 else S_2, the Boolean expression eb is evaluated first. If eb is successfully evaluated, then S_1 is selected, and if instead $\neg eb$ is successfully evaluated, then S_2 is selected.

$$\mathcal{M}(\text{if } (eb) \ S_1 \text{ else } S_2) \stackrel{\text{def}}{=} (\mathcal{M}(eb) \frown \mathcal{M}(S_1)) \vee (\mathcal{M}(\neg eb) \frown \mathcal{M}(S_2)).$$

Instantaneous environment actions are allowed between the evaluation of the Boolean expression and the execution of the statements that follows.

Delay. The delay statement in Verilog is denoted by $\#n$. Its meaning is that when this instruction is reached, the process is blocked for n macro-time units. During this period, other processes may execute discrete state transitions.

$$\mathcal{M}(\#n) \stackrel{\text{def}}{=} \text{idle}_i \wedge \ell \leq n \wedge (\widehat{\text{fin}} \Rightarrow \ell = n).$$

Note that it is possible that before n macro-time units have passed, other processes can execute an infinite number of instantaneous transitions and cause the micro-time to reach infinity.

Iteration. The meaning of a loop **while** (*eb*) *S* is as usual: the statement is executed repeatedly until the boolean expression *eb* becomes false. Its semantics is defined as a greatest fixed point:

$$\mathcal{M}(\texttt{while } (eb)\, S) \stackrel{\text{def}}{=} \nu X.((\mathcal{M}(eb) \frown \mathcal{M}(S) \frown X) \vee \mathcal{M}(\neg eb)).$$

It follows from Theorem 2 that the semantics of the iteration statement contains two parts. The first part is defined by the least fixed point $\mu X.((\mathcal{M}(eb) \frown \mathcal{M}(S) \frown X) \vee \mathcal{M}(\neg eb))$. This describes finite number of iterations, either *eb* becomes false in the end, or the last iteration is infinite. The second part characterises infinite iterations of the loop. Since we assume Boolean evaluation takes one unit micro-time, infinite iterations take infinite micro-time. There are two cases regarding the macro-time. One case is that after some iterations, each iteration takes zero macro-time, then the macro-time will be 'stopped' at that point. The second case is that infinite iterations need infinite macro-time. In V^-, we assume a positive delay has a lower bound, therefore the so-called zeno behaviour is not possible.

The following are some examples about the semantics of iteration statements.

1. $\mathcal{M}(\texttt{while (true) skip}) = (\ell = 0 \wedge \inf \wedge \Box(e.\partial = i \Rightarrow unchanged_{Var}))$
2. $\mathcal{M}(\texttt{while (false) } P) = \mathcal{M}(\texttt{skip})$
3. $\mathcal{M}(\texttt{while (true) skip } \| \ \#1) = \mathcal{M}(\texttt{while (true) skip}) \wedge \text{idle}_2.$

Wait. The wait statement **wait** (*eb*) *S* waits until Boolean expression *eb* becomes true, then the control is passed to the following statement *S*.

$$\mathcal{M}(\texttt{wait } (eb)\, S) \stackrel{\text{def}}{=} (\text{idle}_i \wedge (\lceil \neg eb \rceil \frown (\text{dint} \wedge e.eb))) \frown \mathcal{M}(S)$$

Event Control. Synchronisation can also be achieved by waiting for some events (state changes) to occur. The statement is of the form

$$@(event)\, S$$

where *event* is considered as a binary state predicate, and the control is passed to *S* when *event* is satisfied. An event expression is of the following form

- *v*, indicating waiting for a change of the value in *v*,
- **posedge** *v*, indicating waiting for a positive change of the value in *v*,
- **negedge** *v*, indicating waiting for a negative change of the value in *v*,
- (*event*₁**or** ...**or** *event*ₙ), indicating waiting for any event to be true.

Overloading symbols a little, we define

$$@(v) \stackrel{\text{def}}{=} \mathbf{b}.v \neq \mathbf{e}.v$$
$$@(\textbf{posedge } v) \stackrel{\text{def}}{=} \mathbf{b}.v < \mathbf{e}.v$$
$$@(\textbf{negedge } v) \stackrel{\text{def}}{=} \mathbf{b}.v > \mathbf{e}.v$$
$$@(event_1 \textbf{or} \ ... \textbf{or} \ event_n) \stackrel{\text{def}}{=} @(event_1) \vee ... \vee @(event_n)$$

It is now easy to give the semantics of the statement

$$\mathcal{M}(@(event)\, S) \stackrel{\text{def}}{=} (\text{idle}_i \wedge ((\Box \neg @(event)) \frown (\text{dint} \wedge @(event)))) \frown \mathcal{M}(S)$$

Continuous assignment. A continuous assignment `assign` $w = e$ describes the connection of a wire w to an input. Like a channel, a wire does not store the value, and any change of the input is immediately propagated

$$\mathcal{M}(\text{assign } w = e) \overset{\text{def}}{=} \lceil w = \mathcal{M}(e) \rceil \wedge \text{inf}.$$

The semantics of other V^- statements can be found in [18].

4 Discussion

In this paper, we have given a formal semantics to V^-, a simple version of Verilog. The language contains interesting features like concurrency, timing behaviours, discrete events as well as recursion. Formalising more advanced features of Verilog, such as various other assignments, needs further research. On the other hand, V^- has contained the basics of Verilog, and therefore it will be useful to develop other formal techniques for V^- based on the semantics. However, to support particular techniques, the semantics may need fine tuning; for example, for refinement, the semantics should probably be made insensitive to stuttering.

There has been some related work where semantics of several languages have been formalised using Duration Calculus and its appropriate extensions. He [8], Zhou, Wang and Ravn [3] studied semantics of HCSP in classical DC, which is sufficient because every action is assumed to take some time. Semantics of sequential real-time programs, which may contain instantaneous actions, has been studied in [17] using Super Dense DC (SDC). SDC allows the input/output behaviours of a sequential program to be recorded, but not the intermediate states. SDC is similar to the Relational DC, which has been used by Pace to a subset of Verilog [13]. Hence, Pace also does not record the intermediate states of Verilog programs. To describe the semantics of concurrency adequately, Pandya and Dang proposed to use WDC [15] and applied to an ESTEREL-like language called SL [14]. WDC is extended with infinite intervals in [20] and applied to formalise the semantics of a toy language.

Acknowledgements We would like to thank He Jifeng for introducing Verilog to us, Gordon Pace for discussing his work, and Dang Van Hung, Paritosh Pandya and Zhou Chaochen for their useful comments in the initial stage of this work.

References

1. Zhou Chaochen, C.A.R. Hoare, and A.P. Ravn. A calculus of durations. *Information Processing Letters*, 40(5):269–276, 1991.
2. Zhou Chaochen, Dang Van Hung, and Li Xiaoshan. A duration calculus with infinite intervals. In *Fundamentals of Computation Theory, Horst Reichel (Ed.)*, pages 16–41. LNCS 965, Springer-Verlag, 1995.
3. Zhou Chaochen, Wang Ji, and A.P. Ravn. A formal description of hybrid systems. In R. Alur, T. Henzinger, and E. Sontag, editors, *Hybrid Systems III: Verification and Control*, pages 511–530. LNCS 1066, Springer–Verlag, 1995.

4. Zhou Chaochen, A.P. Ravn, and M.R. Hansen. An extended duration calculus for hybrid systems. In *Hybrid Systems, R.L. Grossman, A. Nerode, A.P. Ravn, H. Rischel (Eds.)*, pages 36–59. LNCS 736, Springer-Verlag, 1993.

5. W.-P. de Roever. The quest for compositionality. In *Proc. of IFIP Working Conf., The Role of Abstract Models in Computer Science*. Elsevier Science B.V. (North-Holland), 1985.

6. M.J.C. Gordon. The Semantic Challenge of Verilog HDL. In *Tenth Annual IEEE Symposium on Logic in Computer Science*, IEEE Computer Society Press, pages 136–145, June 1995.

7. IEEE Computer Society. *IEEE Standard Hardware Description Language Based on the Verilog Hardware Description Language (IEEE std 1364-1995*, 1995.

8. He Jifeng. From CSP to hybrid systems. In A.W. Roscoe, editor, *A Classical Mind, Eassy in Honour of C.A.R. Hoare*, pages 171–189. Prentice-Hall International, 1994.

9. R. Koymans. *Specifying Message Passing and Time-Critical Systems with Temporal Logic*. LNCS 651, Springer–Verlag, 1992.

10. Z. Liu, A.P. Ravn, and X.-S. Li. Verifying duration properties of timed transition systems. In *Proc. IFIP Working Conference PROCOMET'98*. Chapman & Hall, 1998.

11. B. Moszkowski. A temporal logic for multilevel reasoning about hardware. *IEEE Computer*, 18(2):10–19, 1985.

12. B. Moszkowski. Compositional reasoning about projected and infinite time. In *Proc. the First IEEE International Conference on Engineering of Complex Computer Systems (ICECCS'95)*, pages 238–245. IEEE Computer Society Press, 1995.

13. G.J. Pace and J.-F. He. Formal reasoning with Verilog HDL. In *Proc. the Workshop on Formal Techniques for Hardware and Hardware-like Systems*, Sweden 1988.

14. P.K. Pandya. A compositional semantics of SL. Technical report, DeTfoRS Group, UNU/IIST, October 1997.

15. P.K. Pandya and Dang Van Hung. Duration calculus with weakly monotonic time. This volume.

16. P.K. Pandya and Y.S. Ramakrishna. A recursive duration calculus. Technical report, CS-95/3, Computer Science Group, TIFR, Bombay, 1995.

17. P.K. Pandya, H.-P. Wang, and Q.-W. Xu. Towards a theory of sequential hybrid programs. In *Proc. IFIP Working Conference PROCOMET'98*. Chapman & Hall, 1998.

18. G. Schneider and Q.-W. Xu. Towards a Formal Semantics of Verilog using Duration Calculus. Technical Report 133, UNU/IIST, P.O.Box 3058, Macau, February 1998.

19. H.-P. Wang and Q.-W. Xu. Infinite duration calculus with fixed-point operators. Technical Report draft, UNU/IIST, P.O.Box 3058, Macau, September 1997.

20. Q.-W. Xu and M. Swarup. Compositional reasoning using assumption - commitment paradigm. In H. Langmaack, A. Pnueli, and W.-P. de Roever, editors, *International Symposium, Compositionality – The Significant Difference*. Springer–Verlag, 1998.

The ICOS Synthesis Environment

Karsten Lüth

Carl von Ossietzky University, Oldenburg
Department of Computer Architecture
D-26129 Oldenburg, Germany
Lueth@Informatik.Uni-Oldenburg.DE

Abstract. This paper presents an overview of the *ICOS* system, a design environment for control-dominated reactive systems, which is based on a graphical specification language called *real-time symbolic timing diagrams*. ICOS offers a broad set of tools to create, verify, and to synthesize hardware or software code from timing diagram specifications.

1 Introduction

Computer-controlled reactive system are applied in nearly every area of our daily life, but design and implementation of such applications is still a complicated and challenging task. Formal languages and an appropriate tool support are needed when a sound specification of the system under design is desired or –in the case of safety-critical systems– required. The goal of the ICOS project is to develop tools, which are able to generate executable code out from formal declarative specifications. We want to emphasize the following two advantages in using such tools: first, through simulating the specification, the designer can easily *validate* that the stated requirements comply with his intentions. Second, *prototypes* can be generated to demonstrate or test the functionality of the system at all stages of the development process.

The purpose of this paper is to present a brief overview of the concepts and tools of ICOS. Section 2 introduces *real-time symbolic timing diagrams* (RTSTD, for short), a formal graphical specification language that is used in ICOS. Section 3 outlines the basic synthesis steps which are used to compile RTSTDs. The whole tool set of ICOS is presented in section 4. Section 5 concludes this papers and presents ongoing work.

2 Real-time Symbolic Timing Diagrams

RTSTD [2] is a graphical specification formalism similar to the well-known hardware timing diagrams, but in contrast to other timing diagram approaches, RTSTDs have a declarative semantics which is formalized through a mapping to temporal logic formulas. An RTSTD consists of a set of *waveforms* and *constraints*. A waveform defines a sequence of expressions for a signal, which describes a possible temporal evolution. The type of a signal may be bit,

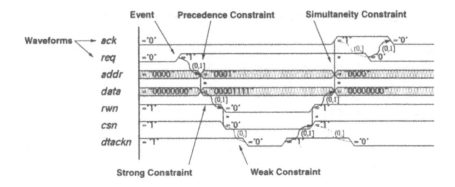

Fig. 1. A real-time symbolic timing diagram.

enumeration, bitarray or (finite subranges of) integer. The point of change from validity of one expression to validity of another expression is called a *symbolic event*. Events are normally not ordered across different waveforms, but *constraint arcs* can be used to impose such an ordering. A constraint can be a *simultaneity constraint* (the two connected events must occur simultaneously), a *conflict constraint* (two events may not occur within a given time-interval), a *leads-to constraint* (an event e_2 may not occur later than t time-units after an event e_1), or a *precedence constraint* (event e_2 may only occur if preceded by event e_1 within a given time-interval). *Strong constraints* express requirements which must be satisfied by the component under design, while *weak constraints* express an expectation on the behavior of the environment. Figure 1 shows a simplified write cycle for an RS-232 transmitter.

Besides RTSTDs, two additional formalism are used in ICOS specifications: a VHDL-alike entity is needed to declare all ports of the component under design, and a VHDL-alike package declaration can be used to define types and constants.

3   Synthesis

The full ICOS synthesis process compiles a set of RTSTD specifications into executable VHDL code in four steps. In the first step, described in [4, 2, 1], real-time symbolic timing diagrams are translated to propositional temporal logic (PTL). These formulae are partitioned into groups, such that for each outport o of the component under design, o is driven in not more than one group. Now, each group can be compiled separately, which in many situations reduces the complexity dramatically. For each of this group we generate a Büchi automaton using standard techniques for deriving semanticly equivalent Büchi-automata from PTL formulae. The interested reader may consult [8, 3] for details about partitioning and Büchi automata generation.

Then we use the Büchi-to-Moore algorithm of Feyerabend and Schlör [3] — a variant of winning strategy construction in regular games [11] — to synthesize a Moore automaton from each Büchi automaton. Finally, these Moore automata are encoded in VHDL using the design styles of *Synopsys* [5]. The resulting VHDL specification can be compiled to FPGA-code or any other low-level hardware description language using VHDL compilers from *Synopsys* or other vendors.

4 The ICOS Toolbox

The complete ICOS system consists of the following set of tools:

- The graphical **User Interface** of the system consists of an *RTSTD Editor* and a *Design Browser* for organizing designs and invoking all synthesis tools. *Syntaxchecker* are used to check RTSTDs, entities or packages for syntactical correctness.
- The **Synthesis Tools**, as discussed in the last section, translate RTSTD specifications into PTL, Büchi- and Moore-automata.
- A static validation of the design can be performed either with the **Analyzer** or the **Tautology Checker**. The Analyzer executes several static analysis queries, while the Tautology Checker is used to verify commitments over specifications.
- The **C Code Generator** generates executable C code from the Büchi automata and is used to simulate the specification. This compiler uses the Büchi-automata rather than the Moore-automata result, since the Moore-automata represents just one possible implementation of the specification and is thus less appropriate for specification validation.
- **VHDL Code Generator.** The VHDL code generator of ICOS produces synthesizable VHDL code from the generated Moore automata.
- The **Testbench Generator** is used to generate testmonitor and testbench-architectures from a specification.

5 Conclusion and ongoing work

The ICOS system offers an extensive set of tools for specifying and synthesizing control-dominated reactive systems. Using symbolic timing diagrams as basic specification formalism, ICOS provides an intuitive but formal language for describing requirements. The synthesis tools of ICOS enable fast validation and prototyping of these specifications.

Related Work. When compared with systems based on operational formalism like *Statecharts* [7] and the *Statemate Environment* [6], the advantage of ICOS lies in the formal semantics and in the compositional nature of RTSTDs. Another environment which is comparable with ICOS is the *RTGIL Environment* [10] which is based on a formalism called *Real-Time Graphical Interval Logic*. But in contrast to ICOS, RTGIL does not offer code generation.

Ongoing Work. Currently, we use ICOS in a project called *EVENTS*, where we apply ICOS and Statemate as specification tools in a cosynthesis environment [9]. The basic idea is to use RTSTDs to specify the control dominated parts of the application under design while using Statecharts to specify the computation dominated parts.

In this project we will enhance the features of ICOS in two ways: first, large-scale timing constraints will be more effectively synthesized by using clocked-automata. Second, abstract domains will be introduced to enable the use of user-defined code and to prevent state-explosions.

References

1. W. Damm, B. Josko, and R. Schlör. Specification and verification of VHDL-based system-level hardware designs. In E. Börger, editor, *Specification and Validation Methods*. Oxford University Press, 1995.
2. Konrad Feyerabend and Bernhard Josko. A visual formalism for real time requirement specification. In *Transformation-Based Reactive System Development*, number 1231 in LNCS, pages 156–168. Springer Verlag, 1997.
3. Konrad Feyerabend and Rainer Schlör. Hardware synthesis from requirement specifications. In *Proceedings EURO-DAC with EURO-VHDL 96*. IEEE Computer Society Press, 1996.
4. Martin Fränzle and Karsten Lüth. Compiling Graphical Real-Time Specification into Silicon. In *Formal Techniques in Real-Time and Fault-Tolerant Systems*, September 1998.
5. S. Golsen. State Machine Design Techniques for Verilog and Vhdl. *Synopsys Journal of High Level Design*, September 1994.
6. D. Harel, H. Lachover, A. Naamad, A. Pnueli, M. Politi, R. Sherman, A. Shtull-Trauring, and M. Trakhtenbrot. STATEMATE: A working environment for the development od complex reactive systems. *IEEE Transactions on Software Engineering*, 16:403 – 414, 1990.
7. David Harel. Statecharts: A visual formalism for complex systems. *Science of Computer Programming*, 8:231 – 274, 1987.
8. F. Korf and R. Schlör. Interface controller synthesis from requirement specifications. In *Proceedings, The European Conference on Design Automation*, pages 385–394, Paris, France, February 1994. IEEE Computer Society Press.
9. Karsten Lüth, Thomas Peikenkamp, and Jürgen Risau. HW/SW Cosynthesis using Statecharts and Symbolic Timing Diagrams. In *Proceedings of the 9th IEEE International Workshop on Rapid System Prototyping*, 1998.
10. L.E. Moser, Y.S. Ramakrishna, G. Kutty, P.M. Melliar-Smith, and Dillon L. K. A Graphical Environment for the Design of Concurrent Real-Time Systems. *ACM Transactions on Software Engineering and Methodology*, 6(1):31–79, 1997.
11. Wolfgang Thomas. On the synthesis of strategies in infinite games. In E. W. Meyer and C. Puech, editors, *Symposium on Theoretical Aspects of Computer Science (STACS 95)*, volume 900 of *Lecture Notes in Computer Science*, pages 1–13. Springer-Verlag, March 1995.

Kronos: A Model-Checking Tool for Real-Time Systems[*]
(Tool-Presentation for FTRTFT '98)

Marius Bozga[1], Conrado Daws[1], Oded Maler[1], Alfredo Olivero[2],
Stavros Tripakis[1] and Sergio Yovine[3]

[1] VERIMAG, Centre Équation, 2 avenue de Vignate, 38610 Gières, France.
e-mail: {bozga, daws, maler, tripakis}@imag.fr
[2] Instituto de Computación, Universidad de la República, Montevideo, Uruguay.
e-mail: yovine@imag.fr, sergio@path.berkeley.edu
[3] VERIMAG; currently visiting California PATH, UC Berkeley.
e-mail: alfredo@ungs.edu.ar

General presentation

KRONOS [8, 10, 7, 11, 20, 16, 4, 3, 9] is a software tool aiming at assisting designers
of real-time systems to develop projects meeting the specified requirements.

One major objective of KRONOS is to provide a verification engine to be
integrated into design environments for real-time systems in a wide range of application areas. Real-time communication protocols [8, 10], timed asynchronous
circuits [16, 4], and hybrid systems [18, 10] are some examples of application
domains where KRONOS has already been used.

KRONOS has been also used in analyzing real-time systems modeled in several
other process description formalisms, such as ATP [17], AORTA [5], ET-LOTOS [8],
and T-ARGOS [15]. On the other direction, the tool itself provides an interface
to untimed formalisms such as *labeled-transition systems* (LTS) which has been
used to exploit untimed verification techniques [20].

Theoretical background

The system-description language of KRONOS is the model of *timed automata* [2],
which are communicating finite-state machines extended with continuous real-
valued variables (*clocks*) used to measure time delays. Usually a system is modeled as a *network* of automata. Communication is achieved by label synchronization à la CCS or CSP (binary or *n*-ary *rendez-vous*), or shared variables (of
bounded integer or enumeration type).

System requirements can be specified in KRONOS using a variety of formalisms, such as the real-time logic TCTL [1, 14], timed Büchi automata, or

---
[*] KRONOS is developed at VERIMAG, a joint laboratory of UJF, Ensimag and CNRS.
http://www.imag.fr/VERIMAG/PEOPLE/Sergio.Yovine/kronos/kronos.html.
C. Daws, A. Olivero and S. Yovine partially supported by European Contract KIT
139 HYBSYS.

untimed LTS. These formalisms are useful for expressing most interesting classes of (timed or untimed) properties about systems, namely, *safety* properties (for example, absence of deadlock, invariant, bounded-delay response, etc), as well as *liveness* properties (for example, time progress, regular occurrence of certain events, etc) [1].

The main verification engine of the tool is based on the *model-checking* approach which comprises both *analysis*: (a) checking whether requirements are satisfied, (b) providing *diagnostic trails* (i.e., execution sequences) demonstrating why a property holds or does not hold; and *synthesis*: adjusting the system (for instance, by computing a restricted sub-system) so that it meets its requirements. Model-checking is done using two methods: (a) the *fixpoint* method, which, given a timed automaton and a TCTL formula, performs a nested fixpoint computation starting from an initial set of states and iterating a *precondition operator* until stabilization (the operator depends on the type of the formula); (b) the *explorative* method, which, given a network of timed automata and a specification (in terms of a TCTL formula or a timed Büchi automaton), generates the reachability graph of the system while checking at the same time whether the property holds. In the case of safety properties a simple (depth-first or breadth-first) search of the reachability graph suffices. In the case of general properties, specified as timed Büchi automata, a double search is performed, refining parts of the graph whenever necessary. Both methods are interesting: the main advantage of the fixpoint method is that it can be implemented in a purely *symbolic* manner, using structures like BDD for efficiency (see below); on the other hand, the explorative method is more suitable for *on-the-fly* verification (see below) and can also provide diagnostic trails.

Apart from model-checking, KRONOS offers the possibility to (a) generate the system's reachable state space (to check, for instance, whether an error state can be reached), and (b) compute the coarsest partition of the state space with respect to the *time-abstracting bisimulation*, an equivalence relating states which lead to the same untimed behavior regardless the exact time delays. This method provides an interface to LTS and verification by bisimulation or simulation equivalences [20] using the ALDEBARAN tool suite [13].

Supported verification techniques

The main obstacle in the applicability of model-checking is the so-called *state-explosion problem* reflecting the fact that the size of the system's state space is often huge. In order to tackle this, KRONOS offers a number of efficient verification techniques, each of which is best suited for different applications.

- *Symbolic* representation of states means dealing with *predicates* representing sets of states rather than individual states. This results into a much more compact representation and storage. In the current KRONOS implementation,

---

[1] To our knowledge, KRONOS is the only real-time verification tool which can handle liveness properties.

sets of clock values are represented using the *difference bounds matrix* (DBM) structure introduced in [12], whereas discrete variables are encoded as *binary decision diagrams* (BDD) [6].

- *On-the-fly* model-checking means dynamically building the state space during the model-checking process, as directed by the model-checking goal (for instance, the property to be verified); this results in saving up space and time, as well as in giving diagnostics as soon as possible.
- *Abstractions* are used for the exploration of a coarser state space than the "real" (*concrete*) one; they result into space and time savings, at the cost of loosing information, so that sometimes definite conclusions cannot be made.
- *Syntactic optimizations* are used to reduce the number of clocks in the model to only the strict necessary; they allow for space and time savings at almost no cost since they are inexpensive to compute.
- *Forward* or *backward* techniques: in the former (typically used in the explorative method) the exploration starts from initial states and tries to reach some target, while in the latter (typically used in the fixpoint method) it is the inverse that happens. Combined with various *search algorithms* (such as depth-first or breadth-first) implemented in the model-checking engine of the tool, these alternative techniques result in a large flexibility with respect to the different application needs.
- *Minimization*: it is used to generate the time-abstracting *minimal model* of the system, which can then be visualized as an untimed graph, compared or further reduced with respect to untimed equivalences, or checked using untimed temporal logics.

Case studies

KRONOS has been used to verify various industrial communication protocols, such as an audio-transmission protocol by Philips [10] (where errors have been found to the previously hand-made proofs) or an ATM protocol by CNET [19] (where a bug was also found relative to the consistency of the network components). Other communication protocols modeled and verified by KRONOS include the carrier-sense multiple-access with collision detection (CSMA-CD) protocol [8] and the fiber-optic data-interface (FDDI) protocol [9]. Well-known benchmark case studies verified by KRONOS include Fischer's real-time mutual-exclusion protocol [9] and a production-plant case study [10]. Finally, the tool has been also applied to the verification of the STARI chip [4] and to the synthesis of real-time schedulers [2].

The most recent enhancements of Kronos include the implementation of different abstraction mechanisms [9], the implementation of a symbolic on-the-fly algorithm for checking timed Büchi automata emptiness [3] and a BDD-based implementation oriented towards the timing analysis of circuits [4]. Table 1 presents some typical experimental results extracted from the cited papers. The measurements were taken on a Sparc Ultra-1 with 128 Mbytes of main memory. Time is

---

[2] Unpublished work.

given in seconds. The size of the state space (when available) is given in symbolic states (i.e., control location plus DBM), BDD nodes, or states and transitions. "OTF" stands for "on-the-fly".

Case study	Method	Time	State space
Production plant	Fixpoint	26	not available
CNET	Forward	3	not available
Philips	Forward	2	not available
Fischer (5 processes)	Minimization	32	3000 states & trans.
Fischer (6 processes)	OTF	2783	164935 symb. states
Fischer (9 processes)	OTF & Abstractions	17098	1096194 symb. states
FDDI (7 stations)	OTF & Büchi aut.	4813	57500 symb. states
FDDI (12 stations)	Forward	1123	13000 symb. states
FDDI (50 stations)	Forward & Abstractions	3900	4000 symb. states
STARI (17 stages)	Fixpoint & BDD	100000	1000000 BDD nodes

Table 1. Some performance results.

It is worth noting that the entire machinery of KRONOS has been useful for handling the above examples. In particular, the fixpoint method has been used in earlier versions of the tool for liveness properties, as well as for synthesis (see, for instance, [10], where initial constraints have been tightened so that the system behaves correctly). Forward model-checking using timed Büchi automata has been recently used for checking liveness on the FDDI protocol for up to 7 processes, as well as to provide diagnostics in the real-time scheduling problem. Minimization has been used for visualizing the behavior of timed automata. On-the-fly techniques have been used whenever syntactic parallel composition could not be applied due to state explosion. Abstractions and clock-reduction techniques have been essential to the verification of the FDDI example for up to 50 processes, and Fischer's protocol for up to 9 processes [9].

Availability

KRONOS is freely available for universities or any other non-profit organisms. It can be obtained through the web at:
http://www.imag.fr/VERIMAG/PEOPLE/Sergio.Yovine/kronos/kronos.html
or by anonymous ftp at:
       host: ftp.imag.fr, directory: VERIMAG/KRONOS/tool/.
The distribution package includes executables for various architectures (Sun5, Linux, Windows NT), documentation and examples.

References

1. R. Alur, C. Courcoubetis, and D.L. Dill. Model checking in dense real time. *Information and Computation*, 104(1):2–34, 1993.

2. R. Alur and D.L. Dill. A theory of timed automata. *Theoretical Computer Science*, 126:183–235, 1994.

3. A. Bouajjani, S. Tripakis, and S. Yovine. On-the-fly symbolic model checking for real-time systems. In *Proc. of the 18th IEEE Real-Time Systems Symposium*, 1997.

4. M. Bozga, O. Maler, A. Pnueli, and S. Yovine. Some progress in the symbolic verification of timed automata. In *CAV'97*, 1997.

5. S. Bradley, W. Henderson, D. Kendall, and A. Robson. Validation, verification and implementation of timed protocols using AORTA. In *Proc. 15th PSTV*, 1995.

6. R.E. Bryant. Symbolic boolean manipulation with ordered binary decision diagrams. Technical report, Carnegie Mellon University, 1992.

7. C. Daws, A. Olivero, S. Tripakis, and S. Yovine. The tool KRONOS. In *Hybrid Systems III*, 1996.

8. C. Daws, A. Olivero, and S. Yovine. Verifying ET-LOTOS programs with KRONOS. In *FORTE'94*, 1994.

9. C. Daws and S. Tripakis. Model checking of real-time reachability properties using abstractions. In *TACAS'98*, 1998. To appear.

10. C. Daws and S. Yovine. Two examples of verification of multirate timed automata with KRONOS. In *RTSS'95*, 1995.

11. C. Daws and S. Yovine. Reducing the number of clock variables of timed automata. In *RTSS'96*, 1996.

12. D. Dill. Timing assumptions and verification of finite-state concurrent systems. In *CAV'89*, 1989.

13. J.Cl. Fernandez, H. Garavel, L. Mounier, A. Rasse, C. Rodriguez, and J. Sifakis. A tool box for the verification of lotos programs. In *14th International Conference on Software Engineering*, 1992.

14. T.A. Henzinger, X. Nicollin, J. Sifakis, and S. Yovine. Symbolic model checking for real-time systems. *Information and Computation*, 111(2):193–244, 1994.

15. M. Jourdan, F. Maraninchi, and A. Olivero. Verifying quantitative real-time properties of synchronous programs. In *CAV'93*, 1993.

16. O. Maler and S. Yovine. Hardware timing verification using KRONOS. In *Proc. 7th Israeli Conference on Computer Systems and Software Engineering*, 1996.

17. X. Nicollin, J. Sifakis, and S. Yovine. Compiling real-time specifications into extended automata. *IEEE TSE Special Issue on Real-Time Systems*, 18(9):794–804, September 1992.

18. A. Olivero, J. Sifakis, and S. Yovine. Using abstractions for the verification of linear hybrid systems. In *CAV'94*, 1994.

19. S. Tripakis and S .Yovine. Verification of the fast-reservation protocol with delayed transmission using Kronos. Technical Report 95-23, Verimag, 1995.

20. S. Tripakis and S. Yovine. Analysis of timed systems based on time–abstracting bisimulations. In *CAV'96*, 1996.

SGLOT: A Visual Tool for Structural LOTOS Specifications

Mario Marrero, Alvaro Suárez, Elena Carrión, and Elsa Macías

Dpto. de Ingeniería Telemática ULPGC
email: mario@cicei.ulpgc.es, alvaro@cic.teleco.ulpgc.es

Abstract. LOTOS is a Formal Description Technique (FDT) that has a strong and obscure textual algebraic notation that is difficult in readability. We have developed a tool that allows to design visual specifications and generate the LOTOS equivalent code. With this tool a lot of time is saved in the specification phase of system simulation.

1 Introduction

FDTs are useful for the specification of complex systems behaviour and its formal verification. LOTOS [1] is an FDT that ensures the precision and tractability of system specifications but has an strong and obscure textual algebraic notation that difficult its readability [2]. In order to solve this problem some graphical tools have been developed for representing LOTOS behaviour and ADTs, and the translation of other FDTs to LOTOS have theoretically been proposed [5][6]. We have put in practice a new graphical representation of the structure of LOTOS specifications finding objects that can represent BASIC LOTOS concepts and its relations.

We have developed the tool SGLOT (Graphic Specificator for LOTOS). It facilitates the rapid generation of LOTOS code, it allows to visually inspect structural relations between processes, hierarchical (at different levels of abstraction) specifications are easily developed and it is an appropiate alternative for introducing students to the study of FDTs and LOTOS. The combination of SGLOT and our EVGC [3] tool forms a powerful method for easily developing LOTOS specifications.

In section two, we present a new proposed graphical representation of LOTOS concepts. In this section three we present the SGLOT tool. In section four an application example is studied and finally we sum up with some conclusions.

2 A new graphical representation proposal for LOTOS concepts

For a graphical representation of BASIC LOTOS specifications, a valid, clear and coherent relation between graphical concepts and textual concepts must be found (a graphical assignment must be found for each of the elements or concepts which form part of the LOTOS specifications). Also, the relation between these elements must clearly represent the behaviour of the systems.

The basic concepts of a LOTOS specification are mainly: Processes, gates, events, synchronization and different levels of abstraction. We consider the graphical representation of those concepts in the following manner: We represent a *process* by a box with a number on the top right-hand corner (#i) and the name of the process on the lower right-hand corner. The hierarchy concept is defined by a *macro* (a box that contains more processes). *Gates* are implemented by black boxes on the border of the processes and finally, synchronization between processes are lines that join different gates. These concepts are represented in figure 1.

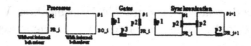

Fig. 1. Equivalences between graphical and textual concepts

Since we are only interested in the structural representation of a LOTOS specification, we are not considering the graphical concept of an event.

3 SGLOT

SGLOT presents a graphical workspace which allows the user to design and analyze complex systems graphically with different levels of abstraction, followed by the automatic generation of the LOTOS code. On the other hand, it allows users to edit the source files (*.lt) of the graphical specifications implemented and the files (*.lot) which contain the LOTOS code specifications which are generated. In figure 2, an image of the graphical workspace is represented. This consists of a main window which includes on the top half, a main menu with five buttons, and the remaining part is composed of the editor's graphical area where the user can design the specification's block diagram.

Also, the SGLOT tool bar contains functions for the graphical representation for the analysis of the system's behaviour, such as the insertion of processes, gates, and the development of macros. There exist other visual objects in the workspace such as the VIPs (Windows of Process' Information), whose information referencing processes or macros, such as their names or dimensions, etc, can be modified depending on the user's needs. Another visual element of the graphical workspace are VCMs (Windows of Macro Contents). With the VCMs the user can design specifications at different levels of abstraction.

To automatically generate LOTOS code corresponding to the graphical specifications, the user must make use of the Application button in the main menu. This button gives the user three options: Specification: Allows the user to assign a name for the specification which will be generated. Specify: Automatically

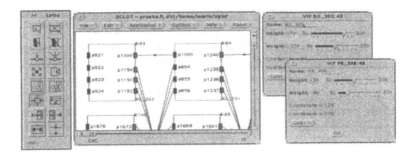

Fig. 2. SGLOT workspace

generates LOTOS code related to the graphical specification. View Specification: Allows the user to view the code generated in the previous step.

4 An application example

In recent years, mobile computing systems have arisen and some wireless networks of computers have been developed and used extensively: terminal equipments can flexibly be located indoors [7]. In *diffuse infrared systems*, the ilumination of the receiver occurs directly by the source or uses bouncing through the surfaces.

The prediction of the behavior of a diffuse infrared system can be obtained through its Formal Specification and the derivation of the parallel simulation (for an interval of time) in a multicomputer with distributed memory [9]. The generation of the parallel deadlock free program is a very difficult problem. For specifying the communication between processes we consider the system consists of n parallel communicating processes. Process P_0 sends initial data to $P_1, ..., P_{n-1}$ which compute power values and communicate among them. Finally $P_1, ..., P_{n-1}$ send the result of the temporary power distribution on the diffuse infrared receivers they compute, to P_0. We consider the following channels (gates in LOTOS): *dat_i*, *trpo* and *trpof* for communicate initial data, power and final power distribution. In figure 3.a we show a SGLOT visual specification of the system.

The processes follow the Compute, Agregate and Communicate parallel programming model. So, for doing the refinement of process behaviour we consider the basic actions: *Compute_p* (computation in processes), *efinal_p* (communication sense: $P_1, ..., P_{n-1} > P_0$) and *blocking* (posibility of a deadlock occurence). Using SGLOT we obtain the code in figure 3.b and next we specify the behaviour of processes (figure 3.c). For considering the strict temporary dependency restrictions of the evolution of processes we consider a parameter in processes $(Compute_p(t))$. This evolution finalizes when t is equal to zero (t eq 0). The action $(Act(t))$ represents the update of time in the system.

Guided by the specification above we generate the parallel program considering the refinement of the actions above. In [4] we present the experimental results

Fig. 3. (a)The example system, (b)Generated code, (c)Final code

of the parallel program that was coded in C with MPI library (using MPI_Bcast and MPI_Allreduce for broadcasting) in an IBM SP-2 multicomputer.

5 Conclusions

In this paper we have presented a tool for visually representing the structure of BASIC LOTOS specifications. It allows to save a lot of time in the specification phase and is very appropiated for students and inexpert designers. Additionally, real time requirements could be considered in the edges of the graphs. We have applied this tool to computer architecture specifications and ATM layer specifications. It greatly facilitates us the specification task. We are working in the integration of SGLOT, EVGC and critical system specifications. We also are working in the animation and debugging of specifications using the above integration.

References

1. Bolognesi, T. Brinksma, E.i: Introduction to the ISO specification language LO-TOS. Conputer Networks ISDN systems, 14 (1987), pp. 25-59.
2. Bolognesi T. Najm E. and Tolanus P.: G-LOTOS: A graphical language for concurrent systems, Lotosphere: Software Develop. with LOTOS, Klummer Academic Publisher, ISBN 0-7923-9528-8, p.p. 391-437, 1995.
3. Marrero Ruiz, Alvaro Suárez: A tool for visualizing LOTOS Behavioural Specifications, 4th FTRTFT, LNCS 1135, pp. 475-478, Sep. 1996.
4. Elsa Macías, Alvaro Suárez, Rafael Pérez, F. J. Lopez Hernandez: Paralelization Of The Temporal Impulse Response Of Infrared Receptors, IEEE-IASTED International Conference on Signal Processing and Communication, pp. 69-72, Febrero 1998.
5. Y. Sun: A translation of Transition Diagrams to LOTOS. Internal Report, The Queens University of Belfast, 1992.
6. Sisto and Valenzano: Mapping Petri Nets onto Basic LOTOS behaviour expressions. IEEE Transactions on Computer, Vol. 44, n. 12, December, 1995.
7. Fritz R. Gfeller, Urs Bapst: Wireless In-House Data Communication via Diffuse Infrared Radiation, Proceedings of the IEEE, vol. 67, no. 11, pag. 1474, Nov. 1979.

Discrete-Time Promela and Spin

Dragan Bošnacki * and Dennis Dams **

Dept. of Computing Science, Eindhoven University of Technology
PO Box 513, 5600 MB Eindhoven, The Netherlands
fax: +31 40 246 3992, e-mail: {dragan,wsindd}@win.tue.nl

Abstract. Spin is a software package for the verification of concurrent systems. A system to be verified is modeled in Promela - Spin's input language. We present an extension of Promela and Spin with discrete time that provides an opportunity to model systems whose correct functioning crucially depends on timing parameters. This extension is completely compatible with all the features of the standard package, in particular the partial order reduction algorithm. We have tested the prototype tool on several applications known from the verification literature and the first results are promising.

The Spin Model Checker. Promela and Spin have been developed for the analysis and validation of communication protocols [10]. The language syntax is derived from C, but also uses the denotations for communications from Hoare's CSP and control flow statements based on Dijkstra's guarded commands. The full presentation of Promela and Spin is beyond the scope of this paper and we suggest [10] as a reference to the interested reader. Following [11] we only give a short overview of the language and validation tools. In Promela, the system components are modeled as *processes* that can communicate via *channels* either by buffered message exchanges or rendez-vous operations, and also through shared memory represented as *global variables*. The execution of actions is considered asynchronous and interleaved, which means that in every step only one *enabled* action is performed. There are no any additional assumptions on the relative speed of process execution.

Given as input a Promela model, Spin can do a random or interactive simulation or generate a C program that performs a verification of the system by scanning the state space using a depth-first search algorithm. This way, both *safety* properties such as absence of deadlock, unspecified message receptions, invalid end states and assertions can be checked, as well as *liveness* properties such as non-progress cycles and eventual reception of messages. The so-called *never claims*, which are best seen as monitoring processes that run in lock step with the rest of the system, are the most general way to express properties in Spin. Being Büchi Automata, they can express arbitrary omega-regular properties. Spin provides an automatic translator from formulae in linear-time temporal logic (LTL) to never claims. When errors are reported, the trace of actions leading to an invalid state or cycle is saved, so that the erroneous sequence can be

---

* On leave from the Institute of Informatics, Faculty of Natural Sciences and Mathematics, University "Sts. Cyril and Methodius", Skopje, Macedonia. Supported by EC ESPRIT LTR Project No. 23498 (VIRES).

** Supported by the Netherlands Computer Science Research Foundation (SION).

replayed as a guided simulation. For large state spaces methods, Spin features state-vector compressing, partial-order reduction and bit-state hashing. The last technique gives only approximate results, which means that there is only a guarantee that some part of the state space is covered.

Xspin is a graphical interface for Spin. It provides an integrating windowing environment for writing Promela models and carrying out virtually all Spin functions in a user friendly manner. The outputs are displayed in various ways, among which are Message Sequence Charts.

Discrete Time Extensions of Promela and Spin. In the timed model that is used in discrete-time Promela and Spin, time is divided into slices indexed by natural numbers. The actions are then framed into those slices, obtaining in that way a good *quantitative* estimation for the intervals between the events belonging to different slices. Within a slice however, we can only have a qualitative relation between the events, as in the untimed case. The elapsed time between the events is measured in ticks of a global digital clock which is increased by one with every such a tick. The actions between two consecutive ticks have the same integer time stamp and only a qualitative time ordering between them can be established. (This model of time corresponds to *fictitious-clock model* from [1] or *digital-clock model* from [9].)

To model timing features, standard Promela is extended with a new variable type timer corresponding to discrete-time countdown timers. Two new additional statements, set and expire, that operate on timers are added. Their syntax is set(tmr, val) and expire(tmr), where tmr is a timer variable and val is of type short integer. These two basic statements are sufficient for modeling all timing features of the system. For instance, a time interval of val clock ticks is denoted in a straightforward way by assigning the value val to a timer with set and waiting with expire until its value becomes 0. Once we have set and expire it is easy to derive new compound statements as Promela macro definitions. For example, using iteration with guarded commands an unbounded nondeterministic delay can be modeled. This is necessary for the modeling of actions that can happen in any time slice. In a similar way, a bounded delay up to val clock ticks can be realized, as well as a delay within a time interval. The two basic statements and the macros that implement the timing features are defined in dtime.h, a header file which is included at the beginning of each discrete-time Promela model. The extension is fully compatible with the standard package and all properties that are on Spin's repertoire can be also validated for discrete-time models. Besides qualitative properties, a broad range of quantitative timing properties can be verified, by using boolean expressions on timer values in the assertions and LTL formulae.

Discrete-time Promela models can be regarded as parallel compositions (networks) of *automata with timers* from [6] assuming our discrete-time instead of the dense-time model, or their equivalent *timed automata* from [1].

Experimental Results. We have tested the implementation on various models known in the literature like the Train Gate Controller, the Seitz Circuit [15], the Parallel Acknowledgment with Retransmission Protocol [14, 12], and the Bounded Retransmission Protocol [7, 5, 4]. We give the results of Fischer's mutual exclusion protocol, which has become a standard benchmark for tools that implement timing. The version of the protocol that was verified is a translation of the same model written in Promela with dense time of [15], with the same timing parameters. The obtained results for the verification of the mutual exclusion property are shown in the table below (N is the number of processes). All tests were performed on a Sun SPARC Station 5 with 64 MBytes of memory. Besides partial order reduction (POR) we used as an additional option *minimized automata*, a technique for reduction of the state space recently included in the standard Spin distribution. In the *options* column of the table, "n", "r" and "ma" denote verifications without POR, with POR, and with POR together with minimized automata, respectively.

N	option	states	transitions	memory [MB]	time [s]
	n	528	876	1.453	0.1
2	r	378	490	1.453	0.1
	ma	378	490	0.342	0.2
	n	8425	10536	1.761	0.8
3	r	3813	4951	1.596	0.4
	ma	3813	4951	0.445	0.3
	n	128286	373968	7.085	15.5
4	r	34157	44406	3.132	2.8
	ma	34157	44406	0.650	33.7
5	r	288313	377032	17.570	36.2
	ma	288313	377032	1.059	332.5
6	ma	2.35×10^6	3.09×10^6	2.118	6246.1

As expected, the state space growth is exponential and we were able to validate the model without using POR up to 4 processes. For 6 processes even POR was not enough and it had to be strengthened with minimized automata. The profit from POR is obvious and even becomes more evident as the number of processes grows. While for $N = 2$ the number of states is reduced to 72% compared to the one in the full state space and the transitions are reduced to 56% of the original number, for $N = 4$ the reduction increases to 27% and 12% for states and transitions, respectively. It is difficult to compare our implementation with the related tools (e.g. [2], [13]), mainly because they are based on a different time model. Although often said to be of the same theoretical complexity as dense time (e.g. [1]), it seems that in practice discrete time often shows an advantage [2]. For instance, having in mind that the property that was checked was a qualitative one, for which discrete time (digital clocks) suffices [9], one can safely say that after $N = 4$ our implementation has better performance in the case of Fischer's protocol compared to [15]. In fact, for $N = 5$ the validator from [15] runs out of memory. Obviously, POR is the decisive factor, because without POR our implementation is also incapable to handle cases for $N > 4$.

An encouraging result is the successful validation of the Bounded Retransmission Protocol, which is a simplified version of an industrial protocol used by Philips. Our verification has the advantage that it can be completely done in Spin, unlike the one in [5] that uses a combination of Uppaal (for the timing properties) and Spin (for consistency of the specification).

Currently, we are working on an extension of Promela and Spin with dense time based on region automata [1], using essentially the same approach as for discrete time. Another possible direction for further development of the tool is the modeling of an interesting class of linear hybrid systems representable by discrete-time rectangular hybrid automata [8]. The first results obtained by the prototype (implemented entirely as Promela macro definitions, without any change of the Spin's source code) are promising [3].

Availability. The tool, together with some additional information and several examples, is available on request from the authors, from http://www.win.tue.nl/~dragan, or via anonymous ftp from ftp.win.tue.nl/pub/techreports/dragan/dtspin. The discrete time extension is portable to all the platforms as the standard Spin distribution - i.e. Unix systems and Windows 95/Windows NT PC's.

References

1. Alur, R., Dill, D.L., *A Theory of Timed Automata*, Theoretical Computer Science, 126, pp.183-235, 1994.
2. Alur, R., Kurshan, R.P., *Timing Analysis in Cospan*, Hybrid Systems III, LNCS 1066, pp.220-231, Springer, 1996.
3. Bošnački, D., *Towards Modelling of Hybrid Systems in Promela and Spin*, Third International Workshop on Formal Methods in Industrial Critical Systems FMICS'98, 1998
4. Dams, D., Gerth, R., *Bounded Retransmission Protocol Revisited*, Second International Workshop on Verification of Infinite Systems, Infinity'97, 1997
5. D'Argenio, P. R., Katoen, J.-P., Ruys, T., Tretmans, J., *The Bounded Retransmission Protocol Must Be on Time!*, TACAS'97, 1997
6. Dill, D., *Timing Assumptions and Verification of Finite-State Concurrent Systems*, CAV'89, LNCS 407, Springer, 1989
7. Groote, J. F., van de Pol, J., *A Bounded Retransmission Protocol for Large Data Packets*, in Wirsing, M., Nivat, M., ed., Algebraic Methodology and Software Technology, LCNS 1101, pp. 536-550, Springer-Verlag, 1996
8. Henzinger, T. A., Kopke, P. W., *Discrete-Time Control for Rectangular Automata*, Proceedings of the 24th International Colloquium on Automata, Languages and Programming (ICALP 1997), LNCS 1256, pp. 582-593, Springer-Verlag, 1997
9. Henzinger, T. A., Manna, Z., Pnueli, A., *What good are digital clocks?*, Proceedings of the ICALP'92, LNCS 623, pp.545-558, Springer-Verlag,1992.
10. Holzmann, G. J., *Design and Validation of Communication Protocols*, Prentice Hall, 1991. Also: http://netlib.bell-labs.com/netlib/spin/whatispin.html
11. Kars, P., *Formal Methods in the Design of Storm Surge Barrier Control System*, Hand-outs of School on Embedded Systems, Veldhoven, The Netherlands, 1996
12. Klusener, A. S., *Models and Axioms for a Fragment of Real Time Process Algebra*, Ph. D. Thesis, Eindhoven University of Technology, 1993
13. Larsen, K. G., Pettersson, P., Yi, W., *UPPAAL: Status & Developments*, Computer Aided Verification CAV 97, LNCS 1254, pp.456-459, Springer-Verlag, 1992.
14. Tanenbaum, A., *Computer Networks*, Prentice Hall, 1989
15. Tripakis, S., Courcoubetis, C., *Extending Promela and Spin for Real Time*, TACAS '96, LCNS 1055, Springer Verlag, 1996

MOBY/PLC – Graphical Development of PLC-Automata *

Josef Tapken and Henning Dierks

University of Oldenburg – Department of Computer Science
P.O.Box 2503, D-26111 Oldenburg, Germany
Fax: +49 441 798-2965
E-Mail: {tapken,dierks}@informatik.uni-oldenburg.de

Abstract. MOBY/PLC is a graphical design tool for PLC-Automata, a special class of hierarchical real-time automata suitable for the description of distributed real-time systems that are implementable on a widely used hardware platform, so-called Programmable Logic Controllers (PLCs). In this paper we sketch the modelling language in use and some features of MOBY/PLC, like several validation methods and code generation.

1   Introduction

MOBY/PLC is a graphical design tool for distributed real-time systems which is based upon a formal description technique called PLC-Automata [6].

This class of hierarchical real-time automata is suitable (but not restricted) to the description of the behaviour of *Programmable Logic Controllers* (PLC) that are often used to solve real-time controlling problems. The automata are tailored to a structural compilation into executable PLC-code and are provided with a formal denotational semantics in *Duration Calculus* [3] as well as an operational semantics in terms of *Timed Automata* [1]. Both semantics are consistent and allow formal reasoning about properties of PLC-Automata [7].

The language of PLC-Automata, developed in the UniForM-project [8], has been applied to real-world case studies of the industrial partner, which produces tram- and railway control systems.

This paper gives a survey of MOBY/PLC by introducing its implemented modelling language (Sec. 2), and by describing some of its features (Sec. 3).

2   PLC-Automata

Programmable Logic Controllers (PLC) are real-time controllers with a cyclic behaviour. In each cycle the PLC polls input values from sensors or other PLCs,

---

* This research was partially supported by the German Ministry for Education and Research (BMBF) as part of the project UniForM under grant No. FKZ 01 IS 521 B3 and partially by the Leibniz Programme of the Deutsche Forschungsgemeinschaft (DFG) under grant No. Ol 98/1-1.

computes the new local state, and generates output values for actuators (or other PLCs). To deal with real-time problems, PLCs are enriched by a convenient timer concept.

A PLC-Automaton describes the behaviour of a PLC by an extended finite state machine with three categories of variables, namely input, local, and output variables. A transition is labelled by a condition on these variables and a list of assignments to local and output variables. In every cycle a PLC-Automaton updates its input variables from the environment and performs (exactly) one transition according to the actual state and values of variables. The execution of a transition may be prohibited according to a state label which consists of a time value d ($\in \mathbb{R}_{\geq 0}$) and a Boolean expression over the input variables. A state can only be left if it is held for longer than for d time units or the state expression evaluates to false.

In order to increase their expressiveness and structuring facilities PLC-Automata are enhanced by a hierarchy concept which is based on state refinement, i.e. a state can represent a set of substates and its label can also restrict the outgoing transitions of the substates.

A system specification consists of a network of PLC-Automata which communicate asynchronously with each other through channels. Each channel links an output variable of one automaton to an input variable of another, i.e. communication is performed implicitly by updating every cycle the input variables of a PLC-Automaton with the current values of the corresponding output variables. The system network may also be structured hierarchically.

In [5] the implemented version of PLC-Automata is related to its formal definition. All extensions implemented in MOBY/PLC, like variables and different kinds of transitions, are interpreted as abbreviations and can be unfolded.

Fig. 1 shows a small part of a case study on securing a Single-tracked Line Segment (SLS) in MOBY/PLC. The case study is a topic within the UniForM-project and deals with the correct control of a single-tracked railway line by distributed PLCs. The right window of Fig. 1 contains the description of the system network and the left window gives the behavioural description of one component in terms of a PLC-Automaton. For further informations about the case study see [5].

3   The MOBY/PLC-Tool

An overview of the main components which are currently implemented in the MOBY/PLC-tool is given in Fig. 2. The central part of the tool is an interactive graphical editor for specifying a real-time system (i). Since the architectural part as well as the behavioural part of a specification may be structured hierarchically the editor comprises several different subeditors, e.g. system editors to describe the network of PLC-Automata or editors to specify automata and subautomata (see Fig. 1).

In MOBY/PLC there are three ways to validate a given specification (ii, iii, iv). A simulator (ii) is able to execute a single or a set of PLC-Automata and to

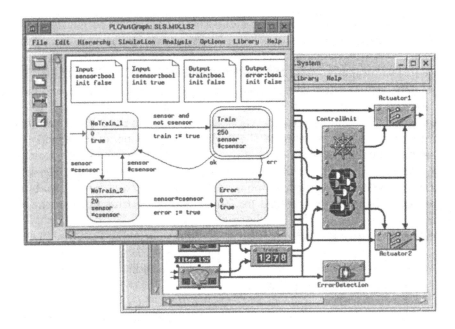

Fig. 1. SLS case study in MOBY/PLC

visualize its results directly in the graphical specification. The simulator is designed to support the interactive simulation of small modules as well as extensive tests of the whole specification in background mode [9].

Special analysis algorithms (iii) which are based on the Duration Calculus semantics of PLC-Automata can be used to statically calculate certain properties of an automaton, e.g. its reaction time on a given combination of inputs.

The Timed Automata semantics defines how to compile a PLC-Automaton into a Timed Automaton. In order to use existing model checking systems for Timed Automata, we have currently implemented two compilers (iv) into the format of the Kronos tool [4] and of Uppaal [2]. The second compiler exploits the fact that Uppaal is able to handle automata extended by variables.

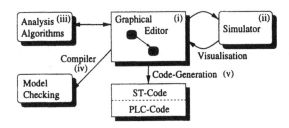

Fig. 2. Components of MOBY/PLC

Furthermore, a given specification can be translated automatically by a structural compilation into a special programming language for PLCs called ST (Structured Text)(v). By the use of commercial compilers the ST-code can be transformed into runnable source code for PLCs.

4 Conclusion

In this paper we have sketched the modelling language and the features of the design tool MOBY/PLC.

Although MOBY/PLC is already usable there are several extensions we are planning to implement. E.g. we want to evaluate and visualize the results of background runs of the simulator. In this context we need a formal description of the environment of a system. This can e.g. be achieved by a non-deterministic variant of PLC-Automata. Furthermore, it seems to be promising to expand the static analysis by further algorithms which calculate interesting properties based on the structure of a PLC-Automaton.

Currently a graphical editor for Object-Z specifications is developed. This editor should be integrated into MOBY/PLC in order to use Object-Z for the description of data aspects in PLC-Automata.

Acknowledgements. The authors thank H. Fleischhack, E.-R. Olderog, and the other members of the "semantics group" in Oldenburg for fruitful discussions on the subject of this paper.

References

1. R. Alur and D.L. Dill. A theory of timed automata. *Theoretical Computer Science*, 126:183–235, 1994.
2. J. Bengtsson, K.G. Larsen, F. Larsson, P. Pettersson, and Wang Yi. Uppaal – a Tool Suite for Automatic Verification of Real-Time Systems. In *Hybrid Systems III*, volume 1066 of *LNCS*, pages 232–243. Springer Verlag, 1996.
3. Zhou Chaochen, C.A.R. Hoare, and A.P. Ravn. A Calculus of Durations. *Inform. Proc. Letters*, 40/5:269–276, 1991.
4. C. Daws, A. Olivero, S. Tripakis, and S. Yovine. The tool Kronos. In *Hybrid Systems III*, volume 1066 of *LNCS*, pages 208–219. Springer Verlag, 1996.
5. H. Dierks and J. Tapken. Tool-Supported Hierarchical Design of Distributed Real-Time Systems. In *Proceedings of Euromicro 98*, pages 222–229. IEEE, 1998.
6. Henning Dierks. PLC-Automata: A New Class of Implementable Real-Time Automata. In *ARTS'97*, LNCS. Springer Verlag, May 1997.
7. Henning Dierks, Ansgar Fehnker, Angelika Mader, and Frits Vaandrager. Operational and Logical Semantics for Polling Real-Time Systems. In *FTRTFT'98*, LNCS. Springer Verlag, September 1998. to appear.
8. B. Krieg-Brückner, J. Peleska, E.-R. Olderog, et al. UniForM — Universal Formal Methods Workbench. In *Statusseminar des BMBF Softwaretechnologie*, pages 357–378. BMBF, Berlin, 1996.
9. Josef Tapken. Interactive and Compilative Simulation of PLC-Automata. In W. Hahn and A. Lehmann, editors, *Simulation in Industry, ESS'97*, pages 552 – 556. SCS, 1997.

Predictability in Critical Systems

Gérard Le Lann

INRIA, Projet REFLECS, BP 105
F-78153 Le Chesnay Cedex, France
E-mail: Gerard.Le_Lann@inria.fr

Abstract. Predictability is crucial in critical applications and systems. Therefore, we examine sources of uncertainty for each of the four phases that span a project lifecycle, from initial problem capture, to system implementation, when conducted according to proof-based system engineering principles. We explore the concept of coverage applied to problems, solutions, assumptions, along with a generic problem that arises with critical applications such as, e.g., air traffic control/management, namely the real-time uniform atomic broadcast problem. We examine two design styles, namely asynchronous and synchronous solutions, and compare the resulting assumptions as well as their coverages. The central issues of overloads and timing failures that arise with synchronous models are investigated in detail.

1 Introduction

We consider X-critical applications and systems, where X can be any such qualifier as, e.g., life, mission, environment, business or asset. Intuitively, an application or a system is critical whenever violating a specification may lead to "catastrophes". Therefore, levels of "confidence" set for such applications or systems are extremely high. For instance, in the case of air traffic control/air traffic management (ATC/ATM), accumulated time durations of inaccessibility to critical services should not exceed 3 seconds a year, which translates into an upper bound of 10^{-7} on acceptable unavailability of critical services. With stock trading or with some defense applications, response times of less than 2 seconds (a timeliness property) are required, 10^{-4} being an upper bound on acceptable rates of lateness. Acceptable failure rates of processors for urban trains should be less than 10^{-12} per hour.

Let Ω be some assertion. Coverage(Ω) is defined as the probability that Ω is true. Assumption coverage has been introduced in [17]. Assumptions relate to the environment where a system is to be deployed or to implementation. We extend the notion of coverage to properties, to problems and to solutions. Such coverages are goals set for designers. For instance, with ATC/ATM, coverage (*availability property for critical services*) should be *shown to be* as high as $1 - 10^{-7}$. Note that an assumption coverage also is a goal set for those who are in charge of "implementing the assumption".

Endowing critical systems with specified properties that hold with such high coverages is a notoriously difficult task. Most often, critical application problems translate into combined real-time, distributed, fault-tolerant, computing problems. Only a small subset of such problems has been explored so far.

There are many examples of systems that have failed to meet such stringent requirements. There is no general agreement on what are the dominant causes of such failures. In the recent past, widespread belief has been that software - noted S/W - must have become the major cause of failures, given that hardware - noted H/W - is so "reliable". However, a growing number of analyses and studies demonstrate that such is not the case. For instance, a study of the failure reports concerning the US Public Switched Telephone Network (PSTN) establishes that S/W caused less downtime (2%) than any other source of failure except vandalism [8]. Overloads are the dominant cause (44%) of downtime measured as the product *number of customers affected·outage duration*. Overloads that occur "too frequently" result into "bad" coverages of such properties as availability or timeliness, which is barely acceptable for the PSTN, and certainly unacceptable for a business-critical system. It turns out that a vast majority of faults that cause overloads are neither S/W originated nor H/W originated. They are system engineering faults.

We have previously argued that, as is the case with H/W engineering and, more recently, with S/W engineering, proof-based approaches (based upon informal or, better, formal methods) should become the rule in system engineering [10]. In this paper, we will make the (extraordinary) assumption that S/W components and H/W components are faultless, i.e. that they actually implement their specifications. Systems would still fail, for the following reasons: (i) specifications may be flawed, due to faulty design and/or dimensioning decisions, (ii) residual assumptions may be violated at run-time.

Ideally, only the initial application problem specification would possibly turn out to be flawed, given that the future cannot be predicted with certainty. Any subsequent specification should be correctly derived from this one, via system design and dimensioning decisions assorted with proofs. With stochastic system engineering (SE) approaches, coverages are involved with design and dimensioning decisions. In this paper, we consider deterministic SE approaches (deterministic algorithms, deterministic analyses). Then, only the coverage of the initial specification does matter.

With critical applications, deterministic proof-based SE is appropriate for an additional reason: Proofs of correctness must be established for worst-case operational conditions, worst-cases being embodied, albeit not explicitly, in an application problem specification.

Residual assumptions (RA) are those needed to prove implementation correctness. Arbitrarily fast faultless sequential processors, or byzantine processors, or absence of H/W metastable states, or bounded broadcast channel slot times, are examples of common RAs. Their coverages can be computed or estimated, by resorting to, e.g., analytical modelling or statistical analysis. Only RAs that have "very high" coverages are acceptable for critical systems - clearly not the case with the first example. Consequently, provably correct system design and dimensioning phases must be conducted until the RAs are acceptable.

Under our assumption, and proof-based SE principles being followed, the only coverages - i.e. uncertainties - left relate to, (i) the capture of an application problem and, (ii) the implementation of residual assumptions.

The basic principles of proof-based SE are introduced in Section 2. In Section 3, we examine sources of uncertainty for each of four important phases that span a project life-cycle, from initial problem capture, to system implementation. Elegant solutions, or efficient solutions, may rest on residual assumptions that have low coverages. For the sake of illustration, in Section 4, we consider a generic problem that arises with critical applications such as, e.g., ATC/ATM, namely the real-time uniform atomic broadcast problem, examine two design styles (asynchronous and synchronous solutions), and compare resulting residual assumptions.

This leads us to revisit popular justifications of asynchronous models, as well as popular approaches to the implementation of synchronous assumptions, to find out that some have low coverages. The central issue of timing failures is explored in Section 5. It is shown that dominant causes of timing failures, namely overloads and excessive failure densities, can be dealt with more carefully than is usually asserted.

2 Proof-Based System Engineering

The essential goal pursued with proof-based SE is as follows: Starting from some initial description of an application problem, i.e. a description of end user/client requirements and assumptions, to produce a global and implementable specification of a system (noted S in the sequel), along with proofs that system design and system dimensioning decisions made to arrive at that specification do satisfy the specification of the computer science problem "hidden" within the application problem.

The notation $\langle Y \rangle$ (resp. $[Z]$) is used in the sequel to refer to a specification of a problem Y (resp. a solution Z). Notation $\langle y \rangle$ (resp. $[z]$) is used to refer to a specification of a set of variables which parameterize problem Y (resp. solution Z). The term "specification" is used to refer to any complete set of unambiguous statements - in some human language, in some formalized notation, in some formal language.

Proof-based SE addresses those three essential phases that come first in a project life-cycle, namely the problem capture phase, the system design phase, and the system dimensioning phase (see figures 1 and 2, where symbol $\Rightarrow$ stands for "results in"). Proof-based SE also addresses phases concerned with changes that may impact a system after it has been fielded, e.g., modifications of the initial problem, availability of new off-the-shelf products. Such phases simply consist in repeating some of the three phases introduced above, and which precede phases covered by other engineering disciplines (e.g., S/W engineering), which serve to implement system engineering decisions.

2.1 The Problem Capture Phase

This phase is concerned with, (i) the translation of an application problem description into $\langle A \rangle$, which specifies the generic application problem under consideration and, (ii) the translation of $\langle A \rangle$ into $\langle X \rangle$, a specification of the generic computer science problem that matches $\langle A \rangle$. A generic problem is an invariant for the entire duration of a project.

Specifications $\langle A \rangle$ and $\langle X \rangle$ are jointly produced by a client and a designer, the latter being in charge of identifying which are the models and properties commonly used in computer science whose semantics match those of the application problem. Consequently, a specification $\langle X \rangle$ actually is a pair $\{\langle m.X \rangle, \langle p.X \rangle\}$, where m stands for models and p stands for properties.

For example, statement "*workstations used by air traffic controllers should either work correctly or stop functioning*" in $\langle p.A \rangle$ would translate as "*workstations dependability property is observability = stop failure*" in $\langle p.X \rangle$. See Section 4 for examples of models and properties.

Variables appear in specifications $\langle A \rangle$ and $\langle X \rangle$. Let us focus on $\langle X \rangle$. Notation $\langle x \rangle$ is used to refer to a specification of those variables in $\langle X \rangle$ that are left unvalued. As for $\langle X \rangle$, $\langle x \rangle$ is a pair $\{\langle m.x \rangle, \langle p.x \rangle\}$.

$$\{\text{description of an application problem}\} \Rightarrow \langle A \rangle \left| \begin{array}{l} \Rightarrow \langle X \rangle \\ \Rightarrow \langle a \rangle \\ \Rightarrow \langle x \rangle \end{array} \right.$$

Fig. 1. Problem Capture

The genericity degree of $\langle X \rangle$ may vary from 0 ($\langle x \rangle$ is empty) to ∞ (every variable in $\langle X \rangle$ appears in $\langle x \rangle$). Of course, any degree of genericity has an associated cost and a payoff.

2.2 The System Design Phase

This phase is to be conducted by a designer. A design phase has a pair $\{\langle X \rangle, \langle x \rangle\}$ as an input. It covers all the design stages needed to arrive at $[S]$, a modular specification of a generic solution (a generic system), the completion of each design stage being conditioned on fulfilling correctness proof obligations. A design phase is conducted by exploiting state-of-the-art in various areas of computer science (e.g., computing system architectures, algorithms, models, properties), in various theories (e.g., serializability, scheduling, game, complexity), as well as by applying appropriate proof techniques, which techniques depend on the types of problems under consideration.

More precisely, one solves a problem $\{\langle m.X(.)\rangle, \langle p.X(.)\rangle\}$ raised at some design stage (.) by going through the following three steps: specification of an architectural and an algorithmic solution designed for some modular decomposition, establishment of proofs of properties and verification that a design correctness proof obligation is satisfied, specification of a dimensioning oracle.

Subproblems result from a modular decomposition. Fulfilling a design correctness proof obligation (see Section 2.6) guarantees that if every subproblem is correctly solved, then the initial problem is correctly solved as well by "concatenating" the individual solutions, which eliminates those combinatorial problems that arise whenever such proof obligations are ignored. And so on. Consequently, a design phase has its stages organized as a tree structure. By the virtue of the uninterrupted tree of proofs (that every design decision is correct), $[S]$ - the union of those specifications that sit at the leaves of a design tree - provably correctly satisfies $\langle X \rangle$. If $\langle X \rangle$ is a correct translation of $\langle A \rangle$, then, by transitivity, $\langle A \rangle$ is provably correctly solved with $[S]$.

Clearly, this approach is based on compositionality principles very similar to those that underlie some formal methods in the S/W engineering field.

Every module of $[S]$ is deemed implementable, or is known (in a provable manner) to be implemented by some procurable product or is handed over to some other designer.

$$\{\langle X \rangle, \langle x \rangle\} \left| \begin{array}{l} \Rightarrow [S] \\ \Rightarrow [s] \\ \Rightarrow [oracle.S] \end{array} \right.$$

Fig. 2. System Design

Another output of a design phase is a specification of a (system-wide) dimensioning oracle - denoted $[oracle.S]$ - which includes, in particular, a set of constraints called (system-wide) feasibility conditions. Feasibility conditions (FCs) are analytical expressions derived from correctness proofs. For a given architectural and algorithmic solution, they define a set of scenarios that, with certainty, includes all worst-case scenarios that can be deployed by "adversary" $\langle m.X(.)\rangle$. FCs link together these worst-case scenarios with computable functions that serve to model properties stated in $\langle p.X(.)\rangle$. Of course, $[oracle.S]$ must be implemented in order to conduct subsequent system dimensioning phases. From a practical viewpoint, $[oracle.S]$ is a specification of a $\{\langle X \rangle, [S]\}$-dependent component of a more general system dimensioning tool.

Lack of FCs is an important source of failures for critical systems, as demonstrated by, e.g., the system shutdowns experienced with the Mars PathFinder probe.

2.3   The System Dimensioning Phase

The purpose of a dimensioning phase is to find a valuation $V([s])$, i.e. a quantification of system S unvalued variables, such as, e.g., sizes of memory buffers, sizes of waiting queues, processors speeds, databuses throughputs, number of databuses, processors redundancy degrees, total number of processors.

$V([s])$ must satisfy a particular valuation $V(\langle x \rangle)$, i.e. a particular quantification of the captured problem-centric models and properties, which is - directly or indirectly - provided by a client.

$V(\langle x \rangle)$: input to $oracle.S$ $V([s])$: output from $oracle.S$

Fig. 3. System Dimensioning

One or several dimensioning phases may have to be run until $[oracle.S]$ declares that there is a quantified S that solves a proposed quantified problem $\{\langle X \rangle, V(\langle x \rangle)\}$ (or declares that the quantified problem considered is not feasible). How many phases need to be run directly depends on the genericity of $[S]$. Consider for example that $[s]$ is close to empty, which happens whenever it is decided a priori that S must be based on specific off-the-shelf or proprietary products. The good news are that a small number of dimensioning phases need to be run, given that many system variables are valued a priori. The bad news are that the oracle may find out (rapidly) that the proposed problem quantification is not feasible (e.g., some deadlines are always missed), no matter which $V([s])$ is considered.

The pair $\{[S], V([s])\}$ is a modular specification of a system S that provably solves problem $\{\langle X \rangle, V(\langle x \rangle)\}$. Modules of $\{[S], V([s])\}$ are contracts between a (prime) designer and those (co/sub) designers in charge of implementing S.

2.4   The System Implementation Phase

If deemed implementable, the set $\{[S], V([s])\}$ is the borderline, i.e. the interface, between system engineering on the one hand, S/W engineering, electrical engineering and other engineering disciplines on the other hand.

S/W engineering serves the purpose of producing correct executable implementations of given specifications, which result from system engineering work. It follows that it is useless or, at best, marginally productive to apply formal methods in the S/W engineering field without applying proof-based methods in the system engineering field, for the obvious reason that provably correct S/W implementations of specifications that are flawed in the first place can only lead to incorrect systems.

Too often, system failures due to SE faults are mistakenly believed to originate in S/W design or S/W implementation errors. See [8], [12] and [13] for counter-examples.

2.5 Final Comments

Models, properties, and algorithms, can be organized into classes. Furthermore, it is possible to structure every class after a hierarchy or a partial order. See [17] for an example with the class of failure models. We will use the terminology introduced in [10]. An element that precedes another one in a hierarchy or a partial order will be said to be *weaker* than its successor (successor is *stronger*). As for models, this is so for the reason that the set of predecessor runs (e.g., behaviors, traces) is included in the set of successor runs. For instance, the *byzantine failure* model [9] is stronger (albeit more "permissive") than the *omission failure* model (which is more "restrictive"). Byzantine failure behaviors include omission-only failure behaviors. The converse is not true.

This is so for properties for the reason that they result from explicitly restricting runs to those of interest (unlike models). For instance, *causal atomic broadcast* is stronger than *FIFO broadcast* [6]. Similarly, *bounded jitters* is stronger than *latest termination deadlines* [10].

Design correctness proof obligations result from class structuring. A solution that solves a problem $\{\langle m.X \rangle, \langle p.X \rangle\}$ is a correct design solution for a problem $\{\langle m.X' \rangle, \langle p.X' \rangle\}$ if $\langle m.X \rangle$ (resp. $\langle p.X \rangle$) is stronger than $\langle m.X' \rangle$ (resp. $\langle p.X' \rangle$). Given some appropriate metrics, one can similarly define dimensioning correctness proof obligations. See [10] for more details.

Note that there are differences between the various sets of assumptions involved with a pair $\{\langle X \rangle, [S]\}$.

The specification $\langle m.X \rangle$ (resp. $V(\langle m.x \rangle)$) states *problem* (resp. *valuation of problem*) assumptions. In many cases, these specifications are predictions on future operational conditions, which must have some coverages.

Specification $[m.S]$ (resp. $V([m.s])$) states *design* (resp. *valuation of design*) residual assumptions (design tree *leaves*), which are to be "implemented". Note that they are the only design (and valuation of design) assumptions whose coverages must be estimated. Indeed, design assumptions embodied in a design tree (design tree *nodes*) are necessarily correctly "implemented", as well as their valuations, a result of fulfilling design and dimensioning correctness proof obligations.

Let $C(X, V(x))$ be the coverage of quantified problem $\{\langle X \rangle, V(\langle x \rangle)\}$. In other words, $Pr\{\langle m.X \rangle$ or $V(\langle m.x \rangle)$ is violated$\} \leq 1 - C(X, V(x))$. This is the coverage of predictions - i.e. assumptions - relative to some future operational environment.

To assess the intrinsic quality of a solution, shown to enforce properties $\langle p.X \rangle$ valued as per $V(\langle p.x \rangle)$, one needs to eliminate from our scope of consideration those uncertainties due to the impossibility of telling the future. The validity of predictions regarding models or their valuations is not discussed. Coverage $C(S, V(s))$, which is the coverage of quantified solution $\{[S], V([s])\}$ for quantified problem $\{\langle X \rangle, V(\langle x \rangle)\}$, serves this purpose.

In other words, conditional probability $Pr\{\langle p.X \rangle$ or $V(\langle p.x \rangle)$ is violated $\mid$ neither $\langle m.X \rangle$ nor $V(\langle m.x \rangle)$ is violated$\} \leq 1 - C(S, V(s))$.

3   Sources of Uncertainty

3.1   Capture Phase

In any of the classes of models that are considered under a deterministic ap-proach, there is one model that is "extreme", in the sense that it reflects a fully unrestricted "adversary" (e.g., the asynchronous computational model, the byzantine failure model, the multimodal arbitrary event arrival model). Picking up these models has a price: One may run into impossibility results or one may end up with "demanding" feasibility conditions (which translates into costly systems). The beauty of such models is that they are "safe": No real future operational conditions can be worse than what is captured with these models. Therefore, the issue of estimating coverages is void with such models. Picking up models weaker than "extreme" ones involves a risk: Operational conditions may be "stronger than" assumed during a capture phase. Again, this is unavoid-able, given that we cannot "tell the future". Picking up the appropriate models for $\langle m.A \rangle$ and $\langle m.X \rangle$ boils down to making tradeoffs between having coverage $C(X, V(x))$ sufficiently close to 1 and retaining models as weak as acceptable.

As for early valuations of problem-centric models (via $V(\langle m.x \rangle)$), comments made for the dimensioning phase apply (see further).

3.2   Design Phase

Coverages do not apply to deterministic design approaches. Properties such as, e.g., serializability, timeliness, are either not ensured or they are, under specific feasibility conditions. There are no "proof coverages" for proofs of properties or feasibility conditions (e.g., lower bounds on a redundancy degree or on a number of modules, upper bounds on response times), even if solutions considered are "complex", possibly due to the fact that strong models appear in $\langle m.X \rangle$.

Fulfilling design correctness proof obligations guarantees that properties and models considered during a design phase are at least as strong as those stated in $\langle X \rangle$. Hence, there are no coverages involved with whether $[S]$ solves $\langle X \rangle$.

This is not necessarily the case with popular design styles. For example, with the problem described in Section 4, one ends up with having to "implement" a synchronous communication module, referred to as Net. Picking up the periodic arrival model for messages submitted to Net would be invalid, given that some of the tasks which generate these messages are activated according to a unimodal arbitrary model, which is stronger than the periodic model. It is legal only to consider unimodal or multimodal arbitrary models. Finding optimal or "good" solutions under such models is definitely more intricate than when considering periodic arrivals, an assumption made by many authors, presumably for the reason that these models are more tractable.

Residual design assumptions $[m.S]$ and $V([m.s])$ must be shown to be im-plementable with "good" coverages. There is an inverse relationship between a "design effort level" and subsequent "implementation effort level".

To continue with the same example: To build Net in such a way that, under unimodal arbitrary arrivals, an upper bound on message delays does hold is not just an "implementation concern". Stated differently: Coverage of residual assumption "synchronous Net exists" is close to 0. This calls for further design work. See [7] for an example where the Hard Real-Time Distributed Multiaccess problem raised with Net is solved considering Ethernets or CableTV networks, technologies whose coverages can be accurately estimated, given their widespread usage, and made very close to 1, given that these technologies are well mastered.

3.3 Dimensioning Phase

Valuations of problem-centric models (via $V(\langle m.x \rangle)$) have related coverages. Assignment of a value to a number of byzantine failures has a coverage, whereas the byzantine model itself has no related coverage.

Under a proof-based SE approach, physical dimensionings of systems have no coverages associated to them. Those numerical values that appear in $V([s])$ specify a "safe" physical dimensioning of a system, a by-product of checking the feasibility of some problem-centric quantification $V(\langle x \rangle)$. Such dimensionings are certainly sufficient (ideally, they should be necessary and sufficient).

Consequently, there are no coverages involved with whether $V([s])$ satisfies $V(\langle x \rangle)$.

Note that, with critical applications, valuation of $C(S, V(s))$ is usually "frozen" by a client when conducting a capture phase. Hence, most often, $C(S, V(s))$ appears in $\langle p.X \rangle$ only (not in $\langle p.x \rangle$).

3.4 Implementation Phase

Which are the coverages involved with implementing $\{[S], V([s])\}$? Recall our assumption that, thanks to some S/W and H/W formal methods, implementation of the architectural and algorithmic solutions embodied in $\{[S], V([s])\}$ is faultless. Given that, as argued previously, the design and the dimensioning of a solution can be faultless, the only issue left is that of implementing residual assumptions $[m.S]$ and $V([m.s])$.

Let ϕ be the smallest of the coverages involved with residual assumptions. It follows that $C(S, V(s)) = \phi$ under proof-based SE approaches.

It derives from this that it is always safer to consider strong models, which bring ϕ - as well as $C(X, V(x))$ - arbitrarily close to 1. For instance, the byzantine failure model or the asynchronous model cannot be "violated" at run-time, and it is very easy to implement them correctly. However, picking up such models may not be feasible because of, e.g., impossibility results, or may be unjustifiable on financial grounds, given that dimensionings - i.e. system costs - may be linear or superlinear functions of models strength.

Conversely, picking up weak (i.e. restrictive) models - while still satisfying design correctness proof obligations - lowers ϕ or $C(X, V(x))$. This is a source of concern with some conventional approaches to the design and construction of critical systems.

4   A Generic Problem with Critical Applications

For the purpose of illustration, let us examine the real-time uniform atomic broadcast problem, noted $\langle RTUAB \rangle$. This problem arises with applications (e.g., ATC/ATM, stock trading, "risky" process control, transportation, protective defense) that need to be run over distributed and/or redundant real-time systems, for the purpose of guaranteeing continuous and timely delivery of critical services despite partial failures.

For instance, in an ATC/ATM cell, an air traffic controller whose workstation "goes down" has immediate access to another workstation - by physical displacement - which should display exactly what would have been displayed by the failed workstation. Such failures "impacting" a given air traffic controller, i.e. surveillance of a given portion of the sky, may occur a number of times before workstations are repaired or replaced with new ones.

Given that within distributed and/or redundant systems, delays are variable, that concurrency is unavoidable - decisions may be made concurrently by different pilots, by different controllers - and that failures impact portions of a system differently and at different times, it is far from being trivial to ensure that redundant workstations do behave identically at all times, or that common knowledge (e.g., of what the "current sky state" is) is indeed maintained among all workstations, in due time, within a cell.

Non real-time versions of this problem have been considered first, such as $\langle UAB \rangle$, the uniform atomic broadcast problem (see [6]) which, informally, is as follows. In a system of processors, some of which may stop unexpectedly and anonymously, *Messages* are broadcast by processors, possibly concurrently, by invoking an Atomic Broadcast (*Message*) primitive, noted ABroadcast. Correct processors must deliver the same *Messages* in the same order. That is, *Messages* are Atomically Delivered, noted ADelivered.

Let $\mathcal{A}$ be an algorithmic solution. $\langle UAB \rangle$ can be solved in various ways, considering computational models and algorithms ranging from synchronous to asynchronous.

Simply stated, in synchronous models - as defined in [4] and [16] - delays are supposed to be bounded, lower and upper bound values being known, or relative speeds of processors, and of links, are supposed to be bounded, or execution steps are supposed to be taken simultaneously, in lock-step rounds. In section 5, we will also consider that processors have access to synchronized clocks [1].

In asynchronous models - as defined in [5] - any execution step may take an arbitrarily long, but finite, time. In other words, delays cannot be bounded.

It has been shown that $\langle UAB \rangle$ has no (deterministic) algorithmic solution in asynchronous models [1], a result derived from [5]. With asynchronous models that are "augmented" with inaccurate failure detectors - noted *FDs* - that exhibit particular properties [1], $\langle UAB \rangle$ can be solved.

---

[1] Models where processors have approximate knowledge of time, of bounds, belong to the class of partially synchronous [4] or timing-based [16] models.

Solving ⟨UAB⟩ only does not help with critical applications. Informally, what is missing is the requirement that *Messages* that are ABroadcast should be ADelivered "in time". Hence ⟨RTUAB⟩.

4.1 Problem ⟨RTUAB⟩

Below is a sketch of ⟨RTUAB⟩, adapted from a simpler problem investigated within the ATR project [2]. A processing module, referred to as a module, comprises a processor, tasks, data structures, system S/W, on top of which some algorithmic solution $\mathcal{A}$ is run.

⟨m.RTUAB⟩
- Finite set Q of modules, interconnected by a network module referred to as Net. Nominal size of Q is $n > 1$.
- Finite set Θ of tasks. Mapping of Θ onto Q (boolean matrix $\Pi(\Theta, Q)$) is unrestricted.
- A task θ is a finite sequence of code that invokes primitive ABroadcast, once or many times. The longest path of execution (in "code length") is known for every task, noted $x(\theta)$ for task θ.
- Finite set E of external event types. Mapping of E onto Θ (boolean matrix $\Pi(E, \Theta)$) is unrestricted. Event $e(\theta)$ - an occurrence of some event type - is the arrival of a request for running task θ.
- External event arrivals:
  - sporadic for some event types (sporadicity interval $sp(t)$ for type t),
  - unimodal arbitrary for others (bounded density $a(t)/w(t)$ for type t).
- For some external event types, causal dependencies exist between events.
- Failure model for modules: stop (correct behavior or immediate crash).
- Failure occurrences: system-wide unimodal arbitrary (bounded density f/W for set Q).

⟨p.RTUAB⟩
- Validity: Every *Message* ABroadcast by a correct module is ADelivered by this module.
- Uniform agreement: If *Message* is ADelivered by a module, *Message* is ADelivered by every correct module.
- Uniform integrity: *Message* is ADelivered at most once by every module, and only if *Message* was previously ABroadcast.
- Uniform total order: If $Message_1$ and $Message_2$ are ADelivered by any two modules, they are ADelivered in the same order.

---

[2] Members of the ATR project are Axlog Ingénierie, Dassault Aviation, École Polytechnique/LIX, INRIA, Thomson-Airsys, Université Paris VII/LIAFA, Université de Grenoble/LMC. The project is supported by Délégation Générale à l'Armement/DSP, Ministère de l'Éducation Nationale, de la Recherche et de la Technologie, and CNRS.

- Uniform external causality: If $Message_j$ causally depends on $Message_i$ and both are ADelivered by a module, $Message_i$ is ADelivered prior to $Message_j$.
- Timeliness: Timeliness constraints are strict relative termination deadlines. A deadline is associated to every task, noted $d(\theta)$ for task θ. If event $e(\theta)$ occurs at time τ, task θ must be completed by time $\tau + d(\theta)$ at the latest.
- Availability: Every task of set Θ should always be runnable within set Q.
- Coverage (solution) = $C(S, V(s))$.

Comments The unimodal arbitrary arrival model is resorted to whenever advance knowledge regarding arrivals is restricted to be an upper bound on arrivals density, noted $a(t)/w(t)$ for event type t, where $w(t)$ is the size of a (sliding) time window and $a(t)$ is the highest number of arrivals of type t events that can occur within $w(t)$.

Messages are arguments of the ABroadcast and ADeliver primitives. These primitives, as well as algorithms $\mathcal{A}$, make use of lower level primitives usually called send and receive, whose arguments are physical messages - referred to as messages in the sequel - processed by module Net. This module is supposed to be reliable, i.e. messages are neither corrupted nor lost.

Variable W is a time window that represents a worst-time-to-repair. For instance, W is an upper bound on a mission duration, an upper bound on a period of regular maintenance/repair activities. The f/W bound is the well known "up-to-f-failures-out-of-n-modules" assumption.

Messages are ADelivered by $\mathcal{A}$ on every module, in a waiting queue, to be read in FIFO order by tasks other than tasks in Θ.

Timeliness constraint $d(\theta)$ specified for task θ induces timeliness constraints for completing each of the ABroadcast invocations (triggered by tasks) and each of the ADeliver operations (performed by $\mathcal{A}$). It is a designer's job to derive a *Message* timeliness constraint from the invoking task's timeliness constraint. If τ is the arrival time of $e(\theta)$, ADelivery (*Message*) matching the latest ABroadcast (*Message*) triggered by θ must be completed by some time smaller than $\tau + d(\theta)$.

Note that, on every module, the execution of tasks and the execution of $\mathcal{A}$ are sequentially interleaved, i.e. the execution of a task may be suspended (its module is preempted) so as to run $\mathcal{A}$.

Observe that, contrary to common practice, availability is not stated as a probability. Similarly, W is not the usual mean-time-to-repair variable handled under stochastic approaches. Indeed, there is no reason to consider that dependability properties should be of "probabilistic" nature, while other properties (e.g., timeliness or total order) are not. Critical services should always be accessible, delivered on time, and should always execute as specified. Why make a special case with dependability properties?

There are reasons why, ultimately, properties - any property - and/or their valuations may not hold with certainty. A coverage is then specified for each of them, separately. This is not the case considered here.

Coverage $C(S, V(s))$ applies to any of the properties or any of their valuations stated as per $\{\langle RTUAB \rangle, V(\langle rtuab \rangle)\}$.

One possibility for specification $\langle m.rtuab \rangle$ would be that it contains all the variables that appear in $\langle m.RTUAB \rangle$. Ditto for $\langle p.rtuab \rangle$, w.r.t. $\langle p.RTUAB \rangle$, to the exception of $C(S, V(s))$ - see Section 3.3. Another possibility is that matrix $\Pi(E, \Theta)$, as well as some of the elements of matrix $\Pi(\Theta, Q)$, would not appear in $\langle m.rtuab \rangle$, neither would some of the variables $d(\theta)$ appear in $\langle p.rtuab \rangle$, for the reason that values taken by these variables are known and cannot be changed, i.e. they conceal "frozen" advance knowledge.

4.2 Solutions

Recall that valuations of $\{\langle m.rtuab \rangle, \langle p.rtuab \rangle\}$, of $C(S, V(s))$, are decided upon by a client or an end user.

Proving that $\{\langle RTUAB \rangle, V(\langle rtuab \rangle)\}$ is solved with $\{[S], V([s])\}$ is conditioned not only on proving that the solution specified is correct, but also on showing that ϕ is at least equal to $C(S, V(s))$.

Let us now consider two design solutions, namely a synchronous solution and an asynchronous solution.

Contrary to commonly held beliefs, a critical problem can be solved with a solution based on an asynchronous algorithm designed considering an asynchronous computational model. For example, for solving $\langle RTUAB \rangle$, one can select an asynchronous algorithm that solves $\langle UAB \rangle$ and that has been shown to have the best worst-case termination time (e.g., in number of phases). This algorithm would be transformed so as to internally schedule $Messages$ according to their timeliness constraints, as well as have the total $Message$ orderings of ADeliveries driven by $Message$ timeliness constraints [3]. Doing this would lead to the best (possibly optimal) timeliness-centric FCs for $\langle RTUAB \rangle$.

The important distinction made here is between *computational* models resorted to during a design phase and *system* models considered for conducting dimensioning and implementation phases. This distinction, which derives directly from proof-based SE principles, has been suggested in [11]. For example, an asynchronous computational model is specified in $[m.S]$, for every processing module, as well as for module Net. These modules are "immersed" in synchronous system models. System models must be synchronous, given that one must know, prior to usage, whether FCs are satisfied.

Is it worthwhile to proceed as described despite the fact that, ultimately, a synchronous system is to be deployed? Why not consider synchronous models up front (at design time)? One major advantage of asynchronous solutions is that they are universally portable. No matter which system they run onto, they retain their safety properties. This is not necessarily the case with synchronous solutions. For example, there are synchronous algorithms that would lose some of the safety properties stated in $\langle RTUAB \rangle$ whenever bounds on delays are violated.

---

[3] Even though neither global time nor absolute deadlines are accessible in an asynchronous system, they can be modelled via (unvalued) variables, which can be used by algorithms to enforce particular schedules.

Conversely, one must keep in mind that some of the properties achieved with asynchronous solutions immersed in a synchronous system, or their valuations, are weaker than those achieved with synchronous solutions. This is the case, in particular, with timeliness properties, shown by the fact that FCs established for an asynchronous solution may be (significantly) more pessimistic than FCs established for a synchronous solution.

Asynchronous Solutions As for $\langle UAB \rangle$, they inevitably rest on such constructs as, e.g., inaccurate *FDs*, which are characterized by their completeness and accuracy properties [1].

It has been shown that $\Diamond W$ (weak completeness and eventual weak accuracy) is the weakest class of *FDs* for solving such problems as Consensus or Atomic Broadcast if less than $\lceil n/2 \rceil$ modules fail [2]. Many algorithmic solutions are based on *FDs* - e.g., $\Diamond S$ - that can be built out of $\Diamond W$. Whenever *FDs* properties happen to hold true in a system, liveness properties enforced by some $\mathcal{A}$ hold true as well.

However, with existing asynchronous algorithms, orderings of computational steps are not driven by timeliness constraints. Furthermore, with *FDs*, values of timers - used by a module to check whether messages are received from others - bear no relationship with timeliness constraints (the $d(\theta)$'s in our case).

Hence, termination (ADeliveries and completion of tasks in Θ in our case) occurs within time latencies that are necessarily greater than achievable lower time bounds. In other words, as observed previously, the resulting timeliness-centric FCs are worse (further away from necessary and sufficient conditions) than FCs obtained when considering a synchronous solution. Timeliness is stronger than liveness.

Let Ω_1 be assertion *"accuracy and completeness properties hold whenever needed"*. Let Ω_2 be assertion *"valuations of FDs' timers ensure specified timeliness property | accuracy and completeness properties hold"*. Examples of issues raised are as follows:

(1) Estimate coverage(Ω_1),

(2) Estimate $\phi_1 = $ coverage(*RAs under which Ω_1 holds*),

(3) Estimate coverage(Ω_2),

(4) Estimate $\phi_2 = $ coverage(*RAs under which Ω_2 holds*),

(5) Check that ϕ_1 and ϕ_2 are at least equal to $C(S, V(s))$.

A problem is that doing (1) or (3) accurately enough is incredibly difficult, if not unfeasible. This is the reason why it is necessary to consider immersion in a synchronous system. Assume for a while that synchronous assumptions are never violated.

Firstly, *FDs* used by asynchronous solutions become perfect detectors (strong completeness and strong accuracy). Therefore, any weaker properties (e.g., strong completeness and eventual weak accuracy for $\Diamond S$) certainly hold. Hence, issue (1) vanishes.

Secondly, *FDs'* timer values can be set equal to the Net delay upper bound. FCs - embedded in a dimensioning oracle - can then be run in order to check whether every (valued) task deadline is met. Whenever the oracle returns a "yes", the specified timeliness property holds for sure. Consequently, issue (3) vanishes.

This is clearly not the case when values chosen for *FDs'* timers are guessed optimistically. Timers values chosen being smaller than the actual upper bound, the timeliness property and/or its valuations are violated, despite positive response from the oracle. If timers values are guessed pessimistically (values greater than the upper bound), then the oracle turns pessimistic as well, i.e. $V(\langle rtuab \rangle)$ which is feasible is declared unfeasible.

Synchronous Solutions These solutions are based on synchronized rounds, whereby messages sent during a round are received during that round, or on bounded message delays; see [16] for examples.

Synchronous solutions can be defeated by timing failures. A timing failure is a violation of proven (under assumptions), or postulated, lower (early timing failure) and upper (late timing failure) bounds on delays.

There are two approaches for addressing issues raised with timing failures in synchronous models. One consists in transforming *algorithms* proved correct in the absence of timing failures [16]. The other consists in transforming the *models*, by imposing restrictions on timing failures. Both have related coverages. We explore timing failures in the sequel.

Comments No matter which design solution is considered, we have to show how to correctly implement synchronous assumptions, i.e. how to address issues raised with timing failures, so as to arrive at residual assumptions that have computable and "very high" coverages.

For the sake of conciseness, we will only focus on how to correctly design, dimension and implement a synchronous Net module, and under which conditions a synchronous Net in the presence of timing failures is not equivalent to an asynchronous Net.

However, let us sketch out how, going through a dimensioning phase, a lower bound on each processor speed - some of the variables in [s] - can be determined, $V([s])$ being needed to implement synchronous (processing) modules. There are two possibilities with respect to variables $x(\theta)$, which are expressed in "code length" by S/W engineers.

Either only variables $x(\theta)$ are provided as inputs for conducting a dimensioning phase. Then, FCs and deadlines $d(\theta)$ - valued by a client - are used to compute an upper bound on acceptable worst-case execution time for every task θ, noted $wcet(\theta)$, such that the valued problem under consideration is declared feasible.

Or, in addition to variables $x(\theta)$, upper bounds $wcet(\theta)$ are also provided by S/W engineers, considering that each task runs alone over its module. Then, FCs serve to tell whether the valued problem under consideration is feasible.

In both cases, the ratio $x(\theta)/wcet(\theta)$ is the lowest acceptable processor speed for task θ [4]. Knowing the mapping of set Θ onto set Q, it is then trivial to compute the speed lower bound for each of the modules [5].

5 Timing Failures

Let b and B be, respectively, the targeted lower and upper bounds of delays for transmitting messages through Net, with $B > b$.

Under our assumption that implementation of $\{[S], V([s])\}$ is faultless, there are two causes for timing failures, namely overloads and excessive failure densities. One easy approach to these issues consists in pretending or assuming rarity (timing failures do not occur "too often"). Typical residual assumptions are as follows:

(RA): it is always the case that every message sent or broadcast by a module is received in at most B time units "sufficiently often" or by a "sufficiently high" number of correct modules.

There are synchronous algorithms that work correctly in the presence of "small" densities of timing failures. They simply ignore late messages. Hence, rigorously speaking, this approach boils down to avoiding the problems raised with timing failures. However, estimating coverage(RA) is hardly feasible.

How often, how long is Net overloaded or impacted by "too many" internal failures? Such phenomena must be under control.

For the sake of conciseness, we will not explore the issue of excessive densities of failures (other than timing failures). Let us briefly recall that any design correctness proof rests on "up-to-f-out-of-n" assumptions (see f/W in $\langle RTUAB \rangle$, which is the assumption that, in W time units, no more than f modules in Q - i.e. among n modules - may stop). Valuations consist in assigning values to variables f only, matching values of variables n (lower bounds) deriving from feasibility conditions.

It is worth noting that, unless proof-based SE principles are obeyed, it is impossible to assert that f cannot become equal to n. This is due to the fact that any SE fault made while conducting a design phase and/or a dimensioning phase is inevitably replicated over the n modules. Whenever this fault is activated, all n modules fail (at about the same time). This is what has happened with the maiden flight of European satellite launcher Ariane 5 [12].

SE faults being avoided, causes of violations of proven bound B are violations of, (i) valuations of variables f (covered by $C(X, V(x))$), (ii) residual assumptions.

Let us now discuss ways of addressing the issue of overload prevention. Then, we will examine how to cope with timing failures via detection.

---

[4] In either case, some of the acceptable bounds $wcet(\theta)$ may be very small, a result of having chosen very small task deadlines or very high external event arrival densities. This could translate into lowest acceptable processor speeds too high to be affordable.

[5] This does not raise scheduling problems. These have necessarily been solved during a design phase, otherwise FCs would not be available.

5.1 Prevention

Overloads should not be viewed as uncontrollable phenomena or as a result of necessarily fuzzy engineering tradeoffs. Module Net has a specification $\langle Net \rangle$, which must be provably derived from pair $\{\langle RTUAB \rangle, \text{solution } \mathcal{A}\}$. For instance, $\langle m.Net \rangle$ should state message arrival models provably derived from the tasks and the external event arrival models stated in $\langle RTUAB \rangle$, from $\mathcal{A}$, and from the analysis of the task schedules produced by $\mathcal{A}$.

With some $\mathcal{A}$s - e.g., periodic algorithms - it is possible to show that message arrivals obey a unimodal arbitrary model. A difficulty stems from the need to establish tight bounds on arrival densities, i.e. ratios $a(message)/w(message)$ for every *message*. Then, it is possible to *prove* that, considering some Net architecture and some message scheduling algorithm (a protocol), message delays are bounded by B.

In fact, it is possible to do even better. For instance, in [7], considering multiaccess broadcast channels (off-the-shelf technology) and tree protocols, one shows how to guarantee delay upper bounds on an individual message basis, i.e. a bound $B(message)$ proper to every *message*. Establishing bound(s) b usually derives easily from establishing bound(s) B.

Many $\langle Net \rangle$-like problems involving periodic or sporadic message arrivals have well known solutions (see [19] for examples).

Proven bound(s) B may be violated if bounds on message arrival densities are violated, i.e. with a probability no greater than $1 - C(X, V(x))$. Indeed, recall that under a proof-based SE approach, such bounds are (exactly or pessimistically) derived from bounds $a(t)/w(t)$ stated in $\langle RTUAB \rangle$.

It follows that coverage (*message arrival densities*) $\geq$ coverage (*external event arrival densities*) $\geq C(X, V(x))$.

Despite the fact that, by its very nature, $C(X, V(x))$ cannot be equal to 1, one can nevertheless enforce bound B, by exercising external admission control (see [14] for example), which amounts to perform on-line model checking. On each Net entry point, incoming message μ is rejected whenever it is found that bound $a(\mu)/w(\mu)$ is violated [6]. In this case, bound B cannot be violated, which comes at the expense of having some messages experience infinite waiting, with a probability at most equal to $1 - C(X, V(x))$.

Consequently, it is possible to *prove* that the delay experienced by every message carried by Net has B as an upper bound, this holding true whenever residual assumptions are not violated. Example of a residual assumption:

(RA): speed of physical signals over man-made passive communication links is 2/3 of light speed at least.

To summarize, SE faults being avoided, a correct specification $\langle Net \rangle$ can be established. A bound B can be proven to hold, and coverage(*proven bound B cannot be violated*) $\simeq 1$, given the RAs usually considered.

---

[6] As for arrival models, one can also perform external on-line model checking for failure models, and "reject" (e.g., stop) a module that would violate its failure semantics.

5.2 Detection

It is granted that timing failures can occur, whatever the causes, albeit not "too often". An approach, suggested by many authors, aims at transforming timing failures into omission failures: A message whose delay does not range between b and B is not "seen" by algorithm $\mathcal{A}$. This implies the existence of a "filtering" algorithm, noted $\mathcal{F}$, sitting in between Net and $\mathcal{A}$. A Net timing failure detected by $\mathcal{F}$ running on module q is transformed into a module q receive omission. There are many synchronous algorithms that work correctly in the presence of bounded omission failures.

Can there be algorithms $\mathcal{F}$ that detect violations of bounds b and B? If not, which bounds can be enforced with certainty? Under which residual assumptions? Densities of "fake" omission failures - i.e., transformed timing failures - must be "under control". How?

The 1W solution Let us review a popular solution, which will be referred to as the 1-way (1W) solution. It is based on the requirement that every module owns a clock (n clocks in Q) and that clocks are ϵ-synchronized [7], that is:

for any two clocks c_i and c_j, for any (universal) observation time T,
$$| c_i(T) - c_j(T) | < \epsilon, \quad \epsilon > 0.$$

Correct clocks are necessary to achieve ϵ-synchronization. A correct clock is a clock whose deviation from physical time is negligible over short time intervals, e.g. intervals in the order of small multiples of B. Clocks must resynchronize more or less regularly, via remote clock readings (message passing), to achieve ϵ-synchronization. This can be done by having each module equipped with a GPS (Global Positioning System) or a radio receiver. In this case, very small values of ϵ can be attained [8]. However, it might not be realistic to assume that each module in a critical system is physically located so that there is an unobstructed line-of-sight path from its antenna to GPS space vehicles. Or ϵ-synchronization must be maintained despite receivers going down or being jammed. In the sequel, we assume that a few modules - called time servers - are equipped with such receivers, and that system-wide ϵ-synchronization is achieved via some algorithm whereby modules remotely read any of these time servers via messages sent through Net (or read their clocks, mutually, whenever no time server is up).

Every message is timestamped with sender's local time (at send time), as well as with a receiver's local time (upon receipt). The difference is the message delay, as observed by a receiver, noted od. Timeliness tests retained for $\mathcal{F}$ are applied by receivers. $\mathcal{F} = 1W/test$ consists in rejecting only those messages that fail *test*.

A message whose real delay - noted rd - lies within interval $[b, B]$ will be said to be correct. Otherwise, a message will be said to be incorrect.

---

[7] ϵ-synchronization is a well known Approximate Agreement problem.

[8] see [18] for a comprehensive presentation of recent results.

Let $u = B - b$. Real lower bound is β, $0 < \beta \leq b$. There is no upper bound for a late timing failure. With critical problems such as $\langle RTUAB \rangle$, early timing failures matter as much as late timing failures. Indeed, in order to establish timeliness-centric FCs, one must identify worst-case scenarios, which is achieved by resorting to adversary proofs and arguments, whereby messages controlled by the "adversary" experience smallest delays, while messages issued by the task under consideration experience highest delays. Any violation of delay lower bounds would invalidate the proofs that underlie the FCs.

With ε-synchronized clocks, for some given od, real delays range between $od - \varepsilon$ and $od + \varepsilon$. Therefore, stricto sensu, the following restrictive timeliness test RTT should be considered:

$$RTT: b + \varepsilon \leq od \leq B - \varepsilon.$$

A problem is that every message, including correct messages, is rejected with $\mathcal{F} = 1W/RTT$. Indeed, it has been shown that ε has $\varepsilon_0 = u(n-1)/n$ as a lower bound with deterministic clock synchronization algorithms, assuming perfect (i.e. non drifting) clocks [15]. With correct clocks, it follows that $\varepsilon = \gamma\varepsilon_0$, $\gamma > 1$.

It can be easily verified that $B - \varepsilon$ cannot be greater than $b + \varepsilon$. Hence, RTT does not make sense.

One could then consider semi-restrictive timeliness tests $SRTT$s, such as:

$$SRTT: b + \alpha u/2 \leq od \leq B - \alpha u/2, \quad 0 < \alpha < 1.$$

With such tests, a correct message whose real delay is δ is accepted only if transmitted while sender's clock is less than $\delta - (b + \alpha u/2)$ ahead of receiver's clock and sender's clock is less than $B - (\alpha u/2 + \delta)$ behind receiver's clock.

Such tests are seldom considered, given that it is generally felt unacceptable to reject correct messages possibly arbitrarily often. With such tests, the initial issue of estimating the coverage of a bounded density assumption relative to timing failures translates into the issue of estimating the coverage of a bounded density prediction relative to accepted correct messages!

Consequently, only permissive timeliness tests are considered. The classical permissive test, PTT, suggested by many authors, is as follows:

$$PTT: b - \varepsilon \leq od \leq B + \varepsilon.$$

Of course, every correct message is certainly accepted. However, incorrect messages may also be accepted, whose real delays satisfy any of the following constraints:

$$max\{\beta, b - 2\varepsilon\} \leq rd < b, \qquad B < rd \leq B + 2\varepsilon.$$

Surprisingly, this appears to be barely addressed in the literature.

In summary:
(1) Assuming ε-synchronized clocks, it is impossible to detect violations of bounds $b - \varepsilon$ or $B + \varepsilon$ with certainty when using the $1W$ solution.

(2) Only early timing failures such that $rd < b - 2\varepsilon$ and late timing failures such that $rd > B + 2\varepsilon$ are certainly detected with $\mathcal{F} = 1W/PTT$.

(3) Bound on message delay uncertainty - initially postulated to be u - can only be amplified with $\mathcal{F} = 1W/PTT$. Actual bound on message delay uncertainty U guaranteed to some algorithm $\mathcal{A}$ by $1W/PTT$ is:

$$U = u[1 + 2\gamma(1 - 1/n)] + (b - \beta), \quad \text{if } \beta > b - 2\varepsilon$$
$$U = u[1 + 4\gamma(1 - 1/n)], \quad \text{if } \beta \le b - 2\varepsilon.$$

(4) With $\mathcal{F} = 1W/PTT$, bounds on tasks response times or, equivalently, feasibility conditions for having the timeliness property stated in $\langle RTUAB \rangle$ hold true, must be established considering that the actual upper bound on Net message delays is $B' = B + 2\varepsilon$, rather than B.

(5) With any filtering algorithm $\mathcal{F}$ based on $1W$ that would use a test more permissive than PTT, the difficult issue of estimating the coverages of the following assertions is raised:
- every timing failure is detected,
- every correct message is accepted.

The ε-synchronization assumption Given that we are assuming timing failures, it is very much appropriate to examine whether those conditions under which ε-synchronization is achieved are or are not invalidated by incorrect messages, when considering clock synchronization algorithms based on message passing. Unfortunately, it is impossible to use $1W$ so as to enforce bounds b and B on delays of clock synchronization messages - which is required to enforce ε - given that restrictive test RTT cannot be contemplated.

Solutions other than $1W$ exist. However, they come at the expense of some amplification of the achievable ε lower bound. In synchronous systems subject to timing failures, ε-synchronization either rests on the *assumption* that synchronization messages exchanged among clocks are correct, and then "small" values of ε can be contemplated, or ε-synchronization holds despite timing failures, provided that "greater" values of ε are acceptable.

Let us explore the coverages involved with ε-synchronization, and compute the "cost" of establishing "guarantees" for one simple example.

Coverage that ε holds true, denoted $C(\varepsilon)$, is an increasing function of $\varepsilon = \gamma\varepsilon_0$. Picking up low values for γ leads to low coverages. Indeed, for $\gamma \simeq 1$, $C(\varepsilon) \simeq 0$. Is there a value ε^* yielding $C(\varepsilon) \simeq 1$? The answer is yes. We sketch out below an example of an algorithm $\mathcal{F}$ that permits to safely detect timing failures impacting clock synchronization messages. This algorithm, denoted $2W/TT$, has previously been proposed for solving the remote clock reading problem [3]. For the sake of simplicity, we neglect factors in time derivatives (which is equivalent to assuming perfect clocks).

Timing failures are detected by each module, by locally measuring message round-trip delays (2-ways, hence 2W). A module q that triggers such a measure, by issuing a request message at time T_1, is to receive a response message *res* from the module being polled, referred to as the sender. Without loss of generality, assume that it takes no time for the sender to generate res. Let T_2 be the time at which res is received by q. Variable rd is the real delay of message res. $T_2 - T_1$ is the (observed, i.e. real) round-trip delay.

Timeliness test TT applied by q is:

$$TT: 2b \leq T_2 - T_1 \leq 2B.$$

Hence, early timing failures experienced by res that are not detected with certainty are such that $\beta \leq rd < b$, whereas late timing failures experienced by res that are not detected with certainty are such that $B < rd \leq 2B - \beta$.

Consequently, clock synchronization message delay uncertainty is $2(B - \beta)$. It follows that $\varepsilon^* = 2(u + b - \beta)(n - 1)/n$.

Knowing a lower bound of guaranteed ε when using $\mathcal{F} = 2W/TT$, it is trivial to re-compute what can be achieved with $\mathcal{F} = 1W/PTT$ w.r.t. messages issued by tasks, as well as to quantify the "cost" incurred with achieving certainty (i.e. $C(\varepsilon) \simeq 1$). Let us examine the "cost" - denoted ΔB - incurred with guaranteeing a message delay upper bound.

$B_0' = B + 2\varepsilon_0$ being the highest upper bound that cannot be considered ($\gamma = 1$), it follows that $\Delta B = B + 2\varepsilon^* - B_0' = 2[u + 2(b - \beta)](n - 1)/n$.

This "cost" has $2\varepsilon_0$ as a lower bound, attained if one makes no mistake in predicting lower bound b.

Note that checking timing failures with $2W$ increases the message load offered to Net. Bounds b and B with $2W$ would then be greater than the bounds considered without $2W$. However, no matter which message-based clock synchronization algorithm is considered, it is possible to resort to piggybacking: Clock synchronization data is transmitted taking advantage of "normal" messages (e.g., those generated by $\mathcal{A}$, by system S/W or application S/W components). In this case, neither bound b nor bound B is affected by clock synchronization traffic.

In summary:

(6) It is possible to achieve ε-synchronization in the presence of timing failures, considering residual assumptions that have coverages higher than usually asserted. Indeed, given that ε-synchronization is known to be achievable in synchronous systems in the presence of a minority f of faulty clocks (e.g., $n > 3f$ with f byzantine clocks), it follows that we have moved from (RA): clocks are ε-synchronized, to (RA): $n - f$ clocks at least are correct. The latter being only one of the assumptions that underlie the former, its coverage is necessarily higher.

(7) Synchronous systems in the presence of timing failures are not necessarily equivalent to asynchronous systems.

(8) With $\mathcal{F} = 2W/TT$ for clock synchronization messages, $\mathcal{F} = 1W/PTT$ for task messages, and under (RA): $n - f$ clocks at least are correct, the actual delay upper bound that is guaranteed - with some coverage $\geq \phi$ - for messages exchanged among modules that own correct clocks is $B^* = B + 4\varepsilon^*$, which has $B + 4\varepsilon_0$ as a lower bound. Claims or proofs of quantified "real-time behavior" based on considering that $B + \varepsilon$ is the actual upper bound are flawed.

Many clock synchronization algorithms could have been considered. Other algorithms $\mathcal{F}$ exist, and other bounds and coverages can be established.

Nevertheless, apart from numerical calculations, these conclusions have general applicability.

5.3 Prevention or Detection?

It is worth noting that there is no choice. It is very risky to resort to timing failure detection only, as there would be no way of showing that a "good" bound B has been picked up, no matter which timeliness test is considered [9]. Therefore, coverage(*no correct message is rejected*) has no significance. The concept of a "correct" message becomes elusive when permissive timeliness test PTT turns out to be unduly restrictive in fact, i.e. bearing no relationship with reality. Would real B be greater than guessed B, proven liveness or timeliness properties would not hold at run-time.

For instance, ε-synchronization is achievable provided that clock synchronization messages are tested correct "often enough" (e.g., once per period, for periodic clock synchronization algorithms). Similarly, algorithmic solutions would serve no real purpose if their messages - as well as those generated by tasks - are not tested correct "often enough".

Consequently, timing failure prevention is mandatory for developing solutions such that coverage(*no correct message is rejected*) and coverage(*every incorrect message is rejected*) are, (i) accurately estimated, (ii) "very high".

For any such problem as $\langle Net \rangle$, which is correctly derived from some higher level problem by applying proof-based SE principles, there exists a matching bound B, which must and can be *established*, exactly or pessimistically, by solving a distributed real-time scheduling problem, as briefly explained under Section 5.1. A proven bound B, noted $\mathcal{B}$, being established, the definition of a *correct* message matches reality. Therefore, messages tested incorrect are incorrect indeed. As a result, it is possible to show that the following coverages can be very close to 1, given the RAs that can be considered:

- coverage(*no message whose real delay is $\mathcal{B}$ at most is rejected*),
- coverage(*every message whose real delay is greater than $\mathcal{B}^*$ is rejected*).

Note also that doing this is the only way to bound densities of "fake" omission failures (with sufficiently high coverages).

With critical systems, there is definitely no choice. Irrespective of which computational models are contemplated for a design phase, synchronous system models must be considered for dimensioning and implementation phases.

With synchronous models, predictability assorted with "very high" coverages is illusory, unless (off-line) prevention and (on-line) detection of timing failures

---

[9] Bounds B estimated via statistical analysis of traffic measurements have poor coverages most often. Furthermore, predictability obligations also apply to systems that are yet to be built.

are resorted to jointly. Hence, the relevance of proof-based SE principles for such systems [10]

6 Conclusions

We have examined issues that arise with critical applications and systems, for each of the four phases that span a project lifecycle, from initial problem capture, to system implementation, when conducted according to proof-based system engineering principles. In particular, assuming correct implementations of H/W and S/W components, we have explored those irreducible sources of uncertainty which restrict predictability, as well as the concept of coverage applied to problems, solutions, assumptions.

A generic problem that arises with critical applications such as, e.g., air traffic control/management, namely the real-time uniform atomic broadcast problem, has been presented. Two design styles, namely asynchronous and synchronous solutions, have been compared in terms of resulting assumptions as well as coverages. This has led us to revisit popular justifications for asynchronous models, as well as popular approaches to the construction of synchronous systems, paying special attention to the issues of overloads and timing failures.

Critical systems raise many open research issues. Examples of areas where further work is needed are formal methods for proof-based system engineering, models and properties class structuring, algorithms for solving combined real-time, distributed, fault-tolerant computing problems, complexity and combinatorial analysis for establishing necessary and sufficient feasibility conditions.

¿From a more general perspective, for generic problems raised with critical systems, it would be very useful to compare design and dimensioning solutions, feasibility conditions, and associated coverages, as obtained under, respectively, deterministic and stochastic approaches.

Acknowledgements
I would like to thank Anders P. Ravn for his comments and suggestions that helped improving the paper.

References

1. Chandra, T.D., Toueg, S.: Unreliable Failure Detectors for Asynchronous Systems. Journal of the ACM 43(2) (March 1996) 225-267.
2. Chandra, T.D., Hadzilacos, V., Toueg, S.: The Weakest Failure Detector for Solving Consensus, 12th ACM Symposium on Principles of Distributed Computing (August 1992) 147-158.

---

[10] Specifications such as ⟨Net⟩ or bounds B are almost never *established* under current SE practice. Therefore, overloads occur at unpredictable rates. It follows that, as stated in the Introduction Section, dominant causes of such overloads are SE faults, rather than S/W or H/W faults.

3. Cristian, F.: Probabilistic Clock Synchronization, Distributed Computing (3) (1989) 146-158.
4. Dwork, C., Lynch, N.A., Stockmeyer, L.: Consensus in the Presence of Partial Synchrony, Journal of the ACM, 35(2) (April 1988) 288-323.
5. Fischer, M.J., Lynch, N.A., Paterson, M.S.: Impossibility of Distributed Consensus with One Faulty Process, Journal of the ACM 32(2) (April 1985) 374-382.
6. Hadzilacos, V., Toueg, S.: A Modular Approach to Fault-Tolerant Broadcasts and Related Problems, Technical Report TR 94-1425, Cornell University (May 1994), 83 p.
7. Hermant, J.F., Le Lann, G.: A Protocol and Correctness Proofs for Real-Time High-Performance Broadcast Networks, 18th IEEE Intl. Conference on Distributed Computing Systems (May 1998) 360 - 369.
8. Kuhn, D.R.: Sources of Failure in the Public Switched Telephone Network, IEEE Computer (April 1997) 31 - 36.
9. Lamport, L., Shostak, R., Pease, M.: The Byzantine Generals Problem, ACM Trans. on Programming Languages and Systems 4(3) (July 1982) 382 - 401.
10. Le Lann, G.: Proof-Based System Engineering and Embedded Systems, in Embedded Systems, Springer-Verlag LNCS on Embedded Systems (G. Rozenberg, F. Vaandrager Eds.) (to appear in 1998) 41 p.
11. Le Lann, G.: On Real-Time and Non Real-Time Distributed Computing, invited paper, 9th Intl. Workshop on Distributed Algorithms, Springer-Verlag LNCS 972 (J.M. Hélary, M. Raynal Eds.) (1995) 51-70.
12. Le Lann, G.: An Analysis of the Ariane 5 Flight 501 Failure - A System Engineering Perspective, IEEE Intl. Conference on the Engineering of Computer-Based Systems (March 1997) 339 - 346.
13. Leveson, N.G., Turner, C.: An Investigation of the Therac-25 Accidents, IEEE Computer (July 1993) 18 - 41.
14. Liebeherr, J., Wrege, D.E., Ferrari, D.: Exact Admission Control for Networks with a Bounded Delay Service, IEEE/ACM Trans. on Networking, 4(6) (December 1996) 885-901.
15. Lundelius, J., Lynch, N.A.: An Upper and Lower Bound for Clock Synchronization, Information and Control 62(2-3) (August-September 1984) 190 - 204.
16. Lynch, N.A.: Distributed Algorithms, Morgan Kaufmann Pub., ISBN 1-55860-348-4 (1996) 872 p.
17. Powell, D.: Failure Mode Assumptions and Assumption Coverage, 22nd IEEE Intl. Symposium on Fault-Tolerant Computing (July 1992) 386-395.
18. Special Issue on Global Time in Large Scale Distributed Real-Time Systems, Schmid, U. Guest Editor, Journal of Real-Time Systems 12(1-2) (1997) 230 p.
19. Tindell, K., Burns, A., Wellings, A.J.: Analysis of Hard Real-Time Communications, Journal of Real-Time Systems 9(2) (1995) 147-171.

Author Index

Springer
and the
environment

At Springer we firmly believe that an
international science publisher has a
special obligation to the environment,
and our corporate policies consistently
reflect this conviction.

We also expect our business partners –
paper mills, printers, packaging
manufacturers, etc. – to commit
themselves to using materials and
production processes that do not harm
the environment. The paper in this
book is made from low- or no-chlorine
pulp and is acid free, in conformance
with international standards for paper
permanency.

Lecture Notes in Computer Science

For information about Vols. 1–1404

please contact your bookseller or Springer-Verlag